Saracens and their World in
Boiardo and Ariosto

# LEGENDA

LEGENDA is the Modern Humanities Research Association's book imprint for new research in the Humanities. Founded in 1995 by Malcolm Bowie and others within the University of Oxford, Legenda has always been a collaborative publishing enterprise, directly governed by scholars. The Modern Humanities Research Association (MHRA) joined this collaboration in 1998, became half-owner in 2004, in partnership with Maney Publishing and then Routledge, and has since 2016 been sole owner. Titles range from medieval texts to contemporary cinema and form a widely comparative view of the modern humanities, including works on Arabic, Catalan, English, French, German, Greek, Italian, Portuguese, Russian, Spanish, and Yiddish literature. Editorial boards and committees of more than 60 leading academic specialists work in collaboration with bodies such as the Society for French Studies, the British Comparative Literature Association and the Association of Hispanists of Great Britain & Ireland.

The MHRA encourages and promotes advanced study and research in the field of the modern humanities, especially modern European languages and literature, including English, and also cinema. It aims to break down the barriers between scholars working in different disciplines and to maintain the unity of humanistic scholarship. The Association fulfils this purpose through the publication of journals, bibliographies, monographs, critical editions, and the MHRA Style Guide, and by making grants in support of research. Membership is open to all who work in the Humanities, whether independent or in a University post, and the participation of younger colleagues entering the field is especially welcomed.

### ALSO PUBLISHED BY THE ASSOCIATION

*Critical Texts*
*Tudor and Stuart Translations* • *New Translations* • *European Translations*
*MHRA Library of Medieval Welsh Literature*

*MHRA Bibliographies*
*Publications of the Modern Humanities Research Association*

*The Annual Bibliography of English Language & Literature*
*Austrian Studies*
*Modern Language Review*
*Portuguese Studies*
*The Slavonic and East European Review*
*Working Papers in the Humanities*
*The Yearbook of English Studies*

www.mhra.org.uk
www.legendabooks.com

# ITALIAN PERSPECTIVES

*Editorial Committee*
Professor Simon Gilson, University of Warwick (General Editor)
Dr Francesca Billiani, University of Manchester
Professor Manuele Gragnolati, Université Paris–Sorbonne
Dr Catherine Keen, University College London
Professor Martin McLaughlin, Magdalen College, Oxford

*Founding Editors*
Professor Zygmunt Barański and Professor Anna Laura Lepschy

In the light of growing academic interest in Italy and the reorganization of many university courses in Italian along interdisciplinary lines, this book series, founded by Maney Publishing under the imprint of the Northern Universities Press and now continuing under the Legenda imprint, aims to bring together different scholarly perspectives on Italy and its culture. *Italian Perspectives* publishes books and collections of essays on any period of Italian literature, language, history, culture, politics, art, and media, as well as studies which take an interdisciplinary approach and are methodologically innovative.

### APPEARING IN THIS SERIES

*Managing Editor*
Dr Graham Nelson, 41 Wellington Square, Oxford OX1 2JF, UK
www.legendabooks.com

# Saracens and their World in Boiardo and Ariosto

❖

MARIA PAVLOVA

*l*

LEGENDA

Italian Perspectives 47
Modern Humanities Research Association
2020

Published by Legenda
an imprint of the Modern Humanities Research Association
Salisbury House, Station Road, Cambridge CB1 2LA

ISBN 978-1-78188-347-1 (HB)
ISBN 978-1-78188-350-1 (PB)

First published 2020

Copy-Editor: Dr Anna J. Davies

The author is grateful for financial support from the Leverhulme Trust

LEVERHULME
TRUST _____

# CONTENTS

❖

# ACKNOWLEDGEMENTS

❖

'[...] a chi nel mar per tanta via m'ha scorto' [to those who have guided me on so long a voyage] (*Fur.*, XL 1,4 AB; XLVI C). Indeed, it has been a long and exciting journey, during which I have contracted many debts, intellectual and otherwise, which I gladly acknowledge.

This book grew out of my doctoral thesis completed at the University of Oxford in 2015. My first and foremost thanks go to the following individuals, who at various stages of my doctoral studies read different drafts of my dissertation and offered me guidance and encouragement: Marco Dorigatti, who introduced me to the world of chivalric literature and who has been very supportive of my work and incredibly generous with his expert advice throughout the years; my examiners Stefano Jossa and Martin Mclaughlin, who encouraged me to turn my doctoral work into a monograph; and my supervisor Nicola Gardini. I am also most grateful to Jane Everson, who read a more recent version of my manuscript and offered me a wealth of useful suggestions on how to improve it. Other scholars, too, have contributed to this book with their insightful comments. In particular, it has benefited from conversations I have had with Shabbir Akhtar, Gloria Allaire, Anna Carocci, Mario Casari, Nicholas Davidson, Daniela Delcorno Branca, Luca Degl'Innocenti, Daniel Javitch, Martin Kemp, Ita Mac Carthy, David Maskell, Annalisa Perrotta, Monica Preti, Giovanni Ricci, Franca Strologo, †Paola Tomè, Gianni Venturi, Alessandra Villa, Michael Wyatt, and Cristina Zampese. Thanks also go to the staff at the Taylorian and Bodleian Libraries in Oxford, the British Library, the Archivio di Stato di Modena, the Archivio di Stato di Mantova (and particularly to its former director Daniela Ferrari), the Biblioteca Comunale Ariostea in Ferrara, and many other libraries in Italy and the UK. The images contained within this book are reproduced by kind permission of the Archivio di Stato di Modena (Figs I.1 and 1.1), the Barber Institute of Fine Arts, Birmingham (Fig. 3.1) and the Wadsworth Atheneum Museum of Art, Hartford (Fig. 5.1). The image on the cover – a fragment of a battle scene between Turks and Turkmens (Persians) painted on a fifteenth-century *cassone* – is reproduced courtesy of the Metropolitan Museum of Art, New York. Moreover, I would like to express my gratitude to Legenda (I could not have found a better home for my book!) and, in particular, to my editors Simon Gilson and Graham Nelson, my copy-editor Anna Davies, as well as to the anonymous readers for their constructive criticism and helpful advice. All mistakes and flaws that remain are obviously my own.

This book was for the most part written during my time at Oxford. St Hilda's College provided a friendly environment in which to complete my doctoral research. The Principal, Fellows and staff at St Hugh's College, where I was a

Joanna Randall MacIver Junior Research Fellow from 2016 to 2018, warmly welcomed me into their scholarly community. I am especially grateful to my inspiring and supportive mentor Giuseppe Stellardi and to my colleagues and friends Genevieve Adams, Janette Chow, Ève Morisi, Susan Valladares and Mimi Zou, whose camaraderie and humour kept me sane when I was editing my thesis into a book. I am also very grateful to my colleagues and friends at the University of Warwick, with special thanks to David Lines, whose intellectual prowess and passion for all things Renaissance were a potent source of inspiration as I was adding the finishing touches to my manuscript, Alberica Bazzoni, Maria Belova, Marta Celati and Julia Hartley. My research has been made possible thanks to the following grants: a Hill Foundation award which enabled me to complete a BA at Oxford (my heartfelt thanks go to Mikhail Khodorkovsky, Alastair Tulloch and Anthony Smith, for without this award my life would have likely taken a different turn); a joint Clarendon and Scatcherd European doctoral scholarship; and research grants from St Hilda's and St Hugh's Colleges. Furthermore, I gratefully acknowledge the generous support of the Leverhulme Trust.

On a more personal note, I would like to thank for their constant support the following friends: Angelica Goodden, who taught me when I was an undergraduate and who strongly encouraged me to pursue graduate studies, Olga Gorbacheva, Kristina Landa, Ayoush Lazikani, and Urooj Shahid. Last but not least, I would like to take this opportunity to express my profound debt of gratitude to my loving and wonderful parents, Larissa Pavlova and Alexey Zlodeev, and my brother Sergey Pavlov, for their faith in me and for always being there for me in good and in challenging times: it is to them that I dedicate this book.

M.P., Warwick, February 2020

# EDITIONS AND ABBREVIATIONS
❖

## A. Boiardo

### (1) Inamoramento de Orlando

Inam.                    *L'Inamoramento de Orlando*, ed. by Antonia Tissoni Benvenuti and Cristina Montagnani with an introduction and comments by Antonia Tissoni Benvenuti, 2 vols (Milan: Ricciardi, 1999)

### (2) Other works

Amorum libri tres        *Amorum libri tres*, ed. by Tiziano Zanato (Turin: Einaudi, 1998)

Istoria Imp. III-IV      *Istoria Imperiale di Ricobaldo Ferrarese nella quale si contiene la divisione dell'Imperio, e la successione de gl'Imperatori dopo Carlo Magno, che primo ottenne l'Imperio Occidentale*, in *Rerum Italicarum Scriptores*, ed. by Ludovico Muratori, 25 vols (Milan: Società Palatina, 1723–1751), IX, books III-IV, pp. 289–342

Historia Imp. I-II       *The 'Historia Imperiale' by Riccobaldo Ferrarese translated by Matteo Maria Boiardo (1471–1473)*, ed. by Andrea Rizzi (Rome: Istituto storico italiano per il Medio Evo, 2008), books I-II.

La pedìa                 *La pedìa de Cyro*, ed. by Valentina Gritti (Novara: Interlinea, 2014)

Pastorale                *Pastorale*, in *Opere volgari. Amorum libri, Pastorale, Lettere*, ed. by Pier Vincenzo Mengaldo (Bari: Laterza, 1962)

Pastoralia               *Pastoralia*, ed. by Stefano Carrai (Padua: Antenore, 1996)

## B. Ariosto

### (1) Orlando furioso

Fur. A                   *Orlando furioso de Ludovico Ariosto da Ferrara* (Ferrara: Giovanni Mazocco dal Bondeno, 1516). The text of *Fur.* A is quoted from *Orlando furioso secondo la princeps del 1516*, ed. by Marco Dorigatti, in collaboration with Gerarda Stimato (Florence: Olschki, 2006)

Fur. B                   *Orlando furioso di Ludovico Ariosto nobile ferrarese ristampato et con molta diligentia da lui corretto et quasi tutto formato di nuovo et ampliato* (Ferrara: Giovanni Battista da la Pigna, 1521). The text of *Fur.* B is quoted from *Orlando furioso secondo l'edizione del 1532: con le varianti delle edizioni del 1516 e del 1521*, ed. by Santorre Debenedetti and Cesare Segre (Bologna: Commissione per i testi di lingua, 1960)

Fur. C                   *Orlando furioso di Messer Ludovico Ariosto nobile ferrarese nuovamente da lui proprio corretto e d'altri canti nuovi ampliato* (Ferrara: Francesco Rosso da Valenza, 1532). The text of *Fur.* C is quoted from *Orlando furioso*, ed. by Cesare Segre, in *Tutte le opere di Ludovico Ariosto*, 5 vols [of which II and V were never published] (Milan: Mondadori, 1964), I

*(2) Other works*

Satire                  *Satire*, in *Carmina, Rime, Satire, Erbolato, Lettere*, ed. by Mario Santoro
                        (Turin: Unione Tipografico-Editrice Torinese, 1989)

## C. Other chivalric texts

Altobello               *Altobello e il re Troiano suo fratello* (Venice: Gabriel di Grassi de Pavia,
                        1481)
Ancroia                 *Libro della Regina Ancroia* (Venice: Petrus de Plasiis, Cremonensis, 1485)
Antiphor                *Antiphor de Barosia* (Venice: Melchior Sessa, 1531)
Aspramonte              *Le battaglie d'Aspramonte* (Venice: Dionysius Bertochus, 1491)
Aspramonte A            Andrea da Barberino, *L'Aspramonte, romanzo cavalleresco inedito*, ed. by
                        Marco Boni (Bologna: per i tipi dell'Antiquaria Palmaverde, 1951)
Aspramonte BL           *Aspramonte*, London, British Library, MS Add 10808
Bradiamonte             *Bradiamonte sorella di Rinaldo* (Florence: Francesco di Dino, 1489)
Cantari d'Aspramonte    *Cantari d'Aspramonte inediti (Magl. VII 682)*, ed. by Andrea Fassò
                        (Bologna: Commissione per i testi di lingua, 1981)
Cantari di Fierabraccia e Ulivieri    *El cantare di Fierabraccia et Ulivieri: Italienische Bearbeitung
                        der Chanson de geste Fierabras*, ed. by Edmund Stengel and Carl
                        Buhlmann, *Ausgaben und Abhandlungen aus dem Gebiete der romanischen
                        Philologie*, 2 (1881)
Cantari di Rinaldo      *I cantari di Rinaldo da Monte Albano*, ed. by Elio Melli (Bologna:
                        Commissione per i Testi di Lingua, 1973)
Chanson d'Aspremont     *Aspremont, chanson de geste du XII<sup>e</sup> siècle, présentation, édition et
                        traduction par François Suard d'après le manuscrit 25529 de la BNF* (Paris:
                        Champion Classiques, 2008)
Chanson de Roland       *La chanson de Roland*, ed. by Cesare Segre (Milan: Ricciardi, 1971)
Ciriffo Calvaneo        Luca Pulci, Luigi Pulci, *Cyriffo Calvaneo* (Florence: Antonio di
                        Bartolommeo Miscomini, before 1490)
Dama Rovenza            *Libro chiamato Dama Rovenza* ('[Q]uando lomo nase') (Venice: Lucas
                        Dominici F., 1482)
Entrée                  *L'Entrée d'Espagne: chanson de geste franco-italienne*, ed. by Antoine
                        Thomas, 2 vols (Paris: Firmin-Didot, 1913)
Falconetto              *Falconetto (1483)*, ed. by Andrea Canova (Mantua: Gianluigi Arcari
                        Editore, 2001)
Fatti di Spagna         *Li fatti de Spagna: testo settentrionale trecentesco già detto "Viaggio di
                        Carlo Magno in Ispagna"*, ed. by Ruggero Ruggieri (Modena: Società
                        tipografica modenese, 1951)
Guerrin Meschino        Andrea da Barberino, *Il Guerrin Meschino, edizione critica secondo l'antica
                        vulgata fiorentina*, ed. by Mauro Cursietti (Rome: Editrice Antenore,
                        2005)
Innamoramento di Carlo    *Innamoramento di Carlo e dei suoi Paladini* (Bologna: Bazaliero di
                        Bazalerii, 1491)
Innamoramento de Guidon Salvaggio    *Libro novo dove si contiene le battaglie dello innamoramento
                        de Guidon Salvaggio che fu figliolo de Rinaldo de Mont'Albano* (Milan:
                        Valerio & Hieronymo fratelli da Meda, after 1550)
Mambriano               Francesco Cieco, *Libro d'arme e d'amore, nomato Mambriano*, ed. by
                        Giuseppe Rua, 3 vols (Turin: Unione Tipografico-Editrice Torinese,
                        1926)
Morgante                Luigi Pulci, *Morgante*, ed. by Franca Ageno (Milan: Mondadori, 1994)

| | |
|---|---|
| *Persiano* | Francesco Cieco da Firenze, *Persiano figliolo de Altobello* (Venice: Cristophoro de Mandelo, 1493) |
| *Quarto libro* | Nicolò degli Agostini, *Quarto libro*, in *Tutti li libri de Orlando Inamorato del Conte de Scandiano Mattheo Maria Boiardo* (Venice: Giorgio de' Rusconi, 1506) |
| *Quinto libro A* | Nicolò degli Agostini, *Il quinto libro dello Inamoramento de Orlando* (Venice: Zorzi di Rusconi Milanese, 1514) |
| *Quinto libro V* | Raffaele Valcieco, *El quinto e fine de tutti li libri de lo Inamoramento de Orlando* (Milan: Nicolò da Gorgonzola, 1518) |
| *Reali di Francia* | Andrea da Barberino, *I Reali di Francia*, ed. by Giuseppe Vandelli and Giovanni Gambarin (Bari: Laterza, 1947) |
| *Sesto libro* | Nicolò degli Agostini, *Incomincia il sesto libro de lo Innamoramento di Orlando*, in *Tutti li libri d'Orlando inamorato, del Conte de Scandiano Mattheo Maria Boiardo* (Venice: Alovise de Tortis, 1543) |
| *Spagna* | *La Spagna: poema cavalleresco del secolo XIV*, ed. by Michele Catalano, 3 vols (Bologna: Commissione per i testi di lingua, 1939–1940) |
| *Spagna F* | *Spagna ferrarese*, ed. by Valentina Gritti and Cristina Montagnani (Novara: Interlinea, 2009) |
| *Trabisonda* | *La Trabisonda* (Bologna: Ugo Rugerius, 1483) |
| *Ugieri il Danese* | *Ugieri il Danese* (Venice: Lucas Dominici, 1480) |
| *Vendetta A* | *Incomenza la vendeta de Falconeto historiata novamente stampata* (Milan: Johanne de Casteliono, 1512) |
| *Vendetta B* | *Libro di mirandi facti di paladini intitulato vendetta di Falchonetto* (Venice, 1513) |

## D. English translations

The English translations of the *Inamoramento de Orlando* and the *Orlando furioso* are based on the following translations (and, where necessary, adapted):

*Orlando Innamorato*, translated with an introduction and notes by Charles Stanley Ross (Berkeley: University of California Press, 1989)
*Orlando Furioso*, an English prose translation by Guido Waldman (Oxford: Oxford University Press, 1974)

All other translations are my own.

### Spelling and punctuation

Original spelling has been maintained in all quotations from manuscripts and early printed books, with the exception of very obvious misprints, contractions and the distinction u/v, which have been normalised. In some cases punctuation has been slightly modernised to facilitate comprehensibility.

### Characters' names

Some character names are spelled differently in different chivalric texts (e.g. Rugiero in the *Inamoramento de Orlando*, Ruggiero in the *Orlando furioso*). I have adopted the spelling of character names as they appear in the editions I quote from. When there are spelling variants within one and the same text (e.g. Argalipha and Argalifa in Boiardo), I use a single name to avoid confusion.

# LIST OF FIGURES

❖

# INTRODUCTION

❖

Like many of his contemporaries, Giordano Bruno was a keen admirer of the *Orlando furioso*. But what was it that he particularly liked about Ariosto's poem? If we look at the references to the *Furioso* scattered throughout Bruno's works, we find that one character is mentioned more frequently than any other. This character is Rodomonte. Bruno developed an 'obsession with the figure of Rodomonte, whose words and acts run through his dialogues as a line of counterpoint'.[1] Not only was this eminent philosopher and theologian fascinated with a character from the *Furioso* — a Saracen — but he came to identify with him. During his imprisonment in Venice, he told his fellow inmates that in his youth he had taken part in a game of drawing lots and that the verse that he had drawn perfectly reflected his nature. The line in question was 'd'ogni legge nemico e d'ogni fede' [an enemy of every law and every faith] (*Fur.*, XXVI 100,8 AB; XXVIII C), which is how Ariosto's narrator describes Rodomonte, a convinced atheist with no respect for any religion. Thus, the rebellious Saracen 'constituted an emblem and a prophecy of the Nolan's tragic destiny'.[2] Like Rodomonte, who in the final canto of the *Furioso* refuses to surrender, Bruno would later choose death over recanting his views, remaining true to himself until the end.

Bruno was not alone in feeling sympathy towards Rodomonte. In his *Considerazioni al Tasso*, Galileo Galilei stressed the Saracen's 'grandezza dell'animo' [nobility of soul].[3] Galileo, however, was impressed by Rodomonte's sense of honour rather than by his lack of religious faith. Other early readers of the *Inamoramento de Orlando* and the *Furioso* admired his physical prowess. Luigi 'Rodomonte' Gonzaga (1500–1532), a renowned *condottiero* and a gifted poet, proudly wore his nickname, which he earned in his childhood because of his extraordinary strength and courage. An enthusiastic reader of the *Furioso*, this real-life Rodomonte wrote stanzas in praise of Ariosto's poem, which were often printed in its sixteenth-century editions.[4]

Rodomonte is just one of the many charismatic Saracen characters that populate the pages of the two *Orlandos*. The fascination that these characters have throughout

---

1    Lina Bolzoni, 'Images of Literary Memory in the Italian Dialogues: Some Notes on Giordano Bruno and Ludovico Ariosto', in *Giordano Bruno: Philosopher of the Renaissance*, ed. by Hilary Gatti (Aldershot: Ashgate, 2002), pp. 121–41 (p. 141).
2    Ibid.
3    Galileo Galilei, *Considerazioni al Tasso*, in *Scritti letterari*, ed. by Alberto Chiari (Florence: Le Monnier, 1970), pp. 487–635 (p. 571).
4    Luigi 'Rodomonte' Gonzaga met and became friends with Ariosto. He is mentioned twice in the 1532 edition of the poem: in cantos XXVI 50,5 and XXXVII 9–11, where he is praised for his virtues.

the centuries exerted over the poems' readers — including members of the Este family — is undeniable. The Ferrarese noblewoman Marfisa d'Este (1554–1608), Torquato Tasso's friend and a famous patroness of arts, was named after the Saracen woman warrior Marfisa. The future Alfonso II d'Este impersonated Mandricardo in the unfortunate joust held in Blois in 1556 (in which he fell from his unruly horse and was badly hurt).[5] The idyllic love of Angelica and Medoro has been a source of inspiration for countless painters, from Simone Peterzano to Giovanni Battista Tiepolo to Eugène Delacroix. Poets and novelists, too, have fallen under the spell of the Saracen world Ariosto 'inherited' from Boiardo. Jorge Luis Borges, whose lifelong interest in Islamic culture pervades his entire *oeuvre*, sensed a deep affinity between Ariosto's Saracens and the characters of the *Arabian Nights*, which he explores in 'Ariosto y los árabes'. David Lodge makes numerous allusions to the *Furioso* in his *Small World: An Academic Romance* (1984), whose main female protagonist, the elusive Angelica Pabst, is partly modelled on Ariosto's Angelica. Similarly, Qara Köz, the enigmatic heroine of Salman Rushdie's *Enchantress of Florence* (2008), is clearly inspired by Angelica.

This book intends to offer a comprehensive insight into Boiardo's and Ariosto's *Paganìa*, or the Saracen world, paying due attention to both the leading protagonists and the seemingly innumerable minor characters that add colour — as well as complexity and depth — to the two *Orlandos*. It is underpinned by two overarching aims. First of all, it seeks to examine the historical dimension of the two poems, that is, the possible points of contact between their fictional universes and real-life interactions between Christians and Muslims. Secondly — and this is the central aim of the present study — it situates the *Inamoramento de Orlando* and its famous sequel within the broader context of late medieval and early Renaissance Italian chivalric literature by highlighting both the original elements in Boiardo's and Ariosto's portrayals of Saracens and the ways in which their poems are indebted to, or influenced by, earlier and contemporary literary representations of cultural and religious Otherness.

For all the important innovations they introduce, both Boiardo and Ariosto owe an immense debt to the literary tradition to which their works belong, a debt that has yet to be fully acknowledged. Although the recent decades have witnessed a significant growth of interest in the vernacular context of Ariosto's poem,[6] the *Furioso* is still often seen as a poem that 'towers over the poems of other Italian chivalric poets' and that can be read, analysed and interpreted without reference to

---

5    See Angelo De Gubernatis, *Torquato Tasso: Corso di lezioni all'Università di Roma nell'anno scolastico 1907–1908* (Rome: Tipografia Popolare, 1908), p. 243.

6    It is a fundamental thesis of Eleonora Stoppino's studies that the *Furioso* must be read in the context of preceding chivalric literature (see, at least, her *Genealogies of Fiction: Women Warriors and the Dynastic Imagination in the 'Orlando Furioso'* (New York: Fordham University Press, 2012)). See also Daniela Delcorno Branca's *L'‘Orlando furioso’ e il romanzo cavalleresco medievale* (Florence: Olschki, 1973); and the first part (namely the essays by Daniela Delcorno Branca, Annalisa Perrotta, Elisa Martini and Maria Pavlova) of the recently published *‘Dreaming again on things already dreamed’: 500 Years of ‘Orlando Furioso’ (1516–2016)*, ed. by Marco Dorigatti and Maria Pavlova (Oxford; New York: Peter Lang, 2019). Moreover, a number of scholars consider Ariosto's vernacular sources when examining specific characters and episodes.

other chivalric texts.[7] It is only relatively recently that scholars have become more willing to consider Boiardo in relation to Ariosto, and, even so, Boiardo is frequently regarded as less sophisticated and aesthetically inferior to his continuator.[8] And yet Boiardo is in many respects a more daring and revolutionary author than Ariosto. Nor is it fair to dismiss other chivalric works of the period (both those preceding and those following the *Inamoramento de Orlando* and the *Furioso*) as lacking in originality and depth. In fact, their quality varies widely. There are many hidden jewels of chivalric literature waiting to be unearthed and brought to the attention of the admirers of Ariosto. Though printed and read throughout the sixteenth century (Galileo, for one, had an impressive collection of chivalric romances, which included copies of the *Ciriffo Calvaneo*, the *Innamoramento de Guidon Selvaggio*, the *Antifor de Barosia*, and the *Aspramonte* as well as a copy of the 1506 Rusconi edition of Boiardo, which comprised Nicolò degli Agostini's *Quarto libro*), many of these works have now been all but forgotten.[9] However, some of them contain flashes of brilliance worthy of Ariosto. In an unpublished interview with Antonino Buttitta (Sicily, March 1984), Borges confessed that his favourite lines of poetry were from the *Furioso*: 'il prode cavalier non s'era accorto, | andava combattendo, ed era morto' [the valiant knight was unaware: | he was fighting on, yet he was dead]. He was wrong: these lines are from Francesco Berni's *rifacimento* [refashioning] of the *Orlando innamorato* (first published in 1541–1542), where they describe the heroic death of a minor yet memorable Saracen character called Alibante di Toledo. Berni, one may add, was inspired by the final moments of the brave Saracen king Sinettore in Luca and Luigi Pulci's *Ciriffo Calvaneo*.[10]

My task has been facilitated by a number of critical works on Saracens in French and Italian chivalric literature. This book is especially indebted to the meticulous scholarship of Paul Bancourt and Norman Daniel, whose monographs are indispensable for the study of Saracens in the Old French *chansons de geste*.[11] These scholars have debunked the myth that in medieval heroic poetry Saracens

---

7    Marianne Shapiro, *The Poetics of Ariosto* (Detroit: Wayne State University Press, 1988), p. 10.

8    On the presence of the *Inamoramento de Orlando* in the *Furioso* see Marco Dorigatti, 'Il boiardismo del primo *Furioso*', in *Tipografie e romanzi in Val Padana fra Quattro e Cinquecento*, ed. by Riccardo Bruscagli and Amedeo Quondam (Modena: Franco Cosimo Panini, 1992), pp. 161–74; Michael Sherberg, 'Ariosto and Boiardo: Poetry and Memory', in Idem, *Rinaldo: Character and Intertext in Ariosto and Tasso* (Saratoga, Calif: Anma Libri, 1993), pp. 13–42; Giuseppe Sangirardi, *Boiardismo ariostesco: Presenza e trattamento dell'*'Orlando Innamorato' *nel* 'Furioso' (Lucca: M. Pacini Fazzi, 1993); Maria Cristina Cabani, 'Considerazioni sul boiardismo del *Furioso* e alcune riflessioni sull'uso degli strumenti informatici nelle indagini intertestuali', *Rivista di letteratura italiana*, 12 (1994), 157–248.

9    Crystal Hall, *Galileo's Reading* (Cambridge: Cambridge University Press, 2013), p. 27. A full list of books in Galileo's library can be found at <//biblioteca.imss.fi.it/acquisti/biblioteca_galileo.pdf> [consulted 16 January 2020].

10    For more information on this interview, see Marco Dorigatti, 'Borges, Ariosto e la vita segreta dei personaggi minori', in *Lettori e interpreti del* 'Furioso': *Atti della giornata di studio (Milano, 3 ottobre 2012)*, in *Carte Romanze: Rivista di Filologia e Linguistica Romanze dalle Origini al Rinascimento*, 1, no. 2 (2013), 377–406 (pp. 378–82).

11    Paul Bancourt, *Les musulmans dans les chansons de geste du Cycle du roi*, 2 vols (Aix-en-Provence: Université de Provence; Marseille: Diffusion J. Laffitte, 1982); Norman Daniel, *Heroes and Saracens: An Interpretation of the Chansons de Geste* (Edinburgh: Edinburgh University Press, 1984).

are invariably demonized, showing that their portrayals are far more complex and nuanced than assumed by critics such as Cyril Meredith Jones.[12] As Daniel argues, 'the songs are not Crusade propaganda [...] but they are good propaganda for a life of daring and adventure'.[13] Although I focus on later chivalric texts, Bancourt's and Daniel's works, as well as those by Lynn Tarte Ramey and Catherine Gaullier-Bougasss (which consider medieval romances), have helped me in writing this book by encouraging me to let go of preconceived ideas about medieval and late medieval literature and sparking my interest in Boiardo's and Ariosto's chivalric sources.[14]

There have been no similar comprehensive book-length studies on the Saracen Other in Italian chivalric literature. William Wistar Comfort, Antonio Franceschetti, and Gloria Allaire have written articles on the evolution of the image of the Saracen in late medieval/Renaissance Italian texts.[15] Scholars have looked at Saracens in individual chivalric works. Claudia Boscolo has examined the portrayal of Islam and Saracens in the Franco-Venetian *Entrée d'Espagne*.[16] Gloria Allaire has analysed Andrea da Barberino's *Guerrin Meschino*, Frej Moretti the *Spagna in prosa*, and Jane Everson Cieco da Ferrara's *Mambriano*.[17] Annalisa Perrotta has recently published a monograph on Saracens in the *Altobello*, the *Persiano*, and the *Falconetto*.[18] Boiardo's

12   Cyril Meredith Jones, 'The Conventional Saracen of the Songs of Geste', *Speculum*, 17 (1942), 201–25.

13   Daniel, *Heroes and Saracens*, p. 267.

14   Lynn Tarte Ramey, *Christian, Saracen and Genre in Medieval French Literature* (New York: Routledge, 2001); Catherine Gaullier-Bougassas, *La tentation de l'Orient dans le roman médiéval: sur l'imaginaire médiéval de l'autre* (Paris: Champion, 2003). Both Tarte Ramey and Gaullier-Bougassas look at the evolution of the image of the cultural Other in the course of the Middle Ages. Tarte Ramey's rather succinct study draws parallels between themes raised in literary texts and changes in Western perceptions of historical Muslims without, however, outlining a clear chronological progression. By contrast, Gaullier-Bougassas's substantial monograph pays special attention to chronology. According to the latter, twelfth-century romances abound in highly positive and very detailed descriptions of the Orient, as they mirror the Western dream of a union between East and West. This dream declined in the thirteenth century, which is reflected in both the disappearance of utopic elements from literary depictions of the Orient and the prominence given to the Holy War theme, still very conspicuous in fifteenth-century romances.

15   William Wistar Comfort, 'The Saracens in Italian Epic Poetry', *PMLA*, 59 (1944), 882–910; Antonio Franceschetti, 'On the Saracens in Early Italian Chivalric Literature', in *Romance Epic: Essays on a Medieval Literary Genre*, ed. by Hans-Erich Keller (Kalamazoo: Medieval Institute Publications, 1987), pp. 203–11; Gloria Allaire, 'Noble Saracen or Muslim Adversary? The Changing Image of the Saracen in Late Medieval Literature', in *Western Views of Islam in Medieval and Early Modern Europe: Perception of Other*, ed. by David R. Blanks and Michael Frassetto (Basingstoke: Macmillan, 1999), pp. 173–84. These critics argue that Saracens are represented more positively in later texts.

16   Claudia Boscolo, 'Representations of Islam', in Eadem, *L'Entrée d'Espagne: Context and Authorship at the Origins of the Italian Chivalric Epic* (Oxford: Medium Aevum, 2017), pp. 153–213.

17   Gloria Allaire, 'Portrayal of Muslims in Andrea da Barberino's *Guerrino Meschino*', in *Medieval Christian Perceptions of Islam*, ed. by John Victor Tolan (New York; London: Routledge, 2000), pp. 243–69; Frej Moretti, 'L'oriente e l'islam nella *Spagna in prosa*', in *Carlo Magno in Italia e la fortuna dei libri di cavalleria: Atti del convegno internazionale di Zurigo (6–8 maggio 2014)*, ed. by Johannes Bartuschat and Franca Strologo (Ravenna: Longo Editore, 2016), pp. 103–24; Jane Everson, 'Il buono, il brutto, il cattivo: figure di regnanti non-cristiani nel *Mambriano* di Francesco Cieco da Ferrara', *Rassegna europea di letteratura italiana*, 44 (2014), 29–43.

18   Annalisa Perrotta, *I cristiani e gli Altri: Guerre di religione, politica e propaganda nel poema cavalleresco di fine Quattrocento* (Rome: Bagatto Libri, 2017). Perrotta's book is based on the following articles:

and especially Ariosto's Saracens have perhaps attracted more scholarly interest than their brothers and sisters in faith in less well-known texts. The present book aims to supplement the findings and challenge some of the conclusions of Jo Ann Cavallo's *The World beyond Europe in the Romance Epics of Boiardo and Ariosto* (2013), which came out even as I was writing up the doctoral thesis that forms the basis of my study. Cavallo's monograph is undoubtedly a valuable contribution to the scholarship on representations of Otherness in Italian narrative poetry. Its principal strength lies in the attention given to the *Inamoramento de Orlando*. Cavallo convincingly shows that Boiardo's representation of Saracens is on the whole remarkably positive. Like Antonio Franceschetti, Denise Alexandre-Gras, Gerhild Fuchs, Angelo Pagliardini, and, more recently, Roberto Galbiati,[19] she maintains that Boiardo does not draw a sharp line of distinction between Christians and Saracens and that there is much communication and interaction between characters of different faiths:

> Regardless of their provenance, Boiardo's characters are motivated by a range of passions — primarily love, ambition, empathy, and the desire for glory or revenge — but not by religious or ethnic differences. The narrative thereby breaks out of the binary opposition of Christians and Saracens typical of Carolingian epic, presenting a broader vision of the globe consonant with a number of ancient, medieval, and fifteenth-century historical and geographical texts that were capturing the attention of the Ferrarese court.[20]

One of the most original features of Cavallo's study is that she distinguishes between Saracens of different origins, analysing them in light of medieval and Renaissance perceptions of various non-Christian peoples. However, while containing a wealth

---

Eadem, 'Alleanze necessarie: cristiani, saraceni e persiani nell'*Altobello*', in *Il cantare italiano fra folklore e letteratura*, ed. by Michelangelo Picone and Luisa Rubini (Florence: Olschki, 2007), pp. 127–44; Eadem, 'Serialità e reinterpretazione: il caso dell'*Altobello* e del *Persiano*', in *Boiardo, Ariosto e i libri di battaglia*, ed. by Andrea Canova and Paola Vecchi Galli (Novara: Interlinea, 2007), pp. 107–26; and Eadem, 'Rifare secondo la norma: il *Falconetto* 1483 e il suo rifacimento in ottave', *Schifanoia*, 34–35 (2008), 251–58.

19  Antonio Franceschetti, 'Cristiani e pagani', in Idem, *L''Orlando Innamorato' e le sue componenti tematiche e strutturali* (Florence: Olschki, 1975), pp. 102–09; Denise Alexandre-Gras, 'Tre figure boiardesche di eroe saraceno: Ferraguto, Agricane, Rodamonte', *Annali d'Italianistica*, 1 (1983), 129–44; Eadem, 'La tolérance envers les païens', in Eadem, *L'héroïsme chevaleresque dans le 'Roland Amoureux' de Boiardo* (Saint-Etienne: Publications de l'Université de Saint-Etienne, 1988), pp. 300–17; Gerhild Fuchs and Angelo Pagliardini, 'La rappresentazione del pagano/musulmano nell'epica cavalleresca rinascimentale', in *Italia e Europa: dalla cultura nazionale all'interculturalismo, atti del XVI Congresso dell'A.I.P.I., Cracovia, 26–29 agosto 2004*, ed. by Bart van den Bossche et al., 2 vols (Florence: Franco Cesati, 2006), II, pp. 579–87; 'Raumkonzepte und Fremdbilder im Zusammenspiel: Zur Darstellungsweise des "Sarazenen" in Texten der italienischen Renaissance-Ritterepik', in *Grenzen und Entgrenzungen: historische und kulturwissenschaftliche Überlegungen am Beispiel des Mittelmeerraums*, ed. by Beate Burtscher-Bechter et al. (Würzburg: Königshausen & Neumann, 2006), pp. 173–209; Angelo Pagliardini, 'Cristiani e pagani nell'epica cavalleresca italiana', *Carte di viaggio*, 1 (2008), 35–58; Roberto Galbiati, 'Cristiani e pagani', in Idem, *Il romanzo e la corte: L''Inamoramento de Orlando' di Boiardo* (Rome: Carocci, 2018), pp. 11–15.

20  Jo Ann Cavallo, *The World beyond Europe in the Romance Epics of Boiardo and Ariosto* (Toronto: University of Toronto Press, 2013), p. 4. The book has been recently translated into Italian: *Il mondo oltre l'Europa nei poemi di Boiardo e Ariosto*, trans. by Corrado Confalonieri (Milan: Bruno Mondadori, 2017).

of interesting information and thought-provoking ideas, her study is weakened by the fact that she is too eager to find references to specific historical events and figures in Boiardo's and Ariosto's poems. Some of her arguments — such as the suggestion that Agramante's war in the *Inamoramento de Orlando* evokes the expansionistic ambitions of Mehmed II, with his ally Marsilio standing for Venice — are not supported by sufficient evidence to make them conclusive.[21] Moreover, she is rather dismissive of Boiardo's Carolingian sources: she mentions a few texts (such as the *Spagna* and Andrea da Barberino's *Aspramonte*) that could have been known to the poet without examining them in any significant depth.

The most controversial part of Cavallo's book is her discussion of the *Furioso* (to which she devotes less space than to the *Inamoramento*). She claims that while Boiardo believes that 'communication and increased knowledge can lead to the enlightenment of the individual and the improvement of human society at large',[22] this worldview is overturned in Ariosto's poem, where the war between the Christians and the Saracens 'increasingly takes on the connotations of a holy war' and the same Saracen characters 'are presented in a less favourable light and are judged more severely'.[23] Stressing the fact that the *Furioso* was composed in a period when Italians felt threatened by their neighbours from beyond the Alps, Cavallo maintains that narrating Agramante's campaign against Charlemagne Ariosto was probably thinking not only of the Turks but also of the European powers that sought to dominate Italy: 'the final defeat and destruction of Biserta may be read as a wish-fulfilment fantasy not simply of western Europe triumphing over Ottoman aggressors but of Italy over European invaders, and of Ferrara over neighbouring enemies on the peninsula'.[24]

Cavallo's stance is not particularly surprising in the context of Ariosto scholarship.[25] Other scholars have in fact argued that Ariosto's Saracens are portrayed negatively, especially in the 'epic' second half of the poem, with some reading the

21    Other scholars too have suggested that Boiardo's portrayal of Saracens could have been influenced by contemporary history. Arguing that Boiardo and his contemporaries abhorred the Turks, Antonio Panizzi does not conceal his own dislike of all things Muslim: he goes as far as to say that the crusades were a necessary act of self-defence. See his 'An Essay on the Romantic Narrative Poetry of the Italians', in *Orlando Innamorato di Bojardo, Orlando Furioso di Ariosto with an Essay on the Romantic Narrative Poetry of the Italians; Memoirs and Notes by Antonio Panizzi*, 9 vols (London: W. Pickering, 1830–1834), I, pp. 50–52; 'Life of Boiardo', ibid., II, pp. lxxiv–lxxvii. And see also Michael Murrin, 'Agramante's war', *Annali d'Italianistica*, 1 (1983), 107–28 (reprinted as chapter 3 in his *History and Warfare* (Chicago: University of Chicago Press, 1994)); Fabio Cossutta, *Gli ideali epici dell'umanesimo e l'*'Orlando innamorato' (Rome: Bulzoni, 1995), pp. 15–24 and pp. 439–64; Pia Schwarz Lausten, 'The Representation of Saracens in Boiardo's *Orlando Innamorato*' (paper given at the Annual Meeting of Renaissance Society of America, Los Angeles, 19–21 March, 2009); Giovanni Ricci, 'Cavalleria e crociata nella Ferrara del Rinascimento: Un piccolo stato davanti a un grande impero', *Italien und das Osmanische Reich*, ed. by Franziska Meier (Herne: Gabriele Schäfer Verlag, 2010), pp. 75–86.

22    Cavallo, *The World beyond Europe*, p. 256.

23    Ibid., pp. 4, 5.

24    Ibid., p. 207.

25    For a review of scholarly interpretations of Saracens in the *Furioso* see Maria Pavlova, 'Ludovico Ariosto and Islam', in *Christian-Muslim Relations: A Bibliographical History (1500–1600)*, ed. by David Thomas and John Chesworth (Leiden: Brill, 2014), pp. 469–83 (pp. 476–78).

poem in light of sixteenth-century anti-Muslim sentiment.[26] Nor is Cavallo's belief that the Saracen warriors represent European 'barbarians' entirely original: similar views have been expressed in studies on Ariosto's representation of warfare.[27] Pio Rajna and Marco Praloran, among others, have emphasized the ideological differences between the two *Orlandos*, contending that if Boiardo treats his Saracen characters with respect and even admiration, Ariosto degrades them.[28]

And yet more positive assessments of Ariosto's Saracens have been put forward too. As we shall see in Chapters IV and V, sixteenth-century interpreters of the poem often made positive comments about individual Saracen characters. Francesco Patrizi, a distinguished Platonic philosopher (who was very conscious of the Ottoman threat and even published a treatise — *Paralleli militari* (1594) — on strategies that could be used to fight the Turks), did not think that Ariosto adopted a binary worldview:

> Nel Furioso molti sono i buoni, Ruggiero, Bradamante, Orlando, Carlo, Brandimarte, Fiordiligi, Isabella, & altri. E pur nel paganesimo, Agramante, Sobrino, Gradasso, Sacripante, Marfisa, & altri se bontà non hanno, sono per certo privi di malizia.

26 According to Roger Baillet, 'les païens sont représentatifs d'une barbarie orientale contre laquelle l'Arioste déclenche une offensive fort proche, dans ces buts et dans ces moyens, des guerres anti-barbaresques de son temps' [the pagans represent an oriental barbarism against which Ariosto launches an attack which closely resembles, in its aims and means, the wars against Barbary fought in his day] (Roger Baillet, 'L'occidentalisme', in Idem, *Le monde poétique de l'Arioste: essai d'interprétation du 'Roland Furieux'* (Lyon: Editions l'Hermès, 1977), pp. 385–424 (p. 424)). See also Pia Schwarz Lausten, 'Saraceni e Turchi nell'*Orlando Furioso* di Ariosto', in *Studi di Italianistica nordica: Atti del X Convegno degli italianisti scandinavi, Università d'Islanda, Università di Bergen, Reykjavik, 13–15 giugno 2013*, ed. by Marco Gargiulo, Margareth Hagen, and Stefano Rosatti (Rome: Aracne Editrice, 2014), pp. 261–86.

27 Adelin Charles Fiorato, for example, argues that 'tra i "giovenil furori d'Agramante" o il brutale furore di Rodomonte, e la "furia francese" degli invasori oltramontani, c'è una relazione tematica e simbolica evidente' [there is an obvious thematic and symbolic relation between the 'youthful rage of Agramante' or Rodomonte's brutal rage and the 'French rage' of the invaders from beyond the Alps] (Adelin Charles Fiorato, 'La "gallica face" nell'*Orlando Furioso*', in *La corte di Ferrara e il suo mecenatismo, 1441–1598*, ed. by Marianne Pade, Lene Waage Petersen and Daniela Quarta (Modena: Panini, 1990), pp. 159–76 (p. 161)). According to Paul Larivaille, 'si potrebbe [...] parlare di una proiezione della realtà contemporanea sulla materia cavalleresca, una proiezione basata su una duplice equivalenza fra cristiani e italiani da una parte, e dall'altra fra saraceni e barbari: spagnuoli, tedeschi, svizzeri, francesi, tutti "lupi di più ingorde brame" venuti "da boschi oltramontani a divorarne" (XVII, 4)' [one could [...] talk of a projection of contemporary reality onto the chivalric subject matter, a projection based on the double association between Christians and Italians on the one hand, and, on the other hand, between Saracens and barbarians: Spaniards, Germans, Swiss, French, all of them 'wolves with even greedier appetites' coming from 'forests beyond the mountains to join in the feast' (XVII, 4)] (Paul Larivaille, 'Guerra e ideologia nel "Furioso"', *Chroniques italiennes*, 19 (2001), 1–20 (p. 4) <http://chroniquesitaliennes.univ-paris3.fr/PDF/web19/Larivailleweb19.pdf> [consulted 16 January 2020]).

28 See Pio Rajna, *Le fonti dell'Orlando furioso* (Florence: Sansoni, 1900), p. 59. According to Marco Praloran, 'In Boiardo [...] i grandi eroi non sono mai malvagi [...]' [in Boiardo [...] the great heroes are never evil], while in Ariosto 'via via si fa progressivamente viva una prospettiva ideologicamente orientata sugli eventi per cui i grandi guerrieri sono investiti da connotazioni etiche opposte [...]' [an ideological prospective on events gradually emerges, because of which the great warriors are given divergent ethical connotations] (Marco Praloran, *Le lingue del racconto: Studi su Boiardo e Ariosto* (Rome: Bulzoni, 2009), pp. 171–72).

[In the Furioso there are numerous good characters, Ruggiero, Bradamante, Orlando, Carlo, Brandimarte, Fiordiligi, Isabella, and others. And even in the pagan camp, Agramante, Sobrino, Gradasso, Sacripante, Marfisa, and others, if they are not good, they are certainly devoid of malice][29]

In 1554 Giovan Battista Pigna hoped that Ariosto's fame would spread beyond Europe and that the Arabs and the Turks would translate the *Furioso* into their languages.[30] Three decades later some Italian intellectuals believed that that the poem had been translated into Arabic and was well known in the Arab world (which, as far as I know, is not true).[31] Nor is it fair to say that modern Ariosto scholars have only offered negative interpretations of the *Furioso*'s Saracens. According to John Patrick Donnelly, the *Furioso* 'reveal[s] no prejudice based on a sense of the superiority of western culture over oriental civilization'.[32] Vincent Cuccaro, in turn, asserts that 'Virtue, heroic valor, wisdom, loyalty, God, are not exclusively Christian, just as bestiality, madness, betrayal, evil, or Satan are not exclusively Pagan'.[33] Fuchs and Pagliardini maintain that the boundary between Christians and Saracens is fluid in all three chivalric masterpieces of the Italian Renaissance, namely in Pulci's *Morgante* and the two *Orlandos*. Moreover, recent years have seen the publication of a number of studies seeking to 'give a voice' to individual Saracen heroes. Gian Paolo Giudicetti, for example, goes as far as to claim that it is characters such as Mandricardo — a carefree, happy-go-lucky knight — who embody the aesthetic values of the poem.[34]

29    Francesco Patrizi, *Parere in difesa dell'Ariosto*, in *Apologia del sig. Torquato Tasso in difesa della sua Gierusalemme liberata* (Ferrara: Giulio Cesare Cagnacini, et Fratelli, 1585), fols L4$^r$-N2$^r$ (fol. M6$^r$).

30    Giovan Battista Pigna, *I romanzi*, ed. by Salvatore Ritrovato (Bologna: Commissione per i Testi di Lingua, 1997), p. 73.

31    In his *Il Carrafa o vero della epica poesia* [1584], Camillo Pellegrino says that 'insino all'Arabica (se vero è quel che si dice) è stata vaga di cantarlo [il *Furioso*], o di ragionarlo: il che non è avvenuto (per quel ch'io sappia) di nessun altro libro nell'età nostra, et forse nelle passate' [even the Arabic [language] (if we believe what people say) has been eager to sing it [the *Furioso*] or recount it: which has not happened (as far as I know) to any other book in our times and maybe not even in the past]. This passage is cited in Lionardo Salviati, *Degli Accademici della Crusca difesa dell'Orlando Furioso dell'Ariosto contra 'l dialogo dell'epica poesia di Cammillo Pellegrino*, in *Apologia del sig. Torquato Tasso*, fols A 1$^r$-G 8$^v$ (fol. B 6$^v$). In reality, Ariosto's fame did not reach beyond the borders of Europe, even if the *Furioso* may have been read by Leone Africano (al-Ḥasan ibn Muhammad al-Wazzān al-Fāsī), a diplomat of the Sultan of Fez, who in 1518 was captured by corsairs and taken to Rome, where he converted to Christianity and wrote *Della descrittione dell'Africa* (1526). In it, he compares 'i fatti d'Orlando' [the Orlando stories] to the Arabic epic tradition, remarking that his compatriots are as fond of Hellul as the Italians are of Orlando (Leone Africano, *Della descrittione dell'Africa*, in Giovanni Battista Ramusio, *Navigationi et viaggi: Venice (1563–1606)*, with an introduction by Raleigh Ashlin Skelton and an analysis of the contents by George B. Parks, 3 vols (Amsterdam: Theatrum Orbis Terrarum, 1967–1970), I (facsimile edition of the 1563 Giunti edition of the first volume), fols 1$^r$–95$^v$ (fol. 49$^v$)). The only partial Arabic translation of the *Furioso* I am aware of is the one by 'Abd al-Fattāḥ Ḥasan (عبدالفتاح حسن), a university lecturer and an *imam*, who translated passages from the poem for his doctoral dissertation on the interplay between reality and fiction in Ariosto (Ain Shams University, Cairo, 2004).

32    John Patrick Donnelly, 'The Moslem Enemy in Renaissance Epic: Ariosto, Tasso and Camoëns', *Yale Italian Studies*, 1, no. 2 (1977), 162–70 (p. 163).

33    Vincent Cuccaro, *The Humanism of Ludovico Ariosto: from the "Satire" to the "Furioso"* (Ravenna: Longo, 1981), p. 146.

34    Gian Paolo Giudicetti, *Mandricardo e la melanconia. Discorsi diretti e sproloqui nell'"Orlando Furioso"*

The very fact that scholars have proposed starkly contrasting interpretations of Ariosto's portrayal of Saracens is intriguing: it testifies to the bewildering complexity of the poem. It is the contention of the present book that this complexity can only be made sense of if we restore the *Furioso* to its original literary context. In order to do so, one must consider not only Ariosto's direct and most obvious chivalric sources (i.e. Boiardo), but also other possible sources that feature thematically — rather than stylistically and textually — in the rich tapestry of the *Furioso* and which may have influenced its portrayal of the Saracen Other in more profound ways than Ariosto's classical models.[35] After all, the figure of the Saracen is absent from Virgil's *Aeneid* and other classical epics, which some scholars see as occupying a higher and more important place in the hierarchy of Ariosto's literary sources. The notion of 'intertestualità cavalleresca' [chivalric intertextuality] — first coined by Antonia Tissoni Benvenuti and subsequently elaborated by Eleonora Stoppino — is central to my methodological approach. The Renaissance Carolingian tradition, to which Boiardo and Ariosto belong, consisted of dozens of texts centred on the same cast of characters — Orlando, Rinaldo, Astolfo, but also the king of Saracen Spain Marsilio, his vassals, and a number of other knights, damsels, and magicians. As Stoppino puts it, 'the characters in these poems were [...], for the early modern public, constellations of literary memories'.[36] An early modern reader would be familiar with the previous incarnations of Boiardo's and Ariosto's characters and would derive pleasure from recognizing the traits that these characters already had in earlier texts as well as any innovative elements in their representations. Moreover, they would be able to appreciate the creativity with which Boiardo and Ariosto incorporated familiar character types (e.g. Orlando's Saracen friend, the Saracen male lover or the Saracen princess) into their stories. In her study of the *Furioso*, Stoppino distinguishes between 'first degree intertexts' (i.e. 'directly imitated' texts) and 'second degree intertexts' (texts that are 'indirectly present' in Ariosto through other texts).[37] Both types of intertexts will be examined in the chapters that follow with an eye to determining what, if anything, is unique in Boiardo's and Ariosto's portrayals of Saracens. The selection of chivalric material for this study is deliberately as inclusive as possible, ranging from more well-known chivalric works (or *libri di battaglia*, as these texts were often called at the time), some of which were composed by rather talented authors and dedicated to powerful individuals, to anonymous *cantari* (which were mostly intended for popular consumption).

(Brussels: Peter Lang, 2010), p. 27. See also Idem, 'Mandricardo a cavallo di due poemi: il suo ruolo nel terzo libro dell'*Inamoramento de Orlando* e nell'*Orlando Furioso*', *Schifanoia*, 36–37 (2009), 103–44.

35   In an important study on intertextuality Cesare Segre distinguishes between different approaches to studying Ariosto's sources, observing that some scholars look for thematic affinities between the *Furioso* and its (mostly vernacular chivalric) sources while others look for direct textual borrowings, mostly focusing on classical texts and the works of illustrious vernacular poets. Segre suggests that Ariosto may have imitated vernacular and classical texts in different ways (Cesare Segre, 'Intertestualità e interdiscorsività nel romanzo e nella poesia', in Idem, *Teatro e romanzo: Due tipi di comunicazione letteraria* (Turin: Einaudi, 1984), pp. 103–18). Eleonora Stoppino uses Segre's hypothesis in her illuminating study of the figure of Bradamante and the dynastic theme in the *Furioso* (Stoppino, *Genealogies of Fiction*).

36   Stoppino, *Genealogies of Fiction*, p 18.

37   Ibid., p. 34.

The present book devotes approximately half of its pages to the *Inamoramento de Orlando*. Chapter II shows that Boiardo's treatment of the Saracen characters he 'borrows' or inherits from earlier chivalric texts and compilations is to a large extent consistent with their earlier literary representations, which are far from simplistic. The intricate stories of these characters reveal that the Christian universe of the *Inamoramento de Orlando* and other Carolingian texts is indebted and inextricably linked to the Saracen universe. Chapter III analyses the Saracens' contribution to the 'revolutionary' chivalric ideology that underpins the *Inamoramento de Orlando*. It also assesses the significance of Agramante's and Rugiero's descent from Alexander the Great in light of the theme of antiquity in Italian chivalric literature, with a special focus on the four Italian versions of the Old French *Chanson d'Aspremont*, whose Saracen characters are related to Alexander. Chapters IV and V are devoted to Ariosto. Chapter IV investigates the elements of rupture and continuity between the representations of Saracens in the two *Orlandos* in order to determine in what ways and to what extent their Saracen worlds can be said to mirror each other. Chapter V deals with the climactic confrontation between Rodomonte and Ruggiero in the final canto of the *Furioso*, arguing that the ending of Ariosto's poem is far more indebted to Boiardo and the chivalric tradition (especially to texts such as the *Aspramonte* and the *Vendetta di Falconetto*) than it is to Virgil. It also suggests that Ariosto's treatment of Ruggiero, the Saracen-turned-Christian dynastic hero, is in some respects similar to how he is portrayed in Nicolò degli Agostini and Raffaele Valcieco, whose sequels to the *Inamoramento de Orlando* were published two years before the first *Furioso*.

Before delving into the rich world of medieval and Renaissance Italian chivalric stories, I consider the influence of contemporary history and Western knowledge of Islam on the two *Orlandos*. Chapter I assesses the degree of realism present in Boiardo's and Ariosto's portrayals of Islam and Islamic culture. Then it broaches the so-called *questione turca*. It is perhaps no coincidence that the 'golden age' of the Italian chivalric tradition — the decades that gave birth to the *Morgante*, the *Inamoramento de Orlando*, the *Mambriano* and the *Furioso*, as well as to a plethora of anonymous poems, many of which are named after their Saracen heroes (the *Altobello*, the *Ancroia*, the *Antiphor de Barosia*, the *Dama Rovenza*, the *Falconetto*, and the *Vendetta di Falconetto*) — was also a period when the relations between Italy and the Islamic world were particularly vibrant.[38] The conquest of Constantinople by Mehmed II (1453) dramatically altered the international political map, bringing the East and the West closer together. The Turkish threat loomed over Christendom already in the second half of the fourteenth and the first half of the fifteenth centuries, but after the capture of the capital of the Byzantine Empire the Ottomans became an integral part of Italian international politics. At the same time, some city-states maintained diplomatic and commercial relations with other Islamic states, such as Egypt (the Venetians' commercial partner since the early thirteenth century), Persia, or Barbary. The Italians probably had more first-hand experience

---

38   The exact dates of composition of these chivalric texts are not clear. Some of them may have been composed earlier.

of the Islamic world than any other European nation (with the exception of the Ottomans' East European neighbours and the Spanish who coexisted with Muslims until 1492, when Granada, the last Islamic kingdom on the Iberian peninsula, fell to the armies of Isabella I of Castile and Ferdinand II of Aragon), but the degree and nature of interaction with the Ottoman Empire and/or other Islamic states and, more generally, the level of interest in non-Christian lands varied considerably from city to city. This must be taken into consideration when looking for possible allusions to contemporary historical events or traces of contemporary knowledge of Islam and Islamic culture in chivalric texts. Although it could be said that most Italian chivalric romances of the late Middle Ages and the early Renaissance were to some extent bound up with the contemporary perceptions of Muslims, some texts were more directly engaged with historical reality than others.

Although this book does not read the two *Orlandos* through a postcolonial lens, analysing the innovative and ideologically pre-conceived elements in Boiardo's and Ariosto's portrayals of Saracens, it engages with a number of recent studies that appropriate postcolonial theory, such as those by Sharon Kinoshita.[39] The postcolonial theoretical model can be a useful tool to study the formation of medieval and early modern identities, provided that one is aware of the pitfalls of applying it to a period that precedes modern colonialism and nationalism. An uncritical application of this theory to pre-modern Europe can easily result in anachronistic and oversimplified interpretations of the history of Europe's relationship the East, especially when this problem is viewed from the perspective of a land such as Italy, which did not exist as a sovereign state before 1861. According to Edward Said's important yet controversial study, Europe, since the days of Homer, has identified the Orient as its Other, portraying it as backward, exotic, sensuous, effeminate, and uncivilized. Said contends that 'European culture gained in strength and identity by setting itself off against the Orient as a sort of surrogate and even underground self' and that, through this misrepresentation, the West sought to establish its hegemony over the East.[40] Tracing the origins of Orientalism to ancient Greece, he suggests that Dante, Ariosto, Milton, and other Western poets contributed to the creation of the Orientalist imagery in Western literatures. While doing so, however, he does not closely examine these poets and the cultural and political contexts from which they emerged, but rather assumes that their portrayals of the East must have been shaped by the centuries-old reductive views. Convinced that there is strong continuity between ancient, medieval, Renaissance and modern Western perceptions of the East, Said extends his theory — which is mostly concerned with the last three centuries — to include all Western literary history, thus failing to do justice to the complexity of cultural exchanges and understandings of identity and alterity in the Middle Ages and the Renaissance.

Unsurprisingly, postcolonial theory has attracted much criticism from scholars

---

39   Sharon Kinoshita, ' "Pagans are wrong and Christians are right": Alterity, Gender, and Nation in the *Chanson de Roland*', in *Race and Ethnicity in the Middle Ages*, ed. by Thomas Hahn, *The Journal of Medieval and Early Modern Studies*, 31, no. 1 (Winter 2001), 79–111; Eadem, *Medieval Boundaries: Rethinking Difference in Old French Literature* (Philadelphia: University of Pennsylvania Press, 2006).

40   Edward W. Said, *Orientalism* (London: Penguin, 1978), p. 3.

of medieval and Renaissance history, art and literature.[41] Lisa Jardine and Jerry Brotton caution against applying it to the Renaissance in no ambiguous terms, maintaining that 'an account of the marginalized, exoticized, dangerous East within Renaissance studies' is 'not only politically unhelpful but also historically inaccurate', being a 'retrospective construction of nineteenth-century ideology'.[42] In her influential monograph on the Renaissance humanists' perceptions of the Turks, Nancy Bisaha notes that 'Renaissance humanists [...] present some important challenges to Said's model', as it 'focuses on colonialism as a key component in the formation of the West-East discourse' and 'does not help explain expressions of relativism' among some humanists.[43] Indeed, delving into the vast body of Italian Renaissance literature dealing with the East and, more generally, with cultural and religious alterity, one is bound to find attitudes that do not fit Said's theory, not least because 'there was no one Oriental "other" in the fifteenth and sixteenth centuries'.[44] As has been brilliantly demonstrated by Margaret Meserve, for fifteenth- and sixteenth-century Italians the East was not one abstract entity, but rather it consisted of 'a bewildering geopolitical chessboard of Islamic polities' with which Italy had diplomatic, commercial and cultural exchanges and which were perceived differently by different groups of people.[45] Despite the fact that Italian chivalric romances often contain stereotypical depictions of Islam and Islamic culture, and that the themes of conquest and conversion are certainly not uncommon in this kind of literature (conversion being a way of dominating the Other, and mass conversions bringing to mind the phenomenon of colonialism), the postcolonial model does not satisfactorily capture the nuances and diversity of literary portrayals of Saracens, or for that matter, of real-life cultural and political contacts between Italian nobles and their Muslim counterparts.

This is not to say it is futile to interrogate medieval and Renaissance texts in the hope of finding attitudes that would later facilitate the emergence of European colonial expansionism and nationalism. Recent decades have seen the publication of a number of monographs — with medieval Britain receiving the lion's share of scholarly attention — that provide thought-provoking insights into the possible medieval origins of European colonial ideologies.[46] But, as Sharon

---

41    For a detailed rebuttal of Said's *Orientalism*, see Robert Irwin, *For Lust of Knowing: the Orientalists and their Enemies* (London: Allen Lane, 2006); Ibn Warraq, *Defending the West: a Critique of Edward Said's Orientalism* (New York: Prometheus Books, 2007).

42    Lisa Jardine and Jerry Brotton, *Global Interests: Renaissance Art Between East and West* (London: Reaktion, 2000), p. 61.

43    Nancy Bisaha, *Creating East and West: Renaissance Humanists and the Ottoman Turks* (Philadelphia: University of Pennsylvania Press, 2004), p. 6.

44    Margaret Meserve, *Empires of Islam in Renaissance Historical Thought* (Cambridge, MA: Harvard University Press, 2008), p. 11.

45    Ibid.

46    Suzanne Conklin Akbari draws upon Said's theory in her *Idols in the East: European Representations of Islam and the Orient, 1100–1450* (New York: Cornell University Press, 2009), albeit with some reservations, observing, for example, that Said does not take into account the fact that in the Middle Ages the East was richer and technologically more advanced that the West. See also *The Postcolonial Middle Ages*, ed. by Jeffrey Jerome Cohen (New York: Palgrave, 2000); Geraldine Heng, *Empire of Magic: Medieval Romance and the Politics of Cultural Fantasy* (New York: Columbia University

Kinoshita states in the introduction to her *Medieval Boundaries: Rethinking Difference in Old French Literature*, 'postcolonial medievalism's disproportionate focus on the English fourteenth century has produced a skewed impression of a proto-modern Middle Ages in which nascent phases of nationalism, colonialism, and Orientalism are always already visible'.[47] In examining representations of alterity in Old French texts, Kinoshita stresses the importance of 'making an initial effort of defamiliarization' when mapping the medieval French-speaking world whose geographical bounds did not correspond to those of modern-day France.[48] When analysing perceptions of the non-Christian Other in Italian Renaissance texts, it is of paramount importance to take into account the political fragmentation of the Italian peninsula. Fifteenth- and early sixteenth-century Italy was not a united country but a collection of duchies and city-states with rivalries — often leading to violent conflicts — between the ruling families. During the upheavals of the Italian Wars the survival of small city-states like Ferrara and Mantua — flourishing centres of Renaissance chivalry and chivalric literature — depended on their alliances with more powerful neighbours, such as Venice and the Papal States, but also France and the Holy Roman Empire. The Ottoman Empire, too, was a powerful player on the international political arena and, as such, it could be both a terrifying enemy and a desirable ally, as can be seen from the enduring friendship between Marquis Francesco II Gonzaga of Mantua (the husband of Isabella d'Este and a keen reader of Boiardo and Ariosto) and the Turkish Sultan Bayezid II, which will be treated in Chapter I. The present study, therefore, starts from the premise that in a period when alliances were formed and broken easily, and political relationships were in a state of considerable flux, identities were often fluid and complex, and the boundary between the self and the Other — both Christian and non-Christian — porous and shifting.

As the Renaissance progressed, identities became more solid and well defined. The Reformation (which, it is worth stressing, started *after* the publication of the 1516 *Furioso*) and the Counter-Reformation strengthened the Catholic identity of the Italian upper classes. As Sergio Zatti observes in the foreword to *La rappresentazione dell'Altro nei testi del Rinascimento*, a pioneering study of representations of Otherness in Italian Renaissance literature, 'L'Altro è, [...] con evidenza sempre crescente, sia colui che è esterno alla nostra storia, sia colui che è escluso dalla nostra società' [The Other is, as becomes increasingly obvious, both someone who is external to our history and someone who is excluded from our society].[49] But the period that is the focus of this book was different, at least if we consider it from the perspective of small Italian principalities that were not under imminent threat from the Turks. As will be shown in Chapter I, Boiardo's and Ariosto's early readers displayed curiosity

Press, 2003); and Eadem, *The Invention of Race in the European Middle Ages* (Cambridge: Cambridge University Press, 2018). As for the 'postcolonial' Renaissance, see Shankar Raman, *Renaissance Literature and Postcolonial Studies* (Edinburgh: Edinburgh University Press, 2011).

47    Kinoshita, *Medieval Boundaries*, pp. 4–5.

48    Ibid., pp. 5–6.

49    Sergio Zatti, 'Premessa', in *La rappresentazione dell'Altro nei testi del Rinascimento*, ed. by Sergio Zatti (Lucca: Maria Pacini, 1998), pp. 7–10 (p. 10).

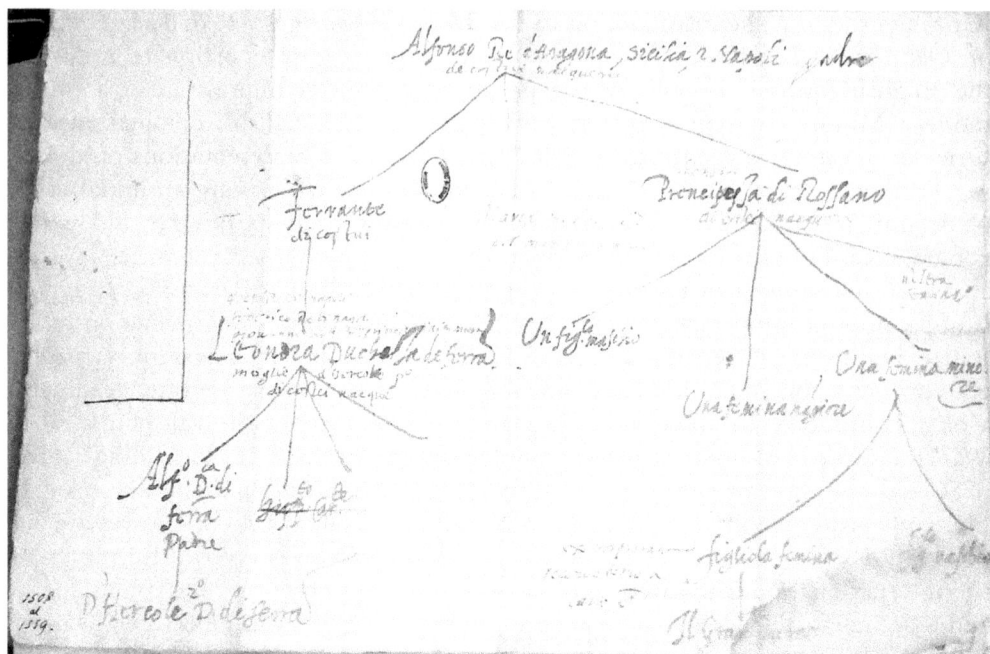

FIG. I.I. Sketch of the Este genealogical tree (1556). Modena, Archivio di Stato, Archivio Segreto Estense, Principi Esteri, busta 1612

and openness towards different parts of the Islamic world, without necessarily constructing a rigidly oppositional self/Other identity.

Nor was this spirit of openness completely stifled even in the wake of the Counter-Reformation. Several decades after the publication of the third and final *Furioso* in 1532, Giovan Battista Giraldi Cinthio, a prominent intellectual and admirer of Ariosto, praised Ercole II d'Este for offering hospitality to the Hafsid Sultan Mohammed Hassan and then to the envoy of the future Ottoman Sultan Selim II, the son of Süleyman the Magnificent.[50] The Este Archive contains

---

50    Having been dethroned and blinded by his own son, Mohammed Hassan arrived in Ferrara in March 1548. Feeling sorry for his plight, 'licet barbari, & à religione nostra penitus alieni' [although he was a barbarian and very distant from our religion], Ercole had him treated (albeit unsuccessfully) by the best doctors and showered him with gifts. Word of this act of kindness and generosity reached the ears of Selim who then sent 'Cassanum Chaus nobilem familiarem suum Corcyrae oriundum cum perhumanis ad eum literis Herculem usque Ferrariam salutatum [...], cum amplissima praeclarissimae illius in eum voluntatis testificatione, quem nuntium, & large, & benignissime Hercules suscepit, & Regiis muneribus liberaliter ornatum ad Principem, qui eum miserat, remisit, cum summa suae erga illum voluntatis, testificatione' [Hassan Chaus, his noble servant born in Corfu, to Ferrara with his most affectionate letters to greet Ercole, with most ample proofs of his immense goodwill towards him. Ercole received this ambassador courteously and most kindly and, having generously given him regal gifts, sent him back to the Prince who had sent him, with supreme proofs of his goodwill towards him] (Giovan Battista Giraldi Cinthio, *Ab epistolis de Ferraria et Atestinis principibus commentariolum ex Lilii Gregorii Gyraldi epitome deductum* (Ferrara: Francesco de' Rossi, 1556), fol. 77ʳ). On Mohammed Hassan's visit to Ferrara, see Giovanni Ricci, *I turchi alle porte* (Bologna: Il Mulino, 2008) p. 156.

little-known letters that shed fascinating light on the latter visit: having been told by Rüstem Pasha Opuković (*c.* 1500–1561), grand vezir to Sultan Süleyman the Magnificent, that he and the Duke of Ferrara were blood relatives, Selim sent a certain Hasan Cavus (from the Turkish word *çavuş,* meaning 'messenger') to find out if there was indeed a blood tie between him and the 'Signior di signiori [...] de gran legniazo degnio di nostra parentella nostro Cl.ᵐᵒ Signor di Ferrara' [Lord of lords [...] of noble lineage worthy of our kinship our illustrious Lord of Ferrara].⁵¹ For his part, Ercole II was happy to oblige his Turkish 'relative': in his reply he explained that 'la mia bassa, e vilissima casa' [my low, and most humble house] and 'la potentissima di Vᵗᵃ Altezza' [the most powerful [house] of your Highness] were related through Selim's 'avia' [grandmother].⁵² As can be gleaned from the sketch of the Este genealogical tree (where we see Cardinal Ippolito next to the 'Gran Turco') [FIG. 1] and some explanatory comments now preserved in ASM, Principi Esteri, busta 1612, this 'avia' was a noblewoman who descended from Alfonso I of Naples (the grandfather of Eleonora d'Aragona, wife of Ercole I d'Este, mother of Alfonso I d'Este and grandmother of Ercole II). She was allegedly kidnapped by the Turks in Schiavonia and then, in a spectacular turn of fortune, became the wife of the Ottoman sultan Selim I.⁵³

This curious episode in the history of the relations between Ferrara and Ottoman Turkey cannot but remind us of the two *Orlandos*: Boiardo makes a Saracen knight the progenitor of the Este dynasty, while Ariosto ends the *Furioso* with the cross-cultural marriage of Bradamante and Ruggiero. Regardless of whether the story of Selim's mysterious grandmother may be true or not, the very fact that a descendant of Cardinal Ippolito and Alfonso I believed that he was related to the Ottoman sultans and was eager to tell a Turkish prince how proud he was of their kinship shows that Renaissance nobles — even during the Counter-Reformation — shared a certain unity despite being 'di fé diversi' [of different faiths] (*Fur.*, I 22,2 ABC).⁵⁴ As we shall see in Chapter I, stories of marriages between Muslims and Christians, of powerful rulers born to parents belonging to different worlds, and of friendships between Italian princes and their Muslim counterparts were possible not only in chivalric literature but also in real life and often in a way that resembled the adventure-packed lives of fictional Christians and Saracens.

---

51   Modena, Archivio di Stato, Archivio Segreto Estense, Principi Esteri, busta 1612. I am citing from an Italian translation of Selim's letter completed on Ercole's request. The Turkish original has been published by Assunta Vitelli (Assunta Vitelli, 'I documenti turchi dell'Archivio di Stato di Modena', *Annali dell'Università degli Studi di Napoli "L'Orientale"*, 54, no. 3 (1994), 317–48 (pp. 333–34)).

52   Modena, Archivio di Stato, Archivio Segreto Estense, Principi Esteri, busta 1644.

53   Ercole seems to be referring to Hafsa Hatun, wife of Selim I and mother of Süleyman the Magnificent, whose origins are shrouded in mystery and who died in 1534. Some historians believe that she was a Christian convert to Islam.

54   Ludovico Muratori, for one, abstains from commenting on the likelihood of this story being true (see Ludovico Antonio Muratori, *Delle antichità estensi continuazione, o sia parte seconda* (Modena: Stamperia Ducale, 1740), p. 381).

# CHAPTER 1

❖

# Between History and Imagination: The Two *Orlandos* and Contemporary Perceptions of Non-Christians

Old French heroic poetry contains highly distorted and often comic representations of Islam and Islamic culture. According to Norman Daniel, this either means that the poets were 'in total ignorance, not only of Arabs and Islam, but of everything Christian writers said about them', or that they were 'completely indifferent to both' and gave free rein to their imagination, aiming, first and foremost, to compose entertaining stories (the latter possibility being, as Daniel puts it, 'surprising', and the former downright 'incredible').[1] This is not to say that the Crusades and contemporary perceptions of Muslims had no influence at all on the development of the genre: Daniel observes that, as a general rule, Saracens are portrayed with more hostility in earlier poems and that occasionally one comes across texts (such as the fourteenth-century Franco-Venetian *Entrée d'Espagne*) that are 'fertile with surprises, clerical, intellectual'.[2] Though in many respects intentionally unrealistic, the *chansons de geste* offer a reflection of some aspects of historical reality. Paul Bancourt's painstaking analysis reveals that the titles of Saracen leaders in the *chansons de geste* often derive from Arabic words and sometimes correspond to real titles, that the conditions in which Christian prisoners are held are not totally unlike those that real prisoners had to endure, and that the poets refer to combat tactics used by historical Muslims. Bancourt contends that Saracen knights become noticeably more chivalrous in poems composed at the end of the twelfth century, which he believes to be the consequence 'd'une découverte accomplie par les Francs au cours de leurs contacts historiques avec les musulmans: celle de l'existence, chez les Arabes, chez Saladin, chez les princes ayyubides, de traditions chevaleresques proches de celles de la chevalerie chrétienne d'Occident' [a discovery made by the Franks in the course of their historical contacts with Muslims: that of the existence, among the Arabs, Saladin, the Ayubbid princes, of chivalric traditions that resemble those of Christian chivalry in the West].[3]

---

1    Daniel, *Heroes and Saracens*, p. 93.
2    Ibid., p. 127.
3    Bancourt, *Les musulmans dans les chansons de geste du Cycle du roi*, p. 1009.

The following question arises at this point: how do Italian medieval and Renaissance *libri di battaglia* [battle books] differ from their French counterparts? Do Italian authors copy their French sources? Or do they offer more realistic and more sympathetic portrayals of Islam? Are they interested in real Muslims and do they ever make references to real history? Did they know anything about chivalry in the Islamic world? These questions will be addressed in the present chapter. I shall begin by examining the interplay between what may be called conventional elements in Boiardo's and Ariosto's representations of the Saracen religion and culture(s) — elements that are already present in the *chansons de geste* — and more realistic elements that clearly depart from accepted ways of portraying Islam and the East. I shall then try to establish whether, to what extent and in which manner the two *Orlandos* reflect contemporary views of Muslims. In order to do so, I shall consider how the Turks and other non-Christian peoples were perceived in Renaissance Ferrara and its neighbouring city-states. Rather than focusing solely on Boiardo and Ariosto, this chapter will analyze these two poems in the light of the representations of Islam and Islamic culture in the Italian chivalric tradition as a whole (thus hoping to provide a useful general discussion of the historical referentiality of Italian chivalric narratives), while also taking into consideration such 'hybrid' texts as *cantari* on contemporary wars belonging to the 'guerre contro il turco' cycle.

Before proceeding further, a brief digression on terminology is necessary. Henceforth I shall use the term *Saracen* to refer to Muslims in chivalric literature both because, together with *pagano*, it is the term most frequently used in chivalric stories and because there are notable differences between fictional Saracens and historical Muslims, of which, as we shall soon see, Boiardo and Ariosto were aware. For the ancients, *Sarakènoi* (in Greek) or *Saraceni* (in Latin) were the members of a nomadic tribe from Arabia which lived on the banks of the Tigris and Euphrates. In the high Middle Ages the term *Saracen* was often applied indiscriminately to all Muslims and even to other non-Christians. The word *Muslim*, by contrast, entered Italian and other European languages relatively late. According to Tullio De Mauro's *Grande dizionario italiano dell'uso*, the first occurrence of *musulmano* dates back to 1557, the year of the publication of Cristoforo Armeno's *Peregrinaggio di tre giovani figliuoli del re di Serendippo*.[4] As a matter of fact, it occurs in a handful of earlier texts too: in the 1517 Italian translation of the account of Selim I's conquest of Egypt written by the Ottoman historian Şemseddin Ahmed (also known as Ibn Kemal),[5] in Giovanni Antonio Menavino's history of the Turkish people (published in

---

4    *Grande dizionario italiano dell'uso*, ed. by Tullio De Mauro, 6 vols (Turin: UTET, 1999–2000), IV.
5    '[...] lo exercito de li boni mussulmani [...]' [the army of good Muslims] (*Storia della distruzione de Mamaluchi ovvero Circassi e battaglie fatte contro di loro per L'Illmo Sig.e Sultan Selim, composta per il Cadi Lascher mandata ad un suo amico in Costantinopoli, tradotta dalla lingua Turca in Lingua Italiana*, Mantua, Archivio di Stato, busta 85, fols 59ʳ-74ᵛ (fol. 60ᵛ)). This translation is also reproduced in Marin Sanudo's *Diarii* (on this latter copy, see Giampiero Bellingeri, 'Turchi e Persiani fra visioni abnormi e normalizzazioni, a Venezia (secoli XV-XVIII)', *Revue des littératures européennes*, 9 (2015), 14–89 (pp. 57–58n)).

1548),[6] and, with many variants, in a number of fifteenth-century texts (*insulmani* in Bernardino Zambotti's *Diario ferrarese*, *monsormino* and *masormino* in the *Trabisonda*, a chivalric poem first published in 1483, and *mussurmanno* in the *Morgante* and the *Ciriffo Calvaneo*).[7] Boiardo and Ariosto, both of whom were familiar with Pulci's *Morgante*, must have come across this term, but they do not use it in their poems. In addition to *saracino* and *pagano*, Ariosto employs the term *moro* when referring to the Saracen warriors: in the *Furioso* and other chivalric texts it can variously mean 'North African', 'black African', 'Arab', 'Spanish Arab' or simply 'Muslim'. In Boiardo it appears only once, at *Inam.*, III vi 7,2. Finally, the term *arabo*, which features in both poems, is used to designate the Bedouins.

## The Saracen religion

One of the most glaring examples of the misrepresentation of Islam in the *chansons de geste* is that Saracen characters are invariably portrayed as polytheists worshipping a pantheon of gods. In addition to their main gods (the 'Saracen Trinity' formed by Machon, Apolin and Tervagan), the Saracens revere a plethora of other deities, including some Greco-Roman gods, such as Mars and Venus.[8] The Saracens erect images of these gods as massive statues of precious metals that are kept in 'mahomeries' (mosques) and often paraded in front of the faithful. While it is possible that some of the poets genuinely believed that Islam was a polytheistic idolatry (after all, as Bancourt points out, Muslims are depicted as polytheists in the chronicles of the First Crusade),[9] it is highly unlikely that all of them were ignorant of the principal tenet of Islam ('la illah ila allah' [لا إله إلا الله], 'There is no god but God'), given that 'serious' medieval authors seldom describe Muslims as idolatrous pagans but rather portray them as heretics.[10]

6    'Se qualche Musulmano venendo a morte vorrà far testamento [...]' [If a Muslim, feeling the approach of death, should wish to make a will [...]] (Giovanni Antonio Menavino, *I cinque libri della legge, religione, et vita de' turchi* (Venice: Vincenzo Valgrisi, 1548), p. 230).

7    On the use of the term in Italian chivalric poetry, see Maria Pavlova, 'I saraceni nella letteratura cavalleresca del Quattrocento, dai rifacimenti di storie medievali all'*Inamoramento de Orlando*', in *Epic Connections/Rencontres épiques: Proceedings of the Nineteenth International Conference of the Société Rencesvals, Oxford, 13–17 August 2012*, ed. by Marianne J. Ailes et al., 2 vols (Edinburgh: British Rencesvals Publications, 2015), II, pp. 577–97.

8    For a list of the Saracen deities in the *chansons de geste* see Bancourt, *Les musulmans dans les chansons de geste du Cycle du roi*, pp. 355–56. Various hypotheses have been advanced as to the etymology of these bizarre names. See at least Paul Casanova, 'Mahom, Jupin, Apollon, Tervagant, dieux des Arabes', in *Mélanges Hartwig Derenbourg, 1844–1908* (Paris: Ernest Leroux, 1909), pp. 391–95; Leo Spitzer, 'Tervagant', *Romania*, 70 (1949), 397–408; Henri Grégoire, 'L'étymologie de Tervagant (Trivigant)', in *Mélanges d'histoire du théâtre du Moyen-Age et de la Renaissance offerts à Gustave Cohen, professeur honoraire en Sorbonne, par ses collègues, ses élèves et ses amis* (Paris: Librairie Nizet, 1950), pp. 45–56.

9    Bancourt, *Les musulmans dans les chansons de geste du Cycle du roi*, p. 357. See also John V. Tolan, 'Saracens as pagans', in his *Saracens: Islam in the Medieval European Imagination* (New York: Columbia University Press, 2002), pp. 105–69.

10    On Islam in medieval Christian thought see Norman Daniel, *Islam and the West: The Making of an Image* (Edinburgh: Edinburgh University Press, 1960) and Tolan's *Saracens: Islam in the Medieval European Imagination*. Neither Dante nor Boccaccio perceive Islam as a form of paganism. For

The Italian Quattrocento and the first decades of the Cinquecento did not witness any significant advances in the understanding of the Islamic doctrine: the humanists tended to rely on the writings of medieval scholars, while travellers were not particularly interested in Islamic theology.[11] However, all educated Italians must have known that Muslims believe in one omnipotent Creator. Basic information on Islam was available not only in polemical works penned by Renaissance and medieval intellectuals, but also in 'lighter' texts, such as the immensely popular *Itinerarius* by Jean de Mandeville of which at least twelve Italian editions had been printed by the end of the fifteenth century.[12] We have very good (irrefutable in Boiardo's case) evidence to say that both Boiardo and Ariosto knew that Islam was a monotheistic religion. In Boiardo's translation or perhaps 'rifacimento' of Riccobaldo's history of the Roman and Germanic emperors (*Historia imperiale*, 1471–1473) there is a section on the birth of Islam, in which it is clearly stated that the Arabs 'uno Idio confessano solo e sancia alcun pari' [worship one and only one God] and that 'Maumetho [è] propheta di quello mandato ad essi ‹per salvarli›, sì come Moyses a' Iudei e Iesù Cristo a noi' [Muhammad [is] his prophet sent to them

Dante Muhammad is a schismatic, a figure similar to Fra Dolcino from Novara; his portrayal in the *Commedia* seems to be influenced by the medieval legend according to which Muhammad was a Christian cardinal who founded a new sect out of spite after his rival had been elected a Pope. According to Nancy Bisaha, Petrarch could be implying that Muslims are polytheists in *Rvf*, XXVIII: 'Turchi, Arabi, et Caldei, | con tutti quei sperano nelli dèi' [Turks, Arabs, and Chaldeans, | with all those who hope in gods] (54–55) (see her *Creating East and West*, p. 20). For a thorough review of scholarly works on Dante and Islam see Paolo De Ventura, 'Dante and Islam', in *Christian-Muslim Relations: A Bibliographical History (1200–1350)* (Leiden: Brill, 2012), pp. 779–87. On Boccaccio see Janet Levarie Smarr, 'Other Races and Other Places in the *Decameron*', *Studi sul Boccaccio*, 27 (1999), 113–36; on Petrarch Enrico Cerulli, 'Petrarca e gli arabi', in *Studi in onore di Alfredo Schiaffini, Rivista di cultura classica e medievale*, 7 (1965), 331–36; and Nancy Bisaha, 'Petrarch's vision of the Muslim and Byzantine East', *Speculum*, 76, no. 2 (2001), 284–314.

11    Only a small number of works specifically devoted to the Islamic faith were produced in this period. Aeneas Silvius Piccolomini penned a letter to Mehmed II, *Epistola ad Mahomatem II* (1461), in which he compared Islam and Christianity, stating among other things that both Muslims and Christians believed in the Old Testament. A close friend of Nicholas of Cusa (the author of *Cribratio Alchorani*, a commentary on the Qur'an composed around 1460), Piccolomini must have been well acquainted with the main medieval Christian writings on Islam, but he was not by any means an original thinker. Guglielmo Raimondo de Moncada, a Sicilian Jew who had converted to Christianity, translated a large section from the Qur'an and dedicated it (together with a list of Arabic terms and names and a few works on Islam) to Federico da Montefeltro. He was Pico della Mirandola's Arabic tutor. Both Marsilio Ficino and Pico attempted to read the Qur'an. Egidio da Viterbo, a Catholic cardinal, commissioned a new Latin translation of the Qur'an in 1518, of which several manuscripts survive. However, the first Italian translation of the Qur'an (published by Andrea Arrivabene in 1547) was based on Robert of Ketton's translation, known as *Lex Mahumet pseudoprophete* (1143), a crucial point of reference for late medieval 'orientalists'.

12    'Chi gli [saracini] domanda de ciò che credeno egli respondeno: "Noi crediamo in Dio creatore del cielo e dela terra e de tutte le altre cose el quale ha facto ogni cosa e senza lui niente è facto; e crediamo che vero sia quello che Dio ha dicto per li sancti propheti."' [When asked about their beliefs they reply: 'We believe in God the creator of heaven and earth and of all things, who created everything and without whom nothing is created; and we believe that what God said through his holy prophets is true'] (John de Mandeville, *Itinerarius* (Bologna: Ugo Rugerius, 1488), fol. eiii^v). Mandeville provides a sympathetic summary of the Islamic beliefs, highlighting the common ground shared by Islam and Christianity. The *Itinerarius* features in the 1495 inventory of the Ducal Library in Ferrara.

for their salvation, as Moses was sent to the Jews and Jesus Christ to us] (*Historia imp.*, I-II, p. 168). Riccobaldo (or indeed Boiardo) also mentions circumcision, the prohibition of pork and wine, Ramadan fasting and the fact that men can have up to four wives and divorce and remarry each of them up to three times. Moreover, he describes the punishments for adultery and theft as well as the rewards that await the faithful in the afterlife, and briefly (and very inaccurately) narrates the story of the schism between Shia and Sunni Muslims, which would later be narrated — albeit in a confusing and equally inaccurate manner — in Sabba da Castiglione's 1506 letter to Isabella d'Este.[13]

Thus, Boiardo undoubtedly had a good knowledge of Islam by the standards of his time. Ariosto, too, in all probability, was aware of the basics of Islam, and so were many of his first readers. However, they deliberately chose not to show this in their poems. Their portrayals of the Islamic faith are deformed and unrealistic, not because of ignorance, but rather because of a centuries-old literary convention.[14] Like in the *chansons de geste*, in both the *Inamoramento de Orlando* and the *Furioso*, 'Macone', or 'Macometto', is one of the Saracen gods and not a prophet of God (as he is, by contrast, in the *Morgante* and in the *Trabisonda*).[15] Boiardo's Saracens sometimes invoke the name of 'dio Macone' [God Macone] in order to lend weight to their words or when they are in distress. By contrast, Ariosto never explicitly calls Macone a god, but his divinity seems to be implied: 'Quanti prieghi la notte, quanti voti, | [Fiordispina] offerse al suo Machon e a tutti i dèi' [How many prayers and vows did she not offer | that night to her Mahomet and all the gods]

13   Sabba da Castiglione (1478–1529), a humanist who joined the Order of the Knights Hospitaller in 1505 and resided in Rhodes until 1508, maintained a correspondence with Isabella d'Este. In a letter dated 1 October 1506 he tells her that he met the son of the dethroned 'Gran Caramano' (i.e. the ruler of Karamania, which corresponds to the southern part of the Central Anatolia) who had been captured by corsairs on his journey from Karamania to Persia, which he had undertaken on the order of the 'Soffi' (the Persian shah), who wanted to know whether the 'Gran Caramano's' former subjects were now loyal to the Turks. Sabba da Castiglione's letter contains an account of what the Karaman prince ('giovane d'anni ventitré, de aspetto assai gentile et de maniere assai urbane' [a young man who is twenty-three years of age, very good-looking and with very refined manners]) told the Knights Hospitallers about the 'Soffi'. The letter states, among other things, that the 'Soffi' is a 'capitale nimico' [sworn enemy] of Muhammad's law, that he follows the teaching of the Prophet Ali, and that his true name is Ismael. It was published by Santa Cortesi: see her *Fra Sabba da Castiglione, Isabella d'Este e altri: Voci di un carteggio 1505–1542* (Faenza: Stefano Casanova, 2004), pp. 29–37 (especially p. 30).

14   It is interesting to note that at least one fifteenth-century poem of the 'guerre contro il Turco' [wars against the Turk] cycle assimilates contemporary history to the old convention by portraying the Turks as worshipping the Saracen gods of the *chansons de geste*. Maffeo Pisano's *Lamento di Costantinopoli* (first printed in 1487) features two references to 'idio Tre(i)vigante' [god Tre(i)vigante] (6,6 and 33,5) despite the fact that the *Lamento* is not about fictional Saracens but real Turks. This clearly testifies to the influence of the chivalric tradition on the ways in which real wars between Christians and Muslims were perceived in the Quattrocento. On the other hand, it would seem that this influence was declining. Many other 'guerre contro il Turco' poems feature only 'Macone' (or 'Maometto'). See Maffeo Pisano, *Lamento di Costantinopoli*, in *Guerre contro i turchi (1453–1570)*, ed. by Marina Beer and Cristina Ivaldi (Modena: Panini, 1988).

15   See *Morgante*, XXV 195,7; *Trabisonda*, XI 97,4–8; 98,1–2 [fol. 72ʳ]. In these poems Macone is similar to Christ insofar as he is both a prophet of the Saracen faith and one of the gods.

(XXIII 42,1–2 A; 44 B; XXV 44 C); '[Agramante] A suasïon di lui [Rodomonte] rotto havea il patto | (così credea) che fu solennemente, | gli dèi chiamando in testimonio, fatto' [it was at his [Rodomonte's] instigation (so he believed) | that he had broken the truce which he had solemnly pledged, | calling the gods to witness] (XXXV 27,1–3 A; 16 B; XXXIX 16 C).

Discussing the representation of the Saracen religion in the *chansons de geste*, Daniel states that 'we must consider the possibility that the multiplicity of Saracen gods is [...] intended, not to deceive, but to amuse'.[16] Indeed, the Saracen religion is an inexhaustible source of humour in many French and Italian chivalric texts. The 'Saracen Trinity' is effectively a grotesque version of the Christian Trinity, and that the Saracens ardently believe in gods with ridiculous names is comical. The fact that they worship idols, confident that these hefty pieces of gold take a personal interest in their lives, provokes a smile; their terrible fits of rage (during which they curse Macone and/or his divine 'brothers' and sometimes physically assault their statues) when they discover that the gods are deaf and indifferent, can be highly entertaining. In short, the reader is invited to have a good laugh at the expense of the naivety and puerile credulity of the infidels. While in the *Inamoramento de Orlando* and in many other Italian chivalric texts Saracen characters' interactions with their deities are occasionally described in a comic fashion, Ariosto's treatment of the Saracen religion is on the whole surprisingly 'respectful'. It is worth pointing out, for example, that the *Furioso* contains only a handful of references to the Saracen gods. In the *Inamoramento de Orlando* Macone (Macometo, Macometto) is mentioned 66 times, Apollino (Appolino, Apolino) 7 times and Trivigante (Travigante) 6. In the *Furioso* Machone (Macometto, Maumete, Maumette) is invoked 10 times (9 in the 1532 version), Trivigante appears only twice (both occurences in rhyme position), while his companion Apollino (not to be confused with the ancient god Apollo) is not honoured with a single mention. It suffices to compare these numbers with those in the much shorter *Spagna ferrarese* (Machone: 83; Apolino: 17; Trivichante: 25), Andrea da Barberino's *Aspramonte* (Maometto: at least 73; Apollino: 13; Trevigante: 15) or Pulci's *Morgante* (Macone: at least 84; Apollino: 19; Trivigante: 11) to see that Ariosto (and to a lesser extent Boiardo) does not attach much importance to Saracen polytheism.[17]

Moreover, it must be said that, though formally polytheists, both Boiardo's and Ariosto's Saracens often address their prayers (or curses) to God *tout court*, rather than to one of the Saracen gods.[18] Thus, at the sight of a centaur carrying a roaring

16    Daniel, *Heroes and Saracens*, p. 121.

17    Significantly, Apollino and Trivigante are banished from the universe of Tasso's *Gerusalemme liberata*, a late Cinquecento poem conceived in accordance with the neo-Aristotelian concept of verisimilitude. On the representation of Islam in Tasso see at least: Alain Godard, 'Le camp païen dans la *Jérusalem délivrée*', in *Quêtes d'une identité collective chez les Italiens de la Renaissance*, ed. by Marina Marietti (Paris: Université de la Sorbonne nouvelle, 1991), pp. 309–429; Maria Pavlova, 'Torquato Tasso and Islam', in *Christian-Muslim Relations*, pp. 592–601.

18    '[...] dans le *Roland amoureux*, le même vocable "Dio", peut désigner à quelques vers de distance le dieu de l'Islam ou celui des chrétiens (ce qui a de quoi décontenancer le lecteur)' [in the *Orlando innamorato*, the same term 'God' may refer to the god of Islam or, just a few lines apart, to that of the Christians (which may well baffle the reader)] (Alexandre-Gras, *L'héroïsme chevaleresque*, p. 316).

lion, Boiardo's Fiordelisa cries out to 'Re celestïale' [Heavenly King] (I xiii 53,6), and Trufaldino calls upon God as his witness ('ma testimonio il ciel e Dio me sia' [let Heaven and God be my witnesses] (I xv 49,3)) when trying to convince Orlando that he betrayed Angelica not out of ill-will but because of the folly of his companions. Boiardo's Rodamonte 'dice contro Dio parole altiere' [utters arrogant words against God] (II vi 30,3) during a storm, and so does Ariosto's Rodomonte when spurring his men to climb the walls of Paris (XII 117,8 AB; XIV C). Having lost his kingdom, Ariosto's Agramante surrenders himself to the will of God, whose ways, as he asserts in his last speech, are mysterious, far beyond the understanding of mortals of whatever faith (XXXVII 44,1–4 AB; XLI C). Many other examples could be given. The fact that Saracen characters seem to believe in one Supreme God, who is perhaps the embodiment of all other deities (and whom they invoke much more frequently than Apollino or Trivigante and, in the *Furioso*, more frequently than Macone), not only reduces the difference between the Christian and Saracen religions but also adds a touch of realism to the portrayal of Islam in both poems.[19]

As far as idolatry is concerned, in the *Inamoramento de Orlando* we come across three statues of Macone: Grandonio has 'd'or scolpito [...] un Macone' [sculpted in gold [...] a Macone] inside his shield (I ii 50,4); beside himself with anger, Orlando cuts to pieces 'un gran Macon di pietra marmorina' [a big marble Macone] (I xxvi 3,2) while waiting to confront his cousin Ranaldo; Orlando accuses Ranaldo of having stolen 'al re Marsilio il suo Macone' [from King Marsilio his Macone] (I xxviii 7,6), which is an allusion to an episode in the *Inamoramento de Carlo Magno*. There are no religious processions with images of Macone or other gods; a temple of Apollino 'in Sericana a lato al mare' [in Sericana by the sea] (II xvii 43,4) and another Saracen temple in Tartary (III i 13,3) are mentioned but not described. In the *Furioso* there appear to be no idols at all, which again could be seen as a move in the direction of greater realism. Neither poet dwells on the Saracen forms of worship. Like the ancients, the inhabitants of the Isole Lontane, a Saracen kingdom ruled by King Manodante, make offerings to their gods: 'chi promete a Macon pecore e boi, | chi darli incenso e chi argento si vanta' [some pledge to Macone cows and sheep, | some promise silver or sweet scents] (II xii 32,5–6).[20] Similarly, Ariosto's Dardinello promises 'al suo Machon, s'udir lo puote, | che se morto Lurcanio in terra getta | ne la moschea ne porrà l'arme vuote' [to his Mahomet (if he has ears) | that if he hurls Lurcanio dead to the ground | he will deposit his untenanted armour in the mosque] (XVI 55,2–4 AB; XVIII C).[21] Just like Christians, Saracens make vows to

19  Although Maomet, Trevegant and Apolin (together with another deity named Jopin) are often on the lips of Saracens in the *Entrée d'Espagne*, Ferragu tells Roland that he believes in one God: 'Ja cro je Alababir | che fist le munde' [I believe in Alababir | who created the world] (3627–28). For an analysis of the theological conversation between Ferragu and Roland see Claudia Boscolo, 'La disputa teologica dell'*Entrée d'Espagne*', in *Les chansons de geste: actes du XVIe Congrès International de la Société Rencesvals*, ed. by Carlos Alvar and Juan Paredes (Granada: University of Granada, 2005), pp. 123–34.

20  In the *Vendetta di Falconetto*, it is the Saracen Pope, 'papa Largalia', who sacrifices cattle to Macone (*Vendetta A*, fol. O iiii^r).

21  Boiardo does not use the term *moschea*. Ariosto uses it once and employs the more archaic word

God when they face mortal danger. In the *Furioso* the prayers of the inhabitants of Biserta echo those of the Parisians:

> Dentro la terra [Paris] suonano a martello
> con spaventevol fretta le campane;
> nanzi alli altari, in questo tempio e in quello,
> donne e fanciulli alzano al ciel le mane.
> Se 'l thesoro paresse a Dio sì bello
> come lo stiman le schiochezze humane,
> questo era il dì che 'l santo Consistoro
> fatto havria in terra ogni sua statua d'oro.

> [In the city [Paris] the bells can be heard
> ringing with frightening fury;
> before the altars, in church after church
> women and children raise their hands to heaven.
> If treasure seemed as beautiful to God
> as it does to our foolish way of thinking
> this is the day when the faithful would have used
> pure gold for every statue dedicated to him.]
>
> (*Fur.*, XII 100 AB; XIV C)

> Dentro a Biserta i sacerdoti santi
> supplicando col popolo dolente,
> battonsi il petto, e con dirotti pianti
> chiamano il lor Machon che nulla sente.
> Quante vigilie, quante offerte, quanti
> doni promessi son privatamente!
> quanto in publico templi, statue, altari,
> memoria eterna de' lor casi amari!

> [In Bizerta the holy priests
> pray with their grieving flock,
> beating their breasts and sobbing
> as they invoke their Mahomet, who hears nothing.
> What vigils, what offerings, what gifts
> are not pledged in private!
> What temples, statues, altars in public —
> eternal monument to their sorry plight!]
>
> (*Fur.*, XXXVI 13 AB; XL C)

It is obvious that Ariosto's irony — a smile tinged with sadness born out of genuine compassion — spares neither the Christians nor the Saracens. Saracens sometimes curse or threaten Macone and other gods, either as a display of bravado (suffice it to think of Rodamonte's rants or of Agramante's intention to conquer the world and then 'ancor nel Paradiso [...] far guera' [wage war in Paradise too] (*Inam.*, II i 64,8)) or in order to vent their frustration when something goes wrong (for example, at the news of the utter rout of his army, Boiardo's Marsilio 'ambe mani se bate in sula fronte | e forte biastemando il suo Macone, | facea le fiche al Ciel a pugne gionte'

---

*meschita* on another occasion (XXXVI 33,6 AB; LX C). By contrast, in the *Morgante* the word *moschea* recurs at least eight times and *meschita* once (but in the Dantesque sense of a tower).

[batters his face with both his hands, | and loudly curses his Macone, | flashing two figs, fists joined, to heaven] (*Inam.*, II xxiii 71,2–4)). While similar outbursts of Boiardo's characters often border on the farcical, the curses of Ariosto's Saracens do not produce any comic effect, not least because the blasphemers (Rodomonte, Feraù, Mandricardo and Marphisa) do not seem to expect any response from the celestial being(s) whom they are insulting.[22] As we shall see in Chapter IV, Ariosto's irony is much more pronounced in octaves devoted to the Christians' relationship with their God.

One may add that, while the Saracen religion is considered a false religion ('la legge falsa di Babelle' [the false law of Babel], as Charlemagne calls it in *Fur.*, XII 71,3 AB; XIV C), it is not represented as an evil cult actively supported by the devil.[23] It is true that both Boiardo and Ariosto often send their dead Saracens to Hell, this being a *topos* in the chivalric tradition. However, they do not insist on the fact that the Saracens receive help from, and unwittingly carry out, the plans of the enemy of mankind.[24] In the *Inamoramento de Orlando* there are a few Saracen villains who seem to put their trust in the devil rather than in Macone: the evil magician Balisardo 'chiama [...] el dimonio con tempesta, | Alïel, Libicoco e Calcabrina' [furiously calls the devil | Alïel, Libicoco and Calcabrina] (*Inam.*, II xi 42,1–2) when he sees that his end is imminent; the robber Barigazo 'al dimonio se racomanda' [calls out for the devil] (II xix 46,2) when Brandimarte mortally wounds him.[25]

22  Unlike Boiardo's Saracens, Ariosto's never lose their dignity when ranting against the supernatural powers. When Boiardo's Marphisa fails to unhorse Ranaldo, her disappointment is extreme: 'chiama iniquo Macone e doloroso; | cornuto e beco Trivigante appella. | "Ribaldi," a lor dicea "per qual cagione | teneti il cavalier in sulo arcione?" || Venga un di voi, e làsciassi vedere, | e pigli a suo piacer questa diffesa, | che io farò sua persona rimanere | qua giù riversa e nel prato distesa! | Voi non voliti mia forza temere, | perché là su non posso esser ascesa! | Ma se io prendo il camino, io ve ne aviso, | tutti vi occido, et ardo il Paradiso!"' [she called Macon unjust and evil, | called Trivigant a horny goat. | She said to them, 'Why do you keep | that baron in his seat, you rogues? || One of you come down! Show yourself! | Select the weapon you prefer. | I guarantee I'll leave your corpse | upside down, stretched along the field. | You do not need to fear my force, | because I can't ascend to the sky, | but if I find a way, be warned, | I'll kill you! I'll burn Paradise!'] (*Inam.*, I xviii 9,5–8; 10). After a similar unpleasant surprise, Ariosto's Mandricardo and Marphisa limit themselves to cursing Heaven: 'bestemmiò il cielo e li elementi il crudo | Pagan [Mandricardo], poi che restar la [Marphisa] vide in sella; | Marphisa, che pensò rompergli il scudo, | non men sdegnosa contra il ciel favella' [the ruthless pagan cursed heaven and the elements | seeing her still in the saddle; | Marphisa, who expected his shield to shatter, | decried heaven no less bitterly] (*Fur.*, XXIV 80,1–4 AB; XXVI 83 C).

23  'Babelle' or Babylon was traditionally seen as the centre of the infidels.

24  It must be said that this is also (partially) true of many other Italian chivalric works. Although religion plays an important role in the *Spagna* and in the *Aspramonte*, it would be wrong to claim that the authors of these texts go to great lengths to show that the war between Christians and Saracens is part of a titanic power struggle between God and Satan (as it will be in Tasso's *Gerusalemme liberata*). The most negative representations of the Saracen religion are to be found in the *chansons de croisade* (a cycle of the *chansons de geste* dealing with the First Crusade), where Saracens are often referred to as 'followers of the devil' and those who kill them are said to cleanse the Earth from sin.

25  As in many *chansons de geste*, in the *Cantari di Fierabraccia et Ulivieri*, the *Dama Rovenza*, and in the fifteenth-century *Aspramonte in ottava rima*, as well as in the *Persiano*, Beelzebub is one of the Saracen gods. In Cieco da Ferrara's *Mambriano*, Beelzebub plays a trick on Bradamante and the Christian paladins by making a dead Saracen seem like Rinaldo (*Mambriano*, XXXI 46–81).

However, the vast majority of Boiardo's Saracens have no contact with the forces of evil.[26] Those infidels who claim to be able to communicate with their gods (for example, the King of Garamantha, a priest of Apollino, who on behalf of 'il dio grande, Apolino' [great God Apollino] (*Inam.*, II i 59,2) tells Agramante and his vassal kings that all of them will perish in France and then accurately predicts his own death) are able to read the future because they are well versed in astrology — a science held in high esteem by Boiardo and his Ferrarese audience — and not because they obtain this knowledge from the devil.[27]

Only on a handful of occasions do Boiardo and Ariosto mention the devil in connection with the Saracens' attempted invasion of France. Describing the panic that has gripped the hearts of the Parisians before the battle for Paris, Boiardo's narrator claims that 'il demonio apena | se ralegrasse a tanta crudeltate' [the devil alone | was pleased to see such cruelty] (III viii 8,3–4), but this comment does not imply that the Saracens are pawns in the hands of Satan. Full of admiration for Rodamonte's superhuman strength, Boiardo wonders 's'el fo piacer del Cielo eterno | donar tanta prodecia ad un Pagano, | o se 'l demonio ussito delo 'nferno | combatesse per lui quel giorno al piano' [if eternal heaven | gave such strength to a Pagan, | or if the devil, come from hell, | fought on the field for him that day] (II vii 2,1–4). In the *Furioso* the 'antiquo Aversario, che fece Eva | al divietato pomo alzar la mano' [the old Adversary, who made Eve | lift her hand to the forbidden apple] (XXV 13,1–2 AB; XXVII C) intervenes in the affairs of men once, when he brings the main Saracen warriors back to Agramante's camp so that they defeat Charlemagne while Rinaldo is away. This is, however, the devil's only appearance; otherwise, the Christians are to some extent helped by their God whereas the Saracens are left to their own devices.[28] Although it is true that in both the *Inamoramento de Orlando* and the *Furioso* Saracen knights are sometimes compared to demons, one should not read too much into such similes, as they are devoid of any religious significance. After all, Christian knights too are occasionally likened to spirits from Hell (as well as to dragons and snakes) because of their terrifying ferocity on the battlefield. Boiardo, for example, does not distinguish between Rinaldo and Rodamonte when they fly into a terrible rage: Christian and Saracen soldiers run away from the two duelists 'sì come dui demonii del'Inferno | fossero

---

26    We must bear in mind that in both poems (and in the chivalric tradition in general) Christian sorcerers and sorceresses (positive characters for that matter) often summon infernal spirits: suffice it to think of Malagigi's or Melissa's magic.

27    It is not uncommon for Saracen idols to be inhabited by demons. In the fifteenth-century *Aspramonte in rima*, for example, Ruggieri tells Almonte that 'd'oro et d'argento son l'idole matte | dentro alle quale sta quel dell'inferno' [the mad idols are made of gold and silver | inside which resides the one from hell] (*Aspramonte*, VIII 26,4–5 [fol. cviii^v]). Not long after, the author gives us a practical proof: Balante's silver Trevigante turns into a frightening demon when a Christian priest orders him to reveal his true essence.

28    It is interesting to note that Ariosto's narrator once suggests that the Almighty is saddened by the loss of life in both camps: 'se non venìa la notte tenebrosa | che staccò il fatto et aquetò ogni cosa; || dal Creator accelerata forse, | che de la sua fattura hebbe pietade' [dark night descended, though, | interrupting the pursuit and bringing a lull — || hastened on, perhaps, by the Creator, | who had pity on his creatures] (*Fur.*, XVI 161,7–8; 162,1–2 AB; XVIII C).

ussiti sopra dela terra' [as if two demons had escaped | from hell, and were at large on earth] (II xv 3,1–2).

It would be fair to say that Christianity and the Saracen religion share the same moral values in the two *Orlandos*, which is true of Italian chivalric literature in general.[29] In both poems, the Saracen creed is to a large extent a mirror image of Christianity with some elements borrowed from ancient Paganism. Its hierarchical structure is unclear, because, unlike the authors of the *Spagna ferrarese*, the *Altobello*, the *Persiano*, and the *Vendetta di Falconetto*, neither Boiardo nor Ariosto explicitly say that Argalipha (Argaliffa) — a very marginal character — is the Pope of the Saracens.[30] However, both religions have priests who provide spiritual guidance and support to the faithful. Lending an Islamic touch to his representation of Saracen clergy, Ariosto mentions *muezzins* ('de li Talacimanni un gridar d'alto' [the muezzins' wailing] (*Fur.*, XVI 7,6 AB; XVIII C)) and the *qadi* of Biserta ('E poi che dal Cadì fu benedetto, | prese il populo l'arme, e tornò al muro' [The qadi blessed the people, | after which they took up arms and repaired to the ramparts] (XXXVI 14,1–2 AB; XL C)).[31] Both Christians and Saracens have holy books: the Bible and the 'Alcorana/o'. Ariosto stages a scene in which, in the presence of a Christian priest and a Saracen 'Papasso', Carlo and Agramante solemnly swear upon their respective holy texts not to interrupt the duel between Ruggiero and his future brother-in-law Rinaldo (XXXIV 81–86 AB; XXXVIII C).[32] The perfect symmetry between the two oaths reinforces the impression that the two religions are underpinned by similar fundamental values. Like Christians (and like real Muslims), Boiardo's and Ariosto's Saracens believe in God and the Devil, in Heaven and Hell. Although their never-ending adventures do not leave them much time to ruminate on the beatitude enjoyed by the souls in Paradise or on the torments that are meted out to sinners, the occasional references to the Saracen Heaven and Hell show that there is little difference between Christian and Saracen views on the hereafter. Thus, ready to die in a doomed attempt to free Prasildo, Iroldo tells Ranaldo that he is not afraid of physical death, as the Almighty saves the righteous: 'sarami quel morir tanto iocondo | che io ne andarò di volo in Paradiso' [that death will be such a joyous thing, | as I will fly to Heaven] (I xvii 16,2–3). A few octaves

29   In Boiardo, Ariosto and other chivalric texts both Christians and Saracens use the chivalric code as their moral guide. However, occasionally characters refer to the values prescribed by their religions. In the *Dama Rovenza* and the *Persiano* we learn that marrying off young ladies without their consent is 'contra la fede de Apolino' (*Dama Rovenza*, III 9,3 [fol. 27ᵛ]). In the *Persiano* Rinaldo tells a Saracen damsel (who thinks that he is a Saracen) that he intends to go to 'Lamech, quella magna cittade, | perho ch'el popul de Macon ho franto | acciò che lui me degia perdonare' [Lamech, this great city, | because I have killed Macon's people | so that he forgives me] (*Persiano*, I 414,5–7 [fol. C viᵛ]).

30   See *Spagna ferrarese*, XVIII 5,2; 22,6–7; *Altobello*, XXIV 50,1 [fol. i vᵛ]; *Persiano*, IV 77 [fol. P iiᵛ]; *Vendetta* A, fol. H iiiʳ. The Saracen Pope performs absolution in *Vendetta B*, fol. F iiiᵛ and *Vendetta A*, fol. F iiiʳ.

31   *Qadis* (Islamic judges) performed a variety of religious (and even political) functions in different Muslim societies. In his *Itinerario* (first published in 1510) the Italian traveller Ludovico de Varthema describes a sermon delivered by a qadi in Mecca. See *Itinerario de Ludouico de Varthema bolognese* (Venice: Francesco di Alessandro Bindone and Mapheo Pasini, 1535), fol. 15ʳ.

32   The word 'papasso' appears in the *Morgante* too, where, unless preceded by the adjective 'gran', it means 'a priest' rather than 'a Pope' (*Morgante*, VI 15,6; XVIII 118,4).

later, having seen Ranaldo slaughter Rubicone's men, Iroldo and his rescued friend
come to believe that the mysterious knight is none other than 'dio Macone' [god
Macone] in person:

> Ciascun de' doi Baron con le man gionte
> come dïo adorarno in gionichione
> e a lui divotamente in voce prompte
> diceano: 'O Re de il ciel, o dio Macone,
> che per pietà in terra sei venuto
> in tanta nostra pena a darci aiuto!
>
> Per cagion nostra giù de il ciel lucente
> hor sei disseso a mostrarci la facia:
> tu sei lo aiuto del'humana gente,
> né mai salvarli il tuo volto si sacia.
> Fa' ciascadun di noi ricognoscente,
> dapoi che ce hai donata cotal gratia,
> sì che per merto al fin si troviam degni
> de star con teco neli eterni regni!'.
>
> [Both of the Barons joined their hands
> and kneeled as to a deity.
> With rapid words, with great devotion,
> They said, 'O heaven's king Mohammed,
> in mercy you have come to earth
> to help us in our tribulation!
>
> You've come down from the shining sky
> and shown your face on our account,
> o Saviour of the human race
> for whom you proffer endless grace!
> Please give each of us a sign
> that you have sanctified our lives,
> that we deserve as our reward,
> to stay with you in your eternal realm!']
> (*Inam.*, I xvii 32,3–8; 33)

It is worth noting that whereas Christian scholars stressed the sensuous delights of
the Saracen Paradise, Boiardo's characters are enraptured at the thought of being
able to contemplate Macone for all eternity ('de star con teco neli eterni regni' [stay
with you in your eternal realm]).[33] Though poking fun at the 'gran simplicitate'

---

33   In Boiardo's (pseudo-)translation of Riccobaldo the Islamic Paradise is described as a beautiful
garden, where 'tra odori suavissimi staranno [the blessed souls] in conviti cum cope d'oro di preciose
pietre adornate e tra belissime donçelle, ‹le quale sempre staranno› vergine, ‹abenché› siecho usino
loro carnalmente, ‹e durarà quello diletto de luxuria quanto serà la voluntade sua [...]›' [surrounded
by delightful scents, the blessed souls will spend their time feasting with gold goblets adorned with
precious stones and in the midst of most beautiful damsels who will stay virgins forever, even if they
lie with them carnally, and this lustful pleasure will last as long as they wish [...]] (*Historia imp.*, I-II,
p. 169). Similarly, Mandeville, mentions rivers of milk, honey, wine, and young virgins (fol. e ii^v).
Pulci alludes to such visions of the Islamic Heaven in the *Morgante*, where the cynical atheist Marsilio
promises his men 'le fonte e' fiumi di latte e di mèle' [springs and rivers of milk and honey] (XXV
192,8) if they die for the sake of their religion.

[great naivety] (I xvii 34,4) of the two Saracens, Boiardo neither demonizes their religion nor represents it as purely concerned with earthly pleasures. Prasildo's and Iroldo's Macone bears much resemblance to the figure of Christ in Christianity: if anything, their mistake shows that they have the potential to become devout Christians, which is immediately clear to Ranaldo who seizes this opportunity to convert them. In the *Furioso* a similar mistake is made by a Christian: Senapo (Prester John) takes Astolfo for a new Messiah and, overcome by religious ecstasy, promises to build him a sumptuous temple and tries to kiss his feet (XXX 85–89 A; 90–94 B; XXXIII 114–18 C). Although Boiardo gently mocks Prasildo and Iroldo, he does not humiliate them. Such emotional sympathy for devout Saracens is rare in Italian chivalric literature. In other chivalric texts Christians sometimes exploit the Saracens' gullibility and religious fervour. The *Vendetta di Falconetto*, for example, contains an episode in which Malagigi arrives in the Saracen camp pretending to be a pilgrim returning from Mecca, where he saw Macone's tomb and had a vision that the Christians would be defeated. He blesses the creduluous Saracens with a donkey's bone, telling them that it is a holy relic, receives alms and a horse, and then returns to Paris and has a good laugh with his friends (*Vendetta A*, fol. H iii^r; *Vendetta B*, fol. H iiii^r).

As for the Saracen Hell, there are references to 'inferno' as the place of eternal sorrow in the amorous laments of Boiardo's Iroldo, Prasildo, Brandimarte (when he despairs of ever finding his beloved Fiordalisa) and Angelica (I xii 51,5; 69,8; 79,7; xxi 47,8; xxviii 36,6). Moreover, the 'cielo' ('Paradiso')/'inferno' antithesis — meaningless concepts for an agnostic leaning towards atheism — features in Rodamonte's blasphemous speeches (II i 65,7; xxii 49,7).[34] It is towards the end of the *Furioso* that the term 'inferno' acquires clear religious overtones. Angrily rejecting Brandimarte's advice to embrace the faith of Christ, Agramante accuses his former friend of being possessed:

> Più presto crederò che tu, ch'in preda
> sai che del Diavol sei, né speri aiuto,
> voresti teco nel dolor eterno
> tutto il mondo poter trarre all'inferno.
>
> [I will sooner believe that you who know
> that you are the Devil's prisoner and have no hope,
> desire to pull the whole world
> down with you to Hell to eternal suffering.]
> (*Fur.*, XXXVII 43,5–8 AB; XLI C)

These lines have been criticized by Tasso, who in his *Apologia* (1585) observes that 'paiano anzi di predicator Christiano, che di Cavalier saracino quelle parole [...]. Perché i Macometani n[on] sogliono usare simili persuasioni, ò simili spaventi; ma spaventano con la morte, con gli incendi, e con le ruine, et in somma con le pene temporali' [those words would be more appropriate coming from a Christian

---

34    In the *Inamoramento de Orlando* Rodamonte appears to be an agnostic rather than a hardcore atheist: 'Se egli è alcun dio nel ciel (ch'io nol sciò certo) | là stassi ad alto, e di qua giù non cura' [If there's a God, which I don't know, | his care is above, not here below] (II iii 22,1–2).

preacher rather than from a Saracen knight [...]. Because the Mahometans do not usually use such reasonings or such threats; but rather they frighten with death, with fires, with disasters, and hence with earthly suffering].[35] Needless to say, Tasso's comment about the inappropriateness of the reference to 'dolor eterno' [eternal suffering] does not point to his deep knowledge of the Islamic faith, but rather reflects the commonly held stereotype that Islam is a less spiritual religion than Christianity. At least one other sixteenth-century scholar (namely Giulio Guastavini) agrees with Tasso on this point.[36] Lionardo Salviati, however, does not think that Agramante's attitude is incongruous with Islam and reminds the author of the *Gerusalemme liberata* of the similarity between the two religions: 'Che minacce, e che spaventi dite voi? [...] Volete voi dir forse, che la legge Macomettana non crede, che dopo morte le buone opere sien ristorate, e le malvage punite per lo contrario?' [What threats, what scares do you mean? [...] Do you perhaps want to say that the Mahometan law does not believe that after death good deeds are rewarded and evil deeds are punished?].[37] One may add that Agramante's reverence for the Creator and his resignation to God's will (which contrasts with blasphemous outbursts of many other Saracen kings in French and Italian chivalric literature) are not in the least incompatible with Islam. Similar attitudes can be found in the Italian translation of Ibn Kemal's account of the conquest of Egypt by Selim I, which enjoyed some circulation in sixteenth-century Italy and may have been known to some of Ariosto's early readers, such as Isabella d'Este and Francesco Gonzaga, considering that there is a manuscript copy of this work in the Gonzaga archive in Mantua.[38]

---

35   Cited from Lionardo Salviati, *Dello Infarinato Accademico della Crusca risposta all'Apologia di Torquato Tasso intorno all'Orlando furioso, e alla Gierusalèm liberata* (Florence: Carlo Meccoli and Salvestro Magliani, 1585), p. 81.

36   See Giulio Guastavini, *Risposta all'Infarinato Accademico della Crusca intorno alla Gerusalemme liberata di Torquato Tasso* [1588], in *Delle opere di Torquato Tasso*, 12 vols (Venice: Steffano Monti e N. N. Compagno, 1735–1742), II, pp. 461–560 (pp. 518–19).

37   Salviati, *Dello Infarinato Accademico della Crusca risposta all'Apologia di Torquato Tasso*, p. 81. In the 1532 *Furioso* the first two lines of the above-quoted passage read as follows: 'Crederò ben, tu che ti vedi in preda | di quel dragon che l'anime devora' [I will more readily believe that you, having fallen prey | to the dragon who devours souls] (XLI 43,5–6). Having assumed that the 'dragon' metaphor refers to Christ, Tasso criticizes it on the grounds that 'i Macometani non biasmano Christo' [the Mahometans do not speak ill of Christ]. Salviati corrects Tasso's mistake, pointing out that Agramante 'intende del Diavolo, non di Giesù Cristo nostro Signore' [Agramante means Devil, not Jesus Christ our Lord] (ibid.).

38   Compare Agramante's words and Selim's speech in the Italian translation of Ibn Kemal's account of his Egyptian campaign: 'Che a vincere habbia o perdere, o nel regno | tornare antiquo o sempre starne in bando, | in mente sua n'ha Dio fatto disegno, | il qual né veder io posso, né Orlando' [Whether I am to win or lose, | whether I am to recover my ancestral kingdom or be forever banished from it –| the decision is known to God, | whose thoughts neither I nor Orlando can search] (*Fur.*, XXXVII 44,1–4 AB; XLI C); 'O glorioso Dio, Gran signor firmo, et constante, sempre quello che è di tua voluntà non pò mancar, ni uno pò reprobar quello tu fai, Io che son schiavo fatto de Terra confidandomi sempre in la tua M.ᵗᵃ voltando il volto a la tua infinita bontà humilmente me racommando' [O glorious God, immutable and constant Great lord, your will can never be frustrated, nor can one reprobate what you do, I, a slave made of earth, always confiding in your Majesty, turning my face [to you], I humbly put my trust in your infinite goodness] (*Storia della distruzione de Mamaluchi*, fol. 60ᵛ).

While Christians and Saracens seem to share identical conceptions of the afterlife, at least on one occasion the Saracen 'inferno' brings to mind the underworld of the ancients. At the beginning of Book III of the *Inamoramento de Orlando*, an old man tells Mandricardo that the soul of his father Agricane will never find peace until Orlando, his murderer, is dead too:

> L'anima del tuo patre è maledetta:
> non pò el mal fiume alo Inferno passare,
> perché scordata s'è la sua vendetta.
> Sopra alla rippa stassi a lamentare,
> stassi piangendo e tien la testa bassa,
> che ogni altro morto sopra li trapassa.

> [The damned soul of your father can't
> traverse the evil stream of hell
> because you have neglected his
> revenge. He moans along the bank,
> head bowed, and he weeps constantly,
> as other dead men pass him by.]
> (*Inam.*, III i 8,3–8)

Here, the grey-haired Saracen seems to be referring to a place similar to Hades; Agricane's suffering makes one think of the state of the unburied dead as described in the *Aeneid* (VI 325–30) and other ancient texts. Cavallo attempts to read the Tartar's speech in light of the Mongol and Chinese religions, stating that Marco Polo's Mongols 'contracted marriages for their deceased children and burnt material possessions they believed would reach the newlyweds in the otherworld' and that 'in China it was traditionally believed that the spirit of someone who died in violence could not be pacified until his assassin was killed in turn'.[39] Although it is not impossible that Boiardo wanted to add a Chinese flavour to his representation of Mandricardo, there is not enough evidence to say that the octave quoted above consciously draws on medieval writings about the Mongols and the Chinese.[40]

---

39    Cavallo, *The World beyond Europe*, p. 63. Cavallo has been unable to find a reference to the Chinese belief in the need to avenge those who suffered a violent death in any source that might have been known to Boiardo.

40    Cavallo finds other allusions to Mongol religious beliefs in Boiardo's portrayal of Tartars. She claims, for example, that Agricane's invocation of the sky and the sun ('ma siami testimonio il ciel e il sole | che darti morte me dispiace e dole!' [but let the sun and heavens see | that killing you displeases me] (I xviii 35,7–8)) 'recalls the Mongolian reverence for the "eternal blue sky" or "heaven" that was believed to keep watch over human events'. According to Cavallo, Agricane's oath 'not only supports the historical context of the episode but keeps the Christian-Saracen binary out of the picture' (*The World beyond Europe*, p. 55), while the fact that his son Mandricardo is referred to as 'saracino' (III i 5,3) 'corresponds historically to the gradual spread of Islam in the Mongol Empire' (ibid., p. 62). Such an interpretation seems far-fetched: had Boiardo wanted to dissociate Agricane from the Saracen faith he would have probably done this in a more explicit way. Agricane believes in Trivigante (I xiv 53,1) and is comfortable with his Saracen identity. There are Tartar characters in the *Altobello* and the *Trabisonda* and their religion is that of the other Saracens. In general, characters in chivalric romances are either Christians or Saracens: very rarely do authors refer to other non-Judeo-Christian religions. Boiardo must have known that the Chinese were 'idolaters'; he could have read this in Marco Polo's *Milione* or in Poggio Bracciolini's *India recognita* (an account of Niccolò

We have to bear in mind that in other chivalric romances, too, the Saracen religion takes on some of the traits of the religions of ancient Romans and Greeks, with Mars and other ancient gods being among the Saracen deities in many chivalric texts.[41] In the *Furioso* Medoro prays to the goddess Moon, asking the 'santa Dea' [holy Goddess] to show him 'ove il Re mio giaccia fra tanti' [where my king lies among so many dead] (XVI 184,7 AB; XVIII C). Although the cult of the Moon was widespread among the Arabs during *asr al-Jahiliyyah* (the 'age of ignorance' or the pre-Islamic period), in pre-Islamic mythology the Moon is a male god, which rules out any possible link with the goddess invoked by Medoro.[42] It is clear that Ariosto draws on Western sources, namely Nisus's prayer to the Moon in *Aeneid*, IX 403–09, and Dymas's prayer in *Thebaid*, X 365–70; as Cavallo observes, the fact that the Saracen comes from Tolomitta (Ptolemais or Tolmeitha), a city whose history stretches back to Greek antiquity, further adds to the Greek atmosphere of this episode.[43] Medoro appears to be seized by genuine religious fervour: Ariosto stresses the fact that his words are animated by 'tanta fede' [such faith] (185,2). The description of Agricane's despair on the shore of the infernal river and Medoro's heartfelt plea to the nocturnal goddess suggest that, in line with the preceding chivalric tradition, in Boiardo's and Ariosto's poems the boundary between the Saracen world and that of the ancients is somewhat blurred. Interestingly, Nicolò degli Agostini blends Christian and mythological elements in the description of afterlife in the *Sesto libro* of his continuation of the *Inamoramento de Orlando*: Rinaldo finds a temple of Minerva, the final abode of the souls of the virtuous closed to Agramante and other Saracens who are desperate to enter it but are unable to do so (*Sesto libro*, II 36–46).

As for the Islamic laws and customs, it must be said that on the whole there are scarcely any cultural differences between Christians and Saracens. Ariosto is more eager to show his knowledge of Qur'anic law. Thus, there is a reference to circumcision in one of the authorial digressions in the *Furioso*: recalling the battles for Bastia (31 December 1511 and 13 January 1512), the poet mentions the tragic death of Vestidello Pagano, a Ferrarese captain who 'senza arme fu fra cento spade occiso | dal popul la più parte circonciso' [was killed, defenceless, by a hundred swords | by for the most part circumcised men] (XXXVIII 5,7–8 AB; XLII C), that is by Spanish soldiers who, as implied in these lines, were mostly Muslim mercenaries.

Conti's travels in the East which constitutes the fourth book of Poggio's *De varietate fortunae*, listed in the 1495 inventory of Ercole's library). He must have known that the Circassians were Christians, as there were Circassian slaves in Ferrara. Yet his Angelica, Gradasso, Galaphrone and Sacripante are Saracens.

41    The author of the *Entrée d'Espagne*, for example, mentions 'uns grant temple de Mart' [a big temple of Mars] (13267). In the *Aspramonte A* Almonte hopes to receive help from 'Marte deo delle battaglie' [Mars god of battles] (*Aspramonte A*, I xiii 16). See also the fifteenth-century *Aspramonte*, XIII 9,6 [fol. giiii^r]; XXII 1,2 [fol. pii^v], and *Mambriano*, XXXIII 53,6.

42    Interestingly, the Arabs used the word الله ('Allah') to refer to the Moon god. Today some radical Christian apologists claim that Muslims worship a false moon god or moon goddess.

43    'Despite Medoro's stated identity as a Moor, Ariosto systematically avoids characterizing him as African and fashions him instead as an heir to ancient Greek culture' (Cavallo, *The World beyond Europe*, p. 32).

Moreover, Ariosto is the first or one of the very few Italian chivalric authors to say that the Qur'an forbids the consumption of wine. Rodomonte kills Issabella when, for the first time in his life, his sharp mind is clouded by alcohol: 'Non era Rodomonte usato al vino, | perché la legge sua lo vieta e danna' [Rodomonte was unaccustomed to wine, | because Moslem law forbids and condemns it] (XXVII 22,1–2 AB; XXIX C). Boiardo's Saracens, by contrast, drink wine without any misgivings: it is the pungent words of a drunken 'tamburino' [drummer] ('ebriaco ognon il iudicava' [they figured he was drunk] (II xxviii 48,4)) that spur Agramante to hasten the preparation for the military expedition against Charlemagne. Wine-drinking is also mentioned at I xxvii 37,4 (where Angelica offers Orlando fruit, sweets and 'bon vino' [good wine]) and II xii 9 (where Orlando and Brandimarte drink drug-laced wine in Manodante's Saracen kingdom). Nor are Boiardo's Saracens alone in indulging in alcoholic beverages; as Daniel points out, in many *chansons de geste* 'there is no hint that wine-drinking is anything but the most natural thing in the world',[44] which is also true of such Italian poems as the *Regina Ancroia* and the *Vendetta di Falconetto*.[45] Besides, some fifteenth-century Italian travellers to Islamic countries reported that Muslims sometimes consumed alcohol. For example, in his memoirs, which were first printed in 1476–1477, the Venetian envoy to Persia Ambrogio Contarini says that the Persian Shah *only* drinks wine.[46]

## Saracen culture(s)

In general in both poems the lifestyle of Saracens is very similar to that of the Christians. Like Saracens in the *chansons de geste* and in most Italian chivalric romances, they are monogamous, if we do not count what seems to be an allusion to the Sultan's harem and the Muslim slave trade in Issabella's story ('m'han promessa e venduta a un mercadante | che portar al Soldan me de' in Levante' [they have promised and sold me to a merchant | who is to take me to the Sultan in the East] (*Fur.*, XI 31 AB; XIII C).[47] The most remarkable difference between Christian and Saracen damsels is that the latter are more mobile (especially in the *Inamoramento de Orlando*): unable to bear even a few months' separation from their men, they follow the Saracen armies, which, as Pigna suggests in his *I romanzi*, could have a

---

44   Daniel, *Heroes and Saracens*, p. 51.
45   See *Ancroia*, VII 194 [fol. e2ᵛ] and *Vendetta A*, fol. hvᵛ.
46   Ambrogio Contarini, *Il viaggio del Magnifico M. A. Ambrosio Contarini Ambasciatore della Illustrissima Signoria di Venetia al gran Signore Ussuncassan Re di Persia nell'anno MCCCCLXXIII*, in Ramusio, *Navigationi et viaggi: Venice (1563–1606)*, II (facsimile edition of the 1583 Giunti edition of the second volume), fols 112ᵛ–125ᵛ (fol. 117ᵛ).
47   The *Guerrin Meschino* and the *Altobello* are notable exceptions to the general rule. Andrea da Barberino informs his readers that the sultan of Persia has more than two hundred spouses because the Saracen religion permits polygamy (*Guerrin Meschino*, III viii 20–21). In the *Altobello* the Saracen king Valerano 'è cento volte maridato: | quando vuol qusta [sic], quando vuol quella' [married a hundred times: | sometimes he wants this one, sometimes he wants that one] (III 40,5–6 [fol. b. iᵛ]]); this is why Fior de spina, the new object of his infatuation, does not want to marry him. Ariosto also mentions the fact that 'appresso l'Indi neri | le donne che non han tanti rispetti, | vivon più liete in lor communi letti' [among the black Indians | women do not have so many inhibitions | and live more happily in their common beds] (*Fur.*, XXXV 3,6–8 A [missing in later editions]).

historical explanation. Attempting to historicize the figure of the warrior woman in chivalric romances, Pigna says that, during their military campaigns in Spain, the North African Arabs took their women with them to war and even allowed them to fight.[48] However, neither Boiardo nor Ariosto can be credited with being the first to introduce this 'custom' into chivalric literature: Saracen ladies accompany Saracen armies in earlier texts too, most notably in the *Aspramonte*.

While Boiardo's giants and monsters have exotic appearances, the dress and manners of 'human' Saracens resemble those of their Christian counterparts, even if occasionally the poets add a few oriental details. Thus, some of Boiardo's and Ariosto's Saracens wear turbans: Baliverno, for example, is defined as 'quel Saracin grosso | ch'avea rivolto al capo una gran fassa' [that hefty Saracen | whose head was wrapped up in a long cloth] (II xxiv 32,5–6).[49] At one point, Falseta, a demon summoned by Malagigi, dresses up as a Persian 'almansore' [lord], pretending to be Gradasso's ambassador:

> le anelle ha nel'orechie e non in ditto,
> e molto drapo al capo ha invilupato;
> la veste longa e d'or tuta vergata
> e di Gradasso porta l'ambassata.
>
> Proprio parea di Persia un almansore
> con la spada di legno e col gran corno.
>
> [his ears, not fingers, now have rings,
> his head is wrapped by lengths of cloth;
> his robe is long, woven with gold
> and he conveys Gradasso's words.
>
> He seemed a Persian *almansor,*
> with wooden sword and a large horn.]
> (*Inam.*, I v 34,5–8; 35,1–2)

Boiardo's vivid verbal portrait of Malagigi's demon bears some resemblance to the painting of an Oriental scribe which might have been executed by Costanzo da Ferrara or Gentile Bellini and which is now kept in the Isabella Stewart Gardner Museum in Boston.[50] Painted in the Persian style, it features a young man wearing

---

48    Pigna, *I romanzi*, p. 39.

49    See also *Inam.*, II i 60,2; *Fur.*, X 84,1–2 AB; XII 80 C; XIV 50,4 AB; XVI C. Neither poet uses the term 'turbante' which appears to have entered Italian relatively late. According to Andrea Canova, the earliest known occurrence of 'turbante' is in a 1466 letter by Luigi Pulci (Andrea Canova, 'Osservazioni lessicali su alcuni romanzi cavallereschi tra Quattro e Cinquecento', in *Carlo Magno in Italia e la fortuna dei libri di cavalleria*, pp. 339–57 (pp. 353–57)).

50    Jerry Brotton attributes the painting to Costanzo da Ferrara (see Plate 7 in his *The Renaissance Bazaar: from the Silk Road to Michelangelo* (Oxford: Oxford University Press, 2002)), while other scholars maintain that its authorship is uncertain. Alan Chong shows that it was most probably executed by Gentile Bellini who worked at the court of Mehmed in 1479–1480 (Alain Chong, 'Gentile Bellini in Istanbul: Myths and Misunderstandings', in *Bellini and the East* (London: National Gallery, 2005), pp. 106–29 (p. 118)). As for Costanzo da Ferrara (who despite his name was not particularly well known in Ferrara), we know about his sojourn in the Ottoman Empire from Battista Bendedei's 1485 letter to Eleonora d'Aragona, in which Battista says that Costanzo spent many years in Constantinople and was knighted by the Turkish Sultan (Maria Andaloro, 'Costanzo da Ferrara: Gli anni a Costantinopoli alla corte di Maometto II', *Storia dell'arte*, 38–40 (1980), 185–212).

a blue kaftan embroidered in gold, a turban, and an earring. There is no evidence to say that Boiardo could have been inspired by this painting, but it is likely that Boiardo and his Ferrarese audience saw or heard stories about Persian ambassadors, given the strong diplomatic ties between the Serenissima and Uzun Hassan (more on this later in this chapter).

The most 'oriental' dress of the *Furioso* is that worn by Ruggiero during his stay on Alcina's island. He is decked out in gold-embroidered silk and has gold hoops with giant pearls in his ears 'qual mai non hebbon li Arabi né l'Indi' [such as no Arabian or Indian ever boasted] (VII 54,8 ABC). Yet his normal attire does not strike the reader as particularly oriental and nor does the armour of most other Saracen superheroes (with the exception of Rod(a/o)monte's invulnerable dragon-skin armour), even if at one point Ariosto draws attention to the 'barbarica pompa' [barbaric splendour] of Agramante's outfit (XXXIV 77,3–4 AB; XXXVIII C). No exotic armour is used in the joust organized by Ariosto's Norandino, as the Syrians 'haveano usanza | d'armarsi a questa guisa di Ponente' [were accustomed | to wear armour after the Western fashion], perhaps because of the 'vicinanza | che de' Franceschi havean continuamente' [proximity | in which they lived with the French] (XV 73,1–4 AB; XVII C).[51] In general, Saracen coats of arms are eye-catching but very few of them feature Islamic symbols or distinctively oriental images. Two notable exceptions are Isolieri's and Mordante's coats of arms: the former 'tre lune d'oro avea nel verde scudo' [had three golden moons on his green shield] (I ii 46,2), while the latter featured 'due lune vermiglie in campo d'oro' [two scarlet moons on gold] (II xxix 17,5). The armour of 'second-class' knights and rank-and-file soldiers is by far inferior to that of Charlemagne's soldiers. In a bid to encourage the allies to do their best, Ariosto's Rinaldo reminds them that the enemy 'gente male experta tutta parmi, | senza possanza, senza cor, senza armi' [they seem to me an untrained host, | timid, weak, and poorly armed] (XIV 38,7–8 AB; XVI C). Boiardo's Rugiero effortlessly kills a Genoese renegade, almost felling him in half, because the latter

> non avea intorno pecio di metallo,
> perché era armato pure a quella usanza
> moresca, dico, essendo genoese,
> ma con la fede avìa cambiato arnese.
>
> [No metal plates protected him
> whose panoply was made in Moorish
> fashion. Although from Genoa,
> he'd changed his arms with his religion.]
> (*Inam.*, III vi 17,5–8)

It is worth pointing out that such disparaging comments can be found in non-fictional texts too. For example, talking about the Turkish, Arabic, Tartar, and Syrian soldiers under the command of the 'ammiraglio' of Alexandria, Lionardo

---

51    Needless to say, this does not correspond to historical reality. As Cavallo, points out, this 'contradicts the fact that Westerners who remained any length of time in the Levant acclimatized to life there by adopting Arab dress' (*The World beyond Europe*, p. 173).

Frescobaldi (a fourteenth-century traveller who wrote a detailed account of his pilgrimage to the Holy Land) observes that 'costoro non vanno armati del dosso né della testa, salvoché certi caporali, e radi di corazza e di panziera' [they do not wear armour on their backs or heads, with the exception of certain corporals, and few of them wear a cuirass and a belly plate].[52]

At the banquet thrown by Charlemagne in the very beginning of the *Inamoramento de Orlando* Marsilio and his barons 'non volsero usar banco né sponda, | anci stérno a iacer comme mastini | sopra a tapeti comme è lor usanza' [had no need of bench or couch; | instead they lay full length like hounds | on carpets, as they always do] (I i 13,5–7). Here, Boiardo is amused by the Saracens' custom, as is the author of the *Entrée d'Espagne* in the episode in which Roland teaches the Persians to use individual plates (*Entrée*, 13961–83).[53] This comment apart, neither Boiardo nor Ariosto portray their Spanish and African Saracens as uncouth and uncultured. It is true that some of Boiardo's Saracens are only interested in fighting (which is of course arguably by far the most important skill for a knight in a chivalric romance): the Tartar Agricane and his monstrous subjects (the Indians, Russians, Norwegians and other 'barbarians') are not particularly learned, which is not surprising taking into account the medieval and Renaissance stereotypes of these peoples.[54] Yet Boiardo's North Africa is an important cultural centre, where such disciplines as philosophy (see the opening of Branzardo's speech at *Inam.*, II i 39), astrology (see the prophecies of the king of Garamantha and Atalante at II i 68–75; iii 25–32; xxi 53–60,5) and navigational science (see the speech of the Moroccan captain Scobrano at II vi 7–9) are clearly flourishing. Boiardo's description of the North African civilization can only be compared to the description of the Saracen Middle East in the *Entrée d'Espagne*: to my knowledge, no other fifteenth-century chivalric poet paints such a nuanced and captivating picture of the Saracens' accomplishments in different branches of knowledge. Although Saracen magicians and learned Saracen

---

52    *Viaggio di Lionardo di Niccolò Frescobaldi fiorentino in Egitto e in Terra Santa con un discorso dell'editore sopra il commercio degl'Italiani nel secolo XIV*, ed. by Guglielmo Manzi (Rome: Carlo Mordacchini, 1818), p. 76.

53    According to Bancourt, Roland 'exerce [...] un rôle civilisateur' [plays a civilising role] in Persia (Bancourt, *Les musulmans*, p. 221). Boscolo disagrees with this, pointing out that 'in order to see Roland in a "role civilisateur" [...] one must accept that he conceived his journey to Persia as a kind of non-violent mission to convert the Saracens', which 'is not Roland's real aim', as he sails to Persia following his quarrel with Charlemagne, and 'ends up in a foreign land where he must literally improvise a way to survive' (Boscolo, *L'Entrée d'Espagne*, pp. 176–77).

54    In the famous nocturnal conversation with Orlando, Agricane admits that he has not received proper schooling: 'io de nulla scïentia sono experto, | né mai, sendo fanciul, volsi imparare | e ròpi il capo al mastro mio per merto, | poi non se pòte un altro ritrovare | che mi mostrasse libro né scriptura, | tanto ciascun avia de mi paura' [I have no skill in any science. | I didn't want to learn when young: | I broke my teacher's head as payment; | they couldn't find another one | to show me books or how to write. | They all were too afraid of me] (*Inam.*, I xviii 42,3–8). Whereas Marco Polo describes Kublai Khan's Northern China as a flourishing civilization, Boiardo's contemporaries had little good to say about the Mongols they knew. Fifteenth- and sixteenth-century Italian travellers were not greatly impressed by Mongolian culture. For example, Ambrosio Contarini was disgusted by the fact that the Mongols from the Kipchak Khanate spent most of their life on horseback and smelt of horses. See *Il viaggio del Magnifico M. A. Ambrosio Contarini*, fol. 114[r].

damsels feature in a variety of chivalric romances, they are usually portrayed in a rather sketchy manner. Boiardo and his early readers certainly knew that Muslims made a very significant contribution to the history of philosophy, with the writings of Averroes and Avicenna (in the *Commedia* both of whom are among the souls relegated to Limbo) being an indispensable point of reference for medieval Western scholars. One may also note that there was a strong interest in Islamic astrology in fifteenth-century Ferrara, 'which was in the vanguard of astrological scholarship during the reigns of both Borso and Ercole'.[55] Pellegrino Prisciani, a renowned Ferrarese astrologer, is greatly indebted to Abū Maʿshar (or Albumasar), a ninth-century Persian astrologer and philosopher, as well as to the *De revolutione annorum mundi* by Masha'allah ibn Atharī, an eighth-century Persian astrologer and astronomer. As has been shown first by Aby Warburg, it is Prisciani's astrological theories that underpin Francesco del Cossa's 'Salone dei mesi' [Hall of Months] in Palazzo Schifanoia.[56]

Ariosto adds a further element to Boiardo's elaborate portrayal of Saracen culture. Among the characters of the *Furioso* there are two Saracen poets, namely Olimpio da la Serra, 'un giovineto che col dolce canto, | concorde al suon de la cornuta cetra, | di intenerir un cor si dava vanto, | anchor che fusse più duro che pietra' [a youth who could sing so sweetly | to the accompaniment of the horn-shaped lyre | that he boasted of softening | even the flintiest of hearts] (XIV 72,1–4 AB; XVI C), and Medoro. The former is a Spaniard while the latter, as already mentioned above, is from Tolomitta, a North African city. Slain before the very eyes of his friend Ferraù (who 'solea amar e haver in prezzo e stima' [loved him well and held him in high esteem], 73,2), Olimpio is partly modelled on Virgil's Creteus, an epic bard who falls in battle (*Aeneid*, IX 774–77). As Marco Dorigatti points out, in the figure of the Saracen poet 'si rispecchia quella dell'autore, a cui pure incombe la necessità di contemperare il "dolce canto" con il suono, ben altrimenti aspro, della battaglia' [is mirrored that of the author, who, too, needs to harmonize his 'sweet song' with the much harsher sound of battle].[57] Medoro, on the contrary, is not a poet by trade, but his prayer to the Moon is imbued with lyricism, and the inscription which he makes at the entrance to a grotto — a passionate celebration of the joys of reciprocated love — is versified: 'Del gran piacer ch'in la spelonca prese, | questa sententia in versi havea ridotta' [The inscription was written in verse | and spoke of the great pleasure he had enjoyed in this cave] (XXI 107,5–6 AB; XXIII C). Medoro's 'epigramma' (which the poor Orlando reads again and again, multilingualism being the norm in chivalric romances) may well be the first written Arabic poem in Italian chivalric literature, even if a number of earlier chivalric texts feature Saracen singers and musicians.[58] Having assured the reader that it must

---

55    Cavallo, *The World beyond Europe*, p. 115.
56    On Pellegrino Prisciani see Antonio Rotondò, 'Pellegrino Prisciani (1435 ca.–1518)', *Rinascimento*, 9 (1960), 69–110. On the Islamic influences on Francesco del Cossa's famous frescoes see Aby Warburg, *The Renewal of Pagan Antiquity: Contributions to the Cultural History of the European Renaissance* (Los Angeles: Getty Research Institute for the History of Art and the Humanities, 1999).
57    Marco Dorigatti, 'Borges, Ariosto e la vita segreta dei personaggi minori', p. 394.
58    In the *Entrée d'Espagne* the Saracen 'stormant' [captain] asks Roland whether he wants to listen

have been a very fine piece in the original Arabic ('che fusse culta in la sua lingua penso' [I believe it was written in his native language] (107,7)), Ariosto provides an 'Italian translation' which takes up two octaves and, as befits a love poem, is replete with Petrarchan reminiscences. Its indebtedness to Petrarch is (perhaps unintentionally) ironic considering that the author of the *Canzoniere* had a very low opinion of Arabic poetry and, more generally, of all things oriental.[59] Like Petrarch, Ariosto must have known that poets and poetry existed in the real Islamic world.[60] However, both Olimpio da la Serra and Medoro are inspired by similar figures in ancient literature and Medoro's poems are patterned after Western literary models, as are Saracen songs in the preceding chivalric tradition.[61]

As far as Saracen cities and palaces are concerned, both Ariosto and Boiardo stress their opulence and beauty, as did many other chivalric authors before them.[62]

to a song about Galiaine and Charlemagne ('mes sergant zantent plus cler e doz qe seraine' [my sergeants sing more clearly and sweetly than a mermaid], 11808) when he sees that his passenger is in very low spirits. In the *Cantari d'Aspramonte* and in the *Altobello* it is Saracen damsels who have angelic voices: in the former poem an anonymous Saracen girl plays the harp and sings about Paris's abduction of Helen (*Cantari d'Aspr.*, XIX 22–23), while in the latter poem Morandina, the daughter of King Morandino (whose other talents include astrology and medicine), sings about the death of Tristan (*Altobello*, XXXII 157–63 [fols oiii^v- oiiii^r]).

59    In one of the *Epistolae seniles* (XII, 2), Petrarch tells his interlocutor (Giovanni Dondi, a doctor) that the Arabs have never produced anything worthwhile. It is highly unlikely that Petrarch had first-hand knowledge of Arabic poetry, but, as Charles Burnett suggests, he must have read Averroes's *Poetria Aristotelis*, in which one particular genre of Arabic poetry is criticized. See Charles Burnett, 'Learned Knowledge of Arabic Poetry, Rhymed Prose and Didactic Verse from Petrus Alfonsi to Petrarch', in *Poetry and Philosophy in the Middle Ages: A Festschrift for Peter Dronke*, ed. by John Marenbon (Leiden: Brill, 2001), pp. 29–62 (pp. 47–51).

60    There are references to Arabic poetry not only in Petrarch and Averroes's *Poetria Aristotelis*, but also in a number of other medieval works. Riccoldo da Monte di Croce, an influential Christian apologist and a travel writer, claims that the Qur'an is a poem in his famous treatise on Islam, *Contra legem saracenorum* (c. 1300): '[...] è da sapere che Alcorano non è lege de Dio: perché non ha stillo né modo consono alla lege de Dio che el stillo suo è metrico [...]' [it must be known that Qur'an is not God's law: because its style and manner are not suitable for God's law, as it uses the style of poetry] (Paulus Angelus, Ricoldus de Monte Crucis, *Epistola ad Saracenos: cum libello contra Alcoranum: pro provida: previaque dispositione conversionis infidelium* (Venice: Alessandro Bindoni, c. 1520), fol. D2^r). Fazio degli Uberti alludes to this passage in his *Dittamondo* (XIII 22–25).

61    It is unlikely that Ariosto had direct knowledge of Arabic literature, even if many critics have noted the striking similarity between the Fiammetta novella (XXVI 1–74 AB; XXVIII C) and the frame story of *The Thousand and One Nights* (see, for example, Rajna, *Le fonti*, pp. 436–40). *The Thousand and One Nights* was first translated into a European language in the eighteenth century, and although some scholars claim that it started to exert its influence on Western literature already in the Middle Ages, thus far no concrete proof of this has been found. Ariosto himself attributes the authorship of the most bawdy story of the *Furioso* to his friend Giovan Francesco Valier (XXV 137,2–7 AB; XXVII 137,2–7 C), a Venetian diplomat and adventurer, who might have heard a version of the Arabic story. The Fiammetta novella also recalls Giovanni Sercambi's *De ingenio mulieris adultere*. According to Margherita Scampinato Beretta, Ariosto's and Sercambi's novellas derive from a common Western source (given that the names Astolfo and Fiammetta feature in both texts), which is related to an Eastern source, but not necessarily *The Thousand and One Nights* (Margherita Scampinato Beretta, 'La cornice delle *Mille e una notte* ed il canto XXVIII dell'*Orlando furioso*', in *Medioevo romanzo e orientale*, ed. by Antonio Pioletti and Rizzo Nervo (Catanzaro: Soveria Mannelli, 1999), pp. 229–49.

62    The opulence of the East (be it Islamic or Byzantine) is a topos not only in chivalric texts but in Renaissance and medieval Western literature in general.

Agramante's palace in Biserta is a splendid piece of architecture: 'il sol mai non ne vide un altro tale | di più richezza e più magnificenza' [the sun had never seen another | richer and more magnificent] (*Inam.*, II i 20,3–4). Its stairs are covered with golden carpets and its main hall is decorated with frescoes that illustrate the exploits of Alexander the Great, an important figure in Islamic culture who is even honoured with a mention in the Qur'an, namely in *Sūrat al-Kahf* (سورة الكهف), 83–99, where he is described as a just ruler and a God-fearing Muslim. Whether or not Boiardo knew about Alexander's reputation in the Islamic world (he could have heard that Mehmed II was 'aspirante a gloria quanto Alexandro Macedonico' [aspiring to glory like Alexander of Macedon]),[63] his main source must be (one of) the *Aspramonte* stories, where the Macedonian conqueror is said to be the founder of the North African dynasty to which Agramante's grandfather Agolante belongs. Moreover, as will be suggested in Chapter III, other chivalric texts contain references to the cult of Alexander in *Paganìa*, which could effectively mean that their authors were aware of Alexander's fame in the Islamic lands.

Ariosto's descriptions of Saracen cities have a fairytale-like feel to them too, but they are slightly more precise and realistic. Thus, talking about Cairo, he notes that:

> Non era grande il Chairo così allhora
> come se ne ragiona a nostra etade:
> ch'el populo capir, che ve dimora,
> non pôn diciotto mila gran contrade;
> e che le case hanno tre palchi, e anchora
> ne dormono infiniti in su le strade;
> e che 'l Soldano v'habita un castello
> mirabil di grandezza, e ricco e bello;
>
> e che quindice mila suoi vasalli,
> che son christiani rinegati tutti,
> con moglie, con famigli e con cavalli
> ha sotto un tetto sol quivi ridutti.
>
> [Cairo was not as large then
> as we are told it is today;
> today its population is too big
> even for its eighteen thousand principal streets:
> its houses are three stories high
> and even so thousands have to sleep in the road:
> the Sultan lives in a castle
> that is remarkable for its size, opulence and beauty;
>
> and he has housed all under one roof
> fifteen thousand of his subjects,

---

63 See Zorzi Dolfin's *Cronaca* (Dolfin draws on the description of Mehmed furnished by his Italian physician, the Venetian Giacomo Langusto). The passage is cited in Jean Colin, *Cyriaque d'Ancône: le voyager, le marchand, l'humaniste* (Paris: Maloine, 1981), p. 381. Nor was Mehmed alone among Muslim rulers in striving to emulate Alexander. In the already-mentioned 1506 letter to Isabella d'Este, Sabba da Castiglione says that he was told by the son of the 'Gran Caramano' that the 'Soffi [...] quanto più po' in tutte le sue operazione si sforza da imitare et emulare el Magno Alexandro, re de Macedonia' [Shah endeavours to imitate and emulate in all his actions, as much as he can, Alexander the Great, King of Macedon] (*Fra Sabba da Castiglione, Isabella d'Este e altri*, p. 31).

all of whom renegade Christians,
with their wives, families and horses.
(*Fur.*, XIII 44; 45,1–4 AB; XV 63–64 C)

According to Luciano Serra, Ariosto could be drawing on Lionardo Frescobaldi's *Viaggio in Egitto e in Terra Santa*.[64] Both Frescobaldi and Niccolò da Poggibonsi (another famous fourteenth-century traveller who recounted his pilgrimage to the Holy Land in his *Libro d'Oltramare*, 1346–1350) say that Cairo is overcrowded (like Ariosto, Frescobaldi observes that some people have to sleep outdoors) and mention the Sultan's castle and the Christian converts to Islam, whose number Frescobaldi estimates at twenty-five thousand and Poggibonsi at thirty thousand: 'Ha nella città del Cairo circa a venti-cinque migliaja di Cristiani rinegati' [In the city of Cairo there are about twenty-five thousand Christian renegades];[65] 'Ora diremo de' tapini miseri che stanno in tale dannazione, quelli che 'l nostro Signore Gesù Cristo ànno rinegato, chi per danari e chi per altra cagione, cioè per sua miseria; e di questi ci à trenta migliaia di persone rinegate' [Now we shall say about the wretches who live in such damnation, those who have renounced our Lord Jesus Christ, some because of money, some for a different reason, that is because of their wretchedness; and there are thirty thousand of such renegades].[66] Even though Frescobaldi and Poggibonsi give the total number of renegades living in Cairo and Ariosto only counts the Mamluks, it is clear that there is a discrepancy between these travelogues and the *Furioso*. Moreover, one cannot help but be struck by the difference in tone: while Poggibonsi's voice is laced with indignation, Ariosto talks about the 'christiani rinegati' in a matter-of-fact manner, without appealing to the readers' emotions.[67]

Whereas Ariosto's description of Damascus (a flourishing city erected on the banks of 'duo fiumi crystallini' [two crystal streams], dotted with ever-green gardens, with beautiful carpets covering the main street and finest draperies hanging from all the doors and windows; a city enveloped in a cloud of fragrance, where women wear sumptuous dresses and luxurious jewellery: XV 18–21 AB; XVII C) is largely consistent with Poggibonsi's, his source for the Cairo stanzas has yet to be identified.[68] There is no unanimity among Italian travellers as to the exact number of Mamluks in Cairo. Don Domenico, the secretary of Marquis Nicolò d'Este's illegitimate son Meliaduse (who had undertaken a pilgrimage to Jerusalem in 1440–

---

64    Luciano Serra, 'Da Tolomeo alla Garfagnana: la geografia dell'Ariosto', *Bollettino storico reggiano, numero speciale*, 4 (1974), 151–84.

65    Frescobaldi, *Viaggio*, p. 94.

66    Niccolò da Poggibonsi, *Libro d'Oltramare*, ed. by Alberto Bacchi della Lega, 2 vols (Bologna: Gaetano Romagnoli, 1881), II, p. 62.

67    While Donnelly claims that Ariosto does not appear to be scandalized (Donnelly, 'The Moslem Enemy in Renaissance Epic: Ariosto, Tasso and Camoëns', p. 165), Cavallo, reads these lines very differently: 'Ariosto's blunt characterization of Mamelukes as "all Christian renegades" [...] not only brings to the fore a centuries-old Christian-Muslim conflict but creates the worrisome impression that in his day thousands of Christians were freely renouncing their religion en masse and joining forces with the Egyptian sultan' (Cavallo, *The World beyond Europe*, p. 162).

68    On Poggibonsi and Ariosto's descriptions of Damascus see Cavallo, *The World beyond Europe*, p. 172.

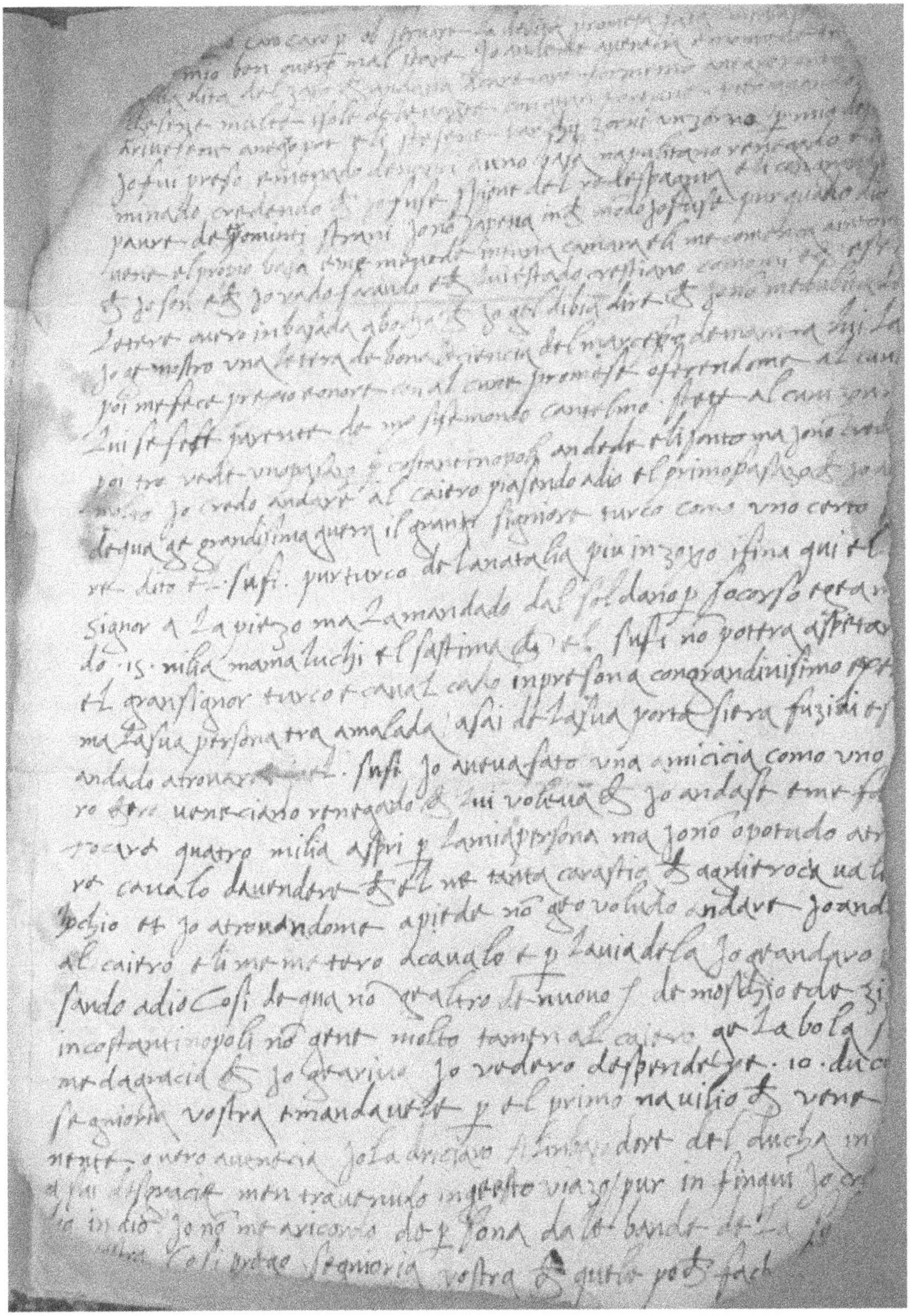

FIG. 1.1. Giulio Sacrati to Cardinal Ippolito d'Este (1507). Modena, Archivio di Stato, Ambasciatori estensi, busta 15/ unica, Egitto

1441, visiting Syria, Lebanon, and Egypt as part of his voyage to the Holy Land) puts their number at ten thousand,[69] while in a letter of 1501 to Vettor Querini, the Venetian Filippo Contarini mentions eleven or twelve thousand Mamluks.[70] In light of this, it is worth noting that there is a reference to fifteen thousand Mamluks in an as yet unpublished letter sent to Cardinal Ippolito d'Este by Giulio Sacrati possibly from Alexandria [Fig. 1.1]: informing Ippolito about a 'grandissima guerra' [huge war] between the Turkish sultan and the 'sufi', or Persian shah, Sacrati says that the former had asked the sultan for help and that 'ge andò 15 milia mamaluchi' [15 thousand Mamluks went there].[71] Although Sacrati does not say that the sultan only has fifteen thousand Mamluks, the fact that the letter features this number is interesting, all the more so considering that it must have been written around 1507, that is when Ariosto was composing his poem.[72] As the cardinal's secretary, Ariosto could have read it or heard about Sacrati's adventures abroad, undoubtedly an exciting topic of conversation for Ippolito's courtiers. Sacrati travelled from Venice to Negroponte and from there to Constantinople, hoping to go to Cairo, where he was planning to spend the ten ducats Ippolito had given him. We do not know whether he ever reached Cairo; nor do we know much about him,

---

69    Don Domenico, *Viagio del Sancto Sepolcro facto per lo Illustro Misere Milliaduxe Estense*, ed. by Beatrice Saletti (Rome: Istituto Storico Italiano per il Medio Evo, 2009), p. 134. Meliaduse was not the first member of the Este family to visit the Holy Sepulchre. Some twenty-seven years earlier, in 1413, his father Nicolò had completed a similar journey, accompanied, among other courtiers, by Boiardo's grandfather Feltrino Boiardo (who was knighted in Jerusalem) and Luchino dal Campo, who was entrusted with the task of chronicling the pilgrimage (see Luchino del Campo, *El viaggio al Santo Sepolcro del nostro Signor Gesù Cristo in Jerusalem, el qual fece lo Illustrissimo Signor Marchese Nicolò da Este con altri gentiluomini suoi compagni*, ed. by Giovanni Ghinassi (Turin: UTET, 1861), pp. 99–160). While Nicolò and his companions had very little contact with Muslims, Meliaduse and his men experienced the local culture in a much more immersive way, developing a sincere appreciation for it, which is manifest, for example, in Don Domenico's admiration of the beauty of the mosques in Cairo (*Viagio del Sancto Sepolcro*, p. 135). Meliaduse had an Arabic-speaking man in his entourage, Folco Contarini, a Venetian who had previously travelled extensively in the Middle East. Thanks to Contarini's knowledge of Arabic and local customs, the pilgrims could go from city to city on horseback disguised as Muslims. This is of course how Boiardo's Orlando travels through Saracen lands: he pretends to be a Saracen knight, Rotolante from Circassia (*Inam.*, II xix 59, 3–7), which also brings to mind the travels of the famous Burgundian spy Bertrandon de la Brocquière who undertook a pilgrimage to the Middle East in 1432–1433. Bertrandon, too, pretended to be a Circassian (see *Le Voyage d'Outremer de Bertrandon de la Brocquière, premier écuyer tranchant et conseiller de Philippe le Bon, duc de Bourgogne*, ed. by Charles Henri Auguste Schefer (Farnborough: Gregg, 1972), p. 105), and, like Boiardo's Orlando, he had a Muslim companion whom he had met by chance and who saved his life on numerous occasions.

70    Contarini's letter was transcribed by Marin Sanudo: see Marin Sanudo, *Diarii*, ed. by Rinaldo Fulin et al., 58 vols (Venice: Visentini, 1879–1903), IV, pp. 167–70 (p. 168).

71    Modena, Archivio di Stato, Ambasciatori estensi, busta 15/ unica, Egitto, Giulio Sacrati, fol. 1ʳ.

72    In this letter Sacrati mentions Kemal Reis (1451–1511), a famous Turkish corsair, and his journey to Alexandria: 'El Gran Signior Turco a mandado dui navili al Soldano carichi de metalo acioché el facia fare da l'artelaria; el portator è stato Camali, el primo corsaro del mondo. El Gran Misto de Rodi si l'a abuto per spia è venuto fora con .60. vele per prenderlo [...]' [The Great Lord Turk sent two ships to the Sultan laden with metal so that he can have artillery made; the carrier was Camali, the first corsair in the world. The Grand Master of Rhodes found out about this from a spy and sailed out with 60 ships to capture him] (Giulio Sacrati, fol. 1ᵛ). Sacrati seems to be referring to events that took place in August 1507.

apart from the fact that he could have been one of the gentlemen in Ippolito's household.[73]

Finally, before moving on to the next section, it is appropriate to add here a note on Boiardo's and Ariosto's use of oriental terminology. Unlike Pulci, the Ferrarese poets use them sparingly. The vast majority of the oriental terms that we find in the *Inamoramento de Orlando* and the *Furioso* feature in earlier chivalric romances too, which could either mean that Boiardo and Ariosto did not have much exposure to oriental languages or that they deliberately chose not to go beyond the conventional 'oriental lexicon' of the received chivalric tradition. Thus, the *Inamoramento de Orlando* contains the following vocabulary:

> *alchena* ('henna', from the Arabic 'al-ḥinā'' [الحناء], III vi 7,3);
> *Alcorana* [*sic*] ('the Qur'an', 'al-qur'ān' [القرآن], I xxii 42,6);
> *algalia* (a type of perfume, a Spanish word probably derived from the Arabic 'al-ghālīah' [الغالية], II xxviii 46,5);
> *almansore* ('lord', from the Arabic 'al-manṣūr' [المنصور], 'the victorious', I v 35,1);
> *Amirante* ('emir', from the Arabic 'amīr' [أمير], I i 4,7 and six more occurrences);
> *alphana* (I iv 31,8 and ten more occurrences) and *afferante* ('horse', from the Arabic 'al-faras' [الفرس], I ix 62,3 and five more occurrences);
> *Argalipha* ('the Caliph', from the Arabic 'al-khalīfah' [الخليفة], I iv 22,4 and seven more occurrences);
> *simitara* ('a sabre with a curved blade', from the Persian 'shamshēr' [شمشير], I v 39,5 and five more occurrences);
> *Soldano* ('Sultan', from the Arabic 'sulṭān' [سلطان], II xviii 6,3 and two more occurences);
> *talabalachi* ('tympans', from the Arabic 'ṭablah' [طبلة], III viii 3,3);
> *torcimano* ('translator', from the Arabic 'mutarjim' [مترجم], I i 17,3).

Moreover, it is possible that the title *sobasso* (Doristella's first husband was 'sobasso [...] di Bursa', II xxvi 31,1) has an oriental origin,[74] while the name of Angelica's fortress, *Albracà*, brings to mind the Arabic word 'al-barakah' [البركة] which translates as 'blessing'.[75]

As for Ariosto, he reuses some of the terms that appear in the *Inamoramento de Orlando*:

> *Alcorano*, XXXIV 81,6 AB; XXXVIII C;
> *Alfana*, II 51,6–7 ABC and three more occurrences;
> *Amirante*, XII 16,3 AB; XIV C;
> *Argalifa*, XII 16,3 AB; XIV C; XVI 44,3 AB; XVIII C;

---

73 Sacrati refers to the cardinal's 'bande' [gangs], which suggests that he took part in Ippolito's parties and other social activities (ibid.).

74 Giovanni Gherardini suggests that *sobasso* might be a corrupt reading for *sobabo*, the Italian form of the French term *soubab*, meaning 'governor of an Asiatic province'. See his *Supplimento a' vocabolarj italiani proposto da Giovanni Gherardini*, 6 vols (Milan: Stamperia di Gius. Bernardoni di Gio., 1852–1857), VI, p. 477. Soubab derives from the Indian word *soubahdâr*, meaning 'master of governor of a large province'.

75 According to Giovanni Ponte, the siege of Albracà could be inspired by Genghis Khan's capture of Bukhara (Giovanni Ponte, *La personalità e l'opera del Boiardo* (Genova: Tilgher, 1974), p. 94). In the comment to I v 72 in her edition of the *Inamoramento de Orlando*, Tissoni Benvenuti states that Boiardo could have also thought of Balac in Marco Polo's *Milione*.

scimitarra, XIV 72,7 AB; XVI C and three more occurrences;
Soldan, XI 31,8 AB; XIII C and four more occurences;

and also adds some new ones, namely:

acque Lanfe ('perfume', from Arabic 'nakhah' [نكهة], XV 19,6 AB; XVII C);
amostante ('an Arab chief', possibly derived from the word 'emir', 'amīr' [أمير], VIII 85,7 ABC);
Cadì ('qadi' or 'judge', from the Arabic 'qāḍī' [قاضي], XXXVI 14,1 AB; XL C);
Califè (like 'Argalifa', 'the Caliph', from the Arabic 'al-khalīfah' [الخليفة], XIII 77,2 B; XV 96,6 C);
Dïodarro ('minister', from the Turkish 'defterdar', 'bookkeeper', XV 97,2 AB; XVII C);
Marano ('converted Jew', a racist insult derived from the Arabic 'muharram' [محرم], 'the anathematized', I 26,6 ABC; X 49,2 AB; XII 45 C);[76]
Talacimanni ('muezzins', from the Persian 'dānishmand' [دانشمند], 'the learned ones', XVI 7,6 AB; XVIII C).

Many of these terms are not only part of the stock vocabulary of earlier Italian chivalric authors but also feature in the *chansons de geste*, having entered Old French at the time of the First Crusade: *almansore*, for example, corresponds to the Old French 'almaçur', *Amirante* to 'amirafles', *Argaliffa* to 'Augalie', *amostante* to 'amustans', *afferante* to 'alferant', *Soldano* to 'Soldan', *torcimanno* to 'trucheman'. The word *simitara* (or *scimitarra*) features in Andrea da Barberino's *Guerrin Meschino* and Pulci's *Morgante* and *Ciriffo Calvaneo*. Other terms are more rare, but not entirely unknown to chivalric authors. In the *Morgante*, for example, we find *acqua lanfa* (XXV 216,2), *marrano* (XXVI 47,3 and five more occurrences) and *talacimanno* (XVII 133,4 and four more occurrences). The term *Cadì* does not seem to appear in any other chivalric text than Ariosto, but it features in non-fictional works, such as the above-mentioned *Itinerario* by Ludovico di Varthema.

As far as the names of Boiardo's and Ariosto's Saracen characters are concerned, we can say with certainty that Nora(n)dino's name has an Arabic origin: 'Norandino' derives from the Arabic name 'Nūr al-dīn' [نور الدين] which translates as 'the light of religion'. Boiardo named his character after 'Noradino padre del pregiatissimo Saladino' [Noradino father of the most worthy Saladin] (Nur ad-Din, emir of Aleppo and Damascus, 1118–1174), who features in his translation of Riccobaldo ferrarese.[77] As for the remaining names, some of them have an Arabic flavour to them thanks to such prefixes as al-, ag-, an- and ar-: Agolante, Agricane, Albrizach, Alfrera, Alibante, Almonte, Alzirdo, Analardo, Archidante, Archiloro, Argalìa, Arganio, Argante, Argesto, Argosto, Ariante.

---

76  Ludovico Castelvetro observes that Ariosto's use of the term 'Marano' is anachronistic, explaining that this insult appeared centuries after Charlemagne's time, when 'i giudei habbitanti in Ispagna furono costretti dalla forza reale o contra loro volontà a mostrarsi di far Christiani, o andar tapinando per lo mondo' [the Jews who lived in Spain were forced by the king's authority to pretend to have become Christians against their will or else to go roaming the world] (Ludovico Castelvetro, *Poetica d'Aristotele vulgarizzata, et sposta* (Vienna: Gaspar Stainhofer, 1570), fol. 341ᵛ).
77  Boiardo, *Historia imp.*, III–IV, p. 351. Boiardo seems to be conflating Nur ad-Din and Saladin's father Najm ad-Din Ayyub.

### Chivalric poetry as a response to the Turkish threat?

Having examined Boiardo's and Ariosto's portrayal of the Saracen religion and culture, the next question that naturally arises is: do the events recounted in the two poems have any basis in history? Seeking to demonstrate that Ariosto did not completely disregard the Aristotelian principle of verisimilitude, some sixteenth-century commentators maintain that the *Furioso* (and chivalric romances in general) has a historical foundation. For example, Simon Fórnari invokes the authority of the Venetian historian Marco Antonio Sabellico to prove that 'nel vero fur già nel mondo et Orlando, et Rinaldo, et gli altri Paladini, et fur valorosi et potenti nelle arme, et hebbero in molte imprese singolari et gloriose vittorie' [Orlando, and Rinaldo and the other Paladins really existed in the world, and they were valorous and strong in arms, and they had singular and glorious victories in many ventures],[78] while Orazio Toscanella asserts that the plot of the *Furioso* is inspired by Charlemagne's wars with 'il Re de i Sarracini appellato Atima' [the King of Saracens called Atima] and the Spanish 'Re Amor; ò come altri vogliono, Machine; et dal volgo Marsiglio' [King Amor, or as others call him, Machine; and Marsiglio as he is called by common people].[79] However, one only has to read the description of Charlemagne's reign in Boiardo's translation of the *Historia imperiale* to realize that Boiardo — and almost certainly Ariosto too — was well aware of the gap between chivalric literature and medieval history.[80] The *Inamoramento de Orlando* and the *Furioso* show very little concern for historical accuracy. Claiming to draw on 'la vera historia de Turpin' [Turpin's true story] (*Inam.*, I i 4,1), the poets certainly do not expect their readers to believe them.

While the issue of historical accuracy needs no further discussion, it remains to be seen whether and to what extent Boiardo and Ariosto engage with contemporary discourses about the Ottomans and other Islamic nations. Having briefly hosted the Ferrara-Florence Council (1438–1439), Ferrara was not actively involved in the Italo-Turkish conflicts during the two poets' lifetimes. Pius II, the only Renaissance Pope who passionately believed that his mission on Earth was to launch a crusade against the Ottomans, doubted Borso's crusading zeal, suspecting that the latter merely wanted the Holy See to confirm his title as Duke of Ferrara.[81] The title was eventually confirmed by Paul II in 1471, and Ercole and his children did not have to pretend to be ardent crusaders. However, the rulers and citizens of Ferrara were certainly conscious of the danger coming from the Ottoman Empire. In the

---

78  Simon Fórnari, *La spositione sopra l'Orlando furioso di M. Ludovico Ariosto* (Florence: Lorenzo Torrentino, 1549), p. 76. The fact that Sabellico thought the Carolingian legends had a solid historical foundation testifies to the enduring appeal of the *Historia Karoli Magni et Rotholandi* (also known as the *Pseudo-Turpin Chronicle*), a twelfth-century forged chronicle recounting Charlemagne's Spanish campaign.

79  Orazio Toscanella, *Bellezze del Furioso di M. Lodovico Ariosto* (Venice: Pietro dei Franceschi, & nepoti, 1574), fol. *6ʳ.

80  Riccobaldo's (Boiardo's) account of the battle of Rencesvals makes no mention of Saracens. Charlemagne's Spanish campaign is narrated without any holy war rhetoric, and Rolando is slaughtered by the Gascons (*Historia imp.*, III-IV, p. 294).

81  See Aeneas Sylvius Piccolomini, *I Commentarii*, ed. by Luigi Totaro, 2 vols (Milan: Adelphi, 1984), I, pp. 510–15.

anonymous *Diario ferrarese* there are entries on the Fall of Constantinople (1453), the Turkish conquest of Negroponte (1470), and public processions and firework displays in Ferrara to celebrate Christian victories over the infidels.[82] The advances of the Ottomans shocked Bernardino Zambotti, as is evident from the 1480–1481 entries in his chronicle. He records, for example, the pact between Ferrara and other Christian states 'a defensione de la fede e a destruxione del Turcho' [to defend our faith and to destroy the Turk] in the aftermath of the conquest of Otranto.[83] Convinced that Otranto is the 'porto e schala al Turcho da pigliare tuta la Italia e cristianitade' [port and ladder for the Turk to conquer all Italy and Christendom], he implores God to save it 'da mane de infedeli e de pessimi cani turchi' [from the hands of the infidels and the most evil Turkish dogs].[84] Moreover, we know from his *Diario* that at the news of one of Alfonso of Calabria's victories 'fu facto fallò e fogi in Piaza per alegreza' [there were bonfires and fires in the square as a sign of jubilation][85] and that the announcements of Mehmed's death and the liberation of Otranto were met with public celebrations.[86]

These entries give the impression that anti-Turkish sentiment was strong in Ferrara, but there is another side to the story. As a conglomeration of states which competed with each other for power, Italy failed to create a united front against the Turks. Not even in the dramatic months following the Ottoman conquest of Otranto did Italian princes forget their rivalries and conflicts. While Bernardino Zambotti was alarmed at the arrival of the Turks on Italian soil, after the initial fear that this might be the beginning of a full-scale invasion, Italian rulers did not see the capture of Otranto as a problem of apocalyptic proportions. Nicolò Sadoleto — Ferrarese envoy to Naples in 1480–1481 — kept Ercole abreast of the latest developments. His encrypted dispatches reveal that in 1481 the Pope and the King of Naples seriously considered negotiating an alliance with Mehmed II and trying to set him against Venice.[87] And in actual fact, Ferrante did enter into an alliance with the Turks during the War of Ferrara (1482–1484): the same Zambotti records that on 16 June 1483, Ferrante's messenger arrived in Ferrara with the news 'como il magno Octomano, Re de' Turchi, hera romaxo in Concordia con soa Maiesta e facta bona pace tra loro e firmati li capitoli, fra li quali prometteva non venire contra dicta Liga a favore de' Veneciani' [that the great Ottoman, King of the Turks, had remained in Amity with his Majesty and made peace and signed the peace agreements, among which was the promise not to attack the said League to help the Venetians]. That day Ferrara celebrated the good news by ringing all the bells in the city.[88]

---

82    *Diario Ferrarese dall'anno 1476 sino a 1504*, in *Diario ferrarese dall'anno 1409 sino al 1502 / di autori incerti*, appendix, ed. by Giuseppe Pardi (Bologna: N. Zanichelli, 1928–1937), pp. 30 [23 March 1447], 37 [1453], 38 [7 August 1456], 64 [31 July 1470].

83    Bernardino Zambotti, *Diario Ferrarese dall'anno 1476 sino a 1504*, in *Diario ferrarese dall'anno 1409 sino al 1502*, fasc. 5/6–9/10 (p. 80 [27 August 1480]).

84    Ibid., p. 86 [end of February 1481].

85    Ibid. [8–9 March 1481].

86    Ibid., pp. 93–94 [3 June 1481]; pp. 95–96 [16 September 1481].

87    See Daniele Palma, *L'autentica storia di Otranto nella guerra contro i turchi: Nuova luce sugli eventi del 1480–81 dalle lettere cifrate tra Ercole d'Este e i suoi diplomatici* (Calimera: Edizioni Kurumuny, 2013), pp. 216, 284–85.

88    Zambotti, *Diario Ferrarese*, pp. 136–37.

Explicit references to contemporary Christian-Muslim wars are scattered throughout the two *Orlandos*. In the *ekphrasis* of Brandimarte's 'bel pavaglione' [fair pavilion] (*Inam.*, II xxvii 50,8) — which a divine Sybil embroidered with 'gran fatti, en degne historie e peregrine' [great deeds, told in worthy and noble accounts] (52,4), including the glorious deeds of the 'duodeci Alfonsi' [twelve Alfonsos] (52,7), that is the Alfonsos of the Aragonese dynasty — Boiardo alludes to the 1432 expedition against Tunisian pirates organized by Alfonso V of Aragon (1416–1458) and to the liberation of Otranto (1481) by the troops of Alfonso Duke of Calabria (1448–1495). Presenting Alfonso the Magnanimous's partially successful campaign (Alfonso failed to conquer the island of Djerba) as a dazzling victory, Boiardo calls him a conqueror of Africa: 'l'Affrica vinta a lui stava davante | ingienochiata col suo popul rio' [before him, beaten Africa | and all its abject people kneel] (54,5–6). However, the poet hastens to add that Alfonso's expansionist ambitions were focused on Italy, of which he 'avìa preso un gran limbo' [had taken a large part] (54,7); 'Italia vinta' [conquered Italy] (55,3) captivated the heart of the Aragonese ruler so that he forgot his native Spain. As for his grandson's victory over the Turks, Boiardo devotes two lines to it, saying that the Sybil's embroidery vividly showed 'sì com'è Italia da' Turchi diffesa | per sua prodecia sola e suo valore' [how Italy is defended | from Turks thanks to his valour and by strength alone] (56bis,3–4).[89] Then, Boiardo moves on to his other exploits, such as the military triumph against Florence and its allies at Poggio Imperiale and the many 'forteze roinate al fondo' [fortresses he'd toppled] (56 bis,5–8).

Is this encomium of Ercole's Aragonese relatives designed to remind the reader of the threat coming from North Africa and the Ottoman Empire? Boiardo looks at contemporary history through the lens of secular chivalry: he portrays the two Alfonsos as perfect knights, paragons of prowess, valour and courtesy in all their undertakings. Their feats of arms against Muslim enemies deserve the highest praise, but their victories against fellow Christians are no less exceptional from the point of view of chivalry. It is interesting to note that in one of his political eclogues (composed in 1482–1483, that is during the war with Venice, in which Ferrante of Naples took Ferrara's side) Boiardo compares Alfonso's re-conquest of Otranto to a victory over a terrifying dragon ('un drago sì crudel [...] | che tuta Ausonia avea già posta in pianto' [a dragon so cruel [...] | that it made all Ausonia, i.e. Italy, weep] (*Pastorale*, II, 41–42)), but hails his triumph at Poggio Imperiale in 1479 — where he fought against the Florentines, who had entrusted their forces to none other than Ercole d'Este — as the high-water mark of his military career, being 'tale | che non se amenta in terra la magiore' [such | that in the whole world no greater one is remembered] (ibid., 50–51). One may add that even though in the *Pastorale* and the Latin *Pastoralia* Boiardo appears more concerned about the bellicose intentions

---

89    This octave, which did not feature in any of the fifteenth-century editions of the first two books, is reproduced in the critical apparatus of Tissoni Benvenuti's edition. According to Tissoni Benvenuti, the octave must have been composed after 1484 (the end of the war with Venice, in which Alfonso was an ally of Ferrara) and added to the first three-book edition of the poem, published in 1495. In Riccardo Bruscagli's edition, which is based on the Trivulziano manuscript, it features in the main text as octave 57.

of the Turkish sultan than in the *Inamoramento de Orlando*, he does not consider the Turks to be the greatest scourge of his age: the claws of the Venetian lion — 'il magior monstro mai non fo veduto' [the greatest monster ever seen] (*Pastorale*, I, 164) — represent a far more serious danger for the future of the Italian peninsula and especially Ferrara.[90] It is true that the Venetians had particularly strong ties with the Turks, with some of their enemies claiming that they had sold Christ for worldly benefits that could be obtained from close relations with the Turkish sultan. However, it is equally true that 'there was yet scarcely a government of any consequence which did not conspire against other Italian states with Muhammad II and his successors'.[91]

Boiardo makes few explicit references to contemporary historical events and one single allusion to the Ottomans. By contrast, deeply anchored in historical reality, the *Furioso* abounds in authorial digressions dealing with matters external to the *fabula*. On two occasions Ariosto interrupts his story to lament the lack of crusading zeal in contemporary Europe, in a way reminiscent of Petrarch (*Trionfo della fama*, 137–48).[92] Recounting Astolfo's visit to Jerusalem, Ariosto says that the paladin visited the churches

> c'hor con eterno obbrobrio e vituperio
> a' Christiani usurpano i Mori empi.
> L'Europa è in arme, e di far guerra agogna
> in ogni parte, fuor ch'ove bisogna.

> [which now, to their eternal shame and ignominy,
> are usurped from the Christians by impious Moors.
> Europe is in arms and aches to do battle
> everywhere, except where battle is needed.]
>      (*Fur.*, XIII 80,5–8 AB; XV 99 C)

Two cantos later, Ariosto delivers a passionate speech on this subject, a fiery diatribe against the unnecessary and unjustified bloodshed in Europe which spans over six and a half octaves (XV 73,7–8; 74–79 AB; XVII C). Decrying the violence of the Italian wars, he urges the Pope (Leo X in all three printed editions of the *Furioso*; Julius II in the lost original manuscript)[93] and other Christian rulers to make peace and join forces against the common enemy:

> S'esser voi Christianissimi volete,
> e voi altri Catholici nomati,
> perché di Chisto li huomini uccidete?
> perché de' beni lor son dispogliati?
> Perché Hierusalem non rïhavete,

90   See also *Pastorale*, I 43–44; X 139–41; *Pastoralia*, I 6–11.
91   Jacob Burckhardt, *The Civilization of the Renaissance in Italy*, trans. by Samuel George C. Middlemore (London: Penguin, 1990), p. 76.
92   Cieco da Ferrara makes a similar digression on the need to liberate the Holy Sepulchre in the proem to canto XXXI of his *Mambriano*.
93   On the original version of XV 79 AB (XVII C), see Marco Dorigatti, 'Il manoscritto dell'*Orlando furioso* (1505–1515)', in *L'uno e l'altro Ariosto in corte e nelle delizie*, ed. by Gianni Venturi (Florence: Olschki, 2011), pp. 1–44 (pp. 31–33).

> che tolto è stato a voi da rinegati?
> perché Constantinopoli e del mondo
> la miglior parte occùpa il Turco immondo?
>
> [If you wish to be called Most Christian,
> if you wish to be called Catholic,
> why do you kill Christ's men?
> Why despoil them of their possessions?
> Why do you not retake Jerusalem,
> seized from you by renegades?
> Why is Constantinople and the better part
> of the world occupied by unclean Turks?]
> (*Fur.*, XV 75 AB; XVII C)

The derogatory epithets applied to the Muslim enemy jar on the ear of the modern reader. However, it is not religious fanaticism that prompts Ariosto to appeal to the European monarchs to launch a new crusade, but rather his earnest belief that a war with the Ottomans or the Egyptian sultan (who will be defeated by the Turks in 1517, with Jerusalem falling under the jurisdiction of the Turkish sultan) would be a lesser evil than mutual slaughter between Christians, that a crusade could be a viable solution to the huge political crisis that has engulfed Italy. The poet has no illusions as to what the driving force of contemporary warfare is: acknowledging that wars are fought primarily for economic reasons, he tells the Swiss and the Germans that if hunger forces them to take up arms, they should turn their gaze to the 'richezze d'Asia [*del Turco* BC]' [the riches of Asia [*of the Turk* BC]] (*Fur.*, XV 77,5 AB; XVII C). Ariosto's real anger is directed not at the Mamluk occupiers of Jerusalem or the Turks but at the rulers of the Italian city-states and in particular the Pope, who do nothing to chase away the foreign (Christian) aggressors:

> O d'ogni vitio fetida sentina,
> dormi, Italia imbrïaca, e non ti pesa
> c'hora di questa gente, hora di quella
> che già serva ti fu, sei fatta ancella?
>
> [And you fetid sink of all iniquities,
> besotted Italy, are you asleep? Does it mean nothing to you
> that now this nation, now that
> lords it over you, when they were once your servants?]
> (*Fur.*, XV 76,5–8 AB; XVII C)

Ariosto will later raise the topic of holy war in his *Satire*, once again from the perspective of Italian politics. In *Satire*, II (1517), we are told that instead of pouncing on the lands of Romagna, Alexander VI would have done better to organize a crusade against the Ottomans. Had he done so, he would have been able both to fulfil his duty as the Head of the Church and satisfy his personal ambitions, for the newly conquered territories could have been used to carve out states for his children and other relatives ('d'Achivi o d'Epiroti | dar lor dominio [...] | de la Morea o de l'Arta far despòti' [give them dominion | over Achaens or Epirotes [...] | make them despots in the Morea or in Arta] (*Satire*, II 211–13)). Needless to say, this suggestion that crusading could be a solution to the problem of nepotism exudes Machiavellian cynicism; it leaves no doubt that for Ariosto peace on the Italian peninsula is far much more precious than the spiritual health of the Catholic Church.

Ariosto started composing the *Furioso* around 1505, and most of the poem was written during the reign of Bayezid II (1481–1512), who was seen — in Italy — as a less dangerous man than his father Mehmed. Paolo Giovio describes him as philosopher-prince, a 'sovrano giusto e equilibrato' [a just and even-tempered sovereign] who 'non era privo di energia combattiva' [did not lack combative energy] but who was well educated and genuinely religious.[94] His son and successor Selim I (1512–1520) had a different personality. Giovio observes that he surpassed Mehmed II both in cruelty and in greatness, adding that 'è ammissibile ritenere che sia stata la provvidenza divina a far sì che una forza indomabile e insuperabile come quella si riversasse verso Oriente per risparmiare un'Europa allora piegata dalle guerre interne' [it is reasonable to believe that it was thanks to divine Providence that such an untamable and unequalled force turned against the Orient, sparing Europe which was then wounded by internal wars].[95] We do not know when Ariosto composed his crusade stanzas, even if the *terminus ante quem* is 1513, given that in the first draft of XV 79 AB (XVII C) he addressed Julius II (who died in 1513).[96] Selim's ascension to power did preoccupy some of the poet's contemporaries (while others hoped that he was well disposed towards the Christians),[97] and Ariosto was not alone in calling for a crusade in those years. In the 1515 draft of the *Libro del Cortegiano*, Castiglione urges Francis I to 'rimover dal mondo una così inveterata e potente setta come la maumetana' [remove from the world such an inveterate and powerful sect as the Muslims are].[98] Unlike Ariosto, Castiglione is careful not to let cynicism leak into his voice: in a tone of deep emotion, he exhorts the French king to lead the Christian world against the Muslim enemy. It is worth observing that this speech was suppressed in the later versions of the *Cortegiano*, whether this being due to the fact that in the 1520s Francis developed a cordial relationship with the Ottomans, or that Castiglione was not wholly convinced by his own words and was merely paying lip service to crusading ideals. What is clear is that despite this emotionally charged crusade speech, both in the early drafts and in the final version of the work, Castiglione's characters make positive comments about the Turks and other oriental peoples, something which will be considered in the next section.

There are three more references to the Turks in the historical digressions of the *Furioso*. Juxtaposing the 'cortesia' [courtesy] and 'gentilezza' [noble conduct] of 'li antiqui guerrier' [the warriors of old] to 'li empii | costumi' [wicked | practices]

---

94    Paolo Giovio, *Elogi degli uomini illustri*, ed. by Franco Minonzio, trans. by Andrea Guasparri and Franco Minonzio (Turin: Einaudi, 2006), pp. 727–31.

95    Ibid., pp. 774–76 (p. 774).

96    See note 93.

97    See, for example, *Tutte le guerre passate in Levante tra el Sophi el gran Turcho el gran Soldano: col nome & tituli delli Reverendissimi Cardinali* (place and date unknown, but printed no later than 1521), an anonymous booklet that narrates Selim's victory over the Mamluks and his kind treatment of the Christians and respectful attitude towards their religion.

98    Cited in Uberto Motta, *Castiglione e il mito di Urbino: studi sulla elaborazione del Cortegiano* (Milan: Vita e pensiero, 2003), p. 47. See also Olga Zorzi Pugliese, *Castiglione's The Book of the Courtier (Il libro del cortegiano): a Classic in the Making* (Naples: Edizioni scientifiche italiane, 2008), p. 184.

of 'li moderni' [present-day warriors] (2,1–4) in the proem to canto XXXIII AB; XXXVI C, Ariosto states that the atrocities perpetrated by the Slav mercenaries of the Serenissima during the 1509 war are equal to 'tutti li crudeli atti et inhumani | ch'usasse mai Tartaro o Turco o Moro' [every cruel, inhuman deed | ever practised by Tartar, Turk, or Moor] (3,1–2). Although the poet hesitates to blame the Venetians for the savage actions of their soldiers, he hints at the fact that they did nothing to restrain their mercenary troops, '*credo* contra 'l voler de' Venetiani, | *forse* con sdegno ben del Leon d'oro' [I *believe* against the will of the Venetians, | *perhaps* to the outrage of the Golden Lion] (3,3–4 AB).[99] Hence, he effectively says that the Venetians are no better than the Tartars or the Turks whose cruelty on the battlefield is proverbial. Then, in the last canto of the *Furioso*, describing the images on the pavilion that Melissa brought from Constantinople, Ariosto mentions the wars between the Turkish sultan and the Hungarian king Mathias Corvinus, at whose court Ippolito had lived between the ages of seven and fourteen (*c.* 1486– 1500):

> o contra Turchi o contra l'Alemanni
> quel Re possente faccia expeditione,
> Hyppolyto gli è appresso, e fiso attende
> a' magnanimi gesti, et virtù apprende.
>
> [if that powerful king makes expeditions
> against the Turks or against the Germans,
> Hippolytus is always beside him, intent on
> performing noble feats and learning valour.]
>     (*Fur.*, XL 60,5–8 AB; XLVI 88 C)

Here, Ariosto does not distinguish between the Turks and the Germans. A chivalric glow is given to Corvinus's military campaigns, which brings to mind the scenes depicted on Brandimarte's tent in the *Inamoramento de Orlando*. Ten octaves later, referring to the highest point of Ippolito's career as a *condottiero*, namely the battle of Polesella (1509), Ariosto tells us that the cardinal defeated 'la più forte armata | che contra Turchi o contra gente Argiva | da' Venetiani mai fusse mandata' [the strongest fleet | that the Venetians ever dispatched | against the Turks or Greeks] (*Fur.*, 70,2–4 AB; 97 C). These lines further prove that the Venetians (as well as other Italian city-states) put more effort into fighting their Christian neighbours than into defending themselves from the Turks.

Judging from the explicit references to historical reality in the two *Orlandos*, neither Boiardo nor Ariosto can be said to be particularly concerned about the Turkish threat. Both acknowledge that Islam is a traditional enemy of the West, but this is a far cry from saying that Europe or Italy are in danger of an imminent invasion. Turning now to the actual stories, it is hard to make a convincing case that they convey a strong anti-Turkish message. Before proceeding any further, it will be helpful to look at a selection of chivalric texts that appear to contain clear allusions

---

99    The italics are mine. In C Ariosto rewrites these lines, removing all ambiguity: '(non già con volontà de' Veneziani, | che sempre esempio di giustizia fôro)' [not indeed by will of the Venetians, | for they have always been of exemplary justice].

to the Turkish problem, namely Andrea da Barberino's *Guerrin Meschino*, the *Storia di Rinaldino da Montalbano*, and the anonymous *Altobello*. Boiardo and Ariosto must have been familiar with these chivalric works, especially with the *Guerrin Meschino* and the *Altobello*, which enjoyed a wide circulation in Renaissance Italy (eleven printed editions of the *Guerrin Meschino* and seven editions of the *Altobello* only by the end of the fifteenth century). Boiardo, as we shall see in Chapter II, alludes to an episode from the *Altobello* in Book I of the *Inamoramento de Orlando*.

There are several prominent Turkish characters in the *Guerrin Meschino* and in the *Rinaldino da Montalbano*, including the Turkish prince Torindo, a namesake of Torindo il Turco in the *Inamoramento de Orlando*.[100] In both romances Torindo is one of the sons of Astilladoro, king of Turkey, who, as we learn in the *Guerrin Meschino*, 'era signore della maggior parte di Romania e per forza tenea quasi tutta la Grecia' [ruled over most of Romania and had conquered by force almost all Greece] (*Guerrin Meschino*, I xv 23). This reflects the geo-political situation at the end of the fourteenth century, while the fact that Astilladoro's sons lay claim to 'sangue trojano' [Trojan blood] (*Guerrin Meschino*, I xxviii 8) is an allusion to the widespread belief that the Turks shamelessly bragged that they had descended from the ancient Trojans.[101] In the *Guerrin Meschino*, Torindo and his brother Pinamonte travel to Constantinople to take part in a tournament in which the main prize is the hand of Elisena, the daughter of the Greek Emperor. They are defeated by the titular hero, but they lie to their father saying that they have won, yet have been denied the prize because they are Turks. Astilladoro lays siege to Constantinople — a bad decision, as he loses the war and is forced to give up 'tutte le terre che [...] tenea e avea tolte a' Greci' [all the lands that [...] he held and he had seized from the Greeks] (I xxviii 4) to ransom his sons. Later, Meschino helps the Persians to wrest the city of Persepolis from the clutches of Astilladoro's brother Galismarte, while towards the end of the romance Astilladoro makes another attempt to capture Constantinople, this time with truly disastrous consequences, paying with his own life for this act of folly. In the *Rinaldino da Montalbano*, Torindo and Pinamonte attack the Syrian king Alipandro (who is married to the Persian princess Elisena and who has converted to Christianity for the sake of his friendship with Rinaldino), but decide to return home when their troops are routed and 'non ci è più uomo che possa durare alla forza di questo Rinaldino' [not a man is left who can withstand this Rinaldino's strength].[102]

The pages devoted to Astilladoro and his Turkish relatives could have been inspired by the fears and dreams of Andrea da Barberino's contemporaries and

---

100 While some scholars believe that the *Rinaldino da Montalbano* was authored by Andrea da Barberino, others think that its author was familiar with Andrea's romances. See Marco Villoresi, *La letteratura cavalleresca* (Rome: Carocci, 2000), p. 86.

101 Luca and Luigi Pulci too allude to this belief in the *Ciriffo Calvaneo*: the poem features a Turkish king called Sinettore who has descended from the Trojans and so claims to be the king of Ilium. For a discussion of the Trojan theme in the humanist writings see Terence Spencer, 'Turks and Trojans in the Renaissance', *Modern Language Review*, 47, no. 3 (July 1952), 330–33; James Hankins, 'Renaissance Crusaders: Humanist Crusade Literature in the Age of Mehmed II', *Dumbarton Oaks Papers*, 49 (1995), 139–43; Margaret Meserve, *Empires of Islam in Renaissance Historical Thought*, pp. 22–64.

102 *Storia di Rinaldino da Montalbano*, ed. by Carlo Minutoli (Bologna: Gaetano Romagnoli, 1865), p. 284.

perhaps, to an extent, by real historical events too, given that the beginning of the fifteenth century was a turbulent period in the history of the Ottoman Empire. In 1402 the Turkish-Mongolian leader Tamerlane (or Timur) defeated the Turks in the battle of Ankara, taking Bayezid I as a prisoner (Tamerlane's victory is probably represented in the fifteenth-century Florentine *cassone* painting on the cover of this book, with the painter conflating the figures of Tamerlane and Uzun Hassan).[103] As a result, the Empire almost disintegrated, sinking into an eleven-year civil war and losing some of its territories in the Balkans. This temporarily slowed the decline of Byzantium, rekindling the almost extinguished hope that Constantinople — the stronghold of the Orthodox Church — could be saved. Guerrino's/Rinaldino's victories over various members of Astilladoro's family seem to reflect precisely this hope.

Andrea da Barberino's relatively realistic portrayal of the Turks is, to my knowledge, unique in the context of the Italian chivalric tradition. Compared to the universe of the *Guerrin Meschino*, that of the *Altobello* (a poem which was probably composed in Venice in the 1460s) has fewer points of contact with reality: the geography of *Paganìa* is vague and the political weight of Turkey is unclear. However, it is significant that Altobello and his elder brother Troiano — Saracen converts to Christianity and allies of the Christians — are Persians. As has been convincingly argued by Annalisa Perrotta, the anonymous poet could have been inspired by the friendship between Venice and Uzun Hassan, the ruler of Persia and an enemy of the Turkish sultan.[104] This friendship started in 1463, when the Venetians sent an ambassador to the Persian shah in an attempt to persuade him to attack the Ottomans. Strikingly, 'Altobello' could effectively be a literal translation (or, more precisely, a calque) of Uzun Hasan's name: 'Uzun' means 'tall' or 'long' (alto) in Turkish, while 'Ḥasan' [حسن] is a very common Eastern name of Arabic origin which translates as 'handsome' (bello).[105] Moreover, it is perhaps significant that the poem features a plethora of Turkish princes and barons (Orlando, for one, kills many a 'gran turco'), including one truly powerful king, Pironello, who falls

103  On this painting see Cristelle Baskins, 'The Bride of Trebizond: Turks and Turkmens on a Florentine Wedding Chest, circa 1460', *Muqarnas*, 29 (2012), 83–100.

104  Perrotta, 'Alleanze necessarie'.

105  We do not know for certain whether the author of the poem was aware of the fact that 'Uzun Hasan' meant 'Alto Bello'. Caterino Zeno, a Venetian citizen and a relative of the Persian ruler (through his marriage to the niece of Uzun Hassan's wife) who was sent as an ambassador to Persia in 1472, writes in his memoirs that 'Ussuncassano [...] in lingua persiana vien a dire magno uomo' [Usssuncassano [...] in Persian means a great man] (*Dei commentarii del viaggio in Persia di M. Caterino Zeno il K. & delle guerre fatte nell'Imperio Persiano dal tempo di Ussuncassano in qua*, in Ramusio, *Navigationi et viaggi: Venice (1563–1606)*, II (facsimile edition of the 1583 Giunti edition of the second volume), fols 219ᵛ–229ᵛ (fol. 220ʳ)). On the other hand, Demetrio Calcondila (a Greek humanist who emigrated to Italy in 1447 and lived there until his death in 1511) says in one of his works that 'Uzun' means 'long': see Pietro Giuseppe Maggi, 'Intorno il libro: *La Repubblica di Venezia e la Persia*, del dottor Guglielmo Berchet', in *Reale Istituto Lombardo di Scienze e Lettere: Rendiconti*, II (Milan: Tipografia di Giuseppe Bernardoni, 1865), pp. 43–56 (p. 47). One should also take into account the similarity between the names 'Altobello' and 'Aldabella' (Alda bella): given that the young Persian knight has a very close relationship with Orlando's wife (the childless woman treats him as her own son, seeing him as a gift from God), it could be that the poet deliberately patterned his name after Alda's.

in love with Orlando's wife Alda and offers her the crown of Turkey, generously allowing her to keep her faith and baptize their future children. The story of Pironello's infatuation with Alda and other wars and adventures narrated in the *Altobello* do not seem to reflect any specific historical events. Yet, without being an allegorical text, the *Altobello* draws inspiration from historical reality, echoing the feelings of the poet's contemporaries.

Can the same be said of Boiardo's and Ariosto's poems? As Giovanni Ponte points out, the geographical map of the *Inamoramento de Orlando* roughly reflects the political situation in the period between the eleventh and fourteenth centuries.[106] This is more or less true of the *Furioso* too. In both poems Turkey is merely one of the many small Saracen states. There are five Turkish knights in the *Inamoramento de Orlando*, but none of them takes part in Agramante's war, which explains why there are no Turkish characters in the *Furioso*. Ariosto, however, mentions the Turks twice in connection with Agramante's attempted invasion of France. Commenting on the violence unleashed by the Saracen soldiers, he says that it could be a divine punishment for the sins of the Christians:

> Deveano allhora haver li excessi loro
> di Dio turbata la serena fronte,
> ch'ogni lor luoco scórse il Turco e il Moro
> con stupri, uccisïon, rapine et onte [...]
>
> [their excesses must have by then
> vexed the serene face of the Almighty,
> for the Turks and Moors had overrun all their lands,
> committing rape and murder, pillage and outrage [...]]
> (*Fur.*, XV 6,1–4 AB; XVII C)

Taken out of context, this passage seems to imply that there are Turkish soldiers in the armies of Agramante and Marsilio. However, since this is not confirmed anywhere else in the poem, it could be argued that Ariosto uses the word 'Turco' as a kind of line-filler, as it is used in other poems.[107] Ariosto's Christians feel no hatred towards the Turks; in fact, they do not even acknowledge their existence. Towards the end of the *Furioso* we learn that the Turks are one of the Saracen nations that are on friendly terms with the African king. When the war is lost, Sobrino tells his despairing king that they will be eager to help him re-conquer his kingdom: 'Armeni, Turchi, Persi, Aràbi e Medi, | tutti in soccorso havrai, se tu li chiedi' [Armenians, Turks, Persians, Arabs and Medes, | you'll have help from all of them if you ask for it] (XXXVI 39,7–8 AB; XL C). Significantly, Ariosto does not distinguish between the Turks and the Persians (who do not take part in Agramante's military campaign either). Nor does Boiardo: the Persian king Framarte, Gradasso's ally in the war with Marsilio, makes a fleeting appearance

106  Ponte, *La personalità e l'opera del Boiardo*, p. 88.
107  Sometimes chivalric poets use the term *Turk* as a synonym for *Saracen*. For example, in the *Entrée d'Espagne*, Ferragu is variously referred to as 'l'Aufricant' (751), 'l'Arabis' (1225) and 'le Turc' (1250; 1280). On the *questione turca* in the *Entrée d'Espagne* see Alberto Limentani, 'Venezia e il "pericolo turco" nell'*Entrée d'Espagne*', in Idem, *L'"Entrée d'Espagne" e i signori d'Italia*, ed. by Marco Infurna and Francesco Zambon (Padua: Antenore, 1992), pp. 358–78.

in canto iv of Book I, only to be killed by Ranaldo several stanzas later. As for the Greeks, Emperor Vatarone's son Costanzo, the only Greek knight in the *Inamoramento de Orlando*, is a minor character, and Leone, Costanzo's counterpart in the *Furioso*, features only in the 1532 edition. While Costanzo is a negative character ('il Greco... era di malicia pieno | come son tuti, d'arte e di natura' [the Greek was full of malice (both | blood and upbringing make Greeks crafty)] (*Inam.*, II xx 37,1–2)), the portrayal of Leone and his family is ambivalent (it is worth recalling, for example, that Ruggiero's rival in love has no scruples about employing dishonest means to get Bradamante).[108] In neither poem is the Byzantine Empire threatened by the Turks or indeed by Agramante.

Boiardo, Ariosto and their early readers knew that there were powerful rulers in the Islamic world. This knowledge added to the appeal of the two *Orlandos* and of the chivalric genre in general, which flourished in fifteenth-century Italy and continued to be popular throughout the sixteenth century. From this perspective, one could argue that, while having much in common with their counterparts in earlier chivalric literature, Agramante and other glory-seeking Saracen kings in Boiardo's and Ariosto's poems are inspired by contemporary history too. However, the fictional universes of the *Inamoramento de Orlando* and the *Furioso* bear little resemblance to the political map of the world in the late fifteenth and early sixteenth centuries, and one should be cautious in looking for allegorical allusions to specific historical figures or events. According to Cavallo, who agrees with Michael Murrin that Boiardo was worried about the Turks when he embarked on the composition of Book II of the *Inamoramento de Orlando*, it is significant that the 'opening of Book Two [...] coincides with the aftermath of the Turkish capture of Negroponte (1470)'.[109] Cavallo suggests that 'Agramante's North African troops are depicted in such a way as to evoke Mehmed's Ottoman Empire', while 'the concomitant aggression of Marsilio's troops against Charlemagne's realm sounds very much like the corollary military action of Venice against Estense Ferrara during the period'.[110] The fall of Negroponte, a Venetian colony, was indeed a devastating loss for Venice and a major blow to Christian Europe. However, Book II opens on a joyful note: having announced the return of 'Alegreza e Cortesia' ['Joy and Courtesy'] (II i 2,3) to Ferrara, Boiardo provides a dazzling description of Agramante's court in Biserta. Agramante is in no hurry to invade Charlemagne's empire: first he has to find his cousin Ruggiero, the progenitor of the Este family, through whom the Este family is related to the North African Saracen dynasty. Only at the end of canto xxviii does Agramante decide to set sail for Europe.

108  Boiardo's and Ariosto's representations of the Greeks are not particularly surprising. Negative stereotypes go back to Roman antiquity. It was during the First Crusade, however, that the relationship between the Byzantine and Western worlds seriously deteriorated. The 1204 Crusade (when instead of attacking Egypt the crusaders attacked and conquered Constantinople) soured the already strained relationship to such an extent that in the years preceding the Fall of Constantinople many Greeks thought that it would be better to live under Turkish occupation than to bow to the Pope.

109  See Murrin, 'Agramante's War', in Idem, *History and Warfare*, pp. 70–73; Cavallo, *The World beyond Europe*, p. 93.

110  Cavallo, *The World beyond Europe*, p. 129.

Recent research has shed new light on the chronology of composition of Boiardo's poem. As has been shown by Tiziano Zanato, the first twenty-one cantos of Book II must have been composed between 1471 and 1473, cantos xxii–xxiii in 1475 or 1476, cantos xxiv–xxvi by mid-1479 and the remainder of Book II by the end of 1482.[111] In April 1471 Borso received the long-coveted title of Duke of Ferrara, and in August of the same year, Ercole, Boiardo's lord and lifelong friend, was elected the new duke. Boiardo's optimistic tone and the introduction of the dynastic theme have been explained by scholars with reference to these two events.[112] Had the poet wanted to alert his readers to the Turkish threat by narrating Agramante's military campaign, he probably would not have made Agramante a relative of his duke. Had he been profoundly shaken by the fall of Negroponte, he probably would not have waited until 1479 to begin narrating Agramante's expedition. Nor is it plausible that Marsilio, Agramante's ally, stands for Venice, given that Marsilio lays siege to Montalbano in canto xxii. If it is true that this canto was composed in 1475–1476, Venice was still at war with the Turks (the fifth Ottoman-Venetian war began in 1463 and only ended in 1479), and the war between Ferrara and Venice (1482–1484) was still six to seven years in the future.

We may add, in closing this section, that most of Boiardo's Turkish characters are portrayed sympathetically. Whereas Torindo, Balsaldo and Morbeco are positive characters, Caramano and Hosbergo may not be among Boiardo's favourite Saracens, but they are not hardened villains either. Torindo's brother, Caramano, disgraces himself when he ignominiously flees from the battlefield (II xviii 29–30), and Hosbergo, Doristela's first husband, 'gagliardo era tenuto e molto ardito, | ma certo che nel leto era un poltrone' [was considered to be a valiant and a mighty man, | but he was negligent in bed] (II xxvi 31,3–4). Boiardo does not tell us much about Balsaldo and Morbeco, a pair of friends who travel to the tournament in Cyprus, apart from the fact that Morbeco 'sopra gli altri si facea mirare' [earned more praise than all the others] (II xx 19,6) until he was unhorsed by Noradino. However, Torindo, the king of Turkey, is one of the most memorable and charismatic minor characters of the poem. In introducing him, as Cavallo puts it, 'Boiardo rehabilitates the name of a non-Christian character previously used negatively in Carolingian epics'.[113] Torindo distinguishes himself by his staunch loyalty to Sacripante. In canto xi of Book I the latter fights with Agricane, with a number of kings and barons, including Torindo, watching the duel. The Circassian king is getting the worst of it. He is losing blood, but will not admit defeat. It is Torindo who convinces the others to intervene:

> 'Né vi crediate di far tradimento
> perché questa battaglia disturbate,

---

111  On the poem's composition, see Tiziano Zanato, *Boiardo* (Rome: Salerno Editrice, 2015), pp. 145–61.

112  See, for example, Dorigatti, 'La favola e la corte: intrecci narrativi e genealogie estensi dal Boiardo all'Ariosto', in *Gli dei a corte: Letteratura e immagini nella Ferrara estense*, ed. by Gianni Venturi and Francesca Cappelletti (Florence: Olschki, 2009), pp. 31–54 (p. 32).

113  Cavallo, *The World beyond Europe*, p. 73.

che tradimento non si può appellare
quel che se fa per suo signor campare!

Sia mia la colpa, se colpa ne viene,
e vostre sian le lode tute quante!'.
Cossì dicendo più non si ritiene,
ma con roina sprona il suo aferante.

['Do not believe it's treachery
for you to interrupt this duel,
since treachery is not the word
for what you do to save your lord.

Let me be blamed, if there is blame,
and let all of the praise be yours!'
So saying, he holds back no more,
but madly spurs his coursing charger.]
(*Inam.*, I xi 17, 5–8; 18,1–4)

This episode ties into the theme of loyalty and betrayal, one of the central themes in both Boiardo and Ariosto, not least because it underpins the respective stories of Rug(g)iero and Rod(a/o)monte, which will be explored in Chapter V. Torindo's hatred of traitors will later lead him to change sides: unable to accept the fact that Orlando has forgiven Trufaldino, who had tried to surrender Albracà to Agricane, he will turn his sword against Sacripante, Orlando and Brandimarte, and will be killed by the latter at II xxviii 29. Endowed with a heightened sense of justice and impressive oratory skills, Torindo has little in common not only with his namesakes in the *Guerrin Meschino* and the *Rinaldino da Montalbano* but also with the figure of the Turk as it emerges from the writings of the humanists or from the 'guerre contro il turco' cycle.[114]

## International chivalry

The *Inamoramento de Orlando* opens with a Pentecostal banquet organized by Charlemagne. The French Emperor has invited Marsilio and Spanish barons, and their presence transforms his court into an international centre of chivalry. In the opening canto of the *Furioso* Ferraù offers to give Rinaldo a lift, as the two knights are pursuing Angelica. Half-amused, half-touched by this courteous gesture, the poet praises, albeit with a hint of irony, the 'gran bontà de' cavallieri antiqui' [great goodness of the knights of old] (*Fur.*, I 22,1 ABC) who were eager to help each other even though they were rivals in love and 'di fé diversi' [of different faiths] (22,2). The two *Orlandos*, as well as other chivalric stories composed in late medieval and Renaissance Italy, contain numerous examples of friendly interactions between

---

114 The treacherousness of the Turks is an important theme in the 'guerre contro il Turco' poems. In the *Lamento di Negroponte*, for example, the Turks have no scruples about violating the chivalric code. At first, they enter into an agreement with Tommaso Schiavo, a Christian traitor who promises to let them into the besieged city. Then, they promise to spare the lives of the citizens if they surrender, but kill them all after the 'rocca' has been delivered up. Both betrayals are based on real events during the Turkish conquest of Negroponte in 1470.

Christians and Saracens. Nor are such gestures limited to chivalric literature. In Boiardo's translation of Riccobaldo we read about the historical Charlemagne's 'grande e precipua amicizia' [strong and singular friendship] with the fifth Abbasid Caliph Harun al-Rashid (*Historia imp.*, III-IV, p. 295). Riccobaldo does not hide his admiration for the gallant Saladin who treats his Christian prisoners with respect (similarly to how Boiardo's Agramante treats Dudone) and who confesses that his aim is 'acquistare Gloria, e non Provincie' [acquire Glory, and not Provinces] (ibid., p. 392), which is what Gradasso tells Charlemagne after he has defeated all his barons (*Inam.*, I vii 41–42).

Although the figure of the chivalrous Saracen features already in the *chansons de geste*, it would be fair to say that Boiardo's passionate glorification of Saracen chivalry is unprecedented in French or Italian Carolingian literatures. While the legend of Saladin certainly influenced his portrayal of chivalry in the Saracen world, he could have been inspired by more recent history too. It is well known that in the fifteenth century the Este rulers amassed an impressive collection of books about non-Christian parts of the world.[115] But not only did they enjoy reading about non-Christian lands; they also sought to establish contacts with Muslim princes. Boiardo makes a North African knight the founder the Este dynasty. If, as Tissoni Benvenuti suggests, the myth of Rugiero was born during Borso's reign, it might have originated in the years when Ferrara developed diplomatic ties with Hafsid Ifriqiya (which comprises present-day Tunisia, where Bizerte, the capital of Agramante's North African empire, is situated).[116] In 1463 Sultan Abu Umar Othman (1435–1488) sent Borso, Marquis of Ferrara, a superb Arabian horse as a token of his good will. Borso was very glad to receive such a present. In April 1464 his squires, Francesco Gattamellata and Giovanni Giacomo della Torre, set out for Barbary carrying gifts for the African sultan. In his detailed *instructio* Borso told them to stay clear of African ladies and to try to make a good impression on the sultan, reminding him of 'lantica amicitia stata tra la prefata nostra casa et sua Maestà' [longstanding friendship between our dinasty and his Majesty].[117] A year later, in 1465, an ambassador of the Tunisian sultan arrived in Ferrara and was lodged in the castle and showered with honours.[118]

---

115   See Donald Lach for a list of texts dealing with the Orient in the Este library, *Asia in the Making of Europe*, 3 vols (Chicago: University of Chicago Press, 1965–1993), II, book 2, pp. 48–49.

116   See Antonia Tissoni Benvenuti, 'Rugiero o la fabbrica dell'*Inamoramento de Orlando*', in *Per Cesare Bozzetti: Studi di letteratura e di filologia italiana*, ed. by Simone Albonico et al. (Milan: Mondadori, 1996), pp. 69–89 (pp. 75–82).

117   *Instructione facta ali Nobili Scudieri de lo Illustrissimo Signore Duca de Modena etc, Gattamellata et Zoanne Iacomo de la Torre, per la loro andata in Barberia*, in *Relazioni dei duchi di Ferrara e di Modena coi re di Tunisi: Cenni e documenti raccolti nell'archivio di stato in Modena*, ed. by Cesare Foucard (Modena: Tipografia Pizzolotti, 1881), pp. 9–19 (p. 12). It is worth mentioning here that Borso's brother Meliaduse could have sought a personal audience with another North African ruler, the Mamluk Sultan Sayf ad-Din Jaqmaq (r. 1438–1453), during his stay in Cairo in 1440. See Beatrice Saletti, *La successione di Leonello d'Este e altri studi sul Quattrocento ferrarese* (Padua: Libreriauniversitaria.it, 2015), pp. 66–70.

118   *Instructione facta ali Nobili Scudieri*, p. 5.

The vainglorious Borso was flattered by the attention of a Muslim monarch of the calibre of Abu Umar Othman and wanted him to know that he was 'Signore in Italia, et non deli inferiori nì deli mediocri' [Lord in Italy, and not one of the inferior or mediocre ones].[119] It could be that, impressed by the squires' descriptions of the splendour of Abu Umar Othman's court, Boiardo or his maternal uncle Tito Vespasiano Strozzi decided to provide Borso with a more honourable genealogy than the one according to which the Este descended from the traitor Ganelon and invented Rugiero/Rugerus, through whom the Este are related to the North African dynasty of the *Aspramonte*.[120] In any case, this exchange of courtesies and gifts between Borso and the Hafsid sultan must have contributed to Boiardo's fascination with Africa, even if, as will be shown in Chapter III, his portrayal of Agramante's court is certainly indebted to preceding chivalric literature.

If the Este family claimed descent from a North African hero, another noble Ferrarese family — the Turchi — were proud of having Turkish blood in their veins: the crest of their coat of arms featured a Turkish archer ready to shoot an arrow.[121] In his wedding oration for Paula Strozzi and Zarabinus Turchi, whose wedding took place in the 1460s, Ludovico Carbone praised the groom's Turkish ancestors, three brothers (Zarabinus, Amorbassanus, and Panzanius), who, according to the family legend, had been sent to Rome as ambassadors and decided to convert to Christianity and begin a new life in Italy.[122] Carbone's praise extended to the whole Turkish nation; he went as far as to say that Mehmed II was one of the greatest emperors of all time. He also admitted that he had been harsh on the Turks in a different speech, as on that occasion he had to conceal his true feelings in order to please the Pope.

The family trees of the Este and the Turchi show that the Ferrarese nobility was not Islamophobic, not even in the aftermath of the Fall of Constantinople. Theirs were invented genealogies, but Ercole d'Este's son-in-law Ludovico il Moro (Duke of Milan from 1494 to 1499) went a step further: at war with Louis XII of France and finding himself completely isolated, the recently widowed Ludovico — whose first wife was Beatrice d'Este — asked Bayezid for the hand of his daughter.[123] Had Bayezid not declined the honour of this alliance, Ludovico would have brought the Turks into Italy several years after he had invited the French.

---

119  Ibid., p. 12.

120  Boiardo could be following the *Borsias* (1460–1470; 1485–1496), an encomiastic poem composed by Tito Vespasiano Strozzi and dedicated to Borso. In Book II of this Latin poem Borso is referred to as 'Rugerius heros' [hero of Rugerus's lineage], while in Book VI (whose composition date is uncertain) Strozzi gives an account of Rugerus's life which resembles Boiardo's story. See Tissoni Benvenuti, 'Rugiero o la fabbrica dell'*Inamoramento de Orlando*', pp. 75–82. Galaciele and her son Rizer are mentioned in Raffaele da Verona's Franco-Venetian prose romance *Aquilon de Bavière*.

121  Giovanni Ricci, *Ossessione turca in una retrovia cristiana dell'Europa moderna* (Bologna: Il Mulino, 2002), p. 93.

122  See Anthony F. D'Elia, 'Genealogy and the Limits of Panegyric: Turks and Huns in Fifteenth-Century Epithalamia', *The Sixteenth Century Journal*, 34, no. 4 (2003), 973–91.

123  Giovanni Ricci, *Appello al Turco: I confini infranti del Rinascimento* (Rome: Viella, 2011), pp. 68–69 (a revised version of this book has been recently translated into English: *Appeal to the Turk: The Broken Boundaries of the Renaissance*, trans. by Richard Chapman (Rome: Viella, 2018)).

It would seem that the Este did not have particularly strong diplomatic ties with the Sublime Porte (at least not until the 1550s, when Ercole II received a Turkish ambassador at his court),[124] but this does not mean that they were not interested in Ottoman Turkey. We know that Ercole was dressed as a Turk in the 'belissima giostra' [most beautiful joust] that was held in Mantua as part of his daughter Isabella's wedding festivities in February 1490;[125] that in 1496 he sent Ambrogio Bucciardo to Constantinople to try and persuade the Turks to attack Venice;[126] and that he followed with keen interest the events unfolding in the Ottoman empire, as is evident from his correspondence with his agents. In a letter sent from Ragusa (Dalmatia) on 30 May 1492, Nicolò Gondula informed Ercole that he had met 'Sangiachbegho Mustaphabegh genero del Gran Turco e nostro vicino' [Sanjakbeg Mustafa Beg, son-in-law of the Great Turk and our neighbour], a very pleasant and well-educated man who thought highly of the Duke of Ferrara as well as of his deceased brother Borso.[127] Gondula says that, talking about Europe and Italy, Mustafa mentioned, among other things, that he wanted to send an ambassador to Venice who was then to travel to Mantua to greet Ercole's son-in-law Francesco Gonzaga. At this point, Gondula asked Mustafa to tell his ambassador to visit Ferrara too, and the Turk promised to send Ercole horses and other gifts 'in signo d'amore' [as a token of love]. Gondula expresses the hope that his Excellence Duke Ercole, 'la qual sempre conobbi essere vagha de gloria' [whom I always knew to be desirous of glory], will be pleased to have contacts with the Turkish gentleman.[128]

The Turkish gentleman in question must have been Mustafa Bey, the governor of Vlorë (a city in present-day Albania) who married Bayezid II's daughter Kamerşâh Hatun in 1490. Gondula had correct information regarding Mustafa's intentions: on 22 May 1492 the latter wrote to Francesco Gonzaga and sent him two horses 'in signo d'amore'.[129] I could not find any evidence that Ercole received the promised gifts in 1492, but Gondula was not wrong in thinking that the Duke of Ferrara would want to befriend Mustafa Bey, for one year later, in July 1493, Ercole offered Kasim Bey, Bayezid's envoy to Mantua, a room in the Castello Estense ('in corte')

---

124 Ercole II first made contact with the Turks around 1553, when he sent to Constantinople a certain Vincenzo, who gave the French ambassador at the Porte a letter for Süleyman. As we learn from Domenico Trevisan, the Venetian bailo in Constantinople, the Duke wanted to 'trattare circa l'appalto delle spezie' [negotiate a spice trade contract] (Domenico Trevisan, *Relazione dell'Impero Ottomano 1554*, in *Le relazioni degli ambasciatori veneti al Senato*, ed. by Eugenio Alberi, 15 vols (Florence: Tipografia all'insegna di Clio, 1839–1863), ser. 3, I, pp. 111–92 (p. 165)). In 1553 Rüstem Pasha Opuković sent Ercole II a letter saying that he was welcome to send an ambassador (the letter is preserved in Modena, Archivio Segreto Estense, Principi esteri, busta 1612).
125 Zambotti, p. 215 [16 February 1490].
126 Ricci, *Appello al Turco*, p. 70.
127 Modena, Archivio di Stato, Ambasciatori estensi, busta 15/ unica, Dalmazia, Nicolò Gondula, fol. 1[r]. Later (between 1499 and 1514, to be precise) Gondula would spy for Venice, sending the Consiglio dei Dieci encrypted letters from Ragusa. On his correspondence with the Serenissima see Paolo Preto, *Servizi segreti di Venezia* (Milan: Saggiatore, 1994), p. 239.
128 Nicolò Gondula, fol. 1[v].
129 See Giancarlo Malacarne, *Il mito dei cavalli gonzagheschi: alle origini del purosangue* (Verona: Promoprint, 1995), p. 53, and Galeazzo Nosari, Franco Canova, *I cavalli Gonzaga della raza de la casa: allevamenti e scuderie di Mantova nei secoli XIV-XVII* (Reggiolo: E.lui, 2005), p. 156.

when he learnt that Kasim had arrived in Ferrara. As Isabella d'Este (who was then visiting family in Ferrara) told her husband in a letter sent on 24 July 1493, Kasim declined that honour, saying that he would rather stay in the local 'hosteria' [inn].[130] This was clearly not a courtesy visit, as Kasim did not meet the Este family and left the following day. As Antonia Gatward Cevizli suggests, the reason for Kasim's coldness towards Ercole might be the closeness of the relationship between Ferrara and France.[131]

Ercole probably did not succeed in establishing direct contact with the Turks, but his son-in-law Francesco Gonzaga — like his wife Isabella d'Este, an avid reader of chivalric literature and a known enthusiast of the two *Orlandos* — developed a fairly close friendship with Bayezid, which lasted from 1491 (when the Marquis of Mantua first sent an ambassador to Constantinople) until Bayezid's death in 1512. Word of their warm relationship spread rapidly throughout Italy: Francesco himself told the Turkish sultan in a letter dated 23 July 1493 that 'per tutta Italia si diceva quella amarmi et havermi nel numero de li suoi chari' [in all of Italy people said that your Majesty loved me and saw me as one of your dear friends].[132] Francesco's ties with Ottoman Turkey earned him the nickname 'il Turco', which he wore with pride, thinking of himself as a 'Turcho non per fede ma per stato | per fama per ingegno per thesoro' [Turk not in his faith but because of his state, | his fame, his intelligence, and his possessions], as his court poet Teofilo da Pesaro calls him in an encomiastic poem.[133] To live up to his nickname, Francesco even started to learn Turkish and commissioned various Turkish-inspired decorations for his palaces, including a 'Camera di Turchi' [Room of the Turks] for the Palazzo del Capitano, and a 'Greek room' with views of the Eastern Meditarranean, a 'sdravizza di Turchi' (a Turkish banquet, where the guests must have been lying on low sofas or cushions, as do the Saracens in the opening canto of the *Inamoramento de Orlando*) and Kasim's portrait for the Marmirolo Palace.[134]

---

130 Archivio di Stato di Mantova, Archivio Gonzaga, busta 2991, libro 3, letter 257, fol. 72$^r$.

131 Antonia Gatward Cevizli, 'More than a Messenger: Embodied Expertise in Mantuan Envoys to the Ottomans in the 1490s', *Mediterranean Studies*, 22, no. 2 (2014), 166–89 (p. 180). Eventually Francis I established an alliance with Süleyman the Magnificent (1536), which would last until Napoleon's Egyptian campaign.

132 Hans Joachim Kissling, *Sultan Bâjezîd II: Beziehungen zu Markgraf Francesco II. von Gonzaga* (München: Max Hueber Verlag, 1965), pp. 24–25. On Francesco Gonzaga's friendship with Bayezid see, apart from Kissling's monograph and Gatward Cevizli's article, Molly Bourne, 'The Turban'd Turk in Renaissance Mantua: Francesco II Gonzaga's Interest in Ottoman Fashion', in *Mantova e il Rinascimento italiano: Studi in onore di David S. Chambers*, ed. by Philippa Jackson and Guido Rebecchini (Mantua: Sometti Editoriale, 2011), pp. 53–64; and Daniela Sogliani, 'The Gonzaga and the Ottomans between the 15th and the 17th Centuries in the Documents of the State Archive of Mantua', in *The Ottoman Orient in Renaissance Culture: Papers from the International Conference at the National Museum in Krakow, June 26–27, 2015*, ed. by Robert Born and Michał Dziewulski in collaboration with Kamilla Twardowska (Krakow: The National Museum in Krakow, 2015), pp. 67–94.

133 This poem is reproduced in Alfredo Saviotti, 'Sonetti di Teofilo da Folengo', *Archivio storico per le Marche e per l'Umbria*, 3 (1886), pp. 328–44 (p. 343).

134 Bourne, 'The Turban'd Turk in Renaissance Mantua', pp. 54–55.

The friendship between Francesco and Bayezid had a pragmatic dimension: the former adored Turkish horses, while the latter wanted to keep an eye on his estranged sibling Cem Sultan (1459–1495) who spent the last thirteen years of his life in Europe, a prisoner of the Christians and hence a source of constant concern for the sultan.[135] Bayezid paid large sums of money to Innocent VIII and his successor Alexander VI so that they would not release his brother, and the Marquis of Mantua helped him to to keep the situation under control. However, their relationship was couched in the language of chivalric romances. Francesco's correspondence with Bayezid and his envoy Kasim Bey is permeated with chivalric vocabulary. Congratulating their Christian friend on his victory against the French in the battle of Fornovo (6 July 1495), the Turks praised his knightly virtues:

> De la qual nova el potentissimo Gran Signor e la Porta et tutti de qui hanno havuto gran contento per lo honore et gran nome che Vostra Signoria si ha acquistato: Et tutti dicono assai de le laudi de Vostra Signoria, la quale Dio mantegni [...] li homeni del mondo vedono al presente con lo effetto in Vostra Signoria essere la gaiardia et virtute che sempre mai io ho parlato, et al potentissimo Gran Signore et alli Signori Bassà, et a tutta la Porta, et de questo ne dago laude a Dio [...].

> [The most powerful Great Lord and the Porte and everybody here were very glad to receive this news because of the honour and the illustrious reputation that Your Lordship has acquired: And everybody here is praising Your Lordship most highly, wishing God may keep you in good health [...] men of the world now clearly see that Your Lordship possesses the audacity and virtue of which I have always spoken to the most powerful Great Lord and to the Lords Pashas and to the entire Porte, and I thank God for this [...]] (Kasim to Francesco Gonzaga, 16 August 1495)[136]

> [...] havemo inteso de la sanitate et gloria vostra, et anche de la valorosità et prodeza vostra: simili opere attendevamo intender de li fatti vostri: Dio ve conservi in simili opere [...].

> [we have heard about your health and glory and also about your valour and prowess: we expected tidings of such deeds performed by you: may God keep you safe in such deeds] (Bayezid to Francesco Gonzaga, November 1495)[137]

Francesco's Turkish correspondents commend him to God, and so does the marquis in his responses. Though professing different creeds, they invoke the

---

135  Much has been written on Cem Sultan. See at least Nicolas Vatin, *Sultan Djem: un prince ottoman dans l'Europe du XVe siècle d'après deux sources contemporaines* (Ankara: Imprimerie de la Société turque d'historire [sic], 1997). After the demise of their father Mehmed II (1481), Cem and his brother Bayezid fought for the throne, and in 1482 Cem decided to seek protection from the Knights of Rhodes who, however, betrayed him and sent him to France. Between 1489 and January 1495 Cem resided at the Papal court in Rome, where he spent his time discussing politics and religion with his captors, writing poetry, hunting and indulging in other pleasurable activities. He liked the company of Juan de Borgia (son of Pope Alexander VI and brother of Lucrezia Borgia, later to become Alfonso's d'Este second wife) and the Romans could see them riding together, Juan dressed in Turkish clothes to honour his Muslim companion. Cem stands close to Lucrezia Borgia (represented as St Catherine) in Pinturicchio's *Disputa di Santa Caterina*, a fresco in the Borgia Apartments.
136  Kissling, *Sultan Bâjezîd II: Beziehungen zu Markgraf Francesco II. von Gonzaga*, p. 53.
137  Ibid., p. 56.

universal God, the supreme Judge of the World who does not distinguish between Christians and Muslims but rewards the virtuous and punishes the wicked. Like Boiardo's and Ariosto's knights, they claim to value courteous conduct and martial prowess above anything else.

Did Ariosto know about Francesco Gonzaga's bond with the Turkish sultan? Almost certainly he did, even if their epistolary exchange became less prolific after Cem's death in 1495. Giulio Sacrati, Cardinal Ippolito's agent whom we mentioned earlier, had a letter written by the marquis of Mantua with him when he embarked on his journey to Egypt around 1507. It saved him from prison or worse: in Negroponte, Sacrati reported back to Ippolito: 'io fui preso e menato dananci a uno basà napalitano renegado e lì minato cridando che io fusse espione del re de spagnia' [I was arrested and taken before a pasha who was a Neapolitan renegade and taken there shouting that I was a spy of the king of Spain]. Trembling with fear ('a li cosi grande paura de trominti strani io no sapeva in che mondo io fusse' [I was so terrified of the strange torments that I did not know in what world I was]), he showed the pasha Francesco's letter and, as if with the wave of a magic wand, the interrogator turned into a welcoming host.[138] Several years later, in August 1509, when Francesco, then the commander of the army of the League of Cambrai, was captured by the Venetians, Isabella did not hesitate to contact Bayezid, asking him for help. And the sultan did not abandon Francesco in time of dire need. As Guicciardini narrates in his *Storia d'Italia*, Bayezid,

> intesa la sua calamità, chiamato a sé il bailo de' mercatanti viniziani che negoziavano in Pera appresso a Costantinopoli, lo ricercò gli promettesse che 'l marchese sarebbe liberato; e recusando il bailo di promettere quel che non era in potestà sua e offerendo scriverne a Vinegia, ove non dubitava si farebbe deliberazione conforme al desiderio suo, Baiset replicandogli superbamente essere la sua volontà che egli assolutamente lo promettesse, fu necessitato a prometterlo: il che essendo significato dal bailo a Vinegia, il senato, considerando non essere tempo a irritare principe tanto potente, determinò di liberarlo; ma per occultare il suo disonore, e riportare qualche frutto della sua liberazione, prestò orecchi al desiderio del pontefice.

> [having heard of his misfortune, summoned the *bailo* of the Venetian merchants then trading at Pera near Constantinople, and asked him to promise him that the marquis would be freed; and the *bailo* refused to promise what he was not authorized to promise and offered to write about it to Venice, where he was certain a decision would be taken in accordance with Bayezid's desire; but as Bayezid haughtily replied that it was his will that an absolute promise be made, he was forced to make it: when the *bailo* had informed Venice, the senate, judging that it was not the right time to displease such a powerful prince,

---

138  Sacrati, fol. 1$^r$. Like his brother-in-law Francesco, Cardinal Ippolito was fond of first-rate Turkish horses. In 1504 and 1505, for example, Luca Antonio Alfani and Pietro Giacomo Meraviglia travelled to the Ottoman Empire to purchase horses for Ariosto's patron. Their as yet unpublished letters to the cardinal are preserved in the Archivio di Stato di Modena, Ambasciatori estensi, busta 15/ unica, Turchia europea. In 1516 Ippolito's agent Francesco Zerbinato (Ariosto briefly mentions him at XXXVI 4 AB; XL C) travelled to the Republic of Ragusa. See Modena, Archivio di Stato, Ambasciatori estensi, busta 15/ unica, Turchia asiatica, Francesco Zerbinato.

decided to free him; but in order to conceal their dishonour and to receive some benefits from his release, they honoured the pope's request.][139]

Borso d'Este's friendship with the Hafsid sultan and Francesco Gonzaga's cordial relationship with Bayezid show that the cult of secular chivalry which underpins the *Inamoramento de Orlando* and the *Furioso* appealed to the two poets' aristocratic readers. Written for 'signori e cavalier' [lords and knights] (*Inam.*, I i 1,1), the two *Orlandos* draw inspiration both from a centuries-long literary tradition to which they belong and from contemporary court culture, which was open to the wider world, including its Islamic parts. This remarkably tolerant culture was not confined to Ferrara and Mantua: suffice it to think of Lorenzo de Medici's friendships with Mehmed and with Ashraf Qaitbay, the Burji Mamluk sultan of Egypt (1468–1496).[140] The spirit of openness towards the Other can be felt in the *Libro del Cortegiano*, too, especially in its early drafts, where, as Olga Zorzi Pugliese puts it, the author is 'acutely aware of the relativity of points of view on cultural questions'.[141] Castiglione's Bernardino Bibbiena, for example, clearly does not see the Turks as uncouth barbarians if he cites the witticisms of Bayezid's brother Cem.[142] In an early draft of the *Cortegiano* (1508–1513; 1515) one of the interlocutors states that if he had more time he would have talked about the courts of the Turkish sultan, the sultan of Alexandria, the Persian *sophi* and Prester John as well as about the Indian kingdoms recently discovered by the Portuguese.[143] In the final version of the same passage Federico Fregoso — whose travels are alluded to in the 1521 and 1532 editions of the *Furioso* (XXXVIII 20 B; XLII C) — mentions the Turkish sultan and the Persian ruler, remarking that he has heard from merchants that Persians are 'molto valorosi e di gentil costumi ed usar nel conversar l'un con l'altro, nel servir donne, ed in tutte le sue azioni molta cortesia e molta discrezione e, quando occorre, nell'arme, nei giochi e nelle feste molta grandezza, molta liberalità e leggiadria' [very valorous and have noble customs and that they show much courtesy and discretion in their conversations, in serving their ladies and all their actions, and, when it is appropriate, in arms, games, and festivities they similarly show much magnificence, liberality and grace].[144]

---

139 Francesco Guicciardini, *Storia d'Italia*, ed. by Silvana Seidel Menchi, 3 vols (Turin: Einaudi, 1971), II, p. 866.

140 Mehmed refused to shelter one of the protagonists of the Pazzi conspiracy and the grateful Lorenzo de' Medici had a medal portrait of the sultan cast to thank him for his cooperation. See Franz Babinger, *Mehmed the Conqueror and his Time*, trans. by Ralph Manheim and William C. Hickman (Princeton: Princeton University Press, 1978), pp. 384–88. In 1486 Ashraf Qaitbay sent Lorenzo a giraffe. Paolo Giovio's biography of Qaitbay is remarkably positive: see his *Elogi degli uomini illustri*, pp. 669–73.

141 Zorzi Pugliese, *Castiglione's The Book of the Courtier (Il libro del cortegiano): A Classic in the Making*, p. 179.

142 See *Cortegiano*, Book II, 66. As Zorzi Pugliese observes, more witticisms are mentioned in the first draft of the book (1509–1513) (Zorzi Pugliese, *Castiglione's The Book of the Courtier (Il libro del cortegiano): a Classic in the Making*, p. 178).

143 Ibid., p. 176.

144 Baldassare Castiglione, *Il libro del Cortegiano*, introd. by Amedeo Quondam, ed. by Nicola Longo (Milan: Garzanti, 2006), III, 2, p. 262.

If the main Christian and Saracen characters of the *Inamoramento de Orlando*, the *Furioso* and other Italian *libri di battaglia* share similar values, this is because already in many *chansons de geste* Christian chivalry is similar to Saracen chivalry. Moreover, Boiardo and Ariosto could find positive representations of the East in various medieval and ancient texts, including Boiardo's own translations of Riccobaldo, Herodotus, and Xenophon.[145] At the same time, however, the fact that the two *Orlandos* abound in episodes of friendly interactions between characters of different faiths can also be explained with reference to the poems' historical background, and it would not be unreasonable to assume that real-life encounters between Italian nobles and their counterparts in the Islamic world added to the popularity of chivalric literature in courtly milieus.

---

145 It is worth noting that Boiardo implicitly compares Ercole to Cyrus in his translation of Xenophon's *Cyropaedia*, where Cyrus, 'saggio signore e [...] valoroso capitano' [wise lord and [...] a valourous captain], embodies the virtues that Boiardo wishes to find in his patron (*La pedìa*, p. 131). Fregoso's positive assessment of Persian culture in the *Cortegiano* brings to mind one of Matteo Bandello's novellas — *Novelle*, I, 2, which is set in ancient Persia and in which the seneschal of King Artaxerxes seeks to surpass his lord in courtesy. Though first published in 1554, this novella could have been written much earlier, as Bandello claims that he heard it from Silvio Savelli at a gathering in Lucio Scipione Attellano's garden, in the presence of Ippolita Sforza Bentivoglio (1481–1520).

# CHAPTER 2

❖

# Who's Who in Boiardo's *Paganìa*

'"[...] se Marsilio è saracino, | ciò non attendo; egli è nostro cognato | et ha vicino a Francia gionto il stato"' [if Marsilio is a Saracen, | that does not matter. He is our brother-in-law | and rules the country that bounds France] (*Inam.*, I iv 14,6–8), says the French Emperor, announcing his decision to help Marsilio against Gradasso, King of Sericana. This statement might puzzle the modern reader, given that nowhere in the *Inamoramento de Orlando* does Boiardo explain why the ruler of Saracen Spain is Charlemagne's relative. However, the poet's early readers did not need any explanation: they knew that Charlemagne's wife Galerana (of whom we catch a brief glimpse at I i 22,1) was the daughter of King Galafro who also fathered Balugante and Falsirone and Marsilio.[1] In Andrea da Barberino's *Reali di Francia* the young Carlotto (or Mainetto, as he calls himself in order to conceal his true identity) falls in love with the Saracen princess Galeana when hiding from his evil half-brothers at Galafro's court in Spain. She runs away with him but is forgiven by her father as soon as he learns that their servant Mainetto is none other than Charlemagne ('Di questo Galafro fu molto allegro, imperò ch'egli seppe come egli voleva tenere Galeana per sua legittima sposa' [Galafro was very glad to hear that, since he learnt that he wanted to take Galeana as his legitimate wife] (*Reali di Francia*, IV xlix)). In the previous chapter, we saw that friendships and even marriages between Christian and Muslim nobles were not unheard of in fifteenth- and sixteenth-century Italy. Nor are they uncommon in chivalric romances that precede, or are contemporaneous with, the *Inamoramento de Orlando*. As will be shown here, the universe which sprang from Boiardo's pen — one in which there is no sharp line dividing characters of different faiths — is steeped in the chivalric tradition, and especially in its Carolingian branch.

This chapter aims to recover some of the chivalric intertextuality of Boiardo's portrayal of Saracens, highlighting the intertextual nature of these characters, with a special, though not exclusive, focus on those that are introduced in Book I. It is divided into two parts. The first is devoted to an overview of Boiardo's Saracens and is more descriptive than the rest of the book (apart from a similar section on Ariosto's Saracens in Chapter IV). It examines, among other things, Saracen names,

---

1    The earliest surviving text containing references to her story is the twelfth-century *Historia Karli Magni et Rotholandi* (the Pseudo-Turpin chronicle). Later texts include the Franco-Venetian *Karleto* and Andrea da Barberino's *Reali di Francia* (see *Reali di Francia*, IV vii-xlix).

a vast and complex topic, considering the sheer size of the corpus of chivalric texts the poet could have been familiar with and the uncertain dating of many of these texts. The second part explores Boiardo's use of the *Spagna* and other Carolingian narratives in his representation of Marsilio, his Spanish subjects as well as other Saracens who figure in the chivalric tradition. What follows is intended as a preliminary part of a larger inquiry (continued in Chapter III) into the ways in which Boiardo engages with his numerous direct and indirect intertexts, at times meeting his audience's expectations and at times deliberately frustrating them.

## Borrowed characters and borrowed names

Two out of every three characters in the *Inamoramento de Orlando* come from the Saracen lands. While Boiardo does not always specify his heroes' faith (which, in itself, points to the fluidity of the boundary between Christians and Saracens), we can assume that, in the absence of compelling evidence to the contrary, characters whom we encounter outside Charlemagne's empire are Saracens. If we count all the so-called infidels featuring in the poem, the total number is at least 218.[2] This number includes figures such as Galerana, i.e. Saracen converts to Christianity from earlier chivalric narratives, whose Saracen past was no secret to Boiardo's early readers. To these daughters and sons of *Paganìa*, we can add Marsilio's treasurer Baricheo, a Jew-turned-Christian-turned-Saracen who, having tried all three Abrahamic religions, 'né credeva in Macon né in Dio divino' [had no faith in Macone or divine God] (*Inam.*, II xxiv 59,6). By contrast, the number of Christians is much smaller: approximately 102, including Theodoro (whom several critics believe to be a Saracen) and the Genoese renegade whose armour was briefly discussed in Chapter I.[3] Such a discrepancy (68% of Saracens versus 32% of Christians) is even more striking if one compares Boiardo's poem to other epic and chivalric texts. Thus, in the *Chanson de Roland*, the numbers of characters of

---

2    For a list of Boiardo's named and nameless Saracens see Appendix I. The number quoted above is an approximation, for, although every effort has been made to count all Saracens, the total number varies depending on the specific edition being used (see note 1 to Appendix I). As far as the nameless Saracen characters are concerned, only those that make some contribution, however small, to the plot have been counted.

3    Both Franceschetti (*L'‘Orlando Innamorato’ e le sue componenti tematiche e strutturali*, p. 104) and Alexandre-Gras, *L'héroïsme chevaleresque dans le ‘Roland Amoureux’ de Boiardo*, p. 308) assume that Theodoro, 'figliol del Re d'Harmenia' [son of the King of Armenia] (*Inam.*, II xxvi 22,5), is a Saracen because he converts to Christianity together with his sweetheart Doristela: 'la gratia dele dame fo cotanta | che dai monti d'Harmenia ala marina | corse ciascuno ala legie divina' [the damsels were so full of grace | that from the mountains to the sea, | all of Armenia joined the divine faith] (II xxvii 35,6–8). However, Varano, King of Hermenia (Armenia) whom we meet in Book I, is not a Saracen but rather a Christian heretic: 'cristïano | (ben che macchiato è forte de heresia)' [a Christian, | though he is severely tainted as a heretic] (I x 38,2). Varano cannot be Theodoro's father: the former dies in battle (I xiv 17,7), while the latter 'morto era [...] a corso naturale' [died [...] of natural causes] (II xxvii 20,4). Yet one could perhaps still argue that, being an Armenian, Theodoro is a Christian heretic who eventually converts to Catholicism. Announcing the conversion of his wife Doristela and her sister Fiordalisa (both of whom had been brought up in the Saracen faith), Boiardo stresses that these two damsels were not just Christians but also Catholic (II xxvii 34,2).

different confessions are more or less equal: around 60 Saracens and 57 Christians. In the *Entrée d'Espagne*, the *Fatti de Spagna* (a prose romance of the late fourteenth or early fifteenth century) and the *Spagna ferrarese* (a shorter version of the *Spagna in rima* preserved in a manuscript commissioned by Borso d'Este) Christians outnumber Saracens. In the *Spagna* the difference is very slight (three characters, as in the *Chanson de Roland*), but in the *Entrée d'Espagne* and the *Fatti de Spagna* it is more perceptible, with Christians constituting about 55–56% of the total number of characters. Similarly, in Andrea da Barberino's *Aspramonte* Christians (54.5%) are more numerous Saracens (45.5%). In Pulci's *Morgante*, there are more Saracens than Christians, but the gap is not as large as in the *Inamoramento de Orlando*: Saracens make up around 54% of the poem's characters.

Out of more than 218 Saracens who populate the pages of the *Inamoramento de Orlando* around thirty-one to thirty-six characters come from earlier chivalric texts. The remainder appear to have been invented by Boiardo, even if many of the names already featured in preceding chivalric literature. The borrowed characters can be divided into two categories: those who actively participate in the plot of the *Inamoramento de Orlando*, and those whom we never see (mostly because they are already dead) but whose exploits are alluded to by the narrator or by other characters. The first category includes:

> the Amirante [Emir]
> the Argalipha (Argalifa, Argaliffa) [Caliph]
> Balugante (Balucante)
> Dudone
> Falsirone (Falcirone)
> Feraguto
> Galerana
> Grandonio
> Isolieri (Isoliero, Isolier)
> Malzarise
> Maradasso
> Marsilio (Marsiglio)
> Morgante
> Ogieri il Danese
> Rugiero
> Serpentino
> Sobrino
> Spinella da Altamonte
> Antiphor de Albarosìa (?)
> Adriano (?)
> Ballano (?)
> Chiarione (?)
> Oberto da il Leone (?)

The following Saracens fall into the second category:

> Agolante
> Almonte
> Balante

Belisandra
Brabante
Caroggieri (Carogiero)
Constantino
Durastante
Galaciella
Mambrino
Pantasilicor
Troiano
Ulieno di Sarza

It only takes a brief glance at these lists to realize that the majority of these characters come either from the *Spagna* (the Amirante, the Argalipha, Balugante, Falsirone, Feraguto, Galerana, Grandonio, Isolieri, Malzarise, Maradasso, Marsilio, Morgante and Serpentino) or from the *Aspramonte* (Agolante, Almonte, Balante, Brabante, Caroggiri, Galaciella, Sobrino, Troiano and Ulieno). As we shall see in this and the following chapter, the *Spagna* is one of the most important chivalric sources for Book I of the *Inamoramento de Orlando*, while the *Aspramonte* is unquestionably the most important source for Book II.

As for the remaining Saracens from preceding chivalric literature, Marsilio's knight Spinella da Altamonte is a Spanish Saracen from the *Trabisonda*, where he is killed by Rinaldo's friend Organtino. The names of Belisandra, Constantino, Mambrino, Durastante and Pantasilicor are brought up during a heated quarrel between Ranaldo and Orlando (*Inam.*, I xxvii 15–22; xxviii 3–12). Mad with jealousy, Orlando spouts a string of accusations (most of them unfair) against his cousin. He claims that Ranaldo violated the chivalric code when he kidnapped the Saracen princess Belisandra (a Saracen beauty who sets on fire Charlemagne's heart and whom Rinaldo and Orlando kidnap for their emperor in the *Innamoramento di Carlo*); when he killed Constantino and Mambrino (Rinaldo kills these powerful Saracen kings in the *Cantari di Rinaldo*); and when he stole King Durastante's treasure after he, Orlando, had defeated Durastante in a fair duel (Durastante's story, to which I shall return in Chapter III, is narrated in the *Altobello*). He also accuses Ranaldo of having treacherously murdered King Pantasilicor: 'né usata fo più mai tanta viltade, | perché esssendo pregion, da te fo impeso' [such cravenness was never seen, | as he was your prisoner and you had him hanged] (I xxviii 6,2–3). It is clear that Pantasilicor must be a character from an earlier chivalric text, yet one which has yet to be identified.[4]

Dudone and Ogieri il Danese — both are Saracen converts to Christianity — appear in many (indeed most) Carolingian chivalric works, the stories of their conversions being narrated in the fifteenth-century *Castello di Teris* (Dudone) and in Andrea da Barberino's *Reali di Francia* (Ogieri). It is possible that Amone's

---

4    In her note to the stanza in question Tissoni Benvenuti observes that 'Un re pagano Pantalicorno si incontra nel *Persiano*, ma la vicenda non ha a che fare' [A Saracen king called Pantalicorno features in the *Persiano*, but this is a completely different story]. We may add that there is a Pantasilicorin in the *ottava rima* version of the *Buovo d'Antona*, and a Pantastalicorno in the *Vendetta di Falconetto*, but again these are different characters.

daughter and Rugiero's sweetheart Bradamante (Bradiamante) is a Saracen convert too, considering that she was born to a Saracen mother and brought up in *Paganìa* according to some Italian chivalric narratives.[5] In Francesco Cieco da Firenze's *Persiano*, a poem first printed in the same year as the first two books of the *Inamoramento de Orlando* and probably composed in Ferrara, Bradiamonte has an excellent relationship with Amone's wife Biatrice and calls her mother, but the narrator explains that her biological mother was a Saracen lady.[6] Finally, Rugiero, the son of the Christian knight Rugiero II di Risa and a Saracen princess, Galaciella, is probably not a completely new character: there are a couple of references to Galaciele and her son Rizer in Raffaele da Verona's Franco-Venetian prose romance *Aquilon de Bavière*, and Rugerus, as we saw in the previous chapter, figures in Tito Vespasiano Strozzi's *Borsias*.[7]

Sometimes it is difficult to say whether Boiardo merely borrows a name or whether the character in question is to be identified with his or her namesake in some other text. Having drunk from the river of oblivion, many a knight loses his memory, 'né saprìa dir alcun quel che lui sia, | né se egli è Saracino o Christïano' [nor can any of them say who he is, | whether he is a Saracen or a Christian] (*Inam.*, I ix 73,4–5). Among Dragontina's victims are 'il forte re Adriano' [the strong King Andriano] (73,1), Antifor de Albarosìa, 'il re Balano, quel mastro di guerra' [the martial expert King Balano] (72,5), 'Chiarïone, il franco Saracino' [the bold Saracen Chiarione] (72,6), and Oberto da il Leone. When the spell is broken, these characters remember who they are, but the reader — especially the modern reader — cannot be certain of anything. It is likely that all of them — not just Chiarione — are Saracens, given that we meet them in *Paganìa*. They keep together as a group and leave the narration at the same time, that is in canto ii of Book II, when Marphisa takes prisoners Chiarione and Adriano, unhorses Antifor de Albarosìa, wounds Balano, and kills Oberto da il Leone. Their names must have had a familiar ring for Boiardo's contemporaries, as their namesakes feature in a number of late fourteenth-century and fifteenth-century Carolingian chivalric texts which very likely precede the *Inamoramento de Orlando*. Thus, there is a character named Adrian in the *Aquilon de Bavière*, where he is the noble son of the Saracen king of Val Perse. In Andrea da Barberino's *Ajolfo del Barbicone* King Adriano rules Pampolona. Another Saracen Adriano appears in the *Drusiano dal Leone*, where he is the King

---

5    In the *Ugieri il Danese* Bradamante (Briamonte in the 1480 incunabulum, Braidamonte in Sara Furlati's edition of the poem, which is based on a fifteenth century manuscript (II.II.31, Biblioteca Nazionale Centrale di Firenze, olim Magliabechiano Cl. VII, n. 1048): *I cantari del Danese*, ed. by Sara Furlati (Alessandria: Edizioni dell'Orso, 2003)) is the daughter of the Soldano, while in the *Castello di Teris* she is the fruit of an extramarital affair between Amone and a Saracen woman. As Rajna points out, 'si è tentati di credere che non senza intenzione il Boiardo taccia della madre' [one is tempted to believe that it is not by chance that Boiardo says nothing about her, i.e. Bradamante's, mother] (Rajna, *Le fonti*, p. 52). On Bradamonte in the *cantari* tradition see Stoppino, 'One Marriage by Duel: Genealogies of the Warrior Woman', in Eadem, *Genealogies of Fiction*, pp. 16–57.

6    The *editio princeps* of the *Persiano* came out in 1483, the year in which the first two books of the *Inamoramento de Orlando* were first published. Its final stanza says that it is printed to celebrate the exploits of Ferrara and its allies in the War of Ferrara.

7    See Tissoni Benvenuti's note to *Inam.*, II i 70.

of Mascona.[8] The author of the *Trabisonda* gives this name to the late father of Ramondo, a young knight who admires Rinaldo, while the author of the *Antiphor de Barosia* gives it to a brave Saracen king who at one point fights with Astolfo.[9] Another Adriano appears in a text that Boiardo was almost certainly familiar with, since, as we saw, he refers to one of its episodes: Adriano who is Rinaldo's friend and the nephew of a Saracen ruler in the *Innamoramento di Carlo*.[10]

As for the namesakes of the friends of Boiardo's Adriano, King Bal(l)ano is one of the most charismatic Saracen characters of the *Trabisonda*, where he is at first Rinaldo's fiercest enemy, but eventually becomes his best friend. A knight called Chiarione is King Durastante's brother in the *Altobello* ('e veramente lui era lustro e chiaro' [and indeed he was brilliant and illustrious], states the anonymous poet, 'mior pagan de lui non adora Macone' [no better Saracen than him worships Macone] (*Altobello*, XXII 4,2–3 [fol. h v^v])).[11] A Saracen king named Antiphor de Barosìa features in the eponymous poem, where he introduces himself as 'lo fiore de tutta Pagania' [the cream of all *Paganìa*] (*Antiphor*, III 27,7), but despite his prowess, is killed by Orlando who then assumes his identity. Finally, as far as Oberto da il Leone is concerned, 'dal Leone' is a rather common 'surname' in chivalric literature. Several cantos after Oberto's first appearance, Boiardo tells us that this 'Baron de alto afare' [nobleman of great renown] was both 'ardito e sagio' [daring and wise] and that he 'tuta la terra intorno ebe a circare, | comme se vede nel suo libro aperto' [had explored the whole world, | as is explained in his book] (*Inam.*, I xiv 41,3–6), thereby implying that his adventures were narrated in some popular chivalric romance.[12]

---

8   The action of the *Ajolfo del Barbicone* and the *Drusiano dal Leone* take places after the death of Charlemagne's paladins.

9   The *Antiphor de Barosia* was certainly composed before 1491, as Isabella d'Este mentions it in a 1491 letter.

10   These namesakes of Adriano (as well as those of Balano and Chiarione) seem to have escaped the attention of Tissoni Benvenuti and other editors of Boiardo's poem.

11   In Pulci's *Morgante*, too, there is a character called Chiarione, a noble Saracen innkeeper who becomes governor of a kingdom (*Morgante*, XXI 19). It is interesting to note that a fair number of Saracens in the French and Italian traditions have names starting with 'Clar' or 'Chiar': we see Clarïen, Clarifan and Clarin in the *Chanson de Roland*, Chiaron in the *Spagna ferrarese*, Chiarello in Andrea da Barberino's *Aspramonte*, Chiariella, Chiariello, Chiaristante and Chiarione in the *Morgante*. Needless to say, many Christian names start with 'Chiar', the most famous one being Chiaramonte. On other evocative names in the *Inamoramento* see Ruggero M. Ruggieri, 'I "nomi parlanti" nel *Morgante*, nell'*Innamorato* e nel *Furioso*', in his *Saggi di linguistica italiana e italo-romanza* (Florence: Olschki, 1962), pp. 169–81.

12   No traces of a romance entitled *Oberto dal Leone* have been found thus far, but a romance called *Drusiano dal Leone* (first printed in 1513) must have circulated in the second half of the fifteenth century. It is preserved in a late fifteenth-century manuscript: MS. Landau Finaly 212, Biblioteca Nazionale Centrale in Florence (see Villoresi, *La letteratura cavalleresca*, p. 94). It is, however, unlikely that Boiardo was thinking of *Drusiano*, given that it narrates the events that happened after the death of Charlemagne's paladins. As Tissoni Benvenuti suggests in her note to I ix 73, 'non si può escludere che Boiardo abbia inventato l'esistenza di questo libro di Oberto dal Leone, per prendersi gioco dell'aggiornata cultura cavalleresca del suo pubblico' [it cannot be ruled out that Boiardo may have invented the existence of this book of Oberto dal Leone in order to tease his audience about their up-to-date chivalric culture], especially considering that his Oberto dies almost by chance, being cut into two pieces by Marphisa.

Whether or not Boiardo was thinking of specific characters from earlier chivalric texts, the names of these five knights link them to the chivalric tradition, where their namesakes are, for the most part, valiant and famous Saracen heroes. Boiardo's Adriano, Antifor, Balano, Chiarione and Oberto are minor characters of whom we only catch fleeting glimpses; they live in the shadow of more prominent Saracens, such as Agricane, Gradasso, Feraguto, and Sacripante. Yet the fact that each one of these seemingly insignificant yet sympathetic characters may have a story to tell reinforces the impression that there is no lack of valour and prowess in the Saracen world of the *Inamoramento de Orlando*.

Boiardo has been much praised for his unbridled imagination, not least for his inventiveness in coining memorable names for his Saracens. Legend has it that he 'faceva suonare le campane ad ogni bel nome che trovava per i suoi personaggi: Fiordispina, Brunello, Sacripante, Gradasso, Rodomonte' [called for the bells to be rung each time he found a beautiful name for his characters: Fiordispina, Brunello, Sacripante, Gradasso, Rodomonte].[13] Charming as it is, it is unlikely that this legend is founded upon fact. Nor should we take seriously Ludovico Castelvetro's claim that Boiardo named 'gli Agramanti, i Sobrini e i Mandricardi' after the peasants of Scandiano.[14] Already the first modern editor of Boiardo, Antonio Panizzi, suspected that most of the Saracen names in the *Inamoramento de Orlando* had literary origins.[15] Below is the list of Saracens whom the poet created *ex nihilo* but whose names are identical or very similar to the names featuring in other chivalric narratives:

Agramante (King Agramonte di Taspi in the *Ajolfo del Barbicone*)[16]
Albarosa (Albarisa di Gallozia in Andrea da Barberino's *Ugone d'Alvernia*)
Alibante (Abilante in the *Spagna ferrarese*, *Innamoramento di Rinaldo* and *Aspramonte A*)
Angelica (Angelica in the *Libro di Rambaldo*, Angelina in the *Antiphor de Barosia*, Anzi(o)lela in the *Altobello*)
Argalìa (King Argalia/Arcalia in *Aspramonte A*, the fifteenth-century *Aspramonte*, the *Altobello* and the *Ugieri il Danese*)
Calabruno di Aragona (Calebrun d'Alessandria in *Aspramonte A*)
Calidora (Calidor in the *Ajolfo del Barbicone*)
Cardorano (Cordoan in *Aspramonte A*)
Dardinello (Dodonello in the *Reali di Francia*, Dondonello in the *Tavola Ritonda*)
Fiordalisa [Fiordelisa, Fiordehelisa] (Fiordalisa in the *Ajolfo del Barbicone*, Fioredalisa in the *Storia di Rinaldino da Montalbano*; Fiordelise in the *Persiano*; Fiore de Lisa in the *Vendetta di Falconetto*)
Fiordespina (Fior de Spina in the *Altobello*, the *Persiano*, and in the *Fioretto dei paladini*)
Folvo di Fersa (Fierse di Folva in the *Spagna ferrarese*)

---

13    Alfonso Burgio, *Dizionario dei nomi propri di persona* (Rome: Hermes Edizioni 1992), p. 256. On the bell-ringing legend see also Ernest H. Wilkins, 'The Naming of Rodomont', *MLN*, 70 (1955), 596–99.

14    See Castelvetro, *Poetica d'Aristotele*, fol. 117$^v$.

15    'Most of the Saracen names mentioned by BOJARDO occur in the *Reali di Francia*, or in the other old books of this description' (Panizzi, 'Life of Boiardo', p. lxxix). Panizzi himself identifies only a handful of borrowings.

16    Antonio Panizzi notes that a certain Agramonte appeared in 'a very ancient chronicle' of the history of Naples (ibid., p. xcix)).

Galaphrone [Galafro] (Galafro in the *Reali di Francia*, Galafrone in the *Spagna ferrarese*)
Gradasso (Gradasso in the *Sala di Malagigi*, the *Visione di Venus* and the *Antiphor de Barosia*; Gradosso in the *Tavola ritonda*; Grapas (Grapaso) in the *Dama Rovenza*)
Grifaldo [Griphaldo, Gryphaldo, Gryfaldo] (Grifaldo in the *Altobello*)
Griphone di Altaripa (Grifone in the *Ugieri il Danese*)
Hordauro [Ordauro] (Ordorieri in Andrea da Barberino's *Storie nerbonesi*)
Horisello [Horrisello] (Orsello in the *Storie nerbonesi*)
Hosbego [Usbergo in the Trivulziano manuscript] (Lusbercho in the *Altobello*)
Lampardo (Lampardo d'Affrica in the *Rinaldino da Montalbano*)
Lucina (Luciana in the *Morgante*, Lucia and Luciana in the *Drusiano dal Leone*)
Malapresa (Malagrappa in the *Storie nerbonesi*)
Malgarino (Malgaria in the *Buovo d'Antona* in octaves)
Marigoto (Margotto in the *Cantari di Fierabraccia e Ulivieri*)
Matalista (Mattalia in *Aspramonte A*)
Mordante (Mordans in *Aspramonte A*; Moradante in the *Antiphor*)
Orione (Orio in the *Buovo d'Antona*)
Pandragone (Uter Pandragone is Artù's father in the *Tavola ritonda* and other Arthurian romances; Pandragone in the *Drusiano dal Leone*)
Piliasi (Piliagi and Pilias in *Aspramonte A*, Pilagi in the *Spagna ferrarese*, Pilias in the *Reali di Francia*)
Radamanco (Rodomanta/Radamanto in the *Morgante*, Rhadamanthus in Virgil's *Aeneid*)
Rodomonte (Rodomanta/Radamanto in the *Morgante*)[17]
Rubicone (Rubican in the *Storie nerbonesi*, Rubicante in the *Morgante* and in the *Altobello*)
Sinagone (Sinagone in *Aspramonte A*, the fifteenth-century *Aspramonte*, the *Fatti de Spagna* and the *Spagna ferrarese*)[18]
Stella (Stelle in the *Aquilon de Bavière*)
Tanfirione (Tanfurone in the *Ajolfo del Barbicone*)
Tibiano (Tidiano in the *Storie nerbonesi*)
Torindo (Torindo in the *Guerrin Meschino* and *Rinaldino da Montalbano*)
Urgano (Urgano lo Velluto in the *Tavola Ritonda*)
Ziliante (Giliante in the *Reali di Francia*, Gilante in the *Antiphor de Barosia*)

Boiardo draws inspiration from Arthurian and Carolingian texts, with Andrea da Barberino's romances (*Ajolfo del Barbicone, Aspramonte, Guerrin Meschino, Reali di Francia, Rinaldino da Montalbano, Storie nerbonesi, Ugone d'Alvernia*) dominating the list. If we add to the names listed above those of the characters taken from the chivalric tradition (such as Marsilio, Galerena, or Sobrino who, contrary to what Castelvetro asserts, is one of the Saracen protagonists of the *Aspramonte*), we will see that more than a third of the Saracen names that feature in the *Inamoramento de Orlando* — seventy-five, to be precise — are either borrowed from or inspired by earlier chivalric works.

The name 'Gradasso' — which, together with that of Gradasso's brother-in-faith

17    On the Pulcian origin of Rodamonte's name see Alberto Casadei: 'Nomi di personaggi nel *Furioso*', *Il nome nel testo: Rivista internazionale di onomastica letteraria*, 2–3 (2001), 229–37 (p. 232). The etymology of this name is also discussed by Eugenio Ragni: cf. his 'Rodomonte e Gradasso: storia incroiata di due "ruganti"', *Letteratura italiana antica*, 8 (2007), 399–413 (p. 401).
18    Like Sinagone in the *Fatti de Spagna*, Boiardo's Sinagone is one of Marsilio's subjects. Both are killed by Oliviero (the former in the battle of Rencesvals, the latter at the beginning of Agramante's war), which is the reason they cannot be one and the same character.

Sacripante, entered the Italian language, giving rise to the idiomatic expression 'fare il gradasso' (to be a boaster, to brag) — deserves to be discussed in some depth. Although it is generally assumed that it was coined by Boiardo, there is good evidence to suggest that, like most other Saracen names that we see in the opening canto of the *Inamoramento de Orlando* (Angelica, Argalìa, Galaphrone, Lampardo, Urgano, as well as the names of the Spanish Saracens), it was borrowed from some other text. Two Gradassos are mentioned in what is probably the most archaic version of the *Sala di Malagigi*, a thirty-nine-octave poem which may have been composed by Antonio Pucci and which is preserved in MS 1091 of the Biblioteca Riccardiana in Florence (copied by Benedetto Biffoli and dated 1460). The *Sala* contains an ekphrastic description of a sumptuous hall whose walls are decorated with portraits of famous warriors. The first Gradasso appears in the company of Saladin, Tarquin, Cicero and Aeneas (*Sala di Malagigi*, 15,8); the second one features in the stanza devoted to Arthurian knights ('Della Ritonda v'era il buon Galasso | [...] | dall'altra parte stava il re Gradasso' [Of the Round Table there was the good Galasso | [...] | King Gradasso was on the other side] (*Sala di Malagigi*, 17,1–5)).[19] The latter Gradasso also appears in some of the fifteenth-century printed editions of the *Sala*[20] as well as in stanza 15 (which is very similar to stanza 17 of the oldest extant version of the *Sala*) of the *Visione di Venus* — a short anonymous poem which, according to Alessandro d'Ancona, dates back to the second half of the fourteenth century or the first decades of the fifteenth century — as preserved in MS 43 of the Biblioteca Comunale in Perugia.[21] Moreover, a knight named Gradasso is mentioned in the *Cronaca di Rimini*. Describing the wedding of Roberto Malatesta and Elisabetta da Montefeltro (1475), the chronicler claims that in the 'rial sala [...] v'erano figurati gran parte delli famosi re e inperadori e baroni e cavalieri de cristiani e pagani, e d'altri valenti homini di scientia' [royal hall [...] many famous kings and emperors and Christian and Saracen knights and other worthy men of science were pictured][22] and inserts a poem which was probably recited at the nuptial celebrations. Clearly inspired by the *Sala*, it mentions the 'alto re Gradasso' [noble King Gradasso] together with Galasso, Palamides, King Marco, and other heroes of Arthurian romances.[23]

19    See *La Sala di Malagigi: Cantare cavalleresco*, ed. by Pio Rajna (Imola: Tip. Galeati, 1871). Rajna's edition of the *Sala* was a wedding gift for his friend and tutor Alessandro D'Ancona. Only a very limited number of copies was printed. Rajna attributes the poem's authorship to Antonio Pucci (*c.* 1310–88), while Ottaviano Targioni Tozzetti suggests that it could have been composed by Antonio da Bacchereto, the author of the *Padiglione di Mambrino* (see Ottaviano Targioni Tozzetti, 'Prefazione', in *Il Padiglione di Mambrino: cantare cavalleresco*, ed. by Pietro Volpini (Livorno: Vigo, 1874), pp. 7–8).
20    An enlarged and slightly rewritten version of the *Sala di Malagigi* was printed at least six times before the close of the fifteenth century: in 1471, 1480, 1483, 1495, and twice in 1500. I have been able to consult four of these editions: the first Gradasso is absent from all of them, while the 'Arthurian' Gradasso features in stanza 23 of the 1480 Florentine edition and in the same stanza in the two 1500 editions (published in Rome and in Florence). The *Sala* that was printed in Bologna in 1483 reads Galasso instead of Gradasso.
21    The *Visione* was published by Alessandro d'Ancona: *La Visione di Venus: antico poemetto popolare*, ed. by Alessandro d'Ancona, *Giornale di filologia romanza*, 2 (1878), 111–18.
22    *Cronaca di Rimini*, cited in Angelo Turchini, *La signoria di Roberto Malatesta detto il Magnifico (1468–1482)* (Rimini: B. Ghigi, 2001), p. 438.
23    Ibid., p. 440.

If the authors of the *Sala*, the *Visione di Venus*, and the anonymous poem cited in the *Cronaca di Rimini* seem to imply that Gradasso was a famous knight from the Arthurian literary tradition, the author of the *Antiphor de Barosia* provides more details. Describing a fierce duel between Rinaldo and Orlando, he compares the former to the most excellent warriors of all time:

> Parea in campo lo forte Galasso
> o vero Tristan o vero Lancilotto
> che liberato ogni tristo passo
> e chi ben fece pagare lo scotto
> quando occise lo forte re Gradasso [...]²⁴

> [In the field he resembled the strong Galasso
> or Tristan or Lancilotto
> who freed every passageway held by the enemy
> and who made him pay the price
> when he killed the strong King Gradasso]
> (*Antiphor de Barosia*, XVIII 10,1–5 [fol. E viᵛ])²⁵

While, to my knowledge, there are no traces of a knight called Gradasso in the extant Arthurian texts, a certain Gradosso figures in the fourteenth-century *Tavola ritonda*: looking for an adventure, Lancilotto 'si ritrovò a un forte passo, lo quale era guardato da due forti gioganti; et facevalo guardare lo re Gradosso di Sansogna, per paura che aveva del conte Liombardo' [found himself near an important crossroads, which was guarded by two strong giants; and it was King Gradosso of Saxony who made them guard it because he was afraid of Count Liombardo].²⁶ Interestingly, the word 'passo', which invariably rhymes with 'Gradasso' in the poems mentioned above, features in this passage too. Could it be that this mysterious Gradosso is the Gradasso mentioned in the *Sala*, that he is one of the central protagonists in some lost Italian romance? Such a possibility cannot be ruled out, even if it is equally possible that Gradosso is a separate character.

We do not know whether Boiardo came across the name 'Gradasso' in the *Sala di Malagigi*, the *Visione di Venus*, the *Antiphor*, or some other chivalric text. He could have read the *Antiphor*, given that an Antifor de Albarosìa does figure among the characters of his poem, but we do not know when the *Antiphor* was composed. On the other hand, in Book III of the *Inamoramento de Orlando* there is a line that brings to mind the thirty-nine-octave *Sala* ('Dal'altra parte el forte re Gradasso' [Strong King Gradasso from the other side] (*Inam.*, III i 43,1)). It is very likely that Boiardo was familiar with the *Sala*, a popular chivalric text that enjoyed a wide circulation in fifteenth-century Italy. That said, he may have read it after he had started

---

24   Rinaldo himself kills a Saracen king named Grapas (Grapaso) in the *Dama Rovenza*, a fifteenth-century chivalric romance first printed in 1482 (*Dama Rovenza*, II-IV [fols a4ᵛ-b4ʳ]).

25   The 1531 edition of the *Antiphor* I cite from probably reproduces the text of the 1493 edition: its last two lines read 'nel anni milli quattrocento tri e nonanta | al vostro honore la historia se stampa' [in the year one thousand four hundred and ninety-three | the story is printed to your honour] (*Antiphor*, XLVII 80,7–8 [fol. iiʳ]).

26   *Tavola Ritonda*, ed. by Emanuele Trevi (Milano: RCS Libri, 1999), ch. 7, p. 109. Trevi based his edition on that prepared by Filippo Luigi Polidori (1864–1866) which for the first eleven chapters follows MS I, VII, 13 of the Biblioteca Comunale in Siena (1478).

Book I. Whatever its provenance, the fact that the name of Boiardo's Gradasso has an Arthurian flavour to it is interesting, considering that, as will be shown in Chapter III, the character's personal chivalric code is remarkably similar to the chivalric ideals of knights in Arthurian literature.[27]

## Borrowed Saracens: between tradition and innovation

### Spanish Saracens

The dead warriors from the *Aspramonte* will be discussed Chapters III and V. Here I shall focus on the Saracens who step into the *Inamoramento de Orlando* well and alive, starting with King Marsilio, his family and his vassals. None of the Spanish Saracens is a particularly prominent character. In general, it would seem that Boiardo treats them with less sympathy than the North Africans or the Saracen kings from Tartary and the Far East. According to Denise Alexandre-Gras, influenced by their representation in the *Spagna*, 'Boiardo n'a pas songé à les racheter et à leur donner une vraie place parmi ses héros' [Boiardo did not intend to redeem them and to give them a real place among his heroes], leaving them in the shadow of the Rencesvals tragedy.[28] This is true to some extent, but it is equally true that the dark shadow of Rencesvals does not swallow them completely, for Boiardo disperses the threatening clouds by changing and omitting some of the details that he would have found in the *Spagna ferrarese* and other chivalric works featuring these characters. Their sinister role in the final chapter of Orlando's life does not prevent Boiardo from highlighting the chivalric virtues practiced at 'la corte di Marsilïone, | di tanto pregio e tal cavalleria' [the court of King Marsilio, | so greatly esteemed and so chivalrous] (II xxiii 9,1–2).

Some of Boiardo's Spanish characters have already been subject to scholarly discussion. Marsilio's nephew Feraguto and his representations in the *Spagna* narratives have been examined by Denise Alexandre-Gras and Franca Strologo, while Luciano Serra and Antonia Tissoni Benvenuti have looked at Grandonio's literary past.[29] Their studies show that Boiardo's portrayal of these characters is less positive than their portrayals in earlier texts. While in the *Entrée d'Espagne*, the *Fatti*

---

27    As we saw earlier, there are other Arthurian names in the *Inamoramento de Orlando*. It was not uncommon for authors of Carolingian romances to borrow names from Arthurian works and vice versa. In the *Altobello* we come across a giant called Galaso; in the *Tavola Ritonda* we see a Ferraguze.

28    Alexandre-Gras, *L'héroïsme chevaleresque dans le 'Roland Amoureux' de Boiardo*, p. 304.

29    Alexandre-Gras, 'Tre figure boiardesche di eroe saraceno: Ferraguto, Agricane, Rodamonte'; Franca Strologo, 'Duels, discours et péripéties de l'ex-géant Ferraù dans l'*Orlando furioso*', in *Lettres romanes* (2008) [special issue], 27–41; Eadem, 'I volti di Ferraù: riprese e variazioni fra la *Spagna in rima* e l'*Inamoramento de Orlando*', *Studi italiani*, 22, no. 1 (2009), 5–27; Luciano Serra, 'Letture boiardesche: storia poetica e geografica di Grandonio', in *Il Boiardo e il mondo estense nel Quattrocento*, ed. by Giuseppe Anceschi and Tina Matarrese, 2 vols (Padua: Antenore, 1998), I, pp. 143–74; Antonia Tissoni-Benvenuti, 'Intertestualità cavalleresca', in *'Tre volte suona l'olifante...': la tradizione rolandiana in Italia fra Medioevo e il Rinascimento* (Milan: Unicopli, 2007), pp. 57–78 (pp. 66–76). Moreover, Cristina Montagnani makes some interesting observations about the Spanish Saracens in the *Inamoramento de Orlando* (especially those who are mentioned at I i 10): see 'Introduzione' to her and Valentina Gritti's edition of the *Spagna ferrarese* (pp. 11–35 (pp. 20–28)).

*de Spagna* and the *Spagna ferrarese* Feraguto (Feragu, Feragù, Feraù) is a formidable warrior, Boiardo's Feraguto loses his status of the strongest knight of *Paganìa* and becomes a half-comic figure.[30] What is more, he loses the good looks he had in the *Spagna*: now he has black hair with red eyes and his face is all smeared with dirt. As for Grandonio, he is a valorous Saracen in the *Chanson de Roland*, one of the most likeable minor Saracen characters in the *Entrée d'Espagne* and a normal human being in the so-called *Spagna maggiore* (the longer version of the *Spagna in rima*). However, the author of the *Spagna ferrarese* turns him into a giant and puts him into the category of evil Saracens. Boiardo too portrays his Grandonio as a repellent giant and a coward.

Boiardo's treatment of Grandonio is not particularly surprising: one could argue that he merely follows the *Spagna ferrarese*, which is probably the version of the *Spagna* he was familiar with. Feraguto's case is more interesting. Both Alexandre-Gras and Strologo underscore the fact that there is a strong parallel between Feraguto and Orlando: both of them are 'epic' characters in the earlier Carolingian tradition and as a consequence are completely inexperienced in love.[31] While they remain valiant knights in the *Inamoramento de Orlando*, Boiardo cannot resist the temptation to poke fun at their clumsy amorous advances to Angelica, stripping them of their epic grandeur. As we shall see in Chapter III, both Feraguto and Orlando are outshone by other prominent members of the Saracen religion.

Turning to the Saracens who, to date, have received scant scholarly attention, Marsilio deserves to be dealt with first. Featuring already in the *Chanson de Roland*, he has a very long literary life behind him. In both French and Italian chivalric literatures Marsilio is neither a villain nor one of the chivalrous Saracens whose only fault is that of believing in false gods. In the *Chanson de Roland* he is represented as terrified of the Franks and incapable of taking decisions. It is his vassal Blancandrins who advises him what to do and brings about the Rencesvals tragedy by playing on Gano's hatred of Roland. Mortally wounded by Roland, Marsile endures a long agony in his palace in Saragossa, hoping that Baligant, the emir of Babylon, will save Spain. In the *Entrée d'Espagne* Marsille is petrified at the thought of a war with the Christians and attempts to persuade Charlemagne that he is his friend, offering him help should he decide to attack other Saracen kingdoms. His uncle Augalie is angry with him for wasting time when he should have been the first to strike. In the *Fatti de Spagna*, too, Marsilio is reluctant to fight with the Christians. In the *Spagna ferrarese* he tells his barons that if Charlemagne wages war on them,

> for de la Spagna converaci fugire
> se noi non vorem morir ciertamente
> per le mani de quel diavol chosante:
> Orlando, figlio di Melon d'Angrante.
>
> [we will have to flee from Spain
> if we do not want to meet certain death

---

30   For a detailed examination of Ferragu in the *Entrée d'Espagne*, see Boscolo, *L'Entrée d'Espagne*, pp. 191–206.
31   See also Cavallo, *The World beyond Europe*, p. 123.

at the hands of that destructive devil:
Orlando, son of Melon d'Angrante.]
(*Spagna ferrarese*, I 22 5–8)

In the light of his representation in the *Spagna* narratives, it is hardly surprising that the first time we hear about him in the *Inamoramento de Orlando* he is in despair. Announcing that Gradasso has attacked Spain, Fiordespina urges Feraguto (who is fighting with Orlando) to return home:

'Il re Marsilio a te solo è rivolto
e te piagnendo solamente noma;
io vidi il vechio Re batersi il volto
e trar de il capo la canuta chioma.'

['Our King, Marsilio, turns to you
alone and calls your name in tears.
I saw the old king beat his face
and tear the grey hairs from his head.']
(*Inam.*, I iv 10,1–4)

Marsilio is being his usual self, even though this time the danger comes not from Charlemagne but from a fellow Saracen. Charlemagne sends him help, but then, carried away by Malagigi's spirits, Ranaldo disappears and the Christian troops flee back to France (worried about his brother, Riciardeto decides to return home and the Christian army leaves in the dead of the night, without saying anything to their Saracen allies). Having been left in the lurch by the Christians, Marsilio decides to surrender:

vene lui stesso, con basso visagio,
avanti al re Gradasso in gionechione:
de' Cristïan raconta lo oltragio,
che fugito è Renaldo, quel giotone.
Esso promette voler far homagio,
tenir il regno comme suo Barone [...]

[He goes himself, with his face lowered,
before Gradasso, and he kneels:
he speaks of Christian perfidy,
of how Ranaldo fled, that swine.
He promises homage and respect,
to hold his land as his baron [...]]
(*Inam.*, I vi 58 1–6)

Again, he behaves in a predictable manner, forgetting about self-respect and falling on his knees before a powerful enemy. Later he will join forces with Agramante who (like Charlemagne) is his relative, as we learn at II i 48,3. Boiardo's reference to their kinship, which has long puzzled critics, can be explained by the fact that in the *Spagna* Marsilio claims to have descended from Alexander the Great (*Spagna*, VIII 22; *Spagna F*, VI 22), who is the founder of Agramante's North African dynasty. Marsilio's alliances with Gradasso and with Agramante recall his willingness 'd'essere con tutto suo sforzo in aiuto del re Agolante [Agramante's grandfather] contro al re Carlo' [to do everything possible to come to the aid of King Agolante in the war against King Charlemagne] in Andrea da Barberino's *Aspramonte* (*Aspramonte A*, I x 12–13). However, Boiardo's readers cannot blame Marsilio for turning his sword against Charlemagne, for the Christian abandoned him at the moment of greatest need, thus transgressing the chivalric code. His bitterness against his Christian brother-in-law is therefore both understandable and justified.

In the preceding chivalric tradition, Marsilio is sometimes seen committing evil acts. In the *Entrée d'Espagne*, he unlawfully strips his vassal of his kingdom (*Entrée d'Espagne*, 10318–21). In the *Spagna*, he has Charlemagne's ambassadors murdered, even if he is initially reluctant to do so. When the Archaliffa of Baldarcha insists on hanging the Christian messengers, Marsilio intervenes, reminding his uncle of their noble lineage:

> [...] 'Caro mio barbano,
> tuti siamo d'Alesandro disesi,
> del più potente signore soprano,
> e più forti che sie in nostri paesi.
> Nostro legnagio non fu mai vilano;
> sempre for tuti gentili e cortexi
> e lealtà usaro in ogni lato.
> Traditor mai nessun non fu chiamato.
>
> Non è usança che nissum messagio
> sie maï fatta nulla villania.
> A sua persona non de' far oltragio
> perché sparli di te in sua diceria.
> Già non dice ello da suo coragio,
> ma da parte di quel ch'el manda via.
> E per lui conpiacier ti convien farlo
> e sì spregiar per ubedir a Carlo.'
>
> ['My dear uncle,
> we have all descended from Alexander,
> the most powerful noble lord
> and the strongest one in our lands.
> Our lineage has never been base;
> all of us have always been courteous and noble.
> and always behaved loyally.
> None of us has ever been called a traitor.
>
> The custom is that no harm
> should ever be done to any messenger.
> You must not mistreat him
> if he speaks ill of you in his speech.
> He does not speak from his heart,
> but on behalf of the one who sends him.
> And to please him, you need to do this
> and tame your pride to obey Charlemagne.']
>                              (*Spagna F*, VI 22–23)

Marsilio's words fail to convince his vassals, and several stanzas later the Christian ambassadors are hanged with his full consent. In the *Inamoramento de Orlando* a Christian character calls him a 'perfido pagano' [treacherous Saracen] (*Inam.*, II xxii 38,7), but he does nothing to deserve this epithet. Boiardo's Marsilio may not cut a very impressive figure, but he is certainly not a bad man. His affection for his family is touching: he adores his nephew Feraguto ('Il Re, che più l'amava [Feraguto] assai che figlio, | oltra a megia hora lo téne abraciato, | basandolo più volte [...]' [The king, who loved him like a son, | embraced him for a half an hour, | kissing him repeatedly] (*Inam.*, II xxiii 4,5–7)) and has a good relationship with his siblings and children. This is consistent with his representation in other chivalric narratives: Charlemagne would not have wedded Galeana (Galerana) had Marsilio not supported his sister in her refusal to marry the middle-aged African king Bramante (*Reali di Francia*, VI xxvii).

Boiardo does not comment on Marsilio's and Galerana's relationship, but they seem to be on friendly terms, at least at the beginning of the poem. Galerana, as we mentioned earlier, appears only once: during the Pentecostal feast in the opening canto of Book I, where Marsilio's barons are Charlemagne's guests. According to Tissoni Benvenuti, the presence of the Spanish Saracens in Paris is 'anomala' [unexpected].[32] However, Charlemagne's hospitality is not without precedent. In the *Reali di Francia* Marsilio and his brothers are invited to Charlemagne's coronation ceremony and his wedding with Galeana (*Reali di Francia*, VI xlix). Encouraged by their father Galafro to attend, they set out for Paris, but turn back when they learn that Charlemagne is fighting Gherardo da Fratta (ibid., VI l). In the *Trabisonda* Marsilio, 'cum soi fratelli e cum li soi baroni' [with his brothers and with his barons] (*Trabisonda*, II 70,1–2), and the Gran Cane are warmly received in Paris. We do not know when exactly the *Trabisonda* was composed and if Boiardo could have read it, but there is an undeniable resemblance between this episode and the Pentecostal festivities in the *Inamoramento de Orlando*: in both poems the Saracens are aware of the mortal hatred between Rinaldo/Ranaldo and Gano; in both poems Gano, together with his relatives, laughs at Rinaldo's poverty. Another example of cultural tolerance can be found in the *Cantari di Rinaldo* (which was almost certainly one of Boiardo's chivalric sources), where Rinaldo organizes 'una fiera per Pasqua d'Ascensione | che vi possa venir d'ogni ragione, | come se saracini o cristïani' [an Ascension Day fair | that anyone can attend, | be they Saracens or Christians] (*Cantari di Rinaldo*, I 35,7–8; 36,1).[33]

Regarding Marsilio's other relatives, it is interesting to note that his children in the *Inamoramento de Orlando* are different from those mentioned in earlier chivalric texts. Boiardo gives him a daughter, Fiordespina, and one or two sons (Folicone and perhaps Matalista who is said to be Fiordespina's brother at I i 48). In the *Fatti de Spagna* his daughter is called Gaydamonte, in the *Spagna ferrarese* Candia, and in Pulci's *Morgante* Luciana. These ladies have little in common with Fiordespina (who unwittingly loses her heart to a woman, Bradamante), apart from the fact

---

32    See Tissoni Benvenuti's comment to *Inam.*, I i 9.
33    On the presence of the *Cantari di Rinaldo* in the *Inamoramento de Orlando* see Michael Sherberg, 'Matteo Maria Boiardo and the *Cantari di Rinaldo*', *Quaderni d'Italianistica*, 7 (1986), 165–81.

that they too are unlucky in love. Gaydamonte and Candia bestow their affections on Orlando: the former damsel brings him food when he is fighting Saracens near Lucerna and even sends a messenger to Charlemagne to warn him of the danger his nephew is running; the latter accompanies Biançardino on his embassy to Charlemagne: 'voglio andare a Carlo | sol per veder Orlando e per amarlo' [I want to go to Charlemagne | so I can see Orlando and love him] (*Spagna ferrarese*, XXVIII 4,7–8). While Orlando remains indifferent to both Gaydamente and Candia, Rinaldo does reciprocate Luciana's love but soon grows bored of her. He visits her on his way to Rencesvals and later ensures that she is spared when the Christian soldiers start slaughtering the inhabitants of Saragossa.

Boiardo introduces Fiordespina in Book III, which was composed between 1485 and 1494.[34] By that time he had certainly read the *Morgante*, which had arrived in Ferrara by 1474 (a manuscript copy of Pulci's poem is mentioned in the 1474 inventory of the Ducal Library).[35] The fact that he does not follow the *Morgante* should not perhaps surprise us, given that there are numerous other discrepancies between the Saracen worlds of the two poems.[36] However, Boiardo's silence with regard to Candia is puzzling. As Strologo observes, 'Sull'assenza di Candia dal poema boiardesco rimane, che ci piaccia o no, un interrogativo irrisoluto' [There remains a question mark, whether we like it or not, about the absence of Candia in Boiardo's poem].[37] Candia's arrival in the Christian camp lightens up the mood of the *Spagna ferrarese* just before the episode of Gano's betrayal, the point of no return after which it becomes clear that there can be no peaceful resolution to the conflict between Christians and Saracens.[38] One possible explanation is that Boiardo

34    See Zanato, *Boiardo*, pp. 159–61.

35    On the reception of the *Morgante* in Ferrara see Neil Harris, *Bibliografia dell''Orlando Innamorato'*, 2 vols (Modena: Panini, 1981–1991), II, pp. 19–20, note 10.

36    There have been several studies on Boiardo's use of the *Morgante*. According to Stefano Carrai, there are numerous allusions to the *Morgante* in Book I of Boiardo's poem, with Boiardo gradually losing his interest in Pulci in the subsequent books (see his 'Primi appunti sulle presenze pulciane nell'*Innamorato*', in *Tipografi e romanzi in Val Padana fra Quattrocento e Cinquecento*, pp. 107–16). By contrast, Raffaele Donnarumma maintains that Book I of the *Inamoramento de Orlando* is Boiardo's defiant response to Pulci inasmuch as he attempts to write a very different poem, while in Book II and especially Book III Pulci's presence is more significant (Raffaele Donnarumma, 'Boiardo e Pulci: per una storia dell'*Innamorato*', *GSLI*, 172 (1995), 161–212). Donnarumma believes that the first two books of the *Inamoramento de Orlando* were composed in the period between 1476 and 1482 and that Boiardo was familiar with the *Morgante* from the very beginning. In fact, as has been shown by Tissoni Benvenuti and Zanato, Book I was composed before in the 1460s, before 1471, which means that Boiardo probably only discovered Pulci's *Morgante* when he was working on Book II.

37    Franca Strologo, 'Le madri di Malagigi e Ferraù, le figlie di Marsilio e le *Spagne* di Boiardo e Ariosto', in *L''Orlando furioso' e la tradizione cavalleresca*, *Versants*, 59, no. 2 (2012), 27–48.

38    According to Strologo, there is a striking difference between the episode of Bianciardino's embassy to Charlemagne in the *Spagna maggiore* and Biançardino's and Candia's embassy in the *Spagna ferrarese*: in the latter poem the Saracens genuinely want peace with the Christians and Charlemagne is open to the idea of peaceful coexistence with unconverted Spaniards ('Mi sembra in effetti che chi scriveva la *Spagna* 'ferrarese' [...] fosse animato da ideali e da interessi diversi rispetto all'autore dei quaranta cantari della *Spagna in rima*: si percepisce facilmente l'accento posto, anziché sull'eroismo bellico e sulla difesa senza quartiere della propria fede, sui benefici della pace e della tolleranza religiosa, con un approccio che poteva parlare alla sensibilità del comitente del prezioso

thought that the story of Candia's unrequited passion for Orlando was too closely linked to the tragic events of the last phase of the Spanish war. One could argue that Boiardo 'forgets' about Marsilio's courageous son Zabueri for the same reason. In both the *Fatti de Spagna* (where he is called Zambuello) and the *Spagna ferrarese* this young man steals the spotlight when he thrusts himself between his father and Orlando, dying a heroic death. Boiardo could have deemed Zabueri marked too heavily by the Rencesvals tragedy to be included in the *Inamoramento de Orlando*. In this respect, it is worth pointing out that Biançardino (Blanzandrino or Blanzardino in the *Fatti de Spagna*) — the cunning Saracen who corrupts Gano in all versions of the *Spagna* and hence a character whom it is virtually impossible to forget — is completely absent from Boiardo's poem.

Like Marsilio himself, his Saracen relatives retain some of their distinguishing traits in Boiardo, but their negative qualities are downplayed. Like the author of the *Spagna ferrarese* (VI 14,3), Boiardo calls Marsilio's brother Balugante 'falso' [false] (*Inam.*, I vii 51,1), but this insult is hardly justified.[39] In fact, we remember him because of his deep affection for his son Serpentino (he cannot take his eyes off Serpentino during the joust in canto ii of Book I of the *Inamoramento de Orlando*) who, as Tissoni Benvenuti points out in her commentary to I ii 40, does not appear to be related to him in any of the surviving versions of the *Spagna*. Similarly, Marsilio's other brother Falsirone (whose name reveals much about his representation in the chivalric tradition) does not show his treacherous nature in the *Inamoramento de Orlando*, where he remains a very marginal character.[40] The Amirante [Emir] and Marsilio's uncle Argalipha [Caliph], too, are little more than names, even if in the *Spagna ferrarese* (as well as in the *Fatti de Spagna*, the *Entrée d'Espagne* and the *Chanson de Roland*, the distant relative of these Italian and Franco-Venetian texts) the latter is a memorable character. As we saw in Chapter I, in the *Spagna* he is the Pope of the Saracens; as such he allows himself to criticize the Spanish king for being too meek. Not only does Boiardo say nothing about his role within the Saracen religious hierarchy, but he also deprives him of his voice. Malzarise, the husband of Marsilio's 'suor carnale' [blood sister] (*Spagna ferrarese*, VI 43,1) and Isolieri's father, is mentioned only once in the *Inamoramento de Orlando* (II

---

manoscritto, Borso d'Este, e che può ancora parlare alla sensibilità di noi moderni' [In fact it seems to me that the person who composed the *Spagna* 'ferrarese' [...] was driven by different ideals and interests than those of the author of the forty cantari of the *Spagna in rima*: one feels that, rather than emphasizing military heroism and the dogged defence of one's faith, he emphasizes the benefits of peace and of religious tolerance, in a way that could appeal to the sensibility of Borso d'Este, who commissioned the precious manuscript, and that can still appeal to the sensibility of modern readers] (Strologo, *La Spagna nella letteratura cavalleresca italiana* (Rome; Padua: Antenore, 2014), pp. 171–72)).

39    Cavallo notes that Boiardo's portrayal of this character is more positive than his representations in the *Reali di Francia* ('nessuna verità si trovava in lui, crudele contro a' nimici, e degli amici non fu misericordioso' [there was no truth in him, he was cruel with his enemies and he was not compassionate with his friends] (*Reali di Francia*, VI xxi)) and the *Spagna* (Cavallo, *The World beyond Europe*, pp. 23–24).

40    Falsaron is a 'felun' [evildoer] already in the *Chanson de Roland* (1216). Though endowed with a brave heart, he has no scruples about violating the chivalric law: in the *Spagna ferrarese* he tells Marsiglio that he will kill himself if he does not have Charlemagne's ambassadors hanged (*Spagna F*, VI 25–26).

xxiii 71,7): it could be that Boiardo was not particularly impressed by his behaviour in the *Spagna*, where he refuses to free Astolfo when Orlando frees his son Isolieri. By contrast, Marsilio's nephews Isolieri and Serpentino — young and chivalrous Saracen knights, one of whom (Isolieri) converts to Christianity in the *Spagna* and the *Fatti de Spagna* — receive some attention from the poet. Isolieri features among Marsilio's warriors at the beginning of Book I (disappearing after stanza 67 of canto iv), and in Book II, where we only catch a few glimpses of him, he falls in love with Calidora and retreats into the world of Arthurian adventures.[41] As for Serpentino, he is described as a 'gioveneto adorno' [handsome youth] (II xxiii 45,7) who takes part in various battles and is often praised for his courage.

As for the remaining Spanish Saracens, Maradasso, King of Andologia, and King Morgante are to be identified with King Moradasse and Margante, King of Siviglia, in the *Spagna ferrarese*. In both poems these are minor characters. In the *Spagna* Moradasse is said to be 'valente' [valorous] (*Spagna ferrarese*, XXVII 7,3) and a 'presto e fiero asalitore' [quick and fierce attacker] (8,2), but his courage fades at the sight of Orlando: 'subitamente el volse il suo destieri | che già nïente el voleva aspetare' [immediately he turned his charger, | for he did not want at all to wait for him] (15,3–4), which does not save him in the end, for the enraged paladin tracks him down and eventually cuts him in half with a mighty blow of his sword Durlindana (16–19). Rewriting this dramatic episode, Boiardo gives it a comic edge: his Maradasso too flees from Orlando and effectively manages to get away ('per tuto 'l campo Orlando lo seguìa, | ma per nïente lui non l'aspetava' [Orlando chased him through the field, | but he was not about to wait] (*Inam.*, II xxiii 63,3–4). However, Boiardo's representation of Morgante contradicts his representation in the *Spagna*. Whereas in the *Spagna* he was said to be 'savio' [wise] because of his reluctance to fight with the Christians (*Spagna ferrarese*, XXVII 34), in the *Inamoramento de Orlando* Morgante is a 'falso pagano' [false Saracen] (*Inam.*, I vii 19,6), even if the poet has to admit that he is 'ben gagliardo e dura ha l'ossa' [a brave man and has tough bones] (I iv 54,5). Finally, Spinella da Altamonte, who comes to Paris to participate in the Pentecostal festivities at the beginning of Book I and then fights in the wars between Marsilio and Gradasso and Gradasso and Charlemagne, is a much more sympathetic figure in the *Inamoramento* than he is in the *Trabisonda*, where he encourages four other Saracens to attack Orlando 'a tradimento' when the paladin has let his guard down (*Trabisonda*, X 40-45 [fol. 63ʳ]). Boiardo's Spinella might not be an outstanding knight, but he certainly cannot be called a traitor.

*Saracen converts to Christianity*

Though indebted to the *Spagna ferrarese* and other 'serious' Carolingian texts, Boiardo's portrayal of the Spanish Saracens has a light-hearted touch. It could

---

41    As Montagnani suggests, 'è forse l'episodio della conversione, sua e del padre, a XII 34–36, che condiziona in qualche modo il suo destino nell'*Inamoramento*' [it is perhaps the episode of his and his father's conversion at XII 34–36 [*Spagna ferrarese*], which in some way determines his fate in the *Inamoramento*], convincing Boiardo to transform him from a fighter into a lover (Montagnani, 'Introduzione', *Spagna ferrarese*, p. 22).

perhaps be argued that some of them (e.g. Marsilio and Balugante) are slightly more humane than they are in the preceding tradition. That said, as we have seen, Marsilio and most of his vassals are certainly not demonized in the chivalric texts Boiardo draws on. Apart from Sobrino, who will be discussed together with other characters from the *Aspramonte* in the following chapters, the remaining borrowed Saracens are in fact Saracen converts to Christianity. Ogieri il Danese and Dudone are among the most prominent of Charlemagne's barons. It is to them that we must now turn our attention.

Boiardo alludes to Ogieri's Saracen roots twice: in Book I, we learn that he has a Saracen cousin, 'il forte Uldano [...] | che fu signor galiardo e ben cortese' [the strong Uldano [...] | who was a brave and chivalrous lord] (*Inam.*, I x 30,6–7); in Book II, Sobrino tells Agramante that he saw Ogieri many years ago: 'conosco Gano e conosco il Danese, | che fo pagan, e par proprio un gigante' [I know Gano, and I know the Danese, | who was once a Saracen, and he looks like a giant] (*Inam.*, II i 51,1–2). The story of his conversion to Christianity is narrated in the *Reali di Francia*: the son of the 'valentissimo signore, chiamato il re Gualfedriano' [the most valiant lord who was called King Gualfedriano] (*Reali di Francia*, VI xxxiv), Uggieri accompanies his father to Saragossa to avenge Bramante who was killed by Galafro's servant Mainetto (Charlemagne); 'invaghito de' belli costumi di Mainetto' [charmed by Mainetto's beautiful manners], Uggieri 'tanto innamorò della sua onestà, ch'egli si puose in cuore d'essere sempre di sua compagnia' [fell in love with his uprightness so deeply that he made up his mind never to part from him] (ibid.), a resolution to which he adheres. Having fought with Mainetto, the old king Gualfedriano returns home, while his son stays and embraces the Christian faith, becoming Charlemagne's best friend.[42]

Uggieri (Ugieri, Ogieri) is represented as a valorous knight in a variety of Italian chivalric texts, including the *Spagna* and the *Aspramonte*. He is greatly respected by his Christian peers, yet one is left with the impression that he is haunted by the ghost of his Saracen past, for he seems to feel a constant urge to prove his loyalty to Charlemagne and the sincerity of his religious belief. Thus, in the *Aspramonte*

---

42    Charles Stanley Ross translates Ogieri's surname as Dane, and this translation is accepted by Jo Ann Cavallo. Indeed, in the French tradition (e.g. *La Chevalerie Ogier de Danemarche*) and in the Franco-Venetian *Entrée d'Espagne* (2375) Ogier is the son of the King of Denmark. However, for Boiardo and his first readers Danese is not Danish. As Andrea da Barberino explains, his surname was acquired in the following way: 'venne nella corte di Carlo una lettera mandata d'Africa a Uggieri, la quale molto lo biasimava perché egli s'era battezzato; e in certa parte diceva: "O Uggieri, tu se' 'danés de l'alma" (cioè tu se' dannato dell'anima). Per queste parole Uggieri se ne rideva, e mostrava la lettera a Carlo e a' baroni [...] quando il papa battezzò Uggieri, egli volle essere chiamato Uggieri Danese' [a letter from Africa to Uggieri was brought to Charlemagne's court, which reproached him bitterly because he had received baptism; and in one part it said: 'O Uggieri, you are *danés de l'alma*' (that is you have damned your soul). Uggieri laughed at these words, and showed the letter to Charlemagne and his barons [...] when the Pope baptized Uggieri he wanted to be called Uggieri Danese] (*Reali di Francia*, VI xlix). On the character's Danish and Saracen origins see Pio Rajna, 'Uggeri il Danese nella letteratura romanzesca degl'italiani', *Romania*, 2 (1873), 153–69 (pp. 155–56). For an overview of the main chivalric texts that develop Ogieri's story, see, apart from Rajna's article, Leslie Zarker Morgan, '"Qe sor les autres è de gran valor": Ogier le Danois in the Italian Tradition', *Cahiers de recherches médiévales et humanistes*, 24 (2012), 423–36.

(both Andrea da Barberino's and the fifteenth-century version) it is he who is most outraged by the arrogant speech of Agolante's ambassador Balante: he would have killed Balante, had Namo, a Christian baron, not prevented him from doing so. Later, Uggieri kills Balante's son Gorante (Gurante): in Andrea da Barberino's *Aspramonte* this happens during a battle and Namo has to intervene to save Balante's life, as Uggieri turns a deaf ear to the Saracen's plea to spare him in exchange for his conversion; in the fifteenth-century *Aspramonte in rima* he kills Gurante after the boy has converted to Christianity, which prompts Balante to abandon Charlemagne.

Uggieri's intolerance towards Saracens shows that conversion can lead to so radical a break with one's past that a feeling of compassion for one's former brothers in faith becomes synonymous with betrayal. Those who were born Christians can allow themselves the luxury of being patient and kind-hearted with Saracens; by contrast, a convert often perceives the religious Other as a threat to his newly acquired identity, and as a consequence his reaction is more extreme. In the *Inamoramento de Orlando* Ogieri's religious zeal manifests itself on a number of occasions. For example, he attempts to stir up hatred between the Christian hosts and their Saracen guests during the Pentecostal joust in Paris. He unhorses a couple of Saracen knights, but when a Christian knight wants to pit his strength against him:

> 'Deh, non faciamo la guerra tra noi,'
> diceva Ogieri 'o popul batizato!
> Che io vedo caleffarci a' Saracini,
> perché faciamo l'un l'altro tapini!'.

> ['Hey, let's not fight among ourselves,
> we who are baptized', Ogieri said.
> 'I see the pagans mocking us
> for giving one another trouble!']
> (*Inam.*, I ii 47,5–8)

Yet Boiardo's Ogieri does not commit any reprehensible or morally ambiguous actions. In fact, he commands our respect as he is a formidable knight, one who lives up to his reputation — earned in texts such as Andrea da Barberino's *Reali* — as a 'brave and worthy combatant'.[43] Grievously wounded, he springs from his bed and thrusts himself at the enemies as soon as he learns that Charlemagne has been taken prisoner and no one is left to defend Paris: 'Giamai non fu un Baron tanto valente!' [No baron ever was so valiant!] (I vii 35,6). Likewise, he is the last and most heroic defender of Paris in Book III:

> Tra' Christïani sol Danese Ugiero
> fiè gran prodeze, la persona degna,
> ché di quel stormo periglioso e fiero
> riportò salva la real insegna.

> [Only the worthy Ugiero Danese

43    Zarker Morgan, '"Qe sor les autres è de gran valor"', p. 432.

> among the Christians did great deeds,
> for through that dangerous, fierce storm,
> he kept the royal standard safe.]
> (*Inam.*, III iv 47,1–4)

Orlando's and Ranaldo's feats of prowess in Agramante's war pale in comparison to Ogieri's heroism. For all his valour, in the previous tradition Ogieri is but one of Charlemagne's many paladins, and although he has his moments in the spotlight, he cannot compete with the French emperor's nephew or the son of Amone.[44] However, in Book III of the *Inamoramento de Orlando*, Ogieri can be said almost to outshine the two famous cousins, both of whom, as will be shown in the next chapter, lose part of their charisma. His unflinching courage is juxtaposed with the tearfulness of his old friend Charlemagne who, instead of encouraging his troops to continue fighting, sinks into despair, making one think of Marsilio's similar behaviour in dangerous situations ('A sassi mossa avrìa compassïone | vegendol lachrimar sì rottamente' [The very stones would have been moved | to pity, witnessing his tears] (*Inam.*, III iv 34,3–4)). Nor is this the first time Ogieri shows exceptional courage in the face of extreme adversity: in the *Ugieri il Danese* (first printed in 1480, but composed around the middle of the fifteenth century) he saves Charlemagne and all his barons when they are defeated by Bravieri, a devil in human flesh.[45]

As far as Ogieri's son Dudone is concerned, Boiardo's early readers would have probably known that he was the fruit of Ogieri's love affair with a giantess. In the *Dodonello di Mombello* Ogieri spends a night with a giantess, and in the *Castello di Teris* she conceives a son, Dodone, who is raised in the Saracen faith but later meets his father and converts to Christianity.[46] The Saracen youth — assures us the author of the *Castello* — 'portava una maza nervata con piastre d'acciaro [...] non fu mai meglio fatto giogamte, dalla natura umana e pieno d'ongni cortesia e gientileza e beleza' [carried a knotty club with steel plates [...] the world had never seen a more handsome giant, of a humane disposition and endowed with courtesy, nobility and beauty].[47] Similarly, Boiardo's Dudone:

---

44    As Rajna points out, even in the *Ugieri il Danese* 'il Danese non ha per nulla una parte più cospicua che Orlando, Rinaldo, od Ulivieri' [Danese does not have a more prominent role than Orlando, Rinaldo or Ulivieri] (Rajna, 'Uggeri il Danese nella letteratura romanzesca degl'italiani', p. 154).

45    The story runs as follows: Charlemagne imprisons Ugieri because he has tried to kill Charlemagne's son Carlotto who had killed his son. Many years after, the Saracens declare war on France. When all the Christian knights have been defeated by Bravieri (who overpowers his opponents with loud shrieks), Ugieri is released from prison and kills the infernal Saracen by plugging his and his horse's ears, as the fairy of Verona advises him to do (*Ugieri il Danese*, IV-IX). This episode resembles that of Astolfo's duel with Gradasso in canto vii of Book I of the *Inamoramento de Orlando*: like Ugieri, Astolfo is thrown into prison by Charlemagne and released when the emperor and his barons have been defeated; if Ugieri is helped by a fairy, Astolfo uses a magic lance to win the duel with Gradasso.

46    Marco Villoresi, 'Supplemento d'indagine su Dodone e altre notizie sui figli di Uggieri il Danese', in his *La fabbrica dei cavalieri: Cantari, poemi, romanzi in prosa fra Medioevo e Rinascimento* (Rome: Salerno Editrice, 2005), pp. 75–100.

47    Cited in ibid., p. 87.

> [...] quasi era gigante di statura,
> dextro e ligiero, a maraviglia forte,
> e con sua maza noderosa e dura
> a molti Saracin dete la morte;
> ma poi di tal bontà si dava il vanto
> ch'era apelato in sopranome il Santo.
>
> [He was of overwhelming size,
> agile, quick, of surpassing strength,
> and with his hard knotty club
> he had slain many Saracens;
> his integrity was praised so much,
> his nickname was 'the Saint'.]
>
> (*Inam.*, II x 13,3–8)

Like his father, Dudone is a superb warrior and a devoted vassal to the French emperor. He is one of the few Christian knights who venture into *Paganìa* and participate in adventures that resemble those of Arthurian romances (even if he does so only because Charlemagne orders him 'ch'el trovi Orlando e 'l Sir de Montealbano' [to find Orlando and the lord of Montealbano] (*Inam.*, II vii 35,8)). Less conspicuous than Astolfo or Oliviero, he nevertheless makes an important contribution to Christian chivalry in the *Inamoramento de Orlando*.

For Boiardo's early readers Ogieri and Dudone had a double identity: on the one hand, they consider themselves Christians; on the other hand, they have Saracen blood in their veins and they grew up into exceptional knights in *Paganìa*, among Saracens. Having converted to Christianity and entered Charlemagne's service, they have enriched the Christian world by injecting into it their valour and energy. Their stories are not unique: in fact, some of Boiardo's Christian characters — characters who figure prominently in Italian chivalric literature — spent their formative years in *Paganìa*. Thus, Rinaldo's cousin Malagise, a Christian sorcerer who tries to outsmart Angelica at the beginning of Book I, learnt the art of magic from his adoptive mother, the Saracen Queen of Belfiore. In the *Cantari di Rinaldo* she finds him in a forest, where he and his brother Viviano (a relatively minor character in Boiardo's poem) are left when their parents are attacked by King Avilante.[48] The queen raises the newborn baby as her own and maintains an excellent relationship with him even after his conversion to Christianity.[49] Viviano too is brought up by a Saracen: he is adopted by King Avilante himself, but their relationship sours after Viviano's discovery of his true identity and subsequent conversion. Moreover, Grifone, as we learn in canto XXVII of the *Ugieri il Danese*, was abducted from his Christian mother by a gyps and grew up in Marsilio's Spain.[50]

---

48  The events recounted in the *Cantari di Rinaldo* chronologically precede those narrated in the *Inamoramento de Orlando*. This does not prevent Boiardo from 'resuscitating' Viviano, even though he had already died in the *Cantari di Rinaldo*. See Franceschetti, *L''Orlando Innamorato' e le sue componenti tematiche e strutturali*, p. 230, and Michael Sherberg, 'Matteo Maria Boiardo and the *Cantari di Rinaldo*', p. 180.

49  See, for example, the episode in which the Queen of Belfiore blesses Malagigi in the name of Trivigante, and Malagigi calls her his mother, knowing full well that she is not his biological mother (*Cantari di Rinaldo*, VI 30–32).

50  For a discussion of Boiardo's references to the story of Aquilante and Grifone, see Anna

In the *Inamoramento de Orlando* Griphone, together with his brother Aquilante, takes part in various romance adventures, including the frustrating fight with Orrilo and his monstrous crocodile in canto iii of Book III. Boiardo does not mention the years he spent in Saracen Spain. Nor does he allude to Malagise's and Viviano's links to the Saracen world. And yet the poems that narrate the events of their childhood and adolescence are part of the literary background of Boiardo's poem. It could be that Malagigi's warm relationship with the Queen of Belfiore influenced Boiardo's treatment of Rugiero's story: like Malagigi, Rugiero is raised by a Saracen magician, Atalante; he too is adored by his adoptive father who decides to follow him to France.[51] Regardless of whether the *Cantari di Rinaldo* was one of Boiardo's sources for the portrayal of Rugiero, the story of Malagigi's youth shows that characters who convert to Christianity do not always completely renounce their past identity in the name of the new Christian faith, as Ogieri il Danese — a bitter enemy of the Saracens religion after his conversion — attempts to do.[52]

Boiardo's poem establishes an intertextual dialogue with a multitude of other chivalric texts, which adds depth and richness to its portrayal of Saracens. His early readers drew on their familiarity with the chivalric tradition to discern and appreciate his allusions to his characters' previous incarnations. They could make connections with other stories even without any prompting on the part of the author. So far, I have focused on how Boiardo's representation of Saracens or 'hybrid' characters with a Saracen past is mostly in line with their representations in previous Italian chivalric literature. In this respect, the world depicted in the *Inamoramento de Orlando* was a familiar one. And yet Boiardo holds quite a few surprises up his sleeve, as we are about to find out in the next chapter.

51   Strozzi mentions the Saracen magician Atlas in Book VI of his *Borsias*, but Book VI may have been written after the publication of the first two books of the *Inamoramento de Orlando*. On Strozzi and Boiardo, see Walter Ludwig, 'Analyse und Kommentar', in *Die Borsias des Tito Strozzi. Ein lateinisches Epos der Renaissance*, erstmals herausgegeben, eingeleitet und kommentiert von Walther Ludwig (München: Fink, 1977), pp. 225-394 (pp. 316–28), and Tissoni Benvenuti, 'Rugiero o la fabbrica dell'*Inamoramento*', pp. 77-81.
52   Malagigi does use his magic to fight Saracens in a number of fifteenth-century chivalric texts, but, unlike Danese, he is not driven by religious zeal.

# CHAPTER 3

❖

# Saracen Chivalry in the
# *Inamoramento de Orlando*

The world of late fourteenth- and fifteenth-century Italian Carolingian literature is one in which Christians and Saracens frequently fight each other. And yet, as we saw in the previous chapter, Saracens are not invariably cast in the role of villains, not even Marsilio and his Spanish barons who, in the *Spagna*, are responsible for Orlando's death. Boiardo's portrayal of the Saracens he inherited from earlier chivalric texts is largely consistent with how they are represented in his chivalric sources, even if at times he plays with his readers' expectations by presenting a well-known character in a somewhat surprising light (for instance, when he mentions Feraguto's strong dislike of bathing!). However, the debt that Boiardo owes to the Italian Carolingian tradition is not limited to borrowed characters and names. He also appropriates themes, situations and stock characters, and in doing so, he often gives them a different meaning, subverting traditional stereotypes. For example, while the figure of the enamoured male Saracen can be found in a variety of fifteenth-century chivalric texts, Boiardo's numerous love-struck Saracen kings and knights are portrayed much more positively than most of their counterparts in earlier and contemporaneous chivalric works.

Building upon Chapter II, the present one continues the discussion of chivalric intertextuality in the *Inamoramento de Orlando*, unravelling the literary memories that are contained within its characters. Its main aim is to assess the extent to which Boiardo's depiction of Saracens is innovative. It shows how Boiardo plays upon his audience's familiarity with the chivalric genre to delight and surprise as he introduces new Saracen characters — such as Agricane, Sacripante or Angelica — that both follow and challenge pre-existing models. It examines how Boiardo engages with the *Aspramonte* as he introduces Rugiero and his African relatives, grafting the dynastic theme onto the fabric of his poem. This chapter consists of two parts. Analysing the representations of some of the most memorable Saracen protagonists of the *Inamoramento de Orlando* (characters that drive its plot forward and that would later reappear in the *Furioso*), the first part looks at how their actions and attitudes contribute to the chivalric ideology that emerges from Boiardo's 'bela historia' [beautiful story]. The second part considers the portrayals of African Saracens in Boiardo and in the *Aspramonte*, his main chivalric source for Book II, by focusing in particular on the connection between the Saracen world and antiquity through the legendary figure of Alexander the Great and its implication for the dynastic dimension of Books II and III.

## Saracens and their 'romance' values

In her monograph on the relation between Old French epic poetry and the romance genre, Sarah Kay points out that in the *chansons de geste* that are contemporary with the birth of romance Saracens 'possess a culture which is more distinctly "courtly" than that of the embattled Franks, sternly settled in their fiefs and dedicated to a life of more or less unrelieved military hardship.'[1] Saracens have sumptuous palaces, gorgeous gardens, and refined and beautiful women. Their somewhat effeminate, exotic world resembles that of Arthurian romances, which had an undeniable fascination for the authors of these later *chansons de geste*. Kay argues that the Saracens' 'availability for conversion marks the possibility of romance values being assimilated to the Frankish world, just as the desirability — and desire — of the Saracen princesses allows for the peaceful appropriation of those values'.[2]

As we saw in the previous two chapters, Franco-Venetian and Italian chivalric texts too feature opulent Saracen palaces and seductive Saracen princesses. Like the second wave of the *chansons de geste*, Carolingian poems and prose romances produced in late medieval Italy absorbed elements from the romance tradition, and it is in their representations of Saracens that the influence of the romance genre is most visible. In many of Boiardo's chivalric sources Charlemagne's knights are drawn to the 'courtly' world of their Saracen neighbours: they have affairs with Saracen damsels, whom they sometimes marry, and they befriend chivalrous young Saracens, who often choose to convert to Christianity. Nevertheless, in the majority of these chivalric narratives Christian chivalry is portrayed as unquestionably superior to Saracen chivalry. In some of the texts that Boiardo must have had on his desk (e.g. the *Spagna* or the *Aspramonte*) the Christians' military prowess is much more impressive that the Saracens' 'courtly' culture, while 'romance' episodes involving Saracen women (who prefer Christian warriors to their countrymen) are relatively brief — if captivating — digressions. Other texts (such as the *Altobello*, which Boiardo almost certainly was familiar with) devote more space to 'romance' episodes and the theme of love, but the 'courtly' values practised by Saracens are viewed with a mixture of admiration, distrust, and contempt. What makes Boiardo's portrayal of *Paganìa* particularly interesting is not so much the fact it is more of a 'romance' space than Charlemagne's Europe, but rather that the Saracens' chivalric ideals shape the chivalric ideology that lies at the heart of the poem.

### Love

The very title of the *Inamoramento de Orlando* reveals that love is one of its main themes. Love, as Franceschetti states, 'costituisce il grande centro ideale intorno a cui si muovono, in linea di massima, i personaggi e le vicende dell'*Innamorato*' [is the

---

1    Sarah Kay, *The Chansons de Geste in the Age of Romance: Political Fictions* (Oxford: Clarendon, 1995), p. 180.
2    Ibid.

big ideal centre around which the characters and events of the *Innamorato* generally revolve].[3] Boiardo — the author of a nominally Carolingian poem — proclaims the superiority of Arthurian chivalry over Carolingian chivalry in one of his most famous authorial digressions:

Fo glorïosa Bertagna la grande
una stagion, per l'arme e per l'amore
(onde ancor hoggi il nome suo si spande
sì ch'al re Artuse fa portar honore),
quando e bon cavalieri a quele bande
mostrarno in più batalie il suo valore,
andando con lor dame in aventura
et hor sua fama al nostro tempo dura.

Re Carlo in Franza poi tienne gran corte,
ma a quela prima non fo somiliante,
ben che assai fosse ancor robusto e forte
et avesse Renaldo e 'l sir d'Anglante:
perché tiéne ad Amor chiuse le porte
e sol se dete ale bataglie sante,
non fo di quel valor o quela estima
qual fo quel'altra ch'io contava in prima.

Però ch'Amor è quel che dà la gloria
e che fa l'homo degno et honorato [...]

[There was a time Great Britain was
illustrious in arms and love
(for which reason her name is celebrated still,
bringing great honour to King Arthur),
when the good knights in those lands
displayed their worth in many battles
and sought adventure with their ladies;
and her fame has lasted to our day.

Later, King Charles held court in France;
his court was no equivalent,
though it was sturdy and strong,
and had Renaldo and the lord of Anglante [i.e. Orlando].
Because it closed its gates to love
and only followed holy battles,
it could not boast the worth, the fame
the former showed, the first I named.

3    Franceschetti, *L''Orlando Innamorato' e le sue componenti tematiche e strutturali*, p. 55. Not all Boiardo scholars agree with Franceschetti. While Domenico de Robertis, Rajna, Emilio Bigi, Franceschetti, Alexandre-Gras, Donnarumma and Riccardo Bruscagli maintain that the cornerstone of Boiardo's poem is a cult of love in its different manifestations, others claim that love is described superficially (Liborio Azzolina, Angelandrea Zottoli), that there is strong didactic message behind many of the love stories (Cavallo: see especially her *Boiardo's Orlando Innamorato: an Ethics of Desire* (Rutherford: Fairleigh Dickinson University Press, 1993)), or that Boiardo's portrayal of love is often ambivalent (Galbiati). Most scholars agree that Boiardo devotes more space to the theme of love in Book I than in Books II and III.

For love is the source of glory
and what brings worth and honour to a man [...]]
(*Inam.*, II xviii 1–3,1–2)

Several cantos later we learn that Saracens, too, just like the Arthurian knights of old who used to take their 'dame in aventura', prefer to travel with their ladies:

Avean usanza tuti i Re pagani,
la qual in questo tempo anco è rimasa,
che campegiando o vicini o lontani
ma' le lor dame lasciavano a casa:
né sciò se lor pensier sian fermi o vani,
ché pur sta mal la paglia con la brasa;
ma d'altra parte anchor per Amore
l'animo crescie e più se fa di core.

[The custom of the pagan kings –
and it remains to this day –
was never to leave their ladies at home
whether camp was near or far:
I don't know what their thinking is,
since embers don't mix well with straw,
but on the other hand, love makes
courage increase and hearts grow great.]
(*Inam.*, II xxiii 11)

Boiardo draws a parallel, albeit an implicit one, between Arthurian knights and Saracen kings. Marsilio's camp is graced by the presence of 'le Regine | quasi di tuta Spagna, e pur le bele' [the Queens | of all Spain, and fair ones] (*Inam.*, II xxiii 12,1–2), among whom Fiordespina, Marsilio's daughter, and Doralice, the daughter of King Stordilano and Rodamonte's sweetheart. Rodamonte carries her portrait embroidered on his banner and performs 'ogni giorno per lei [...] gran prove' [great deeds for her each day] (13,2).

This Saracen custom is not Boiardo's invention: when Agolante sails to Calabria he brings with him 'la reina con ventidue reine incoronate e più di mille donne' [the queen with twenty-two crowned queens and more than a thousand ladies] (*Aspramonte A*, I xiv 16–17). The banners of Ulieno di Sarza, the father of Boiardo's Rodamonte and one of Agolante's best knights in the *Aspramonte*, 'avevano il campo bianco e uno drago nero, e una pulzella che lo teneva a mano con una catena vermiglia, la quale fu figliuola di Lanfras, ed era Ulieno innamorato di lei [...]. Quello amore tolse a molti Cristiani la vita' [featured, on a white background, a black dragon and a damsel who held it on a scarlet chain, and she was Lanfras's daughter and Ulieno was in love with her [...]. Many Christians were killed in the name of that love] (ibid., III lxxvi 5–8).[4] However, whereas in Andrea da Barberino's *Aspramonte* (as well as in its other versions) love is a rather marginal theme and the inspiring presence of beautiful damsels does not save the Saracens from a crushing defeat, in the *Inamoramento de Orlando* love assumes an unprecedented centrality,

---

4    Franceschetti is the first to note the similarity between Ulieno's banner and Rodamonte's (see his *L''Orlando Innamorato' e le sue componenti tematiche e strutturali*, p. 237).

becoming a vital part of the personal chivalric code of most of the main protagonists and less prominent characters. The ideology of 'bataglie sante' [holy battles] is not completely banished from the universe of Boiardo's poem: in Chapter II we saw that Ogieri il Danese, for one, believes that his mission is to defend Christendom from Saracens. Boiardo treats Danese with sympathy, but it is clear that his heart is with the knights and damsels who profess more Arthurian values. These characters are for the most part Saracens.

Most of the characters who figure in the love episodes of the *Inamoramento de Orlando* are Saracens.[5] Apart from Bradamante, who makes her first appearance in Book II and who, as was suggested in the previous chapter, might be a converted Saracen, Boiardo does not introduce any prominent Christian female characters. Galerana, Orlando's wife Alda, Ranaldo's Clarice, and Ogieri's Hermelina are briefly alluded to in the opening canto of Book I and then forgotten both by the narrator and by their husbands. In this respect the *Inamoramento de Orlando* is similar to the *Spagna*, in which Christian women stay at home while their husbands are fighting Saracens in *Paganìa*.[6] Angelica's arrival in Paris in the opening canto does transform Charlemagne's court into an 'Arthurian' space, but only temporarily. All the men present at the banquet — regardless of their age or religion — fall in love with her. However, as far as Charlemagne and his barons are concerned, this *coup de foudre* has a long-lasting effect only on Orlando. Having drunk from the magic fountain of disdain, Ranaldo is immune to love from I iii to II xv and, after regaining his interest in women in general and in Angelica in particular, has little opportunity to prove himself as a lover, since at that point Boiardo gives most of his attention to Agramante's French campaign. The reawakened desire for the Saracen princess makes him fight better, but this is not enough to make up for his past coldness. Charlemagne, Namo and the remaining Christian paladins, including Astolfo who soon forgets Angelica, return to their senses very quickly.

But what about the Saracens? Of the Spanish Saracens who take part in the Pentecostal feast, only Feraguto is deeply smitten by Angelica. Even so, the poet makes it clear that he stands no chance of winning her heart: although he is a valiant knight, he takes no care of his appearance, and so he cannot compete with the elegant

---

5    The Saracens who contribute to the theme of love are: Agricane, Albarosa, Angelica, Ariante, Brandimarte, Calidora, Doralice, Doristela, Feraguto, Fiordelisa, Fiordespina, Folderico, Hosbergo, Iroldo, Isolieri, Larbino, Leodilla, Locrino, Lucina, Mandricardo (who enjoys the physical aspect of love), Marchino, Menadarbo, Noradino, Ordauro, Origille, Polindo, Prasildo, Rodamonte, Rugiero, Sacripante, Stella, Tisbina and Uldarno. By contrast, enamoured Christians are rather few: Astolfo, Bradamante, Griphone, Orlando, Ranaldo, and the Armenian Theodoro, who, in fact, is much closer to Saracens than to Christians.

6    In the *Spagna ferrarese* Charlemagne not only leaves Galerana in Paris when he leads his army into Spain, but he does not have any contact with her for many years. Thanks to the magic book given to Orlando by the Soldano [Sultan] he learns that Machario di Maganza is about to marry the Empress. To save his honour and his empire, Charlemagne makes a Ulysses-like homecoming, transported to Paris by a devil (see *Spagna ferrarese*, XIX-XX). However, Christian women constitute a more active presence in some Carolingian texts, such as the *Reali di Francia* and the *Altobello*, where Orlando's wife Alda is a rather prominent character, or the *Vendetta di Falconetto*, where the Christian damsel Fiore de Lisa steals the hearts of the Christian knight Tiborgo and the Saracen knight Alchero.

Astolfo, a well-groomed English gentleman whose fresh beauty, for a moment, tempts the damsel. Later, we learn that other powerful Saracens are besotted with the princess from Cathay: Sacripante, King of Circassia, and Agricane, Emperor of Tartary. The former is portrayed as a selfless lover: he is ready to do anything for his beloved, without getting much in return. The latter at first comes across as a typical enamoured Saracen: he 'al tuto è destinato | Angelica per moglie ottenire. | Essa ha proposto più presto morire' [is determined | to make Angelica his wife. | She has decided she'd sooner die] (*Inam.*, I ix 39,6–8). Fifteenth-century chivalric literature abounds in Saracen kings who want to marry Saracen or Christian ladies who hate them. Blinded by their amorous desire, they declare war on the fathers or other relatives of their reluctant brides. In the *Dama Rovenza*, for example, Grapas fights with Rinaldo, whom he believes to be Ternau, the father of a Saracen damsel he intends to marry against her will. Rinaldo kills him, saving the damsel from a forced marriage (*Dama Rovenza*, II-IV [fols a4$^v$-b4$^r$]). In the *Altobello* we have two such luckless Saracen lovers. Pironello, the monstrous King of Turkey, falls in love with Orlando's wife Alda and besieges Brava to force her to abandon Orlando and marry him. Predictably, this infatuation costs him his life. Later, Durastante, a valorous yet ugly Indian king, loses his heart to Anzilela, the daughter of the Saracen King Anzelieri. Anzilela, however, prefers the Christian convert Altobello, for he is both stronger and more handsome than Durastante. Durastante's total devotion to his lady inspires respect (he loves her even after she has abandoned him: 'Se con mego Anzilela avesse | de perdanza non cureria un botone' [if only I had Anzilela with me | I would not care at all about losing the battle] (*Altobello*, XXXV 57,1–2 [fol. s vii$^r$]), but he is represented as inferior not only to Altobello but also to the chaste Orlando who eventually kills him. Before dying, Durastante curses love: ' "o falso amore, [...] | tu me tirasti dela dreta via | quando tu me mostrasti Anzilela" ' ['o false love, [...], | you led me astray | when you showed Anzilela to me'] (*Altobello*, XXXV, 160,5–7 [fol. t iiii$^r$]).[7]

Boiardo's Agricane may at first appear to be modelled after Pironello or Durastante. However, this first impression is soon dispelled. Unlike these two Saracens, he is neither black nor ugly. His nobility shines through in his short yet brilliant military career. He earns the reader's respect with his honourable conduct in the Albracà war: when Trufaldino offers to deliver the fortress into his hands, he not only indignantly rejects this infamous proposal (' "Vincer voglio per forza e per ardire, | et a fronte scoperta farmi honore" ' ['I want to win by force and courage, | to gather glory openly'] (*Inam.*, I xiv 53,4–5)), but also promises to hang the traitor and his collaborators.[8] The object of his love might not want to marry him, but his passion for Angelica increases his strength and ennobles him as a person, his story confirming what Boiardo says in the above-cited proem on Arthurian chivalry,

---

7   Sometimes the damsel is capable of defending herself: in the *Bradiamonte sorella di Rinaldo* (first printed in 1498, but probably composed earlier), a monstrous dark-skinned Saracen falls in love with the titular heroine, who agrees to marry him if he overpowers her in a duel. Bradiamonte kills her Saracen suitor (*Bradiamonte*, 6–93 [fols ai$^v$-bvi$^r$]).

8   Initially Durastante, too, wants to win Anzilela by defeating his rival in a joust, but when he loses, he steals Anzilela and then offers money to his rival and effectively buys her (*Altobello*, XXXI [fol. m iiii$^r$]).

namely that 'Amor è quel che dà la gloria | e che fa l'homo degno et honorato' [love is the source of glory | and what brings worth and honour to a man] (II xviii 3,1–2). And Agricane himself is fully aware of the transforming power of love. In fact, he gives the most eloquent formulation of the 'Arthurian' cult of love that is at the core of Boiardo's conception of chivalry: '"ogni cavalier ch'è sanza amore | se in vista è vivo, vivo è sanza core"' ['any knight who despises love | lives heartless — he just looks alive'] (*Inam.*, I xviii 46,7–8). These lines, as has long been pointed out, mirror the last tercet of the opening sonnet of the *Amorum libri tres*, Boiardo's collection of lyric poetry: '[...] chi nel fior de' soi anni | sanza caldo de amore il tempo passa, | se in vista è vivo, vivo è sanza core' [who in the flower of one's youth | spends time without the warmth of love, | leaves heartless — he just looks alive]. Agricane, one could say, becomes the poet's mouthpiece in this episode.

According to Dorigatti, 'È quantomai significativo, oltre che suggestivo, che sia Agricane e non Orlando a pronunciare questa sentenza programmatica [...] perché il saracino evidenzia proprio l'ideale che Orlando non saprà mai realizzare compiutamente ma rappresenta l'essenza più profonda dell'opera boiardesca' [It is both highly significant and suggestive that Agricane and not Orlando makes this proclamation [...] because the Saracen draws attention to the ideal that Orlando will never be able to fully realize but which represents the true essence of Boiardo's work].[9] Indeed, even though during his nocturnal conversation with Agricane Orlando confesses that for the first time in his life he is fighting 'per amore' [for love] (*Inam.*, II xviii 48,3) and not for his religion or honour, he stops short of saying that chivalry is impossible — or incomplete — without love.[10] And he only mentions his feelings for Angelica when the Saracen asks him if he has ever been in love. It is not Orlando but Agricane who brings up the topic of love: the Christian paladin wanted to talk about God's presence in the universe, a topic Agricane refused to discuss, as religion divides the two knights, while love unites them.[11]

Agricane's story ends with his deathbed conversion to Christianity, which recalls Feraù's conversion in the *Spagna ferrarese* and other voluntary deathbed conversions in Carolingian literature, including Troiano's in the *Altobello*.[12] His peaceful death

9    Marco Dorigatti, '"Di novo se comencia la tentione": il duello nell'universo cavalleresco del Boiardo', *Esperienze letterarie*, 40 (2015), 71–93 (pp. 88–89).

10   Riccardo Bruscagli offers a different analysis of the episode. He overlooks Agricane's eloquent defence of love, claiming that it is Orlando who articulates the new 'romance' ideology. See Riccardo Bruscagli, 'Incontrare il nemico: La "gran bontà" degli antichi cavalieri', in his *Studi cavallereschi* (Florence: Società Editrice Fiorentina, 2003), pp. 209–13.

11   According to Franceschetti, 'Boiardo, cavaliere del Rinascimento Ferrarese, non può non condividere gli ideali di cultura di Orlando, la sua più compiuta perfezione' [Boiardo, a knight of the Ferrarese Renaissance, certainly shares Orlando's cultural ideals, his more complete perfection] (*L''Orlando Innamorato' e le sue componenti tematiche e strutturali*, p. 108). Boiardo, of course, values education, but in this particular episode he gently pokes fun at Orlando, who feels most comfortable in his 'conventional' role of a preacher. Orlando surpasses Agricane in erudition, but Agricane surpasses him in his adherence to 'Arthurian' chivalry.

12   It is tempting to agree with Alexandre-Gras who notes that Agricane converts 'più per stima verso Orlando [...] che per vera fede religiosa' [more out of respect for Orlando [...] than because of genuine religious belief] (Alexandre Gras, 'Tre figure boiardesche di eroe saraceno: Ferraguto, Agricane, Rodamonte', p. 134). Cavallo claims that with Agricane's conversion 'Boiardo has [...]

is very different from Durastante's, who dies unconverted and in a state of extreme emotional distress. In the *Altobello* Orlando is saddened by Durastante's demise and even delivers a kind of panegyric in which he praises his enemy's valour. However, although the Saracen inspires compassion, Durastante's story is a warning against the destructive power of love. Agricane's, by contrast, is a celebration of love.

Is Sacripante a victim of love? On the one hand, as Cavallo points out, he is 'a negligent king'.[13] In Book II he learns that Circassia has been invaded by Mandricardo, but decides not to return home because Angelica is still in mortal danger. But does Boiardo use this character to educate the reader about the dangers of love? Sacripante is upset, yet not devastated by the loss of his kingdom. He is prepared to part not only with his material possessions but also with life for the sake of Angelica, her approving gaze being his only reward. There is something extremely touching about his selfless devotion to her. He is perhaps a madman, a lunatic, but a happy one. Unlike Durastante, he does not really suffer, or rather his suffering is bittersweet.[14] His complete dedication to his beloved is similar to Ogieri il Danese's dedication to Charlemagne and the Christian religion. As we saw in Chapter II, grievously wounded, Ogieri springs from his sickbed and re-enters the battle when he learns that Gradasso is about to win. Similarly, the wounded Sacripante leaves his bed and leads his forces to attack Agricane when he is told that this '"maledetto | [...] la citade pone a gran martire!"' ['cursed one [...] is ravaging the city'] (*Inam.*, I xi 36,2–3).[15] Interestingly, Ogieri does not succeed in infusing new courage into the French soldiers, and, after a heroic attempt to cover the retreat of the French army, is taken prisoner by Gradasso. By contrast, Sacripante's courageous defence of Albracà boosts the morale of his troops who massacre Agricane's men and save the city. One could say that love performs a miracle, proving to be a stronger force than religion.[16]

transformed the Carolingian epic's stock conversion episode from a case of coercive proselytism into an invitation to communicate even with one's enemy in a spirit of openness and respect for his autonomy' (Cavallo, *The World beyond Europe*, p. 61). This is true to an extent, but it must be borne in mind that in many other Carolingian texts defeated Saracens convert of their own free will, without their Christian opponents putting any pressure on them. The episode of Troiano's reconversion to Christianity in the *Altobello* may well be one of Boiardo's sources for Agricane's conversion, considering that this episode comes immediately after that of Durastante's death (Troiano, a Persian prince, befriends the Christians and converts to Christianity at the beginning of the poem; he returns to the Saracen faith when he is told that Rinaldo has treacherously killed Altobello; mortally wounded by Rinaldo, he learns that Rinaldo is innocent and decides to reconvert).

13   Jo Ann Cavallo, *The Romance Epics of Boiardo, Ariosto and Tasso: From Public Duty to Private Pleasure* (Toronto; London: University of Toronto Press, 2004), p. 22.

14   Love does cause real suffering in some of Boiardo's characters, but its negative effects are explored not in the main plot but in the novellas, which the poet seamlessly weaves into the narration. The protagonists of the novellas include the lustful and perverse Marchino, the pragmatic Boccaccian Leodilla, the strong-willed Doristela, and the courteous Iroldo and Prasildo. Their stories show that love can take on different forms, but the 'Arthurian' conception of love prevails in the main story.

15   Alexandre-Gras notes the resemblance between these two episodes (see her *L'héroïsme chevaleresque*, p. 311).

16   Maria Pavlova, 'La concezione di cavalleria nei continuatori del Boiardo: Nicolò degli Agostini, Raffaele Valcieco e Ludovico Ariosto', in *Di donne e cavallier: Intorno al primo 'Furioso'*, ed. by Cristina Zampese (Milan: Ledizioni, 2018), pp. 197–227 (pp. 198–99).

Although Angelica loathes Agricane and is totally indifferent to Sacripante, these two Saracen lovers are certainly portrayed in a much more positive light than Durastante. Besides, Orlando, their Christian rival, cannot boast of awakening passion in her either. Here lies a crucial difference between Boiardo's poem and most of its chivalric sources: in the chivalric tradition Saracen damsels tend to fall in love with Christian knights.

In the *chansons de geste* and their Italian *rifacimenti* [refashionings] Saracen princesses often convert in order to marry their Christian lovers, sometimes cutting all ties with, or even betraying, their Saracen families.[17] For example, in the *Cantari di Fierabraccia e Ulivieri* the Saracen princess Fierapace has to endure the death of her father to be able to marry her Christian sweetheart Guido.[18] In such narratives *innamoramenti* serve two purposes: firstly, they show the superiority of Christian men over Saracen men; and secondly, the acquisition of women of royal blood (whose conversion is always voluntary) legitimizes the acquisition of Saracen territories.[19] Marriage does not always crown interfaith love in fifteenth-century Italian chivalric texts, as they are less concerned with the theme of territorial expansion (and hence less willing to exploit the political potential of the theme of conversion). Yet Charlemagne's paladins rarely miss an opportunity to have an affair with some pretty Saracen princess who sometimes dies of despair when her lover leaves her father's kingdom and sometimes reconciles herself to the separation, telling herself that even one night with such a man was worth her virginity.[20] Rinaldo, Astolfo and Ulivieri have a long history of amorous conquests. In the *Cantari di Rinaldo*, Rinaldo has an affair with Fioretta, the daughter of a sultan, who nine months later gives birth to a son. In the *Regina Ancroia* (a fifteenth-century poem first printed in 1479) and in the *Innamoramento de Guidon Salvaggio* (which recounts the events of the first cantos of the *Ancroia*) this son (Guidone Salvagio) travels to Christian Europe to meet his father.[21] Moreover, in the *Ancroia* Astolfo and Ricardo impregnate two Saracen noblewomen. In the *Sala di Malagigi*, a beautiful Saracen princess wants to give her virginity to Astolfo, but is tricked by the astute Malagigi into having sex

---

17    On the theme of cross-cultural marriage in the *chansons de geste* see Bancourt, *Les musulmans dans les chansons de geste du Cycle du roi*, II, pp. 666–827.

18    In the Old French *Fierabras*, Floripas takes the initiative and begs the Christians to kill her father. See Suzanne Conklin Akbari's discussion of this character in her *Idols in the East*, pp. 173–89.

19    See Kinoshita, *Medieval Boundaries*, pp. 46–73.

20    On the representation of women in fifteenth-century Italian chivalric literature, see Marco Villoresi, 'Le donne e gli amori nel romanzo cavalleresco del Quattrocento', *Filologia e critica*, 23 (1998), 3–43, and Stoppino, *Genealogies of Fiction* (in particular, pp. 33–43 on Galiziella in the *Aspramonte*, and pp. 51–57 on the female characters of the *Inamoramento de Carlo Magno*).

21    The name of the Saracen lady and the circumstances in which the child was conceived are (slightly) different in the *Cantari di Rinaldo* and *Ancroia*. The first extant edition of the *Innamoramento de Guidon Salvaggio* was printed around 1516 in Milan by Giovanni di Castiglione and Niccolò da Gorgonzola, but the poem may have been composed earlier. Some scholars attribute its authorship to Giovan Battista Dragoncino (see, for example, Stoppino, *Genealogies of Fiction*, p. 72), but, as Andrea Canova points out, the first surviving edition is anonymous and Dragoncino's name appears in the 1609 edition printed by the Venetian printers Imberti who must have decided that an anonymous work would sell less well. See Andrea Canova, '*Guidone*', *Achademia Leonardi Vincii*, 8 (1995), 186–87 (p. 186).

with him instead.[22] In the *Morgante* Ulivieri proves to be extremely popular with Saracen ladies, and so does Rinaldo who wins the heart of Marsilio's daughter Lucina. Being a married man, Rinaldo can only offer his Saracen mistresses nights of passionate love-making and his help with re-conquering lost kingdoms; in order to safeguard their honour, he sometimes marries them off to Saracen kings, preferably those who have converted to Christianity and who are happy to take them even if they are no longer virgins. In the *Altobello*, for example, Troiano marries Rinaldo's lady Fior de spina.

In the *Inamoramento de Orlando* Angelica's magic-induced infatuation with Ranaldo is the only story that to some extent follows the traditional pattern. Origille's passion for Griphone could also be considered as a variation on the Christian knight/Saracen damsel theme, but, as was mentioned in Chapter II, Griphone has a strong connection to *Paganìa*, having grown up in Marsilio's Spain as Marsilio's adopted son. There are other cases of Saracen women feeling attracted to Christian men, but they do not amount to much, the attraction being caused by a short-lived rush of lust which is soon overcome and forgotten and does not lead to a carnal — or platonic — union. Thus, at *Inam.*, I i 66–67, Astolfo's beauty moves Angelica to pity and probably inspires unchaste thoughts in her.[23] Twelve cantos later Fiordelisa is erotically attracted to the sleeping Ranaldo yet she remains faithful to her Brandimarte and, except for the narrator (and his audience), no one knows about this moment of temptation. Finally, in canto xxi of Book I, Leodilla cannot hide her frustration when Orlando fails to appreciate her good looks and sleeps soundly while she is tossing and turning, unable to close her eyes because of her unreciprocated desire and anger.

The fact that, in a poem where love is one of the central — if not the central (according to the author's own confession in the proem to the opening canto) — themes, Ranaldo does not have a single affair must have surprised and disappointed Boiardo's early readers.[24] As for Orlando, his failure to notice Leodilla's amorous torment is consistent with his representation in earlier chivalric texts. One could of course say that his indifference to Leodilla is a consequence of his love for

---

22   Malagigi has some success with women in the Italian Carolingian tradition. In the *Trabisonda* we learn that he was married to a sibyl and that they had a son (*Trabisonda*, IX). Like his cousin Rinaldo, he enjoys making love to Saracen ladies, but if Rinaldo uses his natural charm to seduce them, Malagigi frequently resorts to magic and his treatment of women is shocking to our modern sensibility. In the *Antiphor de Barosia*, for example, he casts a spell on the enchantress Angelina that makes her sleep and rapes her while she is unconscious (*Antiphor*, XXXIV). Having humiliated her, he offers to find her a husband, but the sorceress rejects the offer and chooses death. As we said in the previous chapter, it has yet to be established when the *Antiphor* was composed. If Boiardo was familiar with this poem, then it could be that he decided to 'punish' Malagise by making him less skilled a magician than Angelica: in the *Inamoramento de Orlando* it is Angelica who overpowers Malagise.

23   Astolfo also conquers the heart of the fairy Alcina: see *Inam.*, II xiii 59–64.

24   As Cristina Montagnani points out, Ranaldo is indifferent to Angelica 'per effetto di magia, giacché il disamore contrasta sia con l'impianto ideologico del poema, sia con la natura passionale del personaggio' [because of magic, as the state of not being in love is at odds both with the ideological foundation of the poem and with the character's passionate nature] (Cristina Montagnani, 'L'incantesimo del *sequel*: fra Boiardo e Ariosto', in *Boiardo, Ariosto e i libri di battaglia*, pp. 41–56 (p. 43)).

Angelica. However, with Angelica he is a timid and hesitant lover who lets good opportunities slip by: Boiardo leaves the reader wondering whether the Saracen princess might have warmed to him had he been bolder when she was giving him a bath (one of the most erotically charged scenes in the *Inamoramento de Orlando*).[25]

Boiardo's Saracens are both braver and luckier in love than their Christian counterparts. The poem features a plethora of noble Saracen couples: Fiordelisa and Brandimarte; Polindo and Albarosa; Stela and Griphone di Altaripa; Larbino and Calidora; Rodamonte and Doralice; Lucina and Noradino; and the wonderful *menage à trois* between Iroldo, Prasildo and Tisbina. By contrast, interfaith and cross-cultural couples are a relatively rare sight: apart from those Boiardo inherits from the chivalric tradition (i.e. Galerana and Charlemagne), we may mention the perfidious Origille and the gullible Griphone, Dorisetela and Theodoro (who may be a Christian heretic), and the nascent love between Bradamante and Rugiero, which is hinted at in Book III. It would not be an exaggeration to say that Fiordelisa and Brandimarte are the most charismatic lovers of the entire poem. Theirs is probably the most positive example of love in the *Inamoramento de Orlando*, one that truly embodies the spirit of Arthurian chivalry.[26] Their devotion to each other is not without precedent. As a Saracen couple they are somewhat similar to Altobello and Anzilela in the *Altobello* and even more so to Falconetto and Duxelina in the *Falconetto* (printed in 1483 but probably composed much earlier), an anomalous — and very interesting — work in the context of Italian fifteenth-century Carolingian literature.[27] Like Altobello and Anzilela, Fiordelisa and Brandimarte convert to Christianity. However, whereas, for all his physical strength and handsomeness, Altobello is a lesser knight than his Christian friends (he cries more often than other characters; he is so naive that he befriends Gano), Brandimarte, as we shall soon see, paradoxically cuts a more impressive figure than Orlando. In this respect, he resembles Falconetto — a chivalrous young Saracen who is deeply in love with a Saracen princess, whose tender feelings are reciprocated, and who is greatly respected by the Christians. Like Boiardo's Saracen knights, Falconetto finds in his passion for Druxelina inspiration for feats of prowess ('"Non temo niente, | ché uno omo innamorato ne vale più de cento"' ['I fear nothing, | because a man who is in love is worth more than a hundred men'] (*Falconetto*, 868–69)). But Falconetto does

---

25  'Stavasi il Conte quieto e vergognoso, | mentre la dama intorno il manigiava | e ben che fosse di questo gioioso, | crescere in alcun loco non mostrava' [The Count was quiet, modest, while | Angelica massaged him, and | he felt tremendous joy, although | no part of him was seen to grow] (*Inam.*, I xxv 39,1–4).

26  It is worth stressing, however, that their love is not adulterous, which sets them apart from some of the most famous couples in the Arthurian tradition.

27  The *Falconetto* stands out from other Italian Carolingian works of the period both for its form and its content. The original version is written in a kind of rhymed prose with no sense of poetic metre (in 1500 a *rifacimento in ottava rima* was published). It is striking to what extent its portrayal of Saracens is positive. As Andrea Canova remarks, 'chi lo scrisse conservò una certa imparzialità rispetto a cristiani e saraceni; e, anzi, talvolta la sua simpatia sembra andare più verso questi ultimi' [the person who wrote it treated his Christians and Saracens with a degree of impartiality; and, in actual fact, sometimes the author's sympathy goes to the latter] (Andrea Canova, 'Introduzione', *Falconetto (1483)*, pp. 25–65 (p. 50).

not convert and so the 'romance' values he incarnates die with him when, poorly armed, he is slain by the invulnerable Rolando. By contrast, through Brandimarte's and Fiodelisa's voluntary conversions their values are assimilated into the Christian world. In connection with their change of religion we may note a curious fact: Fiordalisa abandons the Saracen faith as early as canto xvii of Book I (encouraged by Ranaldo, Iroldo and Prasildo), while her fiancé only does so in canto xii of Book II (we will look at this episode more in the next section). In the twenty-four cantos that separate their respective conversions, Fiordalisa does not mention her spiritual transformation to Brandimarte, despite the fact that they spend time together and even have sex, with Boiardo treating his audience to a titillating description of their love-making on a flowery meadow (I xix 59–64). This alone is a telling illustration of Boiardo's reluctance to use the theme of conversion to express allegorically the Christian West's desire to dominate the Islamic East. Although Brandimarte's and Fiordalisa's decision to convert attests to the superiority of the Christian religion (with the poet paying lip service to the conventions of the genre), it does not in any way prove the superiority of the Christian chivalric model or the Christian way of life. Although later on Brandimarte's and Fiordalisa's parents and their subjects will also convert to Christianity, these mass conversions do not really have any implied cultural or political significance.

### Glory, 'cortesia', audacity, friendship

While it is Agricane who formulates the doctrine of love that informs the *Inamoramento de Orlando*, Gradasso, King of Sericana, draws attention to another key value in the secular chivalric ideology underpinning Boiardo's poem. In an eloquent speech that echoes Saladino's speech in the *Historia imperiale* (see Chapter I, 'International Chivalry'), Gradasso stresses the importance of glory:

> Et a lui [Charlemagne] disse: 'Savio imperatore,
> ciascun signor gientil e valoroso
> de gloria cerca e pasciesi de honore:
> chi atende a far richeza o aver riposo,
> sancia mostrar in prima il suo valore,
> merta de il regno al tuto esser deposo.
> Io che in Levante mi potea possare,
> sono in Ponente per fama acquistare.'

> [He said to him [Charlemagne], 'Sage emperor,
> all valorous and noble lords
> want glory, and they feed on fame.
> Whoever looks for wealth or ease
> instead of showing valour first
> deserves to be deposed from rule!
> I could have rested in the East –
> I'm in the West to win esteem.']

(*Inam.*, I vii 41)

Like Agricane, the character of Gradasso is partly inspired by earlier chivalric literature, where wars between Christians and Saracens are not always fuelled by religious hatred. Sometimes Saracens attack Christians because they want to avenge a dead relative (e.g. Agolante in the fifteenth-century *Aspramonte*), to marry a Christian damsel (e.g. Pironello in the *Altobello*) or simply for the sake of glory (Agolante and Almonte in Andrea da Barberino's *Aspramonte*). As will be shown in the following section, Andrea da Barberino's glory-seeking Saracen kings are presented in an ambivalent way: on the one hand, thirst for glory is proof of a noble character; on the other hand, Agolante and his children do not live up to the ideals they claim to believe in, and lose everything as a result of their recklessness. Gradasso, too, is described as an irresponsible king in the opening canto of the *Inamoramento de Orlando*, where Boiardo tells us that he is one of those 'gran signori | che pur quel voglion che non pòno avere, | e quanto son difficultà magiori | la disiata cosa ad otenere, | pongono il regno spesso in grandi erori' [great lords | who only want what they can't have, | the greater obstacles there are | to reaching what they want to obtain | the more they jeopardize their realms] (*Inam.*, I i 5,1–5). However, this didactic note is not allowed to dominate his story. As it unfolds, it becomes increasingly clear that Gradasso only lacks a sweetheart to be a perfectly 'Arthurian' knight.[28] He wages a war of aggression against Charlemagne, but he is not a negative example of vanity and foolhardiness. He stuns the Christians with his *cortesia*: having taken captive Charlemagne and his barons, he treats them well and declares that he has no intention to establish a Saracen state in France. When he is eventually defeated by Astolfo (who unhorses him with the help of Argalìa's magic lance), he accepts defeat graciously, which earns him the Christians' — and the reader's — respect. His adherence to the pact concluded with Astolfo (he had sworn to release his Christian prisoners and to return to *Paganìa* if Astolfo proved to be a stronger knight) is all the more commendable considering that earlier the Christians broke their agreement with Marsilio despite there having been no provocation on his part (*Inam.*, I vi 56). Although Gradasso has to retreat to Spain empty-handed, he has not been humiliated. Nor is he humiliated later in the poem. His adventure-filled life casts a positive light on the values that he cherishes and pursues.

The fact that Gradasso, a Saracen, is portrayed as a paragon of *cortesia* is remarkable, not least because in most of Franco-Venetian and fifteenth-century Italian chivalric texts Christians tend to be more accomplished knights than their Saracen counterparts. Figures such as Feragu (Feraù) in the *Entrée d'Espagne* and the *Spagna* and Falconetto — who, like Gradasso, are inspired by the myth of Saladin — are rare. Usually Christian knights are not only physically stronger, but also more chivalrous. In many of Boiardo's (possible) chivalric sources *cortesia* is valued by Christians and Saracens alike, but the former are usually better at practising it. Very often it is Christian knights who teach their Saracen opponents how to be *cortesi*. In the *Aspramonte* narratives, for example, Balante's fiery temper is softened by Namo's civility. In the *Spagna*, Orlando gives Isolieri a lesson in chivalry when he frees him, trusting his word that his father will free Astolfo. Sometimes Saracens are so deeply

---

28  Jo Ann Cavallo and Charles Stanley Ross note that Boiardo's Gradasso recalls Galehaut in the prose version of *Lancelot*: 'Introduction' to *Fortune and Romance: Boiardo in America*, ed. by Jo Ann Cavallo and Charles Stanley Ross (Tempe, AZ: Medieval & Renaissance Texts & Studies, 1998), pp. 1–14 (p. 9).

impressed by the chivalrous conduct of Christians that they decide to convert to Christianity out of respect and admiration for individual Christian knights. In the *Trabisonda* Rinaldo colonizes a large part of *Pagania* and converts many Saracens who are swayed by his *cortesia* and prowess. In other chivalric texts it is Orlando who represents the model of a perfect knight. In the *Entrée d'Espagne*, the *Fatti di Spagna* and the *Spagna*, offended by Charlemagne, Orlando leaves the Christian camp and sails to the Middle East, where he converts the Persian sultan together with his family and his subjects, and befriends his son Sansonet (Sansonet(t)o).[29] The young man literally falls in love with the Christian paladin, begging permission from his parents to follow him to Europe: 'mere, ce dit Sanson, n'aiés nulle doutançe, | mais leisiés moi aler veoir les giens de Françe | por aprandre proueçe e largeçe e siançe' [mother, said Sanson, do not worry, | but allow me to go and see the people of France | to learn prowess, magnanimity, and wisdom] (*Entrée d'Espagne*, 14276–78).[30] In all three narratives Orlando's attitude towards the Saracen youth is protective and patronising. He initiates him into chivalry and supervises his education. Sansonet is a good but not exceptional warrior; he is inferior to Orlando in everything, and has to rely on him to survive in a world where danger lurks around every corner.

We see a very different power dynamic in the relationship between Boiardo's Orlando and Brandimarte: it is Orlando who receives practical help and emotional support from his Saracen friend.[31] In canto xi of Book II, Brandimarte succeeds in killing Balisardo who has outwitted Orlando and taken him captive. In the following canto, when both heroes are thrown into prison at Manodante's order, Orlando is overwhelmed with despair, while Brandimarte suggests that they exchange identities so that Orlando can get out and rescue Manodante's son. All Orlando can do is invoke saints ('quanti n'ha il Ciel, e poi del'altri ancora' [all heaven holds, and then some more] (*Inam.*, II xii 10,8)) and make vows — 'per paura' [out of fear] (11,3) — to every icon he can think of. His frantic praying prompts Brandimarte to ask him about his religion, and Orlando uses this opportunity to convert his friend to Christianity. He slips into his familiar role as a saviour of lost souls, but Brandimarte — who retains calm self-possession in the face of danger — emerges as an unquestionably stronger figure as he blackmails Orlando into following through with his plan by telling him that otherwise he will not convert. Later on, Orlando has another fit of panic when he realizes that he, Brandimarte,

---

29    Another good example of a friendship between a Saracen convert and a Christian knight in which the Saracen is clearly inferior to his Christian companion is the friendship between Namo and Balante in the *Aspramonte* tradition.

30    On Sansonet in the *Entrée d'Espagne*, see Boscolo, *L'Entrée d'Espagne*, pp. 182–84.

31    Alexandre-Gras devotes several pages of her monograph to Brandimarte who, as she convincingly shows, is endowed with an extremely important virtue — *prudenza* [prudence] — which distinguishes him from most other Christian and Saracen characters and renders him more mature than Orlando (*L'héroisme chevaleresque dans le 'Roland Amoureux' de Boiardo*, pp. 331–38). See also Maristella De Panizza Lorch, '"Ma soprattutto la persona umana | era cortese": Brandimarte's *Cortesia* as Expressed through the Hero's *Loci Actionis* in Boiardo's *Orlando Innamorato*, Book I', in *La corte e lo spazio: Ferrara estense*, ed. by Giuseppe Papagno and Amedeo Quondam, 2 vols (Rome: Bulzoni, 1982), II, pp. 739–81; and Cavallo, *The World beyond Europe*, pp. 211–34.

and their ladies are being followed by Torindo, Caramano, and other enemies of Angelica. Again, his friend has to reassure him:

> ma Brandimarte se cura nïente,
> anci diceva al Conte: 'Hor t'asicura,
> che piacendoti far quel ch'io te dico,
> quela canaglia non estimo un fico.'

> [but Brandimarte showed not a care.
> He told the Count: 'Now rest assured
> that if you do what I suggest
> that rabble won't be worth a fig.']
> (*Inam.*, II xviii 19,5–8)

It is surprising that a knight of the calibre of Orlando should worry about a bunch of rather mediocre Saracen knights. And yet Boiardo portrays him as hesitant not only in love but also in situations where the reader would expect him to feel in his element. In Book III, when the two friends arrive at the walls of besieged Paris, thinking that all is lost, Orlando begins to weep. It is once again Brandimarte who helps him overcome his puerile self-pity, urging him to dry his tears and start fighting (*Inam.*, III viii 16–18).[32]

According to Jane Everson, what is truly striking about Boiardo's portrayal of Orlando is not so much the fact that he falls in love but his 'unheroic, even anti-heroic behaviour [...] the portrayal of him as a model of what not to do or be, what not to imitate'.[33] Indeed, on his own, Orlando is often reluctant to take risks, as if the chivalric ideal of glory left him indifferent. In canto vii of Book II he is almost persuaded to turn back when Falerina tearfully advises him not to go any further lest Haridano kill him, suggesting that his death would leave her inconsolable: 'il franco Conte a quel dolce parlare | a poco a poco si venìa piegando | e destinava adietro ritornare' [her words were gentle and the brave Count | was yielding to them bit by bit, | almost deciding to turn back] (*Inam.*, II vii 50,1–3). He changes his mind eventually, but his initial reaction to Falerina's speech makes the reader's eyebrows rise in disbelief. In canto xx of Book II Orlando leaves Cyprus only because a treacherous Greek lies to him, saying the king will try to capture him, as Gano has told him that he is Orlando and not Rotolante from Circassia.

Together with the paladin's obvious ineptitude in love, these moments of doubt and hesitation lead one to question Franceschetti's view that Orlando represents the highest example of chivalry in the first two books of the *Inamoramento de Orlando*.[34]

---

32   As Jane Everson notes, 'Orlando is [...] presented, in the context of serious warfare, as somehow enfeebled, lacking the power of command, decisiveness, and courage' (Jane Everson, *The Italian Romance Epic in the Age of Humanism: the Matter of Italy and the World of Rome* (Oxford: Oxford University Press, 2001), p. 246).

33   Ibid., p. 247.

34   'Non c'è dubbio che Orlando rappresenti, almeno nei primi due libri del poema — ché, in seguito, il suo posto sarebbe forse occupato da Rugiero — l'eroe nobile per eccellenza, l'esempio perfetto del tipo di cavaliere vagheggiato dal Boiardo' [There is no doubt that Orlando represents, at least in the first two books of the poem — for later his place would perhaps be taken by Rugiero — the noble hero *par excellence*, the perfect example of the type of knight Boiardo

This is not to say that he is not a good knight.[35] He most certainly is, for he does show his valour in many battles and duels and his deeds are often worthy of the narrator's and readers' admiration. Yet he is going through what may be described as an identity crisis, which prevents him from reaching the pinnacle of chivalry. It is telling that Orlando fails to save Albracà: one night Angelica and her Christian defender flee to France, leaving Albracà to the enemy's fury. The castle is burnt and Angelica becomes the vagabond damsel she is in the *Furioso*. *Paganìa* refuses to fall on its knees before Orlando, who does not quite live up to his fame as the greatest knight in the world.

As for Orlando's cousin Ranaldo, although he does not suffer from self-doubt, one cannot say that Ranaldo towers above all other knights in the poem. On the one hand, Ranaldo's portrayal is often reminiscent of his representations in other chivalric works, where his virtues shine so brightly that they are a beacon for all those who wish to excel in chivalry: suffice it to mention the episode in which he helps Iroldo to save Prasildo and the two Saracen friends are so impressed by his valour that they assume that he is none other than Macone, and then, having discovered the truth, unhesitatingly convert to Christianity. And yet his encounter with Iroldo and Prasildo is not merely a celebration of his *cortesia* and martial skill: it is also a celebration of the extraordinary friendship between the two Saracens. Ranaldo (whose relationship with Orlando is strained over Angelica) is deeply moved by their story (they love the same woman and yet each of them is ready to sacrifice his life for the other), and offers to help them because 'un par di amici al mondo tanto certo | né hora se trova né mai fo trovato: | se io fosse tercio, io me terìa beato' [you two are the truest pair | of friends the world knows, or has known: | I would be honoured to be third] (*Inam.*, I xvii 21,6–7). While Ranaldo saves their lives and their souls, the two Saracens amaze him with their commitment to the ideal of friendship.

In the *Morgante*, the *Cantari di Rinaldo*, and the *Trabisonda* Rinaldo stands out as a noble rebel, an excellent, if short-tempered, knight who is unjustly persecuted by Gano and Charlemagne. In the latter two poems he supplants Orlando as the epitome of chivalry. Boiardo's Ranaldo is an exceptionally valiant knight in a poem that abounds in equally impressive warriors. One of them is the Saracen queen Marphisa, who persuades him to become her ally in the Albracà war. Their relationship is one of equals. Both are endowed with extraordinary strength: they fight a duel but neither is able to defeat the other ('né tra lor se cognosce alcun vantagio' [neither one gaining any edge] (*Inam.*, I xix 35,2)). Both have zero tolerance for traitors. They bond over their mutual hatred of Trufaldino, whom

---

was envisaging] (Franceschetti, *L''Orlando Innamorato' e le sue componenti tematiche e strutturali*, p. 127).

35    On the evolution of the character in the Italian heroic tradition see Marco Dorigatti, 'Reinventing Roland — Orlando in Italian Literature', in *Roland and Charlemagne in Europe: Essays on the Reception and Transformation of a Legend*, ed. by Karen Pratt (London: King's College London Medieval Studies, 1996), pp. 105–26; and also Marco Villoresi, 'Le varianti di Orlando: un personaggio e le sue trasformazioni', in *'Tre volte suona l'olifante': la tradizione rolandiana in Italia fra Medioevo e Rinascimento* (Milan: UNICOPLI, 2007), pp. 72–93.

they want to punish for his crimes (Orlando, in contrast, reluctantly promises Trufaldino his protection if the latter lets him into Albracà). Both admire valour in others and respect chivalric rules of combat. Ranaldo comes to Marphisa's aid when she is attacked by a group of Saracen knights. True to her word, Marphisa does not help Ranaldo against Orlando, even if the thought that Orlando might kill her companion makes her weep.[36] This alliance between a Christian paladin and a Saracen warrior woman is all the more surprising given that in the chivalric tradition unconverted female warriors are usually portrayed in a highly ambivalent fashion. While Galaciella (who marries a Christian man and converts to Christianity in the *Aspramonte*) is treated with sympathy, the eponymous heroines of the *Regina Ancroia* and *Dama Rovenza* are praised for their martial skills, but at the same time aligned with monstrosity and the grotesque.[37] So much so that the Christians do not feel obliged to respect the chivalric code in their dealings with them.[38] Ancroia is killed by Orlando who gives her a copy of his sword Durindana telling her that it is the original. The Christians then quarter her body — out of curiosity, as if she were some kind of monstrous creature — and find four tiny lions near her heart (*Ancroia*, XXIX-XXX). As for the giantess Rovenza, she is slaughtered by Rinaldo who plays dead and treacherously cuts off her foot and then her head (*Rovenza*, IX 3–6 [fol. d4$^r$]). Seen in this light, the companionship between Ranaldo and Marphisa is a subversion of the topos of the grotesque Saracen virago, with Marphisa being an inspiring example of female Saracen chivalry.[39]

One of the most celebrated features of the *Inamoramento de Orlando* is its vitality and dynamism, the *joie de vivre* that exudes from the text. Much of this vitality comes from *Paganìa*. Boiardo's Saracen characters do not know the feeling of inner insecurity which haunts Orlando. They cannot always get what they want, but at least they know what they want and put all their energy into the pursuit of the

36   As Cavallo observes, 'Boiardo portrays Maphisa as a model knight in her unconditional adherence to the chivalric code' (Cavallo, *The World beyond Europe*, p. 73). See Cavallo's discussion of this character at pp. 70–75.

37   On the figure of the Saracen warrior woman in the chivalric tradition see Valentina Denzel, 'La guerrière sarrasine', in Eadem, *Les Mille et Un Visages de la virago: Marphise et Bradamante entre continuation et variation* (Paris: Classiques Garnier, 2016), pp. 259–358; and Stoppino, *Genealogies of Fiction*, especially pp. 18–57.

38   It is true that Pulci's Antea is portrayed more positively. However, as was mentioned in the previous chapter, Boiardo probably only discovered the *Morgante* when he was composing the second book of the *Inamoramento de Orlando*. One crucial difference between Antea and Marphisa is that the former falls in love with Rinaldo (joining the long list of Saracen damsels who cannot resist his charms), while the latter is capable of friendship yet immune to love, foreshadowing in this respect Tasso's Clorinda.

39   Some critics dismiss Marphisa as a comic character. For Pamela Benson, for example, 'Boiardo's Marfisa is a buffoon who spends much of the first book armed and on foot in pursuit of Pinabello, who has stolen her horse and who teases her by keeping the horse out of her reach' (Pamela Benson, *The Invention of the Renaissance Woman: The Challenge of Female Independence in the Literature and Thought of Italy and England* (University Park: Pennsylvania State University Press, 1992), p. 126). Fraught with factual errors (Marphisa's horse is stolen by Brunelo in Book II of the *Inamoramento de Orlando*), Benson's statement reveals the extent to which this heroine has been misunderstood. Boiardo does poke fun at Marphisa in the Brunelo episode, but few characters escape his gentle irony (one thinks of Ranaldo's failed attempt to steal Morgana's treasure or of Astolfo's boastful rants).

objects of their desire, even if they sometimes get distracted by other adventures. It is to a large extent their personal quests that move the narration forward. Agramante wishes to emulate Alexander the Great; Agricane wants Angelica and so does Sacripante; Gradasso has come to France to obtain the sword Durindana and the horse Baiardo; Mandricardo desires Durindana; Marphisa has made a vow to her Macone 'mai non spogliarsi sbergo e piastre e maglia | sin che tre Re non prende per bataglia' [to wear her hauberk, plate, and mail | till she subdued three kings in battle] (*Inam.*, I xvi 29,7–8), that is until she has defeated Gradasso, Agricane, and Charlemagne. None of these Saracen knights is flawless, but neither are their Christian counterparts. It would be wrong to view their stories from a moralistic perspective, for their faults are insignificant in comparison to their virtues and the wars they fight resemble jousts. These and other Saracen protagonists of the poem (Brandimarte, Feraguto, Rodamonte, and of course Rugiero) make important contributions to the chivalric ideology that gradually emerges from it, promoting the ideal of an active life. At various points in the narration they serve as models of knightly behaviour. They are accomplished knights before their encounter with Christian chivalry. They do not look up to Charlemagne's paladins, even if they do acknowledge their valour. In fact, in a number of episodes they outshine their Christian friends and adversaries, and their speeches about love and glory as well as their deeds remain indelibly etched in the readers' memory, influencing our appreciation of the text and its meaning.

The same is true of the plethora of minor Saracen characters that populate the poem. Boiardo takes pleasure in giving them moments in the spotlight. They receive more attention than his minor Christian characters, many of whom — 'Avino, Avorio, Otton e Belengero' (*Inam.*, II vii 18,8) — are little more than names evoked for the sole purpose of obtaining a metrically correct line.[40] As can be seen from Appendix I, Boiardo lavishes praise on countless Saracen kings and barons, of whom we only catch fleeting glimpses. Although his treatment of minor characters is more conventional than his portrayal of the great Saracen warriors insofar as he adopts a disparaging attitude towards some of them (especially towards the giants), it is striking to what extent he is fascinated by their energy and courage.[41] He cannot help expressing his admiration even for those who, as he himself states, lack moral integrity: Baliverzo, for example, is both 'forte e ardito' [strong and bold] (II xxii 19,4) and a 'perfido ribaldo' [faithless villain] (III viii 35,8); Dudrinasso is a 'fior de Paganìa' [the flower of Saracen lands] (II xxvii 25,5) and a 'perfido pagano' [treacherous Saracen] (II xxx 6,6); Radamanco is 'valoroso e franco' [valorous and bold] (I xv 8,2) despite being a 'malvaso gigante e traditore' [treacherous, mean giant] (I xv 9,2).

---

40   Such groupings or quartets of characters are rather frequent in the *Inamoramento de Orlando*. By fitting four Christian knights into a single line the poet deprives them of their individuality. This technique is typical of the *cantari*, where minor characters are often enumerated in a manner that certainly does not underscore their valour.

41   There are twenty-one Saracen giants in the *Inamoramento de Orlando* and all but one die in the course of the narration. The lucky survivor is Gradasso's vassal Alfrera, King of Taprobana, who plays an important role in Gradasso's first military campaign by unhorsing many Christian as well as Saracen knights. Boiardo clearly admires his valour and does not have the heart to kill him.

## Saracen Africa and the legend of Alexander the Great

From a very impressive group of Saracen knights, one character stands out: Rugiero. The future founder of the Este line makes his entrance into the poem in Book II, and immediately his story — closely linked to that of Agramante — becomes one of the main narrative threads, the dynastic theme being one of the most innovative features of the *Inamoramento de Orlando*.[42] Rugiero is a hybrid character, one who belongs to two worlds, and whose family tree goes back to two ancient heroes. Through his Saracen mother, Agramante's aunt Galaciella, he is related to Alexander of Macedon. Through his Christian father he is a descendant of Hector of Troy. As already mentioned in Chapter I, the link between Agramante and Alexander the Great was not invented by Boiardo, but rather inherited from the *Aspramonte*. Boiardo, however, can be credited with the introduction of the Trojan theme.[43] Scholars have explored the connection between Rugiero and Hector of Troy, suggesting that it serves a political purpose: it has been argued that by giving Rugiero an illustrious Trojan ancestor Boiardo celebrates the Este dynasty in a manner that is consonant with contemporary humanist culture.[44] Yet his Saracen roots have been somewhat overlooked. As for Agramante, his connection to Alexander has been interpreted negatively. According to Cavallo, it 'serves to reinforce the negative connotations of his aggressive military expedition'.[45] In the remainder of the present chapter I shall challenge this view by assessing the significance of Agramante's and Rugiero's descent from Alexander in the light of the theme of antiquity in Boiardo's chivalric sources, focusing in particular on the *Aspramonte* narratives.

In Chapter I, we saw that in both the *chansons de geste* and Italian chivalric literature Saracens often worship ancient deities, and that their religious beliefs bear some resemblance to those of the ancients. The heritage of antiquity occupies a special place in Saracen culture. Saracen kings live in palaces decorated with frescoes depicting the lives of ancient heroes and wear armour that once belonged to them. Their closeness to antiquity has various implications. One could argue — and this is especially true of the early *chansons de geste* — that by fighting Saracens Charlemagne's paladins also fight the remnants of paganism.[46] And yet Baligant,

---

42 Boiardo's incorporation of the dynastic theme is a nod to the classical epic tradition (one thinks of Virgil's *Aeneid*), even if we should not lose sight of some Arthurian romances' insistence on genealogy. See, for example, Adrian Stevens, 'Gottfried, Wolfram, and the Angevins: History, Genealogy, and Fiction in the *Tristan* and *Parzival* Romances', in *Romance and History: Imagining Time from the Medieval to the Early Modern Period*, ed. by Jon Whitman (Cambridge: Cambridge University Press, 2014), pp. 74–89.

43 As Tissoni Benvenuti observes in her note to *Inam.*, III v 30, the rulers of Risa do not have Trojan ancestors in any of the extant Italian versions of the *Aspramonte*. However, Strozzi, too, makes his Rugerus a descendant of the Trojans through his kinship with the Trojan Franks.

44 For a discussion of the dynastic theme in the *Inamoramento de Orlando* see Marco Dorigatti, 'Rugiero and the Dynastic Theme from Boiardo to Ariosto', in *Italy in Crisis, 1494*, ed. by Jane Everson and Diego Zancani (Oxford: Legenda, 2000), pp. 92–128; and also Idem, 'La favola e la corte: intrecci narrativi e genealogie estensi dal Boiardo all'Ariosto'.

45 Cavallo, *The World beyond Europe*, p. 88.

46 Jean-Pierre Martin, 'Les références au mythe troyen dans les *chansons de geste* à sujet carolingien', *Bien dire et bien aprandre*, 10 (1992), 101–17. See also Idem, 'Les sarrasins, l'idolâtrie et l'imaginaire de

'le viel d'antiquité' [the ancient old man] who 'tut survesquiét e Virgilie e Omer' [outlived Virgil and Homer alike] (*Chanson de Roland*, 2615–2616), is the most positive Saracen character of the *Chanson de Roland*. Unlike Marsile, he respects the chivalric code, and his refusal to convert and subsequent death sadden the reader.

In the *Entrée d'Espagne*, Marsile's barons often refer to ancient history in their speeches.[47] Nor are such references a mere display of erudition. Courage, loyalty and endurance are fundamental heroic values in ancient epics. By constantly comparing themselves and others to the great men of antiquity (among whom Alexander occupies a prominent place), young Saracen knights (such as Feragu, who, as we mentioned earlier, is a rare example of a perfectly chivalrous Saracen knight) make these values their own and, as a result, grow in chivalry. That said, ancient history has its dark pages. One can imitate the glorious deeds of the Trojans or the treacherous behaviour of the Greeks who used the wooden horse to enter the city of Troy. Moreover, one can overestimate one's strength and attempt to imitate the heroes of the ancient world when one is clearly not in a position to do so. This is the mistake the Africans make in the *Chanson d'Asprement* and some of its Italian versions, to which we shall now turn our attention.

*Alexander in the* Aspramonte *tradition*

Books II and III of the *Inamoramento de Orlando* can be read as a sequel to the *Aspramonte* legend: they continue the story of the *Aspramonte*, bring back some of its characters, and introduce new characters who are related to those who die in Agolante's war. We do not know which of the four extant Italian versions of the *Chanson d'Aspremont* was on Boiardo's desk, as his allusions to the events of the *Aspramonte* do not completely coincide with any of them. According to Franceschetti, Boiardo drew on some lost version which was 'sostanzialmente affine al poema' [essentially similar to the poem], that is the fifteenth-century *Aspramonte*, first published in Florence around 1490.[48] Tissoni Benvenuti, however, remains unconvinced by Franceschetti's conclusion that Boiardo could not have had an in-depth knowledge of Andrea da Barberino's *Aspramonte*, 'testo in proposito molto autorevole, e facilmente accessibile' [a very authoritative text in this respect and an easily available one].[49] Indeed, there are many similarities between the

---

l'antiquité dans les chansons de geste', in *Littérature et religion au Moyen Age et à la Renaissance*, ed. by Jean-Claude Vallecalle (Lyon: Presses Universitaires de Lyon, 1997), pp. 27–46.

47    On allusions to antiquity in the *Entrée d'Espagne* see Leslie C. Brook, 'Allusions à l'antiquité gréco-latine dans l'*Entrée d'Espagne*', *Zeitschrift für romanische Philologie*, 118, no. 4 (2002), 573–86.

48    Franceschetti, 'L'*Orlando innamorato* e la tradizione dell'*Aspremont*', *GSLI*, 147 (1970), 518–33 (p. 525) (later reprinted in his *L'*'*Orlando Innamorato*' e le sue componenti tematiche e strutturali*). On the fifteenth-century *Aspramonte* see Marco Boni, 'L'*Aspramonte* quattrocentesco in ottave', in *Studi in onore di Carlo Pellegrini* (Turin: Società Editrice Internazionale, 1963), pp. 43–59.

49    Tissoni Benvenuti, 'Note preliminari al commento dell'*Inamoramento de Orlando*', in *Il commento ai testi: Atti del seminario di Ascona*, ed. by Ottavio Besomi and Carlo Caruso (Basel: Birkhäuser, 1992), pp. 277–309 (p. 291). Although the first printed edition of Andrea da Barberino's *Aspramonte* appeared only in the twentieth century (Marco Boni's 1951 edition, to be precise), the romance circulated in manuscript form. There was almost certainly a copy of it in the Este Library in Ferrara. On copies of the *Aspramonte* in Borso's and Ercole's libraries see Tissoni Benvenuti, 'Rugiero o la fabbrica dell'*Inamoramento de Orlando*', pp. 69–70, notes 2–3.

*Inamoramento de Orlando* and Andrea da Barberino's prose romance, starting from the fact that both Andrea's Agolante and Boiardo's Agramante have thirty-two vassal kings.[50] Although we cannot rule out the possibility that Boiardo consulted a now lost text, it is very likely that Andrea da Barberino was one of his sources for Book II. In my discussion of the references to Alexander in the *Aspramonte*, I shall pay special attention to both Andrea da Barberino and the fifteenth-century poem. However, in order for the full significance of Boiardo's departure from the *Aspramonte* tradition to emerge, it is useful to begin with the *Chanson d'Aspremont* and to consider the Italian *Aspramonti* Boiardo was less likely to be familiar with.

Agoulant's genealogical claim to Alexander's empire is alluded to, albeit briefly, in the *Chanson d'Aspremont*. Balant, Agoulant's ambassador, arrives in Paris, and tells Charlemagne that his king considers himself Alexander's heir: 'qanque Alixandres conquest an son aage | viaut il tenir, c'est de son eritage' [what Alexander conquered in his day | he wants to keep, it is his inheritance] (*Chanson d'Aspremont*, 428–29). As Keith Busby puts it, 'Charlemagne's victory over Agolant thus represents [...] confirmation of the superiority of the modern West over the ancient East'.[51] Yet the author of this Old French epic only shows a superficial interest in the ancient origins of the African royal family. The desire to recreate Alexander's empire is neither the only nor the main reason behind the Africans' attempted invasion of Europe. More importantly, Agoulant and his son Eaumont want to exterminate Christianity, which is stressed at different points in the narration (see for example, *Chanson d'Aspremont*, 310–13). Ironically, while Alexander was famous for his cosmopolitanism and religious tolerance, his descendant is driven by religious hatred. This is, however, not surprising, considering that the poem was composed at the time of the Third Crusade and that it was most probably conceived as a piece of crusade propaganda. Moreover, while Alexander is presented as an epitome of largesse in medieval romances, Agoulant loses 'his empire, son and own life because of his inability to part with his wealth'.[52]

The medieval poet presents the Africans' connection to Alexander in a somewhat ironic light, possibly intentionally so. The same can be said of the Italian versions of the *Aspramonte* as well as of the *Spagna ferrarese* (where, as mentioned in the previous chapter, the Spanish Saracens are in every respect inferior to their legendary ancestor).[53] In the fragmentary *Cantari d'Aspramonte* (the earliest *rifacimento* to contain the episode of the conquest of Risa) neither Balante's speech nor Agolante's letter to

50    For other points of contact between the two texts see Franceschetti, 'L'*Orlando innamorato* e la tradizione dell'*Aspremont*', especially pp. 227–31, and Tissoni Benvenuti, 'Note preliminari al commento dell'*Inamoramento de Orlando*', p. 291.

51    Keith Busby, 'Post-Chrétien Verse Romance: The Manuscript Context', *CRM*, 14 (2007), 11–24 (p. 17).

52    Joan B. Willamson, 'The figure of the griffin in the *Chanson d'Aspremont*', in *Aspects de l'épopée romane: mentalités, idéologies, intertextualités*, ed. by Hans van Dijk and Willem Noomen (Groningen: Egbert Forsten, 1995), pp. 83–89 (p. 85).

53    On the *Cantari d'Aspramonte* and the anonymous prose *Aspramonte* see Marco Boni, 'Note sul cantare magliabechiano d'Aspramonte e sull'*Aspramonte* di Andrea da Barberino', *GSLI*, 127 (1950), 276–304; and Idem, 'L'*Aspramonte* trecentesco in prosa del manoscritto Add. 10808 del British Museum', *Studi mediolatini e volgari*, 1 (1953), 7–50.

the Christians — which, curiously, is written in Greek and translated into 'latino' (IX 26,1) — mention Alexander. Rather Balante claims that his king has declared war on the Franks 'perché credete in Cristo vostro Idio' [because you believe Christ to be your God] (*Cantari d'Aspramonte*, X 42). However, the Christians are aware of Agolante's desire to emulate Alexander, as we see from Charlemagne's letter to the King of Hungary:

> Agolante, d'Africa un re arguto,
> il pregiat[issim]o Almonte in sua compagnia,
> Rissa m'à tolta e 'n Calavria è venuto.
> Più che Alessandro vuol signoregiare [...]
>
> [Agolante, a canny king of Africa,
> the most valiant Almonte in his company,
> took Risa from me and arrived in Calabria.
> He wants to rule over more lands than Alexander [...]]
> (*Cantari d'Aspramonte*, XII 52,4–7)

Later, Agolante himself declares that the main purpose of his military expedition is to claim back what had once belonged to his noble ancestor, 'cortese Alesandro re saputo' [courteous Alexander, a wise king] (*Cantari d'Aspramonte*, XIX 4,3). But, unlike the chivalrous Alexander of medieval romances, Agolante cannot be described as courteous. Comparing his campaign against Charlemagne to Alexander's war with Porus, he exclaims he will kill the French emperor with his own hands (ibid., 5), forgetting that Alexander not only spared Porus's life but also, impressed by his enemy's valour, reinstated him as a governor of his lost kingdom. The author of the *Cantari* portrays Agolante as a ruthless religious fanatic (he has his own daughter executed for marrying a Christian) and as an irresponsible ruler who foolishly thinks of himself as a new Alexander. As the poet reminds us in the opening octaves of cantare V, it is ill-advised to jeopardize the security of one's state in an attempt to conquer more land. While Almonte is a more likeable character than his father, he is not quite a noble Saracen who only lacks the Christian religion to be a perfect knight. Although he is praised for his chivalric virtues, he falls short of his own heroic ideals when he treacherously kills Riccieri II of Risa (the 'good' son of the lord of Risa and Galaciella's husband), an action that he bitterly regrets. Almonte would have wanted to win by fair means, but, having been overpowered by Riccieri and having sworn not to fight against him, he breaks his oath when he takes part in the conquest of Risa, and, to his own horror, succumbs to the temptation of striking Riccieri where his bare flesh shows. As Riccieri dies, so does Almonte's naive belief that he is the best warrior in the world. From then on he is a broken man who has to live with a shameful secret.

In the anonymous fourteenth-century prose version of the *Aspramonte* (preserved in MS Add. 10808 of the British Library) Agolante attacks the Christians because he wants to give Europe to Almonte. However, the figure of Alexander is not entirely absent. When Balante returns to his lord, he tells him that the French emperor è magiore signiore del monndo e fecemi troppo grande onore, e senpre chon lui mangiavo e factami servire al baroni che ciaschuno rasenbrava re e più son begli quegli che llo servano che no fue vostro padre Alesandro [...]

[is the greatest lord of the world and he received me with great honours, and I always ate with him and he ordered his barons to serve me, each of whom resembled a king and those who serve him are more handsome than your father Alexander was [...]] (*Aspramonte BL*, fol. 7ᵛ).

Here, Alexander is Agolante's father. We do not know if the anonymous author meant Alexander of Macedon, but if so, the distance between Saracens and antiquity is completely erased. In any case, the reader is unlikely to be impressed by Agolante's family tree, as this unspecified Alexander is less handsome than Charlemagne's courtiers. Agolante's lineage pales in comparison to the splendour of the French court (at least in Balante's view). He and his sons are portrayed as arrogant, reckless and short-tempered. They do not, however, stain themselves with truly infamous actions, as the episode of the capture of Risa is absent from this version.

Both Andrea da Barberino and the author of the fifteenth-century *Aspramonte* exploit the dramatic potential of the medieval story, embellishing it with new details and presenting some of the well-known facts in a new light. Both authors show a genuine interest in the ancient origins of the African royal family. In the former romance, the Saracens attack the Christians not so much because of religious intolerance as because they crave glory: a buffoon dares to say that Agolante is a lesser king than Charlemagne, and the Africans are determined to prove him wrong. Andrea da Barberino repeatedly draws attention to Agolante's blood connection to Alexander. Balante tells Charlemagne that the whole world should belong to Agolante because it once belonged to his illustrious ancestor: 'egli à giurato di pigliare tutto il mondo, perché Alessandro ne fu signore e il re Agolante è del suo legnaggio, e del parentado del re Nettenabo d'Egitto; e però tocca a lui el reditaggio' [he swore to conquer the whole world, because Alexander ruled over it, and King Agolante belongs to his lineage, and he is related to King Nectanebo of Egypt; and so it is his by inheritance] (*Aspramonte A*, II x 19–22). We hear this again from Agolante who announces to Namo that 'Franza fu del mio antico Alessandro, figliuolo del re Filippo di Macedonia' [France belonged to my ancestor Alexander, son of Philip of Macedon] (*Aspramonte A*, II xliv 33–34). Later, Agolante repeats this in a conversation with Charlemagne (III xxxiii 26–27), and then Ulieno accuses Charlemagne of having usurped Agolante's lands (III lxvi 10–14). Although the reader knows that had it not been for the buffoon's malicious comment the Africans probably would not have attempted to re-conquer Alexander's empire, their insistence on their descent from Alexander should not be dismissed as merely an excuse to justify their aggression. The Saracens genuinely feel an affinity with the ancients. They are inspired by the great deeds of the heroes of antiquity, so much so that Almonte considers himself a new Aeneas, as is evident from the speech he makes when he and his soldiers are about to set foot on Italian soil:

O valoroso Enea figliuolo d'Anchisse, se gli iddei furono prosperevoli a farti acquistare questa parte d'Italia, siano prosperevoli a me che io l'acquisti, a cui per le terreste forze e le promesse de l'altissima signoria del padre mio credo che i cieli con le loro forze l'abbiano disposto, come io credo che gl'iddii immortali me l'abbino conceduto. E così piglio arme contro a chi difendere la vorrà, e con la speranza di Maometto e di Trevigante e d'Apollino e Iupiter, e' quali sono gl'iddei del padre mio e di Troiano e di me, e con l'aiuto di Marte deo delle battaglie.

[O valorous Aeneas, son of Anchises, if the gods helped you to conquer this part of Italy, may they help me conquer it, since I believe that, by virtue of my father's earthly powers and the promises he made on his highest authority, the heavens in their powers have so decreed, as I also believe that the immortal gods have granted it to me. And so I take up arms against whoever will want to defend it, placing my hope in Muhammad and Trevigante and Apollino and Jupiter, who are the gods of my father and Troiano and my gods, and in the help of Mars, the god of battles.] (*Aspramonte A*, I xiii 9–16).

Almonte firmly believes that, like Aeneas, he has been chosen by gods to accomplish great things. He is determined to follow in the footsteps of both Alexander and Aeneas and to etch his name into the annals of history. While Almonte is endowed with noble traits in the earlier versions of the story, Andrea da Barberino gives even more emphasis to the noble side of his personality. This adds to the drama of his awakening to the bitter truth that he is not the strongest knight and that he can only win by treachery. When his father Agolante accepts the help of Beltramo (one of the sons of the lord of Risa who decides to betray his father and brother in exchange for Galiziella), Almonte is outraged but he reluctantly goes along with the plan ('il re Almonte [...] disse che questo era loro grande vergongna, ma non volle contradire a quello che 'l padre si contentava' [King Almonte [...] said that this brought great dishonour upon them, but he did not want to contradict what his father approved of] (*Aspramonte A*, I xxxv 10–12)). Like his counterpart in the *Cantari d'Aspramonte*, he regrets murdering Riccieri, whom he runs through from behind in the confusion of the night-time battle that breaks out after Beltramo opens the gates of the city to the enemy. Almonte foolishly believed that he was destined to immortal glory, but as his story unfolds, we realize that this self-proclaimed Saracen Aeneas is in reality a tragic anti-Aeneas.

Andrea da Barberino composed his version of the *Aspramonte* in the early fifteenth century, when Florence was the leading centre of humanist thought in Italy. One wonders how Andrea's well-educated readers reacted to the Africans' impressive genealogy and their desire to emulate the heroes of antiquity.[54] The classical, medieval, and late medieval literature on Alexander is a jungle, but, as has been shown by recent studies on the legend of Alexander in Italy, the Macedonian

---

54    As Jane Everson has convincingly shown in her monograph on Italian Renaissance chivalric literature, 'There is [...] no case for continuing to separate critical discussion of the culture of Humanism and the development of the classical revival from the simultaneous development of the vernacular epic', as the boundaries between the two cultures were fluid (*The Italian Romance Epic in the Age of Humanism*, p. 327).

conqueror is often portrayed positively in both 'serious' and 'light' texts.[55] The humanists thought that one's origins shaped one's character, this idea being at the heart of many fifteenth-century panegyric works. Although Almonte has positive qualities, he is a far cry from their famous ancestor. It could be that the author of the fifteenth-century *Aspramonte in ottava rima* presented the African dynasty as tainted by illegitimacy precisely because of his contemporaries' 'obsession' with genealogies. In his version the political foundations of Saracen Africa are fragile, for it has always been ruled by kings born out of wedlock, and the Africans' refined manners are just a disguise for their perfidy and weakness.

The connection between the Saracen rulers' illegitimacy and their inability to live up to their own standards of courtesy and heroism is not immediately evident but becomes increasingly clear in the course of the narration. At first we learn that

> Lo re Agolante con tutte suo genti
> del sangue fo del Re de Macedonia:
> nacque di Philippon, come vi scandro,
> el qual fo decto padre d'Alexandro.
>
> [King Agolante with all his people
> was of the blood of the King of Macedon:
> he was born of Philip, as I'm telling you,
> who was said to be Alexander's father.]
> (*Aspramonte*, V 41,5–8 [fol. bvii$^r$])

Despite the stain of illegitimacy, Agolante and his ancestors are praised for their kingly virtues:

> Bastardi funno suoi antecessori
> et Agolante ancora a tal richiesta,[56]
> ma tucti quanti fur di gran valori
> per l'universo havevan gran podesta;
> d'Affrica et d'Asia fur questi signori
> come la loro historia il manifesta;
> gli altri non hebben come lui paese,
> però Agolante fo tanto cortese.
>
> [All of his ancestors were of illegitimate birth
> and Agolante too was illegitimate,
> but all of them were very valiant
> and had much power in the universe;
> they ruled Africa and Asia,
> as their story goes;
> others did not have as much land as he had,
> and so Agolante was very courteous.]
> (*Aspramonte*, V 42 [fol. bvii$^r$])

55    On the legend of Alexander in Italy, see at least George Cary, 'The Conception of Alexander in Late Medieval and Renaissance Italy', in his *Medieval Alexander* (Cambridge: CUP, 1956, reprinted 1967), pp. 260–72; Roberta Morosini, 'The Alexander Romance in Italy', in *A Companion to Alexander Literature in the Middle Ages*, ed. by David Zuwiyya (Leiden: Brill, 2011), pp. 329–64; Jane Everson, 'Storie di Alessandro Magno nella tradizione volgare: Medioevo, Rinascimento e tempi moderni', *Rassegna europea di letteratura italiana*, 41, no. 1 (2013), 41–58.
56    The meaning of 'a tal richiesta' is unclear. It could be just a line-filler.

Agolante comes across as a rather charismatic ruler in the first cantos of the poem. He is generous and gracious. He seeks his courtiers' opinion before declaring war on Charlemagne (which he does to avenge his dead brother). He gives expensive presents to his vassals, and he takes a magnanimous attitude towards defeated Christians. The barons of Calabria decide to swear allegiance to him as soon they learn that, having conquered Sicily, he is leading his army to invade their lands. And yet his civility and kindness are insincere. When his own people reproach him for being courteous with the Calabrian traitors (his vassals Uliano and Balante think that these Christians deserve to be punished for surrendering to the enemy without attempting any resistance), Agolante replies that wars are won with intelligence and that after he has conquered the whole of Italy, he will force all the Christians to convert to the Saracen religion. He is not the tolerant and open-minded ruler he pretends to be, but a cunning and cynical politician.

Agolante bears only a superficial resemblance to Alexander. His son Almonte has none of the virtues of the Macedonian conqueror. While in the *Cantari d'Aspramonte* and in Andrea da Barberino's prose romance Almonte is a tragic character who arouses the reader's compassion, in the fifteenth-century *Aspramonte* his excessive self-pity and reluctance to accept responsibility for his actions make it hard to feel any sympathy for him.[57] He hides his weakness and baseness beneath the façade of a chivalrous prince, but his true nature soon emerges. Having unhorsed him twice, his Christian opponent Rugieri II of Risa feels nothing but contempt for him, and questions whether he is Agolante's son:

> 'Vatene al padiglion ch'è quasi sera,
> a la tua madre di' senza esser tardo
> che ti dichiari el vero a tal maniera:
> se legiptimo sei over bastardo.'
>
> ['Go back to your tent, as it's almost evening,
> and ask your mother without any delay
> to tell you the truth about the following matter:
> if you are a legitimate son or a bastard.']
>             (*Aspramonte*, VIII 51,1–4 [fol. dii^r])

This is not just an insult hurled in a fit of anger. Rugieri's words remain with the reader. They are echoed later on in the poem when Almonte disgraces himself beyond redemption. If in the previous versions of the *Aspramonte* it is Agolante who negotiates with the traitor Beltramo, here Beltramo approaches Almonte rather than Agolante (the latter is totally unaware of the ignoble pact). After the conquest of Risa and Rugieri's death (he is killed by a poisoned dart in Almonte's presence), Almonte begs his barons not to mention this double betrayal to his father, because if Agolante does find out, 'el mi direbbe vil tristo et bastardo' [he will call me a wretched coward and a bastard] (*Aspramonte*, XI 51,5 [fol. fii^r]). In the same canto Galaciella calls him a 'traditore vil tristo et bastardo' [wretched, cowardly traitor

---

57    His only redeeming feature is his deep love for his sister. For a comparison between the portrayal of Almonte in Andrea da Barberino and in the fifteenth-century *Aspramonte*, see Pavlova, 'I saraceni nella letteratura cavalleresca del Quattrocento', pp. 584–86.

and a bastard] (58,1 [fol. fiii<sup>r</sup>]), claiming that he has brought shame on their family. In Almonte's case the word 'bastardo' may well be used in its literal sense, because Agolante's wife does not observe conjugal faithfulness. She falls in love with Namo when he comes to the Saracen camp as an ambassador. Realizing that she cannot have Namo she develops a passion for Don Chiaro's brother whom she marries, but only after a moment of hesitation during which she considers giving herself to Don Chiaro instead. Nor is she the only Saracen lady to betray her husband: just about a dozen stanzas after the revelation that all of Agolante's ancestors were 'bastardi', we learn that the wife of the 'grande Almansore' [great Almansore] (*Aspramonte*, V 52,1 [fol. bvii<sup>v</sup>]) is a 'meretrice' [prostitute] (56,7 [fol. bviii<sup>r</sup>]) who is madly in love with a servant and secretly hopes that her husband will die in Europe.

Thus, in the fifteenth-century *Aspramonte* the Saracens are inferior to the Christians not only because they believe in false gods, but also because of the impurity of their blood. The poet's insistence on this latter factor reflects his belief in the hereditary transmission of virtue and vice. His attitude to Alexander is much more respectful and sympathetic than his treatment of the Africans who claim to descend from him. His Christian characters are more successful in practising the virtues that made Alexander a great hero: we are told at various points that Rugieri surpasses the Macedonian conqueror in *cortesia*.

## Alexander in the 'Inamoramento de Orlando'

It may seem surprising that Boiardo should decide to provide the Este with a fictional genealogy (or to follow the already existing legend) that links them to the Saracen characters of the *Aspramonte*, whose portrayal, as we have seen, is ambivalent in all surviving Italian versions. On the other hand, in none of the Italian *Aspramonti* are these characters irredeemably evil. Almonte, the central protagonist of the medieval story, is depicted with understanding and compassion in the *Cantari d'Aspramonte* and in Andrea da Barberino's romance. While he cuts a most uninspiring figure in the fifteenth-century *Aspramonte*, his father Agolante, for all his Machiavellian hypocrisy, does not stoop to the same level of moral degeneracy. Connecting his poem to the *Aspramonte*, Boiardo is careful to highlight the most positive traits of the Saracen Africa he inherited from the tradition. In so doing, he devotes more space to Alexander than any of the authors we have considered so far.

Alexander is first mentioned as Agramante's ancestor at the beginning of the opening canto of Book II, where Boiardo explains the origins of the African royal house (*Inam.*, II i 5–16). More information about Alexander's life and death is given in the stanzas devoted to the ekphrastic description of the frescoes that adorn Agramante's palace in Biserta (21–30). Interestingly, Boiardo does not conceal the fact that the Macedonian hero was born from an adulterous union. He is the son of

> [...] l'astrologo prudente,
> qual del suo regno se n'era fugito,
> ch'una Regina in forma di serpente
> avìa gabbata, e prese il suo apetito [...]

> [the wise astrologer
> who'd run away from his own kingdom
> who, pretending to be a snake, had fooled
> a Queen and fulfilled his desire]
> (*Inam.*, II i 22,1–4)

As Bruscagli points out, the legend that Alexander was fathered by the Egyptian ruler Nectanebo and not by Philip of Macedon was very popular in Italy during the Middle Ages.[58] We have seen that Andrea da Barberino also mentions Nectanebo as one of Agolante's ancestors without raising the question of illegitimacy. Boiardo does not seem to attach any importance to this circumstance of Alexander's birth. He does not blame Olympias for betraying her husband, making it clear that she was an innocent victim of the Egyptian sorcerer. Nor does he question the virtue of African women. Needless to say, the legitimacy of Agramante's birth is never called into doubt.

As we saw in Chapter I, it is possible that Boiardo began composing Book II when Borso d'Este was still alive: the lines in which the poet announces the return of 'Alegreza e Cortesia' [Joy and Courtesy] (II i 2,3) to Ferrara could be a reference to Borso's coronation as Duke of Ferrara in April 1471. If so, it is worth bearing in mind that Alexander must have been one of Borso's personal heroes, a fact that has completely escaped the attention of Boiardo scholars. Borso was buried in a magnificent tomb in the Certosa cemetery, which featured his portrait flanked by Latin epitaphs by Tito Strozzi, Rinaldo Cosa, and Battista Guarino il Vecchio. Cosa compared him to Alexander and two other ancient military leaders: 'Caesar, Alexander, tumulo Traianus in isto | clauduntur, nec treis tenet Urna, sed unum [...] [Caesar, Alexander and Trajan are buried | in this tomb, but the Urn contains one body, not three].[59] This was not the first time the vainglorious Borso was likened to the Macedonian warrior. In 1452, at the beginning of his reign, Michele Savonarola (Girolamo Savonarola's grandfather) implicitly compared him to Alexander in his *Del felice progresso di Borso d'Este*.[60] A decade later Ugo Caleffini did so explicitly in his *Cronica de la Ill.ma et Ex.ma Casa da Este* ('Ad uno Alexandro l'è someiante: | peccado a ridopia non habia signoria | per le suo cortesie tamante' [He is similar to an Alexander: | it is a pity that his state is not twice as large | for his many courtesies]).[61] In 1469 Carlo da Sangiorgio, one of Borso's chamberlains,

---

58   Riccardo Bruscagli, 'Prove di commento all'*Orlando Innamorato*', *Studi italiani*, 1 (1989), 5–29. Bruscagli shows that, despite his humanistic culture, in recounting Alexander's life Boiardo mostly draws on medieval rather than classical sources.

59   Marcantonio Guarini, *Compendio historico dell'origine, accrescimento, e prerogative delle chiese, e luoghi pij della città, e diocesi di Ferrara* (Ferrara: Vittorio Baldini, 1621), p. 166.

60   See Michele Savonarola, *Del felice progresso di Borso d'Este*, ed. by Maria Aurelia Mastronardi (Bari: Palomar, 1996), p. 84.

61   Ugo Caleffini, *Cronica de la Ill.ma et Ex.ma Casa da Este*, reproduced in Antonio Capelli, 'Notizie di Ugo Caleffini notaro ferrarese del secolo XV con la sua cronaca in rima di Casa d'Este', *Atti e mem. della R. Deputaz. di storia patria per le province modenesi e parmensi*, 2 (1864), 267–312 (pp. 273–312; see p. 291 for the cited lines). Caleffini traces the Este genealogy to the descendants of Emperor Constantine, mentioning amongst others (Charlemagne, Orlando etc) a certain Aimonte, who may or may not be the Almonte (whose name is sometimes spelt as Aimonte in chivalric romances, including the 1516 *Furioso*) of the *Aspramonte* legend (see *Cronica*, p. 274).

called him 'uno altro Alexandro de Macedonia' [a new Alexander of Macedon] in *Commemoratione del tractato et tradimento facto verso il clarissimo et excellentissimo principe duca Borso*, an account of Giovanni Lodovico Pio and Andrea da Varegnana's conspiracy against the Marquis of Ferrara.[62] Borso's library reflected his strong interest in Alexander: its 1467 catalogue featured an 'Alexandri Maximi Gesta', a 'Liber de Sestis Alexandri Imperatoris', and a 'Liber Alexandreydos'.[63] Nor was he alone in his desire to be celebrated as a new Alexander: his Aragonese relatives, whom Boiardo eulogizes in an ekphrastic digression in canto xxvii of Book II, presented their conquest of Naples as a feat of arms as astounding as Alexander's conquest of the world,[64] while Francesco Gonzaga (another admirer of Boiardo) would later have a series of Alexander frescoes painted in his palace at Marmirolo.[65]

Boiardo provides a glowing portrayal of Alexander. The modern reader of the *Inamoramento de Orlando* may be unduly disturbed by the reference to his 'aroganza' (*Inam.*, II i 5,4), mistakenly assuming that the poet accuses him of that vice. It has been argued that Boiardo sees him as a bad ruler whose boundless arrogance brought much suffering to the world.[66] However, 'aroganza' is not a particularly negative quality in the realm of chivalric literature, where it is often synonymous with 'fierce courage'. Chivalric authors, including Boiardo, use this term in descriptions of battles or duels. Ranaldo, for example, attacks the Saracens 'con molta arroganza' [very boldly] (*Inam.*, I iv 45,6), and Orlando, too, shows 'molta arroganza' [much

---

62    Carlo da Sangiorgio, *Commemoratione del tractato et tradimento facto verso il clarissimo et excellentissimo principe duca Borso*, cited in Marco Folin, 'Appendice 1: L'immagine di Borso in alcuni ritratti encomiaistici del suo tempo', in *Il Palazzo Schifanoia a Ferrara*, ed. by Salvatore Settis and Walter Cupperi (Modena: Panini, 2007), pp. 39–42 (p. 40).

63    For biographies of Alexander in the library of the Este rulers, see Giulio Bertoni, *La biblioteca estense e la coltura ferrarese ai tempi del duca Ercole I, 1471–1505* (Turin: Loescher, 1903), pp. 42, 215, 220–21, 235, 242, 249, 252; and Cavallo, *The World beyond Europe*, p. 273, note 50.

64    In 1443 Alfonso the Great made his triumphal entry into Naples followed by a procession of allegorical figures, 'including one of Alexander standing upon a revolving terrestrial globe' (Roy Strong, *Art and Power: Renaissance Festivals 1450–1650* (Woodbridge: Boydell Press, 1984), p. 44). The future Ercole I d'Este discovered Alexander in Naples, where he spent his youth: he read Pier Candido Decembrio's vernacular translation of Curtius's biography of Alexander while convalescing from an illness (Giovanni Andrea Barotti, *Memorie istoriche di letterati ferraresi* (Ferrara: Giuseppe Rinaldi, 1792), pp. 114–15). In 1473, Ludovico Carbone (the author of the wedding oration for Paula Strozzi and Zarabinus Turchi which we discussed in Chapter I) composed an epithalamium for the marriage of Eleonora of Aragon and Ercole, in which he compared the bride's father, King Ferrante of Naples, to Alexander, praising him for his clemency towards defeated enemies (Anthony F. D'Elia, *The Renaissance of Marriage in Fifteenth-Century Italy* (Cambridge, MA: Harvard University Press, 2004), pp. 60–61).

65    Molly Bourne, *Francesco II Gonzaga: The Soldier-Prince as Patron* (Rome: Bulzoni, 2008), pp. 194–95. Francesco's court poets, too, compared him to Alexander (ibid., p. 69), and in his 1520 oration for the first anniversary of Francesco's death Matteo Bandello stated that the late marquis had been born on the same day as Alexander of Macedon (ibid., pp. 22–23).

66    Cavallo, *The Romance Epics of Boiardo, Ariosto, and Tasso*, pp. 34–44; Eadem, *The World beyond Europe*, pp. 87–88. See also Maiko Favaro, 'Tra "aroganza" e "inclyte vertute": le ambiguità di Alessandro Magno nell'*Inamoramento de Orlando*', in *La 'virtù eccellentissima': Eroe e antieroe nella letteratura italiana da Boccaccio a Tasso*, ed. by Vincenzo Caputo (Milan: FrancoAngeli, 2017), pp. 33–42 (pp. 34–36).

FIG. 3.1. Master of the Griselda legend, *Alexander the Great* (356–323 BC) (*c.* 1493–94). The Henry Barber Trust, The Barber Institute of Fine Arts, University of Birmingham

pluck] (*Inam.*, I xxiv 56,6) on the battlefield.[67] It would be wrong to overinterpret the lines in which we read that Alexander 'ebe il mondo tuto quanto aflito | e visto il mar e il ciel per sua aroganza' [had defeated all the world | and boldly toured the sea and sky] (*Inam.*, II i 5,4–5), as they simply mean that Alexander was a warrior of intrepid heart who conquered the entire world and then tried to pierce the secrets of the sea and the sky. It is true that 'aflito' could be translated as 'devastated', but in the context of a chivalric romance, where war is romanticized, it loses some of its negative charge. In any case, in the frescoes in the palace of Biserta — which recall a similar cycle of frescoes in the Castle of Noble in the *Entrée d'Espagne* (10406–34), but also make one think of the tapestries and other artwork depicting scenes from Alexander's life that decorated the palaces of Renaissance nobles, such the tapestries in the Gran Sala of Castel Nuovo in Naples, those owned by Cardinal Francesco Gonzaga or the *spalliera* portrait of Alexander which was part of the *spalliere* cycle of worthy men in the Piccolomini palace in Siena [FIG. 3.1] — Alexander's military campaigns are presented not as senseless acts of agression but as dazzling feats of arms (each of them is 'bela a·rriguardare' [beautiful to see] (28,2)), and Alexander is portrayed as a bold and chivalrous knight who sees war as an opportunity to show his valour and who abhors traitors.[68] His humanity manifests itself in his treatment of the defeated enemies. He punishes Bessus who treacherously murdered Darius ('ma ben lo paga il Re di tanto errore' [but the king pays him for his fraud] (24,8)), and he treats Porus with utmost *cortesia* ('vivo lo prende e com'hom di valore, | poi che l'ha preso il lassa a grande honore' [takes him alive, but since he's valiant, |

67    Many more examples of the use of the term 'arroganza' in a positive sense can be easily added. In the opening canto of the *Spagna ferrarese* King Salamone enthusiastically supports Charlemagne's decision to declare war on the Spanish Saracens, saying that he will follow Orlando 'con la mia gente. || Otto milia Breton soto mia insegnia, | giente ardita, piena d'arogança, | che di combatar nium no ne sdegnia' [with my people. || Eight thousand Bretons under my banner, | audacious people, full of boldness, | all of them most eager to fight] (*Spagna F*, I 11,8–12,1–3).

68    The 'Alexander the Great' tapestries in Castel Nuovo are mentioned by the Florentine humanist Pier Andrea da Verrazzano in a work dedicated to Beatrice of Aragon (1474–1475). His description of the Gran Sala is reproduced in Bianca de Divitiis, 'Castel Nuovo and Castel Capuano in Naples: the Transformation of Two Medieval Castles into *"all'antica"* Residences for the Aragonese Royals', *Zeitschrift für Kunstgeschichte*, 76 (2013), 441–74 (pp. 471–72). As for Cardinal Francesco Gonzaga's pieces, they could have been similar to the famous tapestries which Philip the Good Duke of Burgundy bought from Pasquier Grenier of Tournai in 1459. One of them depicted the battle between Alexander and Porus. We know that he brought it with him to Bologna (where he moved to in July 1471) and that one Bolognese chronicler was greatly impressed by its beauty and dynamism (see David Chambers, *A Renaissance Cardinal and his Worldly Goods: the Will and Inventory of Francesco Gonzaga (1444–1483)* (London: Warburg Institute, 1992), pp. 81–82, and also pp. 150 and 161 for Alexander-related items in the inventory of Francesco Gonzaga's goods). Boiardo and Tito Strozzi (whose *Borsias*, too, traces Borso's genealogy to Alexander) could have heard about or seen these tapestry panels when they accompanied their lord on his triumphal journey to Rome: in April 1471 the cardinal resided in Rome and he played an important role during Borso's visit. For a detailed overview of the iconographic tradition of Alexander in Renaissance Italy see Claudia Daniotti's forthcoming monograph *Reinventing Alexander: Myth, Legend, History in Renaissance Italian Art* (Turnhout: Brepols, 2021), which is based on her doctoral thesis 'On the Cusp of Legend and History: The Myth of Alexander the Great in Italy between the Fifteenth and Sixteenth Century' (The Warburg Institute, 2016).

he lets him go with many honours] (26,7–8)). There is unmistakable admiration in the narrator's voice when he lists Alexander's many exhibitions of bravery, from his defeat of Darius's enormous armies to his killing of a poisonous basilisk to his descent into the depths of the ocean in a glass case. Further on in the poem, the narrator mentions Alexander in the company of Caesar, rejoicing at the fact that *Memoria* [Memory] has preserved their 'valor [...] | l'ardir e 'l senno e l'inclyte vertute' [valor [...] | their daring, their minds, their famed virtue] (*Inam.*, II xxii 1,6–7).[69]

Boiardo's Alexander and his colourful adventures bring to mind the Alexander of medieval romances. At the same time, he resembles the great Saracen warriors of Book I of the *Inamoramento de Orlando*. Boiardo is much more interested in his chivalric virtues than in the political significance of his conquests. Like Gradasso, Alexander is not motivated by a lust for power. The driving force behind his military campaign is his love of glory and his desire to make the most of life. Like Agricane and Sacripante, he is not insensible to female charms. He gives his heart to the beautiful Helidonia, which is the ultimate proof of his nobility.[70] His death is seen as a tragedy ('poi tuto 'l mondo è in guerra e gran martoro' [then all the world was war and woe] (I i 29,8)), and his murderer, Antipater, is condemned in no ambiguous terms.

Alexander, thus, is a fitting ancestor for the Este. So are his sons — Sonniberra, Atamandro, and Argante — who are born from his union with Helidonia. If Alexander distinguished himself as a warrior, they excel in the art of statesmanship. Together, the brothers unify Africa, a culturally diverse part of the world, without any bloodshed:

> e tre germani presser signoria
> de Africa tuta (comm'ï ho contato)
> e la rivera dela Barbarìa
> e la terra de' negri in ogni lato;
> né per prodeza, né per vigoria,
> né per gran séno acquistàr tuto il stato,
> ma la natura sua, ch'è tanto bona,
> tirava ad obedirli ogni persona.

> [and these three brothers held the rule,
> as I have said, of Africa
> and all the coast of Barbary
> and border lands where black men lived.

---

69    Caesar too enjoyed an excellent reputation in Estense Ferrara. During Borso's coronation in 1471 Pope Paul II compared him to Caesar (Vincenzo Farinella, 'I pittori, gli umanisti, il committente: problemi di ruolo a Schifanoia', in *Il Palazzo Schifanoia a Ferrara*, pp. 83–141 (p. 108)).
70    This story may be Boiardo's invention, as Helidonia (Elidonia) does not appear in any of the known biographies of Alexander. According to the tradition, Alexander's beloved wife is the beautiful princess Roxane. Interestingly, the lavishly illuminated Borso Bible (1455–1461) contains a miniature depicting a white-bearded, aged Alexander dividing his empire between his generals on his deathbed, a figure that could not be more different from the young and passionate lover imagined by Boiardo (see MS 423 of the Biblioteca Estense, Modena, fol. 110ʳ). I am grateful to Claudia Daniotti for bringing this image to my attention.

> They did not win their state by strength,
> by wisdom or by vigour, but
> by excellence of character,
> which prompted men's obedience.]
>               (*Inam.*, II i 11)

*Cortesia*, a virtue they inherited from their father, is key to their political success. It proves to be a more important quality than *prudentia* [prudence], which Boiardo identifies as the cornerstone of Cyrus's rule in his translation of Xenophon's *Cyropaedia*.[71] *Cortesia* is a distinguishing trait of Alexander's progeny. Later in the poem, Boiardo implicitly compares Ercole to Alexander's sons, saying that if he set his mind upon enlarging his state, even birds, let alone men, would eagerly accept him as their lord (*Inam.*, II xxi 59).[72]

The first decades in the history of the 'alta iesta [...] | dela casa affricanna' [noble dynasty [...], | of the great lords of Africa] (*Inam.*, II i 13,4–5) are a glorious period. But how does Boiardo explain the events of the *Aspramonte*? How does he account for the fact that Almonte, Alexander's descendant and thus a distant relative of the Este, murdered Rugiero of Risa? Unwilling to confront the past, he and his characters do not to dwell upon this tragedy. The treacherous conquest of Risa is evoked (and condemned) by the King of Garamantha during the first military assembly in Biserta, but Almonte's role in the death of Rugiero of Risa is never mentioned, as if this were a taboo subject at Agramante's court. Rugiero, the dynastic protagonist of Books II and III, either does not know the full story or thinks that his Christian uncle played a much more sinister role (which, as we have seen, is true of Andrea da Barberino's *Aspramonte*, where Almonte violates the chivalric code in a moment of weakness, while Beltramo carefully plans the betrayal). Recounting his genealogy to Bradamante, he blames Beltramo, his father's brother, for the death of his parents: 'Beltramo, el perfido inhumano, | tradite el patre [Duke Rampaldo of Risa] e il suo franco germano [Rugiero II]' [inhuman, infamous Beltramo | betrayed his father and his brave brother] (*Inam.*, III v 33,7–8). Moreover, in order to distance even further his Africans from the shameful deeds of the protagonists of the medieval legend, Boiardo makes Agramante the son of Troiano, Almonte's brother and a secondary Saracen character who does not take part in the conquest of Risa in any of the Italian *Aspramonti*. In both Andrea da Barberino's romance and in the fifteenth-century *Aspramonte* Troiano's greatest shortcoming is his irascibility, which is an almost excusable flaw in a warrior.[73] His quick temper contrasts with Almonte's civility, but, of the two brothers, it is Troiano who retains his integrity.

71   '[...] sì governò cum tal prudentia Cyrro che da li amici in honorevole amore, da li victi e subditi in amorevole riverenza fu tenuto' [Cyrus governed with such prudence that he was honoured and loved by his friends and held in affectionate esteem by those whom he defeated and his subjects] (Boiardo, *La pedìa*, p. 131).

72   In her comment to the stanza in question, Tissoni Benvenuti suggests that Boiardo could be gently rebuking his duke for not trying to add new territories to his state.

73   Andrea da Barberino describes Troiano as an arrogant man who 'non teneva nessuna religione in sé' [did not believe in any religion] e 'poca verità aveva in bocca' [had little truth in his mouth] (*Aspramonte A*, III ciii 5–7). And yet Troiano does not commit any truly ignoble actions.

In fact, it is his Christian opponents who transgress the chivalric code in his story. Introducing Agramante, Boiardo reminds us that Troiano

> [...] in Bergogna col Conte d'Anglante
> combaté, e con dui altri sopra il piano:
> ciò fo don Chiaro e 'l bon Rugier Vasalo;
> da lor fo morto, e certo con gran fallo.

> [[...] in Burgundy fought the Count of Anglante,
> and then two other knights on the plain,
> namely Don Chiaro and good Rugiero the Vassal —
> these three killed him, a shameful act.]
> (*Inam.*, II i 14,5–8)

In these lines, Boiardo alludes to Orlando's victory over Troiano, one which Orlando is proud of (he boasts about it at *Inam.*, I xviii 47,1–2), but which nevertheless is quite ambivalent, to say the least.[74] In Andrea da Barberino, Orlando challenges Troiano to another duel after Troiano has knocked senseless both him and Don Chiaro; armed with the Durindarda, he chops off the Saracen's hands, but the wounded enemy carries him towards the river with the intention of drowning him. At this point Orlando's friends feel compelled to intervene: Riccieri Vassallo (not to be confused with Riccieri II of Risa) strikes Troiano on his helmet, while Ansoigi d'Avernia cuts off his head. In the fifteenth-century *Aspramonte*, as in the passage from the *Inamoramento de Orlando* cited above, Orlando is rescued by Rugieri Vassalo and Don Chiaro: the former, 'come buon christïan nobile et caro' [as a good Christian, noble and dear] (*Aspramonte*, XXI 79,2 [fol. oviiiᵛ]), plunges his lance into the Saracen's stomach and the latter finishes him off with a blow to his head. By drawing attention to this unheroic episode at the very beginning of Book II, Boiardo shows that Christians too can sometimes fail to observe chivalric laws, suggesting that the conquest of Risa is not the only crime against chivalry in the *Aspramonte*.

It would have been understandable if Agramante had decided to go to war to avenge his father. As mentioned earlier, revenge is the main reason Agolante and Almonte sail to Europe in the fifteenth-century *Aspramonte*. Instead, Agramante's decision to attack the Christians is driven by his belief that a life without glory is not worth living:

> '[...] doppo la morte sol fama ne avanza,
> e veramente son color tapini
> che d'agrandirla sempre non han cura,
> perché sua vita poco tempo dura.'

---

74   Boiardo's disapproval of the manner in which Troiano was killed is shared by Ranaldo who calls it a 'tradimento' [betrayal] during his quarrel with Orlando in Book I: ' "Dàte forsi arroganza il re Troiano? | Né ti vergogni di quella novella, | ch'anchor ferito a morte e senza mano | te trasse a tuo dispetto dela sela? | Tri insieme l'occidesti in su quel piano! | Va', ti nascondi! Va', vil feminella! | Tra li homini apparer haï ardimento, | e sei conduto a tanto tradimento?" ' ['Perhaps you boast of King Troiano? | What a disgraceful episode! | Mortally wounded — and without | a hand! — he still unsaddled you | before you killed him on the field. | Cowering wench! Hide yourself! Leave! | How can you show yourself to men | when you've performed such villainy?'] (*Inam.*, I xxvii 18).

['[...] only renown can outlive death,
and they are truly miserable
who don't incessantly attend
to fame: life hurries to its end.']
(*Inam.*, II i 35,5–8)

Territorial aggrandizement is clearly of secondary importance to Agramante. He does not urge the Africans to regain Alexander's lost empire, but rather urges them to emulate his spirit of adventure. All he wants is martial glory, and in this respect he is similar to his famous ancestor, who is evoked at the culminating moment of his address to his thirty-two vassal kings:

'Né vi crediati che Alexandro il grande,
qual fo principio dela nostra iesta,
per far conviti de optime vivande
vincesse il mondo, né per star in festa.
Hor per tuto il suo nome si spande,
e la sua storia, ch'è qui manifesta,
mostra ch'al guadagnar d'honor si suda
e sol s'acquista con la spada nuda.'

['Don't think that great Alexander, who
was founder of our family's house,
subdued the world for festivals
or banquets of the finest fare.
His name is now known everywhere.
His history, depicted here,
reveals that honour is obtained
by sweat — it is gained with unsheathed blades.']
(*Inam.*, II i 36)

The desire to achieve glory is central to the Africans' military campaign in Andrea da Barberino's romance, but there is an important difference between Almonte's dream of glory and Agramante's. Unlike Almonte, who believes that the Saracen gods have chosen him to be king over Europe, Agramante does not think of himself as a new Aeneas. Although at the very end of his speech he says that the military expedition against the Christians will enable them to 'agrandir la legie di Macone' [aggrandize Macone's law] (37,8), he places his trust in his sword and in his friends' swords rather than in his deities, towards whom he can be shockingly irreverent (in a burst of bravado, he exclaims that he will fight in Paradise after he has conquered the entire world). Though not a hardened atheist, he certainly does not see himself as someone entrusted with a divinely ordained mission. Rather he is determined to follow the ideal of *vita activa* [active life], just as Alexander did in all of his audacious undertakings.

How far does Agramante succeed in his attempt to imitate Alexander? On the one hand, his war is doomed to failure: as his grey-haired vassals warn him already in the opening of Book II, it will bring Africa to ruin. On the other hand, he embarks on an exciting adventure and he and his knights encounter countless opportunities to prove their valour. Forty cantos later, when the poem is abruptly interrupted, the war between Saracens and Christians has effectively just begun and Agramante's defeat is only a distant prospect. In the light of Boiardo's romanticized representation of warfare, his recklessness is, if not forgivable, at least understandable.

Agramante may not be a wise king or an exceptional military leader, but he certainly cannot be called a parody of Alexander. He takes after his forefather in fearlessness, in humanity and in *cortesia*, which is not the superficial *cortesia* practised by some of the Saracen protagonists of the *Aspramonte* narratives, but an earnest commitment to this ideal. He is generous with his wealth (he gives opulent presents to his vassals: 'Quel re cortese avìa tanto donato | che ciascadun de lui ne va contento' [The gracious king has made such gifts | that everyone goes off content] (*Inam.*, II iii 44,5–8)), hospitable to strangers (he receives Brandimarte and Fiordelisa with princely honours), affectionate to friends and relatives (he weeps when he thinks that Rodamonte has died, and he is extremely fond of Rugiero), and not at all cruel despite his 'crudel viso' [cruel face] (II i 15,4).[75] This is what distinguishes him from Xerxes, to whom he has been compared by a number of critics.[76] While, as Michael Murrin shows, Boiardo draws on classical accounts of Xerxes' disastrous war against the Greeks — and in particular on Herodotus, whose *Histories* he translated — in the episodes of the military assemblies and in the catalogue of the African army, Agramante is a much more tolerant and kind-hearted ruler than his Persian counterpart.[77] The latter conforms to the Western stereotype of the Oriental despot. He has the sea whipped and the engineers decapitated when the bridge over the Hellespont is destroyed by a storm. He has a young man sundered into two parts because his father asked him to exempt his son from military service (Herodotus, *Histories*, Book VII). By contrast, Agramante exercises his power with compassion and wants to be loved rather than feared by his subjects. It is revealing that the word 'love' surfaces several times in his very first speech ('quanto cognosco più che voi me amati | [...] | più debo amarvi' [as much, I know, as you love me | [...] | so must I love you] (*Inam.*, II i 34,3–5); 'se amati ponto me, vostro segnore' [if you have love for me, your lord] (37,5)). When a drunken musician reproaches him for postponing his expedition against Charlemagne ('E diceva: "Macon sia maledeto | e la Fortuna trista e mischredente, | qual non riguarda cui facia signore, | et obedir conviensi a chi è pegiore!"') [and cried, 'May God Macon be damned! | May Fortune be cursed and distrusted — | for carelessly she chose our lord! | We must obey the one who's worst!'] (II xxviii 45,5–8)), he does not punish him ('ne fo però batuto né ripreso' [they didn't beat him or detain him] (48,3)), as he understands that the man is intoxicated.

The episode of the drunken musician is not so much Boiardo's response to Herodotus as his attempt to rewrite Andrea da Barberino's *Aspramonte*, his main intertext, where Troiano tries to murder the buffoon who said that Charlemagne was a better ruler than Agolante. Agramante has inherited his father's courage,

---

75    The episode in which Agramanate gives presents to his vassals recalls a similar episode in the fifteenth-century *Aspramonte*, where Agolante distributes gifts at the end of the military council (*Aspramonte*, V 39–41 [fol. bvii$^r$]).

76    See Murrin, 'Agramante's War', and Cavallo, *The World beyond Europe*, p. 88.

77    Murrin, 'Agramante's War', especially pp. 57–68.

but not his explosive and violent temper. He has inherited his uncle Almonte's affability, but not his fear of losing. While Almonte could not come to terms with the fact that he had been defeated by a Christian knight, Agramante accepts his defeat in the joust at the foot of Mount Carena. Unhorsed by Rugiero who is wearing Brunelo's armour, he is saddened by his fall, but he congratulates Brunelo on his victory and praises his prowess, declaring himself lucky to have him in his army. Similarly, Boiardo makes it clear that Almonte's son Dardinello — a minor yet charismatic character — has inherited only his father's positive qualities: he is 'dextro nel'arme come avesse l'ale, | molto cortese, costumato e belo, | né si potrebbe aponervi alcun male' [agile in arms, like one with wings, | handsome, refined, and courteous; | nothing bad can be said of him] (*Inam.*, II xxii 26,4–6), the last line, with its allusion to Almonte's story, reassuring the readers that the young man has no secret flaws.

As for Rugiero, from him Boiardo expects deeds worthy of Alexander: 'se con tieco avrai questo Barone', the King of Garamantha tells Agramante, 'in Franza acquistarai pregio et honore | e cacciarai più volte il re Carlone' [if this Baron comes with you | you'll gain respect and praise in France | and often you'll defeat King Charles] (II i 70,2–4). While Agramante and Dardinello are destined to die, in the unwritten ending of the poem Rugiero's conversion and marriage guarantees the survival of Alexander's bloodline. Boiardo describes him in superlative terms. He is the knight 'che di prodeza in terra non ha pare' [whose prowess is unmatched on earth] (*Inam.*, II i 69,6); he is endowed with an acute sense of justice (he saves Brunelo from the gallows and he rushes to Bradamante's defence when she is attacked by a group of Saracens); his *cortesia* is such that Turpino finds it hard to believe that he is a Saracen ('Né credo mai che tanta cortesia | potesse dar Natura ad un Pagano' [I don't believe that nature gave | such courtesy to a Saracen] (III iv 45,1–2)). Like Alexander, he has a warm heart that is open to love. His meeting with Bradamante reveals the 'Arthurian' side of his personality, making the reader wonder whether the two will eventually tie the knot.[78]

And yet, even though from the very beginning of Rugiero's story we know that he will convert to Christianity, Rugiero is deeply attached to his Saracen identity, more so than his counterparts in the chivalric tradition. Sons of Saracen women and Christians knights are not a rare sight in chivalric literature: Dodone (whom we discussed in Chapter II), Galleant in the *Fatti de Spagna*, and Guidone Salvagio in the *Regina Ancroia* and in the *Innamoramento de Guidon Salvaggio* are just some of them.[79] Such characters grow up in *Paganìa* and are usually unaware of the fact their mother

---

78    As Riccardo Bruscagli points out, 'Ruggiero is a brand new hero [...] He does not need to convert from the exclusive service of war to the service of love, like Orlando and the other paladins: the union of arms and love will come to him as a natural, non-traumatic, non-shocking condition' (Riccardo Bruscagli, 'Ruggiero's Story: the Making of a Dynastic Hero', in *Romance and History: Imagining Time from the Medieval to the Early Modern Period*, pp. 151–67).

79    To these half-Saracens we can add Povero Avveduto in Andrea da Barberino's *Storie nerbonesi*: he even tries to kill his Christian father, but decides to convert to Christianity when a friend tells him that the Saracens will murder him after he has slain all of his Christian relatives. This story forms the basis of the *Ciriffo Calvaneo*.

had a relationship with a Christian knight. In their adolescence they discover the truth and decide to meet their father. They are often portrayed as extraordinarily strong. Galleant, the son of Olivero and a Portuguese princess, is considered one of the best warriors in the world: it is he who inherits Donindarna (that is the famous sword Durindana) after Rolando's death. Guidon Salvaggio is only slightly inferior to his father Rinaldo. When his Saracen mother finally discloses the truth to him, he travels to France to meet Rinaldo and face him in a duel. Waiting for his father to turn up, he fights with many Christians, but not even Orlando manages to defeat him, their strength being more or less equal. What distinguishes Rugiero from Dudone, Guidone, Galleant and others is that Rugiero's Christian father is dead. Rugiero knows who he was and that he died in the Aspramonte war. He is proud of the Christian branch of his family tree, but he has no burning desire to see the part of the world where his Christian relatives lived. Africa is his home and he follows Agramante to France because he, too, is seduced by the dream of glory and eager to emulate their common ancestor Alexander rather than because he is undergoing an identity crisis and wants to find out the truth about his origins. Nor is he particularly interested in his dynastic mission: he may have traits of Virgil's Aeneas, but he does not see himself as such, not in the *Inamoramento de Orlando*.

Rugiero's only living relatives are Saracens: his cousins Agramante and Dardinelo, with whom he has an excellent relationship. He asks Agramante to knight him ('Fami, signor, ti prego, cavaliero' [I beg you, lord, make me a knight] (*Inam.*, II xxi 51,8)), and his request is granted without a moment's delay ('e cossì sarà fato adesso adesso!' [and so this will be quickly done!] (52,6)) and 'con molta festa' [with ceremony] (52,8). Rugiero's pledge of allegiance — the most sacred oath that a knight can swear — binds him to serve his Saracen lord until either of them crosses the great divide. In the final chapter of this study, we shall see whether and in what circumstances Ariosto's Ruggiero breaks it. For now, suffice it to say that, having been dubbed a knight, Rugiero fulfils one of his dreams, and Africa obtains a formidable warrior, one who does not need the Christian religion to reach the pinnacle of chivalry, as his victories against the Christians will take place before his conversion.

By giving a strong Saracen identity to his dynastic protagonist, Boiardo shows that Christian Europe owes a great deal to *Paganìa*, which in turn owes an immense debt to the ancient world. By giving Rugiero another ancient ancestor, Hector of Troy, from whom Rugiero descends through his Christian father, Boiardo departs from the chivalric tradition, where Saracens have a much closer relationship with antiquity than Christians. It is futile to speculate on whether Boiardo considers Hector to be a greater hero than Alexander: both are presented as exceptional warriors.[80] What must be stressed instead is that Boiardo divorces chivalry from religion, as some of the most striking examples of chivalric virtue are those given by non-Christian warriors, with Alexander being one of the most attractive chivalric models of the *Inamoramento de Orlando*.

---

80   Hector is held in high esteem by Christians and Saracens alike. According to Brandimarte, Agramante has earned himself the reputation of 'un altro Hector' [a new Hector] (*Inam.*, II xxviii 2,3).

## CHAPTER 4

❖

# Saracen Chivalry in Ariosto's *Orlando furioso*

Although Boiardo is never explicitly mentioned in the *Orlando furioso*, he had more influence on Ariosto than any other vernacular or classical author. Ariosto's debt to him goes far beyond the *Furioso*'s subject matter. So deep was his admiration for the Count of Scandiano that the task of bringing his poem to an end became the labour of his life. The *Inamoramento de Orlando* was not only his starting point, but also an unending source of inspiration, a text which he must have consulted countless times during the composition of his own poem, which he began in around 1505, eleven years after Boiardo's death. Yet Ariosto is not merely a competent imitator, but an original artist with a unique voice and a complex worldview. The *Furioso* may open with a clear allusion to the values celebrated by Boiardo ('Di donne e cavalier li antiqui amori, | le cortesie, l'audaci imprese io canto' [I sing of the bygone loves, the courteous deeds, | the audacious undertakings of ladies and knights] (*Fur.*, I 1,1–2 ABC)), but its ideological message is far from being straightforward. Ariosto's portrayal of human passions is more modern and realistic; he is more interested in the complexities and ambiguities of human relationships, more aware of the gap between chivalric literature and life. This affects the ways in which he represents both Christian and Saracen characters.

As the reader leaves the world of Boiardo's *Orlando* and steps into the first canto of Ariosto's, he or she is bound to feel slightly disoriented. We need time to get used to the new personalities of Boiardo's characters who, as has been observed by Pio Rajna and other critics, now appear to be older, deprived of their adolescent spontaneity and at times surprisingly cynical.[1] Love emerges as an ambivalent force when Sacripante, a model lover in the *Inamoramento de Orlando*, suddenly decides to take Angelica by force, telling himself that 'a-ddonna non si può far cosa | che più soave e più piacevol sia' [there is nothing that a woman finds | more delectable and pleasing] (*Fur.*, I 58,4–5 ABC). Angelica expects him to continue to serve her faithfully and selflessly, but Sacripante has changed. He is no longer a gullible suitor, a Petrarchan wooer: beneath his 'servitù amorosa [...] bolle il violento

1   According to Rajna, Ruggiero 'si direbbe invecchiato di dieci anni almeno' [seems to be at least ten years older] (Rajna, *Le fonti dell'Orlando furioso*, p. 55). See also Emilio Zanette, *Conversazioni sull''Orlando furioso'* (Pisa: Nistri-Lischi, 1959), pp. 9–60.

impulso sessuale' [amorous servitude [...] burns violent sexual desire].[2] Whilst his gentle, self-sacrificing love made him a perfect knight in Boiardo's poem, this all-consuming physical passion neither increases his strength nor enhances his *cortesia*. Soon after he has made up his mind to pluck Angelica's 'rose', he is unhorsed by Bradamante and, as if that were not enough to undermine Boiardo's belief in the fortifying and ennobling power of love, he encounters Rinaldo and, challenged to combat in canto II, fails to dismount, even though Rinaldo is on foot.

Sacripante is not the only Saracen character to fall short of the chivalric values that underpinned the *Inamoramento de Orlando*. Mandricardo kidnaps Doralice (*Fur.*, XII 39–54 AB; XIV C) and steals Orlando's armour, taking advantage of his madness (XXII 58–59 AB; XXIV C). Rodomonte does not intend to keep his promise to respect Isabella's chastity (XXVII 17–18 AB; XXIX C). Ferraù tells outrageous lies about his past encounters with Orlando (X 48 AB; XII 44 C) and rides away with the paladin's helmet when he accidently finds it (X 64–66 AB; XII 60–62 C). Gradasso fails to bring Baiardo to the spot of his duel with Rinaldo (XXX 61–67 A; 65–71 B; XXXIII 89–95). Agramante breaks his oath when he interrupts the duel between Rugiero and Rinaldo (XXXV 17–18 A; 6–7 B; XXXIX 6–7 C). These episodes have led some scholars to argue that Ariosto establishes a clear-cut boundary between Christians and Saracens, representing the latter as inferior knights. Rajna, to quote but one of the adherents to this view, maintains that most of Boiardo's Saracens are robbed of their charisma in Ariosto's sequel: 'Delle carezze fatte agli eroi cristiani si dovrà sentire il contraccolpo nella rappresentazione dei cavalieri saracini [...] basterà adorare Maometto per essere, o poco o tanto, messi in mala vista' [The praise lavished on the Christian heroes will be counterbalanced by the representation of the Saracen knights [...] all those worshipping Muhammad will be cast in a more or less negative light].[3]

And yet the chivalric universe Ariosto creates is one where characters and events are often open to different interpretations; as John the Evangelist famously tells Astolfo, 'E se tu vuoi ch'el ver non ti sia ascoso, | tutta al contrario l'historia converti' [But if you want to know what really happened, | invert the story] (*Fur.*, XXXII 27,5–6 AB; XXXV C). Taken out of context, isolated from the rest of the poem's intricate plot, the above-mentioned transgressions of the chivalric code may seem to support Rajna's assessment of the portrayal of Saracens in the *Furioso*. However, as soon as one contextualizes them, it becomes clear that these Saracen knights are not necessarily more flawed than their Christian counterparts.

The *Inamoramento de Orlando* is a celebration of a code of chivalry based on love, courage, *cortesia*, honour and desire for adventure and glory, and some of its most charismatic protagonists are Saracens. Ariosto problematizes the concept of chivalry, portraying its ideals in a more critical manner and adopting a somewhat detached attitude towards his characters. The *Furioso* was composed during the Italian Wars, in a period marked by unprecedented violence and great political instability, when a

---

2    Paola Casella, 'Il funzionamento dei personaggi secondari nell'*Orlando furioso*: le vicissitudine di Sacripante', *Italianistica*, 36 (2006), 11–26 (p. 18)).
3    Rajna, *Le fonti dell'Orlando furioso*, p. 59.

number of voices, such as those of Niccolò Machiavelli and Francesco Guicciardini, offered bleak, pessimistic views of human nature. It has been read as a poem of 'crisis and evasion' that both engages with and aesthetically distances itself from the problems and texts of its age.[4] As we shall see, there is a certain undercurrent of sadness running through the *Furioso*, which is especially palpable in its last cantos. But Ariosto does not necessarily dismantle the chivalric ideals Boiardo believed in. We must bear in mind that the 1516 *Furioso*, the 40-canto version that already contains most of the episodes involving Saracens that feature in the 46-canto version, saw the light of day 'in un momento per certi versi festoso, specialmente se paragonato al clima che accompagnerà l'uscita dell'edizione del 1532' [in a moment that in some respects was joyful, especially if compared to the atmosphere in which the 1532 edition will be published].[5] Ferrara joined the League of Cambrai in 1509. In 1510 Pope Julius II excommunicated Alfonso I of Ferrara for refusing to join the Venetians against the French, and until the Pope's death in 1513 the future of Estense Ferrara was most uncertain. This does not mean, however, that a feeling of doom overcame the city. Alfonso and his brother and co-ruler Ippolito were not prepared to go down without a fight, and the wheel of Fortuna did eventually turn their way. In 1513 Ariosto's friend Giovanni di Lorenzo de' Medici was elected Pope Leo X, and although his conduct disappointed both Ariosto and his patrons, the imminent danger to Ferrara passed. In 1515 Francis I became the new king of France. The news of the ascension to the throne of this young and chivalrous king was greeted with enthusiasm in Ferrara, a long-standing ally of the French. In 1515–1516 many hoped — alas, in vain — that Francis would be able to re-establish peace on the Italian peninsula, putting an end to the period of chaos.[6]

These events must have influenced Ariosto's representation of Christians and Saracens, making him aware of how hopelessly romantic Boiardo's worldview was (Boiardo's muse, as is well known, abandoned him in 1482 and 1494, every time the threatening clouds of war gathered on the horizon), without, however, destroying his faith in humanity. That said, it would be misleading to read the *Furioso* as a faithful mirror of contemporary Italian and European history. In the first chapter of this book, I argued that the two *Orlandos* contained relatively few references to the Turkish threat and that the wars fought between Christians and Saracens in these poems had little to do with contemporary wars between Christians and Muslims. Similarly, it would be wrong to claim that Ariosto's Saracens represent the foreign invaders, both because of the close ties between Ferrara and France and because,

---

4    Albert Russell Ascoli, *Ariosto's Bitter Harmony: Crisis and Evasion in the Italian Renaissance* (Princeton: Princeton University Press, 1987); Idem, 'Faith as Cover-up: Ariosto's *Orlando Furioso*, Canto 21, and Machiavellian Ethics', in *I Tatti Studies in the Italian Renaissance*, 8 (1999), 135–70; Idem, 'Fede e riscrittura: il *Furioso* del '32', *Rinascimento*, 43 (2003), 93–130. See also Giorgio Padoan, 'L'*Orlando Furioso* e la crisi del Rinascimento', in *Ariosto 1974 in America: atti del congresso ariostesco, dicembre 1974, Casa italiana della Columbia University*, ed. by Aldo Scaglione (Ravenna: Longo, 1976), pp. 1–29; and Stefano Jossa, *Ariosto* (Bologna: Il Mulino, 2009), pp. 71–74.

5    Marco Dorigatti, 'Il presente della poesia: L'*Orlando furioso* nel 1516', *Schifanoia*, 54–55 (2018), 13–26 (p. 26).

6    For a detailed analysis of how Ariosto engages with contemporary history, see Dorigatti, 'Il manoscritto dell'*Orlando furioso* (1505–1515)'.

as will be shown later, the narrator's historical digressions do not really support such an interpretation. As I shall argue in this chapter, Ariosto neither idealizes nor demeans his Saracen characters, nor uses them as part of a political allegory, but rather he uses them to provide multiple perspectives on issues such as *fides*, love, duty, and honour and to explore a number of themes — including those of death, defeat and betrayal — that are merely hinted at in Boiardo's poem but that come to the fore in the last third of the *Furioso*.

In the previous two chapters we saw that Boiardo owes a huge debt to earlier chivalric literature. Despite the efforts of scholars such as Daniela Delcorno Branca and Eleonora Stoppino,[7] Ariosto is still often read in isolation from the Carolingian chivalric tradition, with some critics assuming that he had little interest in it and that, apart from the *Inamoramento de Orlando*, most of his sources were classical or humanist. My discussion will challenge this view. Although the main focus of this chapter is Ariosto's engagement with Boiardo, it also considers how his portrayal of Saracens could be indebted to other chivalric texts, including Andrea da Barberino's *Aspramonte*, the *Vendetta di Falconetto* (this little-studied sequel to *Falconetto* features in the 1497 inventory of Andreas Belfort's bookshop in Ferrara), Cieco da Ferrara's *Mambriano,* and Nicolò degli Agostini's sequels to Boiardo, that is his *Quarto libro* (1505) and his *Quinto libro* (1514).[8] This chapter is organized into three sections. The first examines the most obvious differences and similarities between the Saracen worlds in Boiardo's and Ariosto's poems, offering a general overview of Ariosto's

---

7    See 'Introduction', note 6.

8    On the *Vendetta di Falconetto* in Andrea Belfort's bookshop, see Andrea Canova, '*Vendetta di Falconetto* (e *Inamoramento de Orlando?*)', in *Boiardo, Ariosto e i libri di battaglia*, pp. 77–106 (p. 78). There is no doubt that Ariosto was familiar with Cieco's *Mambriano* and Agostini's *Quarto libro*, and it could be that he read Agostini's *Quinto libro* before 1516. Enrico Carrara rules out this possibility (Enrico Carrara, 'Dall'*Innamorato* al *Furioso*', in Idem, *Studi petrarcheschi ed altri scritti* (Turin: Bottega d'Erasmo, 1959), pp. 243–76 (p. 270)), but Gioacchino Paparelli suggests that Ariosto could have drawn on both Agostini's *Quinto libro* and Raffaele Valcieco's *Quinto libro* (see his 'Tra Boiardo e Ariosto: le Gionte all'*Innamorato* di Niccolò degli Agostini e Raffaele da Verona', in Idem, *Da Ariosto a Quasimodo: saggi* (Naples: Società Editrice Napoletana, 1977), pp. 34–47 (p. 36n); Idem, 'Una probabile fonte dell'Ariosto: la "Gionta" all'*Innamorato* di Raffaele da Verona', in *Saggi di letteratura italiana in onore di Gaetano Trombatore* (Milan: Istituto Editoriale Cisalpino-La Goliardica, 1973), pp. 343–56), while Rosanna Alhaique Pettinelli highlights a number of striking similarities between the *Furioso* and the *Quinto libro* (Rosanna Alhaique Pettinelli, 'Tra il Boiardo e l'Ariosto: il Cieco da Ferrara e Niccolò degli Agostini', *Rassegna della letteratura italiana*, 79 (1975), 232–78, later reprinted in her *L'immaginario cavalleresco nel Rinascimento ferrarese* (Rome: Bonacci, 1983), pp. 152–230). The relationship between the two sequels has recently been reexamined by Angela Matilde Capodivacca ('"Forsi altro canterà con miglior plectio"': l'innamoramento di Angelica in Ariosto e Niccolò degli Agostini', *Versants*, 59 (2012), 67–84), Anna Carocci ('Stampare in ottave: *Il Quinto libro de lo Inamoramento de Orlando*', *Ecdotica*, 12 (2015), 7–29 (pp. 26–29), and *La lezione di Boiardo: Il poema cavalleresco dopo L'Inamoramento de Orlando' (1483–1521)* (Rome: Vecchiarelli, 2018), pp. 89–94 and 110–27), and Maria Pavlova ('Nicolò degli Agostini and Ludovico Ariosto', in *'Dreaming again on things already dreamed'*, pp. 79–108). Capodivacca and Carocci arrive at opposite conclusions: the former argues that Ariosto draws on the *Quinto libro* in Angelica's story, while the latter suggests that it is Agostini who imitates Ariosto, as the *Furioso* enjoyed some circulation before 1516. My article provides a comprehensive overview of the similarities (including what might be textual echoes) between the 1516 *Furioso* and the *Quinto libro*, concluding that Ariosto could have seen Agostini's second sequel when he was composing his poem.

*Paganìa*. The second section explores the Saracens' contribution to the pivotal theme of love, while the remainder of the chapter is devoted to Agramante's disastrous war. Like the rest of the book, this chapter focuses on the 1516 version of the *Furioso*, taking into consideration all the significant adjustments and additions that we find in the 1521 and 1532 editions. The reason for this is both that the first *Furioso* is chronologically and linguistically closer to the *Inamoramento de Orlando* than the definitive third version, and that most of the changes and additions in the revised versions concern the Christian characters.

## From Boiardo to Ariosto

### Christians, Saracens and the rest

Like the *Inamoramento de Orlando*, the *Furioso* is a densely populated poem. It contains hundreds of characters, with the total number exceeding three hundred already in the first edition. Ariosto uses most of the characters who are still alive when Book III of the *Inamoramento de Orlando* is abruptly interrupted, and occasionally makes references to those who died (or were dead) in Boiardo's poem. At the same time, he introduces a significant number of new characters, many of whom are Christians and some of whom live in strange isolated spaces outside of both Christendom and *Paganìa*, such as the secluded kingdom of Alessandretta or the remote island of Ebuda, where only the gods of the ancients seem to be worshipped.[9] Although the Saracens occupy an important place in the universe of the *Furioso*, they no longer participate in nearly every adventure. Moreover, though painted with vivid colours on Ariosto's map, *Paganìa* is the setting of only some of the stories woven into the rich fabric of the poem.

As we saw in Chapter II, Saracens and Saracen converts to Christianity, including those who died in other chivalric narratives and now live in the narrator's and other characters' memory, constitute approximately two-thirds of the cast of the *Inamoramento de Orlando*. They are more than 218, while the Christians, that is, those who were born into the Christian religion, are about 102. In the *Furioso* there is no such discrepancy between Saracens and Christians. Their respective numbers are more or less equal in the 1516 edition: roughly 142 Saracens and ex-Saracens, and around 147 Christians.[10] In the 1532 version, however, the number

9    The inhabitants of the island of Ebuda believe that Proteus's wrath will be terrible should they fail to feed the Orca with the tender flesh of maidens. The Amazon-like women who live in Alessandretta stay true to the laws established by their Cretan foremothers. Although Ebuda borders with Christian territories (Ireland) and the kingdom of men-haters is geographically close to Saracen lands, the poet does not say whether the religion of Christ or that of Macone have reached these secluded states. All we know is that the laws or customs which go back to pre-Christian times still govern the life of the people who live there. It interesting to note that the connection between the Saracen world and ancient paganism is seriously undermined in Agostini's *Quinto libro*, where pagan gods openly support the Christians: when the remnants of Agramante's army board their ships to sail back to Biserta, the gods unleash a terrible storm in which all the infidels perish (*Quinto libro*, VII 43–59).

10    These numbers include the characters that take part in the story and those that are merely mentioned by the narrator or other characters. I have tried to make note of all the nameless characters

of Christian characters increases by several dozen, as Ariosto adds four stories which are set in Christian lands, namely Olimpia's story, the Rocca di Tristano episode, the Marganorre episode, and Ruggiero's adventures in Eastern Europe. In C, therefore, the Christians (195) outnumber the Saracens (143) by a considerable margin. There are no new Saracens in the 1532 *Furioso*: the number 143 is due to the fact the narrator briefly mentions Truffaldino (*Fur.*, XXIX 41,2 B; XXXI C), the treacherous King of Baldaca who met an inglorious end in the Albracà war when Ranaldo tied him to the tail of his horse and dragged him to death (*Inam.*, I xxvi 46–52). Ariosto's narrator assures us that Aquilante and Griphone (who defended the traitor in the *Inamoramento de Orlando*) no longer hold a grudge against Rinaldo. In A we were merely told that the 'discordie e liti' [disagreements and quarrels] (*Fur.*, XXIX 40,8) between these knights have been forgotten, whereas in B and C the author adds a stanza in which he explains their cause.

It could be that Ariosto was aware of the wide gap between Christians and Saracens in Boiardo's poem and tried to reduce it by giving more prominence to the Christian world. If, together with Tasso, we read the *Inamoramento de Orlando* and the *Furioso* as two halves of one very long chivalric romance,[11] the Christians' numerical superiority in C can perhaps be interpreted as a move towards greater symmetry. Interestingly, not only does Ariosto pay more attention to Christian characters, but he also 'corrects' the map that was drafted by his predecessor. While in the *Inamoramento de Orlando* Christian Europe is very small in comparison to the vast expanses of the Saracen lands, in the *Furioso* it grows in size, absorbing some of the territories of Boiardo's *Paganìa*. Thus, in the huge army that Rinaldo leads to France there are soldiers from the remotest corners of Northern Europe:

> Non dà soccorso a Carlo solamente
> la terra Inglese e la Scotia e la Irlanda,
> ma vien di Svetia e di Norvega gente,
> da Tile, e sin da la remota Islanda:
> da ogni terra, in somma, che là giace,
> nimica naturalmente di pace.
>
> [England, Scotland and Ireland
> are not the only lands to furnish help to Charles:
> troops have arrived from Sweden and Norway, too,
> from Thule and even from distant Iceland –
> in fact from all those regions, where
> the people are by nature warlike.]
>               (*Fur.*, IX 76,3–8 AB; X 88,3–8 C)

The final line of this stanza is borrowed from *Rvf*, XXVIII, where Petrarch expresses the hope that the Germanic peoples will turn their innate rage towards the Muslim enemy. In the context of a story set at the time of Charlemagne, the presence of

---

(hermits, servants, etc.) who make a small contribution to the plot of the *Furioso*. I have not counted the heroes of Arthurian romances (as they belong to a different cycle) or the Christian offspring of Bradamante and Ruggiero. See Appendix II for a comprehensive list of Ariosto's Saracens.
11    Tasso expresses this view in his *Discorsi dell'arte poetica* (see Torquato Tasso, *Discorsi dell'arte poetica e del poema eroico*, ed. by Luigi Poma (Bari: Laterza, 1964), p. 15).

Swedish and Norwegian men in a Christian army strikes us as anachronistic: the first attempts to convert the peoples who lived in the area of modern-day Sweden took place after Charlemagne's death, while the Christianization of Norway only began in 1000 AD. As we saw in Chapter I, chivalric literature is full of historical inaccuracies, but what is remarkable about this particular case is that in the *Inamoramento de Orlando* neither Sweden nor Norway has discovered the Christian faith yet. Their kings are Agricane's vassals and hence Saracens

> Vede là il forte Re dela Gotìa
> che Pandragon per nome era chiamato;
> vedi lo Imperator dela Rossìa,
> che ha nome Argante, et è sì smisurato;
> vedi Lurcone, et il fier Santarìa:
> il primo è di Norvega incoronato,
> il secondo de Sueza, e proximana
> ha la bandera de il Re de Normana.

> [You see Gotìa's mighty king –
> Pandragon he is called — and, there,
> you see the Russian emperor,
> a giant whose name is Argante.
> You see Lurcon and Santarìa:
> the first of these wears Norway's crown,
> the second Sweden's. Nearby is
> the standard of Normana's king.]
> 　　　(*Inam.*, I x 12)

Boiardo's Lurcone, Santarìa, and the King of Normana Brontino are all killed by Orlando five cantos later (*Inam.*, I xv 22–38), but the Christians do not colonize their kingdoms.[12] It remains unclear whether Ariosto was aware of the fact that he was contradicting the *Inamoramento de Orlando* by 'converting' these peoples or whether he simply did not reread carefully enough the cantos devoted to the Albracà war. Had he followed Boiardo, the new rulers of Sweden and Norway would have sent their troops to Mandricardo, Agricane's son and successor.

Although these Northern peoples now believe in Christ, their appearance is monstrous and their lifestyle is that of barbarians:

> Sedice mila sono, o poco manco,
> da le spelonche usciti e da le selve;
> hanno piloso il viso, il petto e il fianco,
> e dossi e braccia e gambe, come belve.
> Intorno a quel stendardo tutto bianco
> par che quel pian di lor lance s'inselve:
> così Moratto il porta, il capo loro,
> che vuol pingerlo poi con sangue Moro.

> [They have come out from their forests and lairs,
> and they number sixteen thousand, or nearly;

---

12   As Tissoni Benvenuti explains in her comment to *Inam.*, I x 12, Normana is part of modern-day Sweden.

they are as hairy as beasts, their faces, chests, flanks,
and backs, their arms and legs are covered in hair.
The plain has all the appearance of a forest
where their spears cluster thickly round their wide standard:
Morath, their chief, carries it,
waiting to dye it in Moorish blood.]
(*Fur.*, IX 77 AB; X 89 C)

Ariosto thus creates a kind of hierarchy of Christian peoples, with the French, the Italians, the English, and the Scots being clearly superior to their Northern co-religionists. The Saracens, especially the Africans and the Spaniards (who, as was shown in Chapter I, are portrayed as highly civilized in both Boiardo and Ariosto), are also unquestionably superior to the Germanic barbarians.[13] Paradoxically, there are more monstrous creatures in the Christian army that defends Paris than in the Saracen army that besieges it. Whereas in the *Inamoramento de Orlando* Saracen armies abound both in valiant knights and in giants and beast-like soldiers, in the *Furioso* the vast majority of Saracens have a human appearance. Even Marbalusto, a 'gigante' [giant] in Boiardo's poem (*Inam.*, II xxx 5,8), for Ariosto is simply a man of unusually large stature: 'quasi era gigante' [well-nigh a giant] (*Fur.*, XII 17,4 AB; XIV C). There are ugly creatures in Ariosto's *Paganìa*, but it is very difficult to tell whether they worship Macone. It is debatable, for example, whether the bloodthirsty giant Caligorante is a Saracen; some readers might think that he is too bestial to have a faith, to be considered a more or less rational creature. Similarly, if Boiardo's Horrilo seems to be a follower of Macone (he is called a 'Pagano' three times), Ariosto's Horrilo, 'che d'un folletto nacque e d'una fata' [offspring of a gnome and a fairy] (*Fur.*, XIII 47,8 AB; XV 66,8 C), is difficult to classify. Fairies, after all, worship their own god, Demogorgone, as Boiardo tells us in *Inam.*, II xiii 27–28.

*Old and new faces*

Although Ariosto does not let his infidels (and ex-infidels) dominate all the plot lines of his poem, their number is still relatively large. Out of the approximately 142 (or 143, counting Truffaldino) Saracens who feature in the *Furioso*, 93 are taken from the *Inamoramento de Orlando*, 5 are borrowed directly from other chivalric texts, and 45 seem to be invented by Ariosto. Boiardo therefore provides Ariosto with roughly two-thirds of his Saracen characters and all of the Saracen leading figures

---

13   According to Walter Moretti, Ariosto creates a dichotomy between Northern fury and Southern courtesy ('Nei termini del codice cavalleresco e umanistico si potrebbe dire che al "furore" delle genti settentrionali è opposta la "cortesia" delle genti meridionali. È infatti la componente letteraria cortese-cavalleresca, nella sua versione umanistica, a privilegiare nella rappresentazione ariostesca la "dolce" terra dei paladini di Carlo Magno, i paesaggi ameni d'Italia, e la Spagna con i suoi ambienti romanzeschi' [From the perspective of the chivalric and humanist code, one could say that the "fury" of Northern peoples is juxtaposed with the "courtesy" of Sourthern peoples. Indeed, it is the courtly-chivalric literary component, in its humanist version, that makes Ariosto prefer the "sweet' land of Charlemagne's paladins, Italy's pleasant landscapes, and Spain with its romance settings] (Walter Moretti, *Ariosto narratore e la sua scuola* (Bologna: Pàtron, 1993), p. 83)).

with the exception of Guidone Selvaggio, a Saracen convert to Christianity, to whom we shall return later. The fact that Ariosto does not enlarge the 'main crew' can be explained by his concern for the poem's structure; even one more Saracen protagonist could have created problems at the structural level, overcrowding the poem and making it harder to control all the narrative threads. Similarly, neither Nicolò degli Agostoni nor Raffaele Valcieco (a less successful continuator of Boiardo whose *Quinto libro* — a sequel to Agostini's *Quarto libro* — came out in March 1514, several months before Agostini's *Quinto libro*) introduce new Saracen 'superheroes' in their sequels, if we do not count Scardaffo, a sympathetic giant modelled on the eponymous hero of Pulci's *Morgante* who enters the narration in canto II of Agostini's *Quarto libro* and leaves it in canto IX of his *Quinto libro*.

Almost a quarter of the 93 Macone worshippers who feature in both Boiardo and Ariosto are already resting in their graves (in Argalìa's case, on the riverbed) when Ariosto reminds us of their exploits or calls them back to Earth as bodiless spirits. Apart from Truffaldino, these characters are: Aimonte (Ariosto's spelling of Almonte in the 1516 *Furioso*), Galaciella, Troiano and their father Agolante; Mambrino, who, as was said earlier, is a character in the *Cantari di Rinaldo*; Agricane and Argalìa, whose deaths are dark clouds on the bright sky of Book I of the *Inamoramento de Orlando*; Argosto, Calabrun d'Aragona, Dudrinasso, Folvirante, Gualciotto, Larbino, Maricoldo, Martasino, Mirabaldo, Pinadoro, Sinagone, Tanfirione and Tardocco, all of whom fall in Agramante's war in Books II and III. While most of these 21 Saracen ghosts receive only a brief mention in the *Furioso*, Argalìa takes part in a mini-episode in canto I, and the names of Agramante's late father and uncle are frequently on the lips of the narrator and other characters.[14]

This leaves us with 72 Saracens from the *Inamoramento de Orlando* who re-appear in Ariosto's poem well and alive. Out of approximately 218 Saracens who feature in Boiardo's poem, more than 100 have not yet departed to the world of shadows when the narration suddenly breaks off. The fact that in the *Furioso* we meet around two-thirds of these 'survivors' shows how attentively he read his predecessor's work, how intimately familiar he was with it. Apart from the main protagonists, these are above all Agramante's and Marsilio's entourage knights (Agricalte, Alzirdo, the Amirante, Analardo, Archidante, the Argalifa, Balinfronte, Balinverno, Baliverzo, Balugante, Bambirago, Baricondo, Bavarte, Branzardo, Brunello, Bucifaro, Dardinello, Doriconte, Dorilone, Doriphebo, Doristone, Falcirone, Farurante, Folicone, Folvo, Grandonio, Isoliero, Languirano, Malabuferso, Malgarino, Malzarise, Madarasso, Manilardo, Marbalusto, Matalista, Morgante, Prusione, Puliano, Serpentino, Sobrino, Soridano and Stordilano) as well as their and their enemies' ladies (Doralice, Horrigille), Ferraù's mother Lanfusa, and the characters who take part in the digressive episodes of Book III (Lucina and Norandino; Marsilio's daughter Fiordespina; Horrilo; Caligorante who is the chained giant we see in *Inam.*, III iii 21,7).[15] Ariosto proves to be a very attentive reader of Books II

---

14   On Argalìa's role in the *Furioso* see Anna Fontes Baratto, 'Fantôme et fantasme: l'apparition d'Argail dans le premier chant du *Roland furieux*', *Chroniques italiennes*, 69–70, nos 2–3 (2002), 39–63.

15   Ariosto makes virtually no mistakes when re-introducing Agramante's and Marsilio's knights

and III insofar as he mentions at least once nearly every Saracen character, however minor he or she might be, who is somehow involved in Agramante's war. Only a handful of such characters (four, to be precise) are left out, and, if truth be said, none of them is particularly important. Thus, the old king of Fiessa (Fez) who recommended Brunello to Agramante, does not make it into the *Furioso*, but in Ariosto's defence it could be said that Boiardo forgets about him after *Inam.*, II v 26. Scombrano, the experienced pilot who tries to persuade Rodamonte to wait a few days before setting sail for the Christian shores (*Inam.*, II vi 5–9), is not in Ariosto's poem either, but it is not clear whether he survived the terrible storm which destroyed part of Rodomonte's fleet. In any case, he is merely a pilot, not a king or a knight. Some readers might be disappointed not to find Larbino's sweetheart Calidora amongst Ariosto's Saracens, considering that her new lover is Isolieri (*Inam.*, II xviii 4), one of Marsilio's knights. It could be, however, that time cured Isolieri of his passion, since there is no mention of Calidora in Book III (even if the fact that neither Doralice nor Horrigille appear in Book III does not prevent Ariosto from using these heroines in the *Furioso*). Finally, Ariosto does not take the trouble to tell us whether Astolfo's *Blitzkrieg* in Africa affected Gordaneto, the King of the Arabs (and head of the nomad tribes), but this rebellious king is merely mentioned *en passant* in the *Inamoramento de Orlando*: Boiardo's narrator observes that he does not participate in Agramante's expedition, as he has not sworn allegiance to him (*Inam.*, II xxii 32–33). Although Gordaneto does not feature in the *Furioso*, there are several references to the 'Arabi' over whom he is supposed to reign.

Many more knights and damsels could have re-appeared in the *Furioso* given that they are not yet dead at the end of Book III. However, Ariosto ignores the vast majority of the Saracen characters who in Boiardo exist outside the plotline centred on Agramante's war. Some of them, it must be said, seem to have been forgotten by Boiardo himself long before Book III. For example, the charismatic giant Alfrera, who is one of the most impressive warriors in Gradasso's army in Book I, is last mentioned in *Inam.*, I vii 50. He probably died of shame or vowed to spend the rest of his days in some dark cave in his native Taprobana after he had had to flee from the enemy because his giraffe, 'bestia pigra molto per natura' [a naturally sluggish beast] (*Inam.*, I vii 22,4), would not obey him. Although, as the narrator reassures

into his continuation of Boiardo's story. One could only note that Boiardo's Alanardo becomes Analardo, Maradasso turns into Madarasso, and that Balinfronte (Ariosto gives Boiardo's Balifronte an extra 'n') is the king of Cosca rather than Mulga. As Emilio Bigi points out in his commentary to XIV 23,1 C, the latter error is probably due to the fact that in *Inam.*, II xxii 22 Boiardo contradicts himself by giving Cosca to Cardorano, a king who is killed by Orlando. Ariosto corrects Boiardo at least on one occasion: in *Inam.*, II xxviii 52 Agramante orders Bucifaro and Folco to stay in Biserta and look after his kingdom in his absence, but in *Inam.*, III viii 11 we see both of them fighting by the gates of Paris; in the *Furioso* these knights do obey their lord's order and are in Biserta when Astolfo lays siege to the African capital. As far as spelling differences are concerned, they are relatively few: Rugiero becomes Ruggiero, Rodamonte turns into Rodomonte, and a few minor characters acquire or lose a consonant. Although most editors of the *Furioso* maintain that Ariosto's changes Boiardo's Argaliffa and Amirante into Largalifa and Lamirante, it is very likely that the letter *l* is merely an article (see Marco Dorigatti's note to XII 16,3 in his edition of the 1516 *Furioso*); if so, Ariosto's spelling remains faithful to Boiardo's.

us in *Inam.*, II vii 40, Gradasso eventually forgave him, Boiardo lost all interest in him after his disgraceful flight from the battlefield. Unsurprisingly, Alfrera does not feature in the *Furioso*. Nor do any of the following Saracens: Giasarte and Pilïasi (the son of the King of Arabia and the ruler of Rosìa who are unhorsed by Astolfo in the joust in Paris at I iii 8–9); Spinella da Altamonte (Marsilio's subject who is last seen fleeing in *Inam.*, I vii 19); Albarosa's brother Horisello (last mentioned at I xiii 34); Pandragon, the King of Gotia (who is grievously wounded by Orlando at I xv 23–24); Tisbina, a Babylonian *femme fatale* (last mentioned in I xvii 12); Uldano, the King of Danna (who is unhorsed by Brandimarte in I xviii 28); Horigilla's suitors Ariante (last mentioned in II v 19), Locrino and Uldarno as well as the evil knight Horingo who killed her brother (all of them are knocked off their saddles by Orlando: 'poi tutti comme morti li abandona' [he leaves them all behind for dead] (*Inam.*, I xxix 43,5)); Polifermo, the King of Orgagna (last mentioned in II ii 40); Adriano, Antiphor, Balano and Chiarione (a group of Saracen knights who fight valorously in the Albracà war and whom we last see in II ii 60–62); Rupardo (Brandimarte's enemy who besieges the Roca Silvana, as we are told in II xiii 12–13); Folderico's wife Leodila (last mentioned in II xiii 46–49, when we learn that she is Brandimarte's sister) and her lover Hordauro (Boiardo leaves him in I xxv 22 and we never find out whether he married Leodila); Caramano (Torindo's cowardly brother who manages to get away from Brandimarte in II xviii 30); the corsair Taridone (who, however, might be already dead when he is mentioned in II xix 22); Balsaldo and Morbeco (two Turkish knights who take part in the tournament in Cyprus in II xxii); Fiordelisa's abductor Fugiforca (last seen in II xxvii 31), her pleasure-seeking sister Doristela (last mentioned at II xxvii 32), their mother Perodia (last mentioned in II xxvii 38) and Doristela's faithful servant Gambone (who waves us goodbye in II xxvi 50).

It is impossible to know whether Boiardo planned to use any of these Saracens at some stage in Book III, but Ariosto decided that there was no need to continue their stories or indeed to remind the readers of their adventures. Only a very small number of similar characters briefly appear or are referred to in his poem: Hiroldo, Prasildo and a few members of Brandimarte's family, all of whom converted to Christianity in the *Inamoramento de Orlando*. These characters are relegated to the fringes of the universe of the *Furioso*. The inseparable friends (they leave Boiardo's poem in II xiv 7) are mentioned twice: when they are freed from Atlante's steel castle (*Fur.*, IV 40 ABC) only to be lured into the sorcerer's second trap (*Fur.*, XX 20 AB; XXII C).[16] We never find out what dream they had been pursuing or what happened to them after a blast of Astolfo's horn had broken the enchantment. In the new poem, Hiroldo and Prasildo are merely two names, but the fact that they join the ranks of Ariosto's Saracens and ex-Saracens means that their story moved him; the friendship between Cloridano and Medoro — Saracen soldiers — is perhaps

---

16    Iroldo and Prasildo also feature in Agostini's *Quinto libro*: in canto XIV they invite Feraguto to stay in their crystal palace, where there is a garden with a magic spring whose waters make one turn into whatever creature one wishes. They re-appear in Valcieco's *Quinto libro*, where their 'romance' adventures run parallel to the main epic plotline.

partly inspired by their devotion to each other (as well as by Virgil and, as I shall attempt to show later in this chapter, by Andrea da Barberino's *Aspramonte*). As far as Brandimarte's family is concerned, his servant Bardino (last seen in *Inam.*, II xiii 44) travels to Africa to tell him that his father Monodante has passed away and that his brother Giliante (who sails back to Damagir in *Inam.*, II xiii 53) wants him to come home and rule their kingdom (*Fur.*, XXXV 73 A; 62 B; XXXIX 62 C). Moreover, Dolistone, Fiordiligi's father, is implicitly referred to in *Fur.*, XXXIX 181 AB; XLIII 184 C.

Having briefly looked at the Saracen characters borrowed from the *Inamoramento de Orlando*, we must say a few words about the five characters whom Ariosto takes directly from the chivalric tradition. They are: Bianzardino, Chiariello, Gostanza, Guidon Selvaggio, and Sansonetto. Bianzardino, as we saw in Chapter II, is the Saracen who persuades Gano to betray Orlando and Charlemagne in the texts that deal with the Roncesvalles tragedy. Chiariello (Chiarello), Mambrino's brother, comes from the *Cantari di Rinaldo*, his name featuring in many other chivalric stories (for example the *Mambriano*: see I 15,2). Gostanza (Costanza) and her son Guidon Selvaggio feature in a number of anonymous fifteenth-century poems and prose romances, including the *Regina Ancroia* and the *Innamoramento de Guidon Salvaggio*, as well as in the *Storie di Rinaldo* (attributed to Andrea da Barberino). As for Sansonetto (Sansonet), he is one of the 'good' Saracens of the *Spagna* narratives, who first appears in the *Entrée d'Espagne*. The inclusion of these characters points to the fact that Ariosto was relatively well-versed in the Carolingian branch of the chivalric tradition and that, in any case, he read beyond the *Inamoramento de Orlando*. However, he does take liberties with some of these Saracens, rewriting parts of their stories and showing a surprising lack of concern for chronology, an attitude which would have scandalized Boiardo's fifteenth-century readers.

Ariosto's treatment of Bianzardino and Chiariello does not seem particularly original. Both of them are minor characters in the *Furioso*. They are mentioned once each: Bianzardino parades his troops in front of Agramante and Marsilio in *Fur.*, XII 14,6–8 AB; XIV C, while at XVIII 6,1–2 AB; XX C we are reminded that Rinaldo killed Chiariello and conquered his kingdom. In the *Chanson de Roland* Blancandrin rules over Valfonde, while the author of the *Fatti de Spagna* gives him Valnoyra. He is simply a 're' [king] in the *Spagna ferrarese* and in the *Morgante*. Ariosto makes him lead the soldiers from Avila, Plancencia, Salamanca, Zamora, and Palencia, adding those from Asturga in the 1532 *Furioso*. There are no references to the sinister role that he will play in the final stage of the war between Charlemagne and Marsilio, which probably means that Ariosto introduced this Saracen character because he happened to remember him rather than out of a desire to link his poem to the Roncesvalles narratives.

Compared to Bianzardino and Chiariello, Guidon Selvaggio and Sansonetto receive much more attention. What is quite striking about Ariosto's portrayal of these characters is that in the *Furioso* both of them come across as more 'Christian' than they are in the chivalric texts from which they are taken. Despite the fact that in the *Spagna* narratives Sansonetto converts to Christianity during Orlando's last adventure in the East, Ariosto's Sansonetto is already a Christian and Charlemagne's vassal when he meets Astolfo and showers him with presents. 'Orlando lo converse a nostra fede, | e di sua man battesmo ancho gli diede' [Orlando converted him to our faith | and even baptized him by his own hand] (*Fur.*, XIII 76,7–8 AB; XV 95,7–8 C), states the narrator, using the past tense where it would have been more correct to employ the future tense. Guidone's case is even more complex and intriguing. As we saw in Chapter III, in the *Regina Ancroia* — a highly popular work that was printed in at least seven editions between 1479 and 1516 — and in the *Innamoramento de Guidon Salvaggio* he sails to Europe to find Rinaldo (who had an affair with his mother Costanza many years ago); after having defeated a fair number of Christian knights and fought with his own father, he embraces Christianity.[17] Not only is Ariosto's Guidone the son of Amone (and therefore Rinaldo's half-brother), but he is comfortable with his Christian identity. In fact, he is very proud to belong to the Chiaramonte family:

> Io son Guidon, che ne le ripe estreme
> del freddo Euxino partorì Gostanza
> del medesmo, onde usciste, inclyto seme,
> che per quanto il sol scopre ha nominanza.
> Per voi [Rinaldo] veder e li altri nostri insieme,
> io mi parti' da la materna stanza [...]

> [I am Guidone, Constance gave me birth
> on the furthest shores of the cold Black Sea;
> I was conceived — like you — from the illustrious seed
> that is famous everywhere where the sun shines.
> I left my mother's house to see you
> and the rest of our family [...]]
> (*Fur.*, XXIX 31,1–6 AB; XXXI C)

Although he fights with Rinaldo and other Christian knights, he does not do so to find out if his Christian relatives are worthy of their fame, but rather, as Rajna puts it, 'giusta il costume degli Erranti, domanda giostra, e l'ottiene' [following the custom of knights errant, he requests a joust and is granted it].[18] When he realizes that the knight whom he could not defeat is Rinaldo, he is filled with joy and immediately apologizes for having dared to challenge him to a duel. Having been reunited with his paternal family, Guidone helps them to drive the Saracens out of France, but, surprisingly enough, there is no mention of his conversion to Christianity. While most early readers would have known that in the *Ancroia* Gostanza is a Saracen queen and that her son has been raised in the Saracen faith, modern readers, who meet Guidone for the first time, might assume that he has always been a Christian, that 'le ripe estreme | del freddo Euxino' [the furthest shores | of the cold Black Sea] are perhaps inhabited by people who believe in Christ. The narrator's silence regarding his Saracen past is puzzling and leaves room for different interpretations.[19]

17   On Ariosto's engagement with the story of Guidon Selvaggio, see Rajna, *Le fonti dell'Orlando furioso*, p. 417, and Stoppino, *Genealogies of Fiction*, pp. 72–73 and 153.
18   Rajna, *Le fonti dell'Orlando furioso*, p. 418.
19   In her discussion of this character, Stoppino suggests that, being a child born out of wedlock,

We should not dismiss out of hand the possibility that Ariosto could be drawing on some chivalric romance(s) in which Sansonetto's and Guidone's stories are different from how they are narrated in the above-mentioned chivalric texts. In any case, we should not automatically assume that his knowledge of the chivalric tradition was superficial, for he is faithful to the tradition in the case of Dudone, one of Boiardo's converted Saracens who becomes a born-and-bred Christian in the *Furioso*. In chapter II we said that Boiardo's portrayal of Dudone is consistent with his representation in the *Castello di Teris* and that he probably expected his audience to know that Dudone's mother was a Saracen giantess. Ariosto, however, turns a blind eye to Boiardo's allusions to this character's Saracen past and claims that his mother is none other than Beatrice's sister: Ruggiero 'sa che Armelina, che produtto havea | Dudone, era sorella di Beatrice, | che fu di Bradamante genitrice' [knows that Armelina, who gave birth to | Dudone, was sister to Beatrice, | who was Bradamante's mother] (*Fur.*, XXXVI 80,6–8 AB; XL C). Dudone's Saracen childhood is obliterated and his family tree is now entirely Christian, but Ariosto does not turn his back on previous chivalric literature: in fact, in the *Ancroia* Dudone says that his father, Danese, 'nel ventre sì me ingenerone / de Armelina, mia madre cortese' [conceived me in the womb / of Armelina, my courteous mother] (*Ancroia*, XIII [erroneously numbered as XII] 96,5-6 [fol. g2ʳ]), while in the *Vendetta di Falconetto* Dudone mentions his Christian mother in a lament ('O madre mia, dolze e cara Armelina' [Oh my mother, sweet and dear Armelina] (*Vendetta A*, fol. N iiiᵛ)). It could be that Ariosto was not aware of the alternative story in which Dudone is the son of a giantess and thus did not see Boiardo's implicit references to the *Castello di Teris* or some other romance that relates that story, but it is also possible that he deliberately chose to stress Dudone's Christian identity and therefore his legitimacy. To this we must add that he dispels all doubts regarding Bradamante's mother, stating clearly that the female founder of the Este dynasty was born to Christian parents who were happily married when they conceived her.[20]

Turning now to the Saracens whose literary lives start in the *Furioso*, they include such memorable figures such as Cloridano and Medoro and Issabella, who will be examined in some depth in the subsequent sections. Other — less prominent — Saracens invented by Ariosto comprise: Agramante's and Marsilio's kings and knights (Arganio, Balastro, Buraldo, Caico, Calamidor da Barcelona, Chelindo, Clarindo, Corineo, Finadurro, Libanio, Malaguro, Mosco, Ormida, Rimedonte, Tesira), rank-and-file soldiers (Altheo, Attalico, Casimiro, Dorchino, Etarco, Gardo, Margano, Olimpio da la Serra), the knights who take part in the joust of Damascus (Carmondo, Corimbo and Tirse from Apamia, Ermophilo, Ombruno,

---

Guidone 'activates an anxiety over legitimacy' (*Genealogies of Fiction*, p. 153). His illegitimacy might be the reason Ariosto decides not to dwell too much upon his childhood and early youth.

20    As Rajna points out, 'L'Ariosto fa senz'altro la fanciulla figliuola di Beatrice, ossia della moglie legittima di Amone. Poté essere ignoranza: fu più verisimilmente proposito. Essere regolati d'una progenitrice bastarda, non doveva garbare gli Estensi' [Ariosto does not hesitate to make this girl the daughter of Beatrice, Amone's legitimate wife. This could be due to ignorance: but it is more likely he did so on purpose. Being ruled by an illegitimately born foremother could not have pleased the Este family] (*Le fonti dell'Orlando furioso*, p. 52).

Salinterno, the rulers of Lodicea, Seleucia, and Sidonia) and a few nameless minor characters. Moreover, Ariosto gives Horrigille a new lover, the cowardly Martano, and mentions at various points the Sultan of Egypt, Agramante's neighbour. While in the *Inamoramento de Orlando* the Egyptian sultan is one of Agramante's vassal kings (Menadarbo, the Sultan of Egypt and Syria, is killed by Brandimarte in *Inam.*, II xviii 26–27), in the *Furioso* Egypt is an independent state, and Agramante's empire is slightly smaller.

Interestingly, most of the new Saracen characters are male. We see only two new female faces: the already mentioned virtuous Issabella and the promiscuous Fiammetta, the heroine of the salacious tale that the narrator tells his female readers to skip. Although Ariosto does not specify Fiammetta's religion, it would seem that she is a Saracen because Valencia, the kingdom where she and her childhood sweetheart Greco first met, is part of Marsilio's Spain.[21] While only two new Saracen damsels appear in the *Furioso*, Ariosto introduces a relatively large number of Christian women, many of whom are actively involved in various 'digressive' episodes. This is remarkable in the context of the Carolingian branch of the chivalric tradition, where, as we saw in the previous chapter, it is unusual for Christian women to have leading roles in romantic adventures (even if occasionally Orlando's Alda or some other Christian lady enters the spotlight). Ariosto's Christian women can compete with their Saracen counterparts. That said, the latter possess an undeniable charisma and are beyond any doubt a conspicuous presence in the poem.

## Love: the Saracen perspective

Saracens make an important contribution to the theme of love in the *Furioso*: suffice to think of the elusive Angelica, the focus of much of the first canto and a heroine whose story is inextricably linked to the stories of many of the male protagonists of the poem. Apart from Angelica, the poem features the following Saracen and Saracen-turned-Christian lovers: Brandimarte, Doralice, Feraù, Fiordeligi (Fiordiligi), Fiordispina, Guidon Selvaggio (who has a loving relationship with one of his 'Amazon' wives), Horrigille, Issabella, Lucina, Mandricardo, Martano, Medoro, Norandino, Rodomonte, Ruggiero, and Sacripante, as well as Fiammetta and her beau Greco. Though united by the bond of a common faith, these characters experience love in different ways and with varying degrees of intensity: Brandimarte, Fiordeligi, Issabella, Lucina, Norandino are models of conjugal

---

21    Boiardo's Doriphebo is the King of Valencia, as we learn in *Inam.*, II xxiii 49,2–3. Ariosto's Marsilio retreats to Valencia after Agramante's defeat (*Fur.*, XXXV 85 A; 74 B; XXXIX 74 C). It is worth noting that half of Ariosto's Saracen heroines (Doralice, Fiordispina, Issabella, and Fiammetta) come from Marsilio's Spain and that, with the exception of Issabella, none of them is a paragon of chastity. It may well be that Ariosto's portrayal of these ladies is partly influenced by his view of Spanish women. According to Remo Ceserani, 'Dalla [...] cultura ispano-aragonese, cara anche a Isabella [d'Este], Ariosto prende varie volte maliziosamente le distanze' [Ariosto at times maliciously distances himself from the Spanish-Aragonese culture that Isabella, too, was fond of], especially with the bawdy story of Fiammetta, who lives in Valencia, the city of the Borgia family. See Remo Ceserani, 'Due modelli culturali e narrativi nell'*Orlando Furioso*', *GSLI*, 161, no. 516 (1984), 481–506 (pp. 504–05).

affection; the surprising union between Angelica and Medoro is open to different interpretations; Feraù's passion for Angelica is not always convincing and, if truth be told, neither is Ruggiero's for Bradamante; Sacripante is unable to suppress his physical desire; Fiordispina's affair with Ricciardetto has comic overtones, while Fiammetta's promiscuity is designed to make the reader laugh; the opportunistic Doralice and Mandricardo inspire mixed feelings; the perfidious Horrigille and the vile Martano earn the readers' contempt. Ariosto uses these Saracen characters to explore the many facets of love and related passions, and he does the same with his Christian lovers. Among the latter, too, there are noble individuals capable of self-sacrifice (e.g. Ariodante), cynical villains (e.g. Gabrina) as well as more or less flawed human beings. One striking difference between the two *Orlandos* is that in the *Furioso* the theme of love is no longer dominated by Saracens. Ariosto's Christian lovers are significantly more numerous than Boiardo's. The long list includes: Adonio, Anselmo, Argeo, Ariodante, Astolfo, Bradamante, Dalinda, Gabrina, Ginebra (Ginevra), Griphone, Melissa, Odorico di Biscaglia, Orlando, Pinabello di Maganza, Polinesso, Ricciardetto, Rinaldo, the knight who offers Rinaldo to drink from the enchanted chalice and his wife, Zerbino, as well as Arbante, Bireno, Cilandro, Drusilla, Leone, Oberto di Ibernia, Olindro di Lungavilla, Olimpia, and Tanacro in the 1532 version. While there were virtually no Christian couples in the *Inamoramento de Orlando*, the *Furioso* features a number of love stories that involve only Christian characters (for example, the stories of Ginevra, Olimpia, and Gabrina, the chalice novella and the judge Anselmo novella).

Another no less striking difference between Boiardo's and Ariosto's poems lies in the fact that more often than not the latter poet does not view love through rose-tinted lenses. Boiardo does not always idealize love (the theme of jealousy, for example, is explored in some of his novellas), but for his main protagonists it is almost invariably a positive, enriching experience and an attribute without which it is difficult, if not impossible, to achieve chivalric perfection. As mentioned earlier, Ariosto problematizes the relation between love and chivalry already in the first two cantos of the *Furioso*. Sacripante's resolution to force Angelica to sleep with him must have been inspired by a similar episode in Agostini's *Quarto libro*, namely Feraguto's attempted rape of Angelica (*Quarto libro*, IX 98–107).[22] If Boiardo's Agricane sets his mind on marrying Angelica without asking himself if she wanted him or not, Agostini's Feraguto and Ariosto's Sacripante go a step further, the former perpetrating a sexual assault and the latter getting ready to do so. Neither of these two characters is portrayed as an unfeeling brute: in a moving speech Feraguto explains to Rinaldo that without Angelica his life loses all meaning ('Io son sì di costei d'amor ferito, | ch'io mi sento senza essa al fin venire [...]' [I am so wounded by my love for her | that without her I feel that I am dying [...]] (*Quarto libro*, X 33,1–2)), while Sacripante's famous Petrarchan lament 'havrebbe di pietà spezzato un sasso, | una tygre crudel fatta clemente' [would have made the very rocks split out of compassion, | and a cruel tigress would have turned gentle] (*Fur.*,

22    On the presence of Agostini's *Quarto libro* in the first canto of the *Furioso*, see Enrico Carrara, 'Dall'*Innamorato* al *Furioso*', pp. 263–65; and Riccardo Bruscagli, ' "Ventura" e "inchiesta" fra Boiardo e Ariosto', in Idem, *Stagioni della civiltà estense* (Pisa: Nistri-Lischi, 1983), pp. 87–126 (pp. 95–96).

I 40,5–6 ABC).[23] And yet, rather than inspiring feats of martial prowess (as it did in Agricane's story), love gives rise to a violent sexual desire; these knights' infatuation with the Saracen princess makes them lose their mind, in a way foreshadowing what will later happen to Orlando.[24]

It would not be accurate to say that Ariosto only uses Saracen characters to show that love can be a dangerous force. His scepticism with regard to the ennobling power of love — which is his response both to Boiardo and his friend Pietro Bembo, the author of *Gli Asolani* (1503–1505) — is also evident in his portrayal of Sacripante's Christian rival, Rinaldo.[25] Fully aware of the fact that Angelica hates him (Sacripante, by contrast, believes that his passion is reciprocated), Rinaldo nevertheless pursues her relentlessly, hunting her as if she were wild game. In other words, by all appearances, he too is a potential rapist. While the narrator — himself a victim of unreciprocated love — seems to be relatively sympathetic towards these hapless lovers, the author distances himself from both of them.[26] Ariosto's irony is even more pronounced in the episodes of Sacripante's encounter with Bradamante and his duel with Rinaldo, in which both the Saracen knight and the Christian knight are brought down from the pedestal where Boiardo set them, without, however, being completely stripped of their chivalric virtue.

---

23   As Giulio Reichenbach wistfully observes, 'il romantico Sacripante degrada nel libertino Mandricardo' [the romantic Sacripante has degraded into the libertine Mandricardo] (Reichenbach, 'L'eroe mal fortunato: Sacripante', in *Atti e memorie dell'Accademia patavina di scienze lettere ed arti*, 75 (1962–63), pp. 159–174 (p. 165)). Ariosto creates an ironic contrast between Sacripante's tearful lament (*Fur.*, I 41–44) and his decision to move from words to action (59). In the 1516 *Furioso* the irony of the episode is further underlined by the fact that Sacripante greets his lady in a most respectful way: 'Pieno di dolce affetto e reverente, | alla sua donna, alla sua diva corse; | lo raccolse ella più cortesemente | che non faria se fusse in India forse' [Brimful of gentle and reverent thoughts, | he ran to his lady, his goddess, | who perhaps welcomed him with more courtesy | than she would have shown if she had been in India] (54,1–4 A). In the second and third editions of the poem the meeting between the two characters is charged with sensuality: 'Pieno di dolce e d'amoroso affetto, | alla sua donna, alla sua diva corse, | che con le braccia al collo il tenne stretto, | quel ch'al Catai non avria fatto forse' [Brimful of gentle, loving thoughts | he ran to his lady, his goddess, | who threw her arms tightly about his neck — | which she would perhaps not have done in her native Cathay] (54,1–4 BC). The difference between this stanza in the first *Furioso* and in the subsequent editions did not escape the attention of Giraldi Cinzio, who in his *Discorsi intorno al comporre dei romanzi* claims that the original version is superior to the emended one, not least because in it Sacripante treats Angelica with the respect that befits her royal status (see Giovan Battista Giraldi Cinthio, *Discorsi intorno al comporre rivisti dall'autore nell'esemplare ferrarese Cl. I 90*, ed. by Susanna Villari (Messina: Centro interdipartimentale di studi umanistici, 2002), p. 126).
24   The theme of love-induced madness is also present in Raffaele Valcieco's sequel, where Orlando's unrequited love for Angelica drives him to the verge of madness, and the lovesick narrator announces that Orlando's torment reflects his own (*Quinto libro V*, III 47). For Valcieco love is an unambiguously negative force that distracts the lover from his or her duty (Orlando threatens to convert to the Saracen religion, destroy the world, and then commit suicide should Charlemagne give Angelica to Rinaldo). See Maria Pavlova, 'La concezione di cavalleria nei continuatori del Boiardo', pp. 213–14.
25   On Ariosto's rejection of Bembo's neo-Platonism, see Sergio Zatti, 'L'Angelica ariostesca, o gli inganni della letteratura', in *Selvagge e angeliche: personaggi femminili della tradizione letteraria italiana*, ed. by Tatiana Crivelli (Leonfronte: Insula, 2007), pp. 95–107 (p. 104).
26   The narrator speaks disapprovingly of Angelica's coldness (*Fur.*, I 49 ABC).

Sacripante's fall in the brief clash with Bradamante is an eloquent proof of the fact that being madly in love does not always increase one's strength.[27] However, this fall is perhaps not as dishonouring as it might appear at first sight. As Angelica suggests in an attempt to console him, this mishap is the fault of his horse: indeed, the poor animal dies in the full-speed collision with Bradamante's steed and Sacripante is trapped underneath. Unlike Boiardo's Astolfo who blames his horse every time he is knocked out of the saddle, the Circassian knight is truly shaken by what has happened, which shows that chivalry and honour are certainly not empty words for him:

> Sospira e geme, non perché l'annoi,
> che piede o braccio s'habbia rotto o mosso,
> ma per vergogna sola, onde a' dì suoi
> né pria né dopo el viso hebbe sì rosso.
>
> [He sighs and groans, not because
> his arm or foot may be broken or sprained,
> but simply for shame: never in his life,
> before or since, was his face so red.]
>                                  (*Fur.*, I 66,1–4 ABC)

Nor is *cortesia* a meaningless term for Sacripante or for Rinaldo, even if in canto II both of them fail to live up to this ideal. Sacripante does not dismount when Rinaldo challenges him to a duel, but, unchivalrous as it may seem, his behaviour is understandable if we only take into account his psychological state: he has just suffered the greatest humiliation of his life, and Angelica has thrown salt on a bleeding wound when, upon seeing her Christian suitor, she suggests that they flee from him. Rather than politely asking the Circassian to return the horse Baiardo (which was not stolen: the readers knows that it ran away to find Angelica), Rinaldo greets him with a torrent of verbal abuse:

> gridò: — Scendi, ladron, del mio cavallo!
> Che mi sia tolto il mio, patir non soglio,
> ma ben fo a chi lo vuol caro costallo;
> e levar questa donna ancho ti voglio,
> che serebbe a lasciartela gran fallo:
> sì perfetto destrier, donna sì degna
> a un ladron non mi par che si convegna. —
>
> [he shouted: 'Thief, get off my horse!
> It is not my custom to allow what is mine to be taken from me:
> he who wants it must pay dearly;
> and I also want to take this damsel from you,
> to leave her to you would be a great mistake:
> it seems to me ill fitting that so superb a charger
> and so noble a lady should fall to the share of a thief.']
>                                  (*Fur.*, II 3,2–8 ABC)

---

27   As Valeria Finucci points out, 'It is almost axiomatic that whenever Angelica appears, male failure follows' (Valeria Finucci, 'The Narcissistic Woman: Angelica and the Mystique of Femininity', in Eadem, *The Lady Vanishes: Subjectivity and Representation in Castiglione and Ariosto* (Stanford: Stanford University Press, 1992), pp. 109–44 (p. 112)).

Sacripante's nerves are on edge, and Rinaldo's insults are the straw that broke the camel's back: blinded by rage, the Saracen forgets about the chivalric code and charges at his enemy to teach him a lesson. The Christian knight, it could be argued, gets what he deserves, for he was the first to act discourteously.[28] It is worth recalling that Boiardo's characters do not always keep their sang-froid in such situations: the furious Rodamonte attempts to kill Baiardo after Ranaldo — angered by the fact that Rodamonte deals blows all around him, without looking where they fall — calls him a 'perfido ribaldo' [treacheous lout] and says that in his 'paese ardente e caldo | [...] vertute e prodecia non vale' [hot, burning land | [...] neither virtue counts nor worth] (*Inam.*, II xiv 48,3–6). Rather than reflecting his disdain for the chivalric code, Rodamonte's extreme reaction shows that undeserved insults can make a knight fly into a terrible rage.[29]

Neither Rinaldo nor Sacripante apologizes to the other when an infernal spirit interrupts their duel by telling them that Angelica is with Orlando. Fuming with anger and fantasising about cutting out his cousin's heart, Rinaldo jumps onto Baiardo and gallops away without saying a word to Sacripante, let alone offering him a lift (as Ferraù did in an analogous situation in canto I). Ariosto refrains from taking sides; his narrator does not intervene with moralizing comments, leaving us free to draw our own conclusions. What is clear is that the episode is infused with comedy. It is highly ironic, for example, that none other than Rinaldo should accuse Sacripante of theft when it is he who has this sin on his conscience: Ariosto's early readers would have known that in times of financial hardship Amone's son frequently resorted to robbing wealthy travellers in order to support himself and his large family.[30] The Saracen of course throws the accusation back in his face ('chi dicesse a te ladro, lo diria | (per quanto n'è la fama) più con vero' [if somebody were to call you a thief, this would be | (such is your reputation) closer to the truth] (*Fur.*, II 4,3–4 ABC)), delighting connoisseurs of chivalric literature. By comparing these lovelorn warriors to 'dui can mordenti | [...] | con occhi bieci e più che bragia rossi' [two ferocious hounds | [...] | with their eyes lit up balefully, redder than hot

---

28   It is interesting to note that Orazio Toscanella, who is much more sympathetic to Ariosto's Christians than to his Saracens, criticizes Rinaldo for his discourteous behaviour. Toscanella's 'Allegoria' to *Fur.*, II states that 'Per Rinaldo, che dice ladrone fuori di proposito à Sacripante, essendo debito di cavalleria di non ingiuriare altrui di parole se non giuridicamente, et (per così dire) sforzatamente, si dà ad intendere che l'huomo il quale si dà in preda al furore amoroso, passa à termini men che convenevoli, et biasemevoli' [In the case of Rinaldo, who improperly calls Sacripante a thief, considering that chivalry forbids insulting others with words, if this is not lawful and (so to say) absolutely necessary, it is shown that the man who is overwhelmed by the fury of love behaves in a way that is inappropriate and blameworthy] (*Bellezze del Furioso di M. Lodovico Ariosto*, p. 23).
29   According to a number of critics, this episode shows that Rodamonte has no regard for the chivalric code. (Alexandre-Gras, 'Tre figure boiardesche di eroe saraceno: Ferraguto, Agricane, Rodamonte', p. 136; Ragni, 'Rodomonte e Gradasso', pp. 407–08). Yet, when not insulted, Rodamonte treats his Christian enemy with *cortesia*. For example, in the episode of his duel with Orlando he patiently waits for Orlando (knocked out by Rodamonte's blow) to come back to his senses: 'Vero è che Rodamonte il Saracino | non lo tocava e staval a mirare' [It's true that Rodamonte, the Saracen, | just looked at him but did not touch] (*Inam.*, II xxv 21,5–6).
30   '"[...] ma sciò ch'a Montealban a nòte scura" — exclaims Orlando in Boiardo's poem — "né al chiaro giorno è la strata sicura!"' ['but I know Montalbano's road | both night and day is dangerous'] (*Inam.*, I xxviii 6,7–8).

coals] (5,1–4) who fly at each other 'con aspri ronchi e rabuffati dossi' [bristling and snarling] (5,6), the narrator mocks both of them; this unflattering simile strips them of any heroic aura, suggesting that these brave warriors are behaving as irrational animals of a rather low species.

Thus, on the one hand, Ariosto undermines Boiardo's idealistic vision of love. On the other hand, he does not adopt a distinctly moralizing tone. If love does not always have a positive impact on the lover's martial prowess and *cortesia* (sometimes it does: Orlando — an ennobled, dignified figure in the *Furioso* — performs many a heroic deed before descending into madness), some love-induced folly can make one's life more exciting. After all, like his contemporary Erasmus, Ariosto seems to believe that folly is intrinsic to the human condition and that, in small quantities, it can even be productive of happiness. That said, not all love stories in the *Furioso* are centred on the theme of unrequited desire. Some of Ariosto's lovers are loved in return. Interestingly, while Boiardo's Saracen male characters are much more successful in love than his Christian male characters, his continuator is kinder to the latter. Boiardo's Saracen damsels had a clear preference for their co-religionists. Ariosto's Saracen princesses sometimes prefer Christian men: Issabella gives her heart to Zerbino, while Marsilio's daughter Fiordispina loses her virginity to Ricciardetto (whom she believes to be Bradamante). Issabella, of course, has many 'sisters' in the earlier chivalric tradition: as was shown in the previous chapter, late medieval chivalric romances abound in Saracen damsels who elope with handsome Christian knights, leaving behind their Saracen families. Similarly, Fiordispina's fling with Ricciardetto reminds us of 'late Carolingian narratives in which lusty [*sic*] Saracen princesses desire paladins who pass through their land and sometimes have love affairs with them but do not establish lasting, legitimate ties'.[31] These two stories of interfaith and cross-cultural love testify to the fact that Ariosto's chivalric models are not limited to the *Inamoramento de Orlando*. It is worth mentioning in this regard that both Cieco da Ferarra and Nicolò degli Agostini are much more sympathetic towards Christian male lovers than Boiardo. In the *Mambriano*, Saracen damsels have a soft spot for Christian knights as they do in the chivalric tradition that precedes Boiardo: Rinaldo, for example, has a passionate affair with Mambriano's mistress Carandina and then marries her off to Mambriano; Astolfo seduces Nilvia and manages to persuade another Saracen beauty, Androsilla, that he is a much better match for her than her Saracen suitor Carmenio. In Agostini's *Quinto libro* Angelica ties the knot with a Saracen man, but her heart belongs to Orlando, who, being unable to marry her (he is, as the reader knows, a married man), blesses her union with Dardinello.[32]

---

31    Cavallo, *The World beyond Europe*, p. 133.
32    Agostini's Angelica declares her love to Orlando after the Christian paladin and his friends have burnt Biserta (*Quinto libro*, IX 28–30). As Agostini explains to his surprised readers, she accepts Dardinello's proposal of marriage because she wants finally to settle down: 'Rispondo che la dama delicata | amava 'l vago giovinetto ardito | con intention di torlo per marito' [I reply that the delicate damsel | loved the handsome and brave youth | with the intention of marrying him] (*Quinto libro*, XIV 45,7–8). Whereas Dardinello is head over heels in love with her, for her this is effectively a marriage of convenience.

And yet, unlike Cieco, Ariosto does not make it easy for Christian men to get the most beautiful Saracen ladies. While Issabella and Fiordispina bestow their affections on Christian knights, Angelica, Doralice, Fiordeligi, Horrigille and Lucina fall in love with fellow Saracens. Angelica rejects the best Christian champion and instead offers herself as well as her kingdom to an obscure African soldier. The fact that Medoro — 'un vilissimo Barbaro' [a barbarian of the lowest sort] (*Fur.*, XXXVIII 36,4 A; 39 B; XLII 39 C) in the eyes of Malagigi and Rinaldo, but, at the same time, an eloquent poet whose unwavering loyalty to his lord Dardinello is virtually without parallel in the universe of the *Furioso* — weds the most coveted Saracen damsel shows that Ariosto's treatment of the love theme is far from being conventional. This unexpected twist of fate has puzzled many generations of readers and critics alike, starting with sixteenth-century continuators of the *Furioso*, some of whom were scandalized by such a denouement, not so much because of Medoro's Saracen faith as because of his low birth.[33] While a number of modern critics have seen this marriage as a disgraceful *mésalliance* and hence a punishment for the arrogant, narcissistic Angelica, others have argued that, by falling in love with a man who was ready to sacrifice his life for his lord, Angelica gains a 'new, more fully human status in desire' that 'brings her pleasure when Medoro returns her love'.[34] Indeed, Angelica and Medoro — a Saracen couple — are among the relatively few characters who are granted genuine happiness, whose love is free from jealousy or fear. It is true that Angelica's exist from the *Furioso* is both dramatic and comic: she and Medoro briefly meet the mad Orlando on their way to Cathay, and in an attempt to escape from him, the invisible Angelica tumbles down from her horse which Orlando then rides to death. But it is equally true that Ariosto's irony does not preclude sympathy. Although her story ends on a near-farcical — even carnivalesque — note, Angelica does not suffer a serious humiliation. A fall from the horse is arguably a small price to pay for what promises to be a happy marriage. However one interprets her return to Cathay, there is no doubt that Ariosto treats his main Saracen heroine with much greater sympathy than does Raffaele Valcieco, whose Angelica is struck by lightning, buried in a ditch and forgotten by her worshippers.[35]

33   Surveying a number of sixteenth-century sequels to the *Furioso*, Bruscagli shows that Ariosto's continuators found it hard to accept that Medoro did not have an illustrious family tree, and either portrayed him negatively, as a vulgar parvenu, or made him discover his royal origins. See Bruscagli, 'Medoro riconosciuto', in Idem, *Studi cavallereschi*, pp. 75–101.

34   Deanna Shemek, 'That Elusive Object of Desire: Angelica in the *Orlando Furioso*', *Annali d'italianistica*, 7 (1989), 116–41 (p. 136). Similarly, Mario Santoro and Ita Mac Carthy argue that Angelica is allowed to experience the joys of love and that Medoro is worthy of her affections (Mario Santoro, 'L'Angelica del *Furioso*: fuga dalla storia', in Idem, *L'anello di Angelica: nuovi saggi ariosteschi* (Naples: Federico & Ardia, 1983), pp. 57–81 (pp. 72–81); Ita Mac Carthy, 'Angelica: Poetry and Desire', in Eadem, *Women and the Making of Poetry in Ariosto's 'Orlando Furioso'* (Leicester: Troubador, 2007), pp. 45–71 (pp. 63–69)). By contrast, according to Peter De Sa Wiggins and Valeria Finucci, Ariosto punishes his heroine by marrying her to a common soldier (Peter De Sa Wiggins, 'Angelica', in Idem, *Figures in Ariosto's Tapestry: Character and Design in the 'Orlando Furioso'* (Baltimore: John Hopkins University Press, 1986), pp. 166–82 (pp. 180–82); Finucci, 'The Narcissistic Woman: Angelica and the Mystique of Femininity').

35   On Angelica in Valcieco's *Quinto libro*, see Anna Carocci, 'Il destino di Angelica: Il

Nor are the stories of Issabella and Fiordispina as conventional as they may appear at first glance. What distinguishes Fiordispina from lustful Saracen ladies in fifteenth-century chivalric texts is that she believes, or pretends to believe, that her beloved is a woman whose sex has been changed by virtue of magic water with the full consent of 'Machon e [...] tutti i dèi' [Mahomet and all the gods] (*Fur.*, XXIII 42,2 A; 44 B; XXV 44 C). It is Bradamante's feminine beauty that she is initially attracted to. Ariosto's debt to Boiardo is obvious: 'Io non credo che fabula si conte | che più di questa historia bella fosse' [I don't believe there can be story | more beautiful than this one] (*Fur.*, XXIII 25,5–6 A; 27 B; XXV 27 C), says Ricciardetto referring to Bradamante's encounter with Fiordispina which took place at the very end of Book III of the *Inamoramento de Orlando*. Ariosto does not portray Fiordispina as an easily available woman. In fact, Ricciardetto started to develop feelings for her before the war with Agramante, but he thought that he had no chance of winning her until his twin sister told him about her bizarre adventure:

> Di Fiordispina gran notitia hebbi io
> in Siragoza, e già la vidi in Francia;
> e piacquer molto allo appetito mio
> li suo' begli occhi e la polita guancia:
> ma non lasciai fermarvisi il disio;
> che l'amar senza speme è sogno e ciancia.
> [...]

> Di questa speme Amor ordisce il nodo,
> che d'altre fila ordir non lo potea,
> onde mi piglia: e mostra insieme il modo
> che da la donna havrei quel ch'io chiedea.
> A succeder serà facile il frodo;
> che come spesso altri ingannato havea
> questo, che a mia sorella mi assimiglio,
> così farà la figlia di Marsiglio.

> [I had heard a great deal about Fiordispina,
> whom I had seen in Saragossa and in France.
> I had been much allured
> by her lovely eyes and smooth cheeks,
> but I had not let my thoughts dwell upon her:
> to love without hope is idle dreaming.
> [...]

> Out of this cord Love prepared bonds for me,
> having no other cord with which to capture me.
> He showed me how to set about
> obtaining what I wanted of this damsel.
> A little deception would procure an easy success:
> the similarity between my sister and myself
> had often deceived others,

destabilizzante femminile nei poemi di primo Cinquecento', in *I cantieri dell'italianistica: Ricerca, didattica e organizzazione agli inizi del XXI secolo: Atti del XVIII congresso dell'ADI*, ed. by Guido Baldassari et al. (Rome: Adi editore, 2016), pp. 1–10 (p. 6).

so perhaps it would deceive Marsilio's daughter too.]
(*Fur.*, XXIII 47,1–6, 48 A; 49–50 B; XXV 49–50 C)

Fiordispina's story is often read as an exploration of questions of sexuality and gender.[36] According to Valentina Denzel, the fact that Fiordispina is a Saracen is not devoid of significance: drawing a parallel between Fiordispina and the Ethiopian man who shamelessly asks Anselmo for sexual favours, Denzel concludes that in the *Furioso* 'le *péché muet* existe surtout dans les pays d'Afrique qui sont loin de l'Europe et dans le cas de Fleurdépine, de la civilisation chrétienne' [the silent sin exists above all in the African lands that are far away from Europe and, in Fiordespina's case, far from the Christian civilization].[37] However, unlike the ugly Ethiopian, the lovelorn and despairing Fiordispina inspires pity rather than contempt.[38] Despite her own claim to the contrary, her impossible homosexual desire for Bradamante is not without precedent in classical and medieval literature. Boiardo's and Ariosto's sources include Ovid's *Metamorphoses* (the story of the love between Iphis and Ianthe in Book IX 666–97), Antonio Pucci's *Reina d'Oriente* (which narrates the marriage between the daughters of the Queen of the Orient and the Roman Emperor), and Piero da Siena's *Bella Camilla* (where the eponymous heroine ignites the fire of love in the heart of another woman, Cambragia, whom she eventually marries).[39] The 'unnatural' yearnings of the female heroines in these texts do not turn them into monsters and the authors are sympathetic towards them: in each of these stories one of the two women is turned into a man and what appears to be an insurmountable obstacle to the lovers' happiness is removed. Ariosto decides not to resort to a *deus ex machina*, but instead to replace Bradamante with her twin Ricciardetto, leaving the reader to wonder whether Fiordispina understood what had happened or whether she genuinely believed that her beloved had metamorphosed into a man.

Both sixteenth-century commentators and modern critics have analysed Fiordispina's passionate yet short-lived affair with Ricciardetto in light of the background conflict between Christians and Saracens. Orazio Ariosto suggests that one should not judge the Christian knight too harshly because 'l'inganno [...] è fatto à Donna di diversa religione, e nimica, se ben Regina' [the victim of the deceit is a Lady of a different religion and an enemy, even if she is a Queen].[40] According to Cavallo, the fact that this romantic relationship does not lead to marriage means that 'the poet seeks to reinforce socially correct national and religious identities'.[41] However, had Fiordispina converted to Christianity and married Ricciardetto,

---

36    See, for example, Finucci, 'Transvestite Love: Gender and Troubles in the Fiordespina Story', in Eadem, *The Lady Vanishes*, pp. 198–225.

37    Valentina Denzel, *Les Mille et Un Visages de la virago: Marphise et Bradamante entre continuation et variation* (Paris: Classiques Garnier, 2016), p. 219.

38    Ethiopia is a Christian country in Ariosto's poem, and its inhabitants are not monstrous.

39    For a detailed analysis of Ariosto's sources, see Franca Strologo, 'Trasgressione, travestimento e metamorfosi nel *Furioso*: intorno alla storia di Ricciardetto e Fiordispina', in *'Dreaming again on things already dreamed'*, pp. 173–98; and Denzel, 'L'identité sexuelle en question dans les épopées italiennes et françaises du XIIIe au XVI siècle', in Eadem, *Les Mille et Un Visages de la virago*, pp. 167–257.

40    Orazio Ariosto, *Difese dell'Orlando furioso dell'Ariosto*, in *Apologia del sig. Torquato Tasso in difesa della sua Gierusalemme liberata*, fols N 3$^r$-P 2$^v$ (fol. O 5$^{r-v}$).

41    Cavallo, *The World beyond Europe*, p. 133.

this would have had repercussions for the on-going war: her conversion would have been a severe blow to her father Marsilio and his ally Agramante who would have perceived it as a betrayal. Unwilling to merge the themes of love and war, Ariosto keeps religion and politics out of this episode. Instead, as Giudicetti puts it, the young lovers embody 'poesia [...] individuale e divertita' [indivualistic and amusing poetry], as they make the most of the opportunities that life throws at them.[42] A similar opinion was expressed by Lionardo Salviati, who, unlike many other Counter-Reformation critics, did not find this story distasteful: 'Era Ricciardetto in età che l'haver fatto altrimenti sarebbe nel poema apparito fallo di sconvenevolezza, sì come anche in Fiordispina, il non aver mostrato di credere à cantafavola sì incredibile [...] sarebbe da molti stata tenuta sciochezza' [Given Ricciardetto's age, had he acted differently, this would have seemed out of place in the poem, and the same is true of Fiordispina, as many would have deemed her stupid had she not pretended to believe such an obvious fib].[43]

Although the episode of Fiordispina and Ricciardetto does not have a happy ending (the lovers are discovered and only the timely arrival of Ruggiero saves Ricciardetto from being burnt at the stake), it does not leave a sad aftertaste either. Their desires are consummated, and the reader hopes that Marsilio (who is portrayed as a loving father in earlier chivalric literature) will eventually forgive his daughter (we know that he has her locked in a tower) and that she will be able to experience love again.[44] The light-hearted tone with which Ricciardetto recounts his adventure prevents us from being too emotionally involved and taking Fiordispina's feelings too seriously.

By contrast, it is difficult not to be moved by the story of Issabella, another Saracen woman who has a relationship with a Christian man. The daughter 'del Re mal fortunato di Gallitia' [of the luckless King of Galicia] (Fur., XI 4,2 AB; XIII C) first notices Zerbino, a valiant Christian knight, at a joust in Baiona. Having set her heart ablaze ('poi che far prove in campo vidi | miracolose di cavalleria, | fui presa del suo amore' [having seen him perform in the field | incredible feats of chivalry | I fell in love with him] (7,1–3)), Zerbino too falls in love. However, the fact that they worship different gods is a serious problem for these star-crossed lovers:

> E perché vieta la diversa fede
> (essendo egli christiano, io saracina)
> ch'al mio padre per moglie non mi chiede,
> per furto indi levarmi si destina.
>
> [As we are of different faiths
> (he a Christian, I a Saracen),
> he cannot ask my father for my hand,

42   Giudicetti, Mandricardo e la melanconia, p. 49. According to Giudicetti, Ariosto juxtaposes Ricciardetto's light-hearted attitude to life to Ruggiero's less appealing gravitas (ibid., pp. 49–52).
43   Salviati, Degli Accademici della Crusca difesa dell'Orlando Furioso, fol. C 8[r–v].
44   In Agostini's Quarto libro Fior de Spina is denied even temporary happiness: she walks away disconsolate from Rugiero and Bradamante, after having offered herself in marriage to Bradamante (thinking that she is a man) and declaring that she will convert to Christianity (Quarto libro, IV 33–48).

but has to resort to abducting me.]
(*Fur.*, XI 10,1–4 AB; XIII C)

So far, Issabella's tale follows a familiar pattern. As with many other Saracen damsels in earlier chivalric works, Issabella is smitten by the valour and gallantry of a Christian man who proves to be superior to his Saracen counterparts. Yet, as in Fiordispina's case, Ariosto decides to avoid (as much as he can) the 'traditional' theme of a Saracen damsel betraying her parents. Maricoldo, Issabella's father, is dead: he was killed in the *Inamoramento de Orlando* (II xxiii 60–61). Issabella does not seem to know about his demise. Nor does she know that the knight who slew him is Orlando, who ironically saves her from the brigands and to whom she narrates her vicissitudes. Having died in Boiardo's poem (Ariosto reminds us of his death in *Fur.*, XII 13,7–8 AB; XIV C), Maricoldo cannot disown his daughter in the *Furioso*. He is virtually absent from Issabella's story, even if she feels a pang of sadness at the thought of him.[45]

What distinguishes Issabella from most Saracen princesses who give themselves to Christian knights in earlier chivalric works is the strength of her love. As we saw in Chapter III, Saracen ladies tend to be quite pragmatic: if they cannot have their first choice, they are happy to marry another Christian man who sometimes has to accept the fact that his bride is no longer a virgin. Doralice would have fitted this stereotype if her lovers had been Christian, but Issabella is anything but pragmatic. Having endured much suffering before being reunited with Zerbino (the ship on which she sails away from Baiona is caught in a terrible storm, Zerbino's trusted friend attempts to rape her, she is captured by brigands and spends months in a cave waiting to be sold to the Sultan's harem), she is a paragon of constancy and faithfulness. When *Fortuna* deals her the most cruel blow and her Zerbino is dying of his wounds before her eyes (unlike Angelica, whose knowledge of medicine helps her save the wounded Medoro, Issabella does not know which herbs to look for — in this heartbreaking episode Ariosto stresses her human fragility), she assures him that she is ready to follow him to the other world:

> [...] — Non vi pensate già, mia vita,
> far senza me quest'ultima partita.
>
> Di ciò, cor mio, nessun timor vi tocchi
> ch'io vuo' seguirvi o 'n cielo o ne lo inferno:
> convien ch'un spirto e l'altro insieme scocchi,
> insieme vada e insieme stia in eterno.
>
> [Do not imagine, my love,
> that you shall make this last journey without me.
>
> Do not fear, my heart, this will not happen:
> I mean to follow you, to heaven or to hell.
> Our two spirits must set forth together,
> and go together and stay together in eternity.]
> (*Fur.*, XXII 80,7–8, 81,1–4 AB; XXIV C)

45   As Emilio Bigi explains in his commentary to *Fur.*, XIII 4,2 C, she calls her father 'mal fortunato' [unlucky] because he has lost his daughter and not because he is dead.

'A me pare — observed Orazio Toscanella — che sia non solamente gran segno d'animo virile, ma grandissimo lo sprezzar la morte, et sprezzarla in tanto, che non si habbia paura di darsela con le proprie mani' [It seems to me that it is not just a great but a tremendous proof of a virile mind if one scorns death and so much that one is not afraid to kill oneself with one's own hands].[46] Issabella does not kill herself with Zerbino's sword, because a hermit intervenes and persuades her to turn her thoughts to the Christian God. However, her conversion to Christianity — or rather her intention to do so — is not entirely convincing, with her garrulous saviour bearing the brunt of Ariosto's irony. Religion does not fill the void that Zerbino's demise has left in her life and her death is only postponed. It will not be long before she tricks Rodomonte into killing her, thereby rejoining her Christian beloved in the 'terzo ciel' [third heaven] (*Fur.*, XXVII 30,3 AB; XXIX C) despite the fact that she has effectively committed suicide and that she dies without having been baptized. It has been argued that Ariosto 'refashions the neophyte Isabella as a Christian martyr who prefers death to the violation of her chastity'.[47] Yet it is not religion that prompts Issabella to devise a way to end her days, but her promise of eternal fidelity to 'quel cavallier ch'in braccio spento | le havea crudele e dispietata sorte' [that knight whom harsh and pitiless fate | had allowed to expire in her arms] (*Fur.*, XXVII 11,5–6 AB; XXIX C). It is his name rather than that of Jesus Christ that she utters as her severed head hits the ground:

> Quel [capo] fe' tre balzi; e funne udita chiara
> voce, ch'uscendo nominò Zerbino,
> per cui seguire, astutia strana e rara
> s'imaginò a schernire il Saracino.
>
> [Her head bounced thrice: from it a voice
> could be clearly heard pronouncing the name of Zerbino,
> to follow whom she had found such a strange
> and novel way to shame the Saracen.]
>                              (*Fur.*, XXVII 26,1–4 AB; XXIX C)

Issabella, thus, literally follows Zerbino to the grave. Her death has provoked mixed reactions from critics and readers. While Giraldi Cinzio claims that it is undeserved (because virtuous characters should not die) and 'contra la religion christiana' [against the Christian religion] since Christ does not want such sacrifices from his faithful,[48] feminist critics see in it a 'triumph for [her] husband [...], whose honour remains intact and whose worth is immortalised'.[49] Today we may find it difficult to understand the high value Issabella places on her chastity, but it is not surprising that many of Ariosto's first readers deemed her a supreme example of virtue, considering how popular the myth of the Roman Lucretia was throughout

---

46   Toscanella, *Bellezze del Furioso di M. Lodovico Ariosto*, p. 200.
47   Cavallo, *The World beyond Europe*, p. 135.
48   See Giraldi's manuscript notes on the *Furioso*: Givan Battista Giraldi Cinthio, *Note critiche all'"Orlando furioso' (Classe I 377 e Classe I 406 della BCAFe)*, ed. by Marco Dorigatti and Carla Molinari (Ferrara: Edisai, 2018), pp. 60–61. The fact that Issabella dies unbaptized is often overlooked by modern critics, but this circumstance did not escape Giraldi's attention.
49   Mac Carthy, *Women and the Making of Poetry in Ariosto's 'Orlando Furioso'*, p. 107.

the sixteenth century. Ariosto's God is so impressed by the Saracen damsel's heroic death as to decree that her name — 'il nome inclyto e degno' [the praiseworthy, illustrious name] (*Fur.*, XXVII 29,6 AB; XXIX C) — be given to none but the most exceptional members of her sex. With these lines the poet pays homage to Isabella d'Este, whose interest in Lucretia is recorded by Bandello.[50] If Boiardo decided that the Saracen Rugiero would be a fitting ancestor for the Este family, Ariosto not only takes over the dynastic theme introduced by his predecessor, but he also weaves the story of the Saracen Issabella into the encomiastic thread of the *Furioso*.

Issabella is not the only Saracen lady who loses the will to live after the tragic loss of her beloved. Fiordeligi does not survive her husband for long, either. She wastes away soon after the death of Brandimarte who drew his last breath with her name on his lips. Boiardo's Fiordelisa became a very devout Christian after her conversion, with the narrator poking fun — albeit in a good-humoured manner — at her newly acquired religious zeal which manifested itself in long prayers. Bringing her story to a close, Ariosto shows that faith is not enough to help her overcome her despair, something which points to God's silence within the universe of the *Furioso*. His Fiordeligi confines herself to Brandimarte's tomb:

> E vedendo le lachryme indefesse,
> et ostinati a uscir sempre i suspiri,
> né per far sempre dire uffici e messe
> mai satisfar possendo a' suoi disiri;
> di non partirsi quindi in cor si messe
> fin che del corpo l'anima non spiri:
> e nel sepolchro fe' fare una cella,
> e vi si chiuse; e fe' sua vita in quella.
>
> Orlando, per voler quindi levarla,
> mandò poi messi, e vi tornò in persona:
> se viene in Francia, vuol compagna farla
> di Galerana, e pension darle buona;
> e vuol sin alla Lizza accompagnarla,
> quando tornare al padre suo prepona;
> edificar le vuole un monastiero,
> quando servire a Dio faccia pensiero.
>
> Ella sta nel sepolchro; e quivi attrita
> da penitentia, orando giorno e notte,
> non durò lunga età, che di sua vita

50    One of Matteo Bandello's novellas (*Novelle*, II 21) is devoted to Lucretia's suicide and the setting of the frame story is Isabella d'Este's palace near Mantua: Isabella asks Bandello to read Livy's account of Tarquin's rape of Lucretia, which gives rise to a heated discussion among Isabella's courtiers as to whether Lucretia was virtuous or insane; Baldassare Castiglione then retells her story, explaining why she should be admired rather criticized. It is interesting to note that an early draft of Castiglione's *Cortegiano* contained a story of a Christian girl who tricked her Turkish captor into chopping off her head by persuading him that she can prepare a potion that would make him invulnerable. According to Maria Cristina Cabani, this story (which does not feature in the published 1528 version) may well be one of Ariosto's sources for the episode of Issabella's death (Maria Cristina Cabani, 'Ariosto e Castiglione', in Eadem, *Ariosto, i volgari e i latini suoi* (Lucca: Maria Pacini Fazzi, 2016), pp. 141–74 (p. 161)).

da la Parca le fur le fila rotte.

[Since her tears were inexhaustible,
her sighs unquenchable,
and since she was quite unable to find emotional satisfaction
in all the offices and masses she had said,
she conceived the wish never to leave this spot
until her soul left with her last breath.
So in the tomb she had a cell built,
in which she closeted herself for life.

Orlando, who wanted to fetch her away,
sent her messengers and went in person:
if she returns to France, he will attach her
to the suite of Galerana with a handsome pension.
Should she ask to return to her father
he will escort her to Laodicea.
Should she wish to serve God,
he will build her a convent.

But she stays in the tomb, where exhausted
by penance and by days and nights of prayer,
she lived only a short while
before Fate cut her life-thread]
(*Fur.*, XXXIX 180–82,1–4 AB; XLIII 183–85 C)

In the 1532 *Furioso* Issabella's and Fiordeligi's example is followed by Drusilla (the main heroine of the Marganorre episode), but in the 1516 and 1521 versions they and Lydia's suitor Alceste — the male protagonist of a novella set in antiquity who dies because of his lady's cruelty — are the only characters who willingly renounce life when the pain of loss becomes intolerable.[51] Zerbino and Issabella and Brandimarte and Fiordeligi recall Tristan and Iseult — the most famous couple in Arthurian literature — who depart this world together, inseparable in death as they were in life. Their deaths also recall and foreshadow those of Orlando and Alda, the most famous couple in medieval Carolingian literature.[52] Alda too dies of a broken heart when she learns of Orlando's death on the battlefield.[53] Ariosto

51    Orlando's sinking into madness can perhaps be seen as a form of death. In the *Furioso* Boiardo's clumsy lover becomes a tragic figure; his all-consuming obsession with Angelica inspires our respect and compassion, even if he loses his charisma when he regains his wits and steps back into his role of the 'chaste Orlando', the best Christian champion.

52    See Angelo Monteverdi, 'Lipadusa e Roncisvalle', *Lettere italiane*, 13 (1961), 401–09. Monteverdi, however, points out that Brandimarte dies with the name of his beloved on his lips, while 'quando Orlando si sente morire [...] il ricordo di Alda nella sua memoria non torna' [when Orlando feels his death approaching [...] he does not remember Alda] (p. 408).

53    In the *Chanson de Roland* Alde drops dead as soon as Charlemagne tells her the tragic news (CCLXVII). In the Italian chivalric tradition she first sees the dead body of her beloved. Thus, in the *Spagna ferrarese* (XXXIV 36–43) Alda asks Charlemagne to see the corpses of her brother Uliviero and her husband Orlando, lies between them and dies with a smile on her face. In the *Spagna maggiore* (XL 10–19) she weeps disconsolately over the sepulchre of her husband and brother, and passes away when, by divine miracle, the dead Uliviero tells her that he is in Heaven. On the death of Alda in the *Spagna in prosa*, the *Rotta*, and the *Tesoro*, see Giovanni Palumbo, *La Chanson de Roland in Italia nel Medioevo* (Rome: Salerno Editrice, 2013), pp. 378–85.

could have also been inspired by the tragic ending of the long version of the *Vendetta di Falconetto* (a possible source that has escaped the attention of Ariosto scholars), where the Christian knight Tiborgo learns of the demise of his beloved Fioredelisa (a namesake of Boiardo's and Ariosto's heroine) during a festive banquet at the court of Charlemagne:

> In quelo ponto che si fasea tale festezare
> in sala si zonse uno mesazero
> da Tiborgo pianzando e disia: 'Sire d'alto afare,
> morta Fioredelisa, sire d'alto afare,
> nela Bergognia, dove ela si havia a stare.'
> Oldando questo Tiborgo, bon bataiero,
> certo in sua vita mai non hebe tale dolore
> e con furia a la sua camera ne ze il signore.
> [...]
> e tosto a lo diserto quelo aschosamente andòe
> e li se misse a far penitentia d'ogni suo pecato;
> parenti e amisi in questo mondo abandonòe
> e sempre stete a servire a Dio padre glorificato.
>
> [While this feast was going on
> a messenger arrived in the room,
> [he went] to Tiborgo weeping and said: 'Noble lord,
> Fioredelisa is dead, noble lord,
> in Bergognia, where she was staying.'
> When he heard this, Tiborgo, a good warrior,
> had certainly never experienced such pain before,
> and the knight stormed out of the room.
> [...]
> and soon he secretly travelled to the desert,
> and there he started to make penance for every sin he had committed;
> he abandoned his relatives and friends in this world,
> and always served God the glorious father.]
> (*Vendetta A*, fol. ddvii^r)

Like Ariosto's Fiordeligi, Tiborgo decides to devote his life to God and dies to the world. In the penultimate line of the *Vendetta*, Antonio, the author, tells us that he 'andò in gloria' [reached beatitude] (ibid.), but this does not dispel the sadness created by the visceral description of his grief. In the preceding tradition it is unusual for Saracens — especially for Saracen women — to die from emotional pain: in the *Chanson de Roland*, Roland's wife refuses to remarry and passes away, while Marsile's wife Bramimonde is baptized after his death.[54] One notable exception is the Saracen princess Duxelina in the *Falconetto*, who like Alde in the *Chanson de Roland*, drops dead when she finds out that Rolando has killed her beloved.[55] In

---

54   In the Italian chivalric tradition, too, there is no shortage of examples of Saracen ladies who remarry after the death of their husbands. In the *Altobello* Anzilella marries Otonelo after Altobello's death, and her new husband adopts her son Persiano. In the *Persiano*, her second husband dies, and although she is saddened by the loss, she does not die with him.

55   In this connection we may also mention Pulci's Forisena, who, like Virgil's Dido, kills herself

Chapter III, we compared Boiardo's Fiordelisa and Brandimarte to Duxelina and Falconetto. Whether or not Ariosto was familiar with the *Falconetto* (as we shall see in this and the following chapter, there is further evidence to suggest he may have read both the *Falconetto* and the *Vendetta*), in the *Furioso*, too, Fiordeligi and Brandimarte bear an undeniable resemblance to the Saracen protagonists of this anonymous chivalric text.

Although the 1516 *Furioso* features an array of noble Christian lovers, the most powerful manifestations of love — love that can override the instinct for self-preservation — are to be found in the stories of Issabella and Fiordeligi. Ariosto's Christian lovers believe themselves to be capable of dying from grief (Ariodante tries to commit suicide by hurling himself from a rock into the sea; Bradamante descends into a pit of despair when she suspects that Ruggiero has left her for Marphisa, as does the knight from the chalice novella when his wife betrays and then rejects him), but in actual fact none of them dies.[56] Christians on the whole are more resilient to life's blows. This may be seen as a positive trait, but at the same this means that Ariosto's most romantic lovers are Saracens. As will be shown in the next section, chivalric idealism is not entirely absent from the representation of Saracen characters involved in the theme of war: although Ariosto certainly does not give a rosy portrayal of Charlemagne's enemies, some of his Saracen warriors prove to be capable of dying for their chivalric values.

## Agramante's war

Far from being merely the backdrop against which individual love stories of Ariosto's knights and damsels unfold, the conflict between Agramante and Charlemagne is an important narrative thread in its own right. As in the *Inamoramento de Orlando*, for the vast majority of Christian and Saracen protagonists of the *Furioso*, the war is above all a thrilling adventure, an opportunity to win glory, to become *primi inter pares*. This is especially true of Saracen characters (such as Gradasso, Mandricardo, Marphisa and Rodomonte) in the first two thirds of the poem.[57] On the other hand, at various points Ariosto does adopt a moralizing stance. His heightened awareness of the gap between fictional and real warfare creates an emotional barrier between him and the story he is narrating, resulting in him viewing characters and events from different — often conflicting — perspectives. In the battle of Paris, for example, Rodomonte is portrayed both as a superb warrior — a 'guerriero artista' [warrior artist][58] — and as a bad military leader whose lack of judgement causes

---

after the departure of her beloved Ulivieri (*Morgante*, V 16–17). However, her death fails to move the reader. As Everson puts it, 'Pulci has done little to motivate psychologically such an extreme reaction, which is not in his source [the anonymous *Orlando*], yet it is the logical outcome of Forisena's linguistic association with death and perhaps also a punning etymology on her name: Forisena: F(u)ori senno [deranged]' (Everson, *The Italian Romance in the Age of Humanism*, p. 186).

56   In the 1532 version of the poem, Olimpia is not destroyed by Bireno's betrayal: she marries another man and rebuilds her life.

57   As Leonzio Pampaloni points out, Saracens do not see the war as a religious conflict (Leonzio Pampaloni, 'La guerra nel *Furioso*', *Belfagor*, 26 (1971), 627–52 (p. 628)).

58   Francesco De Sanctis, *La poesia cavalleresca* (Bari: Gius. Laterza & Figli, 1954), p. 108.

unnecessary loss of life (his soldiers are burnt alive in the ditch where he has forced them to descend (*Fur.*, XIII 1–5 AB; XV C)). The narrator admires his 'gran valor' [great valour] and simultaneously upbraids him for his 'gran crudeltade' [great cruelty] towards his own troops as well as towards the inhabitants of Paris (*Fur.*, XIV 25,7 AB; XVI C).

Ariosto makes numerous references to the military conflicts that rocked the Italian peninsula during the years when he was composing his poem.[59] However, he does not turn the *Furioso* into a full-fledged commentary on the Italian Wars. The beast of Avarice, which Ariosto deems to be the source of the evil in the world (*Fur.*, XXIV 31–50 AB; XXVI 31–53 C), seldom raises its ugly head in the poem itself.[60] While rank-and-file soldiers have their hearts set on looting, Agramante, Charlemagne and their knights (including Rinaldo who, though still plagued with financial problems, seems to have broken free from his 'criminal past') fight for entirely different reasons. They are not always successful in controlling the predatory instincts of their troops, as we see in the episode of the conquest of Biserta, which is extremely disturbing not only in the *Furioso*, but also in Agostini's and Valcieco's sequels. However, they do not encourage, or approve of, pillaging or violence against women.[61] Ariosto's portrayal of war may be less romanticized than it is in the *Inamoramento de Orlando* or in Cieco's *Mambriano*, but it is certainly less cynical than that of the *Vendetta di Falconetto*, where most of Rinaldo's soldiers 'eran robatori e assassini | che haveriano Dio e la matre robato' [were robbers and assassins | who would have robbed God and their own mother] (*Vendetta B*, fol. Bii^v).[62]

---

59    See Stefano La Monica, 'Realtà storica e immaginario bellico ariostesco', *La rassegna della letteratura italiana*, 89 (1985), 326–58; Emanuella Scarano, 'Guerra favolosa e guerra storica nell'*Orlando Furioso*', in *Studi offerti a Luigi Blasucci dai colleghi e dagli allievi pisani*, ed. by Lucio Lugnani, Marco Santagata, and Alfredo Stussi (Lucca: Maria Facini Fazzi, 1996), pp. 497–515; Larivaille, 'Guerra e ideologia nel "Furioso"', pp. 1–20.

60    According to Moretti, the wars fought in the *Furioso* 'non assumono le dimensioni cruente di una conflittualità moderna, non essendo rivolte all'affermazione del potere o alla conquista della ricchezza: i contrasti militari fra cristiani e musulmani sono riducibili alle forme ludiche della tradizione letteraria medievale e umanistica, alle avventure romanzesche nelle quali si celebra la concezione rinascimentale dell'uomo e delle sue "virtù" creative' [do not assume the savage dimensions of a modern conflict, as their goal is not the assertion of power or the acquisition of wealth: the military clashes between Christians and Muslims can be seen as the playful forms of the medieval and humanist literary tradition, as romance adventures that celebrate the Renaissance conception of man and of his creative 'virtues'] (Moretti, *Ariosto narratore e la sua scuola*, p. 85).

61    By contrast, the Christian paladins in Agostini and Valcieco do not appear to be shocked by the actions of their soldiers and participate in the sack of Biserta. See Maria Pavlova, 'Sul finale del *Furioso A*', in *Le 'Roland furieux' de 1516 entre rupture et continuité : Actes du colloque international de Toulouse, 17–19 mars 2016*, ed. by Alessandra Villa (Toulouse: Presses de l'Université de Toulouse — Jean Jaurès, 2018), pp. 29–54 (pp. 49–50); and Eadem, 'La concezione di cavalleria nei continuatori del Boiardo', p. 223.

62    Boiardo's Rodamonte tells his exhausted and demoralized soldiers (who have lost their horses and all their belongings during the storm) that he will lead them to wealthy France, but it is clear that this is not the main reason that he and his men cross the sea (*Inam.*, II vi 49–50). In the *Mambriano* Rinaldo and Orlando prevent their troops from sacking Utica (*Mambriano*, XVII 63–72).

At the beginning of this chapter, I said that it would be wrong to read the *Furioso* as a loose political allegory, in which the Saracens stand for the foreign participants of the Italian Wars. One must not lose sight of the fact that Ferrara sided with France at that time, accepting its protection and thus enraging Julius II who in 1510 swore to drive the 'barbarians' out of Italy. Interestingly, in the proem to *Fur.*, XII AB; XIV C, Ariosto draws a parallel between Agramante's costly victory and that of Ferrara and its French allies in the Battle of Ravenna (1512). As Stefano Jossa suggests, this comparison between the Saracens and the Ferrarese might reflect Ariosto's historical pessimism: 'sono i perdenti, i nemici della storia (entrambi vinti in proiezione)' [they are the losers, the enemies of history (both will later be defeated)].[63] According to Jossa, as early as 1512, Ariosto could have felt that eventually Ferrara and other small Italian states would be defeated by history, losing their independence in a world dominated by large national states. Whether or not Ariosto could foresee the eventual decline of Ferrara, in 1512 the 'warrior Pope' was determined to wrest the Duchy of Ferrara from its Este rulers. Alfonso and Ippolito d'Este managed to keep their state, but things could have gone differently. Ariosto and his contemporaries knew that *Fortuna* was unstable and changeable and that valour did not always guarantee success, and this may be the reason Ariosto devotes so much attention to the theme of defeat and why, as we shall see later, he is secretly sympathetic towards the vanquished. If so, he is not alone. Having narrated the catastrophic defeat of Agramante's forces in canto IV of his *Quinto libro*, Agostini opens the next canto with an emotional stanza on the Italian Wars, in which he complains that the wailing of 'Italia afflitta, sconsolata, e mesta' [suffering, grief-stricken and sad Italy] (*Quinto libro A*, V 1,1–2) has deprived him of the will to live. Contrary to what one would expect, the Christians' glorious victory does not evoke in him optimistic thoughts, but rather reminds him of the sorrowful state of war-ravaged Italy.[64]

*The leaders*

Let us now focus more closely on the characters of Agramante and Marsilio, the initiator of the war and his closest ally. Boiardo's Agramante is a charismatic young king who, although not as strong as Rugiero or Rodamonte, is a worthy descendant of Alexander the Great. Marsilio, on the contrary, is an old man prone to teary fits of despair. In the *Furioso*, too, Agramante eclipses his Spanish counterpart, but the latter undergoes a remarkable personality change. In his representation of Marsilio, Ariosto decisively breaks away from the *Inamoramento de Orlando* and the *Spagna*. Instead, his portrayal of this character may have been influenced by Pulci's *Morgante* or the *Vendetta di Falconetto*, where Marsilio is a strong and uncommonly shrewd political leader.[65] No longer a comic figure, Ariosto's Marsilio is endowed

63   Jossa, *Ariosto*, p. 71.
64   On Agostini and the Italian Wars, see Bruscagli, '"Ventura" e "inchiesta" fra Boiardo e Ariosto', pp. 87–89; and Pavlova, 'La concezione di cavalleria', p. 208.
65   Pulci's Marsilio is an extremely able statesman (which, as we saw in Chapter II, contrasts with his representation in many other chivalric works), but, unlike his counterpart in the *Furioso*, he is an atheist: 'Era Marsilio un uom che in suo segreto | credea manco nel Ciel che negli abissi' [Marsilio

with wisdom, a quality which he lacked in the *Inamoramento de Orlando* and which in the folly-ridden universe of the *Furioso* is as highly valued as it is rare. He who used to weep and shake fists at the sky whenever *Fortuna* turned its back on the Saracens keeps his sang-froid when Dardinello's death sends waves of panic through Agramante's troops:

> Li Mori fur quel giorno in gran periglio
> che in Paganìa non ne tornasse testa;
> ma il giuoco a tempo sa lasciar Marsiglio,[66]
> et se ne va con quel che in man gli resta.
> Restar in danno tien miglior consiglio
> che tutti i denar perdere et la vesta:
> meglio è ritrarsi et salvar qualche schiera
> che, stando, esser cagion ch'el tutto pèra.

> [That day the Moors ran a grave risk
> that not one of their number would return home;
> but Marsiglio knows when it is time to leave the game
> and he withdraws with his survivors.
> To survive defeat, he holds, better counsel
> than to lose his entire fortune and his very clothes:
> it is better to withdraw and save some of their men
> than, by standing fast, expose them to perish one and all.]
> (*Fur.*, XVI 156 AB; XVIII C)

It is Marsilio who saves the Saracen army that day:

> Quel Re [Agramante] che si tenea spacciato al tutto,
> né mai credea più riveder Biserta,
> [...]
> s'allegrò che Marsilio havea ridutto
> parte del campo in sicurezza certa:
> et a ritrarsi cominciò, e dar volta
> alle bandiere, et fe' sonar raccolta.

> [That king who thought that the war was lost
> and never expected to see Biserta again,
> [...]
> rejoiced that Marsilio had brought
> part of the army back into assured safety:
> and he began his own withdrawal, recalling
> the ensigns and sounding the retreat.]
> (*Fur.*, XVI 158 AB; XVIII C)

was a man who deep down | did not believe in Heaven or in hell] (*Morgante*, XXVI 118,1–2). In the *Vendetta di Falconetto*, Marsilio is the only one to realize that the Saracen pilgrim who claims to have visited Mecca is actually Malagigi in disguise who has arrived in the Saracen camp to spy (*Vendetta A*, fol. H iii^r; *Vendetta B*, fol. H iiii^r). Neither Agostini or Valcieco are particularly interested in the Spanish king, even if in Agostini's *Quinto libro* Marsilio features in an important episode that involves Rugiero (which we shall look at in Chapter V). Cieco's Marsilio is a weak and uninspiring figure (see Everson, 'Il buono, il brutto, il cattivo: figure di regnanti non-cristiani nel *Mambriano* di Francesco Cieco da Ferrara', pp. 39–40).

66   In the 1532 version of the poem Marsilio is referred to as 'saggio' [wise] in this line.

Agramante has much respect for both Marsilio and Sobrino who are described as 'li dui più antiqui e saggi' [the eldest and wisest] (*Fur.*, XXXIV 37,8 AB; XXXVIII C) in the Saracen camp. However, while Sobrino — a Saracen borrowed by Boiardo from the *Aspramonte* narratives — genuinely cares about his king, Marsilio puts the interests of Spain before anything else, as we see from the speech in which he advises his ally to ignore the news that the Nubians are ravaging his African kingdom, and to continue fighting Charlemagne (Marsilio 'per util di Spagna dicea cose | poco al bisogno d'Aphrica' [promoted the interests of Spain | rather than those of Africa] (XXXIV 48,7–8 AB; XXXVIII C)).[67] He abandons Agramante after the latter has interrupted the duel between Ruggiero and Rinaldo. At this point we learn that he is not only a cunning politician but also a deeply religious man: Agramante has broken an oath sworn on the Qur'an and Marsilio does not feel guilty about leaving him, as he is terrified that the wrath of the gods will turn on him too. Marsilio's religiosity as well as his concern that Charlemagne might want to take revenge ('ch'alla sua Spagna il fio pagar non tocche' [lest his Spain be made to pay the price] (XXXV 85,2 A; 74 B; XXXIX 74 C)) conjure up the phantom of the battle of Rencesvals, reminding the reader of the catastrophes narrated in the *Spagna*.

As for Agramante, although he does not undergo any dramatic transformation, Ariosto adds new complexity to his portrayal. Linking the *Furioso* to the *Inamoramento de Orlando* (more specifically to *Inam.*, II xxii), Ariosto announces in the first stanza of his poem that Agramante had crossed the sea in order to 'vendicar la morte di Troiano' [avenge Troiano's death] (*Fur.*, I 1,7 ABC). Virtually absent from the world of Boiardo's knights, the motif of revenge is, nevertheless, frequently found in other chivalric works. As mentioned in the previous chapter, in the fifteenth-century *Aspramonte* Agolante sails to Europe to avenge his brother Guernieri who, in turn, lost his life in an attempt to avenge their father. In the *Mambriano* the eponymous hero is resolved to make Rinaldo and Charlemagne pay for the death of his uncle Mambrino who in the *Cantari di Rinaldo* declared war on Charlemagne because Rinaldo had slain his brothers. However, what distinguishes Agramante from Agolante and Mambriano is that, unlike Guernieri and Mambrino, his father Troiano was indeed killed in an unfair duel. Ariosto does not comment on the circumstances of Troiano's death, but some of his first readers may have shared Boiardo's indignation at the unchivalrous behaviour of Orlando and his friends. On the other hand, Agramante does not appear to be obsessed with revenge or to hate Charlemagne or Orlando.[68] He does not seek Charlemagne's death; this

---

67    For an analysis of Sobrino's speech during the war council in Arles see Marco Dorigatti, 'Sobrino ariostesco e misconosciuto', *Belfagor*, 65, no. 4 (2010), 401–14 (pp. 408–09). A rather cynical character in the *Chanson d'Aspremont* (where he advises Agoulant to kill Naimes, a Christian ambassador) and the *Cantari d'Aspramonte* (where he wants to chop off Namo's hands and feet), So(u)brino has a warm and trusting relationship with Agolante in *Aspramonte A* and the fifteenth-century *Aspramonte*. Boiardo highlights the sentimental streak in this old warrior: focusing his affection on the grandson of his late lord, Boiardo's Sobrino assures Agramante that, as his 'servo antico' (*Inam.*, II i 46,7), he will give his life in his service, even if deep down he disapproves of the expedition against the Christians.

68    Although later in the poem the narrator once again describes Agramante as 'ostinato alla vendetta' [stubbornly pursuing his vengeance] (*Fur.*, XXXV 31,5 A; 20 B; XXXIX 20 C), Agramante

is particularly clear in the 1521 and the 1532 versions, where during a military meeting, Agramante talks about capturing, not killing, the French emperor (*Fur.*, XXXIV 40,1–4 B; XXXVIII C).[69] Moreover, in none of the three editions does he wish to confront Orlando: it is *Fortuna* that will bring him to the island of Lipadusa, where he will be killed by the man who also killed his father.

Agramante does appear to be somewhat more mature than he was in the *Inamoramento de Orlando*. He is no longer a starry-eyed young man who dreamed of emulating Alexander. It could be that the new generation of the Este rulers were less interested in the Macedonian conqueror than was Borso: Ariosto's narrator never mentions the fact that Agramante has descended from Alexander, and Agramante himself does not refer to the legendary origins of his family.[70] However, contrary to what has been argued by some scholars, Ariosto does not suppress Agramante's adventurous side.[71] The African king takes part in the battle of Paris, fearlessly flinging himself into the thick of the fighting: 'Caciossi in la battaglia il Re Agramante, | d'uccider gente et far gran prove vago' [King Agramante now flung himself into the fray, | eager to kill people and to perform great feats] (*Fur.*, XIV 75,1–2 AB; XVI C).[72] And 'gran prove' [great feats] he does show, so much so that even Rinaldo is impressed:

> Rinaldo, che havea mente a porre in terra
> hor questo hor quel che più vedea gagliardo,
> la spada contra il Re Agramante afferra,

himself does not seem to be seeking revenge. Critics sometimes tend to exaggerate the significance of the first stanza of the *Furioso*.

69   In the 1516 *Furioso* Agramante talks about 'bringing down the fleur-de-lis' and 'depluming the eagle' (*Fur.*, XXXIV 40,1–4 A).

70   Nor is Ruggiero particularly interested in his Macedonian ancestor, even if, as is evident from Melissa's sarcastic speech in the episode of his flight from Alcina's island, Alexander is one of his role models: 'Quest'è ben veramente alto principio | onde si può sperar che serai presto | un Pyrrho, un Alexandro, un Iulio, un Scipio!' [A goodly beginning, this, | from which we can hope soon to see you become | another Pyrrhus, Alexander, Julius or Scipio] (*Fur.*, VII 59,1–3 ABC). It is worth noting that in the *Mambriano* — which, if we believe Eliseo Conosciuti (who wrote the preface to the 1509 edition of the poem), Cieco wanted to dedicate to Ippolito d'Este — Alexander is an ambivalent figure. In line with his representation in the *Inamoramento de Orlando*, he is admired for his intrepidity. His story is inspiring to young knights such as Rinaldo's son Ivonetto, who invokes Alexander when Rinaldo does not allow him to take part in a joust: 'Non hai tu letto d'Alessandro Magno, | che per sprezzar in gioventù gli affanni | quasi di tutto il mondo fe' guadagno, | prima che avesse trentadue anni?' [Have you not read about Alexander the Great | who, by scorning difficulties in his youth, | had conquered almost the entire world | by the time he was thirty-two years of age?] (*Mambriano*, XXXV 95,1–4). However, he falls short of chivalric perfection. As Orlando tells Astolfo, 'Alessandro fu certo uom di gran pregio, | ma i vizi deturparno la sua immagine' [Alexander was certainly a very valiant man, | but vices marred his image] (*Mambriano*, X 73,1–2).

71   According to Santoro, for example, 'la sua iniziativa viene spogliata di quella brama inesausta e inesauribile di gloria, di avventura e di guerra, e ancorata ad un motivo personale di vendetta' [his venture is stripped of that insatiable and inexhaustible thirst for glory, adventure and war, and linked to a personal motive of revenge] (Mario Santoro, *Ariosto e il Rinascimento* (Naples: Liguori, 1989), p. 28).

72   In the 1532 *Furioso* Agramante's entry into the battle is slightly less impetuous: 'Entrò ne la battaglia il re Agramante, | d'uccider gente e di far pruove vago' [King Agramante now stepped into the fray, | eager to kill people and to perform great feats].

ch'un pezzo egli mirò con fiero sguardo,
che sol più che mille altri facea guerra;
e se gli spinse adosso con Baiardo:
lo fere a un tempo et urta di traverso,
sì che lui col destrier manda riverso.

[Rinaldo, who aimed to lie low
those who seemed most valiant to him,
turns his sword on King Agramante,
whom he watched fiercely for a while,
as all alone he wrought more damage than a thousand;
and so he rode at him on his Baiardo:
and struck him a slanting blow,
knocking him and his mount onto their backs.]
    (*Fur.*, XIV 84 AB; XVI C)

Undeterred by this fall, Agramante jumps back into the saddle and confronts Zerbino, who appears to be more or less his equal in terms of physical strength (*Fur.*, XVI 40,1–4 AB; XVIII C).[73] This episode is reminiscent of the joust at the foot of Mount Carena in the *Inamoramento de Orlando*, where Agramante fights valiantly and does not lose heart when Rugiero proves to be stronger than him. Like Boiardo, Ariosto has great respect for 'ordinary' Saracen knights whose courage is all the more impressive considering that they have neither supernatural strength nor enchanted armour. Such characters include Agramante's and Ruggiero's younger cousin Dardinello, to whom I shall return later, as well as Alzirdo, the young and hot-headed King of Tremisen, and Manilardo, the old King of Noricia who have their moment in the spotlight when they heroically confront Orlando (*Fur.*, X 78–79, 86–88,1–2 AB; XII 74–75, 82–84 C). Ariosto's sympathetic treatment of these Saracens contributes to the continuity between the two *Orlandos*. Both poems abound in dauntless second-level Saracens, even if Ariosto is somewhat less generous with eulogistic adjectives than was Boiardo.[74]

For all his chivalric virtues, Agramante does not quite live up to the ideal of a just ruler. His hanging of Brunello is a morally ambivalent action. He does so to ingratiate himself with Ruggiero's sister Marphisa whose armour was stolen by the virtuoso thief. Marphisa is a valuable ally, and Brunello is a scoundrel, but in following Sobrino's Machiavellian advice to have him executed, Agramante commits an act of ingratitude. Brunello helped him find Ruggiero in the *Inamoramento de Orlando*,

---

73    His courage did not go unnoticed by sixteenth-century readers: in his 'Argomento' [Argument] to canto XVI in the 1556 Valgrisi edition of the poem Girolamo Ruscelli states that 'In Carlo [...], et in Agramante s'ha un rarissimo essempio di due valorosissimi Re, l'uno in combattere, l'altro in valorosamente difendere una Città' [In Charlemagne and in Agramante we see an extremely rare example of two most valorous kings, one of them fighting and the other one valorously defending a city] (*Orlando furioso* (Venice: Vicenzo Valgrisi, 1556), p. 159).
74    Although Ariosto remembers almost every single minor Saracen knight who appears in Books II and III of the *Inamoramento de Orlando*, many of them are merely names in the *Furioso*. Thus, with the exception of Feraù, Marsilio's barons (i.e. Isoliero, Serpentino, Balugante) are now even more marginal characters than they were in Boiardo. The same is true of some of Agramante's less prominent knights (e.g. Malabuferso). For more details see Appendix II.

and the ease with which Agramante sacrifices him is disconcerting.[75] Ironically, Marphisa will later abandon him, converting to Christianity and turning her sword on him. Nor does he succeed in keeping his other key warriors in his army when he most needs them. He fails to make peace between his quarrelling knights in the episode of Discord, antagonizing Rodomonte. He interrupts the judicial duel between Ruggiero and Rinaldo, and, as a consequence, loses Ruggiero. I shall examine these episodes in Chapter V. For now, suffice it to say that in Ariosto's eyes Agramante's most reprehensible action is the fact that he orders the bridges over the Rhône to be cut when retreating into Arles after the final debacle, which leads to many of his soldiers being slaughtered by the enemy. Genuinely outraged, the poet condemns this order in no ambiguous terms:

> [...] Ah sfortunata plebe,
> che dove del tyranno utile appare,
> fu sempre in conto di pecore e zebe!
> Chi s'affoga nel fiume e chi nel mare,
> chi sanguinose fa di sé le glebe:
> molti perîr, pochi restâr prigioni;
> che pochi (a farsi taglia) erano buoni.

> [Alas, unfortunate populace,
> where the monarch's needs are at stake,
> you are always accounted as no better than sheep or goats!
> Some drown in the river, some in the sea;
> others stain the earth with their blood:
> many were slain, few taken prisoner;
> as few were worth a ransom.]
> (*Fur.*, XXXV 82,2–8 A; 71 B; XXXIX 71 C)

Here, Ariosto's gaze falls on the anonymous mass of rank-and-file soldiers whose lives have almost no value in the eyes of kings and renowned knights. Lashing out against Agramante, Ariosto does not contrast his cruelty to the Christians' clemency (as Cieco da Ferrara often does in his *Mambriano*), but rather remarks that Charlemagne's troops only spared those Saracens who were capable of paying a ransom.[76]

On their way back home, Agramante's subjects call him 'superbo' [arrogant], 'crudele' [cruel] and 'stolto' [ill-advised] (*Fur.*, XXXV 86,5–6 A; 75 B; XXXIX 75 C). However, there is a fair degree of exaggeration in these rants, for he is certainly not a bloodthirsty tyrant and his shortcomings are quite insignificant compared

---

75    It is true that Agramante wanted to hang Brunello already in the *Inamoramento de Orlando* (see II xxi 35–38), but there he earnestly believed that his vassal had violated the chivalric code. For an analysis of this character see Luciano Serra, 'La sublimazione del grottesco: Brunello', in *Il Boiardo e la critica contemporanea*, ed. by Giuseppe Anceschi (Florence: Olschki, 1970), pp. 489–97.

76    Cieco's Orlando, for example, is convinced that 'più s'acquista indulgenza porgendo, | che non si fa con la spada uccidendo' [one gains more by being compassionate | than by using one's sword to kill] (*Mambriano*, XIX 28,7–8), and he and Rinaldo often surprise the Saracens with their humanity. There are instances when the Christians act cynically (e.g. *Mambriano*, XXIII 96), but such episodes are few and do not undermine the strong juxtaposition between the Christians' magnanimity and the Saracens' savagery.

to the cruelty of Saracen kings in other chivalric works.[77] He has made mistakes, but, unlike his counterpart in Valcieco's *Quinto libro* (who befriends Gano and from a chivalrous king turns into a treacherous villain), he is not evil. Careful reading of the closing chapter of Agramante's story reveals that rather than adopting a moralizing posture vis-à-vis the Saracen ruler, Ariosto celebrates his unflinching courage and his readiness to die for the chivalric ideals that made him declare war on Charlemagne in Boiardo's poem. Agramante decides not to head straight to Biserta, but to disembark at a different port and then march to the capital of his kingdom:

> Ma suo fiero destin, che non risponde
> a quella intentïon provida e saggia,
> vuol che l'armata che nacque di fronde
> miracolasomente ne la spiaggia
> [...]
> con questa ad incontrar di notte s'haggia [...]
>
> [But his unkind destiny was at variance
> with this wise and provident plan:
> it dictated that the fleet that was created
> miraculously from the leaves on the beach
> [...]
> was to encounter his own by night [...]]
> (*Fur.*, XXXV 89,1–6 A; 78 B; XXXIX 78 C)

Ariosto emphasizes the fact that the sudden appearance of the enemy's fleet could not have been foreseen. In order to imagine such an event one has to believe in miracles and Agramante, like Ariosto himself, does not. Although the *Furioso* is full of magicians and enchanted places and objects, the poet does not hide his skepticism with regard to astrology, occultism and divine intervention in human affairs. It is not by chance that, though proud to be the female founder of the House of Este, Bradamante does not fully trust Melissa.[78] Ariosto's voice is tinged with irony when he tells us of the favours with which the Christian God showers his faithful, such as the transformation of stones into horses ('Oh quanto a chi ben crede in Christo lece!' [Ah, what shall be denied to a man who truly believes in Christ] (*Fur.*, XXXIV 33,5 AB; XXXVIII C)) and that of branches into a first-class fleet, not to mention Archangel Michael's comic search for Discord.

Both Agostini and Ariosto feel sympathy for the defeated African monarch. In Agostini's *Quinto libro* Agramante is portrayed as both the author of his own downfall and a noble knight who meets his death with the fortitude of a hero, rejecting Rugiero's suggestion to surrender (*Quinto libro A*, VII 31–36).[79] He is a lonely figure thrown into tragic relief. Sobrino retreats to a forest to fight Grifone, having criticized his lord for his failure to follow his advice. Sacripante is killed.

---

77    On one occasion Cieco's Mambriano has his own men impaled (*Mambriano*, XIV 85–86), while crucifixion is practised in the kingdom of Fierabraccia's father in the *Cantari di Fierabraccia e Ulivieri*.

78    See, for example, *Fur.*, XI 74 AB, XIII 76 C; XXX 21 A, 25 B, XXXII 25 C; XXXVIII 23 A, 26 B, XLII 26 C.

79    On this episode, see Maria Pavlova, 'Il finale del *Furioso* A', p. 39.

Rodamonte, whom Agramante believes to be dead, simply rides away together with Gradasso and Feraguto, and shortly afterwards Mandricardo leaves too, as he feels no obligation to stay when everyone else has abandoned Agramante.[80] By contrast, Ariosto's Agramante is not alone in the hour of tribulation. When all seems to be lost, the faithful Sobrino stays by his side and prevents him from killing himself. Not a word of reproach escapes Sobrino's lips: he puts on a mask of optimism even if 'dentro di sé Sobrino avverte l'inutilità di ogni iniziativa e l'inevitabilità della catastrofe' [deep down Sobrino acknowledges the pointlessness of any course of action and the inevitability of the catastrophe].[81] Had Ariosto wanted to end Agramante's story on a moralistic note, he would have made all his friends and vassals turn their back on him. Yet Gradasso, whom *Fortuna* has brought to the island of Lipadusa, is happy to see him:

> l'uno e l'altro signor s'abbraccia al sciutto;
> ch'erano amici, e poco inanzi furo
> compagni d'arme al Parigino muro.
>
> [the two kings embrace each other on dry land:
> they were friends, and shortly before this they were
> comrades in arms under the walls of Paris.]
> (*Fur.*, XXXVI 46,6–8 AB; XL C)

Gradasso left Agramante after he had got hold of Baiardo (*Fur.*, XXX 67 A; 71 B; XXXIII 95 C). His decision to sail home at a time when the Saracens were suffering heavy losses strikes us as at odds with his Arthurian personality. The King of Sericana, one could say, temporarily lost his adventurous spirit, forgetting that his quest for Baiardo was but a pretext for showing off his valour. However, his willingness to help Agramante as the story is drawing to a close proves that he is neither a coward nor a traitor and, more importantly, that he still believes in the values that underpinned the notion of chivalry in the *Inamoramento de Orlando*. He brings with him a fresh breeze of optimism, dispelling the clouds of gloom which have gathered around Agramante. Gradasso is confident that he will be able to kill Orlando. His cheerfulness fills Agramante with hope ('ben so ch'in arme ritrovar compagno | di te miglior non si può in tutto il mondo' [I know that I can't find | a better comrade-in-arms than you in the whole wide world] (*Fur.*, XXXVI 53,3–4 AB; XL C)), helping the reader to 'recover' from the highly distressing description of the Christian conquest of Biserta.[82] It is as yet unclear whether Ariosto used

---

80    Similarly, Cieco's Mambriano has no shoulder to lean on following his final catastrophic defeat. After the Christians have routed his troops and his Saracen friends have surrendered to the victors, Mambriano flees into a forest in a state of total despair: 'E sospirando dicea: Poco avante | mi trovai signor di tanta gente, | [...] | e ora non ho meco un vil sargente | che m'accompagni, io non ho pur un fante, | io non ho un paggio, ahi misero dolente!' [And, sighing, he was saying: 'Not long ago | I ruled over so many people, | [...] and now I don't have a lowly menial | with me, I don't have a soldier, | I don't have a page, oh wretched me!'] (*Mambriano*, XXIV 31,1–6).

81    Dorigatti, 'Sobrino ariostesco e misconosciuto', p. 411.

82    It is difficult to agree with Giudicetti, who claims that Agramante's conversation with Gradasso 'avviene sotto l'ombra della sconfitta e della rassegnazione' [takes place under the shadow of defeat and resignation] (*Mandricardo e la melanconia*, p. 95). According to Girolamo Ruscelli's

Agostini's *Quinto libro* in the *Furioso* or if it is Agostini who imitated Ariosto, but there seems to be a curious intertextual echo between the episode of Gradasso's arrival on the island of Lipadusa in Ariosto and the episode in which Gradasso and his companions leave Agramante in Agostini. Ariosto's Gradasso offers his help to Agramante with the following words:

> mi pare al tutto un ottimo *rimedio*
> haver pensato a farti *uscir di tedio*.

> [I think I have hit upon an excellent plan
> to help you get out of these dire straits.]
>     (*Fur.*, XXXVI 47,7–8 AB; XL C)

This is how Agostini describes the departure of the main Saracen warriors after the defeat of the Saracen army:

> Gradasso, e Rodamonte prestamente,
> con Feraguto 'l saracin soprano
> (vedendo perso al campo ogni *rimedio*)
> deliberorno *uscir di* tanto *tedio*.

> [Gradasso and Rodamonte,
> together with Feraguto, the noble Saracen
> (seeing that the battle was lost beyond recovery),
> quickly decided to get out of such dire straits.]
>     (*Quinto libro A*, IV 75,5–8)

Although the rhyme *tedio* | *rimedio* is not rare (it occurs six times in the *Inamoramento de Orlando* and ten times in the *Morgante*), Ariosto only uses it three times in the *Furioso* and only once at the end of a stanza. What, however, makes the above-cited passages particularly interesting, is that the expression 'uscir di tedio' is a hapax in the *Furioso* and that it occurs very rarely in Renaissance and medieval literature.[83] Therefore, it is not unreasonable to hypothesize that the episode of Gradasso's and Agramante's meeting may be Ariosto's response to Agostini whose Gradasso leaves Agramante in the lurch. Or, if it is Agostini who draws on Ariosto, then one could say that in making Gradasso ride away from the battlefield he deliberately undermines the ideal of friendship that Ariosto celebrates in the final part of Agramante's story.

According to Cavallo, 'The systematic degradation of Saracen heroes and the progressive development of the plot towards a holy war narrative' point to Ariosto's complete break with Boiardo.[84] In fact, far from being degraded, Agramante,

---

'Argomento' [Argument] to canto LX in the already mentioned Valgrisi 1556 edition of the *Furioso*, 'In Agramante s'ha l'essempio d'un continuatamente forte, saggio, et valoroso Signore. In Sobrino d'un sapientissimo et amorevolissimo consigliere. In Gradasso d'un sincerissimo amico, et fermo, et stabile in ogni fortuna' [In Agramante we see an example of a continually strong, wise and valiant Lord. In Sobrino we see a wisest and most affectionate advisor. In Gradasso a most sincere friend who is reliable and stable regardless of the situation] (*Orlando furioso* (1556), p. 447).

83    It features in Bernardo Giambullari's sequel to the *Ciriffo Calvaneo* (first printed in September 1514) and in Gasparo Visconti's *Pasitea*. See Pavlova, 'La concezione di cavalleria nei continuatori del Boiardo', pp. 221–22.

84    Cavallo, *The World beyond Europe*, p. 204.

Gradasso, and Sobrino show boundless courage in the face of adversity, remaining true to the spirit of Boiardo's poem. Agramante's refusal to convert (I shall analyse this episode more closely in the next chapter) testifies to his faithfulness to the values he professed the *Inamoramento de Orlando*. His conduct in the Lipadusa duel is impeccable: he fights until the bitter end — that is until the invulnerable Orlando severs his head with the enchanted sword Balisarda, acting as an instrument of the mysterious forces that govern History.

### *Dardinello, Cloridano, and Medoro: Ariosto and the 'Aspramonte'*

In the previous chapter we saw that while Boiardo's portrayal of Saracen Africa is greatly indebted to the *Aspramonte*, his Agramante and Dardinelo surpass their fathers in chivalry. Could we say Ariosto, too, engages with the *Aspramonte*? Or is his main source the *Inamoramento de Orlando*? At first glance, it may seem that Ariosto's knowledge of the *Aspramonte* tradition is superficial. His references to the conquest of Risa and the death of Ruggiero's parents contradict all the extant versions of the medieval legend: Bradamante (*Fur.*, XXXIII 64 A; 60 B; XXXVI 60 C), Atlante (XXXIII 78,3–8 A; 74 B; XXXVI 74 C) and Ruggiero (XXXIII 78,3–8 A; 74 B; XXXVI 74 C) all say that Agramante's father Troiano was one of the murderers, which flies in the face of the *Aspramonte* tradition.[85] It could be that Ariosto read a version now lost, but it is more likely that he deliberately modified the story narrated in the *Aspramonte* in order to give his Ruggiero one more reason to convert to Christianity. While Boiardo chose not to draw attention to the tragic events that followed the conquest of Risa, Ariosto accuses Troiano of a crime he did not commit.[86] However, he does portray Agramante as a more sympathetic character than his father. Similarly, Ariosto's Dardinello is a far cry from his father Almonte. A careful reading of Dardinello's story reveals that Ariosto may have had a better knowledge of the *Aspramonte* than generally believed.

Dardinello is a minor character in the *Inamoramento de Orlando*. In the *Furioso* he steps into the spotlight during the battle for Paris. When the Saracens start to lose heart, he makes a speech to encourage his troops:

> — S'Aimonte meritò ch'in voi si serbe
> di lui memoria, hor ne vedrò l'effetto:
> i' vedrò (dicea lor) se me, suo figlio,
> lasciar vorrete in così gran periglio.
>
> State, ve priego per mia verde etade,
> in cui solete haver sì larga speme:
> deh non vogliate andar per fil di spade,
> che in Aphrica non torni di noi seme.
> Per tutto ne saran chiuse le strade

---

85    On these references to the death of Ruggiero's parents see Maria Pavlova, 'L'Africa nell'*Orlando furioso*', *Schifanoia*, 54–55 (2018), 193–205 (pp. 200–01).

86    Yet later in the poem the narrator states that Ruggiero's father was killed by Almonte (*Fur.*, XXXIV 5 AB; XXXVIII C), which suggests that Ariosto may after all have been familiar with the *Aspramonte*.

se non andiam ben còlti et stretti insieme:
troppo alto muro et troppo larga fossa
è il monte e il mar, pria che tornar si possa.

È meglio qui morir, ch'alli supplìci
darsi a discretïon di questi cani.
State saldi, per Dio, fedeli amici;
che tutti sono altri rimedii vani.
Non han di noi più vita li nemici;
più d'un'alma non han, più di due mani. –

['If Aimonte deserved to leave in your memories,
now let me see proof of it:
let me see', he told them, 'how ready you are
to desert me, his son, in such a perilous pass.

Stand firm, I beg you for the sake of my green years
in which you have placed such hopes:
no, don't allow yourselves to be cut down
so that not one of our seed returns to Africa.
Everywhere the roads shall be closed to us
If we do not hang together as one body:
the mountains are too high a wall, the sea too broad a moat
between us and our home-coming

Far better is to die here than to yield ourselves
to the grim mercies of these dogs.
Stand firm, for love of God, my loyal friends;
as we have no other choice left.
Our foes have no more lives than we have;
they have but one soul, one pair of hands.']
(*Fur.*, XVI 49,5–8; 50–51,1–6 AB; XVIII C)

This rhetorical *tour de force* is deeply moving. The affectionate tone of Dardinello's plea recalls Agramante's speech to his vassal kings in *Inam.*, II i 37. Dardinello, King of Zumara, does not bark orders, but rather appeals to his soldiers' affection by calling them his friends and by reminding them of their African roots and of their love for their late father. He does not rebuke them for their pusillanimity or threaten them with death, as Saracen kings — including Almonte in Andrea da Barberino's *Aspramonte* — often do in similar situations, but rather he explains to them that they will all perish and no one will return to Africa if they do not unite against their enemy.[87] While Almonte's rants in the *Aspramonte* did not have the desired

---

87    Andrea da Barberino's Almonte accuses his troops of cowardice on numerous occasions: 'Almonte rispose adirato: "O falsa gente, uomini ricredenti, per vostra colpa e vostra codardia abbiamo noi perduti e' quattro iddii del padre mio e le bandiere e la mia torre. Voi solavate dire in Africa prima morire che volgere le spalle, e ier mattina meno di diecimila cavalieri cristiani missono in isconfitta centomila cavalieri africani. O gente vile e da poco [...]"' [Almonte replied angrily: 'Oh, treacherous people, faithless men, it is because of you and your cowardice that we lost my father's four gods and the banners and my tower. In Africa you used to say that you would rather die than turn your backs in flight, and yesterday morning less than ten thousand Christians defeated a hundred thousand African knights. Oh, vile, worthless people [...]'] (*Aspramonte*, III i). See also *Aspramonte*, I xli; and II lvi.

effect, Dardinello's words perform a miracle: 'el rimembrar Aimonte così accese | l'exercito Aphrican che fuggea prima, | che di più presto porre in sue difese | le braccia che le spalle fece stima' [the memory of Almonte put such fire | into the hearts of the African fugitives | that they thought better of turning their backs in flight; | they lent their arms to rally to his name] (*Fur.*, XVI 52,1–4 AB; XVIII C).[88] Ironically, the Africans have warmer feelings towards Almonte after his death than when he was alive.

Dardinello is killed by Rinaldo in a duel that can hardly be called fair, considering that the former is little more than a boy and the latter is one of the best knights in the world. Rinaldo is greatly impressed by the valour of this Saracen youth, but he kills him in cold blood, judging that it would be a mistake to let him mature into a superb warrior.[89] As for Dardinello, he is unafraid to confront one of Charlemagne's paladins. The episode of his death could be read a radical rewriting of Almonte's death: in all versions of the *Aspramonte*, Almonte, a world-famous knight, is killed by Orlando, an adolescent. While Dardinello's final moments are painfully beautiful (the poet compares him to a 'purpureo fior' [a purple flower] severed by the ploughshare (XVI 153,1 AB; XVIII C)), Almonte's are grotesque: Orlando finishes him off with the shaft of a lance. In the fifteenth-century *Aspramonte* Almonte disgraces himself by begging for mercy and promising — in vain — to convert to Christianity and to enter Charlemagne's service if Orlando spares his life.

The differences between the son and the father do not end here, for Dardinello's death does not mark the end of his story. When darkness falls, Cloridano and Medoro, two young African soldiers who 'havean ne la seconda et ne l'afflitta | fortuna sempre amato Dardinello' [in good fortune and ill | had always loved

---

88   Modern editors of the *Furioso* (Caretti, Bigi, Ceserani and Zatti, Matarrese, and Praloran) usually cite the speech of Virgil's Pallas (*Aeneid*, X 368–72) as the main source for Dardinello's speech to his soldiers. It is possible, however, that Ariosto also uses a vernacular chivalric text. In the *Vendetta di Falconetto*, Tiborgo, Orlando and other Christians knights make similar speeches during one of the battles, but without managing to raise their soldiers' morale (lexical points of contact are highlighted in italics): 'Tiborgo cridava: "O christiana zente, | *per Dio stati saldi* ora senza menzogna. | Oimè, lo fuzire sì n'è tropo gran vergogna! || *Stati saldi* uno pocho per mio amore | [...]' || Simile Orlando di qua e di là corea | suso Valentino per retenere li christiani, | con humile parole a loro diceva: | "*Amici* mei cari e franchi capitani, | che abandonasti me giamai non lo credea. | Ora stati fermi apresso a me suli piani, | vedete Dunindarna che tengo fra le mane, | la quale è per defendere ogni christiano. || *De'*, stati uno pocho saldi per amore mio, | io ve farò schudo, lanza e brando, | ritornati a ferire sopra il populo rio, | *non vogliate* la fede nostra zire abandonando."' [Tiborgo was shouting: 'O, Christian people, | for the love of God do stand firm now. | Alas, fleeing is too shameful! | Stand firm a bit more if you love me | [...]' || Similarly, Orlando was galloping back and forth | on his Valentino to stop the Christians from fleeing; | he was telling them with humble words: | 'My dear friends and brave captains, | I never thought that you would abandon me. | Now stand firm by my side on the battlefield; | look at Dunindarna that I am holding in my hand, | it is here to defend every Christian. || Please, stand firm a bit more if you love me. | I will be your shield, your lance and your sword. | Come back to strike the evil people; | don't allow yourselves to go away abandoning our faith] (*Vendetta di Falconetto A*, fol. G ii^r).

89   According to Giudicetti, the duel with Dardinello tarnishes Rinaldo's image: it is difficult, he argues, to feel sympathy for Charlemagne and Rinaldo because 'non si esimono [...] dal compiere azioni ciniche, spietate' [they do not hesitate [...] to commit cynical, ruthless acts] (Giudicetti, *Mandricardo e la melanconia*, p. 147).

Dardinello] (165,6–7), attempt to recover his body. This is a much studied episode, one of the most cited and celebrated examples of Ariosto's reworking of classical sources. It is well known that Cloridano and Medoro are modelled on the two most famous male couples in classical epics, namely Virgil's Nisus and Euryalus and Statius's Hopleus and Dymas.[90] And yet there is evidence to suggest that Ariosto also drew inspiration from a vernacular text, using Virgil and Statius to rewrite the episode of Margone's and Asperante's desertion in Andrea da Barberino's *Aspramonte*.

The theme of betrayal is the overarching theme of the *Aspramonte*. In Andrea da Barberino's version Almonte is both a reluctant, remorseful traitor and a man who experiences betrayal. He is particularly close to two of his companions, Margone and Asperante, nephews of the powerful Amostante. Both of them are kings, both are very rich. They owe everything to Almonte: as Ulieno of Sarza explains in *Aspramonte A*, III xlii, he rescued them from prison, where they had been incarcerated on Balante's order. Almonte showers them with honours and gifts, but Margone and Asperante do not love him and repay him with shocking ingratitude. Having been left in charge of Almonte's rearguard, they desert when they are attacked by Gherado da Fratta's men, their betrayal provoking the narrator's indignation:

> Allora Margon disse al fratello Sperante. 'Per mia fe', ecco Franzosi presso a noi! Egli ànno passate le schiere d'Almonte per forza. Ben disse vero Balante che e' franciosi Cristiani sono buoni combattitori. Se noi non ci partiamo noi siamo tutti morti. Male à fatto Almonte a combattere sanza el re Agolante contro a' Franchi. Quanto egli si cura poco di noi, e noi poco ci curereno [*sic*] di lui. Io voglio campare; e tu che farai?' Disse Asperante: 'E io ancora me ne verrò.' E armati montorono a cavallo e confortorono e' cavalieri, e loro tremavano di paura. E inviarono grande gente alla battaglia, e, come gli ebbono messi nella battaglia, ed eglino entrarono per una valle, e sanza fare colpo si fuggirono, abbandonando come cattivi le bandiere del loro singnore; ché, se eglino fussino stati fermi in sul poggio, Gherardo non arebbe potuto mai torre le bandiere.

> [Then Margon told his brother Sperante. 'Upon my faith, here are the Franks near us! They have pushed through Almonte's troops by force. Balante was right when he said that the Christian Franks are good fighters. If we don't leave, we will all die. Almonte shouldn't have fought the Franks without King Agolante. We will care as little for him as he cares for us. I want to escape; and you, what will you do?' Asperante said: 'And I will also go away.' And, wearing their armour, they mounted their horses and reassured their soldiers, and they were trembling with fear. And they sent many men into the battle, and, as they had put them into the battle, and they rode into a valley, and without dealing

---

90    Among the numerous studies on the classical sources of the episode of Cloridano and Medoro, the following may be mentioned: Eduardo Saccone, 'Cloridano e Medoro, con alcuni argomenti per una lettura del primo *Furioso*', *MLN*, 83, 1 (1968), 67–99 (reprinted in Idem, *Il Soggetto del Furioso e altri saggi tra Quattro e Cinquecento* (Naples: Liguori, 1974), pp. 161–200); Daniel Javitch, 'The Imitation of Imitations in the *Orlando Furioso*', *Renaissance Quarterly*, 38, no. 2 (1985), 215–39 (pp. 217–22); Wiley Feinstein, 'Ariosto's parodic rewriting of Virgil in the episode of Cloridano and Medoro', *South Atlantic Review*, 55, 1 (1990), 17–34; Maria Cristina Cabani, 'Ariosto, Tasso e la tradizione cinquecentesca', in Eadem, *Gli amici amanti: Copie eroiche e sortite notturne nell'epica italiana* (Naples: Liguori, 1995), pp. 17–53 (especially pp. 17–35).

a single blow, they fled, shamelessly leaving their lord's banners; for, if they had stood firm on the hill, Gherardo would never have managed to seize the banners.] (*Aspramonte A*, III xviii)[91]

It could be that Ariosto thought of this episode when he was composing the stanzas in which Medoro — a common soldier of humble origins but one who is endowed with uncommon moral integrity and courage — communicates to his friend Cloridano his intention to find their king's body:

> Volto al compagno, disse — O Cloridano,
> io non ti posso dir quanto me incresca
> del mio signor, che sia rimaso al piano,
> per lupi e corbi, ohimè! troppo degna esca.
> A pensar come sempre mi fu humano,
> mi par che quando anchor quest'anima esca
> in honor di sua fama, io non compensi
> né sciolga verso lui l'oblighi immensi.
>
> Io voglio andar, perché non stia insepulto
> in mezo la campagna, a ritrovarlo [...]
>
> [He turned to his companion and said, 'O Cloridano,
> I cannot tell you how much it grieves me
> that my lord has been left in the field,
> to be food — all too dainty, alas! — for wolves and crows.
> When I think how good he always was to me,
> I feel that even if I gave my life
> to serve his fame I could not repay him
> or discharge my immense debt to him.
>
> I mean to go and find him
> so that his body does not remain in the field unburied.]
> (*Fur.*, XVI 168–69,1–2 AB; XVIII C)

The striking contrast between Margone's and Medoro's speeches may not be accidental. Almonte, the father, is betrayed by his companions. Dardinello, the son, is intensely loved by his soldiers even after his death.[92]

---

91    These two characters feature in the fifteenth-century *Aspramonte in rima*, where it is Margone who kills Ruggiero with a poisoned dart. Their story is slightly different, however. They are taken prisoners by the Christians who treat them very well and present them with new armour and new horses. An exchange of prisoners is negotiated, and they return to Almonte, who is very happy see them. They do not take part in the battle in which Almonte's army is defeated: instead, they lie in wait nearby, and so their new armour is without a dent. Then they return to Agolante who, upon seeing their shining armour, decides that they sold his son to the Christians and has them executed. By contrast, the anonymous *Aspramonte* in prose is very close to Andrea da Barberino's version. In it, Almonte at first refuses to believe that his dearest friends have betrayed him, killing the Saracen who tells him the devastating news. When the bad news sinks in, his grief is immense: 'E quando Almonte lo 'ntese, per gran dolore credette morire e stette uno pezzo che quasi non si sentia' [And when Almonte heard it, he thought he would die of the immense pain and for a while he almost lost all self-awareness] (*Aspramonte BL*, fol. 33ᵛ).

92    The character of Medoro could also be modelled on 'il zoveneto bello' [the handsome youth] who finds the body of his dear lord, King Alchero, and, weeping, carries it to the Saracen camp in the longer version of the *Vendetta di Falconetto* (*Vendetta di Falconetto A*, fol. P iiiʳ).

Eventually, Agolante realizes that Margone and Asperante have betrayed Almonte and has them executed. It is Ulieno, Rodomonte's father, who — in the presence of the African barons — accuses them of having abandoned Almonte and urges Agolante to punish them with the greatest severity. In the next chapter, we will consider the similarities between Ulieno and Rodomonte, who throws a similar accusation at Ruggiero in the final canto of the *Furioso*. For now, it suffices to note that the proem to the following canto, in which Ariosto states that princes find out who their true friends are only in times of affliction ('Alcun non può saper da chi sia amato | quando felice in su la ruota siede [...]' [A man riding high on Fortune's wheel | cannot tell who really loves him [...]] (*Fur.*, XVII 1,1–2 AB; XIX C)), could serve as an epigraph both to Almonte's and to Dardinello's stories. But while the former story is a reminder of how untrustworthy and ungrateful people can be, the latter conveys a different message, restoring the reader's faith in chivalry and reaffirming the ideal of *fides* which is central to Ariosto's *Weltanschauung*. This ideal, as has been argued by Eduardo Saccone, is at the heart of the poem.[93] At the same time, as has been shown by Albert Ascoli, it is problematized and questioned in a number of episodes.[94] As we shall see in the final chapter of this book, the complementary themes of *fides* and betrayal dominate the plot centred on the *Furioso*'s dynastic protagonist, who converts to Christianity to fulfil his dynastic function, but at the price of compromising his conscience.

---

93    Saccone, 'Cloridano e Medoro, con alcuni argomenti per una lettura del primo *Furioso*'.
94    According to Ascoli, 'una crisi profonda della fede come imperativo etico si ha sin dal primo *Furioso*' [already in the first *Furioso* we witness a profound crisis of faith as an ethical imperative] ('Fede e riscrittura: il *Furioso* del '32', p. 119; see also Idem, 'Faith as Cover-up: Ariosto's *Orlando Furioso*').

# CHAPTER 5

❖

# Rodomonte and Ruggiero:
# A Matter of Honour

Peggio far non si può sotto le stelle,
che tradir la sua patria e il suo signore.

[One cannot commit a greater evil in this world
than betray one's homeland and one's lord.]
(Francesco Cieco da Ferrara, *Mambriano*, III 79,1–2)

Bringing Boiardo's poem to a close, Ariosto stages the events which Boiardo promised to narrate in Book III. By the last canto of the *Furioso* the prophecies of the King of Garamantha and Atalante are (mostly) fulfilled. Agramante is defeated. Ruggiero, 'la semente | d'ogni vertù' [the seed | of all our virtues] (*Inam.*, II xxi 60,1–2), has converted to Christianity and has married Bradamante, thus becoming the founder of the Este dynasty. Charlemagne throws a sumptuous party for the newlywed couple. True to his reputation, 'Più de li altri valor mostra Ruggiero, | [...] | e così in danza, in lotta et in ogni opra | sempre con molto honor resta di sopra' [Ruggiero shows greater prowess than the rest | [...] | in dancing, in wrestling, in everything | he always emerges the honoured victor] (*Fur.*, XL 74,5–8 A; 73 B; XLVI 100 C). The atmosphere is joyous and serene. And yet, as the curtain is about to fall on the last act of the story that began in Book II of the *Inamoramento de Orlando*, a stranger interrupts the wedding feast. Rodomonte of Sarza has arrived in Paris in order to accuse his former brother-in-arms of having betrayed their lord Agramante. What follows is one of the most dramatic as well as enigmatic duels of the entire poem, the 'pugna incerta' [uncertain battle] (86,2 A; 85 B; 114 C) that will culminate in Rodomonte's death. This death is of fundamental importance for understanding not only the ending of the *Furioso* but also the poem as a whole and its engagement with Boiardo and the preceding chivalric tradition.

Building on the insights gained in the previous chapters, the present chapter is thus devoted to a case study of special significance. It comprises three parts. I shall start by briefly looking at the critical debate surrounding the final confrontation between Rodomonte and Ruggiero. I shall then consider the respective stories of Roda(o)monte and Rug(g)iero in the *Inamoramento de Orlando* and the *Furioso*. This will enable us to approach from a new perspective the events of the final canto, which will be analysed in the final part of this chapter.

## Rodomonte and the ending of the *Furioso*: scholarly perspectives

It would not be an exaggeration to say that the ending of the *Furioso* is one of the most hotly contested topics in Ariosto scholarship. Since the mid-sixteenth century, countless critics have commented on this climactic duel and its meaning. Barely ten years after the publication of the 1532 edition, Tullio Fausto da Longiano and Lodovico Dolce compared it to the single combat between Aeneas and Turnus at the end of Book XII of Virgil's *Aeneid*.[1] According to early commentators, in this episode Ariosto is both a 'vero imitator di Virgilio' [true imitator of Virgil][2] and a more refined poet: Girolamo Ruscelli, for example, claims that the victory of the Christian Ruggiero is less problematic than Aeneas's inasmuch as, unlike 'il misero Turno' [the poor Turnus] who 'non havea di nulla offeso già mai Enea' [had not wronged Aeneas in any way], Rodomonte does not elicit the readers' compassion, 'poi che Rodomonte era venuto con tanto torto et con tanta temerità a disfidar Ruggiero' [since Rodomonte was so ill-advised and so reckless to challenge Ruggiero to a duel].[3] This view is shared by a number of modern scholars, such as Joseph C. Sitterson and James Lawrence Shulman.[4] It has been argued that the ending of the *Furioso* is modelled on that of the *Aeneid*, with the last cantos advocating Christian values and showing a pronounced moralizing tendency.[5] In this perspective, Rodomonte becomes a character represented 'sotto il seme delle negatività' [in a negative light],[6] an 'eroe capovolto' [reversed hero],[7] an antihero.

Not surprisingly, the word 'male' [evil] frequently surfaces in scholarly discussions of the last canto: for Marcello Turchi, Rodomonte stands for the 'violenza del male che assume concreti aspetti di sconvolgente terribilità di cataclisma' [violence of evil that manifests itself in the unsettling horror of cataclysm];[8] according to Roger Baillet, the Saracen knight 'devient le héros de l'ombre, l'un des obstacles majeurs de la croisade contre le Mal' [becomes the shady hero, one of the greatest obstacles

---

1    For Tullio Fausto da Longiano's comparison between the final duel of the *Furioso* and the duel between Aeneas and Turnus, see the 1556 Valgrisi edition of the *Furioso*, fols a3$^r$-a4$^r$ (fol. a3$^v$) (Fausto's commentary on Ariosto's classical sources was first printed in the Francesco Bindoni and Mapheo Pasini 1542 edition of the poem). See also Lodovico Dolce's 'Allegoria' [Allegory] to canto XLVI as well as his *Brieve dimostratione di molte comparationi et sentenze dall'Ariosto in diversi autori imitate*, in *Orlando furioso* (Venice: Gabriel Iolito di Ferrarii, 1542), fols 251$^v$ and ★★iii$^v$, respectively.
2    Fórnari, p. 758.
3    See Girolamo Ruscelli, 'Argomento' [Argument] to canto XLVI, in the 1556 Valgrisi edition of the *Furioso*, p. 520.
4    Joseph C. Sitterson, 'Allusive and Elusive Meanings: Reading Ariosto's Vergilian Ending', *Renaissance Quarterly*, 14 (1992), 1–9 (p. 13); James Lawrence Shulman, ' "Sferza e sprona": The Flight from Authority in the *Orlando Furioso*', in Idem, *'The Pale Cast of Thought': Hesitation and Decision in the Renaissance Epic* (Newark: University of Delaware Press, 1998), pp. 23–55 (pp. 51–54).
5    For an overview of scholarly works on the so-called caesura separating the 'romance' and the 'epic' parts of the poem, see Giudicetti, *Mandricardo e la melanconia*, pp. 43–47.
6    Marco Praloran, *Tempo e azione nell'*Orlando furioso (Florence: Leo S. Olschki, 1999), p. 105.
7    Giuseppe Della Palma, 'L'eroe capovolto: Rodomonte', in Idem, *Le strutture narrative dell'*"Orlando furioso' (Florence: Olschki, 1984), pp. 110–25.
8    Marcello Turchi, *Ariosto o della liberazione fantastica* (Ravenna: A. Longo, 1969), pp. 370–77 (p. 373).

for the crusade against Evil];[9] Daniela Delcorno Branca calls Rodomonte the 'ultima sopravvivenza del male' [the last remnant of evil],[10] while Alberto Casadei asserts that the ending of the poem 'testimonia, eticamente, la vittoria necessaria del bene sul male' [ethically testifies to the necessary victory of good over evil] and at the same time shows that the happy ending was a provisional armistice rather than a definitive victory.[11] A descendant of Nimrod, the arrogant tyrant who supervised the construction of the Tower of Babel, Rodomonte has been compared to Capaneus, Mezentius, Dante's Filippo Argenti, and even Milton's Satan, a rebellious angel invested with an aura of sinister grandeur.[12] For Cavallo, 'all the force of his violence is [...] directed specifically against those of the Christian faith'.[13] David Marsh and Peter Marinelli believe that, through him, Ariosto was adumbrating the Turkish threat,[14] while Peter De Sa Wiggins suggests that Rodomonte is a symbol of the destructive fury that transformed Ariosto's Italy into a battlefield.[15]

9    Baillet, *Le monde poétique de l'Arioste*, p. 403.

10    Daniela Delcorno Branca, 'La conclusione dell'*Orlando furioso*: qualche osservazione', in *Boiardo, Ariosto e i libri di battaglia*, pp. 127–37 (p. 128).

11    Alberto Casadei, 'Il finale e la poetica del *Furioso*', *Chroniques italiennes*, 19 (2011), 1–21 (pp. 9–10) <http:||chroniquesitaliennes.univ-paris3.fr|PDF|web19|Casaseiweb19.pdf> [consulted 12 January 2020]. A similar view was held by Tommaso Porcacchi, who in his 'Allegoria' [Allegory] to canto XLVI claims that Rodomonte's arrival in Paris makes the reader realize that 'niuna felicità in questo mondo pieno di miserie ci può venir compita et perfetta' [in this sorrow-filled world no happiness can be complete and perfect]. See *Orlando furioso* (Venice: Domenico Farri, 1580), fol. NN 2ʳ. Porcacchi's allegories first appeared in the *Furioso* printed by Domenico and Giovanni Battista Guerra in Venice in 1568.

12    See John M. Steadman, 'A Milton-Ariosto Parallel: Satan and Rodomonte (*Paradise Lost*, IV, 181)', *Zeitschrift für romanische Philologie*, 77, nos 5–6 (1961), 514–16; Baillet, *Le monde poétique de l'Arioste*, p. 401. According to Peter De Sa Wiggins, 'If the Good were apparent in Ariosto's world beset with illusion, Rodomonte could be regarded as a Miltonic Satan, but as it is, he must be regarded as exhibiting the blindness in many tragic figures of Renaissance and classical literature' ('The *Furioso*'s Third Protagonist', *MLN*, 98 (1983), 30–54 (p. 40)). Peter V. Marinelli, however, sees Rodomonte as an infernal monster: '[...] because Ariosto remembered the Vergilian interpreters' association of Turnus with the devil, and because he darkens and brutalizes Turnus's energy in Rodomonte, depriving him of heroic qualities in his blood-lust against women and children, we see through to the primal attack on human felicity in Eden' (Peter V. Marinelli, *Ariosto and Boiardo: the Origins of 'Orlando Furioso'* (Columbia: University of Missouri Press, 1987), p. 213). As for more recent studies, Cavallo states that Rodomonte 'want[s] to live and die as a god unto himself' (Jo Ann Cavallo, 'The Pathways of Knowledge in Boiardo and Ariosto: The Case of Rodamonte', *Italica*, 79, no. 3 (2002), 303–20 (p. 314); and Eadem, *The World beyond Europe*, p. 121), while Giuseppe Mazzotta views this character in light of the advent of Protestantism in sixteenth-century Europe: 'through Rodomonte's tragedy of freedom, Ariosto unveils Luther's tragic understanding of faith, which is nonetheless capable of shattering Erasmus's rational, limited understanding' (Giuseppe Mazzotta, 'Italian Renaissance Epic', in *The Cambridge Companion to the Epic*, ed. by Catherine Bates (New York: Cambridge University Press, 2010), pp. 93–118 (p. 110)).

13    Cavallo, *The World beyond Europe*, p. 118.

14    David Marsh, 'Ruggiero and Leone: Revision and Resolution in Ariosto's *Orlando Furioso*', *MLN*, 96 (1981), 144–51 (p. 151); Marinelli, *Ariosto and Boiardo: the Origins of Orlando Furioso*, p. 213.

15    See De Sa Wiggins, 'The *Furioso*'s Third Protagonist', and also Idem, *Rodomonte*, in *Figures in Ariosto's Tapestry: Character and Design in the 'Orlando Furioso'*, pp. 41–66.

And yet, many critics agree that Rodomonte is a memorable — and charismatic — character,[16] with some going as far as to claim that he is superior to his opponent from the aesthetic point of view.[17] It has even been suggested that he is endowed with some positive traits, such as courage and sentimentality. After all, this 'colosso dall'anima sensibile' [giant with a sensitive soul][18] builds a tomb for Issabella, whom he unwittingly kills and who then becomes the object of his adoration. Thus, for a number of scholars, Rodomonte is a barbarian — another word that is frequently used in studies devoted to this figure — who is perhaps capable of noble sentiments, but who lives in his own world and is, in essence, a primitive creature. The ending of the *Furioso*, argues Mario Santoro, 'suggell[a] la naturale conclusione del destino del "barbaro": il quale, nella assoluta, e generosa, fedeltà ai suoi "valori", è incapace di una presa di coscienza della realtà, incapace quindi di misurarsi con l'esperienza' [marks the natural conclusion to the fate of the 'barbarian', who, in his absolute and selfless fidelity to his 'values', is incapable of understanding reality, and therefore incapable of measuring himself against experience].[19]

It would be wrong to claim that Rodomonte is universally seen as an embodiment of evil. Francesco De Sanctis admires his audacity and superhuman strength,[20] while Emilio Zanette contends that Rodomonte — 'un forte che non mente e non manca mai a se stesso' [a strong character who never lies and is always true to himself] — never loses the reader's sympathy and interest, not even in the last canto, where Ariosto allows him to 'grandeggiare accostandolo a Turno' [tower over the rest, likening him to Turnus].[21] Giudicetti, in turn, maintains that the African warrior 'è

16    According to Giuseppina Fumagalli, although this 'gagliarda creatura' [robust creature] is one of the best-drawn characters in the *Furioso*, the poet cannot be said to be emotionally involved (Giuseppina Fumagalli, 'La "bella istoria" di Rodomonte di Sarza', in her *Unità fantastica dell'*Orlando Furioso (Messina: Giuseppe Principato, 1933), pp. 68–117 (p. 116)).

17    'La figura del vincitore [...] — states Giuseppe Raniòlo — ha un eroismo alquanto artefatto' [The figure of the winner [...] displays somewhat affected heroism] (Giuseppe Raniòlo, *Lo spirito e l'arte dell'*'Orlando Furioso' (Milan: Mondadori, 1929), p. 75), while for Thomas Greene, 'Ruggiero, who is meant to embody the most serious heroic ideals of the poem, is lamentably a failure, neither noble, nor believable nor finally very interesting' (Thomas Greene, 'Ariosto and the Earlier Italian Renaissance', in Idem, *The Descent from Heaven: a Study in Epic Continuity* (New Haven: Yale University Press, 1963), pp. 104–43 (pp. 142–43)). See also Franco Pool, *Interpretazione dell'*'Orlando furioso' (Florence: La Nuova Italia, 1968), p. 180.

18    Italo Calvino, *Orlando furioso di Ludovico Ariosto raccontato da Italo Calvino* (Turin: Einaudi, 1970), p. 155.

19    Mario Santoro, 'Rodomonte: la defezione della "ragione"', in Idem, *Ariosto e il Rinascimento*, pp. 263–74 (p. 273); also Ragni, 'Rodomonte e Gradasso: storia incroiata di due "ruganti"'.

20    'Rodomonte ed Orlando sono i due caratteri più originali; ma Orlando non interessa sempre [...] Rodomonte interessa sempre, come un'attrice ottima in mezzo ad una compagnia mediocre' [Rodomonte and Orlando are the two most original characters; but Orlando is not always interesting [...] Rodomonte is always interesting, like an excellent actress in a mediocre theatre company] (De Sanctis, *La poesia cavalleresca*, p. 142). His charisma is due to the fact that he is 'in uno stato perpetuo di pazzia' [in a permanent state of madness] (ibid., pp. 141).

21    Emilio Zanette, 'Rodomonte', in Idem, *Conversazioni sull'*'Orlando furioso', pp. 349–95 (pp. 387, 389). Ragni, too, argues that thanks to the Virgilian reminiscences Rodomonte emerges as a victim, because, like Turnus, he is 'arrogante negli atteggiamenti, violento, ma sventurato, anzi vessato da uomini e dèi' [arrogant in his manners, but unlucky, indeed, persecuted by men and gods] (Ragni, 'Rodomonte e Gradasso: storia incroiata di due "ruganti"', p. 412). See also Giuseppe Ravegnani,

portatore di caos e di vivacità nel poema' [brings chaos and vivacity into the poem] and that, together with Mandricardo, he is viewed positively by the poet.[22]

However, despite these attempts to 'redeem' Rodomonte, few interpreters take his last speech seriously, not least because Rodomonte himself withdrew from the war long before Ruggiero's conversion. '[N]oi comprendiamo e giustifichiamo lo sposo di Bradamante' [we undertand and justify Bradamante's husband], states Zanette, 'ma il saracino non è l'uomo da comprenderlo [...] egli stesso ha abbandonato Agramante, eppure è convintissimo di non averlo tradito' [but the Saracen is unable to understand him [...] he himself abandoned Agramante, and yet he is totally convinced that he has not betrayed him].[23] According to Giudicetti, Rodomonte stays true to his personality — that of a charismatic troublemaker –, while Ruggiero fulfils his duty, assuming his role as the founder of the glorious Este dynasty: his is a morally sound choice, consonant with the (for the critic, alas, not wholly Ariostan) values of the second half of the *Furioso*. For Giudicetti, therefore, 'la vera accusa che il colosso pagano rivolge a Ruggiero è quella di esser venuto meno a se stesso, di aver tradito il proprio lato cortese e avventuroso' [in reality, the Saracen giant accuses Ruggiero of having let himself down, having betrayed his courteous and adventurous side].[24]

Thus, most of Rodomonte's 'apologists' attach little importance to the literal meaning of his last words. But one critic stands out. Far from dismissing the accusation of betrayal as groundless, Attilio Momigliano affirms that Ariosto concedes the moral victory to Rodomonte who — paradoxically — proves to be a better knight than his Christian opponent:

> Non gli passa nemmeno per la mente che il suo popolo ormai è sconfitto, che il duello non giova: Ruggiero ha abbandonato i suoi, e dev'essere punito. Il vincitore del duello sarà Ruggiero, ma l'eroe rimane Rodomonte, che getta la vita per punire un traditore. Qui il cavaliere è, più che il cristiano, il pagano.

> [It does not even cross his mind that his people have been defeated, that the duel is pointless: Ruggiero has abandoned his fellow Saracens, and he must be punished. Ruggiero will win the duel, but Rodomonte is the hero who sacrifices his life to punish a traitor. Here the Saracen is a better knight than the Christian.][25]

Needless to say, Momigliano's interpretation is as surprising as it is original. His thought-provoking view deserves to be further explored, all the more so

'Vita, morte e miracolo di Rodomonte' [1929], in *L'ottava d'oro: La vita e l'opera di Ludovico Ariosto: Letture tenute in Ferrara per il Quarto Centenario della morte del Poeta* (Milan: Mondadori, 1933), pp. 203–23 (p. 223) (later republished in Idem, *Dieci saggi dal Petrarca al Manzoni* (Genua: Emiliano degli Orfini, 1937), pp. 37–72).

22   Giudicetti, *Mandricardo e la melanconia*, p. 168.

23   Zanette, *Conversazioni sull''Orlando furioso'*, p. 389.

24   Giudicetti, *Mandricardo e la melanconia*, p. 176. For a similar interpretation, see entry 'Rodomonte', in *Dizionario Bompiani delle opere e dei personaggi di tutti i tempi e di tutte le letterature*, 11 vols (Milan: Bompiani, 1983), XI, pp. 549–50 (p. 550) and David Quint, 'The Death of Brandimarte and the Ending of the *Orlando furioso*', *Annali d'italianistica*, 12 (1994), 75–85 (p. 83).

25   Attilio Momigliano, *Rodomonte*, in Idem, *Saggio su l''Orlando Furioso'* (Bari: Laterza, 1928), pp. 279–307 (p. 292).

considering that later interpreters of the figure of Rodomonte and his role in the *Furioso* appear to have for the most part ignored it.[26] Not only does Momigliano stress Rodomonte's nobility, but he deems him superior to Ruggiero. Such a claim might appear altogether absurd if we recall that the dynastic theme assumes a central importance in the final canto. Nevertheless, the very fact that some critics have felt the need to defend Ruggiero, to justify his decision to convert, reveals that his innocence is after all not so obvious. If the *Furioso* was not a Christian poem, seems to be saying Andrew Fichter, Ruggiero's conversion would amount to a betrayal.[27] 'No reader can deny that there is a certain literal truth in the charge', asserts De Sa Wiggins, 'whether it is taken to apply strictly to Ruggiero's relations with Agramante or whether it is taken in a more general sense. The charge is outrageous only because it comes from Rodomonte and because it is unjust to Ruggiero's intentions'.[28]

Momigliano reaches his provocative conclusion in a flash of intuition rather than as a result of a painstaking critical analysis of the duel in question and the events that precede it. He does not dwell on the themes of loyalty and betrayal, nor does he discuss the relationship between Rodomonte and Agramante or that between Ruggiero and his lord and maternal cousin. In order to make sense of his interpretation, it is necessary to examine afresh the respective stories of Agramante's best champions, which is what I aim to do presently.

## The duellists

### Rodomonte

As we saw in the previous chapters, the main African knights of the two *Orlandos* are related to the Saracen protagonists of the *Aspramonte*. Rodamonte, states Boiardo, 'fo figliol del forte Ulïeno' [was strong Ulieno's son] (*Inam.*, II i 16,8), Agolante's vassal who took part in his expedition against Charlemagne, and 'pose tuta Franza

---

26   Nancy Lazzaro subscribes to Momigliano's reading, citing his conclusion and adding that 'Rodomonte, paradossalmente pagano, molte volte segue una logica più vera, più onesta degli altri: e alla fine deve morire' [Rodomonte, who, paradoxically, is a Saracen, follows a truer, more honest logic than the others: and in the end he must die] (Nancy Lazzaro, 'Rodomonte e Ariosto nella battaglia di Parigi: Lettura dell'episodio', in *Forma e parola: Studi in memoria di Fredi Chiappelli*, ed. by Dennis J. Dutschke et al. (Rome: Bulzoni, 1992), pp. 235–54 (p. 251)). Ranïolo makes an indirect reference to Momigliano's view when he states that, contrary to what has been argued by some critics, Rodomonte's decision is not an attempt to defend 'l'ideale della fedeltà cavalleresca' [the ideal of chivalric fidelity] but rather 'il capriccio orgoglioso e crudele di un barbaro' [the arrogant and cruel whim of a barbarian] (Ranïolo, *Lo spirito e l'arte dell'*'Orlando Furioso', p. 75).
27   'In one of his aspects Rodomonte is Ruggiero's old carnality; in another Rodomonte is Ruggiero's former adherence to justice in its Old Law formulation as righteousness without charity. Like Ruggiero before his baptism, Rodomonte sees only the literal dimension of justice and so challenges Ruggiero on the grounds that he has betrayed his sworn allegiance to the pagan cause' (Andrew Fichter, 'Ariosto: the dynastic pair, Bradamante and Ruggiero', in Idem, *Poets Historical: Dynastic Epic in the Renaissance* (New Heaven: Yale University Press, 1982), pp. 70–111 (p. 104).
28   Peter De Sa Wiggins, 'Ruggiero', in Idem, *Figures in Ariosto's Tapestry: Character and Design in the* 'Orlando Furioso', pp. 67–108 (p. 107).

in abandono' [put all France within his power] (17,4). Ulien (Ulieno, Uliano) is one of the most important African characters in the twelfth-century *Chanson d'Aspremont* and its Italian *rifacimenti*, his most distinctive trait being his steadfast loyalty to his lord. Though an implacable enemy of the Christians, Ulien, like Baligant in the *Chanson de Roland*, is a perfect knight whose only handicap is not knowing Jesus Christ: 'S'Uliiens fust an Damedex creant, | miauz ne valut Olivier ne Rolant' [If Ulien believed in the Lord God | Olivier and Rolant would not be better knights than he] (*Chanson d'Aspremont*, 8539–40). His death — the Saracen army is routed, but Ulien decides to sell his life dear and is killed by Richier, Duke Berengier's nephew — is one of the gravest blows that destiny deals to Agoulant. In Andrea da Barberino's *Aspramonte* Ulieno is slain by Riccieri Vassallo, while in the fifteenth-century *Aspramonte* he loses his life in a duel with Orlando. Impressed by his valour, the Christian paladin promises to spare him if he converts to Christianity, but the Saracen's reply is an emphatic 'no'.

A paragon of loyalty, Ulien has a strong sense of justice. In the *Chanson d'Aspremont* he urges Agoulant to punish Aprohant and Maragon, Saracen kings who abandoned Eaumont (Almonte) in mortal danger. Lashing out against the traitors, he challenges to a duel anyone willing to defend them; his speech persuades the king to execute the two cowards. In Andrea da Barberino's *Aspramonte*, too, it is Ulieno who convinces Agolante that Asperante and Margone deserve the death penalty. In the fifteenth-century version, Uliano inveighs against Balante who, having decided to renounce Macone during his first encounter with Namo, deserts in the dead of night, abandoning Agolante at a moment when the African camp is torn by internal strife. Uliano's attempt to console Agolante, who sinks into despair upon learning of Balante's betrayal, is touching: 'non temere, signor, né pensar rio: | se ognun ti lassa, non lasseroti io' [fear not, my lord, chase away black thoughts: | I will not leave you even if everybody leaves you] (*Aspramonte*, XIX 164,7–8 [fol. ni$^v$]).

In referring to Ulieno in his poem, Boiardo stresses his physical strength, arrogance and prowess (*Inam.*, II i 17,1–6; 52,4; xiv 34,6–8), qualities that he passed on to his son Rodamonte. In chivalric romances sons often take after their fathers. No wonder, therefore, that the profound bond of friendship and loyalty between Agramante and Rodamonte mirrors that between Agolante and Ulieno, with the former relationship being less formal and deferential, given that there is hardly any age difference between the characters in question. Agramante is twenty-two years old, while Rodamonte too is a 'garzon' [lad] (*Inam.*, II i 16,5), 'un giovene arguto' [a bold young man] (52,3). He is the only knight, so Boiardo tells us, who is not afraid of looking Agramante straight in the eye, which means that right from the beginning Rodamonte is presented as his king's friend, a knight who serves Agramante not out of fear or need but out of affection and admiration. The two Saracens could even be relatives: although Boiardo does not explicitly mention any kinship between them, in Andrea da Barberino's version Ulieno di Sarza[29] is 'nipote del re Agolante, nato della bella Gorianda, sorella carnale del re Agolante' [King

29    In the fifteenth-century *Aspramonte* Uliano is King of Alessandria.

Agolante's nephew, born to the beautiful Gorianda, King Agolante's blood sister]
(*Aspramonte A*, III xc 24–25).[30] If so, Rodamonte is Agramante's and Ruggiero's
second cousin.

Rodamonte's affection for his lord manifests itself in the speech he delivers
before Agramante and the thirty-one kings whom Agramante has summoned to
Biserta in order to discuss his plan to wage a war against Charlemagne. Branzardo
and Sobrino — grey-haired Saracens who have not forgotten Agolante's disastrous
expedition — are convinced that the proposed war is a 'mala impresa' [bad plan]
(*Inam.*, II i 43,1). Rodamonte is the fourth speaker to take the floor; fuming with
rage, he proclaims that Agramante's wish is his wish also, challenging to a mortal
combat anyone who is unwilling to follow the king's banners:

> 'Non vi dimanda consiglio il signore,
> se ben la sua proposta aveti intesa,
> ma per sua riverenza e vostro honore,
> sieco il passagio ala real impresa!
> Qualunque il niega, al tuto è traditore:
> sì che ciascun da me facia diffesa
> qual contradice al mandato reale,
> ch'io lo desfido a guera capitale!'

> ['Your lords asks you not to advise,
> if you've heard his proposal, but –
> for your fame and his reverence –
> to join his royal enterprise!
> All who refuse are traitorous,
> and to each one who goes against
> the royal call, I say, Beware –
> I challenge him to mortal war!']
> (*Inam.*, II i 55)

This is Rodamonte's first speech. Speaking with a gradual crescendo of indignation,
he accuses of betrayal those who dare to disobey Agramante. It is worth noting
that the theme of betrayal (present, as we saw, in Ulieno's story) accompanies the
intrepid King of Sarza from his first appearance in Boiardo's poem. Many critics
have pointed out that Rodamonte's behaviour during the first military council
reveals his boundless arrogance.[31] Indeed, his speech is most insolent, especially its
first two-thirds (53–54), where the impertinent youth implies that Branzardo and
Sobrino suffer from senile dementia. It is clear that Rodamonte considers himself
superior — by a long shot — to the other thirty-one kings. And yet, even if Boiardo
good-humouredly observes that Rodamonte 'fo superbo et orgoglioso tanto | che
dispregiava il mondo tuto quanto' [was so haughty and proud | that he despised the
whole wide world] (52,7–8), it would be wrong to argue that 'sul piano intellettuale
e morale egli [sia] un ribelle che non ammette nessuna legge' [intellectualy and

---

30    To this we may add that Ulieno (Ulien) is the nephew of Agolante in the *Cantari d'Aspramonte*
(*Cantari d'Aspramonte*, IV 7,2) and in the *Chanson d'Aspremont* (8363).
31    See, for example, Bruscagli e Tissoni Benvenuti's comments on the stanzas in question in their
respective editions of Boiardo's poem.

morally, he is a rebel who does not acknowledge any law].[32] For he does recognize Agramante's authority. In fact, this barrage of insults and threats is triggered by the realization that the others have deliberately misinterpreted Agramante's words, failing to treat their king and commander-in-chief with due respect. Exaggerated though it may seem, his reaction is understandable, and it is significant that his speech (in which the key terms *signore* [lord], *honore* [honour] and *traditore* [traitor] are rhyme words) echoes that of Agramante when, earlier, he urged his vassals to follow him, 'se cura vi tien del vostro *honore*, | s'io debo aver di voi giamai speranza, | se amati ponto me, vostro *signore*' [if you are concerned for your honour, | if I can pin my hopes on you, | if you have love for me, your lord] (37,3–5).

Rodamonte, therefore, proves to be an attentive listener, the only knight who correctly understood his king's address. His affection for him is such that he will not allow anyone to criticize him. After Agramante has spoken again, reiterating his intention to sail to France, Rodamonte springs to his feet and swears to stay by his side come what may ('et io te giuro per tute le bande | tenir con tieco la mia mente salda' [I swear to you I'll do your bidding | steadfastly, and in all events] (65,5–6)), thereby setting an example for the other kings, who take the same oath. It is interesting to note that during a similar assembly in the fifteenth-century *Aspramonte* Uliano stood up and advised Agolante to make his barons swear allegiance to him, adding that they will all be happy to give their life to their lord.[33] All those present at the meeting enthusiastically agree, and Agolante starts the preparation for his expedition.

More arrogant than his father (later we discover that the blood of 'Nembroth, il fier gigante' [Nimrod, the proud giant] is boiling in his veins (*Inam.*, II xiv 32,7)), Rodamonte has a total disregard for courtly etiquette. The wise words of the older councillors make him laugh. He wants to be the first to face the enemies ('in Ciel e nel'Inferno il re Agramante | seguirò sempre, o passarogli avante!' [I'll be behind Agramant | through heaven and hell — or lead, in front] (*Inam.*, II i 65,7–8), and

---

32  Alexandre-Gras, 'Tre figure boiardesche di eroe saraceno: Ferraguto, Agricane, Rodamonte', p. 136.
33  'Levossi in piedi lo bon re Uliano | et inverso Agolante alzò lo ciglio, | dicendo: — O signor mio caro et soprano, | voglio che 'l mio parlar fie con artiglio. | Almonte mi perdone e 'l re Troiano | se altrimenti qui hor ti consiglio. | L'amor che porto a te già non s'amorza: | dico che qui si mostri ogni tua forza || et che raccoghi [sic] tucti i tuo campioni | c'havete in tucto quanto l'universo, | principi et duchi con conti et baroni, | che guerra fanno far per ogni verso, | che ad uno ad un in le vostre magioni | vo li vediate per lungo et traverso. | Fategli, signor mio, per tale inditio, | che giurin esser pronti a tal servitio. || Benché mestrier non facia tal tractato: | tucti i baron certo vi serviranno [...]' [Good King Uliano rose to his feet | and turned his eyes to Agolante, | saying, 'O, my dear all-powerful lord, | I want my speech to be harsh. | May Almonte and King Troiano forgive me | if I advise you differently. | The love that I have for you is as strong as ever: | I say that all your might should be shown here || and that you should summon all your supporters | that you have everywhere in the universe, | princes and dukes with counts and barons | [...] | My lord, by this intimation, | make them swear that they are ready for such service || Even if this is not necessary: | all the barons will of course serve you [...]'] (*Aspramonte*, V 36–38,1–2 [fol. bvii*]). Tissoni Benvenuti does not mention this episode in her commentary to Rodamonte's speech (*Inam.*, II i 52–53), which, in her opinion, echoes that of Mardonio in Herodotus's *Histories*, as well as that of Grandonio in the *Spagna ferrarese*.

— it is worth stressing — he does not believe in Rugiero ('Del mio ardito signor mi maraviglio, | che queste cianze possa sopportare!' [I marvel that my daring lord | can bear such tales] (*Inam.*, II iii 24,1–2)). He threatens to sail to France with or without the others ('Stative adunque, e non sia che si mova! | Di là dal mar io vuò solleto gire' [Stay then — don't anybody move! | I'll go across the sea alone] (*Inam.*, II iii 35,5–6)) and then fulfils his threat, leaving 'senza combiato' [with no formal leave] (36,2). His behaviour might seem disrespectful to say the least, but in reality his lord does not mind his being unceremonious.[34] Agramante does not seem to take offence, because he knows that Rodamonte loves him and because both of them are young and believe that glory is the highest ideal worth living for. They are friends, and their relationship is informal. Rodamonte storms out of the palace in Biserta without even bidding farewell to Agramante, and yet he considers himself an obedient vassal, as is evident from the speech he makes as he is about to weigh anchor for the Christian lands:

> 'Soffia, vento,' dicea 'se sai soffiare,
> che questa nòte pur ne vuò gire!
> Io non son tuo vasal, e non del mare,
> che mi possiati a forza retenire:
> solo Agramante mi può comandare,
> et io contento son de l'obedire;
> sol de obedir a lui sempre mi piace
> perch'è guierero e mai non amò pace.'

> ['Blow, wind!' he yells, 'if you know how
> to blow, since I'll set sail this night!
> I'm not your slave, and not the sea's,
> that you can hold me back by force!
> Just Agramante can order me,
> and I'm content with his commands –
> they never fail to please me. He's
> a soldier with no love for peace.']
> (*Inam.*, II vi 4)

Rodamonte is right. Agramante does scorn peace: he will get over the self-predicted death of the King of Garamantha and will cross the sea to fight with the Christians, even if before doing so he will need to find Rugiero. If Rodamonte had offended him by his hasty departure, he would not have burst into tears at the news that some of the African ships returned to Biserta but that the fate of the King

---

34  Some late sixteenth-century commentators saw that beneath his veneer of arrogance, Rodamonte feels a deep affection for Agramante. If, for Camillo Pellegrini, Boiardo's Rodamonte is all 'temerità e fierezza' [recklessness and pride], while Ariosto's is 'rispettoso verso Agramante più d'altro cavaliero' [more respectful towards Agramante than any other knight], Orazio Ariosto maintains that 'E dal Boiardo, e dall'Ariosto è sempre introdotto Rodomonte rispettoso e riverente verso il Re Agramante, e massimamente in quello che spetta alla destruttione de' Christiani' [Both Boiardo and Ariosto portray Rodomonte as respectful and reverent towards King Agramante, and especially in what is needed to defeat the Christians] (Orazio Ariosto, *Difese dell'Orlando furioso dell'Ariosto*, fol. O 7ʳ). See also Lionardo Salviati, *Lo 'nfarinato secondo ovvero dello 'nfarinato Accademico della Crusca* (Florence: Anton Padovani, 1588), pp. 214–16.

of Sarza was unknown: 'Il Re turbato incomenciò gran pianto, | stimando che sia morto Rodamonte' [The king, upset, began to cry, | believing Rodamonte had died] (*Inam.*, II xxii 35,1–2).

As we saw in Chapter III, Rugiero too develops a warm relationship with his maternal cousin. Agramante is convinced that Rugiero — allegedly the most accomplished knight in *Paganìa* — would never break his oath of allegiance, and so dismisses the second part of the prophecy, according to which Rugiero will eventually convert to Christianity.[35] In Biserta the sixteen-year-old knight throws himself into the whirlpool of courtly life, swept away by a rapid succession of amusements and showered with honours and presents. When Brandimarte (whom *Fortuna* brings to the African shores) blows his horn to challenge Agramante to a duel, the latter comes onto the balcony 'apogiandosi al colo al bel Rugiero' [leaning on fair Rugiero's neck] (*Inam.*, II xxviii 4,7), who by now has filled the void left by Rodamonte's departure. Only Brandimarte (whose courage wins him Agramante's respect) and Rugiero are allowed to wear the royal colours: 'd'azuro e d'oro [...] il quartiero' [quartered blue and gold] (43,8).

Rodamonte's and Rugiero's paths cross in Book III of the *Inamoramento de Orlando*, when Rugiero asks Bradamante (who needs to leave in order to succour Charlemagne) if he can fight Rodamonte in her stead. Although the two Africans are equals in terms of physical strength, at one point Rugiero manages to knock his opponent senseless. Conforming to the law of *cortesia*, he does not take advantage of Rodamonte's state but waits until he comes round, a gesture that deeply moves the King of Sarza: 'Ben chiaramente hagio veduto | che cavalier nonn·è di te migliore, | ní tieco aver potrebbe alcun honore' [It's very clear | that you're the world's best cavalier. | No one can win fame fighting you] (*Inam.*, III v 12,6–8). Overflowing with emotions, the arrogant Rodamonte proclaims himself a lesser knight than Rugiero ('di me fa el tuo parere in ogni banda, | come el magior al suo minor comanda' [you may order my service always as | masters command subordinates] (13,7–8)), thus revealing another side of his personality, namely his admiration for *cortesia* and valour in others. Although several critics have argued that the encounter with the future progenitor of the Este dynasty marks a watershed in Rodamonte's story, it is clearly an exaggeration to claim that Ruggiero gives him a life-changing lesson in chivalry.[36] In fact, this is not the first time he acts courteously towards an enemy: in Book II Rodamonte knocked out Orlando and refrained from attacking

---

35    Dorigatti draws attention to 'la possibile contraddizione insita nel fatto che Rugiero doveva sconfiggere Carlo Magno [...] e ciò nonostante convertirsi al cristianesimo' [the possible contradiction lying in the fact that Rugiero had to defeat Charlemagne [...] and nevertheless convert to Christianity] (Dorigatti, 'La favola e la corte: intrecci narrativi e genealogie estensi dal Boiardo all'Ariosto', p. 46)

36    According to Cavallo, the encounter with Rugiero 'change[s] his way of seeing and his way of acting' (Cavallo, 'The Pathways of Knowledge in Boiardo and Ariosto: The Case of Rodamonte', p. 310; see also Eadem, *The World beyond Europe*, pp. 117–18). Similarly, Alexandre-Gras maintains that this duel is fundamental for Rodamonte's moral growth insofar as it marks the 'ultima tappa della sua evoluzione' [last stage of his development] (Alexandre-Gras, 'Tre figure boiardesche di eroe saraceno: Ferraguto, Agricane, Rodamonte', p. 139).

him.[37] If anything, his readiness to admit Rugiero's superiority shows that he is prone to extremes of emotion.

Both Rodamonte and Rugiero serve Agramante faithfully, even if they do not miss the opportunity to participate in 'romance' adventures. The last time we hear about Rugiero is when a hermit tells Bradamante that he has been carried away by demons (*Inam.*, III viii 57). As for the King of Sarza, although he now acknowledges that Ranaldo and other Christian knights are worthy enemies (so much so that he comes close to doubting the success of Agramante's campaign in an interior monologue at *Inam.*, II xv 28–30), he continues to worship his personal god — his sword — and to revere his king. At the end of Book III he shows his military prowess in the battle of Paris. Then he takes part in the military parade, having recently returned from Africa ('tre giorni inante' [three days earlier'], as we learn in *Fur.*, XII 25,8 AB; XIV C), where Agramante had sent him to recruit new soldiers.

Thus, Rodomonte steps into the universe of the *Furioso* when, planning to resume the offensive after a winter lull, Agramante inspects his troops. It is significant that Ariosto mentions his journey to Africa, but not so much because Rodomonte, who thought he was able to conquer France within three days, is forced to return home for reinforcements, as because he crosses the sea *on his king's order*. In perfect continuity with his predecessor, Ariosto highlights the essence of Rodomonte's soul: his touching devotion to Agramante who must consider himself lucky to have him, given the sorrowful state of the Saracen army.

As we saw in Chapter IV, Rodomonte distinguishes himself in the battle for the French capital, with the poet hailing him as the greatest African warrior of all times: 'Aphrica, in te par a costui non nacque, | ben che di Anteo ti vanti e d'Hannibàlle' [Africa, though you may boast of Anteus and Hannibal, | you never bore a man like him] (*Fur.*, XVI 24,3–4 AB; XVIII C). His courage bordering on recklessness, his ferocity and his unshakable self-confidence, all of these traits are ingrained in him by Boiardo and highlighted by Ariosto. But if Rodomonte does not undergo a dramatic transformation in the *Furioso*, the universe which surrounds him is no longer the same. Relegated to the margins of the *Inamoramento de Orlando*, death and suffering are part of the human condition in its famous sequel. Rodomonte will die in the *Furioso*'s last octaves; but before the last act of his drama, before the Saracens' final defeat and the destruction of Biserta, he will have to drink of the bitter cup of rejection. A crucial turning point in his story is his quarrel with Mandricardo, the Emperor of Tartary, a dispute over the fickle Doralice which, with Agramante's consent, will be resolved in Mandricardo's favour. After this humiliation Rodomonte will leave the Saracen camp, withdrawing from the war. In order to decide whether he violates the chivalric code, we must look more closely at this episode.

---

37    As for the fact that Rodomonte was initially reluctant to give Bradamante leave to return to Charlemagne, one could note that the Christians treated him discourteously when he disembarked on the French coast: Rodomonte's horse has drowned in the sea (*Inam.*, II vi 56,1–2) and so he 'sol et a piede la bataglia prende' [makes war on foot and alone] (64,8), fighting with countless Christians, among whom Bradamante e Ranaldo. Bradamante does not even consider dismounting.

as we have seen, has always put his personal interests before those of Agramante.[41] To this we may add that Mandricardo is an unpopular figure in the Saracen camp: apart from Doralice (who, as the poet maliciously suggests, is sad, but not heart-broken), nobody will shed tears when Ruggiero kills him.

The question that naturally arises is whether Agramante could have allowed Rodomonte to challenge Doralice's choice without breaking the chivalric code. Although the author of the *Pareri in duello* seems to rule out this possibility ('essendo ella [the dispute] già stata compromessa, et civilmente decisa, non poteva esser ritornata al giudicio dell'arme' [since it had been already settled and resolved in a peaceful manner, it was not longer possible to return to a trial by battle]), it must be stressed that the King of Sarza refuses to adhere to the pact because he is convinced that Doralice's decision is 'ingiusta e falsa' [unjust and fallacious] (*Fur.*, XXV 108,3 AB; XXVII C), given (as he knows, and we do) that she is almost his wife.[42] In other words, it is the moral law, as he understands it, that makes him break his word. As for the Emperor of Tartary, he is willing to oblige his rival (his laconic reply being 'Vada pur come ti pare' [As you wish] (109,2)), which means that he, too, believes that the cuckolded husband has the right — or rather the obligation — to insist upon resuming the duel. Since Mandricardo does not have any objections, Agramante would be in the position to annul the initial agreement. However, at this point he loses his patience: tired of Doralice and her lovers, he puts an end to the whole matter, moving on to the other quarrels which in his eyes are no less important than the present one.

Trying to come to terms with what has happened, Rodomonte finds solace in thoughts of revenge. Having decided to return to Africa, he wishes terrible calamities to befall Agramante:

> Desidera veder che sopra il regno
> gli cada tanto mal, tanta procella,
> ch'in Aphrica ogni casa se funesti,
> né pietra salda sopra pietra resti;
>
> e che spinto del Regno, in duolo e in lutto
> viva Agramante, misero e mendico;
> e che esso sia che poi gli renda il tutto,
> e lo riponga in l'alto seggio antico,
> e de la fede sua produca il frutto:
> e gli faccia veder ch'un vero amico
> a dritto e a torto esser devea preposto,
> se tutto il mondo se gli fusse opposto.
>
> [He wishes to see such a disaster, such a tempest
> fall upon his kingdom
> that every house in Africa fall to ruin
> and no stone be left upon a stone;
>
> and that Agramante, driven from his kingdom,

---

41    It is true, however, that in the *Inamoramento de Orlando* Mandricardo saves Agramante's life in the battle of Paris (*Inam.*, III viii 47–48,1–2).

42    *Pareri in duello*, p. 326.

> live in sorrow and mourning, a miserable begger;
> and that he, Rodomonte, should be the one to restore his fortunes
> and replace him on the ancestral throne,
> and reap the fruit of his loyalty,
> and make his see that a true friend,
> right or wrong, ought to be favoured,
> even were the whole world against him]
>                    (*Fur.*, XXV 124,5–6; 125 AB; XXVII 125–26 C)

Laden with hurt, anger and resentment, Rodomonte's internal monologue nevertheless conveys a sense of hopefulness. Agramante has turned his back on his most loyal friend, but his ingratitude has not severed the bond between them. Though the wound is still bleeding, Rodomonte has already decided to forgive his king, which reveals how deep his affection for him is. Later, claiming that Tasso is incapable of portraying 'pensier da eroi' [heroes' thoughts], Galileo Galilei would advise him to reread this very passage:

> vi manderei da Rodomonte nel c. 27, st. 125, a sentire quello che dice, sdegnato contro di Agramante per non l'aver egli, a dritto o torto, voluto preporre a Mandricardo; e letto che voi l'avessi, e con infinito stupore della grandezza dell'animo di colui, vi esorterei a ristupirvi di nuovo, e poi a tacere, come disperato di poter mai trovar concetti di quella sorte.

> [I would send you to Rodomonte in canto 27, stanza 125, to hear what he says, angry with Agramante who did not want, rightly or wrongly, to favour him over Mandricardo; and once you have read it, and with infinite astonishment at the nobility of his soul, I would urge you to be astonished again, and then to keep quiet as a man in despair who will never be able to find such concepts.][43]

Nor is Galileo the only critic to show admiration for Rodomonte's attitude. According to Ludovico Muratori, the description of the Saracen's state of mind is among the most beautiful passages in the entire poem: 'non poteva nascere un più nobile, un più bel desiderio in cuore ad un Cavalier, prode, sdegnato, e desideroso di vendicarsi, quanto il bramare, che Agramante fosse spogliato del Regno, e che toccasse a lui il riporlo in trono' [a more noble, more beautiful wish could not have been born in the heart of a valiant, indignant Knight who wants to avenge himself than the wish that Agramante be stripped of his Kingdom and that he be the one to restore him on the throne]. For Muratori, 'un tal sentimento, un tal costume, un tale affetto' [such a sentiment, such conduct, such affection][44] is not only 'nuovo, raro, maraviglioso, e sublime' [new, rare, marvellous, and sublime], but it is 'più maraviglioso, più raro, e più nobile [...] che quel d'Achille' [more marvellous, more rare, and more noble [...] than that of Achilles],[45] given that the ancient warrior is blinded by his thirst for revenge.[46] Indeed, although Rodomonte is often said to be

---

43  Galileo Galilei, *Considerazioni al Tasso*, p. 571.
44  See Ludovico Antonio Muratori, *Della perfetta poesia italiana, spiegata e dimostrata con varie osservazioni*, in Idem, *Opere*, 13 vols (Arezzo: Michele Bellotti, 1767–1773), IX, p. 115.
45  Ibid., p. 117.
46  Salviati, too, maintains that 'chi legge ben que' luoghi truova, che ne anche in quella furia quel Saracino si spogliò in tutto dell'affetto verso il Re suo, poiché desiderava di vederlo mal condotto

FIG. 5.1. Battista Dossi, *The battle of Orlando and Rodomonte* (*c.* 1527–1530).
The Wadsworth Atheneum Museum of Art, Hartford, CT, the Ella Gallup Sumner and
Mary Catlin Sumner Collection Fund, 1949.81

modelled on Homer's Achilles (who withdraws from the war when Agamemnon takes Briseis from him), the resemblance between the two heroes is superficial. As Hegel explains in his essay on chivalry, 'The motif of honour was unknown to ancient classical art', and even though Achilles is beside himself with rage when his king seizes his woman, 'the injury does not pierce right to the very heart of personality as such'.[47] Rodomonte's readiness to forgive Agramante is all the more touching considering that he has been deeply hurt by the latter's failure to appreciate his loyalty.

As far as Doralice is concerned, Rodomonte erases her from his heart. Issabella's beauty will soon make him forget his first love, and her heroic death will teach him that conjugal fidelity is not a myth. Ignoring Agramante's pleas to return, and turning down the offer of 'una cugina sua, figlia d'Aimonte' [his cousin, Aimonte's daughter] together with the 'regno di Oran [...] per dote' [kingdom of Oran for her dowry] (*Fur.*, XXX 5,3–4 AB; XXXII C), Rodomonte will live by Issabella's tomb until his duel with Bradamante. But even so, he will not cease to help the Saracens: all the Christian knights whom he overpowers on the bridge built in memory of Issabella are treated as prisoners of war and sent to Africa. He has not

per averlo à rimettere egli in istato' [if one carefully reads these passages, one finds out that not even in his rage did that Saracen banish from his heart all love for his King, since he wanted to see him ruined in order to restore him to his state] (Salviati, *Lo 'nfarinato secondo ovvero dello 'nfarinato Accademico della Crusca*, p. 216). As for more modern scholars, Zanette is impressed by Rodomonte's behaviour (Zanette, *Conversazioni sull''Orlando furioso'*, pp. 363–66), while Santoro argues that Rodomonte's logic is that of a barbarian (Santoro, 'Rodomonte: la defezione della "ragione"', p. 267).

47    Georg Wilhelm Friedrich Hegel, 'Chivalry', in Idem, *Aesthetics: Lectures on Fine Art*, trans. by Thomas M. Knox, 2 vols (Oxford: Clarendon Press, 1988), I, pp. 552–72 (p. 557).

lost his faith in chivalry, which is evident in Battista Dossi's painting of his fight with the mad Orlando, where we see a handsome man clad in shining armour looking melancholically at the viewer, with the armour of his defeated enemies in the colourful background [FIG. 5.1].[48]

## *Ruggiero*

Though saddened by Rodomonte's departure, Agramante does not seem to realize that he has lost his best champion. In his opinion, his best knight is none other than Ruggiero to whom we must now turn our attention. Picking up his story, Ariosto reminds us that Agramante dotes on his younger cousin. Upon discovering that Ruggiero is held captive by Atlante, Agramante, 'ch'ama Ruggiero e più d'ogn'altro ha a core' [who loves Ruggiero and holds him dearer than anyone else] (*Fur.*, III 69,8 AB; 70 C), sends Brunello to free him from the enchanted castle. Brunello narrowly escapes hanging when he fails his mission.

It is in a state of extreme agitation that Agramante watches the duel between Ruggiero and Mandricardo (who fight over the right to wear the Trojan eagle). When Ruggiero kills the Emperor of Tartary, the relief of the African king knows no bounds:

> Che dirò del favor, che de le tante
> carezze e tante affettüose et vere,
> che fece a quel Ruggiero il Re Agramante,
> senza il qual dar al vento le bandiere,
> né vòlse mover d'Aphrica le piante,
> né senza lui si fidò in tante schiere?
> Hor che del Re Agricane ha spento il seme,
> stima più lui che tutto il mondo insieme.

> [What shall I say of the favours, what of the many
> sincere, affectionate blandishments
> lavished upon Ruggiero by King Agramante?
> Without Ruggiero he would never have trusted himself
> to unfurl his banners to the wind and set forth from Africa
> to venture against such a host.
> Now that Ruggiero has slain King Agricane's offspring,
> he prized him more than the rest of the world put together.]
> (*Fur.*, XXVIII 70 AB; XXX C)

Agramante, maintains the poet, has always believed that Ruggiero's participation was crucial to the success of his expedition against Charlemagne.[49] However, he does not merely see him as the means to defeating the Christians; his friendship for Ruggiero is 'ver[a]' [sincere], born from his admiration for Ruggiero's chivalric accomplishments. Like his predecessor, Ariosto underscores the warmth of their

---

48   Completed in 1528–1530 (and hence before the publication of the 1532 version of Ariosto's poem), this painting is one of the first works of art inspired by the *Furioso*.

49   Boiardo's Agramante, if truth be told, wanted 'ad ogni modo trapassare' [to invade no matter what] (*Inam.*, II iii 37,4), but here Ariosto implies that Agramante would not have set sail for France without Ruggiero.

relationship. Ruggiero is seriously wounded in the fight with Mandricardo, and Agramante surrounds him with his care, doing everything he can to help his recovery:

> Con molta diligentia il Re Agramante
> fece colcar Ruggier ne le sue tende;
> che notte e dì veder sel vuole inante:
> sì l'ama, sì di lui cura si prende.

> [With all diligence King Agramante
> had Ruggiero settled in his royal tent;
> as he wanted to keep an eye on him night and day
> such was his devotion to him, such his care.]
> (*Fur.*, XXVIII 74,1–4 AB; XXX C)

As for Ruggiero, Agramante is not equally central in *his* life. Despite the prophecy of the King of Garamantha, his contribution to Agramante's war is in actual fact modest, as he has been far too eager to pursue 'romance' adventures. While Rodomonte served his king with almost religious zeal, Ruggiero was not in a hurry to return to Paris after taking leave of Logistilla.[50] Very marked already in the 1516 edition, the contrast between Ruggiero's and Rodomonte's attitude to Agramante is further emphasized in the subsequent versions: after the episode in which Rodomonte postpones his duel with Mandricardo, Ariosto adds two new octaves (*Fur.*, XXIII 5–6 B; XXV C), in which Ruggiero too encounters Agramante's messenger. Unlike Rodomonte, he turns a deaf ear to his king's plea, because he has promised to rescue a young man who is about to be burnt at the stake.[51] It is true that the poet tries to justify his decision, observing that, 'da molti pensier ridutto in forse' [perplexed by many thoughts] (6,1), Ruggiero could not decide on his best course.[52] However, it is obvious that he has only a tepid affection for Agramante, all the more so considering that at this point he does not yet know that the young man in question is Bradamante's twin brother Ricciardetto.

Even after saving Ricciardetto, Ruggiero does not return to the Saracen camp, but instead undertakes to free Malagigi and Viviano. Then he decides to find his horse Frontino (whom Rodomonte took from Bradamante's maid Hippalca), judging that 'biasmo e dishonor gli fia | se tôrlo a Rodomonte non s'affretta' [it would be to his shame and discredit | if he did not hasten to retrieve it from Rodomonte] (*Fur.*, XXIV 62,6–7 AB; XXVI 65 C). Ruggiero's and Rodomonte's paths cross again when Rodomonte and Mandricardo are on their way to Paris.

---

50    As is well known, the education that Ruggiero received from Logistilla did not have a lasting effect on him. See Ascoli's illuminating analysis of the crisis of humanistic education in the *Furioso* (*Ariosto's Bitter Harmony*, pp. 121–57 and especially pp. 199–24).

51    By contrast, in A, where these two octaves are missing, Ariosto proceeds straight to narrate Ricciardetto's rescue.

52    If, in the 1521 *Furioso*, Ruggiero does not have time to carefully consider the situation because of his guide 'ch'ad or ad or in modo *l'affrettava*, | che nessun tempo d'indugiar gli dava' [who kept urging him to hasten, | as there was no time to lose] (*Fur.*, XXIII 6,7–8 B), in the 1532 version it is Ruggiero who tells his guide to hasten her pace ('ch'ad or ad or in modo *egli affrettava*, | che nessun tempo d'indugiar le dava' [whom he kept urging her to hasten, | as there was no time to lose] (XXV C)).

The rightful owner of Frontino immediately challenges Rodomonte to a duel, but the latter reminds him of their duty to Agramante, which prompts Ariosto (who is both moved and bemused) to compare Rodomonte to Job: Rodomonte, stresses the poet, would have gone to the ends of the earth to fight with Ruggiero, but now feels compelled to miss this splendid opportunity, 'tanto il desiderio che si giugna | in soccorso al suo Re gli par honesto' [so deserving he finds his ambition | to come to his King's aid] (90,3–4 AB; 93 C).

Ruggiero, however, places his personal honour above that of Agramante: he agrees to postpone the duel, but on condition that Frontino be immediately returned to him (Rodomonte, as the reader knows, refrained from giving Mandricardo a similar ultimatum with regard to Doralice); moreover, he accuses the King of Sarza of having acted infamously, staining his hands with 'cosa indegna a un hom forte' [an action unworthy of a strong man] (94,1–2 AB; 97 C). Predictably, these insults make Rodomonte's blood boil, for he considers them completely unjustified: it is true, as for Frontino, that 'tôrlo a una donzella gli par[eva] fallo' [he deemed it wrong to seize it from a damsel] (*Fur.*, XXI 34,5 AB; XXIII C), but the discovery that the horse's owner was Ruggiero changed everything. Rodomonte convinced himself that he had not stolen Frontino; he had taken it precisely to challenge to a single combat 'sì gran campion' [such a great champion] (35,8) after the sharp-tongued Hippalca had wounded his pride by observing that Ruggiero 'più di te val [...] | né lo pareggia al mondo altro guerriero' [is a far better man than you are | nor is there a warrior alive who can be compared to him] (35,3–4).[53] Ruggiero knows that Frontino was merely a pretext for facing him, Ruggiero, and yet he hurls abuse at his fellow African, provoking him to start a fight.

If Rodomonte is not a new Job, it is equally true that in the Discord episode Ariosto 'lo descrive che egli habbia più rispetto a detto Re, che non hebbe non sol Gradasso, Mandricardo e Marfisa, ma Ruggiero, com'egli vassallo et cavaliero di Agramante' [describes him as more respectful towards the said King than not only Gradasso, Mandricardo and Marfisa, but also Ruggiero, who, like him, is Agramante's vassal and knight].[54] As far as Ruggiero is concerned, by now the reader knows that he no longer wishes to serve Agramante until his last breath: having been freed from the enchanted palace — Atlante's last attempt to save him from his destiny — he had promised Bradamante to receive baptism in order to ask her father Amone for permission to marry her. Standing in the middle of the narration (*Fur.*, XX AB; XXII C), this episode marks an important watershed in his story: one could say that his coldness towards Agramante is ultimately due to the fact that, in his heart, he has decided to convert to Christianity. And yet, on the other hand, he continues to consider himself Agramante's knight. As he explains in a long letter to Bradamante (which he writes on the eve of liberating Malagigi and Viviano), he feels morally constrained to remain with his king until he finds

---

53    As for their duel in the *Inamoramento de Orlando*, on that occasion Rodamonte forgot to ask his opponent's name.

54    So argues Camillo Pellegrini in his *Il Carrafa o vero della Epica poesia* (Florence: Sermartelli, 1584). The passage is cited in Salviati, *Lo 'nfarinato secondo ovvero dello 'nfarinato Accademico della Crusca*, p. 214.

'convenïenti | cagion, che parran giuste, di dar volta' [suitable | reasons, which will seem just, to leave him] (*Fur.*, XXIII 87,5–6 A; 91 B; XXV 91 C).[55]

It is the ideal of knightly honour that makes Ruggiero postpone his conversion, which shows that secular chivalry — at least until this point in the story — is as important for Ariosto as it was for Boiardo. We have seen that some of Boiardo's Saracens (Agricane, Brandimarte and Fiordalisa, Iroldo and Prasildo) have renounced Macone. These conversions cannot be called morally ambiguous, because the characters in question were free to dispose of themselves inasmuch as they were not bound by any feudal or other tie. Different is the case of Balante in the *Aspramonte*, a character whom we referred to numerous times in the course of this study without dwelling, however, on his relationship with his lord. Agolante, as we saw in Chapter III, entrusts him with an embassy to Charlemagne; overwhelmed by the splendour of the Christian court, Balante decides to embrace the Christian faith, but he tells his Christian friend Namo that he cannot do so before the end of the war. Whereas in the fifteenth-century *Aspramonte* Balante betrays his king (we have alluded to this episode when discussing the figure of Ulieno), in Andrea da Barberino's version he remains faithful to him until he is captured by the Christians.[56] Far from condemning his reluctance to abandon Agolante, Andrea da Barberino portrays him as a tragic hero.[57] Moreover, Cieco da Ferrara too seems to subscribe to the view that it is morally wrong to leave one's lord in a moment of extreme danger, whatever the reason for this might be. For example, Carminiano, Mambriano's vassal, asks to be baptized, but immediately after having been admitted into the bosom of the Christian Church, announces his decision to return to the Saracen camp to help his king. And not only do the Christians accept his decision but they even applaud it: 'Turpino per tal grazia il benedisse, | dicendo che da uom giusto facea' [Turpino blessed him for such grace, | saying that he was acting justly] (*Mambriano*, XVII 12,5–6).[58]

---

55    It is worth observing that in BC Ariosto substituted *parran* [will seem] with *sian*: 'cagion, che sian giuste' [reasons, which are just]. One could argue that the former reading betrays the fact that Ruggiero's main concern was to appear noble in the eyes of the others, all the more so considering that in this letter he talks a lot about public opinion.

56    Agolante, observes Andrea da Barberino, has treated Balante as his own son: he raised him, dubbed him a knight, gave him a wife, granted him many kingdoms and the sword Trenzadia (*Aspramonte A*, II xvi 10–11).

57    'El dux Namo domandò Balante s'egli si voleva battezzare. Rispuose: "O signor duca, abbia piatà di me! Io non vorrei essere tenuto traditore contro allo amirante Agolante, ond'io ti priego che tu mi lasci tornare a lui, e domanderogli licenza, e tornerò a battezzarmi". Disse Uggieri: "Tu parli follemente, imperò che tu non puoi essere ripreso di questo; però che l'uomo qual'è nell'altrui forze non è in sua libertà. Tutto questo carico voglio sopra di me"' [Duke Namo asked Balante if he wished to receive baptism. He replied: 'O lord Duke, have pity on me! I don't want to be considered a traitor to Emir Agolante, and so I beg you to allow me to return to him and ask for his permission, and I will return to receive baptism.' Uggieri said: 'You speak madly, as you cannot be reproached for this; for a man who is held captive is not free. I want to take full responsibility for this'] (*Aspramonte A*, III xxviii 5–11).

58    Carminiano will leave Mambriano only after his final defeat and his flight into the forest: 'Carminian, di tal fuga avveduto, | disse ai figliuoli: Noi abbiam serbata | la fede a Mambrian, come è dovuto, | fino a la fin per fargli cosa grata: | ora che lui s'è d'animo perduto | e che gli ha

We may add that even outside the realm of chivalric literature we come across similar statements with regard to the concept of honour. Suffice it to recall the following passage from Federico Fregoso's speech in the *Cortegiano*:

> [...] purché un gentilomo non lassi il patrone quando fosse in su la guerra o in qualche avversità, di sorte che si potesse credere che ciò facesse per secondar la fortuna, o per parergli che gli mancasse quel mezzo del qual potesse trarre utilità, da ogni altro tempo credo che possa con ragion e debba levarsi da quella servitù, che tra i boni sia per dargli vergogna [...]

> [as long as a gentleman does not leave his lord when he is at war or in some dangerous situation, lest he be thought to do so to better his fortunes or because he deemed that he lacked opportunity to receive some gain, I believe that in any other situation he can and ought to leave a service that may disgrace him in the eyes of good men [...]][59]

If Fregoso is right, Ruggiero's fear of being considered a traitor — fear that we sense in his letter to Bradamante — is neither surprising nor groundless:

> – Vorrei (le soggiungea), quando vi piaccia,
> levar al mio signor l'assedio intorno
> acciò che l'ignorante volgo taccia,
> il qual direbbe, a mia vergogna e scorno:
> Ruggier, mentre Agramante hebbe bonaccia,
> mai non l'abbandonò notte né giorno;
> hor che Fortuna per Carlo si piega,
> egli col vincitor l'insegna spiega.

> ['I should like,' he added, 'with your permission,
> to break the siege around my lord,
> so as to silence the ignorant rabble,
> who would otherwise say, heaping shame and scorn on me:
> "Ruggiero, in Agramante's prosperity,
> never abandoned him night or day,
> but, with Fortune favouring Charlemagne,
> he is flying his ensigns on the victor's side"']
> (*Fur.*, XXIII 86 A; 90 B; XXV 90 C)

What is surprising, however, is Ruggiero's haste to convert, especially considering that Agramante is a much better king than Mambriano. If Andrea da Barberino's Balante intends to remain a Saracen 'mentre che dura questa guerra' [until the end of this war] (*Aspramonte A*, II xlviii 38–39) and Carminiano takes part in the decisive

---

totalmente abbandonata | l'impresa, al buon Rinaldo se n'andremo | e fedelmente a lui obbediremo' [Having learnt of that flight, Carminiano | told his children: 'We remained loyal | to Mambriano, as was our duty, | until the end in order to please him: | now given that he is disheartened | and that he has completely abandoned | his undertaking, we shall go to good Rinaldo | and we shall faithfully obey him'] (*Mambriano*, XXIII 91).

59   Castiglione, *Libro del cortegiano*, p. 152. Fregoso's speech is cited by Saccone in a footnote to his discussion of *fede* in the *Furioso* ('Cloridano e Medoro, con alcuni argomenti per una lettura del primo *Furioso*', p. 97). The importance of loyalty is stressed in other treatises on the subject too. See, for example, Giovanbattista Giraldi Cinzio, *L'uomo di corte: Discorso intorno a quello che si conviene a giovane nobile e ben creato nel servire un gran principe*, ed. by Walter Moretti (Modena: Mucchi, 1989), p. 17.

battle, Ruggiero promises Bradamante to receive baptism within fifteen or twenty days, deeming it sufficient to 'comparir [...] una volta, | sì che de li Aphricani alloggiamenti | la grave ossedïon per me sia tolta' [show himself at least once, | so as to raise the dire siege | from the African camp] (*Fur.*, XXIII 87,2–4 A; 91 B; XXV 91 C). In his defence one could say that he does not appear to be wholly convinced by his own reasoning: the sheer length of his letter (seven octaves) as well as its repetitiveness suggest that Ruggiero is more perturbed than he is willing to admit.[60] In twenty days' time he will still be in the Saracen camp. Nor will he abandon Agramante when Bradamante arrives in Arles, where the Saracen army will have retreated after Rinaldo's night-time — and, for that matter, highly unchivalrous — attack.

To Bradamante's immense relief, Marphisa is revealed to be Ruggiero's long-lost sister. At the same time, Ruggiero seems to have found a 'cagione giusta' [just reason] (at least in the eyes of the two warrior-women) to break all ties with his Saracen past. Atlante's voice tells his adoptive children that their father Ruggiero II of Risa was killed by Aimonte and Troiano, who are also responsible for Galaciella's death: 'la fêr, perché s'havesse ad affogare, | s'un debil legno porre in mezo il mare' [they put her in a frail boat | at sea to drown] (*Fur.*, XXXIII 64,7–8 A; 60 B; XXXVI 60 C). This revelation is highly surprising, considering that Troiano, as was mentioned in the previous chapters, is not involved in the treacherous conquest of Risa in any of the versions of the *Aspramonte*, while Almonte sends his sister to Africa in order to *save* her from their father's wrath.[61] Although it cannot be ruled out that Ariosto might have followed some version now lost, it is more likely that he (or his characters) deliberately 'twisted the facts' in order to justify Marphisa's conversion and her resolution to kill Agramante.

Ruggiero, however, does not give in to Bradamante's and Marphisa's exhortations to convert and enter Charlemagne's service. More determined than ever to fulfil his duty, he replies 'che da principio questo far devea; | ma per non haver ben note le cose, | come hebbe poi, tardato troppo havea' [that he should have done so from the outset; | but that, not having well understood the facts | as he afterwards did, he had left it too late] (*Fur.*, XXXIII 84,2–4 A; 80 B; XXXVI 80 C). He then reiterates his promise 'di trovar un modo' [to find a way] so that he can 'partir con ragion' [*con suo onor* in C] [leave with good reason] (85,2–3 A; 81 B; 81 C), preserving his honour. And here we must stress that Ariosto not only approves of his choice (which shows that the author's position does not always coincide with that of his Christian characters), but he also comes close to contradicting what was stated earlier by Atlante, namely that Troiano too was guilty of the murder of Ruggiero II of Risa. The following authorial comment suggests that the (main) guilty party is Ruggiero's and Agramante's uncle, namely Aimonte:

---

60    In BC Ruggiero's uneasiness is further stressed in the octaves devoted to his recollection of his encounter with Agramante's messenger (XXIII 81–82 B; XXV C).
61    Almonte tries to save his sister in the fifteenth-century *Aspramonte*, while Andrea da Barberino leaves the ending of Galiziella's story deliberately ambiguous, saying that she could have been sent to Africa by Almonte.

Fece Ruggiero il debito a seguire
il suo signor, che non se ne potea,
se non con ignominia, dipartire;
che ragion di lasciarlo non havea.
E se Aimonte gli fe' il padre morire,
tal colpa in Agramante non cadea;
ch'in molti effetti havea con Ruggier poi
emendato ogni error de i maggior suoi.

[Ruggiero did his duty to follow
his lord, whom he could only
desert to his shame,
for lack of any sufficient excuse.
If Almonte had murdered Ruggiero's father,
Agramante could not bear the blame;
he had in many ways since made amends
to Ruggiero for his forebears sins.]
(*Fur.*, XXXIV 5 AB; XXXVIII C)

Thus, praised by the author as well as by sixteenth-century commentators, Ruggiero returns to Arles.[62] When under the cover of darkness Rinaldo's troops attacked the Saracen camp, Ruggiero was grievously wounded. Now, however, *Fortuna* has granted him the opportunity to change the course of the war: following Sobrino's advice, Agramante has proposed to Charlemagne to put an end to bloodshed through a judicial duel between Ruggiero and a Christian knight of Charlemagne's choice. The two rulers solemnly swear not to interrupt the single combat, while their respective champions swear to enter the service of the enemy king should their own lord break the oath. The duel will be interrupted by Agramante. And yet, instead of swearing allegiance to Charlemagne, Ruggiero will follow his king to Africa.

Ruggiero's decision may seem puzzling, but, as is often the case in the *Furioso*, the truth lies deeper, and we must focus more closely on this episode, which is of fundamental importance for understanding the events that follow. First of all, it must be stressed Agramante breaks the pact because his champion 'pigro era a menar le mani' [moved his arms half-heartedly] (*Fur.*, XXXV 14,3 A; 3 B; XXXIX 3 C). Ruggiero does not want to kill or wound Rinaldo, his lady's brother. The reader may sympathize with him, but from the point of view of the chivalric code (not to mention the tie of kinship and friendship between him and Agramante) his behaviour is, to say the least, morally ambiguous. As the author of the *Pareri in duello* will later point out, 'Vero è che Ruggiero si mostrò Cavalier di non salda fede, ché, o non doveva accettare il carico del combattere, o doveva combatter con tutte le sue forze' [It is true that Ruggiero showed himself to be a Knight of unsteady faith, because he either should not have accepted to fight or he should have fought with all his strength].[63]

---

62    Suffice it to mention here Lodovico Dolce's 'Allegoria' [Allegory] to canto XXXVIII in Giolito's 1542 edition: 'per Ruggiero, il quale, ancora che amasse Bradamante, non perciò nell'avversa fortuna volle abbandonare il suo re, contiensi la fede di ottimo cavalliero' [in Ruggiero, who, although he loved Bradamante, did not want to abandon his king in adversity, we see the fidelity of an excellent knight] (*Orlando furioso* (Giolito), fol. 204ᵛ).

63    *Pareri in duello*, p. 461. This view is echoed in Tasso's *Apologia in difesa della sua Gierusalemme*

In light of this, it is ironic that the African ruler interrupts the combat following the apparition of 'Rodomonte' (or rather, of Melissa disguised as Rodomonte): Agramante did not let his old friend challenge Doralice's decision, and now he himself breaks an oath sworn on the holy Qur'an, committing the sin of perjury. It is difficult to say if the *real* King of Sarza, rather than Melissa's impersonation, would have advised him to do so... In any case, we should not be too quick to condemn Agramante, for he is not the only character to violate the chivalric code in this episode: 'L'intervento della magia — observes Giovanna Rizzarelli — sovverte ogni logica interna allo scontro codificato e soprattutto rende difficile capire chi non abbia rispettato le regole, se realmente Agramante o i suoi avversari per i quali Melissa è intervenuta' [The intervention of magic subverts the internal logic of the codified combat and above all makes it difficult to understand who did not respect the rules, if that was indeed Agramante or his enemies on whose behalf Melissa intervened].[64] On the other hand, at least one sixteenth-century interpreter went so far as to affirm that 'il rompere il giuramento per la libertà de' suoi sudditi, e per la reputazione de' suoi regni, massimamente contro a popoli d'altra legge, si può forse scusare a grande equità' [breaking the oath for the sake of one's subjects' freedom or for the reputation of one's kingdoms, especially against people of another law, can perhaps be excused in the name of justice].[65]

The interpreter in question is Lionardo Salviati, the principal founder of the Accademia della Crusca. In his opinion, Agramante's action is perhaps less outrageous than it seems at first, while Ruggiero has a moral obligation to remain with Agramante, even if that leads him to break his oath twice.[66] In replying to objections vented by Tasso (who claimed that the progenitor of the Este dynasty committed a most grievous sin 'prepone[ndo] il suo Re al suo Dio, che è quello stesso,

---

*liberata*, where he criticizes Ruggiero for his immaturity and fickleness: 'dopo che egli hebbe accettato di esser campione del suo Re contra un Cavaliero di Carlo, et giurato d'abbandonarlo s'egli disturbasse la contesa, per debolezza, et inconstanza d'animo si mostra tanto inferiore à Rinaldo, che i Rè dell'Africa, et Agramante medesimo dispera della sua vittoria, et si duole d'haver troppo creduto à Sobrino; là onde pare ch'egli tradisca la causa dell'Africa, et il suo Re, del quale mostrava di far tanta stima perché ò non doveva accettar l'impresa, ò accettandola doveva far tutto quel che poteva per vincer l'avversario. Dunque fu 'l fatto medesimo il fedel Ruggiero di Campion publico quasi divenendo publico traditore antepone l'amore all'honore et la sua donna al suo principe assediato [after he had accepted to be his King's champion against Charlemagne's Knight and having sworn to abandon him should he interrupt the duel, he appears, through his weakness and lack of constancy, so much inferior to Rinaldo that the Kings of Africa and Agramante himself loses [sic] all hope that he may win and regrets that he has listened to Sobrino too eagerly; hence it seems that he betrays Africa's and his King's cause, to which he seemed to attach so much importance, as he either should not have accepted this mission, or by accepting it he should have done everything he could to defeat his adversary. And so the fact remains that the faithful Ruggiero puts love before honour, and his lady before his besieged prince, almost turning into a public traitor from being a public Champion] (Torquato Tasso, *Apologia in difesa della sua Gierusalemme liberata*, in *Apologia del sig. Torquato Tasso in difesa della sua Gierusalemme liberata*, fols A1^r–G4^r (A8^v)).

64    Giovanna Rizzarelli, '"Cominciar quivi una crudel battaglia": Duelli in ottave nell'*Orlando furioso*', in *Per violate forme: Rappresentazioni e linguaggi della violenza nella letteratura italiana*, ed. by Fabrizio Bondi and Nicola Catelli (Lucca: Maria Pacini Fazzi, 2009), pp. 79–100 (pp. 92–93).

65    Salviati, *Dello Infarinato Accademico della Crusca risposta all'Apologia di Torquato Tasso*, p. 180.

66    After the interruption of the duel, Ruggiero and Rinaldo repeat their oath (*Fur.*, XXXV 20 A; 9 B; XXXIX 9 C).

che è adorato da i Christiani, et una apparenza di fede alla fede et alla religione, et l'humane opinioni alle divine ragioni' [putting his King before his God who is the one worshipped by the Christians, and a pretence of faith before faith and religion, and human opinions before divine reasons]),[67] Salviati underscores the fact that the hero's decision is dictated by the moral law: 'Quando si giura di far cosa, che non convenga, non si dee il giuramento osservare e à Ruggiero non conveniva, come à civile huomo, abbandonar nel maggior bisogno il Re suo' [When one swears to do what is inappropriate, one must not stay true to the oath and Ruggiero, being a gentleman, could not leave his King at the time of greatest need].[68] This is all the more true because Ruggiero 'si poteva chiamare Affricano, perché era nato, nutrito, e vivuto in Affrica; nato di madre Affricana, e allevato da Affricano; suo padre, né altro suo parente Cristiano non aveva mai conosciuto' [could call himself African because he was born and brought up in Africa and he lived there, born of an African mother and raised by an African man; he had never met his father or any other Christian relative].[69]

These are precisely the thoughts that run through Ruggiero's mind. While foregrounding his fear of dishonour ('molti diran che non se de' osservare | quel ch'era ingiusto e illicito a giurare' [many will say that an oath unjustly and wrongly sworn | should not be observed] (*Fur.*, XXXVI 67,7–8 AB; XL C), Ariosto also, and for the first time, draws attention to his affection for Agramante: 'Ruggiero ama Agramante, e se si parte | per ciò [that is because of the violation of the pact] da lui, far grande error si stima' [Ruggiero loves Agramante, and if he deserts him | over this, he deems it no trifling fault] (65,3–4 ABC). Moreover, a few stanzas later we learn that Ruggiero has warm feelings towards the seven African kings who had been captured by Dudone: 'Ruggier li amava, e sofferir non puòte | lasciarli in la miseria in che trovolli' [Ruggiero was fond of them, and he could not endure | leaving them in the abject state in which he found them] (74,1–2 ABC). Thus, the dynastic hero is more attached to the Saracen world than we thought. At this point his story takes on dramatic overtones: profoundly shaken by Agramante's defeat, Ruggiero comes to resemble Andrea da Barberino's Balante who feels emotionally attached to his king and his brothers-in-arms despite his desire to convert.

Unlike Balante, however, Ruggiero is not completely convinced of the truth of the Christian religion. In reality, though considering himself a believer, like the vast majority of Boiardo's and Ariosto's characters, he has never been particularly devout, neither before nor after his falling in love with Bradamante. Amorous passion has made him renounce Macone ('Non che in l'acqua, ma nel fuoco | per tuo amor porre il capo mi fia poco' [It would be a small thing to place my head in fire, | let alone water, for love of you] (*Fur.*, XX 35,7–8 AB; XXII C)), but it has not led him to Christ. Far from imploring God to help him fulfil his destiny, he continues to live in a world governed by *Fortuna*, hoping that sooner or later it will allow him to marry Bradamante. In fact, he appears to have doubts as to whether the Creator takes any interest in human affairs.[70]

67    Tasso, *Apologia in difesa della sua Gierusalemme liberata*, fol. B1ʳ.
68    Salviati, *Dello Infarinato Accademico della Crusca risposta all'Apologia di Torquato Tasso*, p. 28.
69    Ibid.
70    This is the impression we get from the (irreverent, to say the least) speech in which he declares

Having said that, eventually Ruggiero does recognize God's hand in the chaos of life. Together with the above-mentioned seven African kings, he will set sail for Africa in order to join Agramante, but their ship will by struck by a terrible storm. Fearing that the ship might hit a rock, the crew and the passengers pile into a lifeboat which, overcrowded as it is, sinks. Fighting the furious waves, Ruggiero comes to the conclusion that this storm is Christ's revenge for his reluctance to abandon the Africans:

> Gli ritornano a mente le promesse
> che tante volte alla sua donna fece;
> quel che giurato havea quando si messe
> contra Rinaldo, e nulla satisfece.
> Sì che pentito, a Dio che non volesse
> punirlo qui, tre volte e quattro e diece
> disse; e votosse di core e di fede
> farse christian, se ponea in sciutto il piede;
>
> e mai più non pigliar spada né lancia
> contra a' Fedeli in aiuto de' Mori;
> ma che ritorneria subito in Francia
> e a Carlo renderia debiti honori;
> né Bradamante più terrebbe a ciancia,
> e verria a honesto fin de li sui amori.
>
> [He recalls the promises
> so often made to his lady,
> and the oath he had sworn when he fought
> with Rinaldo, none of which he had honoured.
> Contritely he asked God time and again
> not to punish him now,
> and swore faithfully from the bottom of his heart
> to become a Christian if he set foot on shore,
>
> and never more to take up sword or lance
> for the Moors against the Christians.
> He would return straight to France
> and render due honours to Charlemagne;
> he would no longer dally with Bradamante,
> but would achieve the honourable consummation of his love.]
> (*Fur.*, XXXVII 48–49,1–6 AB; XLI C)

This time Ruggiero keeps his promise: having reached a tiny island, he encounters a hermit who, after having reproached him for his spiritual indolence, teaches him the rudiments of Christian doctrine and then administers the sacrament of baptism.[71] On the surface, it would seem that, identifying with this servant of

---

his willingness to rescue Ricciardetto: 'habbia chi regge il ciel cura di questo, | o la Fortuna, se non tocca a lui' [may He who governs the heavens take care of this | or *Fortuna*, if it is not his affair] (*Fur.*, XX 57,3–4 AB; XXII C).

71  According to Giudicetti, this hermit is 'l'unico eremita del poema non ridicolizzato' [the only hermit in the poem that is not ridiculed] (Giudicetti, *Mandricardo e la melanconia*, p. 55). It can be pointed out, however, that the hermit in the Caligorante episode (*Fur.*, XIII 23–29 AB; XV 42–48 C) is also more or less 'respectable'.

Christ, the author unequivocally condemns Ruggiero's Saracen past. And yet one perceives a sense of detachment in the stanzas devoted to Ruggiero's spiritual purification: his conversion 'si compie come un colpo di scena teatrale, frutto di avvenimenti esteriori e di moventi estranei alla coscienza religiosa' [happens as a *coup de théâtre*, the result of external events and of reasons that are alien to religious conscience].[72] The poet's gaze captures neither Ruggiero's internal crisis nor the infusion of grace into his soul. He limits himself to registering his hero's passive submission to his destiny.

From the psychological viewpoint, it is above all the terror of death — physical demise rather than eternal damnation — that makes Ruggiero promise to God (who, it must be said, does not speak to him directly, as He did in Issabella's case) to cut all ties with his king. From this perspective, he joins the multitude of Saracen knights from the previous chivalric tradition who choose to convert to Christianity when faced with the prospect of death. Yet, at the dawn of his heroic career, burning with the desire to descend from the Mount of Carena and take part in Agramante's joust, Rugiero declared himself ready to die in the name of chivalry ('sarebe la mia zoglia e 'l mio conforto | star sieco un'hora, et esser dapoi morto' [I will be overjoyed and glad | to spend an hour with them, then die] (*Inam.*, II xvi 37,7–8). Moreover, praising the dynastic hero for his resolution to remain with Agramante, Ariosto himself proclaimed on more than one occasion that death with honour was to be preferred to life with disgrace: 'l'honor è di più pregio che la vita, | ch'a tutti li piaceri è preferita' [honour is of greater value than life — | which is preferred to all other pleasures] (*Fur.*, XXXIV 4,7–8 AB; XXXVIII C).

If, threatened with death, Ruggiero forgets about the chivalric code, Agramante can make his own the words allegedly uttered by Francis I of France: 'tout est perdu, fors l'honneur' [all is lost save honour].[73] It may not be a coincidence that at this point in the narration the respective stories of Ruggiero and his king run parallel: using the technique of *entrelacement*, Ariosto leaves the former (still a Saracen) in the tempestuous sea to tell us about the preparations for the Lipadusa duel. On the eve of the combat, Brandimarte tries to persuade the African ruler to convert to Christianity, telling him that if he does so, Orlando will reinstate him as king of Africa. Whereupon Agramante thus replies, giving yet another example of his sense of dignity:

> Che a vincere habbia o perdere, o nel regno
> tornare antiquo o sempre starne in bando,
> in mente sua n'ha Dio fatto disegno,
> il qual né veder io posso, né Orlando.
> Sia quel che vuol, non potrà ad atto indegno
> di Re inchinarmi mai timore; e quando
> fussi certo morir, vuo' restar morto,
> prima ch'al sangue mio far sì gran torto.

72   Ezio Levi, 'L'*Orlando furioso* come epopea nuziale', *Archivum romanicum*, 17 (1933), 459–93 (p. 483). See also Pool, *Interpretazione dell'*'Orlando furioso', p. 180.
73   Admired by Ariosto, Francis I is an important presence in the historical digressions of the *Furioso*, especially in A. See Dorigatti, 'Il manoscritto dell'*Orlando furioso* (1505–1515)'.

[Whether I am to win or lose,
whether I am to recover my ancestral kingdom or be forever banished
    from it —
the decision is known to God,
whose thoughts neither I nor you nor Orlando can see.
Come what may, base terror shall never reduce me
to any act unworthy of a king;
were I certain to die, I should sooner die
than disparage my own blood.]
        (*Fur.*, XXXVII 44 AB; XLI C)

With Agramante's voice still echoing in the reader's mind, the poet suddenly
'remembers' about the drowning Ruggiero and resumes the suspended story. Far
from being fortuitous, the juxtaposition of these two narrative strands adds to the
complexity and ambiguity surrounding the theme of conversion. Agramante does
not have the sin of pride on his conscience;[74] he is willing to surrender to the divine
will, but Brandimarte's proposal (which is, in essence, an injunction to surrender,
appealing to the Saracen's prudence) does not touch his heart. The courage with
which he chooses to sacrifice his life in order to stay true to his values earns him our
respect, making us forget about his shortcomings as a ruler. Already in the sixteenth
century his noble speech was applauded by commentators such as Simon Fórnari,
Clemente Valvassore and Lionardo Salviati:

> In Agramante, che non solamente non accetta la conditione offertagli da Brandi-
> marte, ma contro a·llui gravemente se ne accende, et con parole sdegnose, et
> irate il rimprovera, si dipinge la fortezza dell'animo, che i Re nell'aversa fortuna
> debbono saldamente mantenere, et più tosto andare alla morte certa, che cosa
> commettere indegna, et fuori del real decoro.

> [In Agramante, who not only refuses to accept the condition offered to him
> by Brandimarte, but lashes out at him and with disdainful and angry words
> rebukes him, we see depicted the strength of mind that Kings should firmly
> maintain in adversity and rather face a certain death than commit an ignoble
> action that undermines royal decorum.][75]

---

74  'In fact, even in terms of man's relationship with the divine, Agramante is not presumptuous
as are many paladins, including the newly converted Brandimarte. In the recognition of man's
limitations with respect to divine design he is indeed more human and more wise than his
counterpart' (Cuccaro, p. 147).

75  Fórnari, *La spositione sopra l'Orlando furioso*, p. 666. Clemente Valvassori expresses a similar view
in his 'Allegoria' [Allegory] to the canto in question: 'Nel rè Agramante, che non volle ritornare nel
perduto stato, offertogli sotto conditione, laquale gli pareva essere contro l'honor suo, si mostra che
gli animi forti sempre sono a sé stessi simili, se bene si veggono caduti in estrema fortuna' [In King
Agramante, who did not want to return to his lost state, which had been offered to him with the
condition which he deemed to be contrary to his honour, one sees that strong minds always remain
true to themselves, even when they have fallen into extreme misfortune] (*Orlando furioso* (Venice:
Gio. Andrea Valvassore, 1553), fol. 200ʳ). Moreover, according to Salviati, this is one of the most
eloquent speeches in the entire poem: 'Puossi sentir parlar più magnanimo, più reale, più eroico, e
più accompagnante il decoro della persona, che quel d'Agramante a Brandimarte' [One cannot find
a more magnanimous, more regal, more heroic and more decorous speech than Agramante's speech
to Brandimarte] (Salviati, *Lo 'nfarinato secondo ovvero dello 'nfarinato Accademico della Crusca*, p. 188).

Agramante will die in the Lipadusa duel, while Ruggiero, together with Orlando (who has decapitated Agramante) and the other Christian paladins, will return to France to swear allegiance to Charlemagne and marry Bradamante. But whereas in the first two editions his lady's parents are happy for her to wed such a renowned warrior, in the 1532 version the dynastic couple has to overcome yet another obstacle: Amone has already promised Bradamante to Leone, the son of the Greek Emperor, and will not change his mind, given that Ruggiero, for all his valour, is destitute: 'il qual non ch'abbi regno, | ma non può al mondo dir: questa è mia cosa' [who, far from possessing a realm, | had nothing on earth which he could call his own] (*Fur.*, XLIV 36,5–6 C). Thus, shortly after his conversion, Ruggiero learns that, far from being an idyllic realm of chivalry, Charlemagne's court is infected with the worm of Avarice.[76] This discovery is all the more bitter, considering that Agramante was eager to fulfil his every wish and that no African baron has ever ridiculed his poverty...

It is generally believed that the purpose of the Leone episode is to ennoble the dynastic hero, to render him more interesting and more charismatic. Thus, Ruggiero's penultimate adventure is supposed to celebrate his *cortesia*. Ruggiero's rival happens to save his life; the fear of appearing ungrateful forces the future founder of the Este dynasty to renounce Bradamante. For, however painful this may be,

> pur non è mai per dir che se ne penta;
> che prima ch'a Leon non ubbidire,
> mille volte, non ch'una, è per morire.
>
> [yet he was never to confess that he regretted his word;
> he would have died not once but a thousand times
> sooner than disobey Leone.]
> (*Fur.*, XLV 57,7–8 C)

Be it an act of madness or nobility, 'Ruggiero's adherence to the law of chivalry signals a continuing struggle against any adoption of the Christian foundational narrative'.[77] The sacrament of baptism has not changed his worldview, nor have the long conversations with the hermit strengthened his faith: having lost Bradamante, Ruggiero does not turn to God, but sinks into despair (a mortal sin in the Christian religion), 'né vede, altro che morte, chi finire | possa l'insopportabil suo martìre' [beside death he can see nothing | to put an end to his unbearable torment] (*Fur.*, XLV 86,7–8 C). Needless to say, this renders even more ambivalent the episode of his conversion: Ruggiero, one could argue, wants to depart this life in the name of *cortesia*, because earlier he did not have the courage to die in the name of faithfulness to his liege.

---

76    As Moretti points out, by adding the Leone episode the poet 'coglie l'occasione [...] per "protestare", con voce energica, contro i falsi valori che la società contemporanea antepone agli ideali cortesi e cavallereschi' [takes the opportunity [...] to 'protest', in a vigorous voice, against the false values that contemporary society favours over courtly and chivalric ideals] (Moretti, *Ariosto narratore e la sua scuola*, p. 76).

77    Shulman, '"Sferza e sprona": The Flight from Authority in the *Orlando Furioso*', p. 43.

## From Biserta to Paris

Thanks to Melissa's timely intervention, however, Ruggiero will not die and his story has a happy ending (or so it seems). Having cleared the last obstacle of his dynastic path, he can finally marry his lady. Ruggiero appears to have found peace of mind, but on the last day of his sumptuous wedding celebrations — day nine, to be precise — a knight dressed in black interrupts the closing banquet. This knight is Rodomonte, and so the paths of Agramante's best champions cross again. But this time one of them has to die, given the gravity of the accusation that Rodomonte levels at his former brother-in-arms in the presence of Charlemagne and his entire court: Ruggiero, maintains the King of Sarza, has betrayed Agramante, his legitimate lord, and he, Rodomonte (who has remained true to his oath of faithfulness to the end) has come to confront the traitor.

As we saw earlier, Rodomonte defeated many a knight on the bridge in memory of Issabella. Then, after having been unhorsed by Bradamante, he confined himself to a dark cave (*Fur.*, XXXII 54 AB; XXXV 52 C) to expiate his fault, an undeserved punishment, given that the warrior woman had used Argalìa's lance (even if she was unaware of its magic powers). In the 1516 *Furioso* Rodomonte heads towards Paris as soon as he learns that Ruggiero has converted to Christianity and Agramante is dead. In C, where the dynastic marriage is delayed because of Bradamante's parents, Ariosto informs us that, after the humiliating defeat, the King of Sarza swore 'non porsi arme intorno, | né stringer spada, né montare in sella' [not to wear armour, | hold sword or sit saddle] for 'un anno, un mese e un giorno' [a year, a month, and a day] (*Fur.*, XLVI 102,3–5 C) and that he kept his oath, 'Se ben di Carlo in questo mezzo intese | e del re suo signore ogni successo' [Although in this interval he heard | of all that had happened to Charlemagne and his own lord, his king] (103,1–2). This does not mean, however, that Rodomonte was disloyal or abandoned his lord. We must recall that his intention was to wait until Agramante lost his kingdom, and then help him regain it. Rodomonte could not have foreseen that, instead of going into exile, his friend would challenge Orlando (cured of his madness just in time for the Lipadusa duel). It is futile to speculate on what Rodomonte would have done had the duel taken place before his very eyes. The fact remains that the news of his king's confrontation with Orlando could have reached his cave only after Agramante's death — too late, that is.

Having served his self-imposed penance, Rodomonte thus comes to Paris to challenge Ruggiero whom he deems responsible for the Saracens' defeat. On arrival he feels no need to observe courtly etiquette: he neither dismounts, nor bows down before Charlemagne, nor shows 'segno alcun di reverentia' [any gesture of respect] (*Fur.*, XL 76,2 A; 75 B; XLVI 104 C). It should be noted, however, that he is not breaking the chivalric code. After all, it was Charlemagne himself who unwittingly authorized this intrusion:

> Libera corte fa bandir intorno,
> dove sicuro ognun possa venire;
> e campo franco sin al nono giorno
> conciede a chi contese han da partire.

[He proclaims open court,
where all are welcome in safety;
and he concedes the freedom to fight a duel for nine days
to anyone who has a quarrel to settle.]
    (*Fur.*, XL 47,1–4 AB; XLVI 74 C)

A tense silence settles in the air. Followed by the anxious gazes of the guests, the stranger rides straight to the groom (who is seated at the left hand of his new lord) and announces the purpose of his visit:

— Son — disse — il Re di Sarza, Rodomonte,
che te, Ruggiero, alla battaglia sfido;
et vuo' provarti, prima che tramonte
questo sol d'hoggi, che rebelle e infido
al tuo Signor sei stato, e traditore;
né questo merti, né alcun altro honore.

Ben che tua fellonia si veggia aperta,
ch'essendo hor tu christian non pòi negarla;
acciò si possa ancho saper più certa,
in questo campo vengoti a provarla:
e se persona hai qui che faccia offerta
di combatter per te, voglio accettarla.
S'una non basta, accetto quattro e sei,
provando lor che traditor tu sei. –

[I am — he said — Rodomonte, King of Sarza,
and I challenge you, Ruggiero, to battle;
before the sun sets I want to prove to you
that you have been rebellious and disloyal
to your Lord, and that you are a traitor;
you do not deserve this or any other honour.

Although your treason is transparent,
being a Christian you cannot deny it,
to make it clearer still
I have come to prove it in these lists:
if anyone here offers to fight for you
I shall accept him;
and if one does not suffice, I shall accept four and six —
I shall prove to them that you are a traitor]
    (*Fur.*, XL 77,3–8, 78 A; 76–77 B; XLVI 105–06 C)

This is Rodomonte's last speech. Brimming with indignation, it brings to mind his very first speech, the one that he delivered back in Biserta, when, speaking in front of Agramante and the thirty-one vassal kings, he challenged to a duel anyone who dared to disobey their lord. The thematic similarity between the two speeches is further highlighted by the verbal echoes between the first of the two octaves cited above and *Inam.* II i 55: not only does Ariosto borrow the rhyme words *traditore* [traitor] and *honore* [honour], but also the key terms *signore* [lord] and *[de]sfidare* [challenge]. This specular resemblance between the speeches that open and close Rodomonte's character trajectory creates a sense of circularity, foregrounding the fact that, despite all the blows that life has dealt him, he has remained true to himself, true, that is, to the values instilled in him by his father Ulieno.

But here, in Paris, Rodomonte is alone among enemies. If his first speech was peppered with sarcasm, now his voice is charged with immense bitterness. His hatred and contempt for Ruggiero are such that he does everything to humiliate him in front of the Christians: Rodomonte declares himself willing to fight with anyone who might offer to replace Ruggiero, thereby implying that the latter — reputedly one the most valorous knights on earth — is in reality but a Martano-like coward. On the other hand, for all his apparent arrogance, Rodomonte does not insult the Christians: it is true that they killed his king, but, in his opinion, they did not violate the chivalric code. It is worth noting that in the 1532 version of Rodomonte's speech Ariosto lays even more emphasis on the fact that, far from being driven by religious hatred, Rodomonte subscribes to the ideals of lay chivalry: '[...] *e che non merti, che sei* traditore, | *fra questi cavallieri alcuno* onore' [as a traitor, you deserve | no place of honour amid these knights] (76,7–8 B; 105 C) (emphasis added).

As for Ruggiero, he wastes no time in protesting his innocence, even if first he asks for his new king's permission to do so:

> Ruggier a quel parlar ritto levosse,
> e con licentia rispose di Carlo
> che mentiva egli, et qualunqu'altro fosse,
> che traditor volesse nominarlo;
> e che col Signor suo sempre portosse
> in modo ch'a ragion non può biasmarlo;
> e ch'era apparecchiato sostenere
> d'haver in questo fatto il suo devere:
>
> e ch'a difender la sua causa era atto,
> senza tôrre in aiuto suo veruno;
> e che sperava di mostrargli in fatto
> che assai n'havrebbe e forse troppo d'uno.
>
> [At these words Ruggiero stood up,
> and, with Charlemagne's leave, retorted
> that he lied, as did anyone
> who wanted to call him a traitor;
> that his behaviour towards his liege had always been such
> that no accusation could rightfully be made against him;
> that he was ready to prove that
> he had always done his duty to him;
>
> and that he was capable of defending his cause
> without invoking anybody's help;
> and that he hoped to show him [i.e. Rodomont] that a single opponent
> would be as much as — and possibly more than — he could handle.]
>             (*Fur.*, XL 79–80,1–4 A; 78–79 B; XLVI 107–08 C)

Ruggiero's speech strikes us as being permeated by a sense of vagueness and uneasiness. His reaction is very different from that of Boiardo's Rugiero, who was beside himself with anger when Marchesino and Pinadoro dared to accuse him of betrayal.[78] According to Giudicetti, in his reply 'si nota una sfumatura di esagerazione e di affanno, un'accumulazione di scuse eccessiva, quasi a lasciar trasparire un senso di colpa' [a hint of exaggeration and anxiety, an accumulation of excuses that almost reveals a feeling of guilt].[79]

Ruggiero claims to have fulfilled his duty towards Agramante. And yet his evasive, awkward words do not prove his innocence, especially if one re-examines his case in light of the comments of Renaissance experts on chivalry.[80] Interestingly, while for some the fact that Agramante broke an oath sworn on the Qur'an releases Ruggiero from the obligation to serve his king,[81] others believe that Agramante's violation of the oath is ultimately unimportant. As Giovanni Battista Olevano puts it,

> Ruggiero serve al suo Rè fino all'ultimo estermino, e morte di quello: poscia, spinto da spirito migliore, à miglior legge, et à miglior Principe si accosta. Rodomonte, indomito sprezzatore de' pericoli, e sempre di nuove brighe desideroso, và à ritrovarlo, e sfidandolo gli dice, come intende di provargli con l'armi in mano ch'egli, havendo abbandonato il suo Signore, è stato un traditore. Ruggiero, che con dire ch'egli haveva servito il suo Rè fino alla morte, facilmente lo haverebbe potuto sgannare, e forse fuggir contesa, conoscendo l'orgoglio dell'inimico, per non mostrar viltà, lo mente: onde si stabilisce l'abbattimento.
>
> [Ruggiero serves his King until his last annihilation and death: then, driven by a better spirit, he approaches a better Prince and a better law. Rodomonte, who fearlessly spurns danger and always looks for new quarrels, goes to find him, and challenging him, says that he intends to prove to him with his arms

---

78   A group of African knights attacked Bradamante, prompting the courteous Ruggiero to rush to her defence: 'E Marchesino e Pinador cridarno: | "Tu te farai, Rugier, qua puoco honore! | Contra Agramante èi fato traditore!". || Come quella parola e oltragio intese, | il giovenetto non trovava loco: | e' sì nel cuore e nel viso s'accese | che sfavillava gli ochi come un foco, | e messe un crido: "Gente discortese! | Lo esser cotanti vi gioverà puoco! | Traditor sete voi, io non sono esso, | e mostrerò la prova adesso adesso!"' [And Pinador and Martasino | shouted, 'Rugier! This is dishonour; | you are betraying Agramante!' || When he heard their insulting words, | the young man lost his self-control. | His heart was burning and his face, | and his eyes sparkled like a flame | as he yelled, 'You're discourteous! | That you outnumber us won't help! | You're the traitors here, not me, | and I'll prove it — immediately!'] (*Inam.*, III v 52,6–8; 53).

79   Giudicetti, *Mandricardo e la melanconia*, p. 176.

80   The late sixteenth century witnessed the composition of a plethora of treatises on duels and chivalry. For their discussions of duels in Ariosto and Tasso see Francesco Erspamer, '"E pon la lancia in resta": per una tipologia del duello nei romanzi', in Idem, *La biblioteca di don Ferrante: Duello e onore nella cultura del Cinquecento* (Rome: Bulzoni, 1982), pp. 137–79 (p. 171).

81   '[...] così ode Ruggiero, che Rodomonte lo chiama traditore, e pur sapeva, che così era convenuto, che se veniva impedito, dovesse farsi Cavalliero di Carlo. Agramante havea rotto i patti, che havea fatto con Carlo, e però Ruggiero havea il vero, e la ragione della parte sua; e quando dice à Rodomonte "tu menti", la sua mentita è vera, e data veramente' [so Ruggiero hears that Rodomonte has called him a traitor and yet he knew that such was the agreement, that he had to become Charlemagne's knight if he were impeded. Agramante had broken the pacts that he had made with Charlemagne and therefore Ruggiero was right and the truth was on his side; and when he tells Rodomonte 'you are lying', his *mentita* [identification of insult] is true and rightly given] (Camillo Baldo, *Delle mentite discorso* (Venice: Bartolomeo Fontana, 1634), pp. 31–32).

in his hand that, having abandoned his Lord, he is a traitor. Ruggiero, who could have easily shown to him that he was mistaken by saying that he had served his King until his death, and thereby could have perhaps avoided the duel, knowing his enemy's pride, says that he is a liar in order not to appear a coward: and so the combat is to take place.][82]

In line with what we have argued thus far, Olevano seems to believe that Ruggiero had the moral right to convert to Christianity and enter Charlemagne's service, but only *after* Agramante's death. So did Sobrino, who asked to be baptized *after* the Lipadusa duel.[83] By maintaining that Ruggiero remained loyal to Agramante 'fino all'ultimo esterminio, e morte di quello' [until his last annihilation and death], Olevano suggests that his contention with Rodomonte could have been resolved 'per via di pace' [peacefully],[84] if only Ruggiero had mentioned this circumstance,[85] but that Ruggiero accepted the duel challenge 'per non mostrar viltà' [in order not to appear a coward]. What Olevano does not realize, however, is that Ruggiero did not know about his lord's death at the time of his conversion, that he swore to renounce his African identity before learning about Orlando's victory.

Ruggiero, of course, is no monster of ingratitude. According to Francesco Birago, 'Ruggier non fu traditore, presupposto anco, che abbandonato havesse il suo Rè vivendo' [Ruggiero was not a traitor even if we assume that he abandoned his King when the latter was still alive].[86] Though convinced of the opposite (i.e. that Ruggiero's conduct has always been that of a loyal vassal), Birago goes to great lengths to prove that the accusation of betrayal is groundless from whatever angle one looks at it (which naturally gives rise to the suspicion that, without admitting it, he has doubts as to Ruggiero's innocence):

82   Giovanni Battista Olevano, *Trattato nel quale co 'l mezo di cinquanta casi vien posto in atto prattico il modo di ridurre a pace ogni sorte di privata inimicitia, nata per cagion d'honore* (Venice: Giacobo Antonio Somascho, 1603), p. 23.
83   According to Giuseppe Monorchio, Sobrino's conversion, too, is dictated by opportunism: see Giuseppe Monorchio, *Lo specchio del cavaliere: il duello nella trattatistica e nell'epica rinascimentale* (Ottawa: Canadian Society for Italian Studies, 1998), p. 101n.
84   Olevano, *Trattato*, p. 23.
85   'Dirà Ruggiero a Rodomonte: "Rodomonte, essendo io assicurato, come non per mala volontà, che mi portaste, ma che, come mal informato dell'attioni mie, mi chiamaste traditore, e che ora, accertatovi del vero, mi tenete per fedele al mio Principe, non voglio che la mentita, ch'io vi diedi, vi sia di carico alcuno; anzi vi dico, che se bene diceste quello, che non era vero, non però mentiste: onde desidero, che mi siate amico come prima". Risponderà Rodomonte: "Ruggiero, i falsi altrui riporti, e non altra cagione, ch'io m'havessi, m'indussero à dar nota tale ad un Cavalier honorato, e leale, come voi sete; però, rincrescendomi d'havergli creduto, vi sarò amico come prima"' [Ruggiero will tell Rodomonte: 'Rodomonte, seeing clearly that you called me a traitor not out of ill will towards me but rather because you were misinformed about my actions, and that now, having learnt the truth, you consider me faithful to my Prince, I do not want the *mentita* that I issued to you to trouble you in any way; in fact, I tell you that although what you said was not true, you did not lie: and so I want you to be my friend as before'. Rodomonte will reply: 'Ruggiero, it was because of other people's false reports and not for any other reason that I made such an accusation against an honourable and loyal Knight like you; and so, I regret that I have believed them, and I will be your friend as before] (ibid., p. 26).
86   Francesco Birago, *Discorsi cavallereschi* (Milan: Gio. Battista Bidelli, 1622), p. 23.

io dico, che non colui, che si diparte dal servigio del suo Principe, senza licenza, et senza disubligarsi dal giuramento di fedeltà, et vada al servigio del suo nimico, non è, né si può dimandar traditore; ma sì ben ribello, perché traditore è colui, che insidia nella vita, nell'honor, à chi di lui si fida, overo se manca di sua fede à chi serve, ò sia naturale o adventitio signore, in cosa alla sua fede comessa, per la qual ne seguiti pregiuditio, ò nell'honore, ò nello stato, overo nella vita sua, over de' figliuoli, come rivelar secreti, dar' a' nemici fortezze raccommandate alla custodia sua, et sua fede, et altre simil cose; et in questi casi Ruggier non si trova, sì ché traditor Ruggier non è [...]

[I say that a man who leaves his Prince's service, without permission and without releasing himself from the oath of fidelity, and enters his enemy's service, is not and cannot be called a traitor; but rather he is a rebel, because a traitor is someone who endangers the life and honour of the one who trusts him, that is, who is unfaithful to the person he serves, whether this is his natural or his temporary lord, in a matter that was entrusted to him, which is detrimental to his lord's honour, his state or his life or to his children, such as betraying secrets, handing over to the enemy the fortresses that one was entrusted with and other similar things; and Ruggiero does nothing of the kind, and therefore Ruggiero is not a traitor [...]][87]

Rodomonte, to be precise, does accuse Ruggiero also of having been 'rebelle' [rebellious] to his lord, if only in the 1516 edition (77,6 A). And it is difficult not to agree with him, given that the episode of Ruggiero's spiritual enlightenment chronologically precedes the Lipadusa duel and Agramante's death. It is true that Ruggiero has not betrayed Agramante, if we accept Birago's definition of betrayal. But it is equally true that he abandoned him in time of direst need, fully conscious of the fact that he was violating his personal chivalric code that earlier had made him set sail for Africa.

At this point, we may note that both Agostini and Valcieco — neither of whom continues the dynastic theme of the *Inamoramento de Orlando* — present Rugiero's conversion in an ambivalent light. In Agostini's *Quarto libro* Rugiero converts to Christianity when Bradamante announces that he must do so in order to marry her. He is reluctant to abandon the Saracen faith, not least because he is aware of his duty towards Agramante ('Hebbe di ciò Rugier tanto dolore |che non vorebe al mondo esser mai nato' [Rugiero was so sad to hear this | that he wished he'd never been born] (*Quarto libro*, VII 20,1–2)), but his passion for Bradamante makes him forget everything. In his *Quinto libro*, Valcieco narrates a dramatic encounter between the now Christian Rugiero and Agramante, who reproaches him for having deserted him. Rugiero is overwhelmed with shame and guilt ('"Oimè, per questa dama | privo rimango e d'honor e or fama!"' [Alas, because of this damsel | I've lost my honour and my reputation] (*Quinto libro V*, IV 63,1–8)), but he tries to justify his conversion by saying that he was unable to resist love and that the Christian religion is the true religion. Agostini's *Quinto libro* opens with a no less dramatic series of events. In canto I, Sobrino is sent to Paris to negotiate a truce with the Christians, where he meets Rugiero, who explains to him that he has changed sides because

---

87    Ibid., pp. 22–23.

he grew convinced of the truth of Christianity (which, as the reader knows, is not why he converted). Sobrino rebukes him for his desertion, but speaks courteously to the Christians. Later in the same canto, Agramante and some of his men — who are deeply saddened by the loss of their best knight — attend Rugiero's wedding. During the wedding feast the guests find out that Atlante has hanged himself out of despair, and, while everybody is shocked, Rugiero conceals his distress from the others, as if his conversion made it impossible for him to grieve over his adoptive father's death. Such callousness prompts Marsilio to accuse Rugiero of ingratitude ('Come sei sì d'ingegno privo e stolto | [...] | che non ti duol di chi t'ha nutricato? | Ma tal merto ha chi serve a un cor ingrato!' ['How can you be so mindless and foolish | [...] | that you feel not sorry for the man who raised you? | But this is the reward one gets when one serves an ungrateful heart] (*Quinto libro A*, I 67,5–8)). When Agramante agrees with Marsilio, Rugiero loses his temper and the feast is ruined.[88]

Unlike Valcieco and Agostini, with whose sequels he may or may not have been familiar, Ariosto does not make his Ruggiero meet Agramante. However, he too exploits the dramatic potential of his conversion, leaving the reader to come to his or her own conclusion. Ariosto's Ruggiero tries to justify his passing to the Christians, without, however, mentioning his oath or his belief in the truth of the Christian religion.[89] All the knights present at the banquet take his side; Orlando and many others offer to fight in his stead. But, strangely enough, Rodomonte's speech does not provoke outrage: if anything, the prevailing feeling is fear inasmuch as the memories of his feats in the battle of Paris are still fresh. Nor does anyone dare to accuse Rodomonte of lying; and this silence, one could argue, betrays a certain embarrassment.

And so the duel begins. While for many scholars the final octaves of the *Furioso* are underpinned, on the one hand, by Ruggiero's valour and *cortesia* and, on the other, by Rodomonte's brute force and treacherousness, for some the King of Sarza proves to be superior to Ruggiero. In fact, a close reading reveals that Ariosto exalts Ruggiero's prowess in a half-hearted way, casting his enemy in a surprisingly more heroic light.

Without examining the duel in all its details, suffice it to note that the two duellers are not in a condition of parity. While Ruggiero avails himself of Hector's armour, the horse Frontino and the enchanted sword Balisarda, Rodomonte had left his dragon skin at Issabella's tomb and for this reason:

> Egli havea un'altra assai buona armatura,
> non come quella a gran pezzo perfetta:
> ma né questa né quella, né più dura
> a Balisarda si sarebbe retta;

88    For a more detailed discussion of the figure of Rugiero and his conversion in Agostini and Valcieco, see Pavlova, 'Sul finale del *Furioso* A', pp. 32–40; and Eadem, 'La concezione di cavalleria'. See also Alhaique Pettinelli, pp. 247–49.

89    This omission did not escape the notice of Hyonjin Kim, 'From *La chanson de Roland* to *Orlando Furioso*: the Evolution of the Saracenic Other in the Carolingian epic', *Horizons*, 2 (2011), 97–111 (pp. 106–07).

a cui non osta incanto né fatura,
né finezza d'acciar né tempra eletta.
Ruggier di qua e di là sì ben lavora,
ch'al Pagan l'arme in più d'un luoco fora.

[He had other arms of very high quality
but not as perfect as his usual ones:
not that either the old or the present arms, nor even stronger one
would have resisted Balisarda;
for no enchantment or spell,
nor steel however choice or finely tempered could withstand it.
Ruggiero strives to such good effect
that he pierces the Pagan's armour in a number of places.]
    (*Fur.*, XL 92 A; 91 B; XLVI 120 C)

Thus, Ruggiero wins in no small part thanks to Balisarda and the superior quality of his armour, without which, as the narrator himself has to admit, Ruggiero would have been killed (94,7–8 A; 93 B; 122 C).[90] 'In tutto lo svolgersi del duello,' observes Zanette, 'malgrado la evidente disparità delle condizioni, resta sempre dubbio quale dei due sia il più forte: figuriamoci se i vantaggi fossero stati dalla parte del pagano, o anche solo equilibrati!' [Throughout the duel, despite the obvious inequality of conditions, there always remains a doubt as to who of the two is stronger: what if the advantages had been on the Saracen's side or if they had only been equal!].[91] Ariosto underscores not only Rodomonte's superhuman force, but also his agility (100,1 A; 99 B; 128 C) and, more importantly, his boundless courage.[92] The King of Sarza fights fiercely until his last breath; unlike Gradasso (who is paralyzed with terror when he sees the invulnerable Orlando decapitating Agramante), he is not in the least intimidated by the invulnerability of his adversary. So much so that Ruggiero's 'senno' [prudence] and 'valor' [valour] (105,8 A; 104 B; 133 C) — that is the fact that he is well-versed in freestyle wrestling, which enables him to overpower the Saracen when the latter is greatly weakened by the loss of blood — are eclipsed by Rodomonte's heroism.[93] In this respect, Rodomonte's death is

90    In Andrea da Barberino's *Aspramonte*, too, Ulieno is stronger than Riccieri; but the latter knight wins because of his strategic sense rather than the quality of his armour (*Aspramonte A*, III xc 20–40).
91    Zanette, *Conversazioni sull'*'Orlando furioso', p. 393. Praloran, too, notes that 'a causa della inferiorità delle armi del suo avversario, vero *leitmotiv* del duello, Ruggiero è in vantaggio' [because of the inferiority of his enemy's armour, the real leitmotif of the duel, Ruggiero has an advantage] (Praloran, *Tempo e azione nell'*'Orlando furioso', p. 122).
92    Having been unhorsed by Ruggiero (who, however, had been the first to fall), Rodomonte lands on his feet thanks to 'sua sorte [*forza* in C] o sua destrezza' [his fate [*strength* in C] or his agility] (100,1 A; 99 B; 128 C). The amendment in C contributes to bringing into greater relief Rodomonte's prowess.
93    'Alla conclusione del poema Ruggiero uccide lo "smisurato", antiquato cavaliere Rodomonte in un combattimento che è un capolavoro di astuzia "moderna". E proprio il gigantesco cavaliere viene costretto a combattere appiedato, dissanguato e viene ucciso in un corpo a corpo sanguinoso tanto feroce quanto poco cavalleresco: e muore come il suo modello virgiliano Turno, da vero eroe dei barbari guerrieri vinti' [The poem ends with Ruggiero killing the 'huge', old-fashioned knight Rodomonte in a combat that is a masterpiece of 'modern' cunning. And it is the giant knight who is forced to fight on foot, bleeding to death, and who is killed in a bloody hand-to-hand combat that is as ferocious as it is unchivalrous: and he dies as his Virgilian model Turnus, as a true hero of the

somewhat similar to that of the eponymous hero of the *Falconetto*, who is killed by Rolando only because his armour is inadequate ('perché non aveva se no l'usbergo indosso' [because he was wearing only a hauberk] (*Falconetto*, 3357)).[94]

Rodomonte, as De Sanctis puts it, 'non è vinto da Ruggiero ma dal fato' [is defeated not by Ruggiero but by fate], which effectively means that Ruggiero's reputation for martial prowess is exaggerated.[95] What is true in any case is that Ruggiero's victory does not clear him of the accusation of betrayal. Nor does his *cortesia* redeem him, for in this duel it is forgotten by both knights. Ruggiero, for example, takes advantage of the fact that Rodomonte's sword is broken and he is the first to pull out his dagger.[96] This weapon is rarely used in chivalric romances, but in the longer version of the *Vendetta di Falconetto* — whose portrayal of warfare, as we saw in the previous chapters, is often quite unsettling — the Christian knight Tiborgo seizes his dagger to finish off his Saracen rival in love Alchero. Despite the fact that both of them are wearing enchanted armour, their duel is strikingly similar to the climactic duel of the *Furioso*, which makes one think the *Vendetta* may have been on Ariosto's desk when he was composing the last canto, a vernacular source completely overlooked by critics who have mostly focused on the Virgilian reminiscences. Like Ruggiero and Rodomonte, Tiborgo and Alchero fall to the ground:

> ala fine ala terra andono caschando,
> desoto andò Alchero de la fé pagana.
> 'Rèndete prezone', Tiborgo li va parlando,
> 'e crede in Iesu Christo padre benedeto
> e lasa in tutto Apolino e Machometo.'

> Alchero disia: 'Questo mai non faria,
> avanti taiare me lasaria per bochoni'.
> Quando Tiborgo sì ostinato lo vedia,
> la visera de l'elmo sì levò su li valoni,[97]
> pigliò sua daga che alo lato havia,

vanquished barbarians] (Marina Beer, *Romanzi di cavalleria: Il 'Furioso' e il romanzo italiano del primo Cinquecento* (Rome: Bulzoni, 1987), p. 113).

94    This is not the only instance in the *Falconetto* when a Christian character kills a Saracen character in a somewhat cynical way. Danexe's victory over Cano is also presented in a highly ambivalent light: 'Disse l'actore che se Cano non fusse stato ferito | de quella ferita tanto villana, | morto no lo avereve lo Danexe de Curtana, | ma perché Cano sì aveva perduto la virtude, | così villanamente da lo Danexe fo abatudo' [The author said that if Cano had not been | so treacherously wounded, | Danexe would not have killed him with Curtana, | but because Cano had lost his vigour | he was so treacherously slain by Danexe] (*Falconetto*, 3017–321).

95    De Sanctis, *La poesia cavalleresca*, p. 144.

96    According to Berlingero Gessi, Ruggiero is no paragon of *cortesia* in this episode: 'non la praticò Ruggiero contra Rodomonte, ò per havere ricevuta l'ingiuria gravissima di traditore, ò perché [Rodomonte] tentava di ferirlo ancorche atterrato, ò per essere la sfida di Rodomonte offesa di Carlo' [Ruggiero did not show it to Rodomonte, either because the accusation of treason was a most serious insult, or because he was trying to wound him when he was lying on the ground, or because Rodomonte's challenge was an offence against Charlemagne] (Berlingero Gessi, *La spada di honore. Libro primo delle osservazioni cavaleresche* (Bologna: l'Erede del Barbien, 1671), p. 329).

97    The meaning of 'su li valoni' is unclear.

nela faza lo feria senza fare sermoni:
verso la gola quela daga li cazava
per sì fato modo ch'el pagano schanava.

Cosi morì il pagano bataiero [...]

[at the end they fall to the ground,
Alchero of Saracen faith was underneath.
'Surrender', Tiborgo is telling him,
'and believe in Jesus Christ, our blessed Father,
and leave for good Apolino and Mohammed.'

Alchero was saying: 'I will never do this,
I'd rather let myself be cut into pieces'.
When Tiborgo saw that he was so stubborn,
he lifted the visor of his helm,
and seized his daggar which he had on his side;
he struck him in the face without any further talking:
he thrust the dagger towards his neck
so as to cut the Saracen's throat.

And so the Saracen warrior died]
    (*Vendetta A*, fol. P iii^r)

Similarly, when Rodomonte collapses, Ruggiero

Alla vista de l'elmo gli appresenta
la punta del pugnal c'havea già tratto;
et che si renda, minacciando, tenta,
e di lasciarlo vivo gli fa patto.
Ma quel, che di morir manco paventa
che mostrar di viltade un minimo atto,
si torce e scuote, et per por lui di sotto
mette ogni suo vigor, né gli fa motto.
[...]
Pur si torce e dibatte sì, che viene
ad expedirsi col braccio migliore;
e con la destra man ch'el pugnal tiene,
che trasse *anch'egli* in quel contrasto fuore,
tenta ferir Ruggier sotto le rene:
ma il giovene s'accorse de l'errore
in che potea cader, per differire
di far quel empio Saracen morire.

E due e tre volte in la terribil fronte
(alzando quanto alzar più puote il braccio)
il ferro del pugnale a Rodomonte
tutto nascose, e si levò d'impaccio.

[Ruggiero had drawn his dagger and he is brandishing it
over Rodomonte's visor,
trying with menaces to make him surrender,
offering to spare his life in exchange.
But Rodomonte, less appalled by death
than by the betrayal of the smallest sign of cowardice,

jerks and twists and applies all his strength
to roll on top of Ruggiero, and he answers not a word.
[...]
He twists and struggles nevertheless
until he brings his better arm back into play;
in his hand he clasps a dagger
which he *too* had drawn in the fray
and now he tries to stab Ruggiero beneath his back-plate.
But the young man realized the trap
into which he may fall if he delayed
dispatching the impious Saracen.

And so two or three times he plunged
(raising his arm to its full height)
the dagger to the hilt into Rodomonte's terrible forehead,
thus assuring his own safety.]
(*Fur.*, XL 109–12,1–4 A; 108–11 B; XLVI 137–40 C)

It is unreasonable to accuse Rodomonte of acting treacherously (as a number of scholars have done) if he, too, pulls out his dagger. Like Alchero, his counterpart in the *Vendetta*, he is merely defending himself. He has not for a moment stopped fighting. He has not asked for mercy and he has not tried to deceive his enemy in any way. In this respect, his conduct is as impeccable as Alchero's. As for Ruggiero, he has no choice but to kill his opponent with his dagger, given the latter's determination to fight to the end. Both Tiborgo and Ruggiero are driven by the instinct of self-preservation, and if so, Ariosto's dynastic protagonist is a far cry from Aeneas who kills Turnus for an entirely different reason.[98]

If Tiborgo asks Alchero to convert to Christianity, Ruggiero offers to spare Rodomonte if he surrenders. Is it a courteous gesture? Yes, but only on the surface, for Rodomonte's surrender would have meant acknowledgment of being in the wrong, whereby, by retracting his accusation, he would have legitimized Ruggiero's conversion. Rodomonte, however, remains true to his values until the bitter end. He thereby succeeds in proving — at least to some readers — that Ruggiero has betrayed their lord, paying with his life for this moral victory: paradoxically, Rodomonte's death could be seen as amounting to a triumph of chivalric ethics, a triumph that marks the poem's closure, leaving Ruggiero with a tacit feeling of guilt. Such an interpretation is compatible with the fifteenth- and early sixteenth-century duelling code. If analysed in the light of Paride del Pozzo's seminal treatise on duelling (*De re militari*, originally written in Latin and printed in a vernacular translation around 1475–1478), which may have been known to

---

98   According to Rizzarelli, 'Il gesto compiuto da Enea e da Ruggiero, in apparenza assai simile, si carica di un valore assai diverso, da un lato abbiamo il compiersi di una scelta tragica, ma necessaria, presa per vendicare i torti subiti e la morte di Pallante, dall'altro il manifestarsi di una disposizione ferina alla violenza che riconosce l'incolumità individuale quale unica legge' [Aeneas's and Ruggiero's actions, though seemingly very similar, take on very different significance: on one side, we witness the execution of a tragic yet necessary choice in order to avenge the wrongs that have been endured and Pallas's death, on the other, the manifestation of a beastly inclination to violence that acknowledges individual safety as its only law] (Rizzarelli, '"Cominciar quivi una crudel battaglia": Duelli in ottave nell'*Orlando furioso*', p. 100).

Ariosto and his readers, Rodomonte's defeat and death do not necessarily prove that his accusation was unjust. According to Paride del Pozzo, in fact, the opinion that God always grants victory to the righteous is inaccurate; the two combatants should be equal; and a knight who prefers to die rather than retract his accusation of betrayal dies 'con honore' [with honour], showing rare courage, for 'lo numero è pichulo deli cavalieri che tal prova abiano facta' [the number of knights who have behaved so honourably is small], given the 'gran dolzeza [...] nel vivere' [the great sweetness of life].[99]

Nor would it be fair to accuse Rodomonte of failing to see God's hand in Ruggiero's victory, for God is absent from the final duel of the *Furioso*. It is significant that Ruggiero does not solicit or invoke God's help, while the poet 'forgets' to mention divine grace, without at the same time forgetting to draw attention to the role of *Fortuna* ('Ruggier, c'ha la Fortuna per la fronte [...]' [Ruggiero, who had *Fortuna* by the mane [...]] (*Fur.*, 107,5 A; 106 B; 135 C)). In light of God's silence, the 'squalide ripe d'Acheronte' [dismal shores of Acheron] (112,5 A; 111 B; 140 C), the last abode of Rodomonte's rebellious soul, must bring to mind the underworld of the ancients rather than the 'trista riviera d'Acheronte' [on the sorrowful shore of Acheron] in Dante's Christian Hell (*Inferno*, III 78),[100] especially considering that both Boiardo and Ariosto establish a strong connection between Saracens and classical antiquity. After all, as we saw in Chapter I, the 'inferno' where Agricane's soul is said to reside bears an unmistakable resemblance to Hades. It is in this world of shadows that Rodomonte will finally be reunited with his friend and lord, thus fulfilling the promise he made in Biserta:

> Et io te giuro per tute le bande
> tenir con tieco la mia mente salda:
> in Ciel e nel'Inferno il re Agramante
> seguirò sempre, o passarogli avante!
>
> [And I swear to you I'll do your bidding
> steadfastly, and in all events.
> I'll be behind King Agramante
> through heaven and hell — or lead, in front!]
>                (*Inam.*, II i 65,5–8)

Thus it seems fit to conclude this chapter by recalling Attilio Momigliano's verdict, namely that 'Qui il cavaliere è, più che il cristiano, il pagano' [Here the Saracen is a better knight than the Christian]. We cannot help but acknowledge that Momigliano's reading of the final duel is both insightful and even-handed (even if it goes against the grain of established criticism). Indeed, the concept of knightly honour is the ideological cornerstone of the respective stories of Rodomonte and

---

99    Paride del Pozzo, *Libro de re militari* (Naples: Sixtus Riessinger, [*c.* 1475–1478?]), Book I, chapters 12 and 15; Book IX, chapter 39. This edition has no pagination.

100   As Hyonjin Kim points out, 'The last four lines of *Orlando Furioso*, which describes [*sic*] Rodomont's death, are sadly insufficient either to demonize him or to reestablish the absoluteness of divine justice [...]. Rodomont's soul has not gone to hell; it has flown — at least metaphorically, if not literally — "to Acheron's sad shore," and thus to Hades, the classical underworld beyond the river' (Kim, 'From *La chanson de Roland* to *Orlando Furioso*', pp. 107–08).

Ruggiero, honour being the supreme value for both knights. However, whereas Rodomonte sacrifices his life in order to remain faithful to his king (similar, in this sense, to Cloridano and Medoro), Ruggiero breaks his personal chivalric code when, threatened with death, he converts to Christianity, severing the bond of kinship, friendship and feudal allegiance between him and Agramante. What proves that Rodomonte's accusation is not groundless is that Ruggiero's conversion does not change his worldview inasmuch as even in the final cantos he continues to believe in and live according to the principles of lay chivalry.

In light of this, the claim that the last canto of the *Furioso* rests on the dichotomy between good and evil is quite misleading. Nor should we read too much into the Virgilian reminiscences that are scattered throughout the climactic duel (and indeed the whole poem).[101] It is true that, like Aeneas, Ruggiero has been assigned a dynastic mission and that there is a certain resemblance between Turnus (an unlucky hero, a victim of the gods) and Rodomonte; but that is not enough to turn the *Furioso* into an epic poem. The profound differences between Ariosto's and Virgil's heroes make any similarities pale in comparison.[102] At the core of the ending of the *Furioso* lies the theme of betrayal; absent from the final confrontation between Aeneas and Turnus, it is one of the central themes in the *Aspramonte*, a crucial text for both Boiardo and Ariosto. Viewed from this perspective, the ending of the *Furioso* is far more indebted to Boiardo and the chivalric tradition than it is to the *Aeneid*, with Rodomonte repeating the destiny of his father Ulieno, and Ruggiero (who, devoid of Aeneas's *pietas*, is a tormented hero[103]) coming to resemble Andrea da Barberino's Balante, who converts to Christianity with a heavy heart, feeling deep remorse for abandoning his lord.

Needless to say, Ariosto's treatment of Ruggiero has profound implications for the encomiastic dimension of the poem. If Boiardo establishes a connection between his chivalrous African Saracens and the rulers of Ferrara, his successor renders it most ambivalent by foregrounding the theme of betrayal. We shall have more to say about this aspect of Ariosto's representation of Saracens in this study's final conclusion.

> This chapter is a revised version of my article: Maria Pavlova, 'Rodomonte e Ruggiero: Una questione d'onore', *Rassegna europea di letteratura italiana*, 42 (2013), 135–77.

---

101  As pointed out at the beginning of this chapter, many scholars maintain that Virgil's presence lends an epico-didactic tenor to the last canto of the *Furioso*. For an overview of studies of Virgil in the *Furioso*, see Corrado Confalonieri, 'Quale Virgilio? Note sul finale del *Furioso*', *Parole rubate*, 7 (2013), 56–66.

102  It is worth noting that Daniel Javitch has recently published a stimulating article on the 'romance' elements in the last cantos of Ariosto's poem, in which he argues, among other things, that the points of contact between the final canto of the *Furioso* and the *Aeneid* are of lesser significance than is generally assumed: see his 'Reconsidering the Last Part of the *Orlando Furioso*: Romance to the Bitter End', *Modern Language Quarterly*, 71 (2010), 385–405 (pp. 401–04).

103  Eleonora Stoppino is right to maintain that Bradamante dominates the genealogical theme: see her *Genealogies of Fiction*, p. 13.

# CONCLUSION

❖

# Saracens and their World:
# The Wider Picture

The Gonzaga archive in Mantua contains a document entitled *Descrizione del regno di Granata*, which must have been copied from a letter sent from Granada to the Mantuan court around 1526, some ten years after the publication of the first *Furioso*. It may well be that the addressee of this letter was Isabella d'Este, a woman of wide interests and uncommon intellectual curiosity, who was ever eager to learn more about foreign lands and foreign peoples. The author of this description — or rather, this enthusiastic eulogy — of Granada makes no effort to conceal his sadness at the decline of a once-thriving city following the completion of the Reconquista in 1492:

> Mi è parso essendo hora in Granata donarvj notitia delle cose degne di adviso retrovate in questa Terra che veramente sonno degne da essere desiderate di vedere, et viste donano certa compassione verso quelli rej morj consideran[do] quanto era il vivere loro delicato et grande. Et quanto era questa citade populosa et triumphante a rispecto de hora che pare una cosa perduta [...]

> [As I am now in Granada, I thought it appropriate to write to you about the noteworthy things in this Land, which are truly worthy of one wishing to see them, and once seen, they inspire a certain compassion for those Moorish kings, considering how refined and magnificent their life was. And how populous and thriving was this city compared to now when it seems a lost thing][1]

Rather than rejoicing at the Christian victory over the Muslim invaders, the anonymous author expresses his sympathy and compassion for the so-called Moriscos, the Moorish inhabitants of Granada who were forced to convert to Christianity in the wake of the Christian conquest of the city, going as far as to say that 'quel pocho di bono che vi è restato' [what little good is left][2] is due to their industriousness and the fact that they have more moral integrity than the Castilians ('è tenuta megliore la bona promessa de li novi christiani che de li vechij' [the

---

1 Archivio di Stato di Modena, Archivio Gonzaga, busta 86, fascicolo 18, *Descrizione del regno di Granata*, fols 23$^v$-28$^r$ (fol. 23$^v$). This letter (perhaps a different copy, considering that Portioli's transcription is not always faithful to the document that I have consulted) was published by Attilio Portioli in his *Quattro documenti d'Inghilterra ed uno di Spagna dell'Archivio Gonzaga di Mantua* (Mantova: tip. Eredi Segna, 1868), pp. 27–34.
2 Ibid.

word of the new Christians is considered to be better than that of the old]).[3] He is particularly amazed at the beauty and sumptuousness of the Alhambra ('la più delicata, e bella, e comoda che sia in Christianitade' [the most refined and beautiful and comfortable [citadel] that exist in the Christian world]; 'la casa de le Delitie o di Venere' [house of Pleasures or of Venus]),[4] and provides a very detailed description of its many splendours.

The attitude of this (probably Mantuan) traveller towards the vanquished Moors and their culture is highly positive.[5] In other words, his Christian identity does not prevent him from admiring the achievements of another civilization and acknowledging that in some respects they surpass those of his fellow Christians. He does not exoticize the Other, at least not in a way that implies inferiority to the 'civilized' Christian West. Nor does he see the Moorish kings' love of beauty and pleasure as something reprehensible or excessive. In fact, describing the palaces and gardens that he saw in Granada, he says at one point that he would love to see a similar garden in Mantua. He hopes that his Imperial Majesty Charles V and his spouse Isabella of Portugal ('a quali meritamente queste delitie si convengono' [who truly deserve these pleasure retreats])[6] would be very happy in the magnificent residences that once belonged to the Moorish kings, and that the beautiful setting will help them conceive a long-awaited heir.

The respect for the Spanish Arabs that emanates from the pages of this letter is reminiscent of the attitudes we find in Boiardo and Ariosto, whose portrayals of Saracens are characterized by a similar openness, a similar willingness to recognize the humanity and the valour of the Other. It comes as no surprise, therefore, that the author of this description of Granada was familiar with the two *Orlandos*: 'hor imaginatevi che niuna [porta] se retrova descripta nelo Inamoramento de Orlando o nel Furioso' [now think that one finds no such [door] described in the *Inamoramento de Orlando* or in the *Furioso*],[7] he exclaims as he tries to paint a verbal picture of the Alhambra. Could it be that his readings of these chivalric poems influenced his worldview, making him more open towards cultures other than his own? This is certainly possible, for as we have seen in the course of this book, there exists a complex and fascinating relationship between literature and reality, with each affecting the other in profound and sometimes unexpected ways. If Boiardo's and Ariosto's representations of Saracens are to some extent indebted to the historical interactions between Italy and the Islamic world, it is equally legitimate to suggest that these poems must have contributed to promoting cultural tolerance among their readers.

3    Ibid., fol. 24[r].
4    Ibid., fols 24[r] and 26[r].
5    We know Isabella d'Este's third son Ferrante Gonzaga (1507–1557) spent six months at Charles V's court in Granada in the spring and summer of 1526. It could be that he was the author of this letter. We find a similarly enthusiastic description of Granada in Andrea Navagero's 1526 letter to Giovan Battista Ramusio. Navagero, a Venetian ambassador to the imperial court, too, says that Granada owes everything to the Moriscos, adding that the arrival of the Inquisition is bound to have a catastrophic effect on the city. His letter was published in *Lettere di diversi autori eccelenti* (Venice: Giordano Ziletti, 1556), pp. 718–38.
6    *Descrizione del regno di Granata*, fol. 27[v].
7    Ibid., fol. 25[r].

This book has questioned the assumption that Boiardo and Ariosto must have been seriously preoccupied by the threat coming from the rapidly growing Ottoman Empire and that this is reflected in their treatment of the war theme. It goes without saying that Boiardo was aware of Mehmed II's expansionist ambitions, but his 'bela historia', with its highly romanticized and idealized portrayal of warfare, can hardly be read as a warning about the danger of a Turkish invasion. Similarly, it would be misleading to read Ariosto's *Furioso* as a poem attesting to the anti-Turkish feelings of Ariosto's contemporaries: though abounding in historical digressions, it is above all a nuanced and intricate exploration of chivalry and its ideals, and as such, it offers a very attractive portrayal of Saracen chivalry. The Ottomans were certainly not the main danger facing Ferrara in the period between the 1460s and 1532, at least not in Boiardo's or Ariosto's view. Nor were they the only Islamic nation known in this small Italian city-state, for the Este rulers had a genuine interest in other parts of the non-Christian world. We have seen that in the 1460s Borso — a figure whose importance to the development of the chivalric genre in Ferrara cannot be overemphasized — established a warm relationship with the ruler of Tunisia, Sultan Abu Umar Othman. It is tantalizing to speculate that this long-lasting friendship[8] — a source of pride for Borso, who was flattered by the fact that a powerful North African monarch deemed him worthy of his attention — could have somehow led to the birth of the legend of Rugerus/Rugiero, the half-African forefather of the Este dynasty. In any case, this and other similar 'chivalrous' episodes in the rich history of the interactions between Italian and Islamic princes and noblemen help to explain the fluidity of the boundary between Christians and Saracens in many Renaissance chivalric texts, and especially in the two *Orlandos*.

For rulers such as Borso d'Este and Francesco Gonzaga the North Africans and the Turks were (potentially) powerful allies and useful friends who could supply them with first-rate horses and other precious goods and commodities rather than traditional enemies of the Christians. In fostering closer relationships with their Muslim counterparts, they were unified by their common identity as Renaissance princes. This is not to say that Borso, Francesco, and other Italian statesmen did not also have a Christian identity; they certainly did, and we see it, for example, in the popes' occasional calls for a crusade that produced positive (as far as words went) — if lukewarm (as far as deeds were concerned) — responses. We see it in the derogatory language (typical of the chivalric genre) that is sometimes used to describe Saracen characters in Boiardo, Ariosto, and other chivalric works. However, both in chivalric literature and in real life, common 'aristocratic' identity often proved to be stronger than religious difference. The fact that fifteenth- and early sixteenth-century Italy was a politically fragmented land must have made it easier for Italian noblemen and noblewomen to adopt a more open attitude towards their Muslim neighbours. In a period characterized by an ever-changing kaleidoscope of alliances, yesterday's enemy could become today's valuable friend, which resulted, at least to some degree, in the rejection of rigid identities and stereotypes.

---

8    These ties of friendship survived well into the sixteenth century: see Introduction, p. 14 (esp. n. 50).

Turning now to the literary context, which is of course no less significant than the historical context, this book has shown the extent to which Boiardo's and Ariosto's representations of Saracens are indebted to preceding chivalric literature. Borso was not only a lover of Oriental horses, a shrewd diplomat and a Renaissance prince who liked to be compared to Alexander the Great. He was also an avid reader and collector of chivalric texts. Although only Book I and the beginning of Book II of the *Inamoramento de Orlando* were written before Borso's death, Boiardo's poem is effectively the product of Borso's age, steeped as it is in the chivalric tradition. A large number of Boiardo's Saracen knights and damsels are either borrowed from or modelled on characters from earlier chivalric works, many of whom are endowed with positive traits as well as with an undeniable charisma. However, what distinguishes Boiardo from most other chivalric authors of the period is his decision not to portray Saracen chivalry as in any way inferior to Christian chivalry. While it is not uncommon to find remarkably humane representations of Saracen characters in earlier or contemporaneous texts, their authors usually make a point of portraying Christian knights as stronger, more chivalrous and more attractive to the fair sex, and Saracen damsels as extremely susceptible to the charms of Christian men. Conversely, Boiardo's Saracens show a formidable commitment to glory, adventure, bravery, love, friendship, and *cortesia*, and often emerge as more convincing models of chivalric behaviour than their Christian counterparts. In this respect, Boiardo's undisguised admiration for the chivalric virtues of his Saracens and his wholehearted embracing of the romance ideals they believe in (love being the ideological cornerstone of his poem) are among the most original and striking aspects of the *Inamoramento de Orlando*.

It is important to realize that Boiardo's celebration of Saracen chivalry does not have a political dimension to it. The *Inamoramento de Orlando* is certainly not a critique of contemporary Christian society or contemporary Italy. Quite the opposite is true: it is a poem composed by someone who feels a deep sense of pride in his culture; it draws its inspiration from the cult of chivalry in fifteenth-century Ferrara, one of Italy's most vibrant cultural centres, which sought to keep alive the spirit of medieval chivalry while at the same time embracing the *studia humanitatis* with no less fervour and passion. Yet, since Boiardo's aristocratic readers did not have strong anti-Muslim feelings but, on the contrary, looked at their Muslim neighbours with genuine curiosity and even admiration for their opulence and power, Boiardo allows himself to fantasize about exceptionally valiant knights and extraordinarily beautiful damsels coming from a Saracen *ailleurs*. He takes the liberty of gently poking fun at the French paladins Orlando and Ranaldo, but he does so to play with the expectations of his audience, to produce a surprise effect, without completely toppling these eminent Christian warriors from their heroic pedestals. He knew that his readers would be amused rather than offended.

As for Ariosto, one of the central tenets of this study has been that he owes a far more extensive debt to Boiardo and the chivalric tradition than is usually thought. There is a much stronger continuity between his and Boiardo's portrayals of Saracens than some critics have allowed for, given that many of the Saracen characters of the *Furioso* retain at least in part the personalities they had in the *Inamoramento de*

*Orlando*. Nevertheless, Ariosto distances himself from his predecessor's romantic *Weltanschauung*. His poem is at once an entertaining *comédie humaine* and a profound study of human nature, where characters — and this is particularly true of the Saracen cohort — are not immune from death and suffering, as the author subjects them and their beliefs to various trials and tribulations.

Looking back at the previous chapters, we may say that, after Boiardo, Ariosto's most important chivalric source and intertext is the *Aspramonte*, perhaps in Andrea da Barberino's version, which is a fundamental source for Boiardo too. Not only are many of the protagonists of the two *Orlandos* related to the main African heroes from the *Aspramonte*, but both poets engage with some of the key themes present in the story of Agolante's disastrous attempt to invade Christian Europe. These include the theme of the ennobling power of love (which features, albeit in an embryonic form, in the story of Andrea da Barberino's Ulieno), the theme of glory, and — most crucially — the related themes of *fides* and betrayal, which are explored with great depth and sensitivity in the *Furioso*, as Ariosto probes the moral values and commitments of his Saracen and Christian characters.

Having come to the end our long voyage through some of the finest chivalric works of the Italian Renaissance, we must return to a question prompted by Chapter V: why does Ariosto conclude his poem with a duel in which the dynastic protagonist emerges as a flawed hero? Rodomonte's moral victory somewhat undermines Ariosto's encomiastic project, suggesting that by the time he reached the last canto (and hence well before the 1517 *Satira*) Ariosto could have become disenchanted with Cardinal Ippolito and the Este family. It may not be a coincidence that in his first *Satira* he addresses Ruggiero in a reproachful manner, giving full vent to his disillusionment with his Este offspring. In fact, as has been pointed out by Ascoli and Casadei, an attentive reading of the final canto reveals that the theme of betrayal lurks in its encomiastic stanzas: suffice it to mention the allusion to the conspiracy plotted by Don Giulio d'Este (*Fur.*, XL 68 AB; XLVI 95 C) 'which [...] strikes a dissonant note in its festive context', compromising the idealized image of the Este family.[9] We must not forget that Ariosto will later go on to write the *Cinque canti*, a much more pessimistic work, where the boundary between good and evil is tragically blurred.[10]

Ariosto juxtaposes Dardinello's youthful courage with Rinaldo's cold-blooded cynicism. He allows Agramante to die a heroic death, lending him an aura of tragic nobility in the final chapter of his life. He then lets Rodomonte voice his doubts as to the legitimacy of his former brother-in-arms' conversion. By so doing, Ariosto foregrounds the point of view of the Other. From this perspective, the *Furioso* — or better its last third — foreshadows the *Gerusalemme liberata*, which, as has been argued by Sergio Zatti, is 'the first great example of solidarity

9    Ascoli, *Ariosto's Bitter Harmony*, p. 381; Casadei, 'Il finale e la poetica del *Furioso*', p. 6.
10    In the *Cinque canti*, whose main protagonists are Christians, the 'good' Rinaldo becomes Charlemagne's enemy and Marfisa, Bradamante, and Guidon Selvaggio plot to kill the emperor. Although the paladins are victims of Gano's intrigues, it is still very disturbing to see them turn their swords against their liege. On the *Cinque canti*, see Riccardo Bruscagli, 'I *Cinque canti* dell'Ariosto', in *Carlo Magno in Italia e la fortuna dei libri di cavalleria*, pp. 19–52.

with the "pagan enemy".[11] While rejoicing at Goffredo's victory, Tasso secretly sympathizes with the vanquished. Subscribing to the ideals of honour and secular humanism, his Saracens espouse an alternative ideology to that which governs the behaviour of his Christians, and Tasso's powerful evocation of this alternative system of values almost puts into jeopardy the Christian message of the *Liberata*. Something similar can perhaps be said of the *Furioso*, where Saracen chivalry is a mirror image of Christian chivalry in the first two-thirds of the poem, but where towards the end the Christians seem to embrace the ideology of holy war, as Tasso's Christians would later do. And yet the contrast between the Saracens' and Christians' worldviews is not as stark in Ariosto as it is in Tasso, for the *Furioso* never really becomes a Christian poem, not even in its concluding cantos. After all, the Christians' destruction of Biserta is perhaps less a crusading victory than brutal (and disproportionate) revenge for the havoc that Rodomonte wreaked upon Paris, all the while God remains distant and silent, despite the hasty series of miracles that bring the poem to its close.

The beauty of the *Furioso* lies precisely in its ambivalence. Although no other Italian chivalric text can match the complexity of Ariosto's masterpiece, it would be wrong to assume that Ariosto's multilayered and contradictory treatment of the theme of war is entirely without precedent. Suffice to think of the *Falconetto*, whose eponymous Saracen hero arouses sympathy and respect in the reader, leading us to wonder whether it is the Christians who have forgotten what chivalry is about. Or of Agostini's *Quinto libro*, where at times we sympathize with the Saracens' perspective. These poems are characterized by an interplay of different voices, different points of view, and different meanings. They do not have a definitive conclusion insofar as the triumphs of the 'positive' Christian protagonists (Rolando, Ruggiero) are presented in an ambivalent light. In this respect, they fit — at least to some degree — Mikhail Bakhtin's definitions of a polyphonic text, and display a high degree of 'novelness', to borrow another term coined by Bakhtin.[12] The *Furioso* is a novelized literary work inasmuch as it is characterized by 'an indeterminacy, a certain semantic open-endedness, a living contact with unfinished, still-evolving contemporary reality (the open-ended present)'.[13] In other words, rather than a dogmatic epic underpinned by a sharp dichotomy between good and evil, the *Furioso* is an experimental space, where the concept of chivalry and related ideas — values that were certainly not irrelevant to the ethical code of the Italian nobility at the time — are continually questioned and explored. There is much more to it than a celebration of the Christians' glorious victory over the Saracen invaders and of the Este dynasty.

11    Sergio Zatti, 'Christian Uniformity, Pagan Multiplicity', in Idem, *The Quest for Epic: From Ariosto to Tasso* (Toronto: University of Toronto Press, 2006), pp. 135–59 (p. 154). See also his *L'uniforme cristiano e il multiforme pagano: saggio sulla Gerusalemme liberata* (Milan: Saggiatore, 1983), and 'Dalla parte di Satana: sull'imperialismo cristiano nella *Gerusalemme liberata*', in *La rappresentazione dell'Altro nei testi del Rinascimento*, pp. 146–81.

12    Mikhail Bakhtin, *Problems of Dostoevsky's Poetics*, ed. and trans. by Caryl Emerson (Minneapolis: University of Minnesota Press, 1984).

13    Mikhail Bakhtin, 'Epic and Novel', in Idem, *The Dialogic Imagination: Four Essays*, ed. by Michael Holquist, trans. by Caryl Emerson (Austin: University of Texas Press, 1981), p. 7.

Novelness, of course, is a property common to many literary texts. Even texts that appear to convey an unambiguous moral and religious message often have novelistic traits. One such example is the archetypal Christian epic *Chanson de Roland*. It is fitting to conclude this book with a brief reflection on its most infamous character. Towards the end of his distinguished career as a literary scholar, Cesare Segre published a work that crosses the boundary between fiction and literary criticism: *Dieci prove di fantasia* (2010), ten speeches by characters from some of the most influential texts of world literature. It opens with a monologue by Ganelon, who insists that by selling his stepson to the Saracens he did not betray the Franks but rather performed a great service to them.[14] Ganelon explains that Roland wanted him to perish when he advised Charlemagne to send him as an ambassador to Marsilio's camp and that he, Ganelon, made it clear that he would take his revenge: nobody can blame him if later he stayed true to his word. Roland, continues Ganelon, was a dangerous man, a religious fanatic, a warmonger who would have drowned the world in blood... 'Is Segre being the devil's advocate?', a reader might ask. Not quite, for his defence of Gano is partly authorized by the Old French legend. In fact, in his introduction to Mario Bensi's edition of the *Chanson de Roland* (1985), which he penned twenty-five years before *Dieci prove*, Segre suggests that 'per Gano, l'atteggiamento del narratore è complesso e accattivante' [in the case of Ganelon, the narrator's attitude is complex and captivating] inasmuch as he is portrayed as a handsome and fearless man, who is held in high esteem by Christians knights and hated by his stepson. His insistence on the fact that he had not betrayed Charlemagne is a 'Posizione abbastanza solida se il consiglio di Carlo decide per l'assoluzione' [Rather solid position if Charlemagne's jury decides to absolve him].[15] This does not mean of course that the author of the *Chanson de Roland* wanted his audience to sympathize with Ganelon and condemn Roland. This would be an absurd claim. Even so, its anonymous author does not demonize Roland's implacable enemy (who, by contrast, is almost invariably demonized in the Italian chivalric tradition), and the deliberate ambiguity in his representation adds to the complexity and beauty of the founding poem of European chivalric literature.

This study has attempted to do what Segre does in his *Dieci prove di fantasia* (albeit by means of critical analysis rather than through the medium of fiction): to highlight the perspective of the Other in the two *Orlandos* and other Italian chivalric works. Above all, my hope is that it will give rise to further debate and some rethinking, thus enriching and deepening our understanding of the *Inamoramento de Orlando*, the *Furioso*, and indeed the Italian chivalric genre as a whole.

---

14    Cesare Segre, '"Così ho sacrificato Rolando ai Saraceni"', in Idem, *Dieci prove di fantasia* (Turin: Einaudi, 2010). What might have sparked Segre's interest in Ganelon — one of the most vilified characters in European literature — was his own Jewish background. See Marco Dorigatti, 'Dalla parola al testo: Il cammino di Cesare Segre (1928–2014)', *Rassegna europea di letteratura italiana*, 42 (2013), 11–26 (pp. 25–26).

15    Cesare Segre, 'Introduzione' to *La canzone di Orlando*, ed. by Mario Bensi, trans. by Renzo Lo Cascio (Milan: Rizzoli, 1985), pp. 5–27 (p. 13).

# APPENDIX I

❖

## *A Catalogue of Boiardo's Saracen Characters*[1]

### i. Named characters

1. ADRIANO: 'il forte re Adrïano' [the strong King Adriano] (I ix 73,1); Dragontina's prisoner; valorously fights in the Albracà war until II ii 62, when he is taken prisoner by Marphisa.
2. AGOLANTE: King of Africa in the *Aspramonte*, father of Almonte, Troiano and Galaciella, Agramante's and Rugiero's grandfather; 'con tanto furore, | con tanti armati in nave e nela sella | coperse sì di gente insino in Puglia | che al vòto non capea ponto de aguglia' [with great fury | and many ships and mounted men, | covered Apulia, till its empty | space could not even hold a pen] (III v 31,5–8); died in the Aspramonte war.
3. AGRAMANTE: a 22-year-old 'gioveneto altiero' [haughty youth] (II i 16,1); son of Troiano and hence Ruggiero's cousin; King of Africa who rules over 32 vassal kings; dreams of emulating his ancestor Alexander of Macedon and so wages war on Charlemagne.
4. AGRICANE: 'Re di Tartarìa' [King of Tartary] (I ix 38,7); rules over many Saracen peoples; passionately in love with Angelica who has rejected him; besieges Albracà and dies in a duel with Orlando who baptizes him (I xix).
5. AGRIGALTE: 'Re del'Amonìa' [King of Amonìa] (II xvii 25,1) and hence one of Agramante's vassal kings; 'fior de Paganìa' [the flower of Saracen lands] (II xvii 25,5); takes part in Agramante's war.

---

1   This catalogue is based on Antonia Tissoni Benvenuti's and Cristina Montagnani's edition of the *Inamoramento de Orlando*. The names of the Saracens who are absent from this edition but who feature in Boiardo's poem as edited by Angelandrea Zottoli (1937), Aldo Scaglione (1951; 1963), Riccardo Bruscagli (1995) are preceded by an asterisk. These Saracens are: Arugalte (II xxx 6,4), Balivorne (II xxiv 32,5–8), Barolango (II xxx 6,4), Moridano (II xxx 53,5) and Pulicano (II xxx 52,1). According to Tissoni Benvenuti and Montagnani's critical edition (followed by Andrea Canova's (2011)), Arugalto, Balivorne, Barolango, and Moridano, though present in the earliest extant edition (Venice, 1487), are to be considered errors of the archetype whose correct readings are as follows: Agrigalte, Baliverno, Bardarico, and Soridano [a correction already introduced by Panizzi (1830–34)] respectively, given that Saracens with these names feature in earlier cantos. As for Pulicano, Tissoni Benvenuti and Montagnani opt for Pulïano (a Saracen called Puliano was first introduced at II xvii 6,2), noting in their critical apparatus that the 1487 edition reads 'Plucano'. It is difficult to say to what extent these conjectures are founded. One cannot completely rule out the possibility that the poet may have wanted to have both Baliverno and Balivorne, Barolango and Bardarico, Moridano and Soridano etc, given that a minor character who appears only once is not at all a rare sight in the *Inamoramento de Orlando*. It is worth pointing out that, like the 1487 edition of Boiardo's poem, the one used by Ariosto must have featured Baliverno at II xxiii 73,7 (who remains alive) and Balivorne at II xxiv 32,5 (who is slaughtered by Ranaldo), considering that in the *Furioso* there is a character called Balinverno, whom we see him in the list of Marsilio's knights at *Fur.*, XII 15 AB; XIV 15 C, together with Bavarte, Doriconte, and Langhiran (Ariosto's spelling of Languirano). In general, we must bear in mind that some of Boiardo's Saracens have almost identical names and yet it is clear that we are dealing with distinct characters (e.g. Barigano and Barigazo, Uldano and Uldarno). Other chivalric authors too often give their characters similar-sounding names: for example, in Andrea da Barberino's *Aspramonte* we find a Buteran and a Buterante, two Moadas and two Moadante.

6. ALANARDO: 'Conte in Barzelona' [Count of Barcelona] (II xxiii 49,1) and hence one of Marsilio's vassals; takes part in Agramante's war.

7. ALBAROSA: 'la dama delicata' [the fair damsel] (I xiii 35); Horisello's sister and Polindo's lady; refuses to betray her brother, and is killed by the evil Trufaldino (I xiii 36–45).

8. ALBINA: wife of Manodante, King of the Isole Lontane; Brandimarte's and Ziliante's mother; converts to Christianity.

9. ALBRIZACH: 'il falso nigromante' [the false wizard] (I xvi 15,7); offered an enchanted helmet to Agolante; probably a character in some version of the *Aspramonte*.

10. ALFRERA (ANFRERA): 'un gran gigante, Re di Taprobana, | che ha una zyraffa sotto per alphana' [a huge giant, the King of Taprobana, | whose war-horse is a giraffe] (I iv 31,7–8); Gradasso's subject; disgraces himself when his giraffe takes fright and carries him away from the battle field (I vii 23); Gradasso eventually forgives him (I vii 40,5).

11. ALIBANTE DI TOLEDO: Marsilio's subject: 'non avea la gente saracina | di lui magior ladron e più scaltrito: | Orlando per traverso l'ha partito' [he was the cleverest, | most skilful thief the Saracens had: | Orlando cleaved him across] (II xxiv 58,6–8).

12. ALMONTE: a character from the *Aspramonte*; Agolante's son who participated in the *Aspramonte* war and treacherously killed Riccieri II of Risa; was killed by Orlando who now has his sword Durindana, his helmet, and his 'insegna'; Agramante's and Rugiero's uncle.

13. ALZIRDO: 'il Re de Tremisona | [...] | ha franca persona' [the King of Tremisona | [...] | he is bold] (II i 66,1–3); crosses the sea with his king Agramante.

14. AMIRANTE: Marsilio's subject; a character from the *Spagna* with a long literary life.

15. ANGELICA: daughter of Galaphrone, King of Cathay, who sends her and her brother Argalìa to Paris to destroy France; 'a dir di lei la veritate, | non fu veduta mai tanta beltade' [to tell the truth of her, | never was such beauty seen] (I i 21,7–8); a central character insofar as many male protagonists (Agricane, Orlando, Ranaldo, Sacripante) are madly in love with her.

16. ANTIFOR DI ALBAROSÌA: Dragontina's prisoner; 'fier Antifor' [proud Antifor] (II ii 35,1) fights in the Albracà war until until II ii 61–62, when he is unhorsed by Marphisa.

17. ARCHIDANTE: 'il Conte di Sanguinto' [the Count of Sagunto] (II xxv 16,1); takes part in Agramante's war and is knocked off his horse by Bradamante at II xxv 16–17.

18. ARCHILORO: 'Archiloro il negro, che è gigante' [black Archilor, who is a giant] (I xvi 28,4); Galaphrone's subject; fights in the Albracà war until Agricane cuts off his hands (I xvi 50–51).

19. ARGALÌA: Galaphrone's son and Angelica's brother; pretends to be Uberto da il Leone when he arrives in Paris in the opening canto of the *Inamoramento de Orlando*; 'il forte cavalier di vaglia' [the strong, valorous knight] (I ii 1,3); is killed by Feraguto (I iii 52–67); before dying asks Feraguto to throw his body into a river; allows Feraguto to take his helmet.

20. ARGALIPHA (ARGALIFA, ARGALIFFA): 'Lo Argalipha di Spagna' [The Caliph of Spain] (I iv 22,4); a character from the *Spagna* with a long literary life; Marsilio's subject.

21. ARGANTE: 'lo Imperator dela Rossìa' [the Russian Emperor] (I x 12,3) and hence Agricane's vassal; 'largo sei palmi ha tra le spalle il peto; | mai non fu visto un capo tanto grosso! | Schiazato il naso, e l'occhio picolino, | e il mento acuto, quel bruto mastino!' [his shoulders are six palms across; | no head was ever seen so large! | he has a flat nose, tiny eyes, | and pointed chin, that ugly mastiff] (I x 29,5–8); is mortally wounded by Orlando at I xv 24–25.

22. ARGESTO: 'smisurato' [measureless] (I i 75,4); one of the giants who come with Angelica; is killed by Feraguto at I i 78–79.

23. ARGOSTO DI MARMONDA: 'il Pagan fiero' [the proud Saracen] (II xvii 24,7); Agramante's

vassal; 'stimato è guerier molto soprano' [a warrior much esteemed in war] (II xxii 16,2); follows Agramante to France and is killed by Ranaldo at II xxx 15.

24. ARIANTE (ARRIANTE): one of Origille's lovers; hopes to marry her; 'tanto animoso e di membre aiutante | che forsi un altro par non s'atrovava' [he was bold, | with such handsome limbs | that he was probably unequaled] (I xxix 23,3–4); is condemned to death (II xxix 33).

25. *ARUGALTO: appears in a list of Saracen knights at II xxx 6,4.

26. ATALANTE: 'un barbasor, el qual è nigromante' [a vavasor, who is a sorcerer] (II i 73,7); Rugiero's adoptive father who loves him and does not want him to die in France.

27. BALGURANO: a Saracen killed by Orlando at II XXIV 23.

28. BALANO: 'il re Balano, quel mastro di guerra' [the martial expert King Ballano] (I ix 72,5); Dragontina's prisoner; valorously fights in the Albracà war until II ii 60, when he is wounded by Marphisa.

29. BALANTE: 'il franco re Balante' [the brave King Balante] (I xxviii 11,3); a character from the *Aspramonte* who converts to Christianity and deserts his king Agolante; Ranaldo accuses Orlando of his death at I xxviii 11; father of Boiardo's Pinadoro.

30. BALIFRONTE: 'il nero Balifronte' [the black Balifronte] (II xxii 27,7); King of Mulga and hence Agramante's vassal; 'perfido vechiaro' [faithless old man] (II xxx 40,8); mortally wounded by Charlemagne at II xxx 53, but is seen alive and well in Book III.

31. BALISARDO: a giant at the service of King Manodante; 'malvagio incantator e negromante' [evil sorcerer and necromancer] (II ix 57,8) whom Manodante orders to capture Orlando (II xi 49–50); captures Ranaldo and his companions (Iroldo, Prasildo, Dodone) with a net and sends them to the Isole Lontane, but is killed by Brandimarte who wants to rescue Orlando (II xi 42).

32. BALIVERNO; a Saracen soldier mentioned at II xxiii 73; killed by Ranaldo: 'E Baliverno, quel Saracin grosso | ch'avea rivolto al capo una gran fassa, | de cotal colpo toca con Fusberta | che gli ha la faza insin al colo aperta' [At Baliverno, that hefty Saracen | whose head was wrapped up in a long cloth, | he swung Fusberta with such strength | his face and his neck — both — he rent] (II xxiv 32,5–8).

33. BALIVERZO: 'il Re de Nomandìa' [the King of Normandìa] (II xvii 21,1) and hence Agramante's subject; follows his king Agramante to France; described as 'forte and ardito' [strong and bold] at II xxii 19,4, but in Book III becomes a 'perfido ribaldo' [faithless villain] (III viii 35,8).

34. *BALIVORNE: a Saracen killed by Orlando at II xxiv 32,5–8.

35. BALORZA: King of Ethiopia and Gradasso's vassal; 'un cigante arguto, | che quasi un palmo avìa la boca grossa' [a canny giant, | whose mouth was almost one palm high] (I iv 35,1–2); ordered to capture Feraguto (I iv 35,5); killed by Ranaldo at I iv 64–65.

36. BALSALDO (BASALDO): a Turkish knight who travels to Cyprus to take part in a tournament at II xx.

37. BALUGANTE (BALUCANTE): a character from the *Spagna* with a long literary life; Marsilio's brother and Serpentino's father; 'falso Balugante' [false Balugante] (I vii 51,7).

38. BAMBIRAGO: 'il Re d'Arzila' [the King of Arzila] (II xvii 20,1) and hence Agramante's subject; takes part in Agramante's war.

39. BARBOTA: a highway robber killed by Brandimarte at II xxvi 55.

40. BARDARICO: king of Canara and hence Agramante's subject; 'terribil di persona e ben armato' [fearsome in stature and well armed] (II xxii 31,2); takes part in Agramante's war and is killed by Ranaldo at II xxx 18.

41. BARDINO: Brandimarte's and Manodante's servant; 'pichiato in faza e rosso di colore, | coi denti radi e col naso chiazato' [pock-marked of face and red of hue, | with few teeth and a broken nose] (II xi 47,6–7); 'e quel Bardin per disperacïone | che 'l Re [Manodante]

il battete dal cappo ale piante, | fosse per ira o per sua fallisone, | ciò non so dir, ma via fogì Bardino, | e Bramador [Brandimarte] portò, quel fanciulino' [and Bardino, driven to despair | by the severe beatings he received from the King | (whether driven by anger or his falsety, | I cannot say), had run away, | kidnapping baby Bramador] (II xiii 37,4–8); sold Brandimarte to the Count of the Roca Silvana; forgiven by Manodante at II xiii 44.

42. BARDULASTO: 'Re dela Alganzera' [King of Alcazar] (II xvii 8,2) and hence Agramante's subject; 'quel ribaldo, | di cor malvagio e di persona fiera' [that ruffian, | a proud man with an evil heart] (II xvii 8,3–4); wounds Rugiero 'a tradimento' [treacherously] at II xvii 32; takes flight but Rugiero follows him and kills him at II xvii 35.

43. BARICONDO: King of Majorca (II xxiii 8,8) and hence Marsilio's subject; Orlando throws him and his horse to the ground at II xxiii 62.

44. BARIGANO: King of Bernica and Rasa; 'ha notrito il Re [Agramante] da picolino' [raised the King when he was young] (II xxix 20,2); Bardalusto's cousin; hates Rugiero who killed Bardalusto; is killed by Bradamante at III v 50.

45. BARIGAZO (BARIGAZIO): 'figliol di Taridone; | corsar fo il patre et esso era ladrone' [the son of Taridone; | his father was a pirate and he was a bandit] (II xix 22,7–8); 'proprio un gigante ala sembianza pare' [he seems to be a giant] (II xix 32,3); Brandimarte is impressed by his strength and tries to persuade him to return to honest life at II xix 37–39; mortally wounded by Brandimarte, he refuses to receive baptism and dies within an hour (II xix 46).

46. ★BAROLANGO: features in a list of Saracen knights at II xxx 6,4.

47. BAVARDO (BAVORDO): a king whose tomb is mentioned at I xxiv 37; could be a character from some chivalric romance.

48. BAVARTE: a Saracen king and Marsilio's subject mentioned at II xxiii 73.

49. BELISANDRA: a Saracen princess, Charlemagne falls in love with her in the *Inamoramento de Carlo Magno*; mentioned in Orlando's angry speech (I xxviii 5).

50. BORDACCO: 'Re di Damasco: schiata de cigante' [King of Damascus: from a family of giants] (I x 41,3); comes to Albracà together with Sacripante; challenges Agricane to a duel and is killed by him (I xi 27–30).

51. BRABANTE: 'il possente Brabante, | che in Spagna occiso fo da Carlo Mano' [the mighty Brabante, | who was slain by Charlemagne in Spain] (II i 14,1–2): a character from the *Reali di Francia*, where he is Agolante's brother; Agramante's and Rugiero's relative.

52. BRANDIMARTE (BRAMADORO): son of Manodante, King of the Isole Lontane and his wife Albina; Ziliante's brother; 'un Saracin, che un altro sì perfeto | non ha la tera' [the world has not seen such perfection | in another Saracen] (I ix 49,5–6); Orlando's faithful companion; converts to Christianity out of his own initiative; participates in many adventures; befriends Agramante.

53. BRANZARDO: 'quel vechion, Re di Buggìa' [that old man, King of Buggìa] (II i 38,6); tries to persuade Agramante not to sail to France; is left in charge of Agramante's kingdom (II xxviii 51).

54. BRONTINO: King of Nomana and hence Agricane's subject first mentioned at I x 12; is killed by Orlando at I xv 22.

55. BRUNALDO: 'Imperator di Tribisonda' [Emperor of Trebizond] (I x 38,8); comes to Albracà with Sacripante to defend Angelica; is killed by Radamanco at I xiv 18.

56. BRUNELO (BRUNELLO): 'Egli è ben picoletto di persona, | ma di malicia a maraviglia pieno, | e sempre in calmo e per zergo ragiona; | longo è da cinque palmi o poco meno | e la sua voce par corno che sona. | Nel dir e nel robbar è senza freno; | va sol di nòte e 'l dì non è veduto; | curti ha i capilli, et è negro e rizuto' [He's physically a little man | but is malicious past belief | and always speaks in roguish slang; | he is five palms tall or maybe less, | and his voice seems like a horn that blows. | He's unrestrained in lies

and theft; | he never goes by day, but night; | his hair is cropped short, curly, black] (II iii 40); a virtuoso thief who steals Angelica's ring and to whom Agramante grants the kingdom of Tingitana; finds Rugiero and narrowly escapes hanging when everybody assumes that he has killed Bardulasto.

57. BUCIFARO: new King of Alganzera (II xxii 17–19); 'di prodecia è tra' Baron il terzo' [he's third in prowess among the barons] after Agramante and Rodamonte (II xxii 19,2); is supposed to remain in Africa to help Branzardo look after Agramante's kingdom (II xxviii 52–53), but is in the Saracen army at III viii 11.

58. CALABRUN DI ARAGONA: ''l franco Calabrun, Re di Aragona' [brave Calabruno, King of Aragon] (II xxiii 49,5); Marsilio's subject; killed by Orlando at II xxiii 58.

59. CALIDORA: a damsel who tells knights not to look at the enchanted spring at II xvii 60; Larbino's and Isolieri's lady.

60. CARAMANO: 'il forte Caramano, | che de Torindo è suo carnal germano' [the strong Caramano | who is Torindo's blood brother] (II ii 33,7–8); wants to kill Angelica; disgraces himself when he ignominiously flees from the battlefield at II xviii 29–30.

61. CARDON (CARDONE): an Indian king and hence Gradasso's vassal; all black and 'comme cane baglia' [howls like a dog] (I vi 63,6); is killed by Danese at I vi 67.

62. CARDORANO: King of Cosca and hence Agramante's vassal; described as 'forte' [strong] at II xxix 15,1 and 'tuto peloso' [all hairy] at II xxxi 22,4 (octave in which he is said to be King of Mulga); is killed by Orlando at II xxxi 22.

63. CAROGGIERI (CAROGIERO): 'passò in Italia con molti guerieri: | tutti for morti con pena dolente' [led many men to Italy: | all of them died dismally] (II i 42,5–6); probably a character from the *Aspramonte* (perhaps to be identified with Guernieri in the fifteenth-century *Aspramonte*); Mordante's father and Agramante's and Rugiero's relative.

64. CHIARIONE: 'il franco Saracino' [the bold Saracen] (I ix 72,6); Dragontina's prisoner; fights valorously in the Albracà war until II ii 61, when he is taken prisoner by Marphisa.

65. CONSTANTINO: Mambrino's brother, a character from the *Cantari di Rinaldo*, where he is killed by Rinaldo; mentioned at I xxvii 21.

66. CORBINO: Origille's brother killed by Horingo (I xxix 16).

67. DANIFORTE: King of Tunisia and hence Agramante's vassal, 'homo saputo e di molto consiglio, | gran siniscalco dela real corte' [a sage and knowing councilor, | High Steward to the royal court] (II xxix 19,3–4); sails to France with Agramante; 'pecio di carogna' [foul carrion] (III vi 19,6); wants to kill Bradamante when her horse dies but is outwitted by her; killed by Bradamante at III vi 27.

68. DARDINELO (DARDINELLO): Almonte's son, Agramante's and Rugiero's cousin; 'dextro nel'arme come avesse l'ale, | molto cortese, costumato e belo, | né si potrebe aponervi alcun male' [agile in arms, like one with wings, | handsome, refined, and courteous; | nothing bad can be said of him] (II xxii 26,4–6); Boiardo predicts his death at II xxix 14.

69. DOLISTONE: King of Laleze (Latakia); father of Doristela and Fiordelisa; is reunited with his daughters and converts to Christianity.

70. DORALICE: daughter of the King of Granada; 'era stimata il fior dele dongiele' [she was esteemed the finest flower of all damsels] (II xxiii 12,4); Rodamonte's lady.

71. DORICONTE: a Spanish Saracen mentioned at II xxiii 73.

72. DORIPHEBO (DORIFEBO): 'il fier Pagano, | qual porta di Valenza la corona' [the proud Saracen, | who wears Valencia's crown] (II xxiii 49,2–3); takes part in Agramante's war.

73. DORILONE: King of Septa and hence Agramante's vassal; takes part in Agramante's war; 'copïoso di thesoro' [a wealthy man] (II xxx 41,6).

74. DORISTELA: King Dolistone's daughter and Fiordelisa's sister; her first husband is a Turk; later marries her childhood sweetheart Theodoro and converts to Christianity.

75. DUDONE: a Saracen convert to Christianity; the story of his conversion is narrated in the *Castello di Teris*; in Boiardo he is one of Charlemagne's most valorous knights; taken

prisoner by Rodamonte at II xiv 65–67; taken to Biserta, where he is treated as befits his rank.

76. DUDRINASSO: King of Libicana and hence Agramante's subjet; 'fior de Paganìa' [the flower of Saracen lands] (II xvii 25,5); yet described as 'perfido pagano' [treacherous Saracen] at II xxx 6,6); 'larga la boca avea più d'una spana, | grosso e membruto, e come un corbo nero. | Orlando l'assalì con Durindana | et ispicoli il capo tuto intiero [...]' [his mouth was larger than a span; | he was crow-black, his muscles thick. | Orlando struck with the Durindana | and took his top right off [...]] (II xxxi 24,3–6).

77. DURASTANTE: King of India, a character from the *Altobello* mentioned at I xxviii 7.

78. FALSERONE (FALCIRONE): a character from the *Spagna* with a long literary life; Marsilio's brother and Feraguto's father.

79. FARALDO: 'Re de Arabia' [King of Arabia] (I iv 32,7); a valorous knight killed by Ranaldo at I iv 45.

80. FARURANTE DI MAURINA: 'feroce è lui, ma mal accompagnato' [he is fierce | but he comes with a scraggly band of men] (II xxii 21,5–6); Agramante's vassal; takes part in Agramante's war.

81. FERAGUTO: a character from the *Spagna* with a long literary life; Marsilio's nephew and one of the main Saracen knights in Boiardo's poem; in love with Angelica; 'cima di posancia' [peak of power] (I ii 1,4); 'Aben che Feragù sia gioveneto, | bruno era molto e de orgoliosa voce, | terribile a guardarlo nelo aspetto: | li ochii avea rossi con bater veloce. | Mai di lavarsi non ebe diletto, | ma polverosa ha la facia feroce. | Il capo acuto avëa quel Barone, | tutto riciuto e ner comme un carbone' [Now, though this Feragù was young, | his voice was brassy, he was dark, | his features awful to regard. | His eyes were red and always blinked. | He never cared to wash himself, | but had a dirty, fearsome face. | That baron had a pointed head, | with wiry hair as black as coal] (I ii 10).

82. KING OF FIESSA: 'Il Re di Fiessa, ch'è tutto canuto' [the King of Fez, who's hoary-white] (II iii 39,1); Agramante's vassal and Brunelo's master.

83. FIORDALISA (FIORDELISA, FIORDEHELISA): Brandimarte's lady, Dolistone's long-lost daughter and Doristela's sister; one of the main Saracen women in the poem; converts to Christianity and becomes very religious.

84. FIORDESPINA: Matalista's sister (I i 48) and Marsilio's daughter (III viii 63); falls in love with Bradamante in the last canto of the *Inamoramento de Orlando*.

85. FOLDERICO: Leodila's jealous husband in the novella narrated in I xxi-xxii.

86. FOLICONE: 'del Re [Marsilio] bastardo, e Conte d'Almería' [the bastard of the King [Marsilio], and Count of Almería] (II xxiii 9,6); does not look like a Spaniard because he is blond and fair-skinned (II xxiii 9); 'ben vi posso acertar ch'egli è galiardo!' [I can assure you he is valiant] (II xxiii 48,4).

87. FOLVIRANTE: '(Questo non è spagnol, ma di Levante, || ben che al presente sia Re di Navara, | che 'l re Marsiglio a luï avea donata [...])' [He is not a Spaniard, but he comes from the East, || even if now he is the King of Navarra, | King Marsilio's gift to him] (II xxiii 71,8; 72,1–2); killed by Ranaldo at II xxiv 32.

88. FOLVO: King of Fersa and hence Agramante's vassal; is supposed to stay in Africa to help Branzardo look after Agramante's kingdom (II xxviii 53), yet in Book III takes part in the siege of Paris (III viii 11).

89. FRAMARTE: King of Persia and Gradasso's vassal; 'il Re da valimento' [the valiant King] (I iv 34,3); 'cade morto ala pianura' [falls death to earth] at I iv 48,1.

90. FRANCARDO: an Indian Saracen; King of Elissa and Gradasso's vassal; killed by Charlemagne at I vii 9.

91. FUGIFORCA (FOGIFORCA): a highway robber who attacks Brandimarte, Doristela, and Fiordelisa; taken to King Dolistone (II xxvi 60); confesses that he had stolen Dolistone's daughter, Fiordelisa (II xxvii 4–7); forgiven when the family is reunited (II xxvii 31).

92. GALACIELLA: character from the *Aspramonte*, where she is Agolante's daughter and the wife of Rugiero II of Risa; Rugiero's late mother and Agramante's aunt in Boiardo's poem.

93. GALAPHRONE (GALAFRONE): Angelica's and Argalìa's father; King of Cathay; 'è potente e rico oltre a misura' [infinite are his wealth and power] (I xvi 27,8); takes part in the Albracà war.

94. GALERANA: a character from the *Reali di Francia* with a long literary life; Charlemagne's wife and Marsilio's sister.

95. GAMBONE: Hosbergo's slave; 'a riguardar è proprio un vituperio: | l'un occhio ha guerzo e l'altro lacrimoso, | troncato ha il naso et è tuto rognoso' [a horror to behold: | one eye runs tears, the other crossed, | he is all scabs, his nose clipped off] (II xxvi 33,6–8); betrays his owner by helping Doristela and Theodoro; narrowly escapes being executed.

96. KING OF GARAMANTHA: Agramante's vassal; 'sacerdoto di Apollino: | sagio (e' deli anni avia più de nonanta), | incantator, astrologo e indovino' [Apollino's priest: | a sage of more than ninety years, | astrologer, enchanter, seer] (II i 57,3–4); predicts the Saracens' defeat; advises Agramante to find Rugiero; accurately predicts his own death.

97. GIASARTE: 'Giasarte il brun' [Giasarte the dark] (I iii 8,6); son of the King of Arabia; takes part in Charlemagne's joust and is unhorsed by Astolfo (I iii 8–9).

98. GORDANETO: king of the Arabs (Bedouins); his people are so savage that they do not obey him (II xxii 32).

99. GRADASSO: 'regnava in la terra de Oriente, | di la dal'India, un gran Re di corona, | di stato e di richeze sì potente | e sì galiardo dela sua persona | che tuto il mondo stimava niente' [reigning in the Orient | past India was a mighty king | so powerful in wealth and state | and so impressive in his strength | he held the world of no account] (I i 4,2–6); King of Sericana; one of the main Saracen protagonists of the poem.

100. GRANDONIO: 'il re Grandonio, facia di serpente' [King Grandonio, with his serpent face] (I i 10,3); a character from the *Spagna* with a long literary life; King of Volterna and Marsilio's vassal.

101. GRIFALDO (GRIPHALDO, GRYPHALDO, GRYFALDO): King of Cetula and Agramante's vassal; ordered to hang Brunello and is happy to execute the order (II xxi 39); killed by Oliviero at III viii 41.

102. GRIPHONE DI ALTARIPA: Stela's husband; treacherously killed by Marchino who falls in love with Stela (I viii 28–34).

103. GUALCIOTO DI BELLAMARINA: Agramante's vassal; 'forte nel'arme e di consiglio saggio' [strong in arms and a wise counselor] (II xxii 23,4); sails to France with Agramante and is killed by Brandimarte at III viii 40.

104. HARIDANO: a giant who guards Morgana's lake, throwing damsels and knights into it; 'horrenda creatura' [horrendous creature] (II vii 36,5); whoever fights with him is seven times less strong then him (II vii 37); killed by Orlando at II viii 12.

105. HORDAURO (ORDAURO): Leodila's lover.

106. HORIGANTE: 'di Malica signor era il Pagano' [the Pagan was Malaga's lord] (II xxiv 62,1); killed by Orlando at II xxiv 61.

107. HORINGO (ORINGO): kills Origille's brother Corbino (I xxix 16); condemned to death (II xxix 33).

108. HORRISELLO: Albarosa's brother, Trufaldino's enemy.

109. HOSBERGO: Doristela's first husband; 'turcomano fo de natïone; | gagliardo era tenuto e molto ardito, | ma certo che nel letto era un poltrone' [he as a Turk by birth; | he was thought a valiant and mighty man, | but he was negligent in bed] (II xxvi 31,2–4); extremely jealous; killed by Brandimarte at II xxv 39.

110. IROLDO: a Saracen from Baghdad, Tisbina's lover and Prasildo's friend.

111. ISOLIER (ISOLIERO, ISOLIERI): a character from the *Spagna* with a long literary life;

Marsilio's nephew; King of Pampaluna; 'possente e destro cavalieri' [a strong and agile knight] (I ii 45,8); in love with Calidora.

112. LAMPARDO IL VELUTO: a giant who comes with Angelica; killed by Feraguto at I i 76–77.

113. LANGUIRANO: a Saracen king and Marsilio's subject (II xxiii 73,5–6).

114. LARBIN: 'un Re gentil, acorto e pien d'ardire' [a noble king, courageous, wise] (II xvii 60,6); Calidora's lover; falls victim to the enchanted spring and dies (II xvii 61).

115. LARBIN: 'Larbin di Portugalo, il fier garzone' [Larbin of Portugal, a proud young man] (II xxiii 48,5); Marsilio's vassal; 'il re Larbin avìa molta aroganza, | come han tuti e Portugesi il core' [King Larbino's heart was proud, | like all men's hearts in Portugal] (II xxiii 54,5–6); is killed by Ranaldo at II xxiii 55–57.

116. LEODILA: Folderico's wife and Ordauro's lover; Manodante's daughter; dislikes her jealous old husband who is madly in love with her.

117. LOCRINO: Origille's suitor; condemned to death (I xxix 33).

118. LUCINA: daughter of the King of Cyprus and Noradino's lady; 'a maraviglia bela' [marvelously fair] (II xix 54,3); rescued from an Orco by Gradasso and Mandricardo (III iii 37–60).

119. LURCONE DI NORVEGA: Agricane's vassal; 'perfido' [treacherous] (I x 27,6); killed by Orlando at I xv 34.

120. MALAPRESA: a giant who hates the Dama del Verzier (III i 51); 'portava in mano un gran baston ferato | con la cathena, el malandrin feroce; | in capo avea di ferro un bacineto, | negra la barba e grande a mezzo il peto' [and that fierce rogue was carrying | an iron-covered mace and chain, | and the casque on his head was iron. | Down his chest hung a large, black beard] (III i 59,5–8); wounded by Mandricardo and finished off by a 'sargente' at III i 61–62.

121. MALCOMPAGNO: a highway robber who attacks Brandimarte and Fiordelisa at II xix 16.

122. MALGARINO: a Spanish knight who serves Falserone (II xxiii 29).

123. MALZARISE: an important character in the *Spagna*; Marsilio's vassal in Boiardo; mentioned only at II xxiii 71.

124. MAMBRINO (MEMBRINO): a character from the *Cantari di Rinaldo* where he is killed by Rinaldo; Rinaldo wears his enchanted helmet (I iv 82).

125. MANDRICARDO: Agricane's son; 'tanta forza e tal ardire avìa | che mai non vestì l'arme el più soprano | et era Imperator di Tartarìa; | ma fo tanto superbo et inhumano [...]' [he was of such courage and such strength, | no greater man ever wore armour, | and he was the Emperor of Tartary; | but he was so arrogant and so ruthless [...]] (III i 6,2–5); one of the principal Saracen protagonists of Book III.

126. MANILARDO: King of Norizia and hence Agramante's vassal; 'fior de Paganìa' [flower of Saracen lands] (II xvii 25,5); not very 'gagliardo' [valiant] (II xxix 12).

127. MANODANTE: King of the Isole Lontane; father of Brandimarte, Ziliante and Leodila; 'era di natura humano' [was a civil man] (II xii 22,1); loses both sons but is happily reunited with them in II xiii; converts to Christianity.

128. MARADASSO: 'il Re de Andologìa' [the kind of Andalusia] (II xxiii 5,4); Marsilio's vassal; takes part in Agramante's war.

129. MARBALUSTO: newly crowned King of Orano and hence Agramante's vassal; 'l'anima dannata, | che sieco ha tante gente maledete | e per menarle meglio ala spiegata, | la Franza tuta in preda gli promete' [that damned soul, | who has brought many cursed men, | and to inspirit them the more, | promises them France as their reward] (II xxii 22,2–6); sails to France with Agramante; 'gigante' (II xxx 5,8).

130. MARCHESINO (MARCASINO, MARTASINO): new King of Garamantha and hence Agramante's vassal; 'non avìa il mondo un altro più orgoglioso. | Groseto fo costui, ma

picolino | dela persona e destro e ponderoso, | rosso di faza e di naso aquilino, | oltra a misura altiero e forïoso' [no one was prouder in the world. | He was a heavy man, but short, | agile and ponderous at once, | red in the face, his nose a hook, | and haughty and mad past belief] (II xxix 46,2–6); killed by Bradamante at III vi 14.

131. MARCHINO: 'il sir de Aronda' [the lord of Aronda] (I viii 30,6); falls in love with Griphone's wife Stela; has her husband Griphone killed; in revenge for his infidelity, his own wife kills their children, and tricks him into eating them; Stela shows him their heads; kills Stela and rapes her corpse; is killed by the King of Orgagna (I viii 48).

132. MARFUSTO: one of the three giants who capture Leodila; is killed by Orlando at I xx 31–36.

133. MARICOLDO: 'Re de Galegi' [King of Galizia] (II xxiii 6,1); Marsilio's subject; a giant who does not have a horse because he is too heavy; killed by Orlando at II xxiii 61.

134. MARIGANO: 'Conte de Girona' [count of Gerona] (II xxiii 49,4); killed by Rinaldo: 'fugie al'Inferno l'anima diserta, | rimase in tera il corpo maledeto' [to hell went his abandoned soul, | his cursed body remained on earth] (II xxiii 65,5–6).

135. MARIGOTO: 'il Re di Satalìa' [the King of Satalìa] (II xviii 22,5); 'sembrava proprio al corso una saetta' [he rode fast as an arrow-shot] (II xviii 23,1); killed by Brandimarte at II xviii 24.

136. MARPHISA (MARPHYSA): 'non ha cavalier tutto il Levante | che la contrasti sopra dela sella, | tanto è gagliarda, e ancor non è men bela' [not a knight in all the East | could match her in the saddle, | such is her valour, and she is as beautiful as she is valiant] (I xvi 28,6–8); one of the principal Saracen protagonists of the poem; Angelica's implacable enemy.

137. MARSILIO (MARSIGLIO, MARSIGLIONE, MARSILIONE): a character from the *Spagna* with a long literary life; King of Saracen Spain; one of the most prominent Spanish Saracens; allies himself with Gradasso in Book I; joins forces with Agramante in Book II.

138. MATALISTA: Fiordespina's brother and therefore Marsilio's son or nephew; 'franco Saracino' [a brave Saracen] (I iv 22,3); last appears at I iv 54.

139. MENADARBO: 'Soldano | che tiene Egypto e tuta la Sorìa' [the Sultan who | rules Egypt and all Syria] (II xviii 6,3–4); had been in love with Angelica, but she rejected him and he traveled to Albracà to kill her; is killed by Brandimarte at II xviii 29.

140. MIRABALDO: 'Re di Borga, e di gran iesta' [King of Bolga, of noble lineage] (II xvi 28,5) and hence Agramante's vassal; sails to France with Agramante and is killed by Ranaldo at II xxx 12.

141. MORBECO: a Turkish knight; together with Balsaldo travels to Cyprus to take part in a tournament; 'sopra gli altri si facea mirare' [earned more praise than all the others] (II xx 19,6) until he is unhorsed by Noradino.

142. MORCOLPHO: a giant who 'servìa in corte il re Marsiglïone' [served in King Marsilio's court] (II xxiv 31,2).

143. MORDANTE: King of Tolometta and hence Agramante's vassal; Caroggieri's illegitimate son; 'grande e di persona fiero' [tall and fierce-looking] (II xxix 17,7); sails to France with Agramante; wounds Bradamante; he and Pinadoro 'non han di vergogna alcuna cura' [are both dishonourable] (III vi 29,6); is killed by Rugiero at III vi 31.

144. MORGANTE: a Saracen king; Marsilio's vassal; 'falso pagano' [false pagan] (I vii 19,6).

145. *MORIDANO: features in the list of Saracen knights at II xxx 53,5.

146. MULLABUFORSO (MULABUFORSO, MULABUFERSO): 'Re de Phyzano, | fier di persona e d'ogni cosa experto' [King of Fiziano, | fierce-looking and in all things expert] (II iii 17,1–2); searched for Rugiero but could not find him; sails to France with his king Agramante; 'franco Saracino' [brave Saracen] (II xxxi 41,5).

147. NARBINALE: 'Conte de Algira, quel Saracin fiero | ('ben ch'abia altro mestier, che fo corsale, | era ancor dextro e forte in sul destriero)' [Count of Algeciras, a proud pagan | (even though he is a pirate by his main trade, | on horseback he was strong and dextrous)] (II xxv 19,2–4); participates in Agramante's war; killed by Bradamante at II xxv 20.

148. NORADINO: 'Era Re di Damasco il giovineto | [...] | ardito e forte e di nobil aspeto | quanto alcun altro fosse in quel confino' [This young man was the ruler of Damascus | [...] | his look was noble, strong; he was | as bold as any in that realm] (II xix 53,1–4); in love with Lucina, the daughter of the king of Cyprus; befriends Orlando and invites him to go with him to the tournament in Cyprus (II xix 57–60).

149. OBERTO DA IL LEONE: Dragontina's prisoner at I ix 72; fights valorously in the Albracà war until he is killed by Marphisa at II ii 65.

150. OGIERI IL DANESE: a Saracen convert to Christianity; the story of his conversion is narrated in the *Reali di Francia*; in Boiardo he is one of Charlemagne's most valorous knights.

151. OLIBANDRO: Sacripante's brother; Sacripante learns about his death at II iii 9.

152. OLIVALTO: 'il sir de Carthagena' [the lord of Carthage] (II xxv 16,2); killed by Bradamante at II xxv 16.

153. ORIDANTE (HORIDANTE): one of the three giants who captured Leodila; 'terribil e crudel e di gran possa' [fearful and cruel and powerful] (I xx 14,6); killed by Brandimarte at I xx 30–31.

154. ORIGILLE (HORIGILLA, HORIGILA, HORRIGILLA, ORIGILLA): a perfidious damsel because of whom four Saracen knights are condemned to death; rescued by Orlando who is attracted to her; tricks Orlando twice and every time is forgiven; in love with Griphone, Aquilante's brother; reveals the true identity of Orlando and Brandimarte to Manodante (II xii 5) in exchange for Griphone's liberation; falls ill and is convalescent when Griphone goes to the tournament in Cyprus (II xx 7).

155. ORILO (HORILLO): 'Quel desleale è nominato Horillo | e non ha tutto el mondo el più fellone; | tiene una torre in su il fiume del Nillo, | ove una bestia a guisa di dragone | (che là viene appellata el cocodrillo) | pascie di sangue humano e di persone. | Per stranio incanto è facto el maledetto | che de una Fata nacque e d'un foletto' [Orrilo is this traitor's name — | no villain in the world is worse. | His tower's by the river Nile, | where there's a beast just like a dragon | that feeds on human flesh and blood | (and it is called the crocodile). | A strange spell made this cursed man | who was born of a fairy and a sprite] (III ii 46); Griphone and Aquilante try to kill him.

156. ORÏONE: 'il Re de Machrobia, ch'è gigante, | ch'è tutto negro comme un carbon spento' [the King of Macrobia, who is a giant, | black as a burnt coal] (I iv 34,4–5); Gradasso's vassal; is completely naked but has a very tough black skin (I v 1); killed by Ranaldo ay I v 5.

157. PANDRAGON: 'Re dela Gotìa' [King of Gotìa] (I x 12,1); Agricane's vassal; 'degno di gran fama' [worthy of renown] (I x 48,5); grievously wounded by Orlando at I xv 23–24.

158. PANTASILICOR: a Saracen king from some chivalric romance; Orlando says that Rinaldo hanged him 'a tradimento' [treacherously] (I xxviii 6).

159. PARICONE: 'Conte de Alva [...] | Renaldo lo tagliò tutto a traverso' [the Count of Alva [...] | Renaldo sliced him right across] (II xxiv 39,1–2).

160. PARTHAN: 'Di Cordoba era el Conte' [He was the count of Cordova] (II xxiv 37,5); Marsilio's vassal; killed by Ranaldo at II xxiv 38.

161. PERODIA: wife of King Dolistone; mother of Doristala and Fiordelisa; converts to Christianity at II xxvii 35.

162. PILÏASI: his father 'la Rosìa | tutta avìa presa, e sotto Tramontana | tenea gran parte dela Tartarìa' [had conquered | Russia, and in the northern lands | he governed most

of Tartary] (I iii 9,1–3); takes part in Charlemagne's joust and is unhorsed by Astolfo.

163. PINADORO: 'il Re di Costantina' [the King of Costantina] (II xvii 6,1) and hence Agramante's vassal; Balante's son; 'vago di facia e di cor arrogante, | magior del patre, e più dextro e più forte' [with a handsome face and a proud heart, | and larger, stronger and faster than his father] (II xvii 11,3–4); fights with Orlando at II xxix 34; Orlando defeats him and lets him go; accuses Rugiero of betraying Agramante at III v 52; he and his companion attack Rugiero at III vi 29; 'Rugier li tolse el capo dale spalle' [Rugiero cut off his head from his shoulders] (III vi 32,8).

164. POLIFERNO (POLIFERNE): King of Orgagna; 'di stato è posente e di thesoro | et è gagliardo sopra ala campagna' [lord of a vast and wealthy nation, | and he is valiant in the field] (I x 11,3–4); receives hundreds of damsels every year from a treacherous old man (I xiv 29); in Polifermo's absence his kingdom is governed by the witch Falerina; all travellers who happen to enter the kingdom are fed to a horrible dragon; last mentioned at II ii 40.

165. POLINDO: Albarosa's lover; Trufaldino's victim (I xiii 36–45).

166. PRASILDO: a Saracen from Baghdad, Tisbina's lover and Prasildo's friend.

167. PRUSIONE: 'Re del'Isole Alvarichie' [King of the Alvaracchie [Canary] Islands] (II xvii 19,2); Agramante's vassal; sails to France with Agramante.

168. PULIANO: 'Re de Nasamona' [King of Nasamona] (II xvii 6,1) and hence Agramante's vassal; sails to France with Agramante; 'franco' [bold] (II xxix 10,8).

169. ★PULICANO: fights with Ottone at II xxx 52,1–2.

170. RADAMANCO (Radamanto in Bruscagli): a giant; King of 'Mosca la grande e la terra Comana' [great Moscow, and Comanan lands] (I x 10,8) and hence Agricane's vassal; takes part in the Albracà war; 'valoroso e franco, | et era longo da il capo ale piante | ben vinti pedi, e non è un dito manco' [valorous and bold, | measuring twenty feet in hight | from head to foot, not one inch less] (I xv 8,2–4); 'il malvaso gigante e traditore' [the treacherous, evil giant] (I xv 9,2); killed by Orlando at I xv 21.

171. RANCHERA (RANCHIERA): one of the three giants who captured Leodila; killed by Orlando at I xx 30.

172. COUNT OF ROCA SILVANA: 'Conte de Roca Silvana' [Count of Roca Silvana] (II xiii 10,8) who leaves his fortress and all his possessions to Brandimarte.

173. RODAMONTE: 'figliol del forte Ulïeno' [strong Ulieno's son] (II i 16,8); King of Sarza and Agramante's vassal and friend; 'più fier garzon de lui non fo giamai!' [there never was a prouder boy] (II i 56,3); in love with Doralice; sails to France before Agramante; one of the main Saracen protagonists of Books II and III.

174. RUBICONE: Falerina's soldier; 'seicento libre pesa quel poltrone, | superbo, bestïale e de gran possa; | nera la barba avea come un carbone | et a traverso al naso una percossa; | li ochi avìa rossi e vedea sol con uno. | Mai sol nascente nol trovò digiuno' [that wastrel weighed six hundred pounds, | and he was beastly, proud and strong; | he had a beard as black as coal, | and a scar ran across his nose; | his eyes were red, but just one saw. | No sunrise ever found him hungry] (I xvii 24,3–8); killed by Ranaldo at I xvii 27.

175. RUGIERO: son of Rugiero II of Risa and Galaciella; Agramante's cousin; raised by the Saracen magician Atalante; 'di prodeza in terra non ha pare' [his prowess is unmatched on earth] (II i 69,6); is destined to convert to Christianity; one of the main Saracen protagonists of Books II and III.

176. RUPARDO: Brandimarte's personal enemy; 'crudele et inhumano' [cruel and inhumane] (II xiii 12,6); besieges Roca Silvana in Brandimarte's absence (II xiii 13).

177. SACRIPANTE: 'Re de Circassìa' [King of Circassia] (I v 64,1); Angelica's most devoted suitor; 'altro non ha nel cor che quella dama' [his heart is empty but for her] (I xi 14,5); one of the main Saracen protagonists of the poem.

178. Santarìa: King of Sueza and Agricane's vassal; killed by Orlando at I xv 38.

179. Saritrone: 'il Re de Mongalia' [the King of Mongolia] (I x 10,2) and hence Agricane's vassal; 'non ha il mondo un Baron tanto franco' [the boldest baron in the world] (I x 10,3); killed by Orlando at I xv 21.

180. Savarone: King of Media; travels to Albracà with Sacripante; 'franco' [bold] (I x 46,4); killed at I xiv 17.

181. Scombrano: captain of the ship which takes Rodamonte to France; 'vechione, | experto di quella arte e proveduto' [old, | and skilled in skippering, and provident] (II vi 5,3–4); tries to persuade Rodamonte to wait for better weather.

182. Serpentino della Stella: a prominent character in the *Spagna* with a long literary life; Balugante's son and Marsilio's nephew; 'il gioveneto adorno | ch'avea fatate l'arme tutte intorno' [a handsome youth | who wore charmed armour, a full suit] (II xxiii 45,7–8).

183. Sinagone: 'Re di Calatrava' [King of Calatrava] (II xxiii 5,5) and hence Marsilio's vassal; killed by Oliviero at II xxiii 34.

184. Sobrino: a character from the *Aspramonte*, where he serves Agolante; 'Re di Algoco et ha molto sapere' [Algoco's king, who's very wise] (II i 44,4); 'Sobrin di Garbo' [Sobrin of Garbo] (II xvi 26,5); Agramante's faithful adviser; tries to dissuade his king from travelling to France; crosses the sea with Agramante.

185. Soridano (Sorridano): 'Re dela Hesperìa' [King of the Hesperides] (II xvii 30,1) and hence Agramante's subject; 'rossi ambi gli ochi e 'l viso foribondo, | costui ch'è deto, e i labri grossi avìa' [the said Saracen had red eyes, | a fierce face and fat lips] (II xxii 6,5–6); sails to France with Agramante; 'franca persona' (II xxx 53,5).

186. Spinamacchia: a highway robber; attacks Brandimarte and Fiordelisa at II xix 16.

187. Spinella da Altamonte (Spinela): a character from the *Trabisonda*, Marsilio's subject; takes part in Charlemagne's joust; fights in the war between Charlemagne and Gradasso and is last seen fleeing at I vii 19.

188. Stela (Stella): wife of Griphone di Altaripa; is killed by Marchino.

189. Stordilano: Doralice's father; King of Granada and hence Marsilio's vassal; takes part in Agramante's war; Orlando throws him and his horse to the ground at II xxiii 8.

190. Straciaberra (Straciabera): 'Re de Lucinorco' [King of Lucinorco] (I vii 6,7) and Gradasso's vassal; 'mai non fu la più bruta creatura: | dui denti ha de cinghial fuor dela boca, | sol nela vista ' ognon mette paura' [no creature ever was so ugly: | two boar's tusks issue from his mouth, | his face alone strikes all with fear] (I vi 64,2–4); killed by Oliviero at I vii 7.

191. Tanphirione (Transerïon): King of Almasila; 'anci nomar si può Re del diserto' [properly called the Desert King] (II xxii 7,2); Agramante's vassal; 'horrenda creatura, | che escie oto palmi e più sopra al'arzone | et ha la barba insin ala cintura' [dreadful creature, | who rose more than eight palms above his saddle | and had a beard that reached his belt] (II xxxi 25,2–4); killed or wounded by Orlando at II xxxi 25.

192. Tardoco: 'Re d'Arzila' [King of Arzila] (II xvii 20,1) and hence Agramante's vassal; takes part in Agramante's war; killed by Sigieri at II xxx 25.

193. Taridone: Barigazo's father; a corsair.

194. Tibiano: king of Cyprus and Rhodes; organizes a tournament to find a suitable husband for his daughter Lucina; searches everywhere for Lucina and is reunited with her at III iii 54.

195. Tisbina: a damsel from Baghdad; Iroldo's and Prasildo's lady.

196. Torindo: King of Turkey; travels to Albracà with Sacripante to defend Angelica; saves Sacripante's life (I xi 15–18); outraged when Orlando forgives Trufaldino, who had tried to surrender Albracà to Agricane; turns his sword against Sacripante, Orlando and Brandimarte; killed by Brandimarte at II xxviii 29.

197. TROIANO: a character from the *Aspramonte*; Agramante's father and Rugiero's uncle; 'il feroce re Troiano, | qual in Bergogna col Conte d'Anglante | combaté, e con dui altri sopra il piano: | ciò fo don Chiaro e 'l bon Rugier Vasalo; | da lor fo morto, e certo con gran fallo' [the fierce King Troiano, | who fought Orlando on a plain | in Burgundy and two more knights: | Don Chiaro and good Rugier Vasalo; | these three killed him, a shameful act] (II i 14,3–8).

198. TRUFALDINO: rules 'Babilonia e Baldraca la grande' [Babylon and large Baghdad] (I x 40,6); 'falso traditore' [false traitor] (I x 40,8); takes part in the Albracà war and tries to betray Angelica; is forgiven by Orlando but Ranaldo kills him at I xxv 46–52.

199. TURLONE: a giant who travels to France with Angelica (I i 75); mortally wounded by Feraguto (I i 81–82).

200. ULDANO: 'Il re di Danna' [the Danish king] (I x 13,3); Agricane's vassal; 'ha molto valore' [is very valiant] (I x 13,4); takes part in the Albracà war; unhorsed by Brandimarte at I xviii 28.

201. ULDARNO: Origille's lover; tells Orlando their story (I xxix 1–37).

202. ULIENO: Agolante's vassal in the *Aspramonte*; 'forte Ulïeno' [strong Ulieno] (II i 16,8), Rodamonte's father.

203. UNGIANO: King of Roase; travelled to Albracà with Sacripante; 'molto posente' [very powerful] (I x 39,4); 'forte campïone' [strong champion] (I x 46,2); killed by Radamanco at I xiv 18.

204. URGANO: one of the giants who travel to France with Angelica; killed by Feraguto at I i 78.

205. URGIN: 'savio de Liferno' [a wiseman from Liferno] (II xxiii 73,8); takes part in Agramante's war; killed by Orlando at II xxiv 62.

206. URNASSO: an Indian king and Gradasso's vassal; 'dispietato' [ruthless] (I vi 63,7); killed by Danese at I vii 1.

207. VALIBRUNO: 'il Conte di Medina' [the Count of Medina] (II xxiv 58,2) and hence Marsilio's vassal; killed by Orlando at II xxiv 58.

208. ZAMBARDO: a giant who guards a bridge at I v 80; killed by Orlando at I vi 14.

209. ZILIANTE: Manodante's and Albina's son; Bradimarte's brother; Morgana's favourite prisoner; 'gioveneto bianco e belo, | nel viso colorito e delicato, | negli ati e nel parlar dolcie e iocondo' [a white and handsome youth, | blushing and delicate of face, | merry and sweet in deeds and speech] (II ix 28,5–7); Manodante wants to exchange him for Orlando; rescued by Orlando and reunited with his parents.

## ii. Anonymous characters[2]

1. AN OLD MAN: an old man who 'ogni ano dava di tributo | cento dongielle al forte Re de Orgagna' [every year paid tribute | of a hundred ladies to the King of Orgagna] (I xiv 29,5–6).

2. AN OLD MAN: 'un vechio maladeto' [a malign old man] (I xx 1,6) who kidnaps Fiordelisa (I xx 5–8); 'era quel vechio di mala semenza, | incantator e di malicia pieno; | per Macometo facea penitenza, | credendo gir con lui nel ciel sereno' [that old man was from a wicked brood, | a wizard and full of malice; | he was one of Macone's penitents, | who hoped to join him in high heaven] (I xx 2,1–4).

3. A BOY: a boy who cries for help at I xxii 50.

4. THREE GIANTS: three giants who attack Leodila and her husband at I xxii 55–56.

5. A MUSICIAN: the drunk musician who reproaches Agramante for delaying his expedition against Charlemagne (II xxviii 44–48).

2    Listed in the order of their appearance in the poem.

6. AN OLD MAN: 'un vechio disperato' [a desperate old man] (III i 7,3) who calls Mandricardo 'codardo e ville' [cowardly and vile] (III i 10,5), telling him that he should avenge Agricane's death rather than kill his own people.
7. A GIANT: 'gran gigante' led on a chain by a knight at III iii 21,6–7; Caligorante in the *Furioso*.
8. A SARACEN SOLDIER: 'un moro in su un gianeto bianco' [a Moor riding on a white jennet] (III vi 7,2) killed by Bradamante.
9. A SARACEN SOLDIER: an Arab killed by Bradamante at III vi 7,6.

## iii. Converts to the Saracen faith

1. BARICHEO: 'ha il tesor di Marsilio in suo domino: | costui primeramente fo giudeo, | e dapoi cristïan, poi saracino, | et in ciascuna legie fo più reo, | né credeva in Macon né in Dio divino' [he controls Marsilio's wealth: | he'd been a Hebrew, | then a Christian, then a Saracen, | and he'd become worse in each religion — | he'd no faith in God or Macon] (II xxiv 59,2–7); killed by Orlando.
2. A GENOESE RENEGADE: killed by Rugiero at III vi 17.

# APPENDIX II

❖

## *A Catalogue of Ariosto's Saracen Characters*[1]

### i. Named characters

1. AGOLANTE: a character from the *Aspramonte*; Agramante's and Ruggiero's grandfather.
2. AGRAMANTE: 'si diè vanto | di vendicar la morte di Troiano | sopra re Carlo imperator romano' [boasted | that he would avenge Troiano's death | on Charles, Emperor of Rome] (I i 6–8 ABC); loses the war and is killed in the Lipadusa duel.
3. AGRICALTE: King of Amonia; killed by Rinaldo at XIV 81 AB; XVI C; later 'resurrected'; Dudone's prisoner at XXXVI 73 AB; XL C; freed by Ruggiero; perishes in a storm while sailing back to Africa.
4. AGRICANE: mentioned by Angelica at VIII 43 ABC.
5. AIMONTE (Almonte in BC): 'fiero Aimonte' [proud Aimonte] (I 30,8 ABC): Agolante's son in the *Aspramonte*; Dardinello's father, Agramante's and Rugiero's uncle.
6. ALTHEO: a Saracen soldier killed by Lurcanio at XVI 54 AB; XVIII C.
7. ALZIRDO (ALCIRDO): 'El re di Tremisen, ch'era tenuto | tra li Africani cavallier perfetto' [the King of Tremisen, whom the Africans | esteemed a perfect knight] (X 73,6–7 AB; XII 69 C); challenges Orlando; killed by Orlando at X 79 AB; XII 80 C.
8. AMIRANTE: Marsilio's subject; mentioned at XII 16 AB; XIV C.
9. ANALARDO: Marsilio's subject; mentioned at XII 16 AB; XIV C.
10. ANGELICA: Galaphrone's daughter; 'colei c'ha tutto il mondo a sdegno, | e non par ch'alcun sia di lei degno' [the one who disdained all human kind, | and believed that no man was worthy of her] (I 49,7–8 ABC); marries Medoro; one of the principal female protagonists of the poem.
11. ARCHIDANTE: 'il Sagontino conte' [the Count of Sagunto] (XII 16,4 AB; XIV C); Marsilio's subject.
12. ARGALÌA: Angelica's late brother; his spirit speaks to Ferraù at I 26–29 ABC.
13. ARGALIFFA (ARGALIFA): Marsilio's subject; mentioned at XII 16 AB; XIV C.
14. ARGANIO: Agramante's subject; one of the new captains; leads soldiers from Libicana (XII 18–19 AB; XIV C).
15. ARGILON DA MELEBEA: a knight killed by Guidone Selvaggio on the island of the 'femine homicide' [murderous women].
16. ARGOSTO: Agramante's vassal who died in the *Inamoramento de Orlando*; mentioned at XII 18 AB; XIV C.
17. ATLANTE DI CARENA: Ruggiero's adoptive father; a magician; tries to save Ruggiero from his destiny by luring him into various traps; dies of grief when all his attempts to protect Ruggiero fail.
18. ATTALICO (Artalico in C): a Saracen soldier wounded by Ariodante in XIV 65 AB; XVI C.

---

[1]  This catalogue follows the 1516 edition (A). The only Saracen character added in the 1532 edition (C) is Boiardo's Truffaldino (who is implicitly alluded to in A).

19. Balastro: leads the troops of the late King Tardocco; killed by Lurcanio at XVI 45 AB; XVIII C; later 'resurrected'; Dudone's prisoner at XXXVI 73 AB; XL C [*errata corrige* B: Clarindo]; freed by Ruggiero; perishes in a storm while sailing back to Africa.

20. Balinfronte: leads soldiers from Cosca (XII 23 AB; XIV C).

21. Balinverno: mentioned among Marsilio's knights at XII 15 AB; XIV C.

22. Baliverzo: 'Vien Baliverzo, il qual vuo' che tu tolga | di tutto 'l gregge pel maggior ribaldo' [Next comes Baliverzo, the pick | of the entire host for sheer knavery] (XII 24,3–4 AB; XIV C); 'd'ogni vitio vago' [a compound of every vice] (XIII 6,8 AB; XV C).

23. Balugante: Marsilio's brother; leads 'popul di Leone' [troops from Leon] (XII 12,1 AB; XIV C).

24. Bambirago: King of Arzilla; unhorsed and killed by Rinaldo at XIV 81 AB; XVI C; later 'resurrected'; Dudone's prisoner at XXXVI 73 AB; XL C [*errata corrige* B: Baliverzo]; freed by Ruggiero; perishes in a storm while sailing back to Africa.

25. Bardino: 'un cavallier de la famiglia | del Re di Damogir, Re Monodante, | ch'era venuto un gran numer di miglia, | quando per mar, quando per terra errante, | cercando Brandimarte' [a knight from the household | of King Monodante, King of Damogir, | who had travelled many miles, | wandering over land and sea | in search of Brandimarte] (XXXV 51,3–7 A; 40 B; XXXIX 40 C); finds Fiordeligi.

26. Baricondo: Marsilio's subject; leads soldiers from Majorca (XII 13 AB; XIV C); killed by the Duke of Chiarenza at XIV 69 AB; XVI C.

27. Bavarte: Marsilio's subject; mentioned at XII 16 AB; XIV C.

28. Bianzardino: an important character in the *Spagna* with a long literary life; in Ariosto's poem leads soldiers from Avila, Piagenza, Salamanca, Zamora, and Palenza (XII 14 AB; XIV C).

29. Brandimarte: converted to Christianity in the *Inamoramento de Orlando*; 'Orlando amava a pare | di se medesmo' [he loved Orlando as much | as his own self] (VIII 88,1–2 ABC); sets off to find Orlando; Rodomonte's prisoner; takes part in the battle for Biserta; tries to persuade Agramante to convert; dies in the Lipadusa duel.

30. Branzardo: stays in Biserta to look after Agramante's kingdom; exchanges Dudone for Bucifaro (who has been captured by the Christians); when Biserta falls, 'perduta ogni speranza, ogni conforto, | si uccise di sua mano il Re Branzardo' [having lost heart and hope, | King Branzardo took his own life] (XXXVI 35,3–4 AB; XL C).

31. Brunello: King of Tingitana and Agramante's vassal; falls out of favour when he loses Angelica's magic ring; Agramante hangs him to please Marphisa.

32. Bucifaro: 'Re de l'Algazera' [King of the Algaziers] (XXXV 30,7 A; 19 B; XXXIX 19 C); together with Branzardo stays in Biserta; 'Prigion rimase Bucifar gagliardo' [valiant Bucifar was taken prisoner] (XXXV 32,7 A; 21 B; XXXIX 21 C); 'Fu Bucifar de l'Algazera morto | con esso un colpo da Olivier gagliardo' [Bucifaro of the Algaziers was slain | by a stroke of daughty Olivier] (XXXVI 35,1–2 AB; XL C).

33. Buraldo: Agramante's subject; one of the new *condottieri* mentioned at XII 18 AB; XIV C.

34. Caico: Agramante's subject; new king 'de la gente d'Almansilla' [of the Almansillans] (XII 23,5 AB; XIV C).

35. Calabruno: King of Aragona killed in the *Inamoramento de Orlando*; father of Chelindo and Mosco in Ariosto.

36. Calamidor da Barcelona: Marsilio's subject; 'un che reputato fra' gagliardiera' [one who enjoyed a reputation as a valiant fighter] (XIV 60,3–4 AB; XVI C); 'credendo acquistar gloria e corona' [expecting to win glory and a crown] (XIV 60,6 AB; XVI C), together with Chelindo and Mosco, he attacks Zerbino and kills his horse; when Zerbino kills his horse, 'lascia il cavallo, et via carpone | va per campar, ma poco gli successe; |

che venne caso che'el duca Trasone | gli passò sopra, e col peso l'oppresse' [abandons his horse and crawls away | towards safety, | but to no avail; | Duke Trasone happened by | and rode right over him, crushing him under his weight] (XIV 64,1–4 AB; XVI C).

37. CALIGORANTE: a monstrous giant defeated and tamed by Astolfo during his travels in the Middle East.

38. CARMONDO: 'del mar grande Almiraglio' [High Admiral of the sea] (XV 99,4 AB; XVII C); Norandino's subject; takes part in Norandino's joust in Damascus and is defeated by Griphone.

39. CASIMIRO: a Saracen soldier killed by Ariodante at XIV 65 AB; XVI C.

40. CHELINDO: one of the 'duo figliuol bastardi | del morto Calabrun, Re d'Aragona' [two bastard sons | of Calabrun, King of Aragon] (XIV 60,1–2 AB; XVI C); 'credendo acquistar gloria e corona' [expecting to win glory and a crown] (XIV 60,6 AB; XVI C); he, Mosco and Calamidor da Barcelona attack Zerbino and kill his horse; killed by Zerbino at XIV 62 AB; XVI C.

41. CHIARIELLO: a character from the *Cantari di Rinaldo*, where he is killed by Rinaldo; mentioned at XVIII 6 AB; XX C.

42. CLARINDO: Agramante's subject: leads the troops from Bolga (XII 24 AB; XIV C).

43. CLORIDANO: a soldier in the African army; Medoro's friend; born in Tolomitta; 'cacciator tutta sua vita, | di robusta persona era et isnella' [hunter all his life, robust and agile] (XVI 166,1–2 AB; XVIII C); together with Medoro tries to retrieve the body of their lord Dardinello; slaughters many a sleeping Christian; killed by the Christians.

44. CORIMBO: a Saracen from Apamia; takes part in Norandino's joust in Damascus and is defeated by Griphone (XV 96 AB; XVII C).

45. CORINEO: Agramante's 'fido amico' [loyal friend] (XII 23,4 AB; XIV C); leads the troops from Mulga.

46. DARDINELLO: 'Re de la Zumara [...] | el nobil Dardinel figlio d'Aimonte' [King of Azumara [...] | Almonte's son noble Dardinel] (XVI 47,1-2 AB; XVIII C) and hence Agramante's and Ruggiero's cousin; he and Orlando have the same coat of arms; fights valorously in the battle of Paris, trying to inspire his troops by personal example; Rinaldo challenges him to a duel; killed by Rinaldo at XVI 153 AB; XVIII C; 'fa passar con lui | l'ardire et la virtù di tutti i sui' [his death | ebbed all the courage and strength of his followers] (XVI 153,7–8 AB; XVIII C).

47. DORALICE: beautiful daughter of Stordilano, King of Granada; Rodomonte's fiancée or wife; kidnapped by Mandricardo; grants her virginity to her kidnapper; persuades Mandricardo and Rodomonte to postpone their duel; when Agramante allows her to choose between Rodomonte and Mandricardo 'ella abbassò gli occhi vergognosi, | e disse che più il Tartaro havea caro: | di che tutti restâr maravigliosi' [she bashfully lowered her eyes | and said that she prefered the Tartar; | everyone was astonished at this] (XXV 107,4–6 AB; XXVII C); when Mandricardo is killed by Ruggiero 'Doralice istessa, che con duoli | piangea l'amante suo pallido et bianco, | forse con l'altre ita sarebbe in schiera [to congratulate Ruggiero], | se di vergogna un duro fren non era' [Doralice herself who was bitterly | weeping for her pale, white lover, | might perhaps have joined the other women [i.e. who were congratulating Ruggiero] | were she not inhibited by shame] (XXVIII 71,5–8 AB; XXX C).

48. DORCHIN: a Saracen soldier killed by Lurcanio at XVI 54 AB; XVIII C.

49. DORICONTE: a Spanish Saracen mentioned at XII 16 AB; XIV C.

50. DORILONE: leads the troops from Setta (XII 22 AB; XIV C).

51. DORIPHEBO: Marsilio's subject; leads the Catalans (XII 11 AB; XIV C).

52. DUDRINASSO: King of Libicana who died in the *Inamoramento de Orlando*; mentioned at XII 19 AB; XIV C.

53. ERMOPHILO: Norandino's subject; in charge of 'la militia del Re' [the King's militia] (XV 99,3 AB; XVII C); takes part in Norandino's joust in Damascus and is unhorsed by Griphone.

54. ETARCO (Etearco in BC): a Saracen soldier killed by Ariodante at XIV 65 AB; XVI C.

55. FALSIRONE: 'el fratel di Marsilio [...] | ha seco armata la minor Castiglia' [Marsilio's brother [...] | leads the army of smaller Castille] (XII 12,3–4 AB; XIV C).

56. FARURANTE: Agramante's subject; 'drieto a quello | eran cavalli e fanti di Maurina' [he was followed | by cavalry and infantry from Mauretania] (XII 21,3–4; XIV C); Dudone's prisoner at XXXVI 73 AB; XL C; freed by Ruggiero; perishes in a storm while sailing back to Africa.

57. FERAÙ (FERRAÙ; FERRAUTO): Marsilio's nephew and one of the main Saracen protagonists of the *Orlando furioso*; in love with Angelica; the object of his other quest is Orlando's helmet; 'potea, fra quanti altieri | mai fusser, gir con la corona in testa' [he could be crowned the king | all of the arrogant men who had ever lived] (X 42,5–6 AB; XII 38 C).

58. FIAMMETTA: a promiscuous girl from Valencia.

59. FINADURRO: Agramante's vassal; King of Canaria and Marocco; killed by Zerbino at XVI 45 AB; XVIII C.

60. FIORDELIGI (FIORDILIGI): converted Saracen; Brandimarte's wife; 'Era questa una donna che fu molto | da lui [Brandimarte] diletta, e ne già raro senza; | di costumi, di gratia e di bel volto | dotata, e d'accortezza e di prudenza' [She was the damsel he [Brandimarte] deeply | loved, and he was seldom apart from her; | she was comely, graceful and of gentle manners, | nor she was lacking in shrewdness and wisdom] (VIII 89,1–4 ABC); dies of grief shortly after Brandimarte's demise.

61. FIORDISPINA: Marsilio's daughter; in love with Bradamante; has an affair with Ricciardetto believing (or pretending to believe) that her lover is Bradamante turned into a man.

62. FOLLICON D'ALMERIA: 'di Marsiglio il gran Bastardo' [Marsiglio's illegitimate son] (XII 16,1 AB; XIV C); King of Granada (XIV 67 AB; XVI C); unhorsed by Fieramonte and taken prisoner at XIV 69 AB; XVI C.

63. FOLVIRANTE: King of Navarra killed in the *Inamoramento de Orlando*; mentioned at XII 11 AB; XIV C.

64. FOLVO: Agramante's subject; stayed in Biserta to look after Agramante's kingdom in his absence; dies shortly after the Fall of Biserta: 'con tre ferite, onde morì di corto, | fu preso Folvo dal Duca dal Pardo' [Folvo was captured by the Duke of Pardo [i.e. Astolfo] | with three wounds from which he shortly died] (XXXVI 35,5–6 AB; XL C).

65. GALACIELLA: 'la disperata figlia d'Agolante' [Agolante's despairing daughter] (II 32,4 ABC); Ruggiero's mother; Atalante says that she was killed by Aimonte and Troiano.

66. GALAFRONE (GALAPHRONE): Angelica's father; occasionally mentioned but never seen.

67. GALERANA: Saracen convert to Christianity; Charlemagne's wife.

68. GARDO: a Saracen soldier killed by Lurcanio at XVI 54 AB; XVIII C.

69. GOSTANZA (Costanza in C): Guidone's mother; had an affair with Rinaldo's father Amone; mentioned at XXIX 31 AB; XXXI C.

70. GRADASSO: King of Sericana; one of the principal Saracen protagonists of the poem; 'Era cortese il Re di Sericana, | come ogni cor magnanimo esser suole' [The King of Sericana was chivalrous, | like any man of magnanimous heart] (XXIX 100,1–2 A; 101 B; XXXI 101 C); helps Agramante; sails home after he gets hold of Rinaldo's horse Baiardo; dies in the duel of Lipadusa.

71. GRANDONIO DI VOLTERNA: Marsilio's subject; takes part in Agramante's war; 'el più superbo cavallier di Spagna' [the haughtiest warrior in Spain] (XXXII 71,2 AB; XXXV 69 C); fights with Bradamante at XXXII 71–74 AB; XXXV 69–72 C).

72. GRECO: a young man from Valencia; Fiammetta's childhood sweetheart.

73. GUALCIOTTO: King of Bellamarina who died in the *Inamoramento de Orlando*; mentioned at XII 25 AB; XIV C.

74. GUIDONE SELVAGGIO (SILVAGGIO): a character from the *Regina Ancroia* and the *Innamoramento di Guidon Salvaggio*; Rinaldo's brother in Ariosto's poem; prisoner of the 'femine homicide' [murderous women]; fights in the war on the Christian side.

75. HIROLDO (IROLDO): one of the knights trapped in Atlante's enchanted tower (IV 40 ABC); later mentioned among the prisoners of the palace of illusions (XX 20 AB; XXII C).

76. HORRIGILLE: Griphone's lady; betrays Griphone with the cowardly Martano.

77. HORRILO: a sorcerer and a 'ladron [...] | ch'a paesani e peregrini nuoce, | e sin al Chairo, ognun rubando, scorre' [brigand [...] | who goes about terrorizing villagers and pilgrims, | robbing everybody as far afield as Cairo] (XIII 46,2–4 AB; XV 65 C); fights with Griphone and Aquilante; killed by Astolfo.

78. ISOLIERO: leads the troops from Navarra (XII 11 AB; XIV C); saves Brunello's life when Agramante's wants to hang him (XII 20 AB; XIV C).

79. ISSABELLA: daughter of the King of Gallitia; one of the main female Saracen protagonists of the *Orlando furioso*; falls in love with Zerbino; runs away to marry her beloved; captured by brigands; freed by Orlando; inconsolable after Zerbino's death; tricks Rodomonte into killing her.

80. LANFUSA: a character from the *Spagna ferrarese*; Feraù's cruel mother; wants to give Viviano and Malagigi to Bertolagi di Baiona.

81. LANGHIRANO: 'Langhiran gagliardo' [valorous Langhiran] (XII 16,5 AB; XIV C); Marsilio's subject.

82. LARBINO: King of Portugal; died in the *Inamoramento de Orlando*; King Tesira's relative (XII 13 AB; XIV C).

83. LIBANIO: Agramante's subject; new king of Constantina; mentioned at XII 21 AB; XIV C.

84. LORD OF LODICEA: participates in Norandino's joust; fights with Griphone and manages to stay in his saddle in 'sì fiero incontro' [so mighty a clash] (XV 95,2 AB; XVII C); eventually unhorsed by Griphone.

85. LUCINA: Norandino's wife; captured by an Orco; her husband refuses to abandon her.

86. MADARASSO: leads soldiers from Malaga and Siviglia; mentioned at XII 12 AB; XIV C.

87. MALABUFERSO: Agramante's subject; 'Re di Feza' [King of Fez] (XIV 76,3 AB: XVI C); fights in Agramante's war.

88. MALAGUR: Marsilio's subject; 'havea l'astutie pronte' [he was nible-witted] (XII 16,6 AB; XIV C).

89. MALGARINO: Marsilio's knight; lost his kingdom and was welcomed by Marsilio; mentioned at XII 15 AB; XIV C.

90. MALZARISE: Marsilio's knight; lost his kingdom and was welcomed by Marsilio; mentioned at XII 15 AB; XIV C.

91. MAMBRINO: a character from the *Cantari di Rinaldo*; his armour now belongs to Rinaldo and Danese (XXXIV 79 AB; XXXVIII C).

92. MANDRICARDO: Agricane's son; Emperor of Tartaria; 'né in Ponente era, né in tutto Levante, | di più forza di lui, né di più core' [search East and West, there was not | a man stronger than he, nor more courageous] (XII 30,3–4 AB; XIV C); one of the main Saracen protagonists of the poem; helps Agramante against Charlemagne; kidnaps Doralice; killed by Ruggiero with whom he fights over the right to wear the Trojan eagle.

93. MANILARDO: King of Noricia; 'già fero e gagliardo, | hor miglior di consiglio che d'aiuto' [once upon a time fierce and valorous, | now of greater value as a counsellor]

(X 73,3–4 AB; XII 69 C); heroically confronts Orlando (X 86–88 AB; XII 82–84 C); Dudone's prisoner at XXXVI 73 AB; XL C; freed by Ruggiero; perishes in a storm while sailing back to Africa.

94. MARBALUSTO: King of Oran; 'quasi era gigante' [he was well-nigh a giant] (XII 17,4 AB; XIV C); 'persona povera | [...] di cor, ma d'ossa et polpe ricca' [a man of meagre | courage though well endowed with flesh and bone] (XIV 47,3–4 AB; XVI C); killed by Rinaldo at XIV 48 AB; XVI C.

95. MARPHISA (MARFISA): a warrior woman whose name was 'così temuto per tutto Levante | che facea a molti ancho arricciar le chiome' [so feared throughout the Levant | that it made people's hair stand on end] (XVI 126,2–3 AB; XVIII C); Ruggiero's sister; converts to Christianity and enters Charlemagne's service as soon as she finds out that her father was Ruggiero II of Risa; one of the main Saracen protagonists in the poem; swears to kill Agramante to avenge her father's death.

96. MARGANO: a Saracen soldier wounded by Ariodante at XIV 65 AB; XVI C.

97. MARICOLDO: King of Gallitia; died in the *Inamoramento de Orlando*; mentioned at XII 13 AB; XIV C.

98. MARSILIO (MARSIGLIO): King of Saracen Spain; one of the oldest and wisest Saracens in Agramante's army; abandons Agramante when the latter breaks his oath not to interrupt the duel between Rinaldo and Ruggiero.

99. MARTANO: Horrigille's lover; a cowardly and treacherous knight from Antioch; steals Griphone's armour and slanders Griphone before Norandino; captured by Aquilante and punished by Norandino.

100. MARTASIN: late 'Re de' Garamanti' [King of the Garamants] mentioned at XII 17,8 AB; XIV C.

101. MATALISTA: Marsilio's subject; leads soldiers from Toledo, Calatrava and Guadïano; 'l'audace Matalista' [audacious Matalista] (XII 14,5 AB; XIV C); unhorsed and taken prisoner at XIV 69 AB; XVI C.

102. MEDORO: an African soldier and a poet; Cloridano's friend; born in Tolomitta; 'fra la gente a quella impresa uscita | non v'era faccia più gioconda et bella' [among all the host assembled on the expedition | there was not a comelier or more pleasing face] (XVI 166,5–6 AB; XVIII C); he and Cloridano try to retrieve the body of their lord Dardinello; grievously wounded; found by Angelica who falls in love with him; marries Angelica.

103. MIRABALDO: King of Bolga who died in the *Inamoramento de Orlando*; mentioned at XII 24 AB; XIV C.

104. MONODANTE: King of the Isole Lontane; Brandimarte's father; dies and leaves his kingdom to Brandimarte.

105. MORGANTE: Marsilio's knight; lost his kingdom and was welcomed by Marsilio; mentioned at XII 15 AB; XIV C.

106. MOSCO: one of the 'duo figliuol bastardi | del morto Calabrun, Re d'Aragona' two bastard sons | of Calabrun, King of Aragon] (XIV 60,1–2 AB; XVI C); 'credendo acquistar gloria e corona' [expecting to win glory and a crown] (XIV 60,6 AB; XVI C), he, Chelindo, and Calamidor da Barcelona attack Zerbino and kill his horse; killed by Zerbino at XIV 61 AB; XVI C.

107. NORANDINO: King of Damascus; Lucina's husband; refuses to abandon his wife when she is captured by an Orco; organizes a joust in Damascus; unjustly punishes Griphone but later makes amends.

108. OLIMPIO DA LA SERRA: Marsilio's subject; Feraù's friend; 'un giovinetto che col dolce canto, | concorde al suon de la cornuta cetra, | di intenerir un cor si dava vanto, | anchor che fusse più duro che pietra. | Felice lui, se contentar di tanto | honor sapeasi, et scudo, arco e pharetra | haver in odio, et scimitarra e lancia, | che lo trarro a morir giovene in Francia!' [a youth who could sing so sweetly | to the accompaniment of the

horn-shaped lyre | that he boasted of softening | even the flintiest of hearts. | Happy he, had he known how to rest content | with eminence such as this, and hold in disgust shield, | bow and quiver, lance and scimitar | which had brought him to an early death in France!] (XIV 72 AB; XVI C).

109. OMBRUNO: takes part in Norandino's joust in Damascus; killed by the lord of Seleucia; 'ognun n'hebbe pietà, perch'era molto | buon cavallier, né un altro sì cortese | era in Damasco o in tutto quel paese' [everyone was dismayed at this, for he was | a very good knight as well as the most chivalrous | in Damascus and in all that land] (XV 87,6–8 AB; XVII C).

110. ORMIDA: one of the new African *condottieri*; mentioned at XII 18 AB; XIV C.

111. PINADORO: died in the *Inamoramento de Orlando*; mentioned at XII 21 AB; XIV C.

112. PRASILDO: 'nobil cavalliero' [noble knight] (IV 40,2 ABC); one of the knights trapped in Atlante's enchanted tower; later mentioned among the prisoners of the palace of illusions (XX 20 AB; XXII C).

113. PRUSIONE: Agramante's subject; 'il Re de l'Alvaricchie' [the King of the Alvaricchie] (XII 27,1 AB; XIV C); killed by Rinaldo at XIV 81 AB; XVI C.

114. PULIANO: Agramante's subject; King of Nasamona; dares to confront Rinaldo: 'Re Pulïano sol non muta guancia, | che questo esser Rinaldo non connosce; | né pensando trovar sì duro intoppo, | gli move il destrier contra di galoppo' [Only King Puliano did not change his colour, | for he did not realize this was Rinaldo; | little dreaming what obstacle he was up against, | he made for him at a gallop] (XIV 44,5–8 AB; XVI C); killed by Rinaldo at XIV 45–46 AB; XVI C; Dudone's prisoner at XXXVI 73 AB; XL C; freed by Ruggiero; perishes in a storm while sailing back to Africa.

115. RIMEDONTE: King of Getulia (XII 23 AB; XIV C); Dudone's prisoner at XXXVI 73 AB; XL C; freed by Ruggiero; perishes in a storm while sailing back to Africa.

116. RODOMONTE: King of Sarza; a central protagonist; 'in nessun atto vile' [showing not a trace of fear] (XVI 22,5 AB; XVIII C); one of the strongest knights in the African army; devoted to Agramante; leaves the African camp after Doralice rejects him and Agramante does not allow him to challenge her decision; accuses Ruggiero of having betrayed Agramante; the poem ends with his death.

117. RUGGIERO: the dynastic hero; participates in many romance adventures; unwilling to abandon Agramante; converts to Christianity and marries Bradamante; has to face Rodomonte in the final canto of the poem.

118. SACRIPANTE: King of Circassia; one of the main Saracen protagonists of the poem; in love with Angelica, 'la donna c'havea ognhor fissa nel core' [the woman who was rooted in his heart] (XXXII 58,2 AB; XXXV 56 C).

119. SALINTERNO: 'gran Dïodarro e Maliscalco regio' [Lord Great Chamberlain and Master of the Horse to the king] (XV 97,2 AB; XVII C); takes part in Norandino's joust in Damascus and is killed by Griphone: 'El colpo (eccetto 'l Re) fu a tutti caro; | ch'ognuno odiava Salinterno avaro' [The blow rejoyced everybody, except the king, | for Salinterno was greedy and generally loathed] (XV 98,7–8 AB; XVII C).

120. SANSONETTO DA MECCA: a prominent Saracen character in the *Spagna*; 'oltra l'etade, | (ch'era nel primo fior), molto prudente; | d'alta cavalleria, d'alta bontade | famoso, e reverito fra la gente. | Orlando lo converse a nostra fede, | e di sua man battesmo ancho gli diede' [he was wise | beyond his years (he was in the first flower of youth); | very chivalrous, very generous, | famous and respected by people. | Orlando had converted him to our faith, | and baptized him by his own hand] (XIII 76,3–8 AB; XV 95 C); welcomes Astolfo; Astolfo, Marphisa, Aquilante and Griphone let him win a joust.

121. LORD OF SELEUCIA: participates in Norandino's joust; one of the best knights 'con destrier buono e con arme perfette' [with a good steed and excellent arms] (XV 100,4 AB; XVII C); fights with Griphone.

122. SERPENTINO: King of Gallitia after Maricoldo's death; has enchanted armour; fights with Rinaldo and Bradamante.
123. LORD OF SIDONIA: unhorsed by Griphone in Norandino's joust (XV 93 AB; XVII C).
124. SINAGONE: died in the *Inamoramento de Orlando*; mentioned at XII 14 AB; XIV C.
125. SOBRINO: King of Garbo; Agramante's advisor; it is difficult to find 'più di lui prudente Saracino' [a more prudent Saracen than he] (XII 24,8 AB; XIV C); remains with Agramante until the end; fights in the duel of Lipadusa; converts to Christianity after the death of his king.
126. SORIDANO: leads soldiers from Hesperia; grievously wounded by Rinaldo at XIV 81 AB; XVI C.
127. STORDILANO: King of Granada; Doralice's father.
128. SULTAN OF EGYPT: Agramante's powerful neighbour; Sobrino advises Agramante to ask him for help.
129. TANFIRIONE: died in the *Inamoramento de Orlando*; mentioned at XII 23 AB; XIV C.
130. TARDOCCO: died in the *Inamoramento de Orlando*; mentioned at XII 22 AB; XIV C.
131. TESIRA: 'Fe' Portugal, tolto Larbin dal mondo, | suo Re Tesira, di Larbin parente' [After Larbin had died, Portugal elected | Tesira, Larbin's relative, as its king] (XII 13,5–6 AB; XIV C).
132. TIRSE: a knight from Apamia; unhorsed by Griphone in Norandino's joust (XV 96 AB; XVII C).
133. TROIANO: Agramante's father; Ruggiero's uncle.
134. TRUFFALDINO: died in the *Inamoramento de Orlando*; mentioned at XXIX 41,2 B; XXXI 41 BC.
135. UGIERI IL DANESE: Saracen convert to Christianity; one of Charlemagne's knights.
136. ULIENO: Rodomonte's father.
137. ZILIANTE (GILIANTE): Monodonte's son; Brandimarte's brother; sends a messenger to Brandimarte after the death of their father.

## ii. Anonymous characters[2]

1. A SARACEN KNIGHT: 'uno Amostante' [an Amostant] killed by Orlando 'pochi anni inante' [a few years earlier] (VIII 85,7–8 ABC).
2. A KNIGHT FROM GRANADA: a captain who is entrusted with bringing Doralice to the Saracen camp; killed by Mandricardo at XII 42,2 AB; XIV C.
3. A KNIGHT FROM DAMASCUS: the knight who tells Griphone the story of Norandino and Lucina (XV 25–68 AB; XVII C).
4. DORALICE'S DWARF: 'un Nano piccolino' [a tiny dwarf] (XVI 28,6 AB; XVIII C) who tells Rodomonte that Mandricardo has kidnapped his lady.

## iii. Characters from the *Inamoramento de Orlando* alluded to but not named

1. DOLISTONE: Fiordelisa's father alluded to at XXXIX 181 AB; XLIII 184 C.
2. TIBIANO: Lucina's father alluded to at XV 66 AB; XVII C.

---

2    Listed in the order of their appearance in the poem.

# BIBLIOGRAPHY

❖

## Primary sources

### i. Manuscripts

*London*
    British Library
    MS Add 10808
*Mantua*
    Archivio di Stato, Archivio Gonzaga, busta 85
    Archivio di Stato, Archivio Gonzaga, busta 86
    Archivio Gonzaga, Archivio Gonzaga, busta 2991, libro 3
*Modena*
    Archivio di Stato, Ambasciatori estensi, busta 15/ unica (Egitto, Levante, Turchia asiatica, Turchia europea)
    Archivio di Stato, Principi esteri, vescovi: Gerusalemme (Busta 1731/30), Bethlem (Busta 1730/29); Constantinople (Busta 1730/29).
    Archivio di Stato, Archivio Segreto Estense, Principi Esteri, busta 1612
    Archivio di Stato, Archivio Segreto Estense, Principi Esteri, busta 1644
    Biblioteca Estense Universitaria, Modena
    HERODOTO MS ITAL. 1726 a. H.3.22
    MS 423

### ii. Printed texts

AFRICANO, LEONE, *Della descrittione dell'Africa*, in Giovanni Battista Ramusio, *Navigationi et viaggi: Venice (1563–1606)*, with an introduction by Raleigh Ashlin Skelton and an analysis of the contents by George B. Parks, 3 vols (Amsterdam: Theatrum Orbis Terrarum, 1967–1970), I (facsimile edition of the 1563 Giunti edition of the first volume), fols 1$^r$–95$^v$

AGOSTINI, NICOLÒ DEGLI, *Quarto libro*, in *Tutti li libri de Orlando Inamorato del Conte de Scandiano Mattheo Maria Boiardo* (Venice: Giorgio de' Rusconi, 1506)

——*Il quinto libro dello Inamoramento de Orlando* (Venice: Giorgio de' Rusconi, 1514)

——*Incomincia il sesto libro de lo Innamoramento di Orlando*, in *Tutti li libri d'Orlando inamorato, del Conte de Scandiano Mattheo Maria Boiardo* (Venice: Alovise de Tortis, 1543)

*Altobello e il re Troiano suo fratello* (Venice: Gabriel di Grassi de Pavia, 1481)

ANDREA DA BARBERINO, *L'Aspramonte, romanzo cavalleresco inedito*, ed. by Marco Boni (Bologna: per i tipi dell'Antiquaria Palmaverde, 1951)

——*Il Guerrin Meschino*, edizione critica secondo l'antica vulgata fiorentina, ed. by Mauro Cursietti (Roma; Padua: Editrice Antenore, 2005)

——*I Reali di Francia*, ed. by Giuseppe Vandelli and Giovanni Gambarin (Bari: Laterza, 1947)

——*Le storie nerbonesi: romanzo cavalleresco del secolo XIV*, ed. by Ippolito Gaetano Isola, 4 vols (Bologna: Romagnoli, 1877–1891)

ANGELUS, PAULUS; RICOLDUS DE MONTE CRUCIS, *Epistola ad Saracenos: cum libello contra*

*Alcoranum: pro provida previaque dispositione conversionis infidelium* (Venice: Alessandro Bindoni, c. 1520)

*Antiphor de Barosia* (Venice: Melchior Sessa, 1531)

ARIOSTO, LUDOVICO, *Orlando furioso secondo la princeps del 1516*, ed. by Marco Dorigatti, in collaboration with Gerarda Stimato (Florence: Olschki, 2006)

—— *Orlando furioso secondo l'edizione del 1532: con le varianti delle edizioni del 1516 e del 1521*, ed. by Santorre Debenedetti and Cesare Segre (Bologna: Commissione per i testi di lingua, 1960)

—— *Orlando furioso*, ed. by Emilio Bigi, 2 vols (Milan: Rusconi, 1982) [repr. by Cristina Zampese, 2012]

—— *Orlando furioso*, ed. by Remo Ceserani, 2 vols (Turin: Tipografia Torinese, 1962)

—— *Orlando furioso novissimamente alla sua integrita ridotto & ornato di varie figure* (Venice: Gabriel Giolito, 1542)

—— *Orlando furioso ornato di nove figure & allegorie in ciascun canto* (Venice: Giovanni Andrea Valvassore, 1553)

—— *Orlando furioso, tutto ricorretto, et di nuove figure adornato* (Venice: Vicenzo Valgrisi, 1556)

—— *Orlando furioso* (Venice: Giovanni Andrea Valvassori, 1566)

—— *Orlando furioso* (Venice: Domenico Farri, 1580)

—— *Orlando furioso; delle annotazioni de' più celebri autori che sopra esso hanno scritto, e di altre utili, e vaghe giunte in questa impressione adornato* (Venice: Stefano Orlandini, 1730)

—— *Carmina, Rime, Satire, Erbolato, Lettere*, ed. by Mario Santoro (Turin: Unione Tipografico-Editrice Torines, 1989)

—— *Cinque canti*, ed. by Valentina Gritti (Padova: libreriauniversitaria.it edizioni, 2018)

ARIOSTO, ORAZIO, *Difese dell'Orlando furioso dell'Ariosto*, in *Apologia del Sig. Torquato Tasso in difesa della sua Gierusalemme liberata* (Ferrara: Giulio Cesare Cagnacini, et Fratelli, 1585), fols N 3$^r$-P 2$^v$

*Aspremont, chanson de geste du XII$^e$ siècle, présentation, edition et traduction par François Suard d'après le manuscript 25529 de la BNF* (Paris: Champion Classiques, 2008)

BALDO, CAMILLO, *Delle mentite discorso* (Venice: Bartolomeo Fontana, 1634)

BANDELLO, MATTEO, *Le novelle*, in *Tutte le opere*, ed. by Francesco Flora, 2 vols (Milan: Mondadori, 1942–1943)

BIRAGO, FRANCESCO, *Discorsi cavallereschi* (Milan: Giovanni Battista Bidelli, 1622)

BOIARDO, MATTEO MARIA, *Amorum libri tres*, ed. by Tiziano Zanato (Turin: Einaudi, 1998)

—— trans., *The 'Historia Imperiale' by Riccobaldo Ferrarese translated by Matteo Maria Boiardo (1471–1473)*, ed. by Andrea Rizzi (Rome: Istituto storico italiano per il Medio Evo, 2008), books I-II

—— trans., *Istoria Imperiale di Ricobaldo Ferrarese nella quale si contiene la divisione dell'Imperio, e la successione de gl'Imperatori dopo Carlo Magno, che primo ottenne l'Imperio Occidentale*, in *Rerum Italicarum Scriptores*, ed. by Ludovico Muratori, 25 vols (Milan: Società Palatina, 1723–1751), IX, books III-IV, pp. 289–342

—— *Orlando innamorato. Inamoramento de Orlando*, ed. by Andrea Canova (Milan: BUR, 2011)

—— *L'Inamoramento de Orlando*, ed. by Antonia Tissoni Benvenuti and Cristina Montagnani with an introduction and comments by Antonia Tissoni Benvenuti, 2 vols (Milan: Ricciardi, 1999)

—— *Orlando innamorato*, ed. by Riccardo Bruscagli, 2 vols (Turin: Einaudi, 1995)

—— *Orlando innamorato*, ed. by Aldo Scaglione (Turin: Unione tipografica, 1963)

—— *Orlando innamorato*, in *Tutte le opere di Matteo M. Boiardo*, ed. by Angelandrea Zottoli, 2 vols (Milan: Mondadori, 1936–1937)

—— *Opere Volgari. Amorum Libri, Pastorale, Lettere*, ed. by Pier Vincenzo Mengaldo (Bari: Gius. Laterza & Figli, 1962)

—— *Pastoralia*, ed. by Stefano Carrai (Padua: Antenore, 1996)

——*La pedìa de Cyro*, ed. by Valentina Gritti (Novara: Interlinea, 2014)

——*Le vite degli eccellenti capitani di Cornelio Nepote tradotte da Matteo Maria Boiardo*, ed. by Olindo Guerrini and Corrado Ricci (Bologna: Zanichelli, 1908)

BRACCIOLINI, POGGIO, *De varietate fortunae*, ed. by Outi Merisalo (Helsinki: Suomalainen Tiedeakatemia, 1993)

*Bradiamonte sorella di Rinaldo* (Florence: Francesco di Dino, 1489)

CALEFFINI, UGO, *Diario di Ugo Caleffini* (1471–1494), ed. by Giuseppe Pardi, 2 vols (Ferrara: Premiata Tipografia Sociale, 1938)

CALVINO, ITALO, *Orlando furioso di Ludovico Ariosto raccontato da Italo Calvino* (Turin: Einaudi, 1970)

*Cantari d'Aspramonte inediti (Magl. VII 682)*, ed. by Andrea Fassò (Bologna: Commissione per i testi di lingua, 1981)

CASTELVETRO, LUDOVICO, *Poetica d'Aristotele vulgarizzata, et sposta* (Vienna: Gaspar Stainhofer, 1570)

CASTIGLIONE, BALDASSARE, *Il libro del Cortegiano*, introd. by Amedeo Quondam, ed. by Nicola Longo (Milan: Garzanti, 2006)

CIECO, FRANCESCO, *Libro d'arme e d'amore, nomato Mambriano*, ed. by Giuseppe Rua, 3 vols (Turin: Unione Tipografico-Editrice Torinese, 1926)

CONTARINI, AMBROSIO, *Il viaggio del Magnifico M. A. Ambrosio Contarini Ambasciatore della Illustrissima Signoria di Venetia al gran Signore Ussuncassan Re di Persia nell'anno. MCCCCLXXIII*, in Giovanni Battista Ramusio, *Navigationi et viaggi: Venice (1563–1606)*, with an introduction by Raleigh Ashlin Skelton and an analysis of the contents by George B. Parks, 3 vols (Amsterdam: Theatrum Orbis Terrarum, 1967–1970), II (facsimile edition of the 1583 Giunti edition of the second volume), fols 112$^v$-125$^v$

DAL CAMPO, LUCHINO, *El viaggio al Santo Sepolcro del nostro Signor Gesù Cristo in Jerusalem, el qual fece lo Illustrissimo Signor Marchese Nicolò da Este con altri gentiluomini suoi compagni*, ed. by Giovanni Ghinassi (Turin: UTET 1861), pp. 99–160

*Diario ferrarese dall'anno 1409 sino al 1502 di autori incerti*, ed. by Giuseppe Pardi (Bologna: N. Zanichelli, 1928–1937), fasc. 1–4.

DON DOMENICO, MESSORE, *Viagio del Sancto Sepolcro facto per lo Illustro Misere Milliaduxe Estense*, ed. by Beatrice Saletti (Rome: Istituto Storico Italiano per il Medio Evo, 2009)

*El cantare di Fierabraccia et Ulivieri: Italienische Bearbeitung der Chanson de Geste Fierabras*, ed. by Edmund Stengel and Carl Buhlmann, *Ausgaben und Abhandlungen aus dem Gebiete der romanischen Philologie*, 2 (1881)

*Fioretti dei Paladini* (Venice: Giovanni e Gregorio de' Gregori, 1495)

FÓRNARI, SIMON, *La spositione sopra l'Orlando furioso di M. Ludovico Ariosto*, 2 vols (Florence: Lorenzo Torrentino, 1549)

FRANCESCO CIECO DA FIRENZE, *Persiano figliolo de Altobello* (Venice: Cristophoro de Mandelo, 1493)

GALILEI, GALILEO, *Considerazioni al Tasso*, in Idem, *Scritti letterari*, ed. by Alberto Chiari (Florence: Le Monnier, 1970)

GESSI, BERLINGERO, *La spada di honore: Libro primo delle osservazioni cavaleresche* (Bologna: l'Erede del Barbien, 1671)

GIOVIO, PAOLO, *Elogi degli uomini illustri*, ed. by Franco Minonzio, trans. by Andrea Guasparri and Franco Minonzio (Turin: Einaudi, 2006)

GIRALDI CINTHIO, GIOVAN BATTISTA, *Ab epistolis de Ferraria et Atestinis principibus commentariolum ex Lilii Gregorii Gyraldi epitome deductum* (Ferrara: Francesco de' Rossi, 1556)

——*Discorsi intorno al comporre rivisti dall'autore nell'esemplare ferrarese Cl. I 90*, ed. by Susanna Villari (Messina: Centro interdipartimentale di studi umanistici, 2002)

——*Note critiche all'Orlando furioso (Classe I 377 e Classe I 406 della BCAFe)*, ed. by Marco Dorigatti and Carla Molinari (Ferrara: Edisai, 2018)

GUASTAVINI, GIULIO, *Risposta all'Infarinato Accademico della Crusca intorno alla Gerusalemme liberata di Torquato Tasso*, in *Delle opere di Torquato Tasso*, 12 vols (Venice: Steffano Monti e N. N. Compagno, 1735–1742), II, pp. 461–560

*Guerre in ottava rima: Vol. IV: Guerre contro i Turchi (1453–1570)*, ed. by Marina Beer and Cristina Ivaldi (Modena: Panini, 1988)

GUICCIARDINI, FRANCESCO, *Storia d'Italia*, ed. by Silvana Seidel Menchi (Turin: Einaudi, 1971)

*I cantari del Danese*, ed. by Sara Furlati (Alessandria: Edizioni dell'Orso, 2003)

*I cantari di Rinaldo da Monte Albano*, ed. by Elio Melli (Bologna: Commissione per i Testi di Lingua, 1973)

*Il Padiglione di Mambrino: cantare cavalleresco*, ed. by Pietro Volpini (Livorno: Vigo, 1874)

*Innamoramento di Carlo e dei suoi Paladini* (Bologna: Bazaliero di Bazalerii, 1491)

*Instructione facta ali Nobili Scudieri de lo Illustrissimo Signore Duca de Modena etc., Gattamellata et Zoanne Iacomo de la Torre, per la loro andata in Barberia*, in *Relazioni dei duchi di Ferrara e di Modena coi re di Tunisi: Cenni e documenti raccolti nell'archivio di stato in Modena*, ed. by Cesare Foucard (Modena: Tipografia Pizzolotti, 1881), pp. 9–19

*La Sala di Malagigi. Cantare cavalleresco*, ed. by Pio Rajna (Imola: Tip. Galeati, 1871)

*La Sala di Malagigi* (Rome: Johann Besicken and Martinus de Amsterdam, c. 1500)

*La Sala di Malagigi* (Bologna: Jogann Schriber, c. 1483)

*La Sala di Malagigi* (Florence: Sanctum Jacobum de Ripoli, c. 1480)

*La Trabisonda* (Bologna: Ugo Rugerius, 1483)

*La Visione di Venus: antico poemetto popolare*, ed. by Alessandro d'Ancona, *Giornale di filologia romanza*, 2 (1878), 111–18

*Le battaglie d'Aspramonte* (Venice: Dionysius Bertochus, 1491)

*L'Entrée d'Espagne: chanson de geste franco-italienne*, ed. by Antoine Thomas, 2 vols (Paris: Firmin-Didot, 1913)

*Le Voyage d'Outremer de Bertrandon de la Broquière, premier écuyer tranchant et conseiller de Philippe le Bon, duc de Bourgogne*, ed. by Charles Henri Auguste Schefer (Farnborough: Gregg, 1972)

*Li fatti de Spagna: testo settentrionale trecentesco già detto 'Viaggio di Carlo Magno in Ispagna'*, ed. by Ruggero Ruggieri (Modena: Società tipografica modenese, 1951)

*Libro della Regina Ancroia* (Venice: Petrus de Plasiis, Cremonensis, 1485)

*Libro novo dove si contiene le battaglie dello innamoramento de Guidon Salvaggio che fu figliolo de Rinaldo de Mont'Albano* (Milan: Valerio & Hieronymo fratelli da Meda, after 1550)

LUDOVICO DE VARTHEMA, *Itinerario* (Venice: Francesco di Alessandro Bindone and Mapheo Pasini, 1535)

MANDEVILLE, JOHN, *Itinerarius* (Bologna: Ugo Rugerius, 1488)

MENAVINO, GIOVANNI ANTONIO, *I cinque libri della legge, religione et vita de' Turchi* (Venice: Vincenzo Valgrisi, 1548)

MURATORI, LUDOVICO ANTONIO, *Della perfetta poesia italiana, spiegata e dimostrata con varie osservazioni*, in Idem, *Opere*, 13 vols (Arezzo: Michele Bellotti, 1767–1773), IX

MUZIO, GIROLAMO, *Il duello* (Venice: Gabriel Giolito, 1550)

NAVAGERO, ANDREA, 'A M. Gio. Battista Rannusio', in *Lettere di diversi autori eccelenti* (Venice: Giordano Ziletti, 1556), pp. 718–38

NICCOLÒ DA POGGIBONSI, *Libro d'Oltramare*, ed. by Alberto Bacchi della Lega (Bologna: Gaetano Romagnoli, 1881)

NICCOLÒ DEGLI ODDI, *Dialogo in difesa di Camillo Pellegrini contra gli Accademici della Crusca*, in *Delle opere di Torquato Tasso*, 12 vols (Venice: Steffano Monti e N. N. Compagno, 1735–1742), II, pp. 413–60

OLEVANO, GIOVANNI BATTISTA, *Trattato nel quale co 'l mezo di cinquanta casi vien posto in atto prattico il modo di ridurre a pace ogni sorte di privata inimicitia, nata per cagion d'honore* (Venice: Giacobo Antonio Somascho, 1603)

*Pareri in duello d'incerto auttore*, in *Orlando furioso* (Venice: Giovanni Andrea Valvassori, 1566)

PATRIZI, FRANCESCO, *Parere in difesa dell'Ariosto*, in *Apologia del Sig. Torquato Tasso in difesa della sua Gierusalemme liberata* (Ferrara: Giulio Cesare Cagnacini, et Fratelli, 1585), fols L4$^r$-N2$^r$

PELLEGRINI, CAMILLO, *Il Carrafa o vero della Epica poesia* (Florence: Sermartelli, 1584)

PICCOLOMINI, AENEAS SYLVIUS, *I Commentarii*, ed. by Luigi Totaro, 2 vols (Milan: Adolphi, 1984)

PIGNA, GIOVAN BATTISTA, *I romanzi*, ed. by Salvatore Ritrovato (Bologna: Commissione per i Testi di Lingua, 1997)

POLO, MARCO, *Il Milione*, ed. by Ruggero M. Ruggieri (Florence: Olschki, 1986)

PULCI, LUCA; PULCI, LUIGI, *Cyriffo Calvaneo* (Florence: Antonio di Bartolommeo Miscomini, before 1490)

PULCI, LUIGI, *Morgante*, ed. by Franca Ageno (Milan: Mondadori, 1994).

RAFFAELE DA VERONA, *Aquilon de Bavière*, introd. and ed. by Peter Wunderli, 3 vols (Tübingen: Niemeyer, 1982)

SALVIATI, LIONARDO, *Degli Accademici della Crusca difesa dell'Orlando Furioso dell'Ariosto contra 'l Dialogo dell'epica poesia di Cammillo Pellegrino*, in *Apologia del sig. Torquato Tasso* (Ferrara: Giulio Cesare Cagnacini, et Fratelli, 1585), fols A 1$^r$-G 8$^v$

—— *Dello Infarinato Accademico della Crusca risposta all'Apologia di Torquato Tasso intorno all'Orlando furioso, e alla Gierusalèm liberata* (Florence: Carlo Meccoli e Salvestro Magliani, 1585)

—— *Lo 'nfarinato secondo ovvero dello 'nfarinato Accademico della Crusca* (Florence: Anton Padovani, 1588)

SANUDO, MARINO, *Diarii*, ed. by Nicolò Barozzi, 58 vols (Venice: Visentini, 1879–1903), IV

*Spagna ferrarese*, ed. by Valentina Gritti and Cristina Montagnani (Novara: Interlinea, 2009)

*Storia di Rinaldino da Montalbano*, ed. by Carlo Minutoli (Bologna: Gaetano Romagnoli, 1865)

STROZZI, TITO VESPASIANO, *Die Borsias des Tito Strozzi. Ein lateinisches Epos der Renaissance, erstmals herausgegeben, eingeleitet und kommentiert von Walther Ludwig* (Munich: Fink, 1977)

TASSO, TORQUATO, *Discorsi dell'arte poetica e del poema eroico*, ed. by Luigi Poma (Bari: Laterza, 1964)

—— *Gerusalemme liberata*, ed. by Lanfranco Caretti (Turin: Einaudi, 1971)

*Tavola Ritonda*, ed. by Emanuele Trevi (Milan: RCS Libri, 1999)

TOSCANELLA, ORAZIO, *Bellezze del Furioso di M. Lodovico Ariosto* (Venice: Pietro dei Franceschi, & nepoti, 1574)

*Ugieri il Danese* (Venice: Lucas Dominici, 1480)

VALCIECO, RAFFAELE, *El quinto e fine de tutti li libri de lo Inamoramento de Orlando* (Milan: Nicolò da Gorgonzola, 1518)

*Viaggio di Lionardo di Niccolò Frescobaldi fiorentino in Egitto e in Terra Santa con un discorso dell'editore sopra il commercio degl'Italiani nel secolo XIV*, ed. by Guglielmo Manzi (Rome: per Carlo Mordacchini, 1818)

ZAMBOTTI, BERNARDINO, *Diario Ferrarese dall'anno 1476 sino a 1504*, in *Diario ferrarese dall'anno 1409 sino al 1502 di autori incerti*, Appendix, ed. by Giuseppe Pardi (Bologna: N. Zanichelli, 1928–1937), fasc. 5/6–9/10

ZENO, NICCOLÒ, *Dei commentarii del viaggio in Persia di M. Caterino Zeno il K. & delle guerre fatte nell'Imperio Persiano dal tempo di Vssuncassano in qua*, in Giovanni Battista Ramusio, *Navigationi et viaggi: Venice (1563–1606)*, with an introduction by Raleigh Ashlin Skelton and an analysis of the contents by George B. Parks, 3 vols (Amsterdam: Theatrum Orbis Terrarum, 1967–1970), II (facsimile edition of the 1583 Giunti edition of the second volume), fols 219$^v$-229$^v$

## Secondary Sources

AKBARI, SUZANNE CONKLIN, *Idols in the East: European Representations of Islam and the Orient, 1100–1450* (Ithaca: Cornell University Place, 2009)

ALEXANDRE-GRAS, DENISE, *L'héroisme chevaleresque dans le 'Roland Amoureux' de Boiardo* (Saint-Etienne: Publications de l'Université de Saint-Etienne, 1988)

—— 'Tre figure boiardesche di eroe saraceno: Ferraguto, Agricane, Rodamonte', *Annali d'italianistica*, 1 (1983), 129–43

ALHAIQUE PETTINELLI, ROSANNA, 'Tra il Boiardo e l'Ariosto: il Cieco da Ferrara e Niccolò degli Agostini', *Rassegna della letteratura italiana*, 79 (1975), 232–78

ALLAIRE, GLORIA, 'Portrayal of Muslims in Andrea da Barberino's *Guerrino Meschino*', in *Medieval Christian Perceptions of Islam*, ed. by John V. Tolan (New York; London: Routledge, 2000), pp. 243–69

—— 'Noble Saracen or Muslim Adversary? The Changing Image of the Saracen in Late Medieval Literature', in *Western Views of Islam in Medieval and Early Modern Europe: Perception of Other*, ed. David R. Blanks and Michael Frassetto (Basingstoke: Macmillan, 1999), pp. 173–84

ANDALORO, MARIA, 'Costanzo da Ferrara: Gli anni a Costantinopoli alla corte di Maometto II', *Storia dell'arte*, 38–40 (1980), 185–212

ANTON, CORINA, 'Un principe o un tiranno? Il capo saraceno nell'*Orlando furioso*', in *Limbă, cultură şi civilizaţie la începutul mileniului al treilea*, ed. by Yolanda Catelly, Simona Maziliu, Fabiola Popa, Diana Stoica (Bucharest: Politehnica Press, 2008), pp. 26–32

ASCOLI, ALBERT RUSSELL, 'Fede e riscrittura: il *Furioso* del '32', *Rinascimento*, 43 (2003), 93–130

—— 'Faith as Cover-up: Ariosto's *Orlando Furioso*, Canto 21, and Machiavellian Ethics', in *I Tatti Studies in the Italian Renaissance*, 8 (1999), 135–70

—— *Ariosto's Bitter Harmony: Crisis and Evasion in the Italian Renaissance* (Princeton, Princeton University Press, 1987)

AZZOLINA, LIBORIO, *Il mondo cavalleresco in Boiardo, Ariosto, Berni* (Palermo: A. Reber, 1912)

BABINGER, FRANZ, *Mehmed the Conqueror and his Time*, trans. by Ralph Manheim and William C. Hickman (Princeton: Princeton University Press, 1978)

BAKHTIN, MIKHAIL, *Problems of Dostoevsky's Poetics*, ed. and trans. by Caryl Emerson (Minneapolis: University of Minnesota Press, 1984)

—— 'Epic and Novel', in Idem, *The Dialogic Imagination: Four Essays*, ed. by Michael Holquist, trans. by Caryl Emerson (Austin: University of Texas Press, 1981)

BAILLET, ROGER, *Le monde poétique de l'Arioste: essai d'interprétation du Roland Furieux* (Lyon: Editions l'Hermès, 1977)

BANCOURT, PAUL, *Les musulmans dans les chansons de geste du Cycle du roi*, 2 vols (Aix en Provence: Université de Provence, 1982)

BASKINS, CRISTELLE, 'The Bride of Trebizond: Turks and Turkmens on a Florentine Wedding Chest, circa 1460', *Muqarnas*, 29 (2012), 83–100

BATTAGLIA, SALVATORE, *Grande dizionario della lingua italiana* (Turin: Unione tipografico-editrice torinese, 1961–2009)

BEER, MARINA, *Romanzi di cavalleria. Il Furioso e il romanzo italiano del primo Cinquecento* (Rome: Bulzoni, 1987)

BELLINGERI, GIAMPIERO, 'Turchi e Persiani fra visioni abnormi e normalizzazioni, a Venezia (secoli XV-XVIII)', *Revue des littératures européennes*, 9 (2015), 14–89

BERTONI, GIULIO, *La biblioteca estense e la coltura ferrarese ai tempi del duca Ercole I, 1471–1505* (Turin: Loescher, 1903)

BEZZOLA, RETO, 'L'Oriente nel poema cavalleresco del primo Rinascimento', *Lettere italiane*, 15 (1963), 385–98

BIGI, EMILIO, *La poesia del Boiardo* (Florence: Sansoni, 1941)

BISAHA NANCY, *Creating East and West: Renaissance Humanists and the Ottoman Turks* (Philadelphia: University of Pennsylvania Press, 2004)

—— 'Petrarch's Vision of the Muslim and Byzantine East', *Speculum*, 76, no. 2 (2001), 284–314

—— '"New Barbarian" or Worthy Adversary? Humanist Constructs of the Ottoman Turks in Fifteenth-century Italy', in *Western Views of Islam in Medieval and Early Modern Europe: Perception of Other*, ed. David R. Blanks and Michael Frassetto (Basingstoke: Macmillan, 1999), pp. 185–205

BOLZONI, LINA, 'Images of Literary Memory in the Italian Dialogues: Some Notes on Giordano Bruno and Ludovico Ariosto', in *Giordano Bruno. Philosopher of the Renaissance*, ed. by Hilary Gatti (Aldershot: Ashgate, 2002), pp. 121–41

BOSCOLO, CLAUDIA, *L'Entrée d'Espagne. Context and Authorship at the Origins of the Italian Chivalric Epic* (Oxford: Medium Aevum, 2017)

—— 'La disputa teologica dell'*Entrée d'Espagne*', in *Les chansons de geste: actes du XVI<sup>e</sup> Congrès International de la Société Rencesvals*, ed. by Carlos Alvar and Juan Paredes (Granada: Universidad de Granada, 2005), pp. 123–34

BOURNE, MOLLY, *Francesco II Gonzaga: The Soldier-Prince as Patron* (Rome: Bulzoni, 2008)

—— 'The Turban'd Turk in Renaissance Mantua: Francesco II Gonzaga's Interest in Ottoman Fashion', in *Mantova e il Rinascimento italiano: Studi in onore di David S. Chambers*, ed. by Philippa Jackson and Guido Rebecchini (Mantua: Sometti Editoriale, 2011), pp. 53–64

BROOK, LESLIE C., 'Allusions à l'antiquité gréco-latine dans l'*Entrée d'Espagne*', *Zeitschrift für romanische Philologie*, 118, no. 4 (2002), 573–86

BROTTON, JERRY, *The Renaissance Bazaar: from the Silk Road to Michelangelo* (Oxford: Oxford University Press, 2002)

BRUSCAGLI, RICCARDO, 'I Cinque canti dell'Ariosto', in *Carlo Magno in Italia e la fortuna dei libri di cavalleria*, ed. by Johannes Bartuschat and Franca Strologo (Ravenna: Longo Editore, 2016), pp. 19–52

—— '"Ruggiero's story: the making of a dynastic hero', in *Romance and History: Imagining Time from the Medieval to the Early Modern Period*, ed. by Jon Whitman (Cambridge: Cambridge University Press, 2015), pp. 151–67

—— 'Medoro riconosciuto', in Idem, *Studi cavallereschi* (Florence: Società Editrice Fiorentina: 2003), pp. 75–101

—— 'Incontrare il nemico. La "gran bontà" degli antichi cavalieri', in Idem, *Studi cavallereschi* (Florence: Società Editrice Fiorentina: 2003), pp. 209–13

—— 'Prove di commento all'*Orlando innamorato*', *Studi Italiani*, 1 (1989), 5–29

—— 'Il "romanzo" padano di Matteo Maria Boiardo', in Idem, *Stagioni della civiltà estense* (Pisa: Nistri-Lischi, 1983), pp. 33–86

BURCKHARDT, JACOB, *The Civilization of the Renaissance in Italy*, trans. by Samuel George C. Middlemore (London: Penguin, 1990)

BURNETT, CHARLES, 'Learned Knowledge of Arabic Poetry, Rhymed Prose, and Didactic Verse from Petrus Alfonsi to Petrarch', in *Poetry and Philosophy in the Middle Ages: A Festschrift for Peter Dronke*, ed. by John Marenbon (Leiden: Brill, 2001), pp. 29–62

BUSBY, KEITH, 'Post-Chrétien Verse Romance: The Manuscript Context', *CRM*, 14 (2007), 11–24

CABANI, MARIA CRISTINA, 'Ariosto e Castiglione', in Eadem, *Ariosto, i volgari e i latini suoi* (Lucca: Maria Pacini Fazzi, 2016), pp. 141–74

—— *Gli amici amanti. Coppie eroiche e sortite notturne nell'epica italiana* (Naples: Liguori, 1995)

—— 'Considerazioni sul boiardismo del *Furioso* e alcune riflessioni sull'uso degli strumenti informatici nelle indagini intertestuali', *Rivista di letteratura italiana*, 12 (1994), 157–248

CANOVA, ANDREA, '*Vendetta di Falconetto* (e *Inamoramento de Orlando?*)', in *Boiardo, Ariosto e i libri di battaglia*, ed. by Andrea Canova and Paola Vecchi Galli (Novara: Interlinea, 2007), pp. 77–106

—— 'Osservazioni lessicali su alcuni romanzi cavallereschi tra Quattro e Cinquecento', in *Carlo Magno in Italia e la fortuna dei libri di cavalleria, Atti del convegno internazionale di Zurigo (6–8 maggio 2014)*, ed. by Johannes Bartuschat and Franca Strologo (Ravenna: Longo Editore, 2016), pp. 339–57

—— '*Guidone*', *Achademia Leonardi Vincii*, 8 (1995), 186–87

CARAMELLA, SANTINO, 'L'Asia nell'*Orlando Innamorato*', *Bollettino della reale società geografica italiana*, ser. 5 (1923), 44–59; 127–50

CARDINI, FRANCO, *Europe and Islam*, trans. by Caroline Beamish (Oxford: Blackwell, 2001)

CARDONA, GIORGIO RAIMONDO, 'L'elemento orientale nel *Morgante* e nel *Ciriffo*', *Lingua nostra*, 30 (1969), 95–101

CARNE-ROSS, DONALD S., 'The One and the Many: a Reading of the *Orlando Furioso*, Cantos 1 and 8', *Arion*, 3, no. 2 (1976), 146–219

CAROCCI, ANNA, *La lezione di Boiardo: Il poema cavalleresco dopo L'*'Inamoramento de Orlando' *(1483–1521)* (Rome: Vecchiarelli, 2018)

—— 'Il destino di Angelica. Il destabilizzante femminile nei poemi di primo Cinquecento', in *I cantieri dell'italianistica: Ricerca, didattica e organizzazione agli inizi del XXI secolo: Atti del XVIII congresso dell'ADI*, ed. by Guido Baldassari et al. (Rome: Adi editore, 2016), pp. 1–10

—— 'Stampare in ottave. Il *Quinto libro* de lo *Inamoramento de Orlando*', *Ecdotica*, 12 (2015), 7–29

CARRAI, STEFANO, 'Primi appunti sulle presenze pulciane nell'*Innamorato*', in *Tipografi e romanzi in Val Padana fra Quattrocento e Cinquecento: Atti delle giornate di studio, Ferrara 11–13 febbraio 1988*, ed. by Riccardo Bruscagli and Amedeo Quondam (Modena: Panini, 1992), pp. 107–16

CARY, GEORGE, 'The Conception of Alexander in Late Medieval and Renaissance Italy', in Idem, *The Medieval Alexander* (Cambridge: C.U.P., 1956; reprint. 1967), pp. 260–72

CASADEI, ALBERTO, *Ariosto: i metodi e i mondi possibili* (Venice: Marsilio, 2016)

—— 'Il finale e la poetica del *Furioso*', *Chroniques italiennes*, 19 (2011), 9–10 <http://chroniquesitaliennes.univ-paris3.fr/PDF/web19/Casaseiweb19.pdf> [consulted 16 January 2020]

—— 'Nomi di personaggi nel *Furioso*', *Il nome nel testo: Rivista internazionale di onomastica letteraria*, 2–3 (2001), 229–37

CASANOVA, PAUL, 'Mahom, Jupin, Apollon, Tervagant, dieux des arabes', in *Mélanges Hartwig Derenbourg, 1844–1908: recueil de travaux d'érudition dédiés à la mémoire d'Hartwig Derenbourg par ses amis et ses élèves* (Paris: Ernest Leroux, 1909), pp. 391–95

CASELLA, PAOLA, 'Il funzionamento dei personaggi secondari nell'Orlando furioso: le vicissitudine di Sacripante', *Italianistica*, 36 (2006), 11–26

CAVALLO, JO ANN, *The World beyond Europe in the Romance Epics of Boiardo and Ariosto* (Toronto; Buffalo; London: University of Toronto Press, 2013)

—— 'Talking Religion: The Conversion of Agricane in Boiardo's *Orlando innamorato*', *MLN*, 127, no. 1 (2012), 178–88

—— 'Crocodiles and Crusades: Egypt in Boiardo's *Orlando Innamorato* and Ariosto's *Orlando Furioso*', *Arthuriana*, 21, no. 1 (2011), 85–96

—— *The Romance Epics of Boiardo, Ariosto, and Tasso: from Public Duty to Private Pleasure* (Toronto; London: University of Toronto Press, 2004)

—— 'The Pathways of Knowledge in Boiardo and Ariosto: The Case of Rodamonte', *Italica*, 79, no. 3 (2002), 303–20

—— *Boiardo's Orlando Innamorato: an Ethics of Desire* (Rutherford: Fairleigh Dickinson University Press, 1993)

CERULLI, ENRICO, 'Petrarca e gli arabi', *Rivista di cultura classica e medievale*, 7 (1965), 331–36

CESERANI, REMO, 'Due modelli culturali e narrativi nell'*Orlando furioso*', GSLI, 16 (1984), 481–506

CHONG, ALAN, 'Gentile Bellini in Istanbul: Myths and Misunderstandings', in *Bellini and the East*, ed. by Caroline Campbell and Alan Chong (London: National Gallery, 2005), pp. 106–29

COLIN, JEAN, *Cyriaque d'Ancône: le voyager, le marchand, l'humaniste* (Paris: Maloine, 1981)

CONFALONIERI, CORRADO, 'Quale Virgilio? Note sul finale del *Furioso*', *Parole rubate*, 7 (2013), 56–66

CORTESI, SANTA, *Fra Sabba da Castiglione, Isabella d'Este e altri: Voci di un carteggio 1505–1542* (Faenza: Stefano Casanova, 2004)

COSSUTTA, FABIO, 'Ritornando su Iroldo e Prasildo', in *Il Boiardo e i mondo estense nel Quattrocento*, ed. by Giuseppe Anceschi and Tina Matarrese (Padua: Antenore, 1998), pp. 237–69

——— *Gli ideali epici dell'umanesimo e l'*Orlando innamorato (Rome: Bulzoni, 1995)

CUCCARO, VINCENT, *The Humanism of Ludovico Ariosto: from the 'Satire' to the 'Furioso'* (Ravenna: Longo, 1981)

DANIEL, NORMAN, *Heroes and Saracens: An Interpretation of the Chansons de Geste* (Edinburgh: Edinburgh University Press, 1984)

——— *Islam and the West: The Making of an Image* (Edinburgh: Edinburgh University Press, 1958; reprint. 1960)

DANIOTTI, CLAUDIA, *Reinventing Alexander: Myth, Legend, History in Renaissance Italian Art* (Turnhout: Brepols, 2021), forthcoming

DANNENFELDT, KARL H., 'The Renaissance Humanists and the Knowledge of Arabic', *Studies in the Renaissance*, 2 (1955), 96–117

DAVIS, NATALIE ZEMON, *Trickster Travels: the Search for Leo Africanus* (London: Faber and Faber, 2008)

D'ELIA, ANTHONY F., 'Genealogy and the Limits of Panegyric: Turks and Huns in Fifteenth-century Epithalamia', *The Sixteenth Century Journal*, 34, no. 4 (2003), 973–91

——— *The Renaissance of Marriage in Fifteenth-Century Italy* (Cambridge, MA; London: Harvard University Press, 2004)

DE PANIZZA LORCH, MARISTELLA, '"Ma soprattutto la persona umana | era cortese": Brandimarte's Cortesia as Expressed through the Hero's Loci Actionis in Boiardo's *Orlando Innamorato*, Book I', in *La corte e lo spazio: Ferrara estense*, ed. by Giuseppe Papagno, Amedeo Quondam, 2 vols (Rome: Bulzoni, 1982), II, pp. 739–81

DE ROBERTIS, DOMENICO, 'Esperienze di un lettore dell'*Innamorato*', in *Il Boiardo e la critica contemporanea: atti del convegno di studi su Matteo Maria Boiardo. Scandiano-Reggio Emilia, 25–27 aprile 1969*, ed. by Giuseppe Anceschi (Florence: Olschki, 1970)

DE SA WIGGINS, PETER, *Figures in Ariosto's Tapestry: Character and Design in the* Orlando Furioso (Baltimore: John Hopkins University Press, 1986), pp. 41–66

——— 'The *Furioso*'s Third Protagonist', *MLN*, 98 (1983), 30–54

DE SANCTIS, FRANCESCO, *La poesia cavalleresca* (Bari: Gius. Laterza & Figli, 1954)

——— *Storia della letteratura italiana*, ed. by Benedetto Croce, 2 vols (Bari: G. Laterza & Figli, 1949)

DE VENTURA, PAOLO, 'Dante and Islam', in *Christian-Muslim Relations. A Bibliographical History* (Leiden: Brill, 2012), vol. IV, pp. 779–87

DELCORNO BRANCA, DANIELA, *La conclusione dell'*'Orlando furioso': qualche osservazione, in *Boiardo, Ariosto e i libri di battaglia*, ed. by Andrea Canova and Paola Vecchi Galli (Novara: Interlinea, 2007), pp. 127–37

——— '*L'Orlando furioso' e il romanzo cavalleresco medievale* (Florence: Olschki, 1973)

—— 'L'Orlando furioso e la tradizione romanzesca arturiana', in *'Dreaming again on things already dreamed': 500 Years of 'Orlando Furioso' (1516–2016)*, edited by Marco Dorigatti and Maria Pavlova (Oxford; New York: Peter Lang, 2019), pp. 3-30

DELLA PALMA, GIUSEPPE, 'L'eroe capovolto: Rodomonte', in Idem, *Le strutture narrative dell'*Orlando furioso (Florence: Olschki, 1984), pp. 110–25

DENZEL, VALENTINA, *Les Mille et Un Visages de la virago. Marphise et Bradamante entre continuation et variation* (Paris: Classiques Garnier, 2016)

DESOLE, CORINNA, *Repertorio dei personaggi citati nei principali Cantari cavallereschi italiani* (Alessandria: Edizione dell'Orso, 1995)

*Dizionario Bompiani delle opere e dei personaggi di tutti i tempi e di tutte le letterature*, 11 vols (Milan: Bompiani, 1983)

DONATINI, MASSIMO, 'La corte e l'apertura degli spazi atlantici', in *Storia di Ferrara*, 7 vols (Ferrara: Gabriele Corbo, 1987–2004), VI, pp. 427–36

DONNARUMMA, RAFFAELE, *Storia dell'*'Orlando innamorato'*: poetiche e modelli letterari in Boiardo* (Luca: M. Pacini Fazzi, 1996)

DONNELLY, JOHN PATRICK, 'The Moslem Enemy in Renaissance Epic: Ariosto, Tasso and Camoëns', *Yale Italian Studies*, I, no. 2 (1977), 162–70

DORIGATTI, MARCO, 'Il presente della poesia: L'*Orlando furioso* nel 1516', *Schifanoia*, 54–55 (2018), 13–26

—— '"Di novo se comencia la tentione": il duello nell'universo cavalleresco del Boiardo', *Esperienze letterarie*, 40 (2015), 71–93

—— 'Borges, Ariosto e la vita segreta dei personaggi minori', in *Lettori e interpreti del Furioso: Atti della giornata di studio (Milano, 3 ottobre 2012)*, Carte romanze, I, no. 2 (2013), 377–406

—— 'Il manoscritto dell'*Orlando furioso* (1505–1515)', in *L'uno e l'altro Ariosto in corte e nelle delizie*, ed. by Gianni Venturi (Florence: Olschki, 2011), pp. 1–44

—— 'Sobrino ariostesco e misconosciuto', *Belfagor*, 65, no. 4 (2010), 401–14

—— 'La favola e la corte: intrecci narrativi e genealogie estensi dal Boiardo all'Ariosto', in *Gli dei a corte: Letteratura e immagini nella Ferrara estense*, ed. by Gianni Venturi and Francesca Cappelletti (Florence: Olschki, 2009), pp. 31–54

—— 'Rugiero and the Dynastic Theme from Boiardo to Ariosto', in *Italy in Crisis, 1494*, ed. by Jane Everson and Diego Zancani (Oxford: Legenda, 2000), pp. 92–128

—— 'Reinventing Roland — Orlando in Italian literature', in *Roland and Charlemagne in Europe: Essays on the Reception and Transformation of a Legend* (London: King's College London Medieval Studies, 1996), pp. 105–26

—— 'Il boiardismo del primo *Furioso*', in *Tipografie e romanzi in Val Padana fra Quattro e Cinquecento*, ed. by Riccardo Bruscagli and Amedeo Quondam (Modena: Franco Cosimo Panini, 1992), pp. 161–74

DOROSZLAÏ, ALEXANDRE, *Ptolémée et l'hippogriffe: La géographie de l'Arioste soumise à l'épreuve des cartes* (Alessandria: Edizioni dell'Orso, 1998)

*'Dreaming again on things already dreamed': 500 Years of 'Orlando Furioso' (1516–2016)*, ed. by Marco Dorigatti and Maria Pavlova (Oxford: Peter Lang, 2019)

ERSPAMER, FRANCESCO, '"E pon la lancia in resta": per una tipologia del duello nei romanzi', in Idem, *La biblioteca di don Ferrante: Duello e onore nella cultura del Cinquecento* (Rome: Bulzoni, 1982), pp. 137–79

EVERSON, JANE, 'Il buono, il brutto, il cattivo: figure di regnanti non-cristiani nel *Mambriano* di Francesco Cieco da Ferrara', *Rassegna europea di letteratura italiana*, 44 (2014), 29–43

—— 'Storie di Alessandro Magno nella tradizione volgare: Medioevo, Rinascimento e tempi moderni', *Rassegna europea di letteratura italiana*, 41, no. 1 (2013), 41–58

—— 'The Epic Tradition of Charlemagne in Italy', in *La tradition epique, du Moyen Age au*

*XIX^e siècle, Cahiers de recherches médievales et humanistes*, 12 (2005), 45–81

——— *The Italian Romance Epic in the Age of Humanism: the Matter of Italy and the World of Rome* (Oxford: Oxford University Press, 2001)

FAVARO, MAIKO, 'Tra "aroganza" e "inclyte vertute": le ambiguità di Alessandro Magno nell'*Inamoramento de Orlando*', in *La "virtù eccelentissima": Eroe e antieroe nella letteratura italiana da Boccaccio a Tasso*, ed. by Vincenzo Caputo (Milan: FrancoAngeli, 2017), pp. 33–42.

FICHTER, ANDREW, *Poets Historical: Dynastic Epic in the Renaissance* (New Heaven: Yale University Press, 1982), pp. 70–111

FIORATO, ADELIN CHARLES, 'La "gallica face" nell'*Orlando Furioso*', in *La corte di Ferrara e il suo mecenatismo, 1441–1598*, ed. by Marianne Pade, Lene Waage Petersen, and Daniela Quarta (Modena: Panini, 1990), pp. 159–76

FLORI, JEAN, *Croisade et chevalerie: XI^e-XII^e siècles* (Bruxelles: De Boeck & Larcier s.a., 1998)

FONTES BARATTO, ANNA, 'Fantôme et fantasme: l'apparition d'Argail dans le premier chant du *Roland furieux*', *Chroniques italiennes*, 59–60, nos 2–3 (2002), 39–63

*Fortune and Romance: Boiardo in America*, ed. by Jo Ann Cavallo and Charles Ross (Tempe, Arizone: Medieval and Renaissance Texts and Studies, 1998)

FREELY, JOHN, *The Grand Turk: Sultan Mehmed II — Conqueror of Constantinople, Master of an Empire and Lord of Two Seas* (London: I. B. Taurius, 2009)

FRANCESCHETTI, ANTONIO, 'On the Saracens in Early Italian Chivalric Literature', in *Romance Epic: Essays on a Medieval Literary Genre*, ed. Hans-Erich Keller (Kalamazoo: Medieval Institute Publications, 1987), 203–11

——— *L'Orlando Innamorato' e le sue componenti tematiche e strutturali* (Florence: Olschki, 1975)

FUCHS, GERHILD; PAGLIARDINI, ANGELO, 'La rappresentazione del pagano/musulmano nell'epica cavalleresca rinascimentale', in *Italia e Europa: dalla cultura nazionale all'interculturalismo, atti del XVI Congresso dell'A.I.P.I., Cracovia, 26–29 agosto 2004*, ed. by Bart van den Bossche et al., 2 vols (Florence: Franco Cesati, 2006), II, pp. 579–87

——— 'Raumkonzepte und Fremdbilder im Zusammenspiel: Zur Darstellungsweise des "Sarazenen" in Texten der italienischen Renaissance-Ritterepik', in *Grenzen und Entgrenzungen: historische und kulturwissenschaftliche Überlegungen am Beispiel des Mittelmeerraums*, ed. by Beate Burtscher-Bechter et al. (Würzburg: Königshausen & Neumann, 2006), pp. 173–209

FUMAGALLI, EDOARDO, 'Il volgarizzamento di Erodoto', in *Il Boiardo e il mondo estense nel Quattrocento*, ed. by Giuseppe Anceschi and Tina Matarrese, 2 vols (Padua: Antenore, 1998), I, pp. 399–428

FUMAGALLI, GIUSEPPINA, 'La "bella istoria" di Rodomonte di Sarza', in Eadem, *Unità fantastica dell''Orlando Furioso'* (Messina-Milan: Giuseppe Principato, 1933), pp. 68–117

GALBIATI, ROBERTO, *Il romanzo e la corte: L'Inamoramento de Orlando' di Boiardo* (Rome: Carocci, 2018)

GARDNER, EDMUND GARRATT, *Dukes and Poets in Ferrara: a Study in the Poetry, Religion and Politics of the Fifteenth and Early Sixteenth Centuries* (London: Constable, 1904)

GATWARD CEVIZLI, ANTONIA, 'More than a Messenger: Embodied Expertise in Mantuan Envoys to the Ottomans in the 1490s', *Mediterranean Studies*, 22, no. 2 (2014), 166–89

GAULLIER-BOUGASSAS, CATHERINE, *La tentation de l'Orient dans le roman médiéval: sur l'imaginaire médiéval de l'autre* (Paris: Champion, 2003)

GHERARDINI, GIOVANNI, *Supplimento a' vocabolarj italiani*, 6 vols (Milan: Stamperia di Gius. Bernardoni di Gio., 1852–57)

GIUDICETTI, GIAN PAOLO, *Mandricardo e la melanconia: Discorsi diretti e sproloqui nell''Orlando Furioso'* (Brussels: Peter Lang, 2010)

——— 'Mandricardo a cavallo di due poemi: il suo ruolo nel terzo libro dell'*Inamoramento de Orlando* e nell'*Orlando Furioso*', *Schifanoia*, 36–37 (2009), 103–44

——'I vinti dell'*Orlando Furioso*: Rodomonte e Mandricardo nella struttura del poema', *Studi e problemi di critica testuale*, 76 (2008), 73–101

GODARD, ALAIN, 'Le camp païen dans la *Jérusalem délivrée*', in *Quêtes d'une identité collective chez les Italiens de la Renaissance*, ed. by Marina Marietti (Paris: Université de la Sorbonne nouvelle, 1991), pp. 309–429

*Grande dizionario italiano dell'uso*, ed. by Tullio De Mauro, 6 vols (Torino: UTET, 1999–2000), IV

GREENE, THOMAS, 'Ariosto and the Earlier Italian Renaissance', in Idem, *The Descent from Heaven: a Study in Epic Continuity* (New Haven-London: Yale University Press, 1963), pp. 104–43

GRÉGOIRE, HENRI, 'L'étymologie de Tervagant (Trivigant)', in *Mélanges d'histoire du théâtre du Moyen-Age et de la Renaissance offerts à Gustave Cohen, professeur honoraire en Sorbonne, par ses collègues, ses élèves et ses amis* (Paris: Libraririe Nizet, 1950), pp. 45–56

GREGORY, TOBIAS, 'Providence, Irony and Magic: *Orlando Furioso*', in Idem, *From Many Gods to One: Divine Action in Renaissance Epic* (Chicago: University of Chicago Press, 2006), pp. 102–39

GRITTI, VALENTINA, 'Ercole d'Este come Ciro: un modello di buon governo', in *Il Principe e la storia: atti del convegno scandiano 18–20 settembre 2003*, ed. by Tina Matarrese and Cristina Montagnani (Novara: Interlinea, 2005), pp. 93–115

GUNDERSHEIMER, WERNER, *Ferrara: the Style of a Renaissance Despotism* (Princeton: Princeton University Press, 1973)

HANKINS, JAMES, 'Renaissance Crusaders: Humanist Crusade Literature in the Age of Mehmed II', *Dumbarton Oaks Papers*, 49 (1995), 111–207

HARPER, JAMES, 'Turks as Trojans; Trojans as Turks: Visual Imagery of the Trojan War and the Politics of Cultural Identity in Fifteenth-century Europe', in *Postcolonial Approaches to the European Middle Ages: Translating Cultures*, ed. by Ananya Jahanara Kabir and Deanne Williams (Cambridge: Cambridge University Press, 2005), pp. 151–79

HARRIS, NEIL, *Bibliografia dell''Orlando innamorato'*, 2 vols (Modena: Panini, 1988)

HEATH, J. MICHAEL, 'Renaissance Scholars and the Origins of the Turks', *Bibliothèque d'Humanisme et Renaissance*, 41 (1979), 453–57

HEGEL, GEORG WILHELM FRIEDRICH, 'Chivalry', in Idem, *Aesthetics. Lectures on Fine Art*, trans. by Thomas M. Knox, 2 vols (Oxford: Clarendon Press, 1988), I, pp. 552–72

HENG, GERALDINE, *The Invention of Race in the European Middle Ages* (Cambridge: Cambridge University Press, 2018)

——*Empire of Magic: Medieval Romance and the Politics of Cultural Fantasy* (New York: Columbia University Press, 2003)

HOEPPNER MORAN CRUZ, JO ANN, 'Popular Attitudes towards Islam in Medieval Europe', in *Western Views of Islam in Medieval and Early Modern Europe: Perception of Other*, ed. David R. Blanks and Michael Frassetto (Basingstoke: Macmillan, 1999), pp. 55–81

HOUDEVILLE, MICHELLE, 'Les sarrasins, miroir des chrétiens?', in *La chrétienté au péril sarrasin: actes du colloque de la Section française de la Société internationale Rencesvals, Aix-en-Provence, 30 septembre-1er octobre 1999* (Aix-en-Provence: Publications de l'Université de Provence, 2000), pp. 77–84

HOUSLEY, NORMAN, *Religious Warfare in Europe 1400–1536* (Oxford: Oxford University Press, 2008)

HOWARD, DEBORAH, *Venice and the East: the Impact of the Islamic World on Venetian Architecture* (New Haven: Yale University Press, 2000)

——'The Status of the Oriental Traveller in Renaissance Venice', in *Re-orienting the Renaissance: Cultural Exchanges with the East*, ed. Gerald MacLean; forward by William Dalrymple (New York: Palgrave Macmillan, 2005), pp. 29–49

IBN WARRAQ, *Defending the West: a Critique of Edwar Said's 'Orientalism'* (Amherst, NY: Prometheus Books, 2007)

IRWIN, ROBERT, *For Lust of Knowing: the Orientalists and their Enemies* (London: Allen Lane, 2006)

*Islam and the Italian Renaissance*, ed. by Charles Burnett and Anna Contadini (London: Warburg Institute, 1999)

JAVITCH, DANIEL, 'Reconsidering the Last Part of the *Orlando Furioso*: Romance to the Bitter End', *Modern Language Quarterly*, 71 (2010), 385–405

——*Proclaiming a Classic: The Canonization of* Orlando Furioso (Princeton: Princeton University Press, 1991)

——'The Imitation of Imitations in the *Orlando Furioso*', *Renaissance Quarterly*, 38, no. 2 (1985), 215–39

JOSSA, STEFANO, *Ariosto* (Bologna: Il Mulino, 2009)

——*La fantasia e la memoria: Intertestualità ariostesche* (Naples: Liguori, 2002)

JUBB, MARGARET A., *The Legend of Saladin in Western Literature and Historiography* (Lewiston, NY: Edwin Mellen Press, 2000).

——'Enemies in the Holy War, but Brothers in Chivalry: the Crusaders' View of the Saracen Opponents', in *Aspects de l'épopée romane: mentalités, idéologies, intertextualités*, ed. by Hans van Dijk and Willem Noomen (Groningen: Egbert Forsten, 1995), pp. 251–59

KAPLAN, PAUL H. D, 'Isabella d'Este and Black African Women', in *Black Africans in Renaissance Europe*, ed. by Thomas Foster Earle and Kate J. Lowe (New York: Cambridge University Press, 2005), pp. 125–54

KAY, SARAH, *The Chansons de Geste in the Age of Romance: Political Fictions* (Oxford: Clarendon, 1995)

KIM, HYONJIN, 'From *La chanson de Roland* to *Orlando Furioso*: the Evolution of the Saracenic Other in the Carolingian epic', *Horizons*, 2 (2011), 97–111

KINOSHITA, SHARON, *Medieval Boundaries: Rethinking Difference in Old French Literature* (Philadelphia: University of Pennsylvania Press, 2006)

KISSLING, HANS JOACHIM, *Sultan Bâjezîd II. Beziehungen zu Markgraf Francesco II. von Gonzaga* (München: Max Hueber Verlag, 1965)

LACH, DONALD, *Asia in the Making of Europe*, 3 vols (Chicago; London: University of Chicago Press, 1965), I-II

*La conquista turca di Otranto (1480): tra storia e mito*, ed. by Hubert Houben (Galatina: Congedo, 2008)

*La rappresentazione dell'Altro nei testi del Rinascimento*, ed. by Sergio Zatti (Lucca: Maria Pacini, 1998)

LA MONICA, STEFANO, 'Realtà storica e immaginario bellico ariostesco', *La Rassegna della letteratura italiana*, 89 (1985), 326–58

LANZA, ANTONIO, 'La visione del mondo arabo nelle relazioni dei pellegrini scrittori in Terrasanta del Quattrocento', *Carte di Viaggio*, 1 (2008), 11–32

LARIVAILLE, PAUL, 'Guerra e ideologia nel "Furioso"', *Chroniques italiennes*, 19 (2001), 1–20   <http://chroniquesitaliennes.univ-paris3.fr/PDF/web19/Larivailleweb19.pdf> [consulted 16 January 2020]

LAZZARO, NANCY, 'Rodomonte e Ariosto nella battaglia di Parigi. Lettura dell'episodio', in *Forma e parola: Studi in memoria di Fredi Chiappelli*, ed. by Dennis J. Dutschke et al. (Rome: Bulzoni, 1992), pp. 235–54

LETTS, MALCOLM, *Sir John Mandevile: the Man and his Book* (London: the Batchworth Press, 1949)

LEVI, EZIO, 'L'*Orlando furioso* come epopea nuziale', *Archivum romanicum*, 17 (1933), 459–93

LEVI DELLA VIDA, GIORGIO, 'Fonti arabe dell'Isabella ariostesca', in Idem, *Aneddoti e svaghi arabi e non arabi* (Milan: R. Ricciardi, 1959), pp. 170–90

LIMENTANI, ALBERTO, 'Venezia e il "pericolo turco" nell'*Entrée d'Espagne*', in Idem, *L'Entrée d'Espagne' e i signori d'Italia*, ed. by Marco Infurna and Francesco Zambon (Padua: Antenore, 1992), pp. 358–78

MAC CARTHY, ITA, *Women and the Making of Poetry in Ariosto's 'Orlando Furioso'* (Leicester: Troubador, 2007)

MAGGI, PIETRO GIUSEPPE, 'Intorno il libro: *La Repubblica di Venezia e la Persia*, del dottor Guglielmo Berchet', in *Reale Istituto Lombardo di Scienze e Lettere. Rendiconti*, II (Milan: Tipografia di Giuseppe Bernardoni, 1865), pp. 43-56

MALACARNE, GIANCARLO, *Il mito dei cavalli gonzagheschi: alle origini del purosangue* (Verona: Promoprint, 1995)

MARINELLI, PETER, *Ariosto and Boiardo: The Origins of 'Orlando Furioso'* (Columbia: University of Missouri Press, 1987)

MARSH, DAVID, 'Ruggiero and Leone: Revision and Resolution in Ariosto's *Orlando Furioso*', *MLN*, 96 (1981), 144–51

MARTIN, JEAN-PIERRE, 'Les sarrasins, l'idolâtrie et l'imaginaie de l'antiquité dans les chansons de geste', in *Littérature et religion au Moyen Age et à la Renaissance*, ed. by Jean-Claude Vallecalle (Lyon: Presses Universitaires de Lyon, 1997), pp. 27–46

——'Les références au mythe troyen dans les *chansons de geste* à sujet carolingien', *Bien dire et bien aprandre*, 10 (1992), 101–17

MARTINI, ELISA, *Un romanzo di crisi: Il 'Mambriano' del Cieco da Ferrara* (Florence: Società Editrice Fiorentina, 2016)

——'"Dirò d'Orlando": l'evoluzione della figura del conte di Brava tra il *Mambriano* e il *Furioso*, in *'Dreaming again on things already dreamed': 500 Years of 'Orlando Furioso' (1516–2016)*, edited by Marco Dorigatti and Maria Pavlova (Oxford; New York: Peter Lang, 2019), pp. 59-78

MAZZOTTA, GIUSEPPE, 'Italian Renaissance Epic', in *The Cambridge Companion to the Epic*, ed. by Catherine Bates (New York: Cambridge University Press, 2010), pp. 93–118

MENZIES, GAVIN, *1434: the Year in which a Magnificent Chinese Fleet Sailed to Italy and Ignited the Renaissance* (London: HarperCollins, 2008)

MEREDITH JONES, CYRIL, 'The Conventional Saracen of the Songs of Geste', *Speculum*, 17 (1942), 201–25.

MESERVE, MARGARET, *Empires of Islam in Renaissance Historical Thought* (Cambridge, MA: Harvard University Press, 2008)

MOMIGLIANO, ATTILIO, 'Rodomonte', in Idem, *Saggio su l'"Orlando Furioso'* (Bari: Laterza, 1928), pp. 279–307

MONORCHIO, GIUSEPPE, 'L'ideale di combattere: duello di Orlando ed Agricane nell'*Orlando Innamorato*', in *Lo specchio del cavaliere: il duello nella trattatistica e nell'epica rinascimentale* (Ottawa: Canadian Society for Italian Studies, 1998), pp. 111–26

MONTANARI, ANNA, 'Aquilante e Grifone', *Studi italiani*, 9, no. 2 (1997), 5–25

MONTEVERDI, ANGELO, 'Lipadusa e Roncisvalle', *Lettere italiane*, 13 (1961), 401–09

MORETTI, FREJ, 'L'oriente e l'islam nella *Spagna in prosa*', in *Carlo Magno in Italia e la fortuna dei libri di cavalleria: Atti del convegno internazionale di Zurigo (6–8 maggio 2014)*, ed. by Johannes Bartuschat and Franca Strologo (Ravenna: Longo Editore, 2016), pp. 103–24

MORETTI, WALTER, *Ariosto narratore e la sua scuola* (Bologna: Pàtron, 1993)

MOROSINI, ROBERTA, 'The Alexander Romance in Italy', in *A Companion to Alexander Literature in the Middle Ages*, ed. by David Zuwiyya (Leiden: Brill, 2011), pp. 329–64

MURATORI, LUDOVICO ANTONIO, *Delle antichità estensi continuazione, o sia parte seconda* (Modena: Stamperia Ducale, 1740)

MURRIN, MICHAEL, 'Trade and Fortune: Morgana and Manodante', in *Fortune and Romance: Boiardo in America*, ed. by Jo Ann Cavallo and Charles Ross (Tempe, AZ: Medieval & Renaissance Texts & Studies, 1998), pp. 77–95

——*History and Warfare* (Chicago; London: University of Chicago Press, 1994)

——'Agramante's war', *Annali d'italianistica*, 1 (1983), 107–28

——'Falerina's Garden', in *The Allegorical Epic: Essays in its Rise and Decline* (Chicago, London: University of Chicago Press, 1980), pp. 53–85

NEWTON, ARTHUR PERCIVAL, 'Travellers' Tales of Wonder and Imagination and European Travellers in Africa in the Middle Ages', in *Travel and Travellers in the Middle Ages*, ed. by Arthur Percival Newton (London: Routledge & Kegan Paul, 1949, repr. 1968), pp. 159–73

NORI, GABRIELE, 'La corte itinerante: Il pellegrinaggio di Nicolò III in Terrasanta', in *La corte e lo spazio: Ferrara estense*, ed. by Giuseppe Papagno and Amedeo Quondam, 2 vols (Rome: Bulzoni, 1982), I, pp. 233–46

NOSARI, GALEAZZO; CANOVA, FRANCO, *I cavalli Gonzaga della raza de la casa: allevamenti e scuderie di Mantova nei secoli XIV-XVII* (Reggiolo: E.lui, 2005)

PAGDEN, ANTHONY, *Worlds at War: the 2,500-Year Struggle between East and West* (Oxford: Oxford University Press, 2008)

PAGLIARDINI, ANGELO, '*Repetitio* e *variatio* nella denominazione del nemico/straniero nell'epica cavalleresca del Rinascimento', in *Anaphora: Forme della ripetizione*, ed. by Gianfelice Peron (Padua: Esedra, 2011), pp. 229–42

——'Cristiani e pagani nell'epica cavalleresca italiana', *Carte di viaggio*, 1 (2008), 35–58.

——'Procedimenti di denominazione lessicale e onomastica del pagano/musulmano nell'epica cavalleresca del Rinascimento', in *Prospettive nello studio del lessico italiano*, ed. by Emanuela Cresti, 2 vols (Florence: FUP, 2006), I, 229–33

PALMA, DANIELE, *L'autentica storia di Otranto nella guerra contro i turchi: Nuova luce sugli eventi del 1480–81 dalle lettere cifrate tra Ercole d'Este e i suoi diplomatici* (Calimera: Edizioni Kurumuny, 2013)

PALUMBO, GIOVANNI, *La 'Chanson de Roland' in Italia nel Medioevo* (Rome: Salerno Editrice, 2013)

PAMPALONI, LEONZIO, 'La guerra nel *Furioso*', *Belfagor*, 26 (1971), 627–52

PANIZZI, ANTONIO, *Orlando Innamorato di Bojardo, Orlando Furioso di Ariosto: With an Essay on the Romantic Narrative Poetry of the Italians; Memoirs, and Notes by Antonio Panizzi*, 9 vols (London: W. Pickering, 1830–1834)

PAPARELLI, GIOACCHINO, 'Tra Boiardo e Ariosto: le Gionte all'*Innamorato* di Niccolò degli Agostini e Raffaele da Verona', in Idem, *Da Ariosto a Quasimodo: saggi* (Naples: Società Editrice Napoletana, 1977), pp. 34–47

——'Una probabile fonte dell'Ariosto: la "Gionta" all'*Innamorato* di Raffaele da Verona', in *Saggi di letteratura italiana in onore di Gaetano Trombatore* (Milan: Istituto Editoriale Cisalpino-La Goliardica, 1973), pp. 343–56

PARIDE DEL POZZO, *Libro de re militari* (Naples: Sixtus Riessinger [*c.* 1475–1478?])

PAVLOVA, MARIA, 'Nicolò degli Agostini and Ludovico Ariosto', in *'Dreaming again on things already dreamed': 500 Years of 'Orlando Furioso' (1516–2016)*, ed. by Marco Dorigatti and Maria Pavlova (Oxford: Peter Lang, 2019), pp. 79–108

——'La concezione di cavalleria nei continuatori del Boiardo: Nicolò degli Agostini, Raffaele Valcieco e Ludovico Ariosto', in *Di donne e cavallier: Intorno al primo 'Furioso'*, ed. by Cristina Zampese (Milan: Ledizioni, 2018), pp. 197–227

——'L'Africa nell'*Orlando furioso*', *Schifanoia*, 54–55 (2018), 193–205

——'Sul finale del *Furioso* A', in *Le 'Roland furieux' de 1516 entre rupture et continuité: Actes du colloque international de Toulouse, 17–19 mars 2016*, ed. by Alessandra Villa (Toulouse: Presses de l'Université de Toulouse — Jean Jaurès, 2018), pp. 29–54

——'L'immagine del regnante saraceno nell'*Orlando furioso*', in *Par deviers Rome m'en renvenrai errant: Atti del XXème Congrès International de la Societé Rencesvals pour l'étude des épopées romanes*, ed. by Maria Careri e Stefano Asperti (Rome: Viella, 2017), 131–41

——'Rodomonte e Ruggiero: Una questione d'onore', *Rassegna europea di letteratura italiana*, 42 (2013), 135–77

——'Ludovico Ariosto and Islam', in *Christian-Muslim Relations: A Bibliographical History (1500–1600)*, ed. by David Thomas and John Chesworth (Leiden: Brill, 2014), pp. 469–83

——'Torquato Tasso and Islam', in *Christian-Muslim Relations: A Bibliographical History (1500–1600)*, ed. by David Thomas and John Chesworth (Leiden: Brill, 2014), pp. 592–601

——'I saraceni nella letteratura cavalleresca del Quattrocento, dai rifacimenti di storie medievali all'*Inamoramento de Orlando*', in *Epic Connections / Rencontres épiques: Proceedings of the Nineteenth International Conference of the Société Rencesvals, Oxford, 13–17 August 2012*, ed. by Marianne J. Ailes et al., 2 vols (Edinburgh: British Rencesvals Publications, 2015), II, pp. 577–97

PERROTTA, ANNALISA, *I cristiani e gli Altri. Guerre di religione, politica e propaganda nel poema cavalleresco di fine Quattrocento* (Rome: Bagatto Libri, 2017)

——'Paladini in Pagania: Vero e falso, buggie e camuffamenti nei personaggi cavallereschi tra Quattrocento e Cinquecento', in *'D'un parlar ne l'altro': Aspetti dell'enuncizione dal romanzo arturiano alla 'Gerusalemme liberata'*, ed. by Annalisa Izzo (Pisa: ETS, 2013), pp. 51–70

——'Rifare secondo la norma: il *Falconetto* 1483 e il suo rifacimento in ottave', *Schifanoia*, 34–35 (2008), 251–58

——'Alleanze necessarie: cristiani, saraceni e persiani nell'*Altobello*', in *Il cantare italiano: fra folklore e letteratura*, ed. by Michelangelo Picone and Luisa Rubini (Florence: Olschki, 2007), pp. 127–44

——'Serialità e reinterpretazione: il caso dell'*Altobello* e del *Persiano*', in *Boiardo, Ariosto e i libri di battaglia*, ed. by Andrea Canova and Paola Vecchi Galli (Novara: Interlinea, 2007), pp. 107–26

PONTE, GIOVANNI, *La personalità e l'opera del Boiardo* (Genua: Tilgher, 1974).

——'Storicità e immaginosità del Boiardo nella versione di Ricobaldo Ferrarese', *Rassegna della letteratura italiana*, 76, no. 7 (1972), 203–14

POOL, FRANCO, *Interpretazione dell'*'Orlando furioso' (Florence: La Nuova Italia, 1968)

PORTIOLI, ATTILIO, *Quattro documenti d'Inghilterra ed uno di Spagna dell'Archivio Gonzaga di Mantua* (Mantua: tip. Eredi Segna, 1868)

PRALORAN, MARCO, *Le lingue del racconto. Studi su Boiardo e Ariosto* (Rome: Bulzoni, 2009)

——*Tempo e azione nell'*'Orlando furioso' (Florence: Leo S. Olschki, 1999)

QUINT, DAVID, 'Palaces of Enchantment: the 1516 *Orlando Furioso*', *MLN*, special issue (*Orlando Furioso at 500, 1516–2016, Selected Papers of Symposium held in Baltimore, MD*, ed. by John C. McLucas, April Oettinger, Leslie Zarker Morgan, preface by Walter Stephens) (2018), 9–31

——'The Death of Brandimarte and the Ending of the *Orlando furioso*', *Annali d'italianistica*, 12 (1994), 75–85

——'The Figure of Atlante: Ariosto's and Boiardo's Poems', *MLN*, 94 (1979), 77–91

RABY, JULIAN, 'East and West in Mehmed the Conqueror's library', *Bulletin du Bibliophile*, 3 (1987), 297–321

RAGNI, EUGENIO, 'Rodomonte e Gradasso: storia incrociata di due "ruganti"', *Letteratura italiana antica*, 8 (2007), 399–413

RAJNA, PIO, *Le fonti dell'*'Orlando furioso' (Florence: Sansoni, 1900)

——'*Il Cantare dei cantari* e il serventese del maestro di tutti l'arti', *Zeitschrift für romanische Philologie*, 2 (1878), 220–54, 419–37

——'Uggeri il Danese nella letteratura romanzesca degl'italiani', *Romania*, 2 (1873), 153–69

——'Rinaldo da Montalbano', *Il Propugnatore*, 3, no. 2 (1870), 58–127

RAMEY, LYNN TARTE, *Christian, Saracen and Genre in Medieval French Literature* (New York: Routledge, 2001)

RANIÒLO, GIUSEPPE, *Lo spirito e l'arte dell'*'Orlando furioso' (Milan: Mondadori, 1929)

RAVEGNANI, GIUSEPPE, 'Vita, morte e miracolo di Rodomonte' [1929], in *L'ottava d'oro: La vita e l'opera di Ludovico Ariosto: Letture tenute in Ferrara per il Quarto Centenario della morte del Poeta* (Milan: Mondadori, 1933), pp. 203–23 [republished in *Dieci saggi dal Petrarca al Manzoni* (Genua: Emiliano degli Orfini, 1937), pp. 37–72]

REICHENBACH, GIULIO, *Matteo Maria Boiardo* (Bologna: Zanichelli, 1929)

———'L'eroe mal fortunato: Sacripante', in *Atti e memorie dell'Accademia patavina di scienze lettere ed arti*, 75 (1962–63), pp. 159–174

RICCI, GIOVANNI, *Appeal to the Turk: The Broken Boundaries of the Renaissance*, trans. by Richard Chapman (Rome: Viella, 2018)

———*Appello al Turco: I confini infranti del Rinascimento* (Rome: Viella, 2011)

———'Cavalleria e crociata nella Ferrara del Rinascimento: Un piccolo stato davanti a un grande impero', in *Italien und das Osmanische Reich*, ed. by Franziska Meier (Herne: Gabriele Schäfer Verlag, 2010), pp. 75–86

———*I turchi alle porte* (Bologna: Il Mulino, 2008)

———*Ossessione turca in una retrovia cristiana dell'Europa moderna* (Bologna: Il Mulino, 2002)

RIZZARELLI, GIOVANNA, '"Cominciar quivi una crudel battaglia": Duelli in ottave nell'*Orlando furioso*', in *Per violate forme: Rappresentazioni e linguaggi della violenza nella letteratura italiana*, ed. by Fabrizio Bondi, Nicola Catelli (Lucca: Maria Pacini Fazzi, 2009), pp. 79–100

ROSA, PIETRO, 'Un personaggio dell'*Orlando innamorato*: Agricane', in Idem, *Note di critica letteraria* (Milan: Editrice Dante Alighieri, 1930), pp. 61–73

ROTONDÒ, ANTONIO, 'Pellegrino Prisciani (1435 ca.–1518)', *Rinascimento*, 9 (1960), 69–110

RUGGIERI, RUGGERO M., 'I "nomi parlanti" nel *Morgante*, nell'*Innamorato* e nel *Furioso*', in Idem, *Saggi di linguistica italiana e italo-romanza* (Florence: Olschki, 1962), pp. 169–81

SACCONE, EDUARDO, *Il soggetto del Furioso e altri saggi tra Quattro e Cinquecento* (Naples: Liguori, 1974)

———'Cloridano e Medoro, con alcuni argomenti per una lettura del primo *Furioso*', *MLN*, 83, 1 (1968), 67–99

SAID, EDWARD W., *Orientalism* (London: Penguin, 1978)

SALETTI, BEATRICE, *La successione di Leonello d'Este e altri studi sul Quattrocento ferrarese* (Padua: Libreriauniversitaria.it, 2015)

SAMARRAI, ALAUDDIN, 'The idea of fame in medieval Arabic literature and its Renaissance parallels', *Comparative Literature Studies*, 16 (1979), 279–93

SANGIRARDI, GIUSEPPE, *Boiardismo ariostesco: Presenza e trattamento dell'*'Orlando Innamorato' *nel 'Furioso'* (Lucca: M. Pacini Fazzi, 1993)

SAVARESE, GENNARO, *L'Ariosto e la cultura del Rinascimento* (Rome: Bulzoni, 1984)

SANTORO, MARIO, 'Rodomonte: la defezione della "ragione"', in Idem, *Ariosto e il Rinascimento* (Naples: Liguori, 1989), pp. 263–74

SCAMPINATO BERATTA, MARGHERITA, 'La cornice delle *Mille e una notte* ed il canto XXVIII dell'*Orlando furioso*', in *Medioevo romanzo e orientale*, ed. by Antonio Pioletti and Rizzo Nervo (Catanzaro: Soveria Mannelli, 1999), pp. 229–49

SCARANO, EMANUELLA, 'Guerra favolosa e guerra storica nell'*Orlando Furioso*', in *Studi offerti a Luigi Blasucci dai colleghi e dagli allievi pisani*, ed. by Lucio Lugnani, Marco Santagata, and Alfredo Stussi (Lucca: Maria Facini Fazzi, 1996), pp. 497–515

SCARCIA, GIANROBERTO, 'Venezia e la Persia: tra Uzun Hasan e Tahmasp (1454–1572)', in *Commémoration Cyrus: actes du Congrès de Shiraz 1971 et autres études rédigées à l'occasion du 2500e anniversaire de la fondation de l'Empire perse*, 3 vols (Tehran: Bibliothèque Pahlavi, 1974), III, pp. 419–38

SCHWARZ LAUSTEN, PIA, 'Saraceni e Turchi nell'*Orlando Furioso* di Ariosto', in *Studi di Italianistica nordica: Atti del X Convegno degli italianisti scandinavi Università d'Islanda Università di Bergen Reykjavik 13–15 giugno 2013*, ed. by Marco Gargiulo, Margareth Hagen, and Stefano Rosatti (Rome: Aracne Editrice, 2014), pp. 261–86

———'The Representation of Saracens in Boiardo's *Orlando Innamorato*' (a paper given at the Annual Meeting of the Renaissance Society of America, Los Angeles, 19–21 March 2009)

SCHWOEBEL, ROBERT, *The Shadow of the Crescent: the Renaissance Image of the Turk (1453–1517)* (New York: St Martin's Press, 1967)

SEARLES, COLBERT, 'Some Notes on Boiardo's Version of the Alexander-Sagas', *Modern Language Notes*, 15, no. 2 (1900), 89–95

SEGRE, CESARE, *Dieci prove di fantasia* (Turin: Einaudi, 2010)

——'Introduzione' to *La canzone di Orlando*, ed. by Mario Bensi, with an introduction by Cesare Segre, trans. by Renzo Lo Cascio (Milan: Rizzoli, 1985) pp. 5–27

——'Intertestualità e interdiscorsività nel romanzo e nella poesia', *Teatro e romanzo: Due tipi di comunicazione letteraria* (Turin: Einaudi, 1984), pp. 103–18

SERRA, LUCIANO, 'Letture boiardesche: storia poetica e geografica di Grandonio', in *Il Boiardo e il mondo estense nel Quattrocento*, ed. by Giuseppe Anceschi and Tina Matarrese, 2 vols (Padua: Antenore, 1998), I, pp. 143–74

——'Da Tolomeo alla Garfagnana: la geografia dell'Ariosto', *Bollettino storico reggiano, numero speciale*, 4 (1974), 151–84

——'La sublimazione del grottesco: Brunello', in *Il Boiardo e la critica contemporanea*, ed. by Giuseppe Anceschi (Florence: Olschki, 1970), pp. 489–97

SETTON, KENNETH M., *The Papacy and the Levant, 1204–1571*, 4 vols (Philadelphia: American Philosophical Society, 1976–1984)

SHERBERG, MICHAEL, 'Ariosto and Boiardo: Poetry and Memory', in Idem, *Rinaldo: Character and Intertext in Ariosto and Tasso* (Saratoga, Calif: Anma Libri, 1993), pp. 13–42

——'Matteo Maria Boiardo and the *Cantari di Rinaldo*', *Quaderni d'italianistica*, 7 (1986), 165–81

SHULMAN, JAMES LAWRENCE, ' "Sferza e sprona": The Flight from Authority in the *Orlando Furioso*', in Idem, *'The Pale Cast of Thought': Hesitation and Decision in the Renaissance Epic* (Newark: University of Delaware Press, 1998), pp. 23–55

SINOR, DENIS, 'The Mongols and Western Europe', in Idem, *Inner Asia and its Contacts with Medieval Europe* (London: Variorum Reprints, 1977), pp. 513–44

SITTERSON, JOSEPH, 'Allusive and Elusive Meanings: Reading Ariosto's Vergilian Ending', *Renaissance Quarterly*, 14 (1992), 1–9

SMARR, JANET LEVARIE, 'Other Races and Other Places in the *Decameron*', *Studi sul Boccaccio*, 27 (1999), 113–36

SOGLIANI, DANIELA, 'The Gonzaga and the Ottomans between the 15th and the 17th Centuries in the Documents of the State Archive of Mantua', in *The Ottoman Orient in Renaissance Culture: Papers from the International Conference at the National Museum in Krakow, June 26–27, 2015*, ed. by Robert Born and Michał Dziewulski in collaboration with Kamilla Twardowska (Krakow, The National Museum in Krakow, 2015), pp. 67–94

SORRENTINO, ANDREA, 'La leggenda troiana nell'epopea cavalleresca di Matteo Maria Boiardo', *Bulletin italien*, 17 (1917), 22–35

SOUTHERN, RICHARD WILLIAM, 'Dante and Islam', in *Relations between East and West in the Middle Ages*, ed. by Derek Baker (Edinburgh: Edinburgh University Press, 1973), pp. 133–45

SOUTHERN, RICHARD WILLIAM, *Western Views of Islam in the Middle Ages* (Cambridge, Massachusetts: Harvard University Press, 1962)

SPENCER, TERENCE, 'Turks and Trojans in the Renaissance', *Modern Language Review*, 47, no. 3 (1952), 330–33

SPITZER, LEO, 'Tervagant', *Romania*, 70 (1949), 397–408

SQUILLACE, CATERINA, 'L'Oriente fra erudizione e realtà: il *De Asia* di Enea Silvio Piccolomini', in *Pio II Umanista Europeo: Atti del XVII Convegno Internazionale (Chianciano-Pienza 18–21 luglio 2005)*, ed. by Luisa Secchi Tarugi (Florence: Cesati, 2007), pp. 261–80.

STEADMAN, JOHN, 'A Milton-Ariosto Parallel: Satan and Rodomonte (*Paradise Lost*, IV, 181)', *Zeitschrift für romanische Philologie*, 77, nos 5–6 (1961), 514–16

STOPPINO, ELEONORA, *Genealogies of Fiction: Women Warriors and the Dynastic Imagination in the 'Orlando furioso'* (New York, Fordham University Press: 2012)

STEVENS, ADRIAN, 'Gottfried, Wolfram, and the Angevins: History, Genealogy, and Fiction in the *Tristan* and *Parzival* Romances', in *Romance and History. Imagining Time from the Medieval to the Early Modern Period*, ed. by Jon Whitman (Cambridge: Cambridge University Press, 2014), pp. 74–89

STROLOGO, FRANCA, Trasgressione, travestimento e metamorfosi nel *Furioso*: intorno alla storia di Ricciardetto e Fiordispina', in *'Dreaming again on things already dreamed': 500 Years of 'Orlando Furioso' (1516–2016)*, ed. by Marco Dorigatti and Maria Pavlova (Oxford: Peter Lang, 2019), pp. 173–98

—— *La* Spagna *nella letteratura cavalleresca italiana* (Rome; Padua: Antenore, 2014), pp. 171–72

—— 'Le madri di Malagigi e Ferraù, le figlie di Marsilio e le *Spagne* di Boiardo e Ariosto', in *L''Orlando furioso' e la tradizione cavalleresca*, *Versants*, 59, no. 2 (2012), 27–48

—— 'Ai margini delle due *Rotte di Roncisvalle*', *Rassegna europea di letteratura italiana*, 38 (2011), 149–77

—— 'I volti di Ferraù: riprese e variazioni fra la *Spagna in rima* e l'*Inamoramento de Orlando*', *Studi italiani*, 22, no. 1 (2009), 5–27

—— 'Duels, discours et péripéties de l'ex-géant Ferraù dans l'*Orlando furioso*', in *Lettres romanes*, special issue (2008), 27–41

SUARD, FRANÇOIS, 'Les héros chrétiens face au monde sarrasin', in *Aspects de l'épopée romaine: mentalités, idéologies, intertextualités*, ed. by Hans van Dijk and Willem Noomen (Groningen: E. Forsten, 1995), pp. 187–208

*The Postcolonial Middle Ages*, ed. by Jeffrey Jerome Cohen (New York: Palgrave, 2000)

TISSONI BENVENUTI, ANTONIA, 'Intertestualità cavalleresca', in *'Tre volte suona l'olifante...': la tradizione rolandiana in Italia fra Medioevo e il Rinascimento* (Milan: Unicopli, 2007), pp. 57–78

—— 'Rugiero o la fabbrica dell'*Inamoramento de Orlando*', in *Per Cesare Bozzetti: Studi di letteratura e di filologia italiana*, ed. by Simone Albonico et al. (Milan: Mondadori, 1996), pp. 69–89

—— 'Note preliminari al commento dell'Inamoramento de Orlando', in *Il commento ai testi. Atti del seminario di Ascona*, ed. by Ottavio Besomi and Carlo Caruso (Basel: Birkhäuser, 1992), pp. 277–309

TOLAN, JOHN V., *Islam in the Medieval European Imagination* (New York: Columbia University Press, 2002)

—— 'Muslims as pagan idolaters in chronicles of the First Crusade', in *Western Views of Islam in Medieval and Early Modern Europe: Perception of Other*, ed. by David R. Blanks and Michael Frassetto (Basingstoke: Macmillan, 1999), pp. 97–117

TREVISAN, DOMENICO, 'Relazione dell'Impero Ottomano 1554', in *Le relazioni degli ambasciatori veneti al Senato*, ed. by Eugenio Alberi, 15 vols (Florence: Tipografia all'insegna di Clio, 1839–1863), 3rd series, I, pp. 111–92

TRISTANO, RICHARD M., 'The *Istoria Imperiale* of Matteo Maria Boiardo and Fifteenth-century Ferrarese Courtly Culture', in *Phaethon's Children: the Este Court and its Culture in Early Modern Ferrara*, ed. by Dennis Looney and Deanna Shemek (Tempe: Arizona Center for Medieval and Renaissance Studies, 2005), pp. 129–68

TUOHY, THOMAS, *Herculean Ferrara: Ercole d'Este, 1471–1505, and the Invention of a Ducal Capital* (Cambridge: Cambridge University Press, 1996)

TURCHI, MARCELLO, *Ariosto o della liberazione fantastica* (Ravenna: A. Longo, 1969)

TURCHINI, ANGELO, *La signoria di Roberto Malatesta detto il Magnifico (1468–1482)* (Rimini: B. Ghigi, 2001)

VAN ESSEN, CAREL CLAUDIUS, *Cyriaque d'Ancône en Egypte* (Amsterdam: Noord-Hollandische Uitcevers Maatschappij, 1958)

VATIN, NICOLAS, *Sultan Djem: un prince ottoman dans l'Europe du XVe siècle d'après deux sources contemporaines* (Ankara: Imprimerie de la Société turque d'historire [*sic*], 1997)

VILLORESI, MARCO, 'Le varianti di Orlando: un personaggio e le sue trasformazioni', in *'Tre volte suona l'olifante': la tradizione rolandiana in Italia fra Medioevo e Rinascimento* (Milan: UNICOPLI, 2007), pp. 72–93

—— *La fabbrica dei cavalieri: cantari, poemi, romanzi in prosa fra Medioevo e Rinascimento* (Rome: Salerno, 2005)

—— *La letteratura cavalleresca* (Rome: Carocci, 2000)

—— 'Le donne e gli amori nel romanzo cavalleresco del Quattrocento', *Filologia e critica*, 23 (1998), 3–43

VINCENZO, AHMAD 'ABD AL WALIYY, 'La *futuwwa*: la cavalleria spirituale', in Idem, *Islam: l'altra civiltà* (Milan: Mondadori, 2001), pp. 261–81

VITELLI, ASSUNTA, 'I documenti turchi dell'Archivio di Stato di Modena', *Annali dell'Università degli Studi di Napoli 'L'Orientale'*, 54, no. 3 (1994), 317–48

VITKUS, DANIEL, 'Early Modern Orientalism: Representations of Islam in Sixteenth- and Seventeenth-Century Europe', in *Western Views of Islam in Medieval and Early Modern Europe: Perception of Other*, ed. David R. Blanks and Michael Frassetto (Basingstoke: Macmillan, 1999), pp. 207–30

WARBURG, ABY, *The Renewal of Pagan Antiquity: Contributions to the Cultural History of the European Renaissance* (Los Angeles: Getty Research Institute for the History of Art and the Humanities, 1999)

WATT, MONTGOMERY W., *The Influence of Islam on Medieval Europe* (Edinburgh: Edinburgh University Press, 1994)

WILKINS, ERNEST H., 'The naming of Rodomont', *MLN*, 70 (1955), 596–99

WISTAR COMFORT, WILLIAM, 'The Saracens in Italian epic poetry', *PMLA*, 59 (1944), 882–910

WOLFF, ANNE, *How Many Miles to Babylon? Travels and Adventures to Egypt and Beyond, 1300–1640* (Liverpool: Liverpool University Press, 2003)

ZAMPESE, CRISTINA, *'Or si fa rossa or pallida la luna': la cultura classica nell''Orlando Innamorato'* (Lucca: Maria Pacini Fazzi, 1994)

ZANATO, TIZIANO, *Boiardo* (Rome: Salerno Editrice, 2015)

ZANETTE, EMILIO, *Conversazioni sull''Orlando furioso'* (Pisa: Nistri-Lischi, 1959)

ZARKER MORGAN, LESLIE, '"Qe sor les autres è de gran valor": Ogier le Danois in the Italian Tradition', *Cahiers de recherches médiévales et humanistes*, 24 (2012), 423–36.

—— 'War is Hell (for Saracens): A Footnote to *Aspremont*'s Afterlife in Italy', in *'Moult a sans et vallour': Studies in Medieval French Literature in Honor of William W. Kibler*, ed by Monica L. Wright, Norris J. Lacy, and Rupert T. Pickens (Amsterdam: Rodopi, 2012), pp. 289–304

ZATTI, SERGIO, 'L'Angelica ariostesca, o gli inganni della letteratura', in *Selvagge e angeliche: personaggi femminili della tradizione letteraria italiana*, ed. by Tatiana Crivelli (Leonfronte: Insula, 2007), pp. 95–107

—— 'Christian Uniformity, Pagan Multiplicity', in Idem, *The Quest for Epic: From Ariosto to Tasso* (Toronto: University of Toronto Press, 2006), pp. 135–59

—— 'Dalla parte di Satana: sull'imperialismo cristiano nella *Gerusalemme liberata*, in *La rappresentazione dell'Altro nei testi del Rinascimento*, ed. by Sergio Zatti (Lucca: Maria Pacini, 1998), pp. 146–81

—— *L'uniforme cristiano e il multiforme pagano: saggio sulla Gerusalemme liberata* (Milan: Saggiatore, 1983)

ZIPPEL, GIUSEPPE, 'Un pretendente ottomano alla corte dei Papi: il "turchetto"', *Nuova Antologia*, 5 (November 1912), 69–84

ZORZI PUGLIESE, OLGA, *Castiglione's The book of the Courtier (Il libro del cortegiano): A Classic in the Making* (Naples: Edizioni scientifiche italiane, 2008)

ZOTTOLI, ANGELANDREA, *Di Matteo Maria Boiardo, discorso* (Florence: Sansoni, 1937)

# INDEX

❖

www.ingramcontent.com/pod-product-compliance
Lightning Source LLC
Chambersburg PA
CBHW081423090426
42740CB00017B/3164